D0172249

REAL UTOPIA
Participatory Society for the 21st Century

EDITED BY CHRIS SPANNOS

PRESS
EDINBURGH · OAKLAND · WEST VIRGINIA

Real Utopia: Participatory Society for the 21st Century

© 2008 Chris Spannos
This edition © 2008 AK Press (Oakland, Edinburgh, West Virginia)

ISBN-13 9781904859789

Library of Congress Control Number: 2007939199

AK Press	AK Press
674-A 23rd Street	PO Box 12766
Oakland, CA 94612	Edinburgh, EH8 9YE
USA	Scotland
www.akpress.org	www.akuk.com
akpress@akpress.org	ak@akedin.demon.co.uk

The above addresses would be delighted to provide you with the latest AK Press distribution catalog, which features the several thousand books, pamphlets, zines, audio and video products, and stylish apparel published and/or distributed by AK Press. Alternatively, visit our web site for the complete catalog, latest news, and secure ordering.

Printed in Canada on acid free, recycled paper with union labor.

Cover by Herb Thornby
Interior design and layout by ZB

ADVANCE PRAISE FOR *REAL UTOPIA*

"This is a spectacular book of ideas—brave, adventurous, intriguing ideas that reclaim perhaps the greatest human asset of all, political imagination, and help us realize once again that another world is indeed possible." —John Pilger, author of *New Rulers of the World* and *Freedom Next Time*

"Chris Spannos has assembled a volume of hard-hitting, thought-provoking essays that address a critical need on the Left: the creation and elaboration of new theory. Whether in agreement or disagreement, readers will be both excited and challenged by the contents of this book. So pick it up right now!" —Bill Fletcher, Jr., cofounder of the Black Radical Congress and the Center for Labor Renewal, and former president of TransAfrica Forum

"This book captures what's best in past, and most promising in future, social practice; no one-size-fits-all miracles but practical suggestions and a huge and warranted display of confidence in peoples' skills and imagination. It's a compendium of healthily head-in-clouds (where the air is purer) but feet-on-ground utopias, and it reinforces our belief that the story of human emancipation is far from over." —Susan George, Board Chair of the Transnational Institute

"This excellent book fills a huge gap in the thinking and writing about the creation of a better society. It not only outlines how such a society might be organized in theory but also looks at concrete applications of these ideas around the world, in recent history and in the U.S., and at how we might organize to get there. This book is essential reading for all those who firmly believe that a better world is possible and who want to engage with some of the best ideas and practices for bringing about such a world."—Gregory Wilpert, author of *Changing Venezuela by Taking Power: The Policies of the Chavez Presidency* and editor of Venezuelanalysis.com

"Now that the idea that 'there is no alternative' has been challenged by the idea that 'another world is possible,' it behooves us to debate what that 'other world' could and should be. This book presents a coherent school of thought with provocative answers to that question—answers that go beyond the traditional shibboleths of the left." —Jeremy Brecher, historian and author of *Strike!*

"There comes a time in every anarchist's life when she must decide whether her value system has application in the real world or is simply an ideology of lament. For those not content with the low-mileage of the latter, *Real Utopia* is an inspiring interim report—collated from the four corners of the Earth—on the evolution of the complex adaptive system we commonly refer to as 'anarchism.'" —Chris Hannah, Propagandhi

Dedication

This book is dedicated...

To the innocence, curiosity, and wonder of early childhood, before society's defining institutions warp and corrupt.

To youth resistance and rebellion—another world is possible!

To all adults struggling to change the world, living lives knowing everything is broken while new and better lives are waiting.

To older folks and those before them whose struggles offer lessons so we may stand on their shoulders to grab victory.

To human consciousness and potential waiting within, sometimes impatiently, for liberation.

To all revolutionaries everywhere and the lessons their efforts offer so we may win a new society and world.

TABLE OF CONTENTS

ACKNOWLEDGMENTS   1

INTRODUCTION: WHAT IS REAL UTOPIA?   3
Chris Spannos

Part 1: Defining Spheres of a Participatory Society

CHAPTER 1: PARECON TODAY   14
Chris Spannos interviews Michael Albert

CHAPTER 2: PARPOLITY: A POLITICAL SYSTEM FOR A GOOD SOCIETY   25
Stephen R. Shalom

CHAPTER 3: THE ART (AND SERENDIPITY) OF KINSHIP: IDEAS ABOUT
FAMILY, SEXUALITY, AND CAREGIVING IN A BETTER WORLD   32
Cynthia Peters

CHAPTER 4: POLYCULTURALISM AND THE GOOD SOCIETY   49
Justin Podur

CHAPTER 5: PARTICIPATORY ECONOMICS AND THE ENVIRONMENT   56
Chris Spannos interviews Robin Hahnel

Part 2: Revolutionizing Everyday Life

CHAPTER 6: A CALL TO ARTISTS: SUPPORT PARECON   76
Jerry Fresia

CHAPTER 7: FROM SELF-MANAGED MOVEMENTS TO SELF-MANAGED CITY   83
Tom Wetzel

CHAPTER 8: TECHNOLOGY OF THE NEW SOCIETY   88
Nikos Raptis

CHAPTER 9: PARTICIPATORY PLANNING IN LIFE AFTER CAPITALISM   95
Barbara Ehrenreich interviews Michael Albert

CHAPTER 10: EDUCATION FOR A PARTICIPATORY SOCIETY   106
Chris Spannos interviews Noam Chomsky

Part 3: Assessing Parecon Internationally

CHAPTER 11: AFRICA: LIFE AFTER COLONIALISM   112
Mandisi Majavu

CHAPTER 12: LOCAL PLANNING: THE KERALA EXPERIMENT   130
Richard W. Franke

CHAPTER 13: PARTICIPATORY BALKANS   136
Exchanges between Andrej Grubacic and Michael Albert

CHAPTER 14: THE ORGANIZATION OF SAC AND ITS COMPANIES   145
Anders Sandström

CHAPTER 15: PROJECT FOR A PARTICIPATORY SOCIETY—UNITED KINGDOM   151
Mark Evans interviewed by U.K. Watch

CHAPTER 16: FASINPAT (FACTORY WITHOUT A BOSS): AN ARGENTINE EXPERIENCE
IN SELF-MANAGEMENT   155
Marie Trigona

CHAPTER 17: VENEZUELA'S PATH   169
Michael Albert

Part 4: Looking Backward, Looking Forward: History's Lessons for the Future

CHAPTER 18: WORKERS' POWER AND THE RUSSIAN REVOLUTION   182
Tom Wetzel

CHAPTER 19: THE SPANISH ANARCHISTS, THROUGH A PARTICIPATORY LENS   194
Dave Markland

CHAPTER 20: WINNOWING WHEAT FROM CHAFF: SOCIAL DEMOCRACY
AND LIBERTARIAN SOCIALISM IN THE 20th CENTURY   204
Robin Hahnel

Part 5: Theory and Practice: Institutions and Movement Building

CHAPTER 21: THE MAKING OF SOUTH END PRESS AND Z   264
Lydia Sargent

CHAPTER 22: PARECON AND WORKERS' SELF-MANAGEMENT: REFLECTIONS ON
WINNIPEG'S MONDRAGÓN BOOKSTORE & COFFEE HOUSE COLLECTIVE   275
Paul Burrows

CHAPTER 23: THE NEWSTANDARD: A PARECON WORKPLACE IS POSSIBLE   306
Jessica Azulay

CHAPTER 24: VANCOUVER PARECON COLLECTIVE: FOUR YEARS OF ORGANIZING   313
Marla Renn

CHAPTER 25: CAPES: THE CHICAGO AREA PARTICIPATORY ECONOMICS SOCIETY   323
Matt McBride, Lloyd Philbrook, and Mitchell Szczepanczyk

CHAPTER 26: DOING VISION: THE AUSTIN PROJECT FOR A PARTICIPATORY SOCIETY 330
Marcus Denton

Part 6: Moving Toward a Participatory Society

CHAPTER 27: PRAXIS MAKES PERFECT: THE NEW YOUTH ORGANIZING   338
Madeline Gardner and Joshua Kahn Russell

CHAPTER 28: AUTONOMOUS POLITICS AND ITS PROBLEMS: THINKING THE PASSAGE
FROM SOCIAL TO POLITICAL   346
Ezequiel Adamovsky

CHAPTER 29: U.S. SOCIAL FORUM: VISION AND STRATEGY PROPOSAL   363
Z Staff and Marcus Denton

CHAPTER 30: WHICH WAY FOR THE NEW LEFT?: SOCIAL THEORY, VISION, AND
STRATEGY FOR A REVOLUTIONARY YOUTH AND STUDENT MOVEMENT   364
Pat Korte and Brian Kelly

CHAPTER 31: DID YOU JUST SAY CLASS?   373
John J. Cronan Jr.

CHAPTER 32: FROM HERE TO PARECON: THOUGHTS ON STRATEGY FOR
ECONOMIC REVOLUTION   380
Brian Dominick

CHAPTER 33: BUILDING A PARECONISH MOVEMENT   396
Michael Albert

CONTRIBUTOR BIOS   406

INDEX   400

ACKNOWLEDGMENTS

REAL UTOPIA HAS BEEN over three years in the making. In April 2005 I left Vancouver to work on an expedition boat off the coast of Maine. While docked one weekend I received an email from Michael Albert saying AK Press was trying to track me down. I had sent around my book proposal months before moving east, and after some time, thinking there was no publisher interest, set up all new contact info, canceling the old. I vividly remember talking with Zach Blue, now my editor at AK, on a cell phone, he in Oakland and I off-shore in the north-east Atlantic. From the first manuscript proposal till publication in May 2008 I have steadily revised the book's content and shape numerous times. Any acknowledgments truly indicative of all who have made this book possible would be overkill in these pages. However, there are a few people I would like to thank who helped along the way, as well as those who had a formative effect, without which the cause of transforming the world, and consequently this book project, would have passed me by.

The Redeye Collective, where I was a participant from 1999 to 2006, is a radical current affairs program heard on Vancouver Co-op Radio, CFRO. The show's egalitarian structure and decision-making process provided an education like no other, sending me on a trajectory committed to radical societal transformation, along with the confidence and belief that winning is only a matter of time. I would like to thank my dear friends Mordecai Briemberg, Alison Brown, Val Cavers, Leela Chinniah, Lorraine Chisholm, Karen Mackintosh, Peter Royce, Jane Williams, and the late Mark Dickson. At various times they have provided support, direction, inspiration, and guidance without which my path would have led any number of other places, but certainly not here. From 2001 to 2006 I was a social service worker of various capacities in Vancouver's Down Town East Side, working with homelessness, mental health, and addictions. It was an honor to have worked and built relationships with all those who came to me for assistance but who in turn passed along enough insight for me to reflect on for a whole lifetime. I owe them much more than I was able to give, and it was through my experiences with them that I gained the resilience necessary to complete a project of this scale.

The Vancouver Parecon Collective is a group where dreams are chased and caught. I'd like to thank Bryan Berndt, Matt Grinder, Dave Markland, and Marla Renn for making possible more than any of us ever expected while also laying ground for further hopes to realize.

While crewing with the expedition vessel *Wanderbird* the captains provided material support, enabling me to work on early drafts of the manuscript while in my bunk below deck. And thanks to my crew mates who put up with the nightly glow of my laptop that emerged from behind my bunk curtain, lighting the whole crew quarters, while they were trying to catch valuable sleep.

After a brief period back in Vancouver, I moved east again to Woods Hole, Massachusetts where I joined Z as fulltime staff in September 2006, working mostly on ZNet. My prior media work, activism, and organizing put me in contact with many of this books contributors long before it was ever conceived. However, joining Z has placed me among a larger global community, working directly with many contributors to this book. In particular the Z Sessions on Vision and Strategy, June 2006, then the Z Media Institute, July 2007. Both these events provided opportunity to connect with people already contributing chapters, meet new people whose work I thought exceptional, and so asked to come aboard, as well as lead to further contacts with people whose work helped round out the entire project and with whom I have since become acquainted.

I would like to thank my family and friends, of course, for helping in ways only they could.

I would also like to thank everyone at Z for welcoming me into the fold. I have always looked up to the various Z projects; from Z Magazine when I was a subscriber, and ZNet when I was a sustainer, as a participant in the 2001 Z Media Institute, and now finally as fulltime staff. It is a dream come true to finally work with, and directly contribute to, a project I have long admired. And it is a positive coincidence that this book is being published in 2008, after we have completed a total overhaul of Z's web operations for its 20th anniversary. The year looks promising.

After sending this book proposal to numerous publishers, AK Press and Zach Blue were the most enthusiastic, supportive, and encouraging. It is an honor to have my first book published by AK. Special thanks go to them.

Finally, I would like to thank all contributing authors. I can honestly say that without them this book would not have been possible. On top of their own chapter contributions many made helpful suggestions on the rest of the manuscript. It is a privilege and honor to work with such an amazing group of people. Thank you all for trusting me with your work. I hope I have done it justice. Any weaknesses in this book fall squarely on my shoulders as editor.

Chris Spannos, January 1, 2008
Woods Hole, Massachusetts.

Introduction

WHAT IS REAL UTOPIA?

Chris Spannos

UTOPIAS HAVE A LONG, mixed history in Left movements. Sometimes they have propelled our imagination toward what better worlds might look like. Other times they have trumpeted heaven on earth, a world for angels rather than mortals, a far fetched leap to the impossible, where birds can play guitar and human beings are able to flap their arms to fly. *Utopia*, the word, has its origins in Greek, meaning "nowhere," suggesting that it doesn't—and maybe cannot—exist. Still, it has been conceived as an island perfectly designed in all ways societal and moral, and an ideal place or state of being where no wrong can be done. Where utopia offers vision escaping reality it has rightly been rejected by serious Leftists. But even when vision is not pie in the sky, objections are made that any long-term goals can become a blueprint that carries inherent danger of authoritarianism with people reacting as spellbound children naively following the Pied Piper. In this book,[1] we hope to transcend all such problems by drawing from history and real-world conditions, offering vision and strategy for what is possible in transforming society's defining institutions and in revolutionizing human existence in all spheres of life.

The book's contributors are a diverse range of novice and veteran activists, organizers, writers, and intellectuals. The content is derived from and addresses many different regions of the world: from Africa, Asia, and Europe, as well as North and South America. *Real Utopia* addresses politics, economics, gender, sexuality, parenting, culture, race, education, technology, ecology, cities and architecture, art, history, theory and practice, as well as institutions and movements. Taken together the content shows how classlessness, self-management, diversity, and solidarity are all desirable and attainable. "Another world is possible!" does not have to be a vague claim never solidifying compelling visions of a better world, nor a demand glossing over the structural roots of capitalism, patriarchy, racism, imperialism, and un-sustainability. Instead we need and should want convincing vision and strategy that reaches into the roots of today's problems and seeks to replace them with emancipatory alternatives. The proposals in this book are only partial, and require effort by all who care, to further develop and refine a mutually agreed upon and widely shared vision of a future participatory society and world.

Where Does this Book Come From? Why Now?

We want to attain victory in the 21st century and luckily for us 21st century move-ments are born with a silver spoon in their mouths in so far as they are poised to draw from the wealth of experience offered by Classical and New Left revolutionaries who have come before them. We do not have to reinvent their wheel. Nor do we have to repeat their mistakes. We hope to leave behind our forbearers' baggage but carry for-ward their wisdom and courage. Our efforts are made easier by both the gains previ-ous struggles have won as well as their previous failures. We owe it to our forbearers, ourselves, and future generations to carry past progress forward to victory.

So where do we start in this new century, to identify what still needs to be done, un-done, and redone? When looking back, we only need to turn to a period as recent as last century when movements that sought to change the world were predominant-ly concerned with class struggle and transformation of the economic system. Class was considered by many as the lone focus that could yield progressive social change. This conception was held by many on the Left and articulated primarily by orthodox Marxists. And though the sixties and seventies saw the emergence of "neo-Marxists," even these variations on Marxism still emphasized a core of economics with class struggle being the driving force of history and society.

In the last third of the 20th century many social movements arose whose principle concerns were in other spheres of social life including the women's and gay libera-tion movements, and the civil rights and Third World national liberation struggles. These movements did not fit so easily into Marxist conceptual frameworks, at least not without considerable overhaul, with results yielding something little resembling the old Marxism. For those of us concerned with societal transformation and emanci-pation, the best of these New Left efforts yielded new social formations, experiences, and insights which some in turn used to inform their vision and strategy. The worst of this period, despite being rightly disillusioned with deterministic and mechanical approaches toward social change, wrongly jettisoned emancipatory aspirations and at-tempts to seek out understandings guiding us to a better future; and in some cases even consciously rejected truth, reason, and rationality, claiming these concepts were actually part of the problem (post-modernism).

In line with the best of this period, one approach retaining much value for today's social movements, and prefiguring the kind of thinking that people will need to use to reach a future good society, was articulated first in the book *Liberating Theory*[2] (SEP, 1986), collectively authored by Michael Albert, Leslie Cagan, Noam Chomsky, Robin Hahnel, Mel King, Lydia Sargent, and Holly Sklar. As the book's description says, the authors attempted to "combine and transcend various theories of history (marxism, anarchism, feminism, and nationalism) to develop an alternative conceptual frame-work…." and apply "this framework to questions of economics, politics, gender, race, and culture for… understanding society and strategizing its transformation."[3]

This conceptual re-working, largely a response to overly mechanical and econ-omistic approaches of the past, offers today's movements insight to draw from, how-ever we should avoid throwing the baby out with the bath water. Class analysis is something offered by Classical and New Left anti-capitalist theory to understand so-ciety and history. Yet, class analysis is largely absent among today's social movements, and to the extent that it is present, is usually a variation not straying too far from clas-sical two-class economic determinism. Oddly, the forward moving debates about class analysis in the sixties and seventies, which saw many reformulations and innovations (albeit some better than others), has been largely set aside. One such debate, mostly overlooked at the time and since, was captured in *Between Labor and Capital*, a book organized around the lead essay "The Professional-Managerial Class" by Barbara and John Ehrenreich.[4] The Professional-Managerial Class (PMC), as the Ehrenreichs saw it, was a third class between capitalists and workers with its own relations and inter-ests.[5] The PMC approach differed from popular notions of the "middle class" in that it saw this third class as being structurally as important as capitalists and workers. The PMC as the Ehrenreichs describe it includes doctors, managers, "cultural workers," teachers, and others who do largely conceptual and empowering work. The PMC thus differs from capitalists who own and control society's productive assets, as well as from workers who do mostly manual labor on assembly lines, agricultural work, sales, bus-ing tables, etc. The relations and antagonisms between these three classes persist and, according to the Ehrenreichs, cause us to need to consider "the historical *alternative* of a society in which mental and manual work are re-united to create whole people."[6] What is consequential, but rarely if ever stated, is that this insight provides a frame-work for envisioning how work can be re-organized for a classless society where the division of labor is balanced for both empowerment and desirability.

Michael Albert and Robin Hahnel made their own contribution to the same book, "A Ticket to Ride: More Locations on the Class Map," where they first outlined their proposal for a three-class analysis introducing what they call the "Coordinator Class," thereby laying the groundwork for what would become their vision of a classless and participatory economic system. Paraphrasing Albert and Hahnel's essay, the Coordi-nator Class, like the PMC, is positioned above workers who do rote and unempow-ering tasks, who want higher wages, better working conditions, more control over their work, etc., and below capitalists who own the means of production and want to lower wages while extracting more labor and progressively weakening the bargaining power of workers in order to gain more profit. Standard two-class analysis, concerned mostly with class struggle as the propelling force shaping society and history, not only abstracts away *core* concerns of diverse racial and ethnic groups, gender and sexuality, as well as power and political considerations, but also, ironically, overlooks strategic actors within its own realm of economics: the Coordinator Class. On the one hand, coordinators have authority and power over workers. They do mostly empowering and conceptual work, and so benefit from their elite position. On the other hand, workers below them do mostly rote and executionary work. This matters not only in the unjust distribution of desirable work, but also in so far as the kinds of work we do help shape and inform our skills and capacities for decision making and participation both in our work places as well as in the institutions of society more broadly. Again, the thrust of this recognition pushes toward seeking classlessness, not only regarding ownership relations, but also relations of power and empowerment. This in turn bears upon how social movements perceive their own organizational structures today as well as regarding what we seek to win. Standing fast in seeking a classless society necessitates holding a modern day three-class analysis highlighting relations between workers, coordinators, and capitalists. Putting a three-class analysis in the conceptual tool box of today's social movements is only one of the many tasks critical to developing widely shared vision and strategy for the kind of classless and participatory society proposed in this book.

Another change indicative of our times is that today's social movements are seemingly much more adept at relating to one another than in the past, not just by avoiding conflicts among movements and not compromising the needs and interests of any for others, but by positively acknowledging and accepting diverse concerns and strategies and acting out of solidarity. However, this is due more to intuition and lingering gains made by the New Left than to any explicit and widely shared understanding of autonomy, mutual aid, and solidarity for societal transformation.

There is also another difference today that makes having widely shared vision and strategy for a new world necessary. Here in the U.S., across North America, Western Europe, and in many parts of the world, the passion for radical societal transformation is not present in our social movements. We are not excited about the prospects of human liberation, of fundamentally altering society's core defining institutions—of Revolution. Where is this passion among today's movements? Does the international anticorporate globalization movement have a widely shared desire not only to fundamentally transform corporate hierarchies, markets, class structures, and property relations, but also to develop complimentary vision and strategy regarding emancipatory transformation in other spheres of life? Where is this desire among our anti-war, labor, or other social movements? Does anyone believe, as they should, that we can transcend the policies and institutions which warp our society in racist, sexist, and classist ways?

To illustrate the point, consider Venezuela. The Venezuelan population is excited about the massive structural reforms leading them to more control over the institutions which affect their lives. Nobody knows where it will lead. It could all unravel and fall apart next month. But right now Venezuelans are aroused about the possibility of winning a new society. It is not just in Venezuela, but wherever structural transformation empowers the population, that hopes and desires surface. Passion seemingly deepens and spreads as moves toward empowerment and structural change deepen and spread. Venezuelans believe they can win.[7] Our own efforts should also propose vision and strategy able to inspire our movements so that we too believe we can win—one of the many reasons for *Real Utopia*.

When conceiving of this book, I wanted it to be useful in the sense that it should serve a practical purpose and rise from a movement need: the need for vision and strategy. My hope is that it can empower us and enable us to make insightful decisions, to be open to others, learn from mistakes, and move forward. I hope it will shed new light on history, society, and human beings. I hope it will help us become more of a self-conscious movement.

In choosing essays for this book, one of the goals was to assure that *Real Utopia* would be broadly accessible. If we are going to achieve social transformation in accord with widely held vision, and for many people to participate in shaping that vision, proposals offered in these pages have to be easily understood, simple to grasp, and feasibly employed. Having vision and strategy which only a small group of people understand, no matter how class-, race-, gender conscious, and participatory that movement is, runs the high risk of a small group gaining, retaining, and exercising disproportionate power and control over the trajectory of our movements. Consciousness and good will alone will not protect us against the potential rise of elite rule. We need vision and strategy that we all can understand and that is user friendly, so that everyone is able to participate in the process of self-consciously affecting the course of our social movements.

Totality: A Holistic Approach

Our vision and strategy should inform our understanding of who the agents of social change are, of what guides and shapes them, and should not send us down a century-long dead end. Looking back, the predominant view among Left movements of the 20th century was historical materialism: that class struggle was the lone driving force shaping history, society, and people. We want our vision and strategy to incorporate a modern understanding of class struggle, enriching the insights of class analysis but also accounting for other factors that shape people and society. Therefore this book aspires to present vision for all spheres of a future participatory society on equal footing.

To contrast, a *monist* approach would look at one sphere of society and attribute primary importance to how that sphere affects the rest of social life. Someone looking at the economy might say we need to focus on class struggle because it is the primary force affecting all other spheres—gender, cultural, political relations, and so on.

Alternatively, someone looking at power and culture would use a *pluralist* approach combining the political and cultural spheres seeing authoritarianism and racism as the primary forces shaping society. The same *pluralist* approach could be applied again using any other two focuses, say, kinship and economics, to see class struggle and patriarchy as the determining factors shaping society.

A third approach, and the one guiding this book, argues for a *complimentary* and *holistic* orientation which does not assume *a priori* the primary dominance of any of the spheres over any of the others, but instead seeks to understand how parts of the whole are interdependent and relate to one another. It understands that a variety of interactions among the different spheres can occur and that careful observation and assessment will often reveal differing results from society to society.[8]

A Note on Parecon

Of all the visions presented in this book, the participatory economics model proposed by Michael Albert and Robin Hahnel is most developed. Nothing in this book is final and all its ideas require further elaboration. However, the works presented in Part 1, "Defining Spheres of a Participatory Society," and Part 2, "Revolutionizing Everyday Life," should been seen as preliminary sketches. Much more work needs to be done developing and experimenting in these areas. The parecon model, on the other hand, has already undergone much assessment. That is not to say that it should be embraced without critical consideration. On the contrary, more assessment is precisely what is needed to gather popular approval and acceptance. If you are a reader not already familiar with parecon, this book will serve as an introduction, but it is highly recommended that you also check out the many other books fully outlining participatory economics.[9] If, on the other hand, you are a reader already well versed in parecon's underlying values and defining institutions then you will find this book a useful refresher and accessible orientation to how parecon overlaps and has complementary relations with other spheres of societal life.

Now, On with the Show!

People throughout civilization have related to one another so as to carry out certain social functions seeking to meet their needs, wants, and desires. To aid in this, people have created institutions to facilitate their religious, spiritual, and cultural identifications and beliefs; procreation, child rearing, and socialization of future generations; political adjudication, law making, and legislation; and economic production, consumption, and allocation of the material means of life. All of this rests on an ecological foundation that all species interact with and rely on.

Society's core defining institutions thus span the spheres of culture and community, kinship, the polity, and the economy; and provide interrelated roles and relationships that establish patterns of recurring behaviors and outcomes. Over time, these patterns shape human beings and generate a wide array of social groupings, producing and reproducing race and culture, gender and sexuality, class, and political outcomes with both desired and undesired characteristics. The outcomes can be more or less sexist, more or less racist, more or less equitable, and so on. An emancipatory world would eliminate the totality of oppressions that afflict us today and, as *Real Utopia* attempts, focus on producing liberation in all spheres, not any one alone.

Part 1 of this book, "Defining Spheres of a Participatory Society," opens with me interviewing Michael Albert, outlining participatory economics, explaining briefly how parecon handles production, consumption, and allocation, where it comes from, and what its implications for today are. Next, Stephen R. Shalom presents his model of "ParPolity," a political system designed as a nested council structure complimentary to parecon handling disputes, lawmaking, adjudication, legislation, and society's political matters more broadly. Cynthia Peters offers a vision for kinship in a better world, in particular ideas about family, sexuality, and caregiving. "Polyculturalism" is the subject of Justin Podur's essay, where he explores possible interactions between different cultures and identities in accordance with the principles of participatory society. This section wraps with me interviewing Robin Hahnel about how a participatory economy would handle ecological considerations in a sustainable and judicious way.

Part 2, "Revolutionizing Everyday Life," begins with Jerry Fresia's call to action for artists to support parecon while also looking at how parecon would handle art. Tom Wetzel examines what a self-managed city might look like as well as strategic implications. Technology and civil engineering of the new society are explored by Nikos Raptis. Barbara Ehrenreich interviews Michael Albert about the day-to-day intricacies of parecon's decentralized participatory planning process. I interview Noam Chomsky about "Education for a Participatory Society" to close this section.

"Assessing Parecon Internationally," Part 3, presents a wide array of international movements and assessments of revolutionary possibilities opening the 21st century. Africa, postcolonial theory, and development are examined by Mandisi Majavu, who discusses the implications of pan-Africanism, black nationalism, black Marxism, and more generally the relationship between race, class, and gender for vision and strategy in Africa. Richard W. Franke overviews good village-level public planning in Kerala, a southwestern province of India with a population of 32 million.[10] Then, a two-part interview between Andrej Grubacic and Michael Albert on Participatory Society vs. Civil Society in the Balkans as well as the relevance of parecon for workers in a Serbian pharmaceutical factory struggling to take back their workplace. Anders Sandström of Stockholm uses the parecon model to assess the strategic direction of the Central Organization of the Workers of Sweden (SAC), a union based on libertarian socialist values with approximately 8,000 members. Mark Evans is interviewed about the Project for a Participatory Society—United Kingdom. Marie Trigona takes a close look at Argentina's movement of worker-run factories and their example for workers around the world. Also in South America, and closing this section, Michael Albert presents his assessment of the national transformation unfolding in Venezuela based on his visit to that country in 2005.

Part 4, "Looking Backward, Looking Forward: History's Lessons for the Future," tours some of the high-water marks of 20th century Left history. Tom Wetzel reviews workers' power and the Russian Revolution, Dave Markland looks at the Spanish Revolution through a participatory lens, and Robin Hahnel weighs the shortcomings as well as the strengths of Libertarian Socialism and Social Democracy in the 20th century.

Efforts to implement and build participatory structures and movements are presented in Part 5, "Theory and Practice: Institutions and Movement Building." Lydia Sargent outlines the origins of the book publishing house South End Press as well as of Z, with its print magazine, website, and other media operations. Paul Burrows draws both theoretical and practical insights from his experience working in a nonhierarchical worker-run bookstore and restaurant in Winnipeg, Canada. Jessica Azulay passes along lessons learned and process defined at the hard hitting, but ultimately under financed, alternative newswire service, The NewStandard. Marla Renn overviews four years of grassroots parecon organizing by the Vancouver Parecon Collective. Matt McBride, Lloyd Philbrook, and Mitchell Szczepanczyk overview the Chicago Area Participatory Economics Society and the work they do, including having organized a "Chicago School of Participatory Economics" at that university's neoliberal breeding ground. Down in Texas, the efforts of the Austin Project for a Participatory Society are presented by Marcus Denton, along with a discussion of the role he hopes it can play within Left movements today.

Getting from here to there, Part 6 "Moving Toward a Participatory Society," is opened by Madeline Gardner and Joshua Kahn Russell who write about today's youth movement, this century's SDS, and the strategic relation between theory and practice, claiming "praxis makes perfect." Ezequiel Adamovsky explores the potential of Assembly Organizing as a strategic vehicle for emancipation. The U.S. held its first ever national Social Forum in 2007, where Marcus Denton presented a vision and strategy proposal for the 2010 U.S.S.F. at the closing Peoples Movement Assembly. Pat Korte and Brian Kelly offer vision and strategy for a revolutionary youth and student movement. John J. Cronan Jr. argues that Left movements of today are afflicted by class crisis, highlighting the consequences for today's youth, students, and young adults while outlining the three-class analysis explaining relations between workers, coordinators, and capitalists. Brian Dominick proposes steps "From Here to Parecon," utilizing a grassroots dual power strategy. The final chapter in this section, and of the entire book, presents ten claims offered by Michael Albert about the vision and strategy of participatory economics and the implications for building a "pareconish movement."

Finally, it is my hope that this book, my first, will contribute to the growth and development of a movement aspiring to win a participatory society in this century.

(Endnotes)

1   This book, although unrelated to either "The Real Utopias Project" or Erik Olin Wright's forthcoming book *Envisioning Real Utopias* (Verso), and our proposals are quite different, they are motivated by similar concerns.
2   Michael Albert, Leslie Cagan, Noam Chomsky, Robin Hahnel, Mel King, Lydia Sargent, and Holly Sklar *Liberating Theory* (South End Press, 1986)
3   Ibid.
4   Pat Walker, ed., *Between Labor and Capital* (South End Press, 1979)

5   In fact, early opposition to orthodox Marxism's two-class analysis can be found in Michael Bakunin, who not only critiqued the workplace division of labor between mental and manual labor, but also predicted the rise of the "Red Bureaucracy" in revolutionary Russia.

6   Ibid.: 17

7   See the contribution on Venezuela by Michael Albert in Part 3 of this book.

8   There is much more to be said about using a complimentary and holistic approach, and this book can only provide an introduction. See Albert et al *Liberating Theory*, Michael Albert *Thought Dreams: Radical Theory for the 21st Century* (Arbeiter Ring Publishing, 2004), and *Michael Albert Realizing Hope: Life Beyond Capitalism* (Zed Books, 2006).

9   Michael Albert and Robin Hahnel *Looking Forward: Participatory Economics for the Twenty First Century* (South End Press, 1991). See also Albert and Hahnel's companion volume for a technical explanation of the same ideas aimed at economists, *The Political Economy of Participatory Economics* (Princeton University Press, 1991), Michael Albert *Parecon: Life After Capitalism* (Verso, 2003), and Robin Hahnel *Economic Justice and Democracy: From Competition to Cooperation* (Routledge, 2005).

10   2007 estimate.

PART

I

Defining Spheres of a Participatory Society

Chapter 1

PARECON TODAY

Chris Spannos interviews Michael Albert

Spannos: Where did parecon come from? What is its history?

Albert: Participatory economics, or parecon, came mainly from cumulative struggles of diverse populations trying to win liberation from capitalism. Parecon owes, in particular, to the anarchist and libertarian socialist heritage and to the most recent experiences of the New Left of the Sixties, but also to every historical uprising and project aimed at eliminating class rule, from the beginning to present. It has learned from successes and from failures. I once heard about a strike, billed as the first, by Egyptian peasants against a Pharaoh who moved from requiring six days labor on the pyramid a week to requiring seven days, and from providing food to providing nothing. I think parecon harks back all the way to that uprising. I think it owes to every essay, speech, and book, and to every activist project and movement that has tried to shed light on the meaning or practice of classlessness.

Parecon, meaning most broadly classlessness, was born when revolutionaries of various camps began imagining and seeking a classless economy. Kropotkin, Rocker, Bakunin, Pannekoek. That's what parecon is, a classless economy. It is not capitalism, but it is also not an economy ruled by roughly a fifth of the population that monopolizes empowering conditions. In parecon a few participants don't dominate the remaining participants.

Parecon itself, the model, came into being more recently, however, with a particular conception of defining institutions, when Robin Hahnel and I thought through our reactions to various schools of anti-capitalist activism, and set out our views in a book titled *Looking Forward*,[1] about seventeen years ago. Since then parecon has been repeatedly refined, partly in its conception, but mostly in how to communicate about it.

Spannos: Sometimes people talking about participatory economics sound like they are talking about something in their head. Sometimes they sound like they are talking about a thing that exists out there in the world. Is it an intellectual model or is it an actual system like a place we haven't yet visited? What is participatory economics, a creation we define, or a thing we uncover?

Albert: Both. Parecon is a thing we uncover in the sense of being the name of an economy that will someday exist, with real workers and consumers, flesh and blood, who produce and consume. In that sense, yes, parecon has properties like a place that we haven't yet visited. We think about it, guess the properties, and finally uncover them. Parecon in that sense is something out there, not in space but in time.

Parecon is also, however, the name of a specific economic model, a free creation of the mind, that claims to capture the essence of the real future classless economy that we will enjoy. The model called parecon is in people's heads. The economy called parecon is in the future. The in-the-mind model seeks to describe the in-the-world economy. The economy is what we will enjoy, to be revealed in the future. The model in our heads now may need to adapt and alter as we learn more about the system it seeks to clarify.

I think the model is accurate regarding broad defining features. I think we need the model for the help it can give us in attaining the system. We don't need the model for entertainment. We don't need it to exercise our thinking. The model has a more immediate and practical purpose. It exists to provide hope by making real the demand for a new economy. It exists to provide a goal that can help us embody the seeds of the future in our current efforts. It exists to help us orient our demands and activism toward where we want to end up, rather than only toward opposition. The model exists to envision an alternative economy and help us attain it. For that, the model needs to capture the skeletal image of the future participatory economy. It needs to reveal the defining byways. It can, however, ignore more detailed tributaries, which will vary from case to case in any event.

Spannos: What are the central institutional features of parecon which, if they were absent, then an economy wouldn't be a parecon anymore? And beyond the features essential to being a parecon, what range of variety and choice is there in any specific participatory economy?

Albert: The central features of the model called parecon are workers' and consumers' self-managed councils, balanced job complexes, remuneration for duration, intensity, and onerousness of socially valued labor, and participatory planning.

I think these institutional features are to the parecon model what private ownership, corporate divisions of labor, remuneration for property, power, and output, and market allocation are to capitalism. You can't have a classless economy without these defining features.

But just as capitalism comes in many shapes, often dramatically different from one instance to the next, and just as this diversity of capitalism is not due solely to countries having different populations, resources, levels of technology, or differences in other parts of social life, but also owes to countless variations in the implementation of key economic features and in the implementation of endless second, third, and fourth order economic features as well, the same will hold for actual participatory economies.

Thus, different instances of participatory economy will differ in the details of how labor is measured, how jobs are balanced, how councils meet and make decisions, how participatory planning is carried out, and, beyond that, in all manner of less central attributes within and between workplaces and communities.

It is a debilitating mistake to get caught up in seeking an inflexible, unvarying blueprint. Parecon is not inflexible or unvarying. It no more specifies the details of all future parecons than any broad description of capitalism's defining features tell us everything about the U.S., Sweden, Chile, and South Africa. The model shows central defining features, no more, no less.

Spannos: What is the shortcut logic by which you understand the centrality of each of parecon's defining features? Can you start by explaining why you see self-managed workers' and consumers' councils as unavoidable if an economy is to be a parecon?

Albert: One of the pivotal aims of defining a post-capitalist economy is to establish within it an appropriate approach to decisionmaking. If the economy is going to be classless and fulfill our highest aspirations and those of Kropotkin and Rocker and all the rest, then it has to promote each worker and consumer participating in the decisions that affect their lives.

Most succinctly, if no one is to occupy a more privileged position than others occupy, then each person must have the same broad relation to decisionmaking. There are various ways to achieve that. We could have every person get one vote in every decision, for example. But that's patently absurd. Many decisions have near zero impact on me. Why should I have the exact same say as people directly involved and far more affected?

On the other hand, regarding decisions where I am highly involved, I should have more say than people tangentially affected. When I think that simple insight through, guided by requiring that the same norm apply to everyone, what emerges as a norm is that every actor should have a say in economic decisions in proportion as he or she is affected by them. This formulation provides an ideal we reach for. The norm, I call it self-management, is not true or false. It is a value that we like, or not, taking into account its implications.

The next step in my shorthand thinking about this is, if workers and consumers are going to have an influence in outcomes proportionate to how they are affected by them, where are they going to exert this influence? It may be a lack of imagination, but I find it hard to conceive of any answer other than that workers and consumers will have to do so in gatherings and connections with other workers and consumers, acting sometimes singly and often in groups, using relevant information and means, and having relevant confidence and skills as well.

Sometimes, it seems obvious; we will make decisions as individuals, sometimes in small groups, sometimes in larger ones. We will have more or less say in decisions, either individually or in groups, depending on how much outcomes affect us relative to how much they affect others. This is the logic that leads to the idea of workers and consumers as specific individuals, in little teams, in whole workplaces or neighborhood councils, as well as in nested aggregates of councils, expressing and manifesting their preferences via self-managing methods.

That the councils and other levels if participation should be self-managing means that they should utilize means of sharing information, discussing options, and then tallying preferences that give each worker and consumer a say proportionate to the degree they are affected. Full discussions of the meaning of self-management would describe different cases, methods, and so on. But the overall idea is simple. Sometimes people determine that democracy is best. Sometimes they determine that different vote tallies may be called for, like two-thirds or three-quarters. Sometimes they decide consensus is best. Sometimes preferences are expressed by one person, or a few people, or all workers in a plant or consumers in some locale, but it always occurs in the context of the whole larger determination of economic inputs and outputs, so that everyone has influence in all outcomes, as appropriate.

The idea of workers' and consumers' councils, I should add, has a long and elevated history in labor struggle and workplace revolution, and at times in community organizing, as well. That may be why I can't imagine anything but self-managed workers' and consumers' councils as the main site of decisionmaking. Workers and consumers gravitate to this option themselves every time they rise in widespread resistance. Parecon's explicit clarification of self-management as a decision-making norm is an innovation that has long been implicit in popular inclinations.

Spannos: What about remuneration for effort and sacrifice for socially valuable labor? What simple logic reveals that that is the only way to determine income if an economy is to qualify as a parecon?

Albert: We want two things from a remunerative norm. On the one hand, we want it to apportion society's output in an ethically sound way. Everyone should get an amount that reflects appropriate moral preferences rather than their violation. Second, however, the remuneration scheme should give people economically sensible incentives. It needs to propel society's assets being utilized well to meet needs, without waste.

The ethical advisory is why parecon gives you more if you work longer, harder, or at more debilitating conditions and why you don't get more for having more power, or for owning property, or because you happen to be in an industry making something more valuable, or you have highly productive workmates or better tools to work with. That this is the ethical way to proceed can't be proven valid. It is a matter of values. We can say what this approach leads to, and what this approach prevents, which you may ethically like or not. But the liking or not, that's just the way it is.

What this approach leads to is equity. We all earn at the same rate. We all earn with the same prospects. We don't exploit one another. No one earns excessively more because no one can work too much longer or harder than others, and when someone does earn more, for those reasons, everyone agrees it is warranted. Of course, a full discussion addresses finer points, but the values underlying the norm should be pretty clear. Rather than remunerating property, power, or even output, parecon opts to remunerate how hard and how long we work, and the discomfort we endure at work. Parecon claims that this is what we are contributing that deserves to receive payment.

The incentive part of the proviso regarding remuneration is what makes parecon declare that work that gets income must be socially valuable. If I say pay me for the hours I spent composing music, or digging people's lawns, or playing shortstop for a ball team, I won't be convincing. Such work, at least done by me, is not socially valued because I am unable to do it socially usefully. I just don't have those capacities. If I say, instead, pay me for the hours I spend producing bicycles, or producing medicine, or maybe even writing social commentary, and it is a product that society wants and that I am capable of usefully producing, then I can get paid at the standard rate for my effort, but I can't just stand around and say, hey, I worked, pay me. I have to generate output commensurate to the time I claim to have spent. I don't get paid for the value of the output I generate, but along with my council mates, my work does have to generate valued output if it is to count as being worthy of remunerating.

Without getting too detailed, I think this remunerative norm is necessary for classlessness because it is hard to see the generation of equity and proper incentives with a different approach. Regarding ethics, duration, intensity, and onerousness of work deserve to be remunerated. Regarding incentives, these are the attributes that incentives can draw forth. And regarding outcomes, to ensure that what is produced makes economic sense, work needs to be socially desired and efficient.

Spannos: You say balanced job complexes are also central to classlessness, and that classlessness can't do without them. How do you arrive at that claim?

Albert: We want classlessness, and by definition of what classes are, that means that we can't have our economic institutions giving some producers more power that they use to accumulate excessive wealth, better conditions, and so on.

We know that if we let people own means of production and determine its use they will dominate outcomes and accumulate extreme wealth. Parecon, seeking classlessness, excludes that. That much is straightforward.

But it also turns out that if some people do only rote and tedious, obedient labor, while other people do only work that involves empowering conditions, the former traditional workers will be dominated by the latter group whom I call the coordinator class. The logic of seeking balanced job complexes stems from this observation.

If we reject having some people monopolize empowering conditions and roles, then we require a division of labor that doesn't give only some people empowering, and most people disempowering, work. That's the advisory underlying the choice to have balanced job complexes that are simply a positive way to avoid a class-divided distribution of tasks.

With balanced job complexes, we honor expertise, of course, but each worker does a mix of tasks—not solely rote or solely empowering—so that everyone is comparably and sufficiently prepared by their economic position to participate in self-managing councils. We have to have balanced job complexes, in which we all have a mix of tasks of comparable empowerment impact, to avoid a division of labor that separates a co-ordinator class above from a working class below.

Spannos: Finally, why must an economy have participatory planning to be a parecon? Wouldn't it be easier to stick with markets or to opt for central planning from the top down? What is the logic that implies such an inviolable need for this new type allocation?

Albert: Well it would certainly be an easy approach, yes, but I think a wrong one. Both markets and central planning have intrinsic flaws which would compel workers and consumers to make choices contrary to maintaining self-management, solidarity, classlessness, etc. It is a long story when all evidence is presented, but the logic is simple enough. Central planning by its very definition gives excessive influence to planners and diminished influence to others. Planners turn out to need loyal allies inside plants, so when the dust settles we are back to empowered and disempowered producers—coordinators and workers. Additionally, the former bend decisions to advance their interests, not those of workers. With markets the story is similar, but in some respects even worse. Where central planning could arguably arrive at quite accurate valuations, markets cannot, mis-specifying prices regarding public and social goods, ecological impact, etc. Markets also enforce that actors behave individualistically, self-ishly, in the worst sense. Solidaritous behavior is punished. And markets induce class rule, again. In the rush to capture market share, to compete and avoid being out competed, it is necessary to cut costs. This can only be done, after a point, at the expense of workers and consumers. To carry it out well requires a group that is callous to general needs and doesn't suffer the losses penny pinching imposes. This is the coordinator class, hired by firms to ensure surpluses, even against desires for self-management. The above, more fully explored, provides reason to be a market abolitionist, and to join the generalized chorus against central planning, too. But why adopt participatory planning?

Again, the underlying argument is not complex. We want social behavior, not antisocial behavior. We want self-management, which means informed participation with appropriate levels of say. We want all the true social costs and benefits to be accounted for in decisions among options. These desires lead toward having those affected by decisions—the workers and consumers in their councils—cooperatively negotiate outcomes. This impetus is pretty much sufficient, I suspect, to narrow our search to participatory planning as outlined in models of parecon, or something very much like it, at any rate. Workers and consumers express preferences. That can't possibly be avoided if we want self-management. They have to take into account what others express and modulate accordingly. There is thus a back and forth dynamic to it. Once you have that much in mind, the rest is essentially driven by the constraints of having accurate pricing and appropriate say for actors, I think. That's how Hahnel and I drew out the contours, at any rate, putting in steps and facilitating structures as needed to make the operations viable and effective.

Participatory planning is just the long-term anarchist and decentralized socialist injunction that workers and consumers should decide production and consumption themselves, in accord with their needs and desires, not compelled by some narrow elite or ruling class, with parecon's self-management norm appended—made real by giving it institutional content.

Spannos: Why should anyone take seriously even just the possibility that these four features you identify might be desirable? If that claim was true, for example, shouldn't many more people be discussing, debating, and advocating parecon—beyond this book? If parecon is worthy, why aren't there more reviews, essays, advocacy, and support?

Albert: When first presented, parecon was utterly invisible, as is true with any conceptual model or argument at its outset. A decade and a half later, it is still nearly invisible, on a grand scale, but if we look just at the world of anti-capitalists, things are now changing for the better as steadily more people come into contact with parecon and begin to assess it for themselves—most, as far as I can tell, finding it worthy. But why has this process taken so long, and why, even now, is there noticeably little print discussion and debate even as growing numbers of activists at the grassroots are taking parecon seriously?

One possible answer, benign and without broader implications, is just that new ideas and formulations often require a lot of time to percolate into view, and even more time to get serious public assessment. I think there is no doubt that this is part of the story. But I also think it isn't the whole of the story. Why, for example, haven't there been major reviews and essays about parecon, either highly critical, or gently or aggressively supportive? I think there are two parts to the answer.

The first part is that there is relatively little written, whether as a review or otherwise, about any economic vision, period. It isn't just parecon that goes underdiscussed even in alternative media, but also, by and large, other economic visions (and, really, any kind of vision at all). In fact, one could make a case that parecon is getting more ink than other formulations, by a large margin, at this point. So I suspect vision aversion is a big part of the problem. Make some new claim about how capitalism, or racism, or whatever, works, and it will be dissected ad nausea. Make some claim about what should replace capitalism, racism, or whatever, and there will be a crescendo of silence. This is true regardless of what the claims are.

But I think, while nonspecific vision aversion explains a long, slow haul for any visionary claims, the second part of the answer, in the case of specifically parecon, is that parecon has attributes that work against its being taken seriously by people who run review outlets and other print publications. That is, if parecon becomes widely advocated on the Left, there will arise pressure for changes in Left institutions in pareconish directions. There is a loose but instructive analogy to the rise of feminism or black power. As those broad perspectives gained strength there arose great pressures to reduce sexism and racism in Left movements and projects and to actively propel in their place feminism and cultural diversity. There also arose considerable resistance to these frameworks, not least from people who saw them as threatening their situations. I think the same holds for parecon. Those who own or administer Left projects, publications, and movements, often realize either implicitly or explicitly that if pareconish economic views become preponderant, their current agendas for Left efforts will be disrupted by a drive toward equity, self-management, and particularly balanced job complexes.

There was a time when a periodical that didn't have reviews of parecon, or any kind of visibility for parecon at all, could legitimately claim it was because parecon was a sidebar set of notions, without much support, and because the periodical hadn't, in fact, received any writing about parecon. Their not soliciting writing would hardly evidence active resistance, just a disposition away from vision in any form, or even just honest ignorance of its existence. But nowadays at least a good number of Left periodicals have received, in some cases, many submissions, and have actively rejected them. I think that is very plausibly a different situation than benign neglect.

I agree with you, that whatever the causes may be, the relative absence of people seriously debating parecon's merits in diverse print venues greatly hinders its spread. A potential reader thinks to him- or herself, Should I wade through this book, should I immerse myself in this website, should I work to understand these ideas? Well, perhaps I shouldn't. After all, my favorite journals haven't said anything about it. I will wait and see if parecon gains in credibility before I invest my time in assessing it. Indeed, I think this kind of reader reticence to take parecon seriously, given the absence of serious print debate about it, has operated for over a decade. The rise in the number of people relating to parecon despite the absence of print discussion and debate is arguably remarkably quick, rather than slow, seen that way. At any rate, slow or fast, hindered or natural, the attention parecon is getting is now reaching a scale that will propel collective adjudication of the merits of the model, I think—or hope, at any rate.

Spannos: What difference can parecon make now? Is this vision just for the future, or can it matter in the present, and if so, how?

Albert: If it was just for the future, why work on it now? No, I think parecon has tremendous implications right now, today, as well as in coming periods as we get further along in our activism.

For me, indeed, the main point of endlessly advocating the need for vision and arguing the merits of parecon is precisely that I think current practice, if it is to have greater success, depends in considerable part on incorporating vision.

We need vision, economic and otherwise, to overcome the cynicism that there is no alternative to oppressive conditions. We need vision, economic and otherwise, to give us insight permitting us to incorporate the seeds of the future in our present organization and activism. And we need vision, economic and otherwise, to orient and inform both our critique of what exists and our demands and practices at changing what exists so that our efforts lead where we want to wind up—rather than taking us in circles, or, worse, toward a new world we didn't anticipate or desire.

Parecon implies in the present that we ought to make demands around income that move us toward equity, and demands about power that move us toward self-management. It suggests the need to win changes leading toward balanced job complexes. It suggests fighting for adaptations of and restraints on markets leading toward participatory planning. It makes obvious the desirability of establishing workers' and consumers' councils, and of having our movements internally pareconish regarding their decision-making procedures, roles, and modes of remuneration. It suggests restructuring our institutions in accord with our economic aims, as much as we can within the current limiting context, to learn more about future implementation, and also to inspire and benefit people in the present. And it has much to say not only about what we fight for—demands, campaigns, etc.—but especially how we talk about our efforts. We should be discussing our projects and demands in ways that lead toward ever greater comprehension of and desire for pareconish structures and outcomes. I am baffled when people say vision has no implications. To me it is like saying to someone looking for their terminal at the airport, Hey, where you want to go has no relevance, just tell me how you are feeling about where you are, that is enough to decide your terminal. You see the problem. You can't have good activist strategy, good organizational structure, good policies in the movement, or good policies regarding the broader society unless you know what you are trying to attain. Without vision, you can make your strategy fit your current means and assets. You can make it oppose what you dislike. But you can't orient it to arrive at a preferred destination. How many times must people suffer the disasters of directionless activism before we elevate having a destination to priority importance?

Spannos: After clearing that hurdle, what are the strategic implications of embracing positive economic, political, cultural, and kinship perspectives? How does parecon inform these other social spheres? How do these spheres affect parecon organizing?

Albert: Well there are way too many implications in both directions to do more than skirt the surface here. Most broadly, if we are seeking new relations for race, religion, and culture; kinship, family, and socialization; and for legislation, adjudication, and government, as I certainly think we ought to, a much needed step is to arrive at convincing and inspiring shared vision for each realm, not just for the economy. Once we attain such vision, it will greatly inform our immediate efforts, orienting us toward demands consistent with moving forward around race, gender, and power, and with consistent ways of organizing and structuring our movements while we do so. Some of what will arise is easy to predict. We will better incorporate feminist and anti-racist features in our organizational present. Likewise, once we have goals for how to adjudicate disputes, establish shared norms, and implement collective projects, surely it would follow that we should both demand government innovations moving toward these goals and also, as best we can, implement those ways of making decisions and acting in our own political organizations in the present.

Parecon points toward various possible values that might transfer well to these other realms from the economy, including solidarity, diversity, self-management, and probably also variants on equity, such as justice. We have to ask of parecon, are its features such that they would be compatible with and even help propel visionary aims regarding family, culture, and polity? Do parecon's economic features help attain desired aims regarding those other realms? Can the requirements of those spheres of life, addressed by new preferred institutions, be met by parecon? And vice versa, can they meet parecon's demands? Actually, all this is the subject matter of my 2006 book *Realizing Hope*,[2] which addresses participatory economics in the broader social- and world setting, including exploring some possible aims for that broader setting.

Spannos: Finally, what are the next steps for parecon? What do you see happening that could lead to parecon playing a major role in current practice and in how we live in a new world?

Albert: The thing about history is that it isn't even a little like chemistry or physics that we implement in a lab. In real life there are countless possibilities. There are endless circles of variables piled on variables. Even tiny and quite unpredictable shifts and occurrences can magnify into huge implications. So, I have to honestly say, the main answer is: Who knows? Shit happens. So do good things. And stuff comes unexpectedly, often.

But, for purposes of your question, let's assume what we don't yet know, but what I claim—that parecon the model is, indeed, a close description of the defining features necessary to have a classless economy. In that case, there are a number of scenarios I can see possibly unfolding.

Perhaps some major advocacy will occur that will greatly accelerate the process of people gaining the requisite interest to judge parecon, and, I hope, arrive at supporting it. Then it will grow in prominence quickly. What might this be? Perhaps some major movement will adopt parecon as an economic aim, propelling it into sight and assessment. Or perhaps some very prominent individuals or periodicals will in one big act together push it into much wider visibility. Or maybe there is some other escalation that might occur.

In the absence of all that, however, I think the path forward is quite likely to extend the path of the past few years. This would mean more advocates taking time to write and to organize around pareconish ideas, as you and a growing number of other people have begun doing. It might mean caucuses or groups beginning to form specifically to advocate and educate about parecon within larger movements or projects. It would hopefully mean grassroots support continuing to grow, which leads to growing pressure for public debate. And so on.

One can imagine as well the possibility of some kind of participatory economy or participatory society project, domestic or international, to help activists coordinate in such endeavors. These have begun to form, indeed, in a few places already. One can even imagine pareconish activist groups, movements, or an international, but it still seems a ways off. So I guess the bottom line is that we will see what occurs, or, more accurately, we will try things and will experience the results.

(Endnotes)

1   Michael Albert and Robin Hahnel *Looking Forward: Participatory Economics for the Twenty First Century* (South End Press, 1991). See also Albert and Hahnel's companion volume for a technical explanation of the same ideas aimed at economists, *The Political Economy of Participatory Economics* (Princeton University Press, 1991).

2   Michael Albert *Realizing Hope: Life Beyond Capitalism* (Zed Books, 2006), a very insightful effort that could be read as a companion volume to this book.

Chapter 2

PARPOLITY: A POLITICAL SYSTEM FOR A GOOD SOCIETY

Stephen R. Shalom

WHAT SORT OF POLITICAL institutions and practices would be appropriate for a good society? Let me exclude executive and judicial institutions, and narrow the question down to ask, What sorts of decision making institutions and practices would be appropriate for a good society? Over the years, the Left has offered a variety of answers to this question, all of which in my view are seriously flawed in one respect or another, even though they each have valuable insights to offer.

Leninism

One popular answer on the Left has been Leninism. While naïve Russian peasants in the early 20th century used to say "If only the Czar knew ," Lenin said instead "If only I were the Czar." When Lenin declared that "unquestioning submission to a single will" is necessary for modern large-scale industry, he was reflecting the perspective and interests of the coordinator class, not the working class. The Bolsheviks established a political system that evolved into the horrors of Stalinism, but even earlier it was inconsistent with basic democratic values.[1]

Leninists replied to those who criticized their lack of democracy by arguing that society ought to serve the objective interests of the working class, not its perceived interests, not what the working class with its false consciousness believes to be its interests. So the vanguard—who have true revolutionary consciousness—often have to impose their will on the ignorant population. This notion of false consciousness has been used to justify some of history's most grotesque dictatorships, but the concept is not entirely phony. The Leninist error was not in thinking that there is lots of ignorance out there; nor in thinking that debilitating life circumstances often interfere with people understanding their true interests. Their mistake was in assuming that they were free of self-interest or ignorance, and that they knew the interests of others, with enough certainty to warrant suppressing those who disagreed.

Editor's note: This paper was prepared for the June 1–7, 2006, Z Sessions on Vision and Strategy, held in Woods Hole, Massachusetts. The session brought together activists from around the world to share ideas and experiences regarding social vision and strategy.

So while we must reject the dictatorial Leninist position, we want a political system that doesn't just take people's attitudes as fixed, but as a work in progress, improving as people function in a humane society.

Representative Democracy

A second political system is representative democracy, a system whereby people vote for other people—representatives—who will rule in their names. Representative democracy has several serious defects.

First, it treats politics as strictly instrumental—that is, as a means to an end, instead of a value in its own right. But political participation is intrinsically worthwhile: it gives people the experience of controlling their own lives. The more that the task of thinking about how we can collectively manage our lives is delegated to others, the less knowledgeable we become regarding our society, the less we determine our own destinies, and the weaker our ties of solidarity to our fellow citizens.

A second problem with representative democracy is that representatives for many reasons don't in fact represent their constituents. Representatives say one thing to get elected and then change their positions once in office. They have no real connection to the hundreds of thousands of people they represent. Their different life circumstances lead them to develop different interests from those of their constituents.

Now it's true that we could mandate representatives to keep their campaign promises. But what happens when circumstances change? Do we want representatives to be required to carry out policies that new developments have made inappropriate or even harmful? Alternatively, we could mandate all representatives to follow the evolving wishes of their constituents as reflected in public opinion polls. But if we do this, then the representatives are rendered technically irrelevant. There is no need for representatives to study or debate the issues because it doesn't matter what they think. All that matters is that they vote according to their constituents' stated wishes. In short, mandated representatives could simply be replaced by a computer that compiles the opinions of the people and then votes accordingly. But this is really nothing more than a system of direct (referendum) democracy. So if representatives are mandated, they are irrelevant, and if they are not mandated then they will often not be truly representative of their constituents. Advocates of representative democracy do make some legitimate arguments, however. They claim that it would take too much time for everyone to decide everything. I think this point is often exaggerated—people's tolerance for meetings, for example, cannot be judged by their reaction to meaningless meetings today where they have no real power—nevertheless, it is true that not everyone has, or ever will have, the same enthusiasm for politics as do political activists. We don't want a political system that requires everyone to value political participation as much as full-time politicos do today. But though we'll want a lesser degree of participation than that favored by political fanatics, this is not an argument against institutionalizing substantially more political participation than is experienced by most citizens of capitalist democracies.

A second argument on behalf of representative democracy is that representative legislatures are deliberative bodies that debate and negotiate complex resolutions that fairly capture the essence of an issue, whereas the citizenry as a whole would be incapable of such fine tuning. They have to vote a ballot question up or down; they can't reword or amend, even though we know that the precise wording of a ballot question can often skew the results. This is a valid point, one which any alternative to representative democracy needs to take account of.

Referendum Democracy

Direct democracy is an alternative to representative democracy. Under direct democracy people make decisions themselves rather than choosing others to do it for them. There are several variants of direct democracy. One of these is referendum democracy, where every issue is put to the population as a whole. In the past such an approach was simply impossible: there was no mechanism for allowing millions of people to cast ballots on a near-daily basis. But modern technology makes this possible. People could use the internet first to access as much background information as they wanted and then to vote on their preferred options.

But even if technically possible, would you really want to spend all this time exhaustively studying the many hundreds of issues that national legislatures currently take up each year? Those legislators are doing this more or less full-time. Do you want to invest that same amount of time (while doing some other job as well)? Legislators typically have a staff to make the work manageable. Would each citizen have a staff person? Clearly some means is needed to separate the important issues out from all the rather routine issues that legislators currently deal with.

Beyond this time problem, referendum democracy suffers from the defects noted previously. When people make decisions that do not emerge from participation in some sort of deliberative process, their off-the-cuff opinions are more likely to be intolerant and uninformed. While deliberation encourages people to seek common ground and find ways to take seriously the opinions of others, voting in a referendum encourages people to express their pre-existing views on polarized positions. In referendum democracy, when you lose a vote you don't feel better for having participated; you feel trampled on, that no one gave serious consideration to your concerns. When you win a vote you feel self-righteous, with no need to consider the concerns of those you defeated.

Autonomous Communities

A second type of direct democracy is where all decisions are made directly by the people living in fully autonomous small communities. Here we can have the benefits of participation and the benefits of deliberation. But there are nevertheless serious shortcomings.

First, not all problems are susceptible to small-scale solutions. Avian flu calls for a global solution. Environmental problems need a large-scale response. Small communities cannot afford their own MRI equipment. (Yes, I like Echinacea too, but who can doubt that life expectancy has been enhanced by access to modern, high-tech medicine compared to societies that depended solely on herbs and roots.) It is true that some large-scale technologies—like nuclear power plants—create great harm and that much technology is horrendously misused in current society to serve the interests of elites. But this is no reason for us to reject technology entirely. Technology—one of our species' great accomplishments—has the potential to reduce human drudgery and provides us the opportunity of undertaking more creative work and leading fuller lives.

Advocates of autonomous communities often reply that their preference for small scale does not prevent communities from cooperating, whether to address environmental problems or to share an MRI machine. But how do we decide how to share scarce medical resources among communities if not with some decision-making procedure involving multiple communities? And if we have such procedures, then we no longer have autonomous communities.

A second problem with small autonomous communities involves the question of how small is small. Kirkpatrick Sale, for example, recommends communities of about 10,000 people each. These, it seems to me, will be too small to accomplish many important social purposes and too boring to provide adequate variety. At the same time, however, they are too large to permit face-to-face direct democracy. A meeting of the community's 5,000 adults would not be a very participatory experience. Few would get to speak, to share their insights and concerns, or to participate. No doubt, after several of these alienating mega-meetings, attendance would drop off sharply, eventually reaching a manageable size, but this might result in participation rates even lower than currently obtained in the United States.

Nested Councils

A third type of direct democracy is to reject both the self-sufficiency and the referendum models and instead have small councils, linked to one another. The logic of this system of nested councils is three-fold.

First, everyone gets to participate in a council that is small enough for face-to-face decision making and for real deliberation. Second, many decisions will be made in these councils. That is, there are many decisions that should be made at this lowest level council because the decision affects only or overwhelmingly the members of that council. Third, because there are many decisions that affect more than the people in a single council, the councils affected will have to coordinate their decision making. This means that councils will have to send delegates to a higher level council. (And, if the decision affects more than one of these higher level councils, they would in turn send delegates to a third-level council. And so on.)

How would these higher level councils operate? We don't want to have delegates mandated by their sending councils, for then the higher level councils will not be deliberative bodies. As noted previously, there would be no point to anyone speaking or trying to persuade others, or passionately explaining one's special concerns, because all the delegates would have zero leeway—they have to vote the way their sending council told them to. This means that no one from council A gets to hear the perspective of people from council B, and there is no possibility of coming to a better position than either A or B alone proposed. On the other hand, if the delegates are not mandated and just do what they want, then we have the problem of delegates becoming like the unrepresentative representatives that characterize representative democracy.

What makes more sense is to send a delegate who, because she or he has been part of a council and participated in a deliberative process with its members, understands their sentiments and concerns, and is authorized to deliberate on their behalf with other delegates. But what will prevent this unmandated delegate from becoming an unrepresentative representative? First, the connection between delegates and their sending councils is an organic one, not at all like the connection between members of the U.S. Congress and their 600,000-member constituencies. The delegates are part of—and constantly returning to—their sending council. Second, delegates will be rotated; no one will be permitted to serve continuously as a council's delegate. Third, delegates will be subject to immediate recall. If ever a council believes that its delegate no longer adequately reflects its concerns and sentiments (and all higher level council meetings are videotaped and easily monitored), then it may immediately replace the delegate with someone else. Fourth, the higher level councils will only vote on matters that are relatively non-controversial. Whenever a vote is close (or when enough lower councils insist), the decision is returned to the lower councils for a decision.

It might be asked, why not send all issues back to the primary level councils for a vote? But this is where our concern to avoid overdoing participation with excessive time demands comes in. By sending back contentious issues or those so requested by the lower level councils, we have a check on abuse of power by the delegates to the higher level councils. But to send everything back would simply be a waste of time.

Voting

I've used the word "voting" several times, but this raises the question of whether the decision-making procedure requires consensus, majority rule, or some other percentage.

Consensus decision making—where discussion continues until everyone agrees—has much to recommend it. It allows and encourages mutual respect, deliberation, and tolerance. An impassioned minority should not be ignored. Consensus particularly works well in small groups with a common outlook. But to rely exclusively on consensus doesn't make sense for a large scale society, or even for smaller groups which did not come together on the basis of common views. To reject consensus is to override the often deeply held concerns of a few. But to insist on consensus is to override the often deeply held concerns of the many.

Take the issue of abortion, an issue not likely to disappear even after the establishment of a new society based on humane, including feminist, values. A proposal is made to open a new abortion clinic. A small minority opposes the proposal on the basis that they sincerely consider abortion to be murder. The others, however, hold equally sincere views that to prohibit abortion is to violate women's most fundamental rights. They talk, they debate, they respect the moral seriousness of one another, they find some areas of common agreement (say on the need to provide resources for women who choose to carry their pregnancies to term), but at the end of the day they cannot reach a consensus. In that case, a vote, decided by majority rule, is the only just option. To allow the few dissenters to block action is to deny the overwhelming majority ultimate authority to decide their own fates. There is nothing magical about 50 percent plus one, but it does deserve more moral weight than 50 percent minus one.

Decision making in councils should proceed by consensus when possible, majority rule when not. That said, in fact, the dynamics of small groups strongly incline toward consensus. People who find themselves in the minority on some issue are likely to be willing to go along with the majority because they know they'll be in the majority on some other issue. In large, anonymous groups, this sense of reciprocity is unlikely to be as strong, but where there is face-to-face contact, social pressure will tend to encourage people to avoid votes and to go along with the sense of the meeting. But on some occasions this will not be the case, and then it makes sense—after appropriate deliberation—to have a vote. The vote is of benefit not just to the majority, which gets its policy preference, but to the minority as well, which can officially register its dissenting view. The minority is not forced into the position where it has to either block the majority or falsely indicate its agreement with the majority view.

Protecting Minority Rights

Given that I've proposed following majority rule in contentious cases, how will the rights of minorities be protected in such a system? Many societies have constitutions that spell out limitations on the authority of the majority: the majority cannot tell people what religion to practice, what they can say, what they can think; the majority cannot deny individuals the right to a trial, the right to vote, and so on. A good society would of course have some sort of charter that specified these sorts of limitations. But the best constitution in the world is not going to be specific enough to define and resolve every circumstance that might arise. If a council votes that hate speech is illegal, is this a violation of free speech? If a council votes that parents cannot send their children to religious schools that preach sexism, is this a violation of religious freedom? These sorts of issues will need to be decided on a case-by-case basis. But by whom? If the decisions are made by the councils, then the majority is essentially charged with providing a check on itself—which won't be very reassuring to minorities. In many societies, these decisions are made by judges, but then the question is: How are the judges chosen?

If judges are elected, then they are likely to be subject to the same majoritarian passions as the council that made the contested decision. Judges in the United States who campaign for election promising to be tough on crime, to clamp down on immorality, and so on, are hardly the most reliable defenders of minority rights against an intolerant majority. On the other hand, if judges are appointed for life terms (as a way to remove them from the immediate whims of the majority), then they are an undemocratic body, often sticking up not for the oppressed minority but for the privileged minority. This problem of how to check the abuse of power by the majority has been a vexing one in democratic theory. If majorities oppress minorities, that's not democracy. Yet if minorities can block majorities, that too is undemocratic.

The approach I propose is analogous to the jury model. Choose a small group at random from the population to constitute what I call the council courts. These courts will review decisions made by councils to see if they interfere with basic rights and constitutional protections. Each level council above the primary level will be assigned a court, with the High Council Court being the court assigned to the highest level council. Like current-day juries, these courts will be deliberative bodies, though unlike juries they would have a term longer than a single case—perhaps staggered two year terms. As a cross-section of the population, these will be democratic bodies: democratic bodies serving to check the democratic councils.

Why won't these randomly chosen council courts simply reflect the worst prejudices of the majority? No system can guarantee that justice will always prevail, but there is good evidence that when people deliberate together, more intelligent and more tolerant views emerge. This would be the case especially in a society without serious economic deprivation.

To sum up my position: I reject Leninism, representative democracy, referendum democracy, and small autonomous communities. Instead I urge us to support a system of nested councils. At each level, councils proceed not by consensus, nor by strict majority rule, but by a deliberative process that seeks consensus where possible, and majority rule where necessary. My proposal includes a court system that limits the majority, thereby protecting minority rights, but these courts are neither elected nor appointed, but chosen randomly from the population to constitute a deliberative body modeled on the jury system.

I am sure that my proposals can use many refinements and perhaps serious revisions. But at a first approximation I think they show how we can have a political system that incorporates the values we would like to see in a good society.

(Endnotes)

1   For more on this aspect of Lenin and the Bolsheviks see Tom Wetzel's contribution in Part 4 of this book, "Workers' Power and the Russian Revolution."

Chapter 3

THE ART (AND SERENDIPITY) OF KINSHIP: IDEAS ABOUT FAMILY, SEXUALITY, AND CAREGIVING IN A BETTER WORLD

Cynthia Peters

Introduction

"IS LOVE AN ART?" Erich Fromm asks in *The Art of Loving*.[1] "Then it requires knowledge and effort. Or is love a pleasant sensation, which to experience is a matter of chance, something one 'falls into' if one is lucky?" Fromm's book is premised on the idea that it is the former, and I started out wanting to say the same about kinship. The institutions, the sets of practices that define how we "do kinship," are a matter of choice and intentionality. They are not accidents of biology or institutions whose rules are written in stone. Through collective process and ongoing practice, we can determine what kinship looks like.

As much as I believe that the kinship sphere is socially constructed, the fact of the matter is: kinship is *also* something you "fall into." You don't choose what family to be born into or what years you will live or what gender you will most identify with. You don't choose who will first love you when you are born or whether, indeed, you will be loved at all. The fact that the most vulnerable portion of the population—babies—have no choice about the "luck" of their early kinship attachments is all the more reason why we have to think hard about how to construct this sphere. It has to work not just for the people who, later in life, make choices about how they interact with it, but also for those who have no choices about it whatsoever.

Furthermore, the activities and relationships that make up the kinship sphere are some of the most important activities and relationships of our entire lives. In the kinship sphere:

- People create family and all the lifelong attachments and commitments that are implied with that. People create intimacy that is somehow separate from the public sphere of work, politics, culture, etc., even though there is also continuity with those spheres.

- People raise children and give them their first experiences with gender identity, language, race/ethnic identity, geographic identity, and religious identity.

• People have sex and learn to express sexuality (though these activities are not limited to the family; they also happen in the community/culture/society, as well as in the economic sphere—e.g., the production of erotic literature, movies, sex toys, sex work, etc. Also, I don't mean to imply that sex and sexuality are 100 percent "learned" behaviors. They have roots in biology as well.)

• People care for children, elders, and each other, tuning in to specific needs and being intimately able to respond to those needs.

Writing about kinship vision is challenging because getting it right will be a process. Furthermore, it may never be exactly right for everyone, but it could be always evolving toward what is more right for most people. There's no way to give exact prescriptions of what should be. As people function in a better society, and continue to do so for generations, surely the family will evolve accordingly. Minds freed from oppressive work and oppressive culture will make much better choices about how to organize family.

Judging by the names "participatory economics" and "participatory politics," *participation* is a cornerstone quality of those spheres. Perhaps the same is true of the kinship sphere. Although the family is a more private sphere than economics or politics, society-wide participation is still essential to creating safe, healthy, thriving families. Although not everyone will be in families in the same way and not everyone will choose to be a parent, all of society has an interest in working together to make sure the kinship sphere is rooted in and helps reproduce the values that we hope would guide our new society—liberty, justice, solidarity, participation, and diversity/tolerance.

Lifelong Attachments, Commitment, and Intimacy

Perhaps in a better world, with things like solidarity, justice, tolerance, participation, and liberty running rampant in our economic and political institutions, the family as we know it will simply wither away. Who needs a "haven in a heartless world" if the world is not heartless at all? Who needs the protective bonds of family intimacy if the workplace, the culture, and the political sphere are not constantly assaulting your humanity? Who says there is even anything necessarily positive about family intimacy when it seems so often to be a cloak for family dysfunction? At best, some might argue, parents create families in desperate attempts to somehow meet their own unmet needs for love and connection. At worst, parents' approach to children as pawns in their emotional game leads to wholesale oppression of young people, including physical and emotional abuse. Today's political and social structures give few rights to children, protecting them only from the most egregious forms of abuse, and doing that poorly.

Why have families at all if there is so much danger of them acting as sealed breeding grounds for unhealthy relationships and possibly even extreme oppression?

One of the most important components of family life, I would argue, is the opportunity to experience lifelong attachment and intimacy. In families, people have the potential to experience and to feel unconditional love. That seems to me to be an inherent good that we should protect and nurture in a better society. You don't have to earn love; simply being born should put you in direct touch with it. And that first love you feel in your family should give rise to lifelong attachments that meet many emotional needs but also make you a responsible actor in the equation.

Consider the love and attachment between a parent and child. Parents might feel overwhelming love for children, but that doesn't mean they simply bask in the connection that it makes them feel and leave it at that. Instead, they also do the things that children need to have done for them. They feed them in the middle of the night, change their diapers, and listen to their stories. In the process, they make sacrifices, which are often rewarded by deeper relationships and connections, but are still sacrifices nonetheless.

Meanwhile, children—sponges for love and attention that they are—learn something about the responsibility that comes with love and attachment. They see that sometimes making sacrifices leads to a greater good, and that while love is an unconditional right, it's not something that happens automatically. They have intimate role models for the delicate balancing act of enjoying rights and taking responsibility for them—a balancing act that is key to the success of any sphere in a better society—and which is nonetheless an inherent good. Being loved and giving love back, sometimes sacrificing a part of yourself in the process, puts you in the human community. It's your first experience of being connected to others, and if everyone had loving, trustful first attachments, you might wonder how much easier it would be to manage things in all the other spheres.

In fact, a guideline for every other sphere could be: Are we organizing systems in this sphere in the ways that are most conducive to nurturing families' ability to sustain loving, trustful, non-oppressive relationships that help everyone involved hone the great human right to be loved alongside the equally great human responsibility to give back?

If not, think again.

Learning about Gender Identity, Language, Race/Ethnic Identity, Geographic Identity, and Religious Identity

Children, obviously, do not have any choice about what family they are born into, what language they will grow up speaking, what name they will be given, what spiritual practices they might be included in, what city or town or rural area they will live in. All these things will have a big impact on a child, but s/he will have no choice in them, so society has to act as another layer of protection for the child. A child's emotional development might be centered in the family, but it should not be confined to it, and society has to take responsibility for that.

Say, for example, parents regularly expose their children to a certain religious practice. Those children will participate in rituals, be taught a certain belief system, and take on a community identification—such as Catholic or Jewish. By definition, it seems to me, children can't choose a religious practice. They are born into one if their parents have one. But society takes some responsibility for what happens in these communities or cultural practices. While there is respect for diverse cultural practices, oppression is not allowed. Intervention into a community's cultural practice would have to follow certain guidelines and would be based on the level of potential injustice.[2]

Say parents want to baptize their one-year-old. They do this by having the minister dab water on her forehead and participating in the ritual of welcoming the baby into the church community. Clearly, the baby has no choice in this matter, but society might judge that there is nothing terribly oppressive about it. As she grows up, she gains the ability to make more and more choices about her religious practices and she lives in a society that affirms her ability and freedom to make changes. But what if she is psychologically tortured by wretched ideas of heaven and hell coursing through her consciousness her whole damn life? Or what if the gory sight of Jesus hanging from the cross is a constant source of nightmarish guilt and fear forever imprinted on a young mind? Well, that's a problem. The trouble is, there's *no reversing the way she was raised* (and we have to acknowledge that that is a significant power that parents have over children). Still, society can and should mitigate the potential for oppressive practices and it can and should seek to nurture diverse cultural/religious practices that flourish freely and transparently.

Consider the religious practice of circumcision. The baby has no choice in the matter but must live with the lifelong and irreversible choice that someone else made on his behalf. Perhaps society might decide that circumcision is something that should only be chosen by the boy himself when he is old enough to be equipped to make a decision he will have to live with his whole life. Some Jews, for example, attach great emotional importance to the ritual of having their sons circumcised, so I imagine a lot of difficult debate on this topic and others like it. Enforcing a ban on circumcision might drive the practice underground in some unhealthy way or drive a whole community to isolate itself from a society that is trying to control its practices. Furthermore, who's to say that circumcision performed in infancy is not easier to live with in the long run than the gory Christ images imprinted on the brain?

As we all figure out how to function in a better society, there will be a constant balancing of tolerance, justice, etc., and the knowledge that injustice happens along a continuum.

Most would argue, for example, that female circumcision is at the extreme end of the injustice continuum and should not be allowed. It is a much harsher and deeply disabling form of genital cutting than male circumcision is. However, even with that, questions remain. Should adult women be allowed to choose it? Should it be allowed in some less invasive form? Is any form of ritual scarring or cutting acceptable? Does it depend on the nature of the cutting? The age at which it is done?

I am thinking of the lyrics to a song that Bernice Johnson Reagon sings,

Your children are not your children.
They are the sons and daughters of
Life's longing for itself.
They come through you
but they are not from you,
and though they are with you
yet they belong not to you.[3]

To whom do children belong, then, if not their parents? A feeling of "belonging" is likely a most fundamental human need. So, while society must make it possible for children to be freed from oppressive practices, society must also ensure that children have access to cultural practices, communities, religions, families, etc. that they feel they are an integral part of.

To achieve this, society has to balance privacy with transparency as far as families are concerned. Like religions, families get to make choices about their practices, but there should be many opportunities for family members to air issues that are internal to the family.

Say a heterosexual couple wants to start a "traditional" nuclear family. Some members of society might want to argue that such a family structure would give rise to sexist gender dynamics, which are unjust and should not be tolerated. Or say a commune of adults might want to adopt a child, but some members of society feel this would not give the child an opportunity to develop the necessary attachment to people who were clearly responsible for him or her.

In an effort to respect diverse family choices, society should allow scenarios like the above (despite potential risks to children), but should have supports in place for families to evolve, function well, and continually choose the most healthy ways forward. The heterosexual, nuclear family might indeed find itself recreating sexist practices. Rather than disbanding their unit or somehow reversing their decision, the family should have opportunities to ameliorate the situation, rethink assumptions, change patterns, expose their children to alternatives, etc. Quite simply, society should provide resources for parents to continually figure out what they're doing. In oppressive societies, our minds are so *un*-free to make good decisions. In a better society, we won't dictate right and wrong as much as we will find ways to support everyone's *more freed* minds to keep thinking, solving problems, and evolving.

Concretely, society should support voluntary peer support groups—networks that give adults and children a chance to reflect on family practices, get perspective from others, and figure out ways to make changes if need be.

Familiar current examples of these sorts of networks include Alcoholics Anonymous, La Leche League, consciousness-raising groups of various sorts, social clubs, etc. These groups have some sort of a clear mission, yet they are volunteer run, voluntarily attended, diverse in ideologies and norms, open to anyone who wants to attend, and easy to drop out of. In a better society, they could be supported by public money and/or resources—all decided by a participatory decision-making process.

Sex and Sexuality

Sex and sexuality are fundamental to who we are. Although they are spheres of life where people have experienced enormous pain and victimization, they also have found many powerful and beautiful expressions. Unlike economic and political structures, which are harder to imagine, we could actually fairly easily access some decent ideas about sexuality just by looking around, seeing what we like, noticing our own desires, noticing what others like, and caring enough to imagine what it would take to cause these things to thrive in a way that felt fun, freeing, rewarding, and non-oppressive.

The following subsections identify an attribute of healthy sexuality and then discuss what sort of society we would need to be able to give rise to and continually nurture such conditions. This is not meant to be exhaustive, obviously, for two reasons: (1) One would need multiple volumes to be thorough on this topic, and (2) I just don't think it could be done well anyway without the participation of many folks, feedback, processing, and rethinking—all of it evolving over time as we learn things we didn't know before.

(1) Healthy sexuality is a powerful and necessary form of expression in which we act independently and interdependently, and which is fundamental for every human being.

Sex and sexuality can be a means toward an end—i.e., reproduction (at least as far as heterosexuals are concerned), but with technology being what it is, you don't need sex to fertilize an egg and you don't need to be a biological parent to make a family. So, while many people use sex at least in part as a way to make babies, it seems most useful to think of sex and sexuality as something we do for pleasure, to deepen our understanding of who we are, and to create intimacy. Just that right there practically makes it a radical undertaking.

Sex is both a need and a want, and so it has something in common with other things we need and want—like solidarity, diversity, equity, artistic expression, delicious food, engaging work. Sex doesn't enrich anyone; it doesn't impoverish anyone; it doesn't create ownership or disenfranchisement. Instead, it's a place you go to just be or to experiment with your being or to experiment with what it means to be close to another being. Often, it's a process more than an event, but maybe sometimes it is just an event. In any case, sex is where you claim your needs/wants either alone or in conjunction with others. In the process, you express some part of your deepest self—not because you have to, but because you want to, and claiming that want is empowering and life-affirming.

(2) Healthy sexuality is sometimes fluid and includes a wide spectrum of behaviors and feelings—from genital-oriented sex acts to other activities that are erotic, sensual, or sexual, such as dancing, singing, touching, and playing.

If sex and sexuality are where we pursue pleasure, a sense of self, and a sense of belonging and connection to others, then we must put a lot of care into the forums where it is carried out and where it is learned. It is a precious part of ourselves and an integral part of being human, so it deserves utmost care and attention.

Parents and families must get great quantities of support so they can pass on great quantities of the same to their children who will need it so they can be loved unconditionally, their bodies treasured and kept safe, their minds allowed to roam but also seek guidance, their desires affirmed, reflected on, and never shamed. Assuming parents are also sex partners, they'll keep their actual sex life private, but the sexual energy they emanate, which they surely will and which any kid with half the typical kid-radar will pick up on, should broadcast respect, care, and appropriate degrees of lust, too. Right? Why not? If parents are not sex partners, if they have sex with various partners or in some other configuration, they too will have to think about how to communicate to their children messages about this private part of their lives. Whatever the sex lives of the parents, children should get lots of physical love and attention that walks a very special line between pure abandonment and clear boundaries. How do we achieve all these tricky, challenging, nuanced goals? The only way I know is through experience, seeing how others do it, reflecting on how it was done to you, and learning from others. This kind of learning happens when communities and families make time to talk and share.

Schools and community centers must offer engaging, empowering education around sex and sexuality. Understanding how the reproductive system works, along with the mechanics of birth control and sexual health are vital, but only small parts of sex education. Through mentoring, creative writing, artistic projects, and kid-led support groups, kids should have the opportunity to explore sexuality. All along the way, kids should receive powerful messages that their bodies (and everyone else's) are precious, that sharing a sexual experience with someone should be respectful, mutual, safe, and fun. And there should always be older kids or peers or adults available for kids to talk to about whatever they want.

By reorganizing work and reducing the degree to which caregiving work is done privately in the home, society must do away with rigid gender roles and definitions of sexuality so that people are free to seek identity and intimacy in whatever way(s) they see fit. The culture must support art and music so that those channels are available to all for expression and reinforcement of diverse sexuality. Work cannot be so boring, alienating, or demeaning that it's impossible to feel desirable or desire after a long day. In fact, there shouldn't be long days of work. Maybe one of the principles around which work should be organized is: Does it leave people enough time and energy to go home and have sex?

Finally, it should be understood and reinforced in various ways in the culture and society that a person's sexual identity might change over time—opening and closing the door on various practices or approaches. Or a person might take a lifelong "polyamorous" approach to sex and sexuality, holding onto many identities and forms of expression at one time. Or a person might be happily monogamous, and all these choices can be affirming expressions of sexuality.

(3) Healthy sexuality is powerful, but it does not victimize. It is always safe, even if it sometimes causes pain.

When I was in college, my politically correct lesbian friends used to joke about how they tried to have politically correct sex. They took turns, each getting five minutes "on top." But sex isn't like a political meeting, where everyone should have an equal opportunity to talk or a balanced job complex where everyone does similar amounts of empowering and disempowering work. It seems to me that sex is a place you go to work out deep, pleasurable, and even painful feelings about vulnerability, power, being in control and not. Maybe you're a lifelong "bottom" who's found a devoted "top" as a soul mate, and you discarded the stop-watches a long time ago. Maybe hovering along the line between pleasure and pain is exactly what turns you on the most, and you and your partner have communicated well about this and so sometimes you feel pain (exquisitely), but you are not a victim.

No matter what kind of society we create someday, there will be emotional and physical hurts that we might look to resolve through sexuality.

I have a friend who was in a terrible car crash when she was a young child. Her brother died and she experienced severe burns over much of her body. The emotional and physical pain from this experience figure prominently in her life. She told me once about getting her labia (or was it her clitoris?) pierced. I cringed. "Doesn't that hurt?" I asked. She didn't answer with a simple yes or no, but rather with some background on how she has a long, complicated relationship dealing with hurt and loss in her life, and with her body being worked on, and operated on, and treated in various ways. At that time in her life, she was using her sexuality, and specifically piercing her vulva, to work out that relationship to pain. I don't pretend to fully understand, but I support her choice of expression.

In a book I read about Borneo, the writer describes how men implanted their penises with various hard barbs or sticks (or something!) in order to increase the sexual pleasure of their female partners during intercourse. Presumably, they checked in with the women about this, and the women did in fact agree that there was some benefit in it for them. (For my part, I was just cringing again.)

The golden rule, "Do unto others as you would have them do unto you," does not apply when it comes to sex. What you would do unto others they may have no desire to do unto you. And you can't make them. And that's okay. Sexuality should play itself out in wide open (emotional) spaces with very few prohibitions. If what someone does in her private life makes you uncomfortable, then don't do it yourself.

However, it may be worthwhile to pause and *pay attention* to what makes us cringe. There may be something to learn from it, and we may have something to offer to each other. Being non-judgmental doesn't mean turning off your brain. If we care about others, we should be present for them. I could be available to listen to my friend as she works through her issues around pain. I could be what various people have referred to as a "fair witness" (see Patrick Carnes)—someone who offers a reality check, a warm embrace, a willingness to bring a different perspective if someone is seeking that. In a society that supported these types of informal exchanges, maybe even encouraged them using available communication channels—schools, the media, etc.—maybe people would be less likely to replicate their hurts in sexual encounters. Or at least maybe they would have more true choice about it.

(4) Healthy sexuality is learned in families and in societies and cultures that embrace diverse feelings and expressions, but also constantly reinforce the need to balance rights and responsibilities.

No matter what kind of society we create someday, it may be that we are never completely rid of rape, sexual abuse, or coercion. Progressives should support a strong and fair judicial system that enforces legal protections, but the first line of defense against these crimes should be the existence of institutions—e.g., the family, schools, the workplace, the civic community—that stress the mechanisms by which people both experience their rights but also take responsibility for the rights of others. In the family, in the community, on the job, and in the political sphere, people should continually have the opportunity to practice getting their wants/needs met, and making sure others are as well.

So, if, for example, you have learned in the workplace that a guiding principle is that decisions should be made by people who are most affected by them, then you have some practice at this concept. It is a fair principle that is just as true in the bedroom as it is in the workplace. If you are off on some sexual adventure that involves only you, then you have 100 percent decision-making power. Go for it, as they say. However, if you are with a partner who will be affected by your desires, now you have to modulate your adventure, allowing it to be changed and affected by the other person. If you would be enormously turned on by strutting naked down the street with a peacock feather in your hair, well, now, your adventure affects all the people who have to look at you, and so you are not the sole decision maker in the matter.

In a better society, all the ways we practice solidarity, equity, and diversity in all the various spheres of life will provide the greatest disincentive to violent, coercive, or even just inappropriate behaviors when it comes to sex and sexuality. We will be schooled in how to act according to these principles, and we will bring that knowledge to our private relationships and our roles as mentors, "fair witnesses," parents, peers, and community members.

(5) Healthy sexuality takes a certain amount of work (for lack of a better word). Let's call it intentionality.

I think we live with a certain myth that sex and sexuality spring unbidden from deep biological urges (mostly) in men or are tied to romantic swoons (mostly) in women. Sure, sex has something to do with biology and sexual pleasure can be tied to love, but it's okay to be a little more *intentional* about it as well! Maybe that's why these myths persist—to *save* us from being intentional about our sexuality. It is so embarrassing, after all. It would be a lot easier to consign it to some murky part of ourselves that we can claim to have no control over.

A friend of mine who was steeped in motherhood, full-time work, and the demands of home and community told me recently she had zero sexual drive. She missed it. I suggested she try reading some erotic literature to see if that might spark her interest. She looked shocked. I think she thought that if it didn't happen on its own accord, there was nothing she could do. But there's a lot we can do to fully embrace being sexual, and in a better society this sort of renewal would be expected and supported.

There would be a wide range of erotic literature, movies, and music. There would be support groups, how-to books, mentors, friends, and enough *time* to keep in touch (!) with this important part of yourself.

But when I say "wide range," surely there must be parameters. What if someone seeks sexual "renewal" in a way that others consider oppressive? This raises the question of pornography and the long and sickening history of male power being used to sexually subjugate and objectify women (and sometimes children), often violently. Perhaps participatory economics will deal partly with this. Women won't need to be sexual slaves to husbands for economic reasons; women won't need to earn a living as sex workers; women and their sexuality and everything about them will constantly be reinforced as autonomous and inviolate. Furthermore, men will be liberated from the need to use women's bodies as the battleground on which they prove their masculinity.

But what if rape still exists? What if there is some drive (which our better society has not yet foiled) for men to see women as "other," which they might then seek to act on through sexual abuse and/or rape? It goes without saying that non-consensual sex of any kind would be illegal. But what about pornography or erotica that suggested non-consensual sex or showed images of it—for the express purpose of turning people on? Obviously, there can and should be prohibitions against certain acts (such as non-consensual sex), but should there be prohibitions against fantasies, stories, and images?

To answer these questions, we need open dialogue and society-wide problem solving. We need positive, sex-and-sexuality-affirming people to consider the sensible parameters in the sex trade. On Susie (the sexpert) Bright's website, she mentions viewing some pornography that left her unsure whether to cry or masturbate. Clearly, a whole society (even a "better" society) of people "being intentional" about sexuality will have to muck around in exactly such a gray area to figure out the parameters of sex-positive intentionality.

Caring for Children, Elders, and Each Other

The costs of sexist divisions of labor are high, and in a good society, all the spheres—political, economic, community, and kinship—will have to puzzle over how not to allow sexism to emerge in our institutions and daily practices. The family is where children have their first experiences with "gendered" behavior.

In a better society, families might aim to have balanced job complexes within the family—aiming to make sure men and women evenly share the typically gendered tasks, such as caregiving. Even if families were to master the sharing of caregiving across gender lines, there still may be pressure on women to do more than their fair share of the mostly invisible mothering work. The costs of this imbalance are high. Women hone the selflessness that seems to be an integral part of mothering. Their radar is finely calibrated to pick up and respond to the needs of others. Men, meanwhile, seem to screen out some of the incoming neediness messages. They have more time for themselves.

There's nothing wrong with either of these qualities; in fact, they are both necessary. All parents, whether men or women, need time when they are fully present for and tuned into their children. They also need a break from that—the opportunity to be cared for themselves and/or to follow pursuits outside the parenting role. The problem with these qualities is when they are monopolized (or nearly monopolized) by one gender or another.

How, in a better society, might we ensure that everyone has more equal access to care—both the giving *and* the receiving of it? Parecon lays out in great detail the ways that work would have to be structured in a better society in order for it not to unfairly concentrate power and decision-making ability in the hands of a few. A similar effort needs to be made in the kinship sphere. How could family life be organized to ensure that caregiving work is not concentrated in the hands of women?

The principles that guide a pareconish society would do a lot of the heavy lifting when it comes to addressing gender imbalances outside the home. In a participatory economy, if there were any income inequality, it would favor those doing the most tedious and difficult work. There would be no question of women being financially dependent on men, so a major cause of the systemic pressure on women to agree to stay in domestic situations that were unfair or imbalanced would be eliminated. The structure of institutions would ensure equal access to decision making, so women and men would be equally experienced at taking on empowered roles. Parecon would create outside systemic pressures that would help put men and women on equal footing in the home, but I'm not sure it would fully address the intimate and very gendered nature of caregiving in the home.

Part of the problem is finding structural solutions to private, familial configurations. One thing I hope for in a good society is that there are diverse family configurations—with very little public input about what is right or wrong about how to be a family. There would have to be prohibitions on certain things, of course, such as child neglect and child abuse. But I hope we would avoid prescribing how people might choose to love each other, make commitments to each other, raise children or not together, grow old together, etc. I hope we would embrace diverse models, trusting that there are probably nearly infinite ways that people can positively interact over the short- and long-term.

I would not even want to prescribe equal amounts of mothering and fathering work in heterosexual couples. Even if it could be proved that equally sharing the mothering and fathering across gender lines would produce a whole generation of non-gendered caregivers, I would still not support it. Who am I (or anyone, for that matter) to know what is right and sensible for any given family at any given time? When a baby is first born, the nursing mother will be doing most of the mothering work. That's obvious and is dictated by biology (assuming the baby is breastfed). Fathers can do a lot of nurturing in this context, so the imbalance does not have to be enormous, but the fact remains that a nursing mother is going to tune into her child's basic needs in a direct biological way that a man is not likely to experience. Perhaps a mother will choose not to nurse, and perhaps a father will be the primary caregiver and so develop the intense bond that comes from being constantly tuned in to a baby's needs. Or maybe the parents will equally share this work, and maybe even share it with others, too.

It's not the job of the public to decide how families carry out these roles.

But it is the job of the public to make sure that each new generation has more than just private family to depend on. Why? Because it will help de-gender caregiving work, which is a key way that sexism reproduces itself. Socializing caregiving work but preserving individual liberty in families will begin the process of unraveling sexist kinship structures at the same time that it supports diversity in families (see *New Family Values*, by Karen Struening).[4] It's a process that will take generations and that will require (obviously) other efforts in other realms of society as well, but it should be a key focus of attention for a society that is committed to non sexist practices in all levels of daily life. Here are five reasons why we should socialize caregiving work:

(1) Children represent the future.

The next generation—whether your offspring are included in it or not—will inherit our collective messes and triumphs. They will be the engineers that sort out what to do with the garbage we leave behind. They'll have to figure out how to preserve whatever treasures we create. They are the ones who will take care of us when we are old. They are tasked with nothing less than carrying on. Not only is it their right to be born into a society that looks out for them, but we *better hope* they have such a society, if only in our own self-interest.

(2) We need women's contributions in the public sphere.

We also *better hope* we can find effective ways to de-gender the caregiving work. If women are doing the lion's share, the simple fact of the matter is that they will be more worn out and less able to participate in other aspects of society, and so we will miss out on their contribution. Just as there can be no true democracy if some groups of people are ill-equipped to participate because they do un-empowering work all day, so there can be no true democracy if some groups of people are sleep-deprived or are overwhelmed by private caregiving responsibilities. We care about democracy not just because of the principle that says everyone *should* have a say, but because we can do with nothing less than our collective imagination and will in the ongoing work of making a better world.

> (3) No matter what the gender configuration of caregiving in each family, every person needs access to caregiving work via public institutions (in the same way they need access to empowering work).

Michael Albert and Robin Hahnel have argued that a balanced job complex should include a fair mix of empowering and un-empowering work so that everyone is equally empowered to participate in decision making. But what if this leaves out another whole kind of work—caregiving?

Caregiving is neither tedious nor empowering. It is both and neither. It requires both creative energy as well as endless patience. It is in a league of its own because the caregiver, although often performing rote and repetitive tasks, is in a position of responsibility regarding the emotional well-being of the person being taken care of. This responsibility has unfairly fallen on women. Nancy Folbre in *The Invisible Heart*[5] defines "caring labor" as work that "is done on a person-to-person basis, in relationships where people generally call each other by their first names, for reasons that include affection and respect. ... Much of this work is done on behalf of family members ... Much, though not all of it, has an explicitly compassionate dimension."[6]

There have to be publicly structured ways to share caregiving work or else the bio-logical/gendered pressure for women to monopolize it will win out. We can't dictate what private families do, but we can make sure that all individuals, no matter how they were "mothered" or "fathered," have access to the work of caregiving—and so learn about it themselves and hone those skills.

Would everyone perform direct one-on-one caregiving? Probably not. Some people may not have the disposition, and those people could engage in any number of indirect ways of providing care. But my guess is that almost everyone could find a way to participate in direct caregiving. Given the wide range types of caregiving, it would be hard not to find a way to fit in. Whether changing diapers, coaching a sports team, teaching chess, setting up an apprenticeship at your workplace, or simply providing an extra pair of arms to hold your neighbor's baby when needed, you would be contributing to the meeting of human needs.

In the process, all the young ones would have access to caregiving from a great variety of sources. Thus they would experience it as a non-gendered activity, and as they grow up, they would be better able to pursue their own inclinations and proclivities in that field in a way that was at least not defined by gender.

(4) The more caregiving is socialized, the less invisible it will be.

Another benefit of including caregiving in a balanced job complex is that the work of caregiving becomes structurally impossible to make invisible. This is not to say that everyone has to help raise everyone's children, but they do have to participate in creating a safe, nurturing, educational space for the next generation to grow into. They have to be part of the web that makes sure that other people's needs are getting met. Thus, they have to be tuned into and aware of the mechanics of caring. This will lead to better decision making in the same way that if you experience rote and empowering work you make better decisions about how to organize work because you are more invested in fairness, etc.

A society that sees caring for children as a collective responsibility and that creates institutions that share caregiving work will make better decisions about how to organize daily life, the economy, politics, etc. (For now, my focus is on children, but clearly there are many other age groups and types of people that would benefit from caring. Indeed, I can't think of group or type of person who would not.)

(5) Finally, if successive generations receive caring (in some form or another) from all adults, caregiving work will become less and less woman-centered.

Even in a society that embraces diverse families, women are still the ones who give birth and have the capacity to nurse. These biological pressures alone will probably mean more women being the primary caregivers in the early months or years of a child's life. Women's potential to be the primary caregiver, however, does not have to mean that caregiving is seen or experienced as "women's work." Nursing moms could have food delivered and prepared by men. Men (or women) whose balanced job complex included supporting and nurturing families with newborns would mostly support and nurture the mother and/or other family members—cleaning, cooking, caring for siblings, reading out loud, playing music, preventing a new mother's isolation, etc.

If there are social supports for old people to stay in families, then there could be another lap nearby, another set of arms, another source of lullabies—great assets for any family with a newborn.

Outside the home, there could be emotional support for people in the newborn's family. People working as playground monitors would help solve disputes, keep kids safe, apply Band-Aids when needed, and walk children home when they are tired. Sufficient teachers, tutors, and mentors could mean older siblings arrive home relaxed and confident rather than in desperate need of maternal support.

The nursing mother would be providing one element of nurturing in what should be an elaborate web of nurturing. Children growing up in this context would perceive nurturing as gender neutral, even if it is sometimes at least partly informed by biology (as in the case of breastfeeding). Children would learn caregiving skills from men and women. It would be seen as a valued and integral part of everyone's work. This would be true whatever the family configuration might be—single mother, heterosexual parents, homosexual parents, multiple parents, extended families, whatever.

Conclusion

The kinship sphere is where people go to practice the special "arts" of loving, experiencing intimacy, expressing sexuality, raising children, and both giving and receiving care. It is more private than economic, political, and cultural spheres, but it still requires the participation of everyone to ensure it nurtures rather than hinders liberty, justice, solidarity, diversity, and tolerance.

Negotiating the porous boundaries between private and public will be key to evolving better practices in the kinship sphere. Consider the case of my friend who is in her fifties and is having trouble in her love life. Her longtime lesbian partner has identified that she is transsexual. She feels that she is a man inside, and she wants to be loved and appreciated as a man. Where does this leave my friend (let's call her L), who says, "I'm a lesbian. I'm not interested in men."

She's wishing her partner (let's call her T) would just embrace being butch. "Why does she have to want to be a man?" By the same token, one might wonder, why does it matter so much to L? Why not just keep loving T even as her gender identity evolves?

If we had a better society where gender categories were less rigidly enforced, would people be freed up from the gender assigned to them by biology? Would fluid androgyny make terms like heterosexual and lesbian obsolete because the categories male and female play less of a role in determining who you are attracted to? Would we, in fact, discourage the use of strong labels, which in turn give rise to pairings based on gender identity? Would there be a sort of falling-away of gender all together? My fifteen-year-old daughter says that she and her peers are embracing the idea of being pan-sexual, which apparently means loving the person for whomever s/he is, unrelated to gender.

But what "is" a person? For some, like my friend L, gender identity is part of what makes her who she is. She is a woman who loves women. She insists that she is only attracted to the female body and to what she considers female qualities. But clearly it is possible for others (like the pan-sexuals) to experience sexual attraction in ways that are not rooted to gender. Furthermore, in a better society, lesbians would not be an oppressed group attempting to survive on the margins of society and often forced into defensive positions—in order to protect the degree of freedom won through decades of organizing, building alternative institutions, and fighting in the political realm. The way we address many questions about sexuality and identity will be informed by the society we live in. If we live in a homophobic society, a person is less free to claim a lesbian identity and also less free to be non-defensive about possibly giving up aspects of that identity if something (like what happened to L and T) transpires.

Furthermore, in the context of a society where men have more power, is it to possible to embrace a male identity as if it is unrelated to *relationships of power* that clearly exist between men and women?

The "private" evolution of my friend's relationship, in other words, is not so private after all. While elements certainly are individual, the political, social, and cultural context that they are trying to love each other in plays a big role in their options. How could society support them in the art of loving?

How could society support all of us—parents, families, lovers, in all our various arrangements to create kinship as the loving, nurturing sphere it should be?

My friends L and T, anyone who's ever cared for a child, every person who's worked to sustain friendships and humane relations with others, all those who dare to explore sexuality and live sexually fulfilled lives—all of us, in other words would benefit from a society that took seriously a mission to develop the personal "arts."

First of all, in a better society, the art of kinship will not be relegated to dark and private recesses of the family. As we work to ensure that all spheres (economics, community, and politics) enhance liberty, justice, solidarity, participation, and diversity, we should also ask if they enhance our ability to love and nurture each other. Family and personal relationships will of course be more or less private, but they will happen in a context that honors and supports the importance of the human work of social reproduction and that actively combats the systemic oppression that cause distress in personal relationships. Imagine a world where racism, sexism, homophobia, and classism don't divide us and where we see each other for who we are rather than through the toxic filter of stereotypes and defenses against stereotypes. Absent these negative aspects of others spheres, the kinship sphere will automatically improve.

But no matter how positive the other spheres are, the kinship sphere will need a second key ingredient, and that is ongoing sustained attention by every future generation. This essay provides a cursory look at what that attention should include: the role of the family in creating lifelong attachments and intimacy; the fact that children are vulnerable to parents who exercise tremendous power and authority over many aspects of their lives; the need for people to have sex and express sexuality; and the importance of social ties in the caretaking of children, those with more needs, and the elderly. In all of these areas, it will be the public's task to encourage participation, balance privacy with transparency, and focus on what must be proscribed (rather than prescribing certain behaviors). As we grow and change in what will be a constantly improved environment, our minds will be more and more freed to meet these admittedly difficult challenges, so we should be prepared to constantly revisit the challenges of the kinship sphere, allowing our responses to evolve over time.[7]

(Endnotes)

1   Erich Fromm *The Art of Loving* (Harper & Row, Inc., 1956)
2   See Justin Podur on polyculturalism in the next chapter of this section.
3   From a song by Bernice Johnson Reagon, with lyrics drawn from Khalil Gibran.

4   Karen Struening *New Family Values: Liberty, Equality, Diversity* (Rowman & Littlefield Publishers, Inc., 2002)

5   Nancy Folbre *The Invisible Heart: Economics and Family Values* (The New Press, 2001)

6   Ibid.: xi

7   Thanks to the many folks who talked to me about these issues and/or commented on various drafts: Michael Albert, Paul Kiefer, Justin Podur, Lydia Sargent, Steve Shalom, and Karen Struening, as well as the participants at the Z Strategy and Vision Sessions in Woods Hole, Massachusetts, June 2006. I also drew from the following:

Dorothy Allison *Talking About Sex, Class and Literature* (Firebrand Books, 1994)

Patrick Carnes *Sexual Anorexia: Overcoming Sexual Self-Hatred* (Hazelden, 1997)

Nancy Folbre *The Invisible Heart: Economics and Family Values* (The New Press, 2001)

Erich Fromm *The Art of Loving* (Harper & Row, Inc., 1956)

Inga Muscio *Cunt: A Declaration of Independence* (Seal Press, 1998)

Karen Struening *New Family Values: Liberty, Equality, Diversity* (Rowman & Littlefield Publishers, Inc., 2002)

Shari Thurer *The Myths of Motherhood: How Culture Reinvents the Good Mother* (Penguin Books, 1994)

Chapter 4

POLYCULTURALISM AND THE GOOD SOCIETY

Justin Podur

IN A SOCIETY WITH equitable, cooperative, and free economic arrangements such as those of participatory economics, the problem of the interaction of different cultures and identities in accordance with *principles of equality*, solidarity, and liberty still arises. The following are some thoughts of how to address this problem.

Definitions

Discussing the problem of culture and identity in a good society requires the definition of some terms. My definitions will stick fairly closely to what I think people mean when they use these terms, but I am going to select meanings in order to make it easier for me to make my points.

I define a *community* as a group of people who share something in common. Who is in or out of the community is determined by the community and by those outside it. The Black community, for example, is not one based solely on self-identification. Who is Black has been defined, historically, by whites, not blacks. The journalistic or scientific "community," a very different kind of community, is not defined from the outside—or is defined from the outside to a much lesser extent.

Identity is most simply membership in a community or group. Like the boundaries of community, identification happens in two ways. One's own consciousness is important. But so too is that of the group—in many cases, membership in a group is contingent upon the group's acceptance. Additionally, identity can be imposed from the outside, i.e. by states who confer "status" or "non-status" identity on their subjects.

I am going to define *culture* differently from anthropologists. To anthropologists culture is everything that is not defined by biology. But I will define culture as the shared language—not only verbal language, but nonverbal cues, assumptions, norms, customs—that enables members of a group to communicate internally and to strengthen the identification of individuals with the community. But the capacity to communicate is moderated through cultural institutions—media, educational, religious, etc. Indeed every institution has a cultural element, which is the reason for phrases like "working-class culture."

Race is just a particular kind of group identity, correlated with continent of origin and physical features like skin color. In North America "racial" identifications are basically: Asian (sometimes divided into East, West, and South), Indigenous, Latin@, Black, and white. *Ethnicity* is a more nuanced understanding of the concept, relying on country or language of origin.

Next is *racism*. Leftists used to have some control over the definition of this word but have since lost it, leading to some of our problems. Common usage of the word racism is that racism is bigotry, prejudice, and resort to stereotypes. In this common usage, Blacks can be just as "racist" as whites. Another idea is that racism is simply the irrational hatred of Black people. In this usage, "racism" is reserved for anti-Black prejudice, and differentiated from anti-semitism, Islamophobia, and hatred against other groups. This usage leads to the idea of "reverse racism," which in common usage is discrimination against whites and is usually suggested as an argument against affirmative action programs.

Leftist usage of the word racism is different from common usage. In Leftist usage, *racism* is either a system of *power* that one group (whites) holds over others, or any individual or institutional behavior or pattern that reinforces this system of power. This is the most useful definition of racism, but it has been rejected in favor of the common usage because of its limitations. I will discuss these limitations below.

Multiculturalism is a proposed solution to racism. In a multicultural framework, all cultures are respected and indeed, all cultures are equal. Groups are free to express their cultural preferences and dominant groups are to have special respect for minority groups. Tolerance and diversity are the order of the day. Cross-cultural understandings are sought. Multiculturalism posed as the counter to the common-usage form of racism.

Multiculturalism is not, however, a solution to racism as Leftists refer to it. Indeed, if a system of power is still in place, multicultural ideals of respect, tolerance, and diversity can be used as arguments against mobilization aimed at identifying or redressing power imbalances (as divisive or intolerant). Ideas of fairness and equality developed as an antidote to bigotry become arguments against affirmative action. Multiculturalism is official policy in Canada, and it plays out in perverse ways: it is a table built on dispossession at which the gatekeepers of the different communities compete for resources based on their ability to convince the others that they "represent" their communities. The result is that the dominant group, presumed to have no "culture" (having to settle for wealth and power instead) gets to wield strict fairness and equality arguments against these "cultures," who sound like they want "special rights."

At the same time, Leftists helped develop multicultural analysis and the multicultural ideal. That it has become mainstream speaks to its basis in good values (fairness, equality, diversity). That it is used as a weapon against oppressed constituencies speaks to its limitations.

Limitations of Multiculturalism by Leftists

The limitations of the Leftist definition of racism are related to the limitations of multiculturalism. Both are highlighted by the proposed solutions to the problem. If we are against power differentials between groups, do we eliminate the differentials but preserve the groups? Or do we eliminate the groups?

If we want to preserve the groups neatly and separately, we have a separatist solution.

If we want to eliminate the groups, we are after assimilation.

Both such solutions—and in its crudest form, multiculturalism is a separatist solution, albeit with an injunction to "tolerance" between the separate groups—are solutions based on cultural homogeneity. They are based on a flawed idea that people live their lives as members of a single group or a single identity.

The flaw and its application in multiculturalism is described by Vijay Prashad in his book *Everybody was Kung Fu Fighting*.

> Are cultures discrete and bounded? Do cultures have a history or are they static? Who defines the boundaries of culture or allows for change? Do cultures leak into each other? ... To respect the fetish of culture assumes that one wants to enshrine it in the museum of humankind rather than find within it the potential for liberation or for change. We'd have to accept homophobia and sexism, class cruelty and racism, all in the service of being respectful to someone's perverse definition of culture.[1]

Adding to Vijay's list of rhetorical questions are two posed by Michael Rabinder James's book *Deliberative Democracy and the Plural Polity*. Do individuals choose their cultural identities, do they inherit them, or are they imposed from without? A group's claim on resources or restitution may depend on this question. When we are talking about resources, we are talking about the economy, and class, and perhaps of conflict between classes. Why should a group based on self-definition have any special claim on resources? The truth is, Rabinder James argues, choice and inheritance, internal group acceptance, and external imposition all play a role in identity formation, in virtually all cases.[2]

Most of our views about culture and multiculturalism underestimate diversity within groups. They overlook how group boundaries can shift over time.

Amartya Sen's book, *Identity and Violence*, also makes this argument. He makes two main points. First, individuals have multiple identities that overlap and can change. Second, there is always some role for choice in how identity plays out in any given situation.[3]

This is not a matter that requires great imagination. It merely requires recognition of daily reality. It is in front of all of us. But it has some important consequences.

Polyculturalism

Robin Kelley, in *ColorLines*, describes this recognition as "polyculturalism," which he counter-poses with "multiculturalism."

> We were and are "polycultural." By "we," I'm not simply talking about my own family or even my 'hood, but all peoples in the Western world. It is not our skin

or hair or walk or talk that renders black people so incredibly diverse. Rather, it is the fact that most black people in the Americas are products of a variety of different "cultures"—living cultures, not dead ones. These cultures live in and through us everyday, with almost no self-consciousness about hierarchy or meaning. In this respect, I think the term "polycultural" works a lot better than "multicultural," since the latter often implies that cultures are fixed, discrete entities that exist side by side—a kind of zoological approach to culture. Such a view of multiculturalism not only obscures power relations, but often reifies race and gender differences. While this may seem obvious, for some people it's a dangerous concept. Too many Europeans don't want to acknowledge that Africans helped create so-called Western Civilization, that they are both indebted to and descendants of the very folk they enslaved. They don't want to see the world as One—a tiny little globe where people and cultures are always on the move, where nothing stays still no matter how many times we name it. To acknowledge our polycultural heritage and cultural dynamism is not to give up our black identity or our love and concern for black people. It does mean expanding our definition of blackness, taking our history more seriously, and looking at the rich diversity within us with new eyes.[4]

Consequences for the Future

Just economic and political arrangements necessitate the elimination of power and class differentials between groups. So restitution—programs that pay attention to history with a view to eliminating equality and fairness in the present—is important, for example in North America for Blacks and indigenous peoples in particular. Inequalities cannot be justified on the basis of tolerating diversity. A reparations program that decreases inequality should not be viewed as "special treatment." Two caveats are necessary. First, such programs have to be carefully designed so they actually do decrease inequality. Second, wanting to eliminate inequalities between groups does not mean tolerating inequalities within groups.

This is where a possible tension emerges between cultural autonomy and solidarity. This is not a plea for cross-cultural tolerance, because we do not live in a single identity. We can have solidarity with others on the basis of shared identity, even if we have only our shared humanity as a basis for solidarity. But if we don't want to use cultural relativism as an excuse to tolerate injustice within groups, we also don't want to allow powerful groups to violate the autonomy of weaker or smaller groups based on their own values or norms.

But what does it mean in the real world of institutions, groups, and populations to say we cannot "allow powerful groups" to do something? What kind of protection is there for a minority within a country, or for a small independent national community in the family of nations? There are legal, political, and media protections that could help society deal with this problem—formal legal protections in constitutions and international law—protections that require consensus or huge majorities to change. But these can be violated by powerful groups.

Voting systems can be arranged to provide incentives to politicians and campaigners to reach out across obvious community divisions. But these, too, could be ridden with conflict.

Major media institutions could be encouraged to operate based on fairness criteria. These criteria include:

- Representing all subgroups in the wider community

- Presenting all different positions in the wider community

- Being accessible to anyone

- Facilitating communication or translation between groups

- Developing the "common culture" of the wider community

Smaller, community media institutions might have a more specialist role. These might not be held to the same standards of fairness. Nor would they have the same levels of public support or access to public space. They would just be independent media, available to anyone and protected by free speech laws.

This sketch, for media institutions, suggests an important principle for a polycultural framework. Wider society has a responsibility to make its institutions representative of the diversity of communities within it. But it should also encourage and help the creation of autonomous institutions for those communities: institutions that are not held to the same strict criteria of fairness, because, unlike society-at-large, people are free to exit them.

Michael Rabinder James, in his *Deliberative Democracy and the Plural Polity*, suggests fairness criteria for judging democratic processes: aggregative equality (each person has roughly the same voting power), deliberative equality (each different position is represented regardless of its popularity), aggregative autonomy (choice between different candidates and positions), deliberative autonomy (a chance to develop positions free of coercion and with full information), aggregative reciprocity (equal coalition-building opportunities), and deliberative reciprocity (a tendency to view others as partners and understand their positions). He also suggests voting systems that would encourage people to seek votes across identity groups.[5]

Legal, political, and media protections can all facilitate a polycultural framework. But in spite of them, powerful groups could wield control over resources shutting out or misrepresenting alternative views, or consign them to the margins.

Beyond institutionalized protections, the ultimate protection is the development of a "common culture" in which people do not "vote," or even think, reliably or consistently as a member of their "community"—only as opposed to the larger society. This is the best protection against communalism and in India it has been the main brake on communalism. People do not vote, or live, in a single identity. A sound society would not ask them to.

What about across societies? What if cases of oppression or violence are occurring within a community or a nation? When does the wider society—or the family of nations, or an external agent of any kind—have the right to intervene?

In the most extreme cases, this can be resolved with a simple rule, proposed by Arthur I. Waskow in his book *Keeping the World Disarmed*.[6] The rule is simply this: intervention is allowed, but more force requires more consensus. So any country could send a single unarmed observer or investigator to investigate claims that a country was arming or committing rights violations against its people. To send more would require more consensus and full armed intervention would require some super majority.

Consequences Today

I argue above that people do not vote, or live, in a single identity. A sound society would not ask them to, nor would a sound political movement. Unfortunately, Leftists do ask people to, and that is a mistake.

There is no such thing as a homogeneous group or movement. The idea of representativeness in common spaces and the creation of autonomous spaces can almost always be applied. Criteria of deliberative and aggregative autonomy, reciprocity, and equality can always be adapted. Left institutions and processes can, and should, be evaluated according to these criteria. Anti-racist work would gain from the recognition of the multiple, overlapping identities and the element of choice in them, and from avoiding the error of asking people to live or think in a single identity.

This framework leads to a skepticism about the label "people of color" used by Leftists. "People of color" is a flimsy identity, externally imposed. It lacks the elements of shared history, language, experience, or territory that make for coherent communities. It obscures power differentials and oppression within its too-wide boundaries. Anti-racists do better to rely on stronger bonds of solidarity, whether based in coherent communities or in shared principles and practice. I do not believe that the benefits of excluding whites are so great that they make up for what is lost. For racial identity, I am in favor of more precise labels: Black, Indigenous, East, West, or South Asian, Latin@, and white—these, too, however, are subject to fluid and shifting boundaries and internal (class, power, gender) diversity.

I also believe that Leftists' analysis of "privilege" is either too often used or too selectively used. Especially in the absence of positive aims and political strategy, it is common Leftist practice to attack individuals on grounds of identity and consequent privilege. Without positive aims or objective criteria, critiques on the basis of identity have the potential to destroy any group and any organizing effort that is not completely homogeneous or atomized. While this is not an argument for denial, silence, or complicity in the face of inequalities or hypocrisy, such attacks need to be evaluated on a case-by-case basis, on the basis of their strategic value and on basis of the likelihood they will advance positive anti-racist aims of decreasing power differentials, strengthening solidarity, or expanding freedom. Many are made instead for sake of self-expression or because they are easy to make. Attackers are too often unreflective of their own privilege. This is the experience of many Leftists trying to function in activist circles, particularly in privileged North American contexts. Indeed, Michael Rabinder James suggests criteria for when a minority group would be justified in political struggle against the majority. The majority has to have failed the tests of deliberative and aggregative equality, reciprocity, and autonomy. It is worth keeping this in mind, too, when we are deciding whether or not to struggle against one another.

Conclusions

Material and political inequalities between individuals and groups are absent in a good society, but cultural and identity differences are not. Neither separation nor assimilation are viable frameworks for cross-cultural interaction. The alternative to these is a "polycultural" framework in which multiple, overlapping identities are recognized and celebrated and minorities are protected not only by constitutional arrangements but also by the development of a "common culture." Institutions can be evaluated on fairness criteria to determine whether they facilitate just, equitable, and polycultural outcomes. The recognition of multiple, overlapping identities and the element of choice that individuals have in determining identity can serve to protect individuals from groups, small groups from large groups, and the general interest from narrow interests.

(Endnotes)

1   Vijay Prashad *Everybody was Kung Fu Fighting: Afro-Asian Connections and the Myth of Cultural Purity* (Beacon Press, 2001)

2   Michael Rabinder James *Deliberative Democracy and the Plural Polity* (University Press of Kansas, 2004)

3   Amartya Sen *Identity and Violence: The Illusion of Destiny* (W. W. Norton, 2006)

4   Robin Kelly *ColorLines* (1999)

5   James, *Deliberative Democracy and the Plural Polity.*

6   Arthur I. Waskow *Keeping the World Disarmed* (Center for the Study of Democratic Institutions, 1965)

Chapter 5

PARTICIPATORY ECONOMICS AND THE ENVIRONMENT

Chris Spannos interviews Robin Hahnel

Chris Spannos: Participatory economics is an economic vision, just one part of society. What role do environmental considerations have in visions of a future society?

Robin Hahnel: I think you raise two important issues I would like to address separately. One issue has to do with the fact that historically, most Leftists have proposed economic visions as if they were sufficient visions for all spheres of social life. The second issue has to do with environmental vision and how that relates to economic vision.

I believe that by conflating economic vision with social vision in general, most Left visionaries have been guilty of unwarranted "economism." However, in this regard, I do not think Michael Albert and I were guilty when we wrote about participatory economics. Participatory economics was proposed as an economic vision—not as a substitute for political and cultural visions, nor for a vision of non-patriarchal gender relations. Moreover, Michael Albert and I never presumed that economic vision was more important than visions for new and better social institutions in other spheres of social life—quite the contrary—and I think we made that very clear in everything we ever wrote about participatory economics.

It's true we wrote much more about economic vision than visions for other spheres of social life. But we did so only because we thought that we, personally, had more insights to offer regarding economic vision, not because we ever believed that emancipatory visions for other spheres of social life were any less important than economic vision. Even in this regard, when we wrote about what we called at the time "socialism tomorrow" in Part III of *Socialism Today and Tomorrow*,[1] we wrote separate chapters on "socialist politics," "socialist economics," "socialist kinship," and "socialist community" because we did not want to conflate vision for a truly socialist economy with vision for a desirable society in general—which we, like everyone else at that time, called "socialism." In short, since the two of us were already sensitive to economistic biases on the Left before we ever wrote about economic vision, I think we did manage to avoid the mistake of conflating economic vision with social vision.

However, regarding the relationship between our vision of a participatory economy and the environment, I'm afraid I must plead guilty. As a whole the Left was a "Johnny-come-lately" to environmental awareness. That includes not only the old Left, but much of the new Left as well—which is where Michael Albert and I both grew to political awareness in the 1960s. As a result, I believe most economic visions coming out of the Left—including ours—have failed to adequately address environmental concerns.

When we first wrote about participatory economics we believed that a participatory economy would treat the environment far more wisely than capitalist, communist, or market socialist economies, and we briefly pointed out why we believed that was the case in broad generalities. We mentioned that externalities, such as pollution, and public goods, such as environmental preservation, would be more efficiently accounted for by participatory planning than by markets, but we did not propose specific procedures to protect the environment, nor explain concretely how particular features of a participatory economy could be expected to lead to a more judicious relationship with the natural environment. In other words, we failed to address serious questions about participatory economics and the environment when we first published *The Political Economy of Participatory Economics*[2] and *Looking Forward: Participatory Economics for the Twenty-First Century*[3] in 1991.

Therefore, it was not surprising that serious environmentalists took us to task at the time and remained skeptical of claims that remained vague. Carl Boggs wrote: "It is unclear precisely how Albert and Hahnel's participatory economy establishes mechanisms for determining overall ecological impacts, for setting limits to the production of harmful goods, or for ascertaining how much industrial growth is desirable."[4] And Howard Hawkins reported: "One Left Green who read *Looking Forward* scoffed at it as 'industrialism with a human face.' He wondered how in the world—given our contemporary situation of ozone depletion, greenhouse effect, radioactive and toxic poisoning, and general ecological breakdown—can one lay out an economic vision without going into some detail on ecological issues?"[5] Boggs and Hawkins were completely justified in demanding to know what "mechanisms" would determine ecological impacts and set limits on harmful production and growth.

It took over ten years, but I think we now have some concrete answers for environmentalists about precisely how the environment can be protected in a participatory economy. However, these answers are just getting out there. I also propose and discuss concrete procedures to protect the environment in a participatory economy in chapter eight of my book *Economic Justice and Democracy: From Competition to Cooperation*.[6]

While I look forward to reactions from environmental activists and scholars to what we now propose about how a participatory economy can handle environmental issues, I hasten to point out that we have not proposed an environmental vision as that is usually understood. Explaining how decisions regarding the environment can be made in a participatory economy is not the same as describing what wise interaction with the natural environment will actually look like. In other words, there is nothing forthcoming that will satisfy environmentalists who want to know what specific technologies will be chosen or banned in a participatory economy, what the rate of growth of production will be, or how great the division of labor between different communities and regions will be in a participatory economy.

In their great 19th century utopian novels *Looking Backward*[7] and *News from Nowhere*,[8] Edward Bellamy and William Morris each attempted to motivate a desirable alternative to capitalism not only by describing new economic institutions and patterns of behavior, but also by describing new products and technologies they presumed their post-capitalist economies would feature. In that regard, Bellamy and Morris did provide a technological and environmental vision as part of their attempt to motivate readers to think positively beyond capitalism. I think greens who research and write about new products and technologies that are more environmentally friendly in the energy, transportation, agricultural, and industrial sectors are doing crucial intellectual work. I think activists who experiment with environmentally friendly modes of production and consumption are an important part of the hope for the future. But I am neither an expert on green technologies, nor competent to judge which ideas about environmentally friendly technologies and products are more fruitful and which will prove to be less so. I must leave the job of pointing out the advantages of particular technologies and products to scientists and engineers, and the task of conveying what life might be like in ecotopia to more talented novelists and science fiction writers than I am. I think this work—offering environmental vision—is very important. I'm just ill-equipped to do it myself.

Instead, the focus of my attention is on whether or not basic economic institutions afford creative ideas and proposals about how we relate to the natural environment a fair and friendly hearing. In that vein, in the past I have tried to explain why the profit motive ignores crucial environmental effects unmeasured in the commercial nexus, why markets are biased in favor of economic activities that pollute and biased against activities that preserve and restore valuable ecological systems, and why capitalism promotes private consumption over social consumption and leisure to the detriment of the environment. In other words, I have tried to explain why capitalism is incapable of granting ideas about how to better relate to the natural environment a fair and friendly hearing. Now I am trying to explain, more concretely than a decade ago, how particular features and procedures in a participatory economy can create an institutional setting and incentives that promote judicious relations with our natural environment. In other words, when ideas that environmentalists (and I) think are promising—ideas like recycling, organic farming, locally grown produce, smart growth, de-automobilization, solar and wind power, and more leisure instead of more consumption—are proposed in a participatory economy, why is there good reason to believe they will receive a friendly hearing rather than be discarded as they are in capitalist economies today.

Let me state my views regarding the environment clearly. I do not believe environmentalists should ever be satisfied that any proposal for how to conduct human activities will adequately protect the environment. Unlike other species, we humans proved so adept at shifting from preying on one species to others, that even before we invented agriculture we were already a bull in the ecological china shop for whom the normal ecological constraints on overhunting and grazing were largely absent. The agricultural and industrial revolutions greatly compounded the damage we have wreaked on the natural environment. And as we enter the third millennium AD, none should doubt that the six billion humans on earth can damage the biosphere irreparably in a number of different ways, and that most of us are still blissfully ignorant of the havoc we create and the dangers we court.

But environmentalists must be satisfied with something less than zero pollution and no depletion of nonrenewable resources. Zero pollution usually means not producing and consuming goods and services whose benefits far outweigh their social costs—including the damage pollution associated with producing and consuming them does to the environment. Never tapping nonrenewable resources is a debilitating constraint when it proves possible to develop substitutes before a nonrenewable resource runs out. Unless we plan to vacate planet earth, zero pollution and no resource depletion are impossible. But fortunately they are also unnecessary. A sustainable economy does not mean going back to scattered clans of hunter gatherers—who hunted most large mammal species to extinction in short order wherever they spread in any case! Humans will affect the environment—but we must learn to do so in ways that do not produce catastrophic climate change. Human activity will drive some species to extinction—but we must learn to do so in ways that minimize species extinction and do not destroy vital ecosystems. Human activity will affect fauna and flora—but we need to learn how to affect the living environment in ways that preserve a biosphere capable of sustaining human and non-human life of the same or higher quality that we presently enjoy. It would be foolish as well as impossible to strive to have no impact whatsoever on the biosphere. Instead our goal should be to have a benign impact instead of the malignant effect we have at present.

Our present interaction with the environment is not sustainable, and will not be sustainable as long as global capitalism persists. At present we are consigned to fighting rear-guard actions to minimize the environmental damage capitalism wreaks while organizing to replace the unsustainable economics of competition and greed with a sustainable system of equitable cooperation. By calling them "rear-guard actions" I do not mean to demean their importance. Without effective rear-guard actions there may be no tropical rain-forests to preserve by the time capitalism is replaced, and there may be no way to avert climate change if it has proceeded past the point of no return. After global capitalism is replaced, we will certainly need to prioritize immediate changes to prevent environmental collapse. But we will also need to plan the transition to a sustainable interaction with the environment with both efficiency and inter-generational equity in mind. Even if collapse is avoided, if the transition is too slow it will unfairly advantage the present generation at the expense of future generations, and unwisely reject opportunities to achieve future environmental benefits that exceed present social costs. But besides being impractical, insisting on a sustainable end state immediately imposes unnecessarily high costs on the present generation. Once capitalism has been replaced, we will need to calibrate non-zero levels of pollution and resource depletion over long periods of time, and the question will be if our new economic institutions are suited to helping us do this. I look forward to discussions with environmentalists of whether the specific features we have recently proposed in participatory economics are appropriate.

Spannos: What would be considered a judicious use of natural resources? And how would a participatory economy adjudicate pollution levels, resource depletion, and sustainability?

Hahnel: A judicious use of natural resources is one that preserves a natural environment that not only continues to be capable of supporting human and non-human life on the planet but provides future generations with a natural environment that is at least as beneficent as the one we enjoy today. However, this does not mean that every aspect of today's natural environment must be preserved exactly as it is today. As I explained above, that is impossible in any case, but fortunately unnecessary. New technologies must be developed to replace existing ones before the raw materials they require are used up. Stocks of renewable resources must be increased to compensate future generations for nonrenewable resources that are depleted. New technologies must be developed to replace existing ones that overtax the capacity of the environment to absorb waste from human activity. Ecological economists are correct to point out that depletion of natural "capital" cannot be substituted for entirely by more human produced "capital." On the other hand, a judicious use of the environment does include substituting some renewable forms of natural capital for some nonrenewable forms, and substituting some kinds of human made capital for some kinds of nonrenewable natural capital. But mostly a judicious use of the environment requires further development and rapid substitution of renewable energy systems for fossil fuels and nuclear energy, rapid de-automobilization of our mode of transportation, and rapid changes in consumption and living patterns.

A participatory economy determines levels of pollution and resource depletion through the participatory planning process. How does participatory planning internalize the negative external effects of pollution? In each iteration in the annual planning procedure there is an indicative price for every pollutant in every relevant region representing the current estimate of the damage done by releasing a unit of that pollutant into the region. What is a pollutant and what is not is decided by federations representing those who live in a region, who are advised by scientists employed in R&D operations run by the residents' federations. For example, if only the residents of Ward 2 of Washington, DC, feel they are adversely affected by a pollutant released in Ward 2, then Ward 2 is the relevant region. But if the federation representing residents of all wards of Washington, DC, decide that residents of all wards are affected by a pollutant released in Ward 2, then the entire city of Washington is the relevant region.

Whereas if the federation representing all who live in the Chesapeake Bay watershed feels that all who live in the watershed are adversely impacted by a pollutant released in Ward 2, then the relevant region includes the District of Columbia, Maryland, and parts of Virginia, West Virginia, Delaware, Pennsylvania, and New York.

If a worker council located in an affected region proposes to emit x units of a particular pollutant they are "charged" the indicative price for that pollutant in that region times x—just as they are charged y times the indicative price of a ton of steel if they propose to use y tons of steel as inputs in their production process, and just as they are charged z times the indicative price of an hour of welding labor if they propose to use z hours of welding labor. In other words, any pollutants the worker council proposes to emit are counted as part of the social cost of their proposal, just as the cost of making the steel inputs and the opportunity cost of the welding labor they propose to use are counted as part of the social cost of their proposal—all to be weighed against the social benefits of the outputs they propose to make. The consumer federation for the relevant region looks at the indicative price for a unit of every pollutant that impacts the region and decides how many units it wishes to allow to be emitted. The federation can decide they do not wish to permit any units of a pollutant to be emitted—in which case no worker council operating in the region will be allowed to emit any units of that pollutant. But, if the federation decides to allow x units of a pollutant to be emitted in the region, then the regional federation is "credited" with x times the indicative price for that pollutant.

Spannos: What does it mean for a consumer federation to be "credited?"

Hahnel: It means the federation will be permitted to buy more public goods for its members to consume than would otherwise be possible given the effort ratings of its members. Or, it means the members of the federation will be able to consume more individually than their effort ratings would otherwise warrant. In other words, residents of a region have a right not to be polluted if they so choose. On the other hand, if they choose to permit a certain amount of pollution to occur in their region, they are compensated for the damage they choose to endure. This procedure allows people in different regions to choose different tradeoffs between less pollution and more consumption.

Spannos: Can you explain the reasoning behind these tradeoffs?

Hahnel: Citizens in different communities might have different opinions about how damaging pollution is or beneficial consumption is. Or, even if all effects could be estimated with certainty, not all people feel the same about how much they value environmental preservation versus consumption, and citizens in different regions may feel differently on average as well. However, it is important to consider if this procedure would create the kind of "race to the bottom" effect environmentalists point out that local, as opposed to national, standards do in today's economies.

First, we should be clear what we are talking about. We are *not* talking about allowing a local community to set standards for pollutants that emanate from their community but affect other communities as well, i.e. affect a larger community. Our proposal is that in all cases the federation representing all those affected by a pollutant set the standard for that pollutant. Instead, we are talking about whether or not different communities of all those affected by any pollutant should be allowed to set different standards, or if standards for local pollutants should be set nationally. What we have proposed is that local communities be empowered to set their own standards, which may therefore differ from one another. And the question we are considering is whether or not this would generate a race to the bottom effect in local pollution standards.

The reason I do not think this would occur is because in a participatory economy there will be no significant differences in income and wealth between communities. In my opinion the reason a race to the bottom occurs in today's economies when local communities are allowed to set their own standards is that poor communities are unfairly tempted to permit greater environmental destruction to attract jobs and income, while only wealthy communities can afford the luxury of strict pollution controls. That is why I generally support national standards over local standards in today's economy—it is necessary to protect poorer communities from becoming dumping grounds. But in a participatory economy there will be no poor or rich communities, and therefore I believe any differences in local pollution standards communities might choose should simply reflect differences of opinion or values between residents of different communities.

Spannos: How effective is decentralized participatory planning in accounting for this?

Hahnel: The procedure I just described in the annual planning process protects the environment sufficiently only if present residents in the region of impact are the only ones who suffer adverse consequences. While this is the case for some pollutants, it is often the case that future generations bear a great deal of the cost of pollution today. The interests of future generations must be protected in the long-run participatory planning process and by an active environmental movement, as I explain below. However, before moving on to the long-run planning process and other features of a participatory economy that help protect the environment, I hasten to point out how much improvement the annual participatory planning process provides compared to market systems. Under traditional assumptions the procedure we have proposed will: (1) reduce pollution to "efficient" levels, (2) satisfy the "polluter pays principle," (3) compensate the actual victims of pollution for the damage they suffer, and (4) induce worker councils and consumer federations to truthfully reveal the benefits and costs of pollution. In other words, the procedure is what economists call "incentive compatible."

The fact that a participatory economy can treat pollution and environmental preservation in an "incentive compatible" way is crucial. When producers or consumers have incentives to ignore damaging effects on the environment of their choices about what and how to produce and consume, it is not incentive compatible. And when polluters and pollution victims lack incentives to reveal the true costs of pollution to victims, or the true benefits of pollution to consumers of the products produced jointly with the pollution, it is not incentive compatible. But in a participatory economy, since producers are charged for harmful emissions, the damage from pollution is included in the cost of a worker council proposal—giving producers just as much incentive to reduce pollution as any other cost of production. And since the indicative prices consumers are charged for goods in participatory planning include the costs of pollution associated with their production and consumption, there is just as much incentive for consumers to reduce consumption of goods that cause pollution as there is for them to reduce consumption of goods that require scarce productive resources or unpleasant labor to produce.

Spannos: But does the procedure yield an "efficient" indicative price for pollutants, i.e. a price that permits pollution as long as the benefits outweigh the costs, but prevents pollution whenever the costs outweigh the benefits?

Hahnel: In most cases it is reasonable to assume that as emission levels increase the costs to victims of additional pollution rise and the benefits to producers and consumers of additional pollution fall. In which case the efficient level of pollution is the level at which the cost of the last unit emitted is equal to the benefit from the last unit emitted. What will happen if the Iteration Facilitation Board, IFB, quotes during the planning process a price for a pollutant less than the "efficient" price, i.e. less than the price at which the last unit of emissions causes damage equal to its benefits? In this case the pollution victims, represented by their federation, will not find it in their interest to permit as much pollution as polluters would like, i.e. there will be excess demand for permission to pollute—and the IFB will increase the indicative price for the pollutant in the next round of planning. If the IFB quotes a price higher than the efficient price the federation representing pollution victims will offer to permit more pollution than polluters will ask to emit—and the IFB will decrease the indicative price in the next round. There is no incentive for pollution victims to pretend they are damaged either more or less than they really are, or for polluters to pretend they benefit more or less than they really do from being allowed to pollute, because each would fare worse by responding untruthfully than by responding truthfully to the indicative prices quoted by the IFB. Consequently, when the IFB adjusts the indicative prices for pollutants until requests to pollute equal permission to pollute, the efficient level of pollution is reached.

Spannos: What is the contrast with how markets handle pollution levels?

Hahnel: Uncorrected markets accomplish none of the four goals above. Markets corrected by pollution taxes could only reduce pollution to efficient levels and satisfy the "polluter pays" principle if the taxes were set equal to the magnitude of the negative external effect. But because markets are not incentive-compatible for polluters and pollution victims, markets provide no reliable way to estimate the magnitudes of efficient taxes for pollutants. Ambiguity over who has the property right, polluters or pollution victims; free-rider problems among multiple victims; and the transaction costs of forming and maintaining an effective coalition of pollution victims—each of whom is affected to a small but unequal degree—all combine to render market systems incapable of eliciting accurate information from pollution victims about the damages they suffer, or acting upon that information even if it were known. A participatory economy, on the other hand, awards victims an incontestable right *not* to be polluted, and arms them with a federation that includes every victim to express and represent their interests. Moreover, the participatory planning procedure makes it in the best interests of a federation's members for their federation to truthfully express the magnitude of the damage pollution does to its collective victims.

Since the market system contains no mechanism for generating accurate estimates of the damage from pollution, how can levels for pollution taxes be set in a market economy? Leaving the level of pollution taxes to be determined by the relative power of polluters and victims to influence politicians clearly has no claim to efficiency, and in an age of overweening corporate power invariably leads to taxes that are too low, and to too much pollution.

The crucial difference between participatory planning and market economies in this regard is that the participatory planning procedure generates accurate quantitative estimates of the costs and benefits of pollution while markets do not. Consequently, even "good faith" efforts to internalize the cost of pollution through taxes or tradable permit programs in market economies are "flying blind," and opportunities for "bad faith" intervention are ever present. Estimates from surveys and studies sometimes used to determine appropriate levels for pollution taxes are less accurate than the indicative prices for pollutants that would be automatically generated by the participatory planning procedure. Moreover, because everyone knows estimates based on surveys and studies are unreliable, it is possible for interested parties in market economies to challenge estimates they find inconvenient. Interested parties frequently finance alternative surveys and studies that arrive at predictably different conclusions regarding the damage from pollution and benefits from environmental preservation. Since, unlike participatory planning, market systems generate no "objective" estimates that could serve as arbiters, debates over the size of pollution taxes in market economies, or the number of pollution permits we should print up, invariably devolve into a cacophony of "he said, she said."

Spannos: While participatory planning may "settle accounts" efficiently and equitably concerning the environment for all those taking part in the various councils and federations, what protects the interests of future generations who cannot speak for themselves? How can we avoid intergenerational inequities and inefficiencies while preserving economic democracy when a great deal of the adverse effects of environmental deterioration are born by people who cannot be part of the democratic decision making process today?

Hahnel: The interests of future generations—which include the future state of the natural environment—must always be protected (or ignored) by the present generation. This is true whether it is a political or economic elite in the present generation that weighs the interests of the present generation against those of future generations, or a democratic decision-making process involving all members of the present generation that weighs the competing interests of different generations.

In a participatory economy intergenerational efficiency and equity regarding the environment must be achieved in the same way intergenerational efficiency and equity are achieved in all other regards—by means of restraints the present generation places on itself in its democratic deliberations concerning the long-run plan. In a participatory economy the same rules and procedures are used to determine the long-run plan as are used for the annual plan. Federations rather than individual worker and consumer councils play a larger role in long-run planning, as do R&D facilities attached to federations. But federations of workers propose and revise investments they would like to make in their own industries, together with federations of consumers who propose and revise what they would like to be able to consume more and less of in the future, in a process that settles on particular investment priorities and time tables. The long-run planning process also generates estimates of what economists call the marginal user costs of scarce resources, just as the annual planning process generates estimates of the social opportunity costs of using productive resources in a given year. When it is agreed through the long-run planning process that consumers five and fifty years down the road will have particular levels of consumption, long-run plans translate that commitment into a commitment to have particular amounts of scarce natural resources available five and fifty years from now, and these resource commitments are in turn translated into estimates of user costs for resources in annual plans distributing their depletion judiciously over time. In broad terms, each annual plan is hammered out within constraints imposed by choices already agreed to in the long-run planning process, which is where issues of intergenerational equity and environmental sustainability are settled.

For example, if the long-run plan calls for more overall investment, this decreases the amount of consumption available in this year's annual plan. If the long-run plan calls for reducing the automobile fleet and expanding rail and bus service in the future, this reduces the amount of investment and productive resources this year's annual plan is permitted to allocate to worker councils making automobiles, and increases the amount of investment and resources to be allocated to worker councils making trains. And if the long-run plan calls for a 25 percent reduction in carbon emissions over five years, the national consumer federation must reduce the amount of carbon emissions it permits accordingly in each of the next five annual plans. Major changes in the energy, transportation, and housing sectors, as well as conversions from polluting to "green" technologies and products, are all determined by the long-run planning process. When consumer federations demand more green space and improvements in air and water quality for the future during this process, investment priorities in energy, transportation, and housing are affected, and time tables for phasing in "green" technologies and products are settled on.

Spannos: Sometimes, when the present generation draws up the long-run plan, they are making choices that affect only the future generation, i.e., sticking with the cars and trains example, which will people of the future transport themselves in? But often when the present generation agrees on the long-run plan they make choices that favor one generation over another. Will the present generation consume less so more can be invested and future generations will be able to consume more? Will the present generation consume less so carbon emissions can be reduced more and future generations will suffer less from climate change? Will the present generation consume less so "green" technologies and products can be phased in more quickly and future generations can enjoy increased environmental amenities sooner rather than later?

Hahnel: I can think of no way to guarantee that members of the present generation will take the interests of future generations sufficiently to heart, or, for that matter, choose wisely for them even when there is no intergenerational conflict of interest. Whether or not the present generation decides on a long-run plan democratically or autocratically, there is no way to guarantee they will not make mistakes that damage future generations: maybe replacing cars with trains for our descendants is a mistake because solar powered cars would be as environmentally friendly as trains and more convenient. Nor is there any way to make sure the present generation will not behave like Louis XV and simply decide, *apre mois l'deluge*. I can hope that people who practice economic justice diligently among themselves, as a participatory economy requires, will · practice it on behalf of their children, grandchildren, and great-grandchildren as well. I can hope that people used to permitting pollution only when the benefits outweigh the costs will apply the same principle in their long-run planning and include the costs to those they know will follow them. And I can hope that, when people have choices posed in ways that make perfectly clear when they would be favoring themselves unfairly at the expense of their descendants, they will be too ashamed to do so. Long-run participatory planning is designed to make issues of intergenerational equity and efficiency as clear as possible. It is also designed to estimate the detrimental and beneficial effects of economic choices on the environment accurately and incorporate them into the overall costs and benefits that must be weighed. But even so, there is no guarantee that future generations and the environment might not be slighted. Some will have to speak up in the long-run participatory planning process when they think others in their generation are unmindful of future generations. And some will have to speak up during long-run planning when they think others are neglectful of the future of the environment.

Finally, there are other features of a participatory economy that favor environmental protection. (1) An egalitarian distribution of wealth and income means nobody will be so poor and desperate that they cannot afford to prioritize environmental preservation over material consumption. There will be no destitute colonists cutting down and burning valuable rain-forests because they have no other way to stay alive. There will be no poverty-stricken local communities who acquiesce to host unsafe toxic waste dumps because they are desperate for additional income. An egalitarian distribution of income and wealth also means nobody will be so rich they can buy private environmental amenities while lobbying and voting to permit the public environment to deteriorate. (2) A system that minimizes the use of material incentives and emphasizes rewards for social serviceability greatly diminishes the environmentally destructive effects of conspicuous consumption. (3) An allocation system that provides productive resources to workers as long as the social benefits of their work exceed the social costs—including the environmental costs and the cost of lost leisure—eliminates the competitive rat race for producers to accumulate and grow despite the environmental consequences, and despite the fact that after a certain point our extra consumption is not worth the leisure we sacrifice. In other words, unlike capitalist economies, and communist economies ruled by leaders who chose to compete with them in a "growth race," there is no bias toward injudicious growth in a participatory economy. In two books, *Overworked American: The Unexpected Decline of Leisure*[9] and *The Overspent American: Why We Want What We Don't Need*,[10] Juliet Schor dissected the irrationality of over work and over consumption in America, tracing its causes to incentives embedded in the economic system. None of the perverse incentives she documents would be present in a participatory economy.

However, in the end there is nothing a democratic economy can do to prevent environmental abuse if people make unwise or selfish choices. This can happen because people are simply unaware of the detrimental environmental consequences of their choices, or underestimate their severity. This can occur because the present generation is selfish and cares more about itself than about future generations. Or, if one believes that other species have rights or interests that deserve to be taken into account, it can be because humans refuse to do so. An active environmental movement educating and agitating for its causes will be necessary in a participatory economy, and the health of the biosphere will depend on this movement's wisdom, strength, and persuasive powers.

Spannos: Radical environmentalists and others have proposed small scale, self-reliant, community-based economics; even "bioregionalism." What is the logic of environmental sustainability in these proposals and how do they compare with parecon?

Hahnel: Some who reject capitalism, authoritarian planning, and market socialism offer a vision of largely self-reliant, local economies governed by the kind of direct democracy once used in New England town meetings. A growing number of radical environmentalists and young anarchists argue that only reducing the scale of economic institutions, and increasing self-sufficiency of local communities, can satisfy libertarian goals, reduce alienation, and promote ecological balance. They seek to avoid the negative repercussions of both markets and planning by eliminating the "problem" these allocation mechanisms address—coordinating a division of labor among geographically dispersed groups. By decentralizing large, national economies into small, autonomous economic communities they also hope to promote face-to-face democratic decision-making and create incentives for local communities to take the environmental effects of their activities into account. They argue that, while participatory democracy doesn't work in large groups where people do not know one another and cannot discuss things in person, it can work in small communities. They also reason that once the consequences of choices all fall "in my back yard," the IMBY principle will force local communities to protect their environment. Of course, just as there are different models of market socialism and democratic planning, community-based economics comes in different flavors: Social Ecology and Libertarian Municipalism (see Murray Bookchin, *Post Scarcity Anarchism*,[11] Murry Bookchin and Janet Biehl, *The Politics of Social Ecology*,[12] and Howard Hawkins, "Community Control, Workers' Control, and the Cooperative Commonwealth")[13] an ecological society through democratic pluralism (See David Korten, *The Post-Corporate World: Life After Capitalism*,[14] and Paul Hawken, *The Ecology of Commerce*;[15] Buddhist Economics (See E. F. Schumacher, *Small Is Beautiful*,)[16]; bioregionalism (See Kirkpatrick Sale, "Principles of Bioregionalism")[17]; ecological economics (See Herman Daly and Joshua Farley, *Ecological Economics*);[18] and eco-socialism (See Joel Kovel, *The Enemy of Nature*,[19] and Roy Morrison, *Ecological Democracy*)[20] are some of the versions, and they all differ from one another in significant ways. While I sympathize with the participatory and ecological goals of radicals who propose small scale, democratic autarky, all versions of community-based economics suffer from a major problem. Unlike many versions of market socialism and democratic planning, no "model" of community-based economics is a real model in the sense that it specifies rules and procedures for how to make all the decisions that must be made in any economy. For this reason all versions of community-based economics are really "visions," not coherent "models."

Sometimes proponents are blissfully unaware that they have failed to address important issues that will inevitably arise. Sometimes proponents refer to the lack of specific, concrete answers regarding how something would be decided as a virtue compared to what they criticize as "deterministic" models of market socialism and democratic planning. But this response misses the point. It is impossible to evaluate a proposal for how to run the economy until it is a full and complete proposal. This failure should not be confused with the problem of explaining how to move from today's capitalist system to a community-based economy. Advocates of community-based economics often address this issue more extensively than they answer exactly how they propose particular issues be decided once we get to a community-based economy. Nor should the failure be confused with lack of speculation about what kinds of decisions they imagine people will make in a community-based economy. Since proponents of community-based economics are motivated by strong convictions that people need to choose radically different technologies and products, need to change their priorities regarding leisure versus work, and need to accept the necessity of zero growth of "material throughput," authors usually write at length about the differences between the decisions they believe will be made in their community-based economy and the decisions made in today's capitalist economies. The problem is that any professional economist knows there are certain categories of decisions that must be made in any economy, and until a proposal is comprehensive enough to specify how a proponent suggests these necessary decisions be made—i.e. until we have what economists call a formal model—it is literally impossible to evaluate whether or not the economy would do what its proponents claim it would.

One manifestation of this problem is that when push comes to shove, no version of community-based economics proposes that communities be entirely self-sufficient— for understandable reasons. In other words, it turns out that autonomous communities are only semi-autonomous. And when it comes down to explaining precisely how the "semi" part be handled, we invariably find no answer beyond hand waving and declarations of faith that democratic communities can work this out between themselves satisfactorily. Of course if communities were completely self-sufficient there would be inefficient duplication of efforts and inequities. But in the likely event that communities rediscovered the advantages of some division of labor, no proposal in this literature—precisely because they are not truly models—provides an answer to the question of how communities which are no longer completely autonomous should arrange their division of labor. How do communities decide how much a division of labor they want to engage in? What if one community wants a greater division of labor than another community wants? For example, a careful reading of Bookchin's vision of Libertarian Municipalism[21] reveals that no community must acquiesce to a greater division of labor than it wants to. While this is a specific rule, it is a problematic one. This rule means the community that wants the least division of labor among communities can impose its preference over the preferences of all other communities. Why a community that is better endowed with natural, human, and/or physical capital would not be tempted— even if unconsciously—to take unfair advantage of this veto right is unclear.

Even if communities can agree on a division of labor with other communities, how do they go about deciding how to distribute the burdens and benefits of this division of labor? How do they jointly manage the division of labor? Should goods and services not produced by every community be traded in free markets? If so, why would this not lead to the usual litany of inequities, instabilities, and inefficiencies that advocates of community-based economics criticize in capitalism and market socialism? Should communities attempt to plan mutually beneficial economic relations? If so, how would they go about it, and how would the authoritarian dynamics of central planning be avoided? Simply asserting that communities will decide all this "democratically" is not a good enough answer.

Joel Kovel's "model" of eco-socialism, defined as an expanding network of "ecological ensembles," is in many ways even more opaque than other so-called models in this literature. In truth it is more an interesting and insightful proposal about movement strategy than a coherent post-capitalist economic model. But Kovel provides an excellent critique of the disadvantages of extreme localism:

> A pure community, or even "bioregional" economy is a fantasy. Strict localism belongs to the aboriginal stages of society: it cannot be reproduced today, and even if it could, it would be an ecological nightmare at present population levels. Imagine the heat losses from a multitude of dispersed sites, the squandering of scarce resources, the needless reproduction of effort. ... This is by no means to be interpreted as a denial of the great value of small-scale and local endeavors. ... It is rather an insistence that the local and particular exists in and through the global whole; that there needs to be, in any economy, an interdependence whose walls are not confinable to any township or bioregion; and that, fundamentally, the issue is the relationship of parts to the whole.[22]

Proposals for community-based economics simply fail to address this fundamental issue. In the end, the problem of devising desirable allocation mechanisms to coordinate the division of labor between communities that are not completely self-sufficient won't go away, and advocates of autonomous economic communities provide no coherent or satisfactory answer to how they would coordinate cooperation between communities that always turn out to be only "semi-autonomous" under careful cross examination.

Advocates of community-based economics also fail to provide concrete answers to crucial questions about how communities would make different kinds of internal decisions. Even in a community of several thousand people there will be different groups of workers and consumers. There will be different kinds of economic decisions to make. It is impractical for the whole community to vote on each and every economic question that comes up. What would the agenda for such a meeting look like? Who would be responsible for setting this agenda? Moreover, a democratic vote of a community does not provide its citizens with decision-making power in proportion to the degree they are affected in cases where not all members of the community are equally affected by a particular economic choice. Nor can all decisions be left to the work groups who form within these communities. Many of the decisions groups of workers make affect other groups of workers and must be coordinated with consumers in the community as well. Proponents of community-based economics unfortunately have precious little to say about how these internal decision-making problems should be solved. Saying that ultimate power over all economic decisions resides in the community assembly where all have voice and one vote is not a good enough answer.

Not all proponents of community-based economics reject private enterprise and markets altogether. Some whose vision includes space for private firms alongside worker-owned cooperatives, and for markets when "properly socialized," seem to do so because they confuse what we must tolerate during the transition from today's economic system based on competition and greed with economic relations that are truly consistent with equitable cooperation itself. Others seem to mistakenly believe that private enterprise and markets are compatible with equitable cooperation. They fail to realize, in the words of Joel Kovel, that combining private enterprise and market forces with people seeking to practice equitable cooperation is like trying to raise weasels and chickens in the same pen. More radical visions of community-based economics do reject private enterprise and markets entirely. Like those of us who support participatory economics, advocates of libertarian municipalism, eco-socialism, and communitarian anarchism all argue that there is no place for either private enterprise or markets in a truly desirable economy.

However, all who espouse community-based economics—whether inclined to abolish or to retain markets and private enterprise to some degree—are staunchly democratic, egalitarian, and pro-environment. Because advocates of community-based economics and supporters of participatory economics share these same values, I believe as discussion continues we will become even closer allies than many of us already are. I see nothing in a participatory economy that I believe should displease proponents of community-based economics. In fact, I think those attracted to community-based economics will find that many problems for which they lack solutions are nicely resolved by some features of a participatory economy. In my opinion there is little if any disagreement over values, and much of the criticism of participatory economics voiced by advocates of one or another version of community-based economics is based on a misreading and misinterpretation of participatory economics. In other words, I regard most modern, libertarian, communalist visionaries as allies—like our council communist, syndicalist, anarchist, and guild socialist forbearers—and ask them to consider the procedures of participatory planning when they think further about how they would coordinate economic relations among semi-autonomous communities, and how they would propose communities comprised of different groups of workers and consumers apportion decision-making authority internally as well.

Spannos: What role would environmental activism, groups like Greenpeace, or future environmental political parties, say the Green Party, have in a future participatory society?

Hahnel: Substituting the institutions of a participatory economy—worker and consumer councils and federations, participatory planning, jobs balanced for empowerment and desirability, and remuneration on the basis of effort or sacrifice—for the institutions of capitalism—private enterprise, markets, hierarchical decision making, and remuneration according to the market value of the contribution of the capital one owns—does not guarantee that the environment will be adequately protected, much less restored. A participatory economy gives people decision-making power to the degree they are affected. A participatory economy eliminates perverse incentives that make it in the individual interest of decision-makers to overexploit and despoil the environment. Unlike capitalism and communism, each of which contain powerful incentives for decision-makers to ignore adverse affects on the environment—and unlike market socialism, which is little better suited to accounting for environmental externalities, avoiding conspicuous consumption, and avoiding injudicious growth—in a participatory economy it is in the individual interests of decision makers to treat the environment wisely. There is no bias favoring growth of output over growth of leisure. Status cannot be achieved through conspicuous consumption. There are no perverse incentives that make it in the interest of producers or consumers to over pollute because of effects that are neglected by market decision making but accounted for by decision making in the participatory planning process. Instead, those who benefit from environmental preservation have the power necessary to protect their interests. Long-term plans place constraints on annual plans in ways that balance the interests of present and future generations. And the interests of future generations—which depend on environmental preservation—are given every opportunity to receive their due in the long-run participatory planning process. But a participatory economy provides no guarantee that people will treat the environment wisely, which is to say it does not make the environmental movement obsolete. A participatory economy merely eliminates perverse incentives that create biases against environmental preservation and restoration on a playing field where people weigh their competing goals democratically and fairly.

Therefore, an active environmental movement will be necessary in a participatory economy to argue for the importance of environmental protection and restoration. Many who a participatory economy empowers for the first time will be ignorant of their own true interests regarding the environment. The environmental movement will have to teach newly enfranchised voters in a participatory economy why environmental preservation is important to their well-being. Environmentalists will have to speak up in worker and consumer councils and federations, pointing out the true benefits of environmental preservation and the magnitude of the costs of environmental degradation. When consumer federations decide how much local pollution they are willing to tolerate for a given level of compensation, environmentalists in those federations must point out all the damage the pollution causes, and convince their fellow citizens not to permit too much. During the long-run planning process environmentalists must speak up when they believe others are insufficiently prioritizing the interests of future generations by failing to prioritize environmental restoration. Whenever environmentalists believe that people are being overly anthropocentric—i.e. considering only effects of decisions on humans rather than considering the interests of other species and the biosphere itself as well—they will have to argue their case and try to convince others. And if there are going to be environmentalists to do all this in worker and consumer councils and federations and long-run planning sessions, there will have to be an active environmental movement to sensitize, educate, and empower its members to effectively carry out the work of environmental consciousness raising.

Finally, if environmentalists believe that exemplary actions to obstruct mistakes, or to call attention to environmental concerns they believe are going unheeded by an ignorant or selfish majority are necessary, then organizations like Greenpeace that are willing to engage in civil disobedience in defense of the environment will have an important role to play in a participatory economy as well. Real-world economic democracy means more than voting power in proportion to the degree one is affected. It also means discussion and debate when there are differences of opinion, and civil disobedience can be an important part of "discussion and debate" in a real economic democracy as well. When we chant "this is what democracy looks like" while marching in the streets and engaging in civil disobedience, we need to realize that we really mean it! That is also what democracy will look like in a participatory economy and society as well.

But I should also point out another aspect of the relationship between the environmental movement and participatory economics: participatory economics will never replace capitalism until a number of progressive social movements come to see replacing capitalism with participatory economics as necessary to achieve their goals. Until the labor movement, the consumer movement, the anticorporate movement, the poor people's movement, the global justice movement, the civil rights/anti-racist movement, the women's movement, the gay/lesbian/bisexual movement, the peace movement, and the environmental movement all grow in size and come to support something like a participatory economy, we will not succeed in replacing the unsustainable economics of competition and greed with the sustainable economics of equitable cooperation in the first place. Strengthening the environmental movement and environmental activism are necessary parts of a successful strategy for achieving participatory economics, and the environmental movement and environmental activists must continue to function once a participatory economy is established to achieve environmental protection and preservation.

(Endnotes)

1   Michael Albert and Robin Hahnel *Socialism Today and Tomorrow* (South End Press, 1981)
2   Michael Albert and Robin Hahnel *The Political Economy of Participatory Economics* (Princeton University Press, 1991)
3   Michael Albert and Robin Hahnel *Looking Forward: Participatory Economics for the Twenty-First Century* (South End Press, 1991)
4   Carl Boggs "A New Economy," *The Progressive* (May, 1992): 40
5   Howard Hawkins "Review of Looking Forward and The Political Economy of Participatory Economics," *Left Green Notes* (August–September 1991): 14
6   Robin Hahnel *Economic Justice and Democracy: From Competition to Cooperation* (Routledge Press, 2005)
7   Edward Bellamy *Looking Backward: 2000–1887* (William Ticknor, 1888)
8   William Morris *News From Nowhere* (*Commonweal*, 1890)
9   Juliet Schor *Overworked American: The Unexpected Decline of Leisure* (Basic Books, 1992)
10 Juliet Schor *The Overspent American: Why We Want What We Don't Need* (Basic Books, 1998)

11   Murray Bookchin *Post Scarcity Anarchism* (AK Press, third ed., 2004, original 1970)
12   Murray Bookchin and Janet Biehl *The Politics of Social Ecology* (Black Rose Books, 1998)
13   Howard Hawkins "Community Control, Workers' Controls, and the Cooperative Common-
      wealth" *Society and Nature*, Vol. 1 no. 3 (1993)
14   David Korten *The Post-Corporate World: Life After Capitalism* (Kumarian Press, 1999)
15   Paul Hawken *The Ecology of Commerce* (Harper Collins, 1993)
16   E. F. Schumacher *Small is Beautiful* (Harper and Row, 1973)
17   In J. Mander and E. Goldsmith, eds. *The Case Against the Global Economy* (Sierra Club Books,
      1996)
18   Herman Daly and Joshua Farley *Ecological Economics* (Island Press, 2004)
19   Joel Kovel *The Enemy of Nature: The End of Capitalism or the End of the World?* (Zed Books,
      2002)
20   Roy Morrison *Ecological Democracy* (South End Press, 1995)
21   Bookchin and Biehl *The Politics of Social Ecology*
22   Kovel *The Enemy of Nature*

PART

II

Revolutionizing Everyday Life

Chapter 6

A CALL TO ARTISTS: SUPPORT PARECON

Jerry Fresia

A HISTORY OF ART over the last hundred years, not as the history of the product, the piece, but as the history of decision making within our industry, is the history of investors acquiring greater control over the distribution, definition, and making of art products—and thus over who we are. It is the history of power slipping further from the people who make the piece to the people who profit from the piece. Yes, there are individual art stars aplenty. But as workers in an industry, we are being ground into dust.

I would argue that our responsibility as artists is to help invent institutions that protect and expand the opportunity for autonomous creative work. Our responsibility, in light of our current situation, is to help build an economy sympathetic to the notion that art, as access to a creative life, is the province of every human being.

With this in mind, let the following commentary serve as a call to artists to endorse the idea of a participatory economy and in particular the institutional design laid out in Michael Albert's *Parecon: Life After Capitalism*.[1]

Unless we make building socially just institutions part of our understanding of what it means to be an artist, all the verbiage about "content" and all the pieces of art dedicated to peace, equality, and a better way of life will, in the end, serve only as evidence that we got it wrong, that we fundamentally misunderstood what it is we do. All that stuff will serve as evidence that when we needed to and when we were called upon to build better ways of being creative as a people, we thought that art was simply about things.

A Commentary and Call to Action

For the past fifteen years I have made my living entirely as a visual artist. I have been able to do this only by exhibiting outside of the institutionalized academic-museum-gallery system. I exhibited outdoors in the parks of San Francisco so I could control the distribution of my work and enjoy direct and personal relationships with my audience. Additionally, for a ten-year period, I worked with public and private officials and artists in reinventing this mode of exhibition to the point where it was something quite unexpectedly professional, wonderful, enchanting, and lucrative—as opposed to the conventional "swap meet" set of exhibitions that one might expect to find outside established venues.

However, the model was impossible to sustain for a simple reason. Too few artists wanted to take time from their work to build an organization. Most artists had only one set of interests: making their art and promoting themselves within established institutions. In other words, the dominant modus operandi of the artist, as I know it, is the artist as individual and as entrepreneur. However, within the art industry today, entrepreneurialism cannot lead to ownership of any consequence. Decision making with regard to distribution (exhibition), what counts as important art, and what gets funded is not in our hands no matter how "good" any of our art might be. The decisions that structure our life chances are in the hands of an investor class, an oligarchy, that exercises substantial influence over boards of trustees, both academic and museum, non-profit foundations, public art commissions, and the galleries and auction houses that follow in their wake.

The individualist/entrepreneurial approach cannot lead but to utter dependency—a dependency on those who own galleries and control exhibition spaces, on critics, on those who control foundations or access to education, on those who direct competitions, on curators. This list is endless. And because we have become so thoroughly dependent on the institutions within the art industry, we are compelled to adopt as our own the very ideas, assumptions, and practices that the oligarchy uses within those industries that require our marginalization in the first place.

If we provide free inventories to galleries before they take 50 or 60 percent of any sale, we say that that is the nature of things. If the work we make following art school is not saleable it is because the public is uneducated. If the cognoscenti define important work as conceptual—that is, a nonvisual visual art—we make an effort to understand, not to challenge. When we are told that only twelve of us in a city of nearly one million people (San Francisco) can make a living in the gallery system because we have chosen a difficult way of life, we believe it.

It gets worse. According to these cognoscenti, art is not *a* thing of value, it is *the* thing of value. We produce that incredibly valuable thing and we are tagged as a class of workers with the moniker "starving." And we accept it! Unlike other trained professionals, we have no expectation of having health insurance, a modicum of security, the ability to buy a home, have kids, send them to college, go out to dinner regularly, or even travel comfortably. Instead, our expectation is that we will have a second job or a partner to support us in order to do the work that transforms the filthy rich into better people.

My argument is that we toil in isolation and buy into the notion that the average person cannot really understand our noble sacrifice, or that it is beyond the intelligence and aesthetic sensibility of the public, because we have lost touch with the history of our profession, particularly as it relates to our life outside the studio. In order to become free artists we need to become free from the institutions that require our marginalization. We need to get back into the game of defining art ourselves, of teaching art independently of universities, of building movements with other members of the community and other artists, of controlling exhibitions, and of enjoying direct and personal relationships with the public that artists from Michelangelo to the Abstract Expressionists enjoyed. In short, we need to build alternative institutions that permit us to have say over what we do, what we make, and how it is distributed.

Let's take a look, then, at parecon, a well-thought-out proposal for a participatory economy that would better serve the interests of artists as artists and as living, breathing members of communities. Briefly, I would like to touch upon the concepts of Worker Councils, Balanced Job Complexes, and Participatory Planning, and how each might impact our lives.

Worker Councils

Another word for participatory economics is democracy. Together with other artists and members of the community in which we live, we would decide what work would be produced and for what purpose. I can hear artists screaming bloody murder as I type: we don't want a "big brother" telling us what to do. Agreed. But we haven't been doing too well with the director either. In fact, it would be hypocritical to inveigh against a workers' council without first knowing something about how we are bossed around right now. Consider this, following World War II, a tiny handful of economic elites, by virtue of their right as property owners, together with their political and cultural allies, were able to direct and shape the lives of visual artists in the following ways:

• Important art and important careers—read a modicum of remuneration— had to be divorced from European influences.

• Art that suggested political commentary had to be displaced by art that suggested psychological angst—read abstraction.

• The teaching of art had to be removed from the studio and jurisdiction of the master artist and placed into the hands of corporate representatives or boards of trustees and into the university.

• The studio itself, once a locus of social and public activity, a place of exhibition and distribution, had to become the studio of the isolated, angst-probing artist. By the 1970s, the studio, as the workplace of the individual artist, was transformed further. It now resembled a factory, where the studio floor was the work site of artists' assistants who followed the direction of artists who in turned collaborated with the investor/collector.

• By the late 1960s painting and easel painting, as far as "important work" was concerned, were declared "dead," thus weakening the individual artist's access to and control over his or her means of production.

The question is this: What is it that we want? With worker councils, we, as participant decision makers, would enjoy far more power over our work and our lives than we have yet experienced.

Balanced Job Complexes

The principle central to this concept is a principle that most artists probably already accept: creative work is the province of every human being. As an artist interested in finding more people responsive to what I do, I find it a terribly exciting possibility that everyone might have the opportunity to engage in creative work themselves. Indeed, if my chances of making a living as a creative person are under assault, as in fact they are, it is in my interest to have involved as many people as is possible in creative work; work not only where workers also make decisions but work where the creative process is central to the work process.

In helping to design balanced job complexes we would have much to contribute. Our work is not governed by the clock. We make time for reflection. An aesthetic dimension is always paramount. Mind and body are not separate. Could it be a rewarding experience to play a meaningful role helping to construct ways of working rooted in the knowledge we possess? Might it be fulfilling to have this kind of ongoing discussion with the broader community? Might it broaden the interest in what we do? Would these types of personal contacts be a welcomed balance to the isolation of the studio?

Besides, artists are already deeply involved in what could be described as a balanced job complex. If we are painters, we are already photographers, web designers, mailing list managers, marketers, promoters, frame-makers, grant writers, and expert application makers. If we have jobs in addition to making art we are even more extended. In a participatory economy, much of the competitive work, such as making applications, might be reduced in favor of teaching and sharing our knowledge of design, color, writing, song, dance, theater, and various other aesthetic considerations with a population who have not had the opportunity, in their everyday lives, to explore the various ways they could creatively and rewardingly accomplish socially useful tasks.

Participatory Planning

Participatory Planning is the negotiation among workers' and consumers' councils that is intended to replace the market system of distribution, a system of distribution based upon price and one's ability to pay. It is important to recognize that while various market relations have existed practically forever, for most of human history social relations (kinship, communal, religious, and political) existed apart from the relationships of buying and selling. But we happen to live in a very unusual period, historically—one where virtually all social relations are embedded within the market, where decisions about what we make, who gains access to it, how we live and use our time are determined by the impersonal imperatives of price and profit. But this is an historical anomaly, a convention that can be changed.

Second, the irony for artists in this regard is that the market relations that we enter in order to gain access to the material means of life are skewed to the advantage of the very wealthy largely because planning mechanisms already have been inserted within the market. But these planning mechanisms, unlike the participatory model that Albert and Hahnel advocate, are exclusionary and elitist. If you have strong misgivings about challenging market forces of distribution, as an artist you ought to be quite upset already. The investors and owners of culture are quite adept at using an array of planning mechanisms—art commissions and auction houses that utilize market forces, for example—to control the goose that lays the golden egg.

The question becomes, If market-planning mechanisms are already in place, why do we permit them to be controlled by a few whose interests run counter to ours? And arguably against the interests of many? If we are the goose that lays the golden egg, how does it come about that our precious golden egg is taken from us? With our cooperation?

My suspicion is that we are too busy making art to take a good look at the institutional matrix that has us by the short hair. One example, along these lines, is our acceptance of one planning mechanism that was designed to mitigate against popular influence in the arts: the public benefit corporation, better known as the non-profit.

Non-profits are planning mechanisms. They are run by community elites, generally with artist representation, for the purpose of protecting culture within a market environment from popularizing influences. The sociologist Paul DiMaggio notes that non-profits, while claiming service to the entire community, actually function to mystify art and separate the community from the world of art and artists.[2] Alice Goldfarb Marquis concurs and points to the "high-art" worlds of museums, operas, and symphonies where financial and social elites use the non-profit planning mechanisms for the same purpose. She notes that this capturing of culture is often accomplished by "pasting an altruistic, morally chase veneer over basically self-serving activities."[3] Wealthy donors and trustees, she explains further, have long aligned themselves with "liberal, reformist intellectuals and critics who see themselves as guardians of high culture" and who have campaigned "against almost every artistic innovation of the past two centuries."[4]

The non-profit as planning instrument by the investor class may be most visible in the creation of "art centers." In the creation of the Lincoln Center in New York City and the Yerba Buena Center for the Arts in San Francisco, for example, redevelopment interests, together with cultural elites and non-profits, use the rhetoric of public access around art to acquire monopoly control over the distribution of the art product. Their "art centers" then become the site for glitzy chic-chic art events in order to anchor the array of upscale hotels, restaurants, and retailers that return competitive dividends to real estate investors. Many of us work with non-profits and do our best to make them function in a way that serves the community. But I ask, Is it not the case that we are always poor? That we are always beseeching the rich? That our non-profits are not dedicated to challenging the starving artist paradigm or amplifying public involvement as decision makers?

Artists today cannot have it both ways. We cannot run from parecon-type market alternatives in the name of artistic freedom and at the same time play our role as sidekicks within existing planning mechanisms that permit the wealthiest among us to direct and control all that we do.

Summary

I am not criticizing the intention of artists. We contribute much to rallies, marches, and the numerous exhibitions, plays, music, and stories that inveigh against war and injustice. My concern is that this art spirit is not part of an institutional critique. We need a critique of our institutions so that we can develop a concrete strategy to build new ones. Artists opposed to war, to use one example, might be more effective by using their creative talents to build institutions that make the kind of war in Iraq impossible. The good artist and the justice good artists seek cannot exist unless we first create institutions that require both.

Our history is replete with such transformations. While the Impression period is often referred to as the movement where visual art was first ridiculed and later accepted as prescient, let us recall that it was ridiculed not by the unsophisticated masses in need of education but by the educated and powerful whose control over culture had to be eliminated. Impressionism was a frontal assault by artists upon art institutions that, in the words of the rebellious artists, erected artificial barriers between themselves and the public.

Ditto jazz, rock n' roll, and Beethoven. Recall also that Michelangelo said of a statue that it was only by the "light of the public square" that it could be judged. The point is that we as artists are of the public and we are of the community. No better. No worse. And together it is necessary for us to regain control over our lives in order to become the artists we wish to become. Our best chance is to create the institutions necessary to give our voice best purchase. Democratic institutions. Participatory economics. Parecon.

Finally it is important, I believe, to explore further the artistic sensibilities that were widespread one hundred years ago, sensibilities that suggested revolutions required dancing, that suggested that, if what we create is not a better world, what is the point of our work? Creating better institutions, ones in which our voices are heard meaningfully, is both our responsibility and a pragmatic solution. It must also be our art. As Bertolt Brecht said:

Canalising a river
Rafting a fruit tree
Educating a person
Transforming a state
These are instances of fruitful criticism
And at the same time instances of art."[5]

(Endnotes)

1   Michael Albert *Parecon: Life After Capitalism* (Verso, 2003)
2   Paul DiMaggio, ed., *Nonprofit Enterprise in the Arts: Studies in Mission and Constraint* (Oxford University Press, 1986): 46–47
3   Alce Goldfarb Marquis *Art Lessons: Learning from the Rise and Fall of Public Arts Funding* (Basic Books 1995): 4
4   Ibid.
5   John Willet and John Manheim, eds. "On the Critical Attitude," *Bertolt Brecht, Poems 1913–1956* (Methuen, 1976): 308–309

Chapter 7

FROM SELF-MANAGED MOVEMENTS TO SELF-MANAGED CITY

Tom Wetzel

IN THE EARLY 20th century, radical workplace activists put forward the idea that, in building workplace organizations or unions self-managed by rank-and-file workers, and in challenging the bosses for control of production, they were "building the new society in the shell of the old." They envisioned rank-and-file self-management of the union or organization of workplace struggle as foreshadowing grassroots bodies through which workers would manage production in a non-market, post-capitalist society.

The assumption is that self-management, having control over your life, having a say over the decisions that affect you, should be central to our vision of a post-capitalist future.

But self-management isn't relevant only to our control over our work, the sphere of production, but to the sphere of consumption as well. What sorts of housing do we want to live in? What sorts of services do we want available in our neighborhoods? What do we want the layout of the city to be? What products do we want produced? Our economic vision needs a means of providing people with a say over consumption decisions that affect them.

This idea is reflected in the participatory economics vision which proposes both workers' councils and neighborhood consumption councils as building blocks of self-management. For cities, participatory economics poses the possibility of a horizontal, self-managing regionalism in planning investment in transportation and other infrastructure as well as in meeting social needs such as housing, child care, and health care.

Participatory planning would mean that people, starting in their local councils, would develop proposals for what they want to be produced. Both as individuals, for private consumption, as well as for items of collective consumption, we figure out what we want to consume, and what work we want to do. These proposals filter outward through organizations over a larger geographic scope insofar as they have impact on a larger area. Through a process of give-and-take between workers and consumers, proposals would be refined into a comprehensive agenda for social production.

Land use decisions are also a part of this give-and-take process, and issues like the relationship between housing and worksites become a negotiated process among production groups and neighborhood councils. For example, would people most prefer to move back in the direction of the pre-capitalist artisanal city, with work and housing in close proximity? Well, if so, we would expect that to be reflected in decisions about investment in the built environment.

Participatory economics implies elimination of some of the main forces that shape the capitalist city.

Worksite decisions would not be simply a question of what the CEO thinks best. Spatial sorting of the population by class and race in the capitalist city is built on huge disparities in income and power that would no longer exist in an economic system where remuneration is based on work effort or sacrifice and where corporate-style hierarchies no longer rule.

From a participatory economic point of view, the principle of self-management says that each person is to have a say over decisions that affect them in proportion as they are affected. This implies there can no longer be external negative impacts like air pollution that are simply imposed dictatorially on people without those people having a say about it. The huge environmental burden of polluting uses, such as over-reliance on private auto transport, will have to be properly taken into account in a self-managing, participatory economy.

We can envision participatory economics emerging as a real alternative through the development of mass, self-managing social movements, from a resurgent, self-managed form of worker unionism in the sphere of production to self-managed tenant organizations and mass organizations of all kinds.

Housing is a major area of consumption that is also a source of much conflict, from people securing shelter by squatting in vacant buildings, to renters organizing tenant unions and rent strikes. Within capitalism, the status of land and housing as a commodity, and the cycle of investment in the built environment, generate both periods of decay and deterioration of working-class neighborhoods, as well as displacement, when professional and business people use their higher incomes to outbid the working class for housing.

Peter Marcuse writes: "The opposite of gentrification should not be decay and abandonment but democratization of housing."[1] An interesting tactic for democratization of housing that has emerged in the U.S. in the last two decades is community land trusts, which are typically formed in response to either rising rents and displacement or in response to deterioration and decay.

Community land trusts are land cooperatives that enroll members in a geographic area and act as a non-profit developer of resident-controlled housing. As a democratic membership organization, the community land trust can empower people in a neighborhood to control what is done with the land there, what services are provided in the neighborhood, and to ensure that an adequate supply of housing is provided at prices working people can afford.

The basic concept is that the community land trust holds land in a community in perpetuity, taking it off the speculative market. Dwellings are typically sold to residents in some form of limited equity ownership. Long-run affordability of the housing is enforced by a ground lease. A departing household must sell their house or apartment back to the community land trust at a restricted price to keep housing prices low. The community land trust approach thus works at decommodifying land and buildings.

Self-management is implemented along two dimensions: residents have control over the buildings they live in, but the community is empowered to control housing prices and land use.

At various times labor unions, and other groups in the U.S., have formed limited equity housing co-ops to provide working-class housing at affordable prices. The community land trust model was developed in the sixties to overcome problems that tended to destroy limited-equity housing cooperatives in the U.S.

The problem is someone who owns a share in a housing co-op has a personal self-interest in getting the maximum possible price when selling. For this reason, co-op share owners eventually figure out ways to break the limits on equity. The housing then becomes just another real estate commodity.

This happens because the larger working-class community, who have a stake in preserving low housing prices, are not a party to the market transaction between seller and buyer. In fact, this is a case of a negative externality.

The community land trust solution to this problem is to organize the people who would be externally impacted so that they do have a say over this decision. Community land trusts have separate categories of membership: owners of limited equity dwellings versus others in the community who are not owners. Each elects the same number of representatives to the council or board of directors and split votes can be taken in general assemblies on major issues. The effect is to ensure that people who would be adversely impacted by breaking the limits on equity are represented and can prevent conversion of the housing into unrestricted commodities.

There is a second problem that limited-equity co-ops have encountered in the U.S. Given the concentration of expertise about economic management at the top of the social pyramid and huge inequalities in U.S. society, not everyone has the opportunity to acquire knowledge that would be relevant to effectively managing buildings. If low-income people are set loose in a stand-alone co-op, they may be taken advantage of by unscrupulous building contractors or property management firms. Management by untrained amateurs sometimes creates problems like this even for condominium associations of professional people.

The more traditional approach to social housing, either run by state entities or by non-profit community development corporations, overcomes this problem by concentrating the expertise and decision making in a corporate-style hierarchy. The problem is that the relationship to the tenant is paternalistic, and the residents have no control over the places where they live or the shape of the built environment around them.

By contrast, the community land trust solution to this problem is to do training of residents and develop in the residents the skills for effective management of their buildings. The community land trust is there to provide guidance and backup in case problems are encountered. The "you're-on-your-own" approach of the market is replaced by a more collaborative approach in which knowledge and risks are shared.

The community land trust thus acts as a buffer to protect the housing co-ops against the corrosive effects of the surrounding capitalist economy.

We can imagine various ways in which the community land trust model could be extended. People who are going to live in buildings could be actively involved in the design of the buildings so that new ones are customized to meet their particular needs and tastes.

Community land trusts can try to secure powers of eminent domain, to dislodge properties from speculators and absentee landlords. For example, through political struggle, Dudley Street Neighbors, a Boston community land trust, was able to get a limited power of eminent domain.

In cities where large-scale squatting of buildings has occurred, community land trusts could be used as the means to regularize or legalize the resident's control of their buildings in a way that prevents the land and buildings from becoming real estate commodities.

Tenants organized in tenant unions could work with a community land trust to buy out the landlord and gain control, collectivizing the building.

In situations where public housing projects are under threat of being privatized, the tenants could use the community land trust approach to keep the land off the speculative market and gain control over their buildings.

These last several examples illustrate ways that community land trusts can be used as a tactic in the ongoing class struggle over the built environment.

Some community land trusts in the U.S. have provided spaces for health clinics and child care centers. Space could also be provided for work collectives.

The principle of self-management can be applied to services that are developed for communities so that immediate gains are consistent with the long-run vision of a self-managed society. A city-wide network of community land trusts might provide spaces for a city-wide network of worker-collective groceries or worker co-op child care centers, for example.

The example of the community land trust suggests that we can develop organizations that begin to play, in an embryonic way, the sort of role envisioned for the Neighborhood Council in participatory economics, where we have a participatory, democratic body to decide what sorts of services or what sorts of economic development or what sorts of housing we want in a neighborhood.

Right now funding for social housing in any form is scarce in the U.S. Prospects for changing this depend upon the trajectory of social change. Workplace organizations of struggle, the unions, will continue to be a crucial force for change because of their size and position in the economy.

I would envision a people's alliance of unions, tenant groups, and other mass organizations coming together around a multiplicity of concerns that affect city dwellers in their daily lives—not only housing but health care, transportation, child care, schools, and other issues.

If organizations are not to be simply run by professional cadre or reduced to a hard core of committed activists, we need to figure out ways that make it easier for the average working person to be involved in movements. When people must work two jobs or sixty hours a week to make ends meet, it is hard to find the time to be involved in organizations. This brings out the importance of efforts to gain more free time for people, such as reviving the movement to shorten the workweek without loss in pay. Affordable childcare is also important if parents are to find the time to be involved in community organizations.

The way in which we organize for change is important in shaping what the outcome will be down the road. If we develop organizations that simply implement a corporate-style hierarchy internally, how is that consistent with participatory self-management as a goal? That form of organization sends the wrong message and develops the wrong habits.

If our aim is a society based on self-management, we need to work to develop movements and organizations now that are self-managed, organizations based on participation and democratic control, such as unions self-managed by rank-and-file workers. Through the experience of direct control of these organizations, people can develop skills, self-confidence, and better knowledge of the system they are up against.

We build the self-managed city in the process of the struggle for change.

(Endnotes)

1   Peter Marcuse, "In Defense of Gentrification," *Newsday* (Dec. 2, 1991)

Chapter 8

TECHNOLOGY OF THE NEW SOCIETY

Nikos Raptis

IN 1829, IN A series of lectures at Harvard, the physician Jacob Bigelow observed:

> There has probably never been an age in which the practical applications
> of science have employed so large a portion of talent and enterprise of the
> community, as in the present. To embody... the various topics which belong
> to such an undertaking, I have adopted the general name of Technology, a
> word sufficiently expressive, which is found in some older dictionaries... Under
> this title is attempted to include an account... of the principles, processes, and
> nomenclatures of the more conspicuous arts, particularly those which involve
> applications of science...[1]

Thirty-two years later, in 1861, the Massachusetts Institute of Technology was
established in Boston. The word "Technology" in the title was proposed by Bigelow
himself "to indicate that the study of science at MIT, rather than being a form of po-
lite learning, would be directed toward practical ends."[2]

Science had always been separate from technology. In classical times science "belonged" to the aristocrat-philosophers. Technology was the task of the manual workers. Similarly, during the 18th century in England, "science became an activity for a
cultured, moneyed and leisured class." Indeed, "the term 'scientist' did not exist in
Britain until the mid-19th century; the phrase actually used was 'a cultivator of science.'"[3]

The meeting of science and technology took place only in the middle of the 19th
century although the roots of technology go back to the Middle Ages.

Thus, if we define technology as the "practical application of scientific knowledge," we have a variety of technological fields: medical technology, computer technology, etc. Of all these fields the one that arguably has the most direct and the most
important significance for ordinary people is engineering.

Of all the branches of engineering there is one that is involved with almost every
aspect of human life on earth. Let us try to substantiate the validity of this statement.

Imagine an ordinary person getting up in the morning in his house. That house
was designed and constructed by engineers of this critical branch of engineering (let
us call it "C. Engineering," or C. E. for short). The design was done on the basis of the
scientific knowledge of a division (or subdiscipline) of C. E.: the *structural* division.

Next, the person goes to the toilet. C. E. engineers designed and constructed the water supply and the sewage system. C. E. divisions involved *hydraulics, sanitary, water resources, soil mechanics* (dam design).

Our hero or heroine eats breakfast: cereals and other farm products. C. E. divisions involved: *irrigation and drainage, pipeline, energy division.*

He or she gets into a car, train, or plane to go to work. The highway, railway, or airport used was designed and constructed by C. E. engineers. C. E. division involved: *transportation.*

Their workplace is situated in a city, town, etc. C. E. division: *urban planning.*

No need to go on following our heroes and heroines. A (partial) listing of the more than two dozen (!) C. E. divisions suffice to show the importance of C. Engineering in the life of ordinary persons. The listing of C. E divisions: *aerospace, cold regions, computing in C. E., construction engineering, engineering mechanics, environmental engineering, materials, professional issues, surveying, water port coastal*, etc.

The letter C. in C. E. stands for "civil," therefore we are talking about "civil engineering." That is, the engineering that has to do with a major part of the life of a civilian population. However, this civilian population has only a very vague idea of what a civil engineer deals with. For (a not so strange reason) most people think that all the above activities are performed by architects. The reason for that could be that architects, like lawyers and doctors, are considered by Hollywood to be more glamorous than the engineers. Even dictionaries give a rather wrong definition of architecture as "the art or science of designing and building structures and esp. habitable ones." (See below for some comments on this.) Engineers are mostly considered as uninteresting, unethical developers, etc.

Things are a bit different. "Only certain persons choose to become engineers and are willing to undertake the rigors of the demanding college curriculum that allows them entrance to the field."[4] "Engineers have chosen to join a profession that is dedicated to honesty and the public's welfare."[5] Actually, civil engineers through their work in sanitary engineering have doubled the life expectancy of people.

My fifty-year long experience in the field of civil engineering dictates me to agree with both the above quoted statements. That Kurt Prufer, an engineer, built the ovens at Auschwitz, or that (chemical) engineers produced Agent Orange does not reflect on the overwhelming majority of engineers. However, there is a real problem with engineers in the existing social system. It has to do with their lack of courage not to yield to external (political, etc.) influences and pressures. As for architects, they have nothing to do with the "design and the construction" of all the above. Even for the "habitable ones" all they do is deal with aesthetics.

The core of the parecon vision is the values that guide this vision, that is, its moral foundation. The characteristics of the pareconish analysis (moral foundation, rationality, and honesty) are pushed to their limits. Specifically, the moral base of the parecon proposition is far more advanced than anything that has been suggested up to now.

Thus, if we accept that civil engineers are people "dedicated to honesty and the public's welfare" (i.e. have pareconish qualities), then it is reasonable to choose civil engineering as the object of the analysis of the "Technology of the New Society"; the topic of this chapter.

We shall base our assessment on three areas: participation, decision making, and the need for innovation.

Participation

We examine on the one hand the participation of the layman in the work of the civil engineer and on the other hand the participation of the engineer in the social process.

A civil engineer is a professional with very specialized knowledge. Consequently, can lay people participate in his work?

Let us examine the historical record. "Almost all the environments in human history have been designed by lay people. Many of the most wonderful places in the world… were not designed by architects."[6] In the free city-states of medieval Italy citizens participated in the planning of technical projects through citizens' committees. "Dante served on the Florentine committee, and during his term of office took part in making arrangements for widening via San Procolo."[7]

Christopher Alexander, Professor of Architecture at the University of California, Berkeley, wrote "Let us begin by asking what exactly 'participation' means. It can mean any process by which the *users* of an environment help to shape it"[8] (emphasis added). It is quite remarkable that this "definition" of participation dates from 1973.

To say that the need of humans to "shape" their environment is almost instinctive seems not to be an exaggeration. But can ordinary people communicate meaningfully with a civil engineer and make a substantial contribution to the work of the engineer? It is up to the engineer to present his work in a way intelligible even to a layman. Furthermore, all humans have an innate ability to use their minds to apply their knowledge in a practical manner, that is, to act *technologically*. What is not innate to humans is to use their minds "scientifically."

Here is a rather "dramatic" example of this *technological* (or *tacit*) way of thinking: At one U.S. aircraft company they engaged a team of four mathematicians, all of Ph.D. level, to define in a program a method of drawing the afterburner of a large jet engine. This was an extremely complex shape. They spent some two years dealing with this problem and could not find a satisfactory solution. When, however, they went to the experimental workshop of the aircraft factory, they found that a skilled sheet-metal worker, together with a draftsman, had actually succeeded in drawing and making one of these. One of the mathematicians observed, "they may have succeeded in making it but they didn't understand how they did it."

Thus, the statement that ordinary persons (users) have the right and the ability to shape their environment by helping in the work of an engineer seems to be valid.

Let us now examine the case of the participation of the civil engineer in society. A civil engineer is an expert. However, after offering his expertise to the community he is simply an ordinary citizen with the same rights and responsibilities as any other citizen.

What is the situation today? "For too long engineers have failed to take part in the moral debates that help to shape our society. We avoid these debates in the name of ethics and professionalism. Conveniently, we seem to forget that our technical and analytical skills can be used for many types of problems. Unfortunately it is more common not to stand up for what is socially right."[9]

Dennis A. Randolph, the civil engineer who wrote the above quoted opinion, is a Member of ASCE (American Society of Civil Engineers) and Chief Highway Operations in Fairfax County, Virginia. It is engineers (or, better, citizens) like Randolph that give hope to all ordinary people in the world.

Of course, there are civil engineers like Ronald A. Chadderton, Professor at the University of Villanova, who laments the economic crisis in the U.S. writing that "few would admit... the crisis is, fundamentally, philosophical. An *altruist-collectivist* view is prevalent [in the U.S.!]"[10] (emphasis added). One should not ignore the fact that there are quite a few anti-altruist individualists of the Chadderton ilk in the world.

At this point it is interesting to dwell a bit on the work of ASCE. As a Greek civil engineer, all my professional life I had relied on the precious (this is the right word) knowledge deposited in the publications of ASCE since 1852, the date of its founding. In essence the ASCE is the syndicalist organ of the American civil engineers, a rather conservative sector of U.S. society. However, life is pushing people to be "altruistic-collectivist." "So extensive was the devastation and so ominous the residual risk, that today—nearly two years later—the future of New Orleans is clouded. [ASCE's] Hurricane Katrina External Review Panel (ERP) has an obligation to share its findings and insights... so that others may learn from this tragedy and prevent similar disasters from happening again, not just in New Orleans but in other communities."[11]

An interesting (pareconish!) detail: the ERP was composed of 14 members (13 from the U.S. and 1 from the Netherlands) and was associated with a group of 150 experts from government, academia, and industry who represented more than 40 organizations—an example of democratic collaboration of at least 164 people.

> The concept of moral excellence goes far beyond the contractual ethics of the relation engineer—the customer. It needs to be a moral compact between the engineer and society, and not only one's national society, but world society. We as civil engineers have done much to help the development of poor regions of the world. But the core of the concept of moral excellence in civil engineering should be a passionate commitment to put all our knowledge, skills, and influence in society to the task of providing housing for the homeless, from Calcutta to New York City; of eliminating the horrors of the favelas.[12]

Could it be that even the (rather conservative) civil engineers, members of the "coordinator class," are ready to adhere to the parecon vision? As a matter of fact, one of these engineers, C. R. Pennoni, writes, "Visioning is a look at the past, present, and future, a study of change—thinking beyond today's reality... A vision often provides inspiration where a plan may only provide a detailed action agenda."[13]

Decision Making

In his book *Realizing Hope: Life Beyond Capitalism* (2006) Michael Albert writes: "[We] must conceive a mechanism that can properly and efficiently determine and communicate accurate information... that can then apportion to workers and consumers influence over choices proportional to the degree they are *affected*," (emphasis added).[14]

In a 1993 article in an ASCE journal we read:

The engineer shall:

1. Honor the right of all individuals affected by an engineering project to participate to the appropriate degree in the decisions concerning the project.

2. Provide complete, accurate and understandable information to all parties concerning all engineering decisions that may affect them.

3. Refuse to sanction or participate in, and encourage others to do likewise, projects that, even when approved by the appropriate clients or superiors, will cause unjustifiably harmful consequences."[15]

It appears that *Homo sapiens,* having lived only 100,000, years on this earth left his progeny with an almost identical way of thinking. Notice the coincidence of even the words in the above texts which are fourteen years apart.

To substantiate his thesis, the writer of the 1993 quote offers a tragic example, the *Challenger* accident:

The engineers of Morton-Thiokol who argued against the launch clearly followed the third point in the foregoing code, since they refused to participate in an action that they saw as having a high chance of causing unjustifiable harm. Unfortunately, they were caught in the internal contradictions of the engineering code of ethics [a different code than the above], which instructed them to also remain loyal to the company [!]... If the engineers had been governed by the proposed [code], they would have recognized that one of the parties with the greatest interest in this decision was the astronauts, and the astronauts would then have been brought into the decision-making process... The astronauts would have been told the facts, and a decision—which affected them foremost—would have included their contribution."[16]

Here is another example of the application of parecon in the new society: Let us suppose that for the buildings in a town, it is necessary that they be constructed according to method A, which is structurally and socially correct. However, with the existing social system in the town, a small group of powerful people decides to construct the buildings according to method B, which is structurally incorrect but profitable.

If, instead of the existing social system in the town, parecon had taken effect, the decision to build would have been taken in a participatory manner and the choice would have been method A, which is the correct one (and not the profitable one).

The example is not hypothetical. The town is the town of Volos, in central Greece. The next big earthquake in this town (an earthquake-prone area) will probably prove the value of the fundamental moral logic that is the core of parecon.

Innovation

Engineers in general, and specifically civil engineers, have been rather "indifferent" to innovation. Most of their work, though extremely beneficial to society, has been, and is, routine. Yet when obliged to innovate, for example to save the life of a relative, engineers have proved to be extremely efficient, as attested to by their innovative contributions to medicine.

In a new, parecon society the need for innovation is vital. We think that the fields where innovation by engineers is possible and necessary could be the following:

• Earthquakes kill tens of thousands of people every year (only war is equally destructive to human life). Most of the deaths happen in houses with masonry bearing walls, especially in third world countries. It is imperative that, at last, civil engineers invent light weight houses that can be mass produced from local materials. The participation of local people in the design and construction of this new type of house cannot be emphasized enough. This mass-produced type of house can also be the solution for residents of non-earthquake-prone areas—the homeless of Calcutta, or the people of the Favelas. Also, time is overdue for civil engineers to reexamine the quake-resistance of multistory buildings with steel reinforced concrete frames. The brittle nature of these structures is more than proven. A survey of the history of failed structures of this type since the beginning of the 20th century all over the world should not be ignored.

• We propose that there should be an additional separate division or department, or course in the universities, the ASCE, etc. for failures in civil engineering works. It is possible that the August 2007 failure of the bridge in Minneapolis could have been avoided if local civil engineers were trained to be failure-conscious through the study of failures during the last century.

• The "timidity" of civil engineers has in great measure let the car become the worst enemy of the earth and its inhabitants. It is time that engineers and honestly informed and participating citizens reexamine the case of the car. The solution was and is the use of steel wheels on steel rails for mass transportation.

• Katrina, floods, and other natural destruction due to climate cannot be controlled. What can be controlled are the man-made structures that protect humans. One should put the question to engineers and to citizens: Has there been a serious investigation of the problem?

• On June 11, 1976, a hearing took place before a subcommittee of the House of Representatives of the 94th Congress. The title of the subject discussed was "Converting Solar Energy into Electricity: A Major Breakthrough?" The (possible) breakthrough discussed was an idea of the American physicist Joseph C. Yater for the conversion of solar energy into electricity through the use of extremely miniature devices with dimensions as small as a molecule (the term 'nanotechnology' was only two years old). Thirty-two years later, no such devices are in use. It is about time that the solar-energy problem should be priority number one. The people in Silicon Valley, in the schools of engineering, in the research institutions, etc. should tackle this vital problem instead of spending their energy to invent "glamorous" mobile phones.

We think that besides the participatory way of decision-making, the most important factor for a beneficial technology is the moral dimension of a parecon society. Engineers will not be obliged to succumb to the dictates and pressures by the barbaric ruling elites of existing societies to invent and produce mines, napalm, and cluster bombs. They will be free to use their intelligence to satisfy the rational and morally right needs of their fellow humans.

Also, in a parecon society engineers (especially civil engineers) will have the means to honestly devote their knowledge and their expertise to the safety of ordinary people. For example, they will be given a chance to face the (dominant) problems of earthquakes worldwide and of the aging infrastructure. In a parecon society, instead of murderous stealth aircraft, people will have safe bridges.

(Endnotes)

1   David F. Noble, *America by Design* (Oxford University Press, 1977): 3,4
2   Ibid.: 23
3   Rita Arditti, *Science and Liberation* (Black Rose Books, 1980): 18
4   Aarne P. Vesilind "Why Do Engineers Wear Black Hats," *Journal of Prof. Issues, American Society of Civil Engineers* (ASCE from now on) (Vol. 119 No.1, Jan. 1993): 2
5   Mark J. Holliday "Ethical Responsibilities of Engineering Profession," *Journal of Prof. Issues, ASCE* (Vol. 120 No. 3, Jul. 1994): 271
6   Christopher Alexander *The Oregon Experiment* (Oxford University Press, 1975): 45, 46
7   Ibid.: 158, 159
8   Ibid.: 39
9   Dennis A. Randolph "Civil Engineering Shaping Society: Our Social Responsibilities," *Journal of Prof. Issues, ASCE* (Vol. 118 No. 1, Jan. 1992): 13
10   Ronald A. Chadderton "Praxeology and Engineering," *Journal of Prof. Issues, ASCE* (Vol. 109 No. 3, Jul. 1983): 159
11   "The ERP Report: What Went Wrong and Why," *ASCE, Civil Engineering Magazine* (Vol. 77 No. 6, June 2007): 54
12   George Bugliarello "Ideal of Civil Engineering," *Journal of Prof. Issues, ASCE* (Vol. 120 No. 3, Jul. 1994): 293
13   C. R. Pennoni "Visioning: the Future of Civil Engineering," *Journal of Prof. Issues, ASCE*, (Vol. 118 No. 3, Jul. 1992): 221
14   Michael Albert *Realizing Hope: Life Beyond Capitalism* (Zed Books, 2006)
15   Vesilind "Why Do Engineers Wear Black Hats"
16   Ibid.: 6

Chapter 9

PARTICIPATORY PLANNING IN LIFE AFTER CAPITALISM

Barbara Ehrenreich interviews Michael Albert

Ehrenreich: Though I call myself a socialist, I am unpersuaded of the wisdom of abolishing the market in all areas. Health care, housing, and other basic things should be freed from the market for some kind of public control. But cosmetics, stylish clothing, and other things that could be construed as nonnecessities—why not leave all that to the market? Call me a vain, petty, capitalist running dog, but I certainly don't want a bunch of committees deciding how long skirts will be or what lipstick colors will be available.[1]

Albert: Of course capitalism can be better or worse. The relative bargaining power of contending classes determines just how draconian income distribution, concentrations of power, investment patterns, and conflicts among economic classes are. With more bargaining power, we can raise wages, improve work conditions, increase social investments, and win many other innovations. So yes, we can certainly win and defend improvements against capitalism's socially reinforced greed and power, and we must—but why not simultaneously seek a new system that has desirable outcomes as its norm?

To avoid miscommunicating my desires, I don't call myself a socialist, and I certainly would never call you petty, vain, or a capitalist running dog—but about markets, the big choice is not markets versus a bunch of committees. That's a false polarity.

The big choice is do we want competitive markets that depend on each actor fleecing the rest, that misaccount the relative value of all items and distort preferences, that lead workplaces to seek maximum surpluses and deliver unjust remuneration, that apportion decision-making influence hierarchically, and that produce class division and class rule—or do we want cooperative participatory planning that produces equity, enhances solidarity, enlarges diversity, and facilitates self-management, even as it also helps us meet needs and develop potentials?

Having markets for some items and not for others as you suggest might have relative benefits if markets had significant virtues that no alternative allocation system could match and exceed, and if markets had no huge debits for the proposed items, and if a market in some items but not in others was viable, for that matter.

But markets have no virtues that participatory planning won't match and dramatically exceed. Markets lack all kinds of virtues that participatory planning incorporates.

Markets have numerous disastrous faults that apply not only to markets in labor, or to markets in huge investment projects, but to markets in any item at all, including dresses, all of which faults are absent in participatory planning. And finally, if you don't have labor markets the entire argument that marketeers put forth for having any kind of market collapses.

Applying all this to skirts, we should want the tastes and preferences of all workers and consumers, and particularly of people who wear and of those who produce skirts, to interactively, proportionately influence their length and colors, as well as their number and composition, their method or production, and so on—instead of profit seeking determining these results. But to have a market in skirts not only violates these desires, it means skirt prices will diverge from the true social costs and benefits of their production and consumption, that skirt factories will seek surpluses as their guiding motive and will remunerate their workers unjustly, and that these factories will utilize ill-conceived methods of production and also incorporate class division, among many other faults.

All items involved in economic life are connected. Producing more of any one item leaves fewer assets for producing all other items. Items that seem relatively simple on the consumption side can utilize all kinds of inputs with wide-ranging ramifications. Mispricing any item induces a ripple effect that misprices the rest. Having antisocial motives at play in any one item's production and consumption skews the context for other items' production and consumption. Excessive or inferior remuneration levels generate harmful incentives.

In other words, markets aren't a little bad, or even just very bad, in some contexts. Instead, in all contexts, markets instill antisocial motivations in buyers and sellers, misprice items that are exchanged, misdirect aims regarding what to produce in what quantities and by what means, misremunerate producers, introduce class division and class rule, and embody an imperial logic that spreads itself throughout economic life.

If eating, having shelter, and having desirable additional items to express and fulfill our potentials and enjoy life's options—including skirts—couldn't be had by some system better in its material and human implications than markets, then yes, we would have to settle for markets and try to ameliorate their ills as our highest aim. But luckily for humanity, there is a system that is much better than markets, so that we can strive to attain participatory planning even as we also ameliorate current market ills.

Ehrenreich: I don't want to prolong the skirt discussion (I hardly ever wear them myself), but I am confused about the way you conflate markets with capitalist exploitation. There were markets of one kind or another for thousands of years before capitalism, so they can't be the same thing. Do you totally reject all attempts to create nonexploitative enterprises within capitalism, for example—like "No Sweat" in L.A., various micro-enterprises throughout the world, etc?

Albert: I certainly don't mean to conflate markets with capitalism. They differ. Capitalism has markets in labor power, and in most though not all goods. But you can certainly have markets without having private ownership of the means of production, as, for example, in Yugoslavia not long ago. I think I was actually quite careful in my list above to pinpoint faults of markets per se, not of capitalist markets. Markets always compel pursuit of surplus for example, but it won't go to owners as profits if they are not capitalist markets.

Having helped create nonexploitative South End Press among other institutions, I certainly advocate creating better institutions now. Pushing existing institutions in desirable directions as well as creating new and more desirable institutions can make life better for people working in and consuming products from those institutions now, and can make life better later for everyone if we can make the efforts part of a process leading to a whole new economy.

But it is also important to note that when we create desirable institutions like South End Press, if we do it short of winning a whole new economy, they will exist in a sea of counter pressures pushing hard on us to return our activities to an oppressive logic. There is counter pressure on our new institutions—if they are in a market environment—to advertise, to cut and slough off costs, and have managers impose the cost cutting and dodging policies, to lengthen the work day regardless of people's desires for leisure, and so on. Thus we should seek not only reforms but a whole new economy.

Ehrenreich: Before proceeding to other matters, my big reason for wanting some things to remain marketized is that it would reduce the burden of planning. As you know, some have complained that parecon condemns us to endless meetings, so why not leave "nonessentials" to the market?

Albert: Opting for some markets in order to reduce the burden on participatory planning doesn't, in fact, reduce that burden. What is planned would have to use items from the marketized industries and also deliver items to them. Managing those interfaces would add a whole new and disruptive dimension to participatory planning. Moreover, supposing this interfacing could even exist, it would condemn the participatory planning process to arrive at false plans by undermining its capacity to determine true exchange values.

Markets compel competition for market share and revenues. What would it mean to say that some workplaces should compete to sell as much as possible in order to accrue surpluses, but that they shouldn't then disperse those surpluses to their employees? On the one hand, if they do disperse surpluses to their employees, then the entire remuneration scheme of participatory planning—to remunerate not for output, or for bargaining power, or for property, but only for effort and sacrifice—is laid waste. On the other hand, if they don't disperse their surpluses to employees, then the firms aren't really operating in a market fashion and, what's more, have no basis for deciding their level of production, length of workday, etc.

I therefore wonder what you have in mind when you say you want nonessential production decisions to be decided by markets. It wouldn't mean that people wouldn't make choices for those items. It would mean people would make their choices under the institutional pressures of market competition. Why would you want to have allocation decisions made with institutionally imposed surplus-seeking motivations, using wrong prices as guides, engendering unjust remuneration, imposing antisocial behavioral incentives, and with actors exercising inappropriate levels of influence—instead of having participatory planning in which people make the decisions based on true prices exercising proportionate, say, in pursuit of social well-being and development rather than surplus accumulation?

If markets are accompanied by capitalist ownership relations, then the pursuit of revenues that markets induce, after meeting costs and investing in equipment, is largely allotted to profits for the owners. If markets exist with public- or state-owned property, then the pursuit of revenues they induce, after meeting costs and investing in equipment, is largely allotted to a surplus for what I call a coordinator class. There are elements of progress in this alteration, but much less than I seek as my aims.

When you say we should marketize inessential goods—what qualifies something as being inessential? Inessential goods would include a huge array of items if it includes dresses, but aren't all products essential if we consider that they are all created by people, headed for consumption by people, utilizing assets which could be put to other ("more essential") ends, and so on?

Are sneakers inessential? If so, does that mean it is okay for firms pursuing market share and surpluses via cutting the cost of production of sneakers to run sweat shops and spew pollution? Is soda pop inessential? If it is, and we have it operate via market exchange, is it okay for the soda pop firms to gobble up all the available quinine so that millions die of malaria? Is it okay for all the workers in the soda pop firms to be overseen by bosses and reduced to only rote labor just because they aren't producing milk?

Economies are general equilibrium systems. What happens in one place is inextricably bound to influence and be influenced by what happens elsewhere. If you feel that housing is essential and clothes aren't, how do planned housing decisions get made unless clothes decisions are being taken interactively at the same time, and how can the housing decisions be good decisions unless the valuations of clothes are correct? If clothes decisions are being taken by market dynamics, then the planning of housing is undermined by the inaccuracy of clothing choices. Too much or too little productive time, energy, and resources may be going to clothes instead of housing.

Markets lead to corporate divisions of labor and to remuneration that diverges from measures of effort and sacrifice—which is the type of remuneration participatory planning advocates—even without private ownership of productive assets.

Likewise, markets misprice goods and services due to their failing to account for external and public effects, again, even without private ownership. The fact that dresses are "inessential" doesn't tell us that their production involves no external environmental effects. What if producing dresses uses important resources, or generates damaging pollution? And producing dresses most certainly impacts workers. Markets induce individualist behavior of the narrowest sort, again, even without private ownership. Markets give an incentive to dump pollution and to otherwise ignore the effects of one's actions on those who aren't buying and selling. Why do we want people who produce dresses to be motivated by greed, not the fulfillment of themselves and consumers? Why would we want to accept market ills for any item in the economy?

If a particular industry operates on a market, say the dress industry, it means that that industry seeks to sell as many of its products as possible, at as high a price as it can extract as possible, regardless of the implications of those sales on buyers or more broadly. Dress producers will advertise. They will want to buy cheap and sell dear. They will prefer production techniques that cost them less even if they pollute more. The dress industry will produce in light of incorrect valuations of the product. It will cut costs of production regardless of whether doing so hurts workers more than it benefits consumers. The dress industry will do all these things, and much more, to get market share and stay in operation.

When you say leave non essentials to a market—I also think perhaps you have in mind central planning and markets, and you are thinking why not augment one with some of the other, since neither has stupendous virtues compared to the other? But my claim for participatory planning, which I can't make in full in an interview without abusing length even more than I already am, is that participatory planning does have stupendous virtues compared to either markets or central planning. Participatory planning produces solidarity by creating conditions in which, to get ahead, actors must take into account the well-being of those who produce what they consume or consume what they produce. It facilitates actors having appropriate decision-making power by its modes of decision making and proper pricing. It is consistent with and facilitates remunerating effort and sacrifice. It respects and expands diversity. It establishes a dynamic consistent with classlessness by not requiring a layer of coordinators controlling outcomes.

Ehrenreich: Have you ever tried to calculate the human labor costs of all the planning involved in parecon? Or maybe I should say "time" not dollar "costs."

Albert: Yes, in the various books the issue of time allotment is certainly addressed. And the discussions not only look at the time it takes to plan, which is only one side of the coin, but also at the time gained due to eliminating diverse kinds of no- longer-needed activity when we change to a parecon.

Some people, especially when hearing a brief summary of parecon, worry that self consciously deciding on what to produce and consume by a negotiated cooperative process will take too long. I have two answers. First, no, it won't. The planning process in a parecon is confined to a couple of weeks and only takes part-time attention over that span. But, second, even prior to that answer, we have to decide what would count as being too long. That is, when someone asks me about the cost of planning in time expended, I want to try to communicate that this is at worst a trade off.

Let's say the total time that you as a consumer have to spend thinking about and implementing your consumption choices would go up in a parecon by a factor of two, or even three or four, depending on how much time you spend now—which, I think, is quite exaggerated, unless you spend very little time now. Okay, that would be a cost, to be sure.

But would it be a deal breaker? To know that, you have to look at both sides of the equation. You have to weigh the new time costs (which I deny). But you also have to weigh countervailing gains—such as having no ruling class, having equitable work conditions and income distribution, having accurate pricing, having no drive toward individualism, no poverty, no products designed to wear out, and so on, through many more gains.

Okay, let's say someone really values time a whole lot. For this person spending extra time on consumption outweighs attaining classlessness and all the rest. Even in that case, he or she would still need to consider the countervailing implications of having participatory planning for time savings and not just its implications for new time expenditures.

For example, parecon affects the length of the workday. Where markets increase workday length by their competitive logic regardless of the wills of actors to have more leisure, participatory planning leaves the choice entirely in the hands of actors in light of their preferences for leisure versus income. Likewise, there are time savings due to the absence of class struggle, the elimination of the IRS, the end of redundant and wasteful production, the end of having to clean up the messes produced by market competition in the ecology, etc. And even regarding consumption itself, there are very substantial time savings due to actors having accurate information, and, in particular, due to sensible collective consumption obviating the need for quite a lot of individual consumption as we now know it, as well as by producing for durability rather than market-induced built-in obsolescence.

So, okay, in light of all this would planning in a parecon take inordinately longer than consuming does now plus the time for other activities that parecon replaces? In a parecon, you have to spend some time over the course of a week or two entering your budget and interacting with the overall process. I suspect this won't take longer than people now spend doing tax returns, say, and worrying about how to pay bills, or recuperating from purchases made due to false advertising, or having to do personal consumption that would be rendered irrational in a parecon, or producing or cleaning up wasteful and useless outputs, and so on. After the plan exists, time spent making adaptations as the year proceeds really isn't significantly different than time spent nowadays on consumption or production decisions, though it is carried out very differently, with different implications.

My reaction to averting time expenditures by utilizing markets is therefore two-fold. Markets are harmful. Even if they are utilized for one product, which isn't what would occur, the price of that product will be wrong and that wrong price will enter in every other industry incorrectly. The workers in the market-driven industry will be motivated to seek surplus and will be unfairly remunerated as compared to all other workers who are motivated by fulfilling needs and remunerated for effort and sacrifice. The marketized workplace structure will push toward class division. More, it makes no sense to have an infrastructure for "market exchange" and have only a few goods marketed. In fact, it only makes sense to both consume via the participatory plan and also via markets if there are lots of things to buy on the market. But then all the associated ills of markets would be spreading—and we may as well have markets for everything and say goodbye to classlessness. And second, the purported time gain is false, in any event.

Ehrenreich: That response raises all kinds of questions and sets off some alarm bells in my mind. To start with one of them, which may seem trivial, but is actually very central to our differing visions of a utopian arrangement: When you say "let's say someone really values time a whole lot," I cringe. Is there anyone who doesn't? What's important to me is my work and time with friends and family. In my vision of the good society, there is more time for these things, not less. So I want as little time devoted to planning as possible. Maybe I'm just a deadbeat, but I do think this issue needs to be taken seriously unless parecon is to be run, by default, entirely by weirdly obsessed nerds.

Albert: I referred to someone really caring about time a whole lot referencing someone valuing time so much that saving even a little would outweigh eliminating class division, exploitation, mispricing, misdirection of motives, and so on. I pointed out that even such a person, and I don't think that is you by a long shot, would have no reason to worry about parecon's time implications, because parecon in total frees time rather than robbing it.

To not care about time would be odd, I agree with you. We should value saving an extra hour a week, but not so much as to sacrifice equity, solidarity, diversity, self-management, sustainability, and an end to class division to attain that extra hour.

Suppose having a dictator would save time. Suppose allotting supreme power to an owner of some firm and derivative power to some managerial henchmen keeping others completely subordinate would save time. Suppose utilizing markets would save time. Time concerns shouldn't trump all other concerns. That said, in fact, in parecon to participate in decision making rather than to obey decisions taken by others takes some time, but other time reductions more than offset this.

I indicated diverse factors bearing on time reduction last answer. But let's concretize one. In the mid 1950s, which was generally considered the golden age of capitalism, as our mutual friend Juliet Schor points out,[2] the per capita output in the U.S. was nearly exactly one half what it rose to about forty years later. That means by the mid-1990s we could have worked one week on and one week off, or a month on and a month off, or a twenty hour work week, and produced the same total output per person as we had available in that earlier golden age. Market competition ensured, instead, that the total time allotted to work went up instead of down. Participatory planning would have let us choose. And that immense gain isn't the whole story. Parecon would also save time no longer allotted to producing excess advertising and packaging, to producing shoddy individual goods replaced by collective durable ones, and of course time no longer allotted to military production.

I should add, I don't think there is anything nerdy about people deciding their own lives.

Ehrenreich: OK, let's forget about slackers vs. nerds and approach the time issue in a more socially serious way. On a panel you organized at the 2003 World Social Forum, a former mayor of Porto Alegre described a real-life experiment in something like parecon—the city's "participatory budget," introduced by the Workers' Party (PT). For a year, hundreds of ordinary citizens representing different neighborhoods and themes—health, welfare, housing, transportation, etc. (but n.b.—not lipstick colors or skirt lengths!)—met repeatedly to devise the next year's budget, or at least that half of the budget other than fixed expenses. Then the Brazilian radical economist Paul Singer observed that, if it took hundreds of people a year to plan 50 percent of the budget for one medium-sized city, the process of planning for a nation could be cumbersome beyond imagining. Doesn't that give you pause?

Albert: The Participative Budget project in Brazil is a fascinating and important experiment. But it certainly does not give me pause. It came about because when the Brazilian Workers' Party (PT) began to win city and even state government elections, the legislature was hostile and likewise the judiciary. The PT had unchallenged control of only the government budgets where they held mayoralties and governorships, such as in Porto Alegre and the state called Rio Grande Del Sol. When the governor there planned to raise minimum wages, the legislature quickly organized to pass a law that any raise given at the lower levels of income had to be matched by a proportionately identical raise at every other level of income, thus obviating the gain. Given this type of obstruction, the PT decided that a campaign they could embark on without sabotage from other branches of government was to incorporate public involvement in deciding what the PT-led governments would spend taxes on.

So the participative budget program was initiated as a kind of consultation between government ministries and sectors of the populace brought together for the purpose of discussing about 10 to 15 percent of the government budgets. It is certainly a pareconish direction to move in, though it didn't explicitly reject markets or private ownership or propose any alteration to workplaces, etc. Indeed, it was really a political innovation. It diverged from parecon not only in scale, not only in having no aspect on the producer side—not only isn't it about numbers of dresses or lipsticks to be produced, it isn't about deciding any production outputs at all—and not only in being a government project, but also in its entire infrastructure and methodology.

That the participative budget is slow (though I think it actually runs on the schedule set for it, and though much of the slowness may be attributable to the government side of the equation, rather than running long because it must take that long or because the public is the problem) tells us no more about how participatory planning would operate than the fact that a half a bridge won't get us rapidly across a river tells us about the affectivity of a whole bridge to get us quickly across a river, or then the travails of central planning tell us about participatory planning's prospects, for that matter.

Skirts, and now you mention lipstick too, keep resurfacing. In participatory planning what is addressed by the cooperative negotiation between consumers and workers during planning is their quantities. Inside firms, rather than a boss deciding their composition, colors, etc., this is handled however workers' councils choose, though without class division. Consumers don't enter consumption proposals enumerating the lipstick shades they want, colors, sizes, etc. Just how many lipsticks, broadly. They later pick what they like at distribution outlets. Teasing details from the amounts they desire is handled statistically.

All this is elaborated in more detailed discussions of the procedures in various books on parecon and elsewhere.[3] But parecon doesn't require that the consumer explore the detailed issues associated with lipstick colors, or even pay attention to lipstick colors other than how they do now—which is by choosing, on the spot in a store, which color he or she likes. And the same holds for skirt sizes, colors, lengths, etc. But to accomplish all this easily, parecon doesn't make the mistake of marketizing lipstick and skirts (and so much else) and thereby consigning the larger issues of how many to produce, by what methods, using what techniques, and with what remuneration for those doing the work, to market motivations and dynamics. Instead, it uses statistical averaging techniques to avoid nitpicking detail, while keeping the driving dynamics of decision making under the purview of workers and consumers who cooperatively negotiate the outcomes with proportionate influence.

Would a working participatory planning be efficient in reaching decisions and in getting them to reflect self-managed preferences in light of the true social costs and benefits of competing options? I have said that yes, it would, and I have offered some modest evidence for it, but the real and compelling case requires presenting and assessing the full participatory planning model as, for example, in the book *Parecon*.[4]

I guess what I would say here is that if readers would like there to be an alternative to class-dominated markets or centrally planned allocation, and if they would like to be able to advocate such an alternative knowing its properties (or improving them as they see fit), they ought to look at the more complete description of participatory planning's procedures and institutions and judge its properties for themselves.

Ehrenreich: Singer also asked, What do you do when changed conditions, say a natural disaster, require instant decision making? How do you answer this question?

Albert: The question about responding to changes in people's preferences or in material conditions, whether modest or major, is very important, of course. Any economy needs to be flexible or it will be disastrous in various respects. Indeed, there is a full chapter in the *Parecon* book,[5] even after the full presentation of the model, exploring this issue in detail. Both markets and participatory planning have to reply to changes and shocks. Markets do it via actors seeking to exploit the new situation to increase profits or surplus using prices that reflect bargaining power rather than social costs and benefits and little concern for who goes without missing outputs or other possible ramifications. Effects ripple out from the affected industry. Results accrue. And this takes time and involves diverse implications, often moving outcomes even further from just and desirable results.

In participatory planning, effects are also systemic, and also ripple outward from centers of change. Sometimes they are modest and have damped ripple effects, as when slack planning covers the changes or when industries in question can increase output with overtime. Sometimes, as with a big disaster or a major breakthrough in productivity, real juggling and resetting of options must occur, or if it is more efficient and desirable, changes must wait a new planning·period.

There are many ways this can happen. It can be that valuations of items change and that some people go without affected items when prices climb, shifting their expenditures elsewhere, while others get what they sought, though at increased cost. It can be that, instead, valuations are held steady but some people go without due to shortfalls—either randomly or perhaps in accord with assessments of need—as production comes back into accord with desires. The details of alternatives and why one or another would be preferred in different situations would take too long to elaborate here. The point is, the norms guiding the situation are workers' and consumers' preferences. The process is self-managed. And the results occur with only modest dislocation, even in difficult cases.

I guess the answer for this interview, then, is yes, responding to shocks is very important. If it turns out participatory planning is inadequate in this regard, it would certainly need refinement, though it certainly wouldn't be an argument to employ markets or central planning, which react to shocks like they react to everything else, in the interest of dominant classes and therefore with horrible repercussions. As to whether participatory planning has failings in this regard, I think when readers examine the whole parecon system they will see that it very closely addresses these issues, and can handle them adroitly as well as in accord with parecon's guiding values.

(Endnotes)

1   This interview is a selection from a longer exchange between Barbara Ehrenreich and Michael Albert "Parecon?" ZNet (April 26, 2004): www.zcommunications.org/znet/viewArticle/8665

2   Juliet Schor *The Overworked American: The Unexpected Decline of Leisure* (Basic Books, 1992)

3   Michael Albert and Robin Hahnel *Quite Revolution in Welfare Economics* (Princeton University Press, 1991)

Michael Albert and Robin Hahnel *The Political Economy of Participatory Economics* (Princeton University Press, 1991)

Michael Albert and Robin Hahnel *Looking Forward: Participatory Economics for the Twenty-First Century* (South End Press, 1991)

Robin Hahnel *The ABCs of Political Economy: A Modern Approach* (Pluto Press, 2002)

Michael Albert *Parecon: Life After Capitalism* (Verso, 2003)

Robin Hahnel *Economic Justice and Democracy* (Routledge, 2005)

4   Michael Albert *Parecon*

5   Ibid.

Chapter 10

EDUCATION FOR A PARTICIPATORY SOCIETY

Chris Spannos interviews Noam Chomsky

Spannos: In societies with class, race, gender, and power hierarchies, people must come to expect or at least to put up with, and be prepared for and able to fulfill, the requisites of their positions, whether high and hypocritical or low and degraded. If not, society would not function. In your view, how has current schooling and education generally been bent to fulfill these functions?

Chomsky: In its revealing study *The Crisis of Democracy*,[1] the Trilateral Commission criticized what they called the institutions responsible for "the indoctrination of the young" for failing to carry out their necessary tasks. That failure they regarded as an important factor contributing to the "crisis" of the 1960s, as young people became seriously concerned about justice and freedom, and actively engaged in doing something about these concerns—and more generally people outside of privileged sectors sought to bring their concerns to the political arena, an "excess of democracy" from their perspective. The Commission's call for more "moderation in democracy" included warnings that something must be done to restore discipline and obedience, particularly in the crucial institutions responsible for indoctrination of the young.

It is of no slight interest that the years that had a notable civilizing effect on the society are commonly lamented as "the time of troubles" in elite circles.

Recall that the Commission is at the liberal internationalist end of the elite spectrum; the Carter administration, for example, was largely drawn from their ranks. Their description of the schools and universities as institutions responsible for the indoctrination of the young is more brutally frank than the norm, but they were talking to each other; the words were not intended for public consumption. And the description is too extreme, though it captures important elements of the educational system, which have been reinforced in recent years in the course of the elite backlash against the "excess of democracy" and other threatening features of the 1960s.

These perceptions, and the actions that flow from them, do indeed have to do with ensuring that society will function—in a particular way: a way that supports hierarchy, domination, and unaccountability of power systems, state and private.

Spannos: In what ways do you think it is true, in current society, that the more education you have, the dumber you are? What is the purpose of Harvard, of MIT, where you teach, of lower-tier universities, public and state colleges, vocational schools, high schools and primary schools, now? Do the exceptions prove the rule, or disprove it?

Chomsky: The generalization is too sweeping, but it has a thread of truth, perhaps an important one. Though the matter has not been carefully studied, there is evidence in the academic political science literature that "the opinions of the highly educated may actually be the most easily manipulated by policy makers."[2] For many reasons, that would not be surprising, and it accords with a good deal of experience. On the rest, I think that here too we should be careful of brushstrokes that are too broad. There is a natural tendency for elite institutions to seek to socialize students to the norms and expectations of management: political, economic, and doctrinal management. Others tend to induce attitudes of conformity and acceptance of authority, and to provide skills to enable students to function successfully in society as it is, not to challenge what is. But it's not uniform. The natural sciences survive on challenge to received doctrines, and educational practice in these fields—ideally, and often in reality—encourages innovation, challenge, and independence of mind. A physicist of world renown at MIT was famous for his answer to students in his introductory freshman physics class who asked, "what will this course cover?" His (highly appropriate) answer was: "It doesn't matter what we cover. What matters is what you discover." Maybe you will discover that what your book and I are saying is wrong, a welcome outcome. To the extent that precepts such as these are observed, we are entering the domain of serious education.

Just to add a personal reminiscence, one of the most exciting courses I ever took was a graduate math course in modern algebra. The professor, a fine mathematician, would come into the class, write down something on the blackboard, stare at it, and then turn to the class and ask whether or not it is a theorem. He'd then expect the students to discover the answer, following false leads if they were brought up, while he would make suggestions here and there to guide the inquiry on the right path.

These are not modern ideas. In the imagery of centuries ago, education is not a matter of filling a vessel with water, but of laying out a thread along which students will proceed in their own ways, coming to understand how to use the resources available to them for discovery, creation, and enriching their lives.

Some educational programs are designed to induce conformity and passivity: programs geared to passing tests, for example "No Child Left Behind"—which perhaps might more accurately be called "Every Child Left Behind." Focus on passing tests is filling a vessel with water—and most of us know, from experience, how quickly it leaks, often without leaving a trace. Learning that derives from one's own initiative is quite different. And that is what should be stimulated by serious educational programs, which should seek to encourage creativity, understanding, discovery, and moral and ethical commitment.

Spannos: In societies of the future where all people freely participate in collectively self-managing life without hierarchies of influence and income, presumably people will need very different capacities and attributes than they would to rule or be ruled while preserv-

ing inequitable hierarchies at all costs. What do you think these new capacities and attributes are, broadly?

Chomsky: The question virtually answers itself. People would have to make use of capacities and attributes that are suppressed, undermined, often explicitly denigrated in institutions devoted to "the indoctrination of the young": the capacities for free creative thought, for questioning authority, for planning constructively in association with others, and other capacities required to fulfill personal and collective goals. I know of no reason to doubt that such capacities and attributes are pretty much a common human possession, latent in everyone, ready to flourish if opportunity is provided—which is what education should be about in societies of the kind you envision.

Spannos: How do you think desirable education, in a desirable society, would convey or nurture these capacities?

Chomsky: It doesn't seem to me much of a mystery. Children are naturally curious, and seek to understand the world around them—the physical, social, and personal worlds. These natural tendencies can be supported in many ways. The same goes on throughout life, unless natural tendencies have been effectively suppressed. Advanced education in the sciences is one illustration—again, ideally, and often actually.

Spannos: Is there a danger of losing quality or excellence to attain equity and universality? Or would we, instead, gain on every level of expertise and range, with new modes of education?

Chomsky: In a world in which all people were clones, I'd prefer suicide. I think most people would. Variety of talent and achievement is nothing to be feared. On the contrary. It's greatly to be welcomed. I have no musical, athletic, literary, artistic, or other talents, but my own life is greatly enriched by the opportunity to appreciate what is done by those who have and exercise such talents, just as it's exhilarating to learn about deep insights that others have achieved in the sciences, mathematics, the arts, and other domains. We each have only to gain if abilities, talents, interests that are suppressed or distorted by authoritarian institutions are encouraged to flourish, in their own individual and (luckily) unpredictable ways.

Spannos: Finally, what do you think might be sensible and worthy things to seek now, in the present, in educational settings—in public schools presumably with parents and kids and teachers seeking the changes, in colleges with students and some faculty seeking them—as part of a process of social struggle for a better world?

Chomsky: Short-term goals are sometimes dismissed as "reformist," a serious error I think. Just from my own personal experiences in the educational system, in various capacities—student, parent, grandparent, friend, colleague—I can think of countless ways in which educational practice could have been improved. And I don't doubt that everyone else can add their own examples. That alone offers a great variety of sensible and worthy things to do. And small improvements become more sensible and worthy if they are guided by longer-term commitments, which in my view, for what it's worth, should be along the lines we've been discussing.

(Endnotes)

1   Michel Crozier, Samuel P. Huntington, and Joji Watanuki *The Crisis of Democracy* (Trilateral Commission, New York University Press, 1975)
2   Benjamin I. Page with Marshall M. Bouton *The Foreign Policy Disconnect: What Americans Want from Our Leaders But Don't Get* (University of Chicago Press, 2006)

PART

III

Assessing Parecon Internationally

Chapter 11

AFRICA: LIFE AFTER COLONIALISM

Mandisi Majavu

THE ONE ISSUE THAT remains the main problem in post-colonial Africa is the failure of African revolutionary movements to articulate a truly liberatory political and economic vision. The word "liberatory" is used in this essay in an anarchist sense; meaning, I am a fanatical lover of liberty.[1] According to Michael Bakunin, liberty is the only context in which people's intellect, dignity, and happiness can increase and grow, as opposed to the formal liberty doled out, measured, and regulated by the State. Further, as Bakunin reminds us, it is important to keep in mind that the State, as we know it, represents and is there to serve the interests of the privileged few in reality.[2]

Post-colonial thinkers have yet to conceptualise a liberatory State structure that does not facilitate a mere replacement of the old colonial ruling class with the new post-colonial ruling elite. Other obstacles we face in our struggle to achieveing a decolonized Africa are, for example, the theoretical concepts we use to describe what we are fighting for and the assumptions we make when talking of decolonisation. The roots of this problem can be traced to limiting political ideologies; some of these political ideologies include pan-Africanism, black nationalism, and black Marxism.

Another problem encountered by writers is the challenge of talking about race in the post-colony. Many post-colonial writers make a mistake of prioritizing class over race, or vice versa, instead of using both viewpoints.

It seems to me that if we are serious about winning social changes, then it is crucial that these issues are discussed openly and honestly. A sensible point of departure for our debate ought to begin by critically reviewing some of the widely read post-colonial political literature on the topics of decolonization, post-colonial society, and racism.

The objective is not to merely highlight the wrongs and flaws of different political ideologies. The ultimate goal is to present an alternative ideology that is consistent with our values and aspirations. So in Part Two of this essay I present an alternative political theory that relates sensibly to post-colonial socioeconomic conditions. This alternative political theory is based on the logic of participatory politics. I use post-apartheid South Africa as my case study to discuss political and economic challenges faced by post-colonial Africa and to show how a liberatory political theory could be implemented in practice. The reason I chose South Africa as my case study for this essay is simply because I know South African history and politics very well, and, in addition, I am South African.

PART ONE: LITERATURE REVIEW

Frantz Fanon is regarded as one of the key post-colonial theorists, and so it makes sense to first review his work. For the purpose of this study, the *Wretched of the Earth* by Fanon is an appropriate text to review.[3] Regarding the issue of race versus class, the literature review will focus solely on post-apartheid South African writing.

Defining Decolonization

Fanon argues that decolonization is always a violent phenomenon. "The naked truth of decolonization evokes for us the searing bullets and bloodstained knives which emanate from it."[4] According to Fanon, decolonization is a program of "complete disorder" which aims to change the social order of the colonial world. It is a meeting of two forces, opposed to each other by their very nature, and their first encounter was marked by violence, and their existence together was carried on by dint of a great array of bayonets and cannon.

It is a truism to point out that the colonial society is by its very nature violent. It does not, however, necessarily follow that decolonization is a revolutionary programme that is violent in nature. It might be true that most countries that have been colonized have achieved freedom through a violent struggle; however, that says more about the arrogance of colonial power than it says about the decolonization program itself. The misconception of decolonization as violent in nature characterizes the false assumptions that underlie Fanon's thinking about where the decolonization process ought to begin.[5] It must be emphasized that Fanon's understanding of the colonial world is profound; however, some of his assumptions regarding decolonization hinder how we might relate sensibly to the possibilities of moving forward to the liberated, decolonized society that is not a source of pathology.[6]

Instead of decolonization evoking for us the searing bullets and bloodstained knives which emanate from it, we could conceive of decolonization as a fundamental societal change, a radical change in both the economy and the broader societal values regarding social relations such as race relations and class relations, to paraphrase Albert.[7] It is through such a program that colonized people find their freedom. It is not, as Fanon claims, through violence that the colonized people find their freedom.

Fanon argues that violence for the colonized is therapeutic, that it is a "cleansing force."

In reality, as Albert points out, violence has horrible effects on its perpetrators; it compels people to devalue human life.[8] Colonial societies serve as evidence to support this view. And, there is no evidence to make us believe that violence perpetrated by the other side will not have the same effects.

Fanon, however, argues that violence frees "the native from his inferiority complex and from his despair and inaction; it … restores his self-respect."[9] Fanon does not provide evidence to support this perspective, nor does he explain his assumption regarding the "native inferiority complex." He (Fanon) seems to assume that simply because blacks in the colony are subjected to all sorts of racist humiliation, this automatically results in inferiority complex and self-hatred in blacks.[10]

In his book *Shades of Black,* William Cross argues that there are at least four factors that explain why the mental health of blacks, including any propensity toward self-hatred, are not and have never been easily predicted by measures of racial identity.[11] These are:

• The limited generalizability of results of racial-preference studies conducted with three- and four-year-old children.

• The effects of Black biculturalism, acculturation, and assimilation on Black monoracial preference trends in racial identity experiments.

• The problem of interpreting the meaning and salience of racial preference and racial identity for Black adults operating with a multiple reference group orientation.

• The historical failure of students and scholars of racial identity to differentiate between concepts and measures of ascriptive RGO [Reference Group Orientation] and concepts and measures of self-defined RGO.[12]

The point one wants to highlight is that some of Fanon's assumptions vis-à-vis what decolonization represents, the motivations that inspire natives to violently rebel against a colonial regime, and the supposedly rampant inferiority complex that is said to drive the natives into a blood frenzy, are completely unfounded. If we are concerned with building a sound post-colonial theory that explains more than hinders the comprehension of reality, then that theory ought to at least be based on sound assumptions. What is needed rather is a post-colonial theory that explains social events and psychological phenomena, a theory that explains political and psychological trends sufficiently for us to situate ourselves, explain to others, and understand the way things are.[13]

The Pitfalls of National Consciousness

This is perhaps the most important chapter in the *Wretched of the Earth,* for in it Fanon discusses ways a new government of the liberated post-colonial state could betray the revolution. Fanon argues that the middle-class of the new post-colonial state is under-developed because it is reduced in numbers, has no capital, and is totally opposed to the revolutionary path. Eventually it falls into deplorable stagnation. For this middle-class, nationalization of the economy simply means the transfer into native hands of those unfair advantages which are a legacy of the colonial period. Also, this middle-class "will be quite content with the role of the Western bourgeois's business agent, and it will play its part without any complexes in a most dignified manner."[14]

Fanon adds that after independence this middle-class does not hesitate to invest the money it makes out of its native soil in foreign banks. Further, the new middle-class will spend large sums of money on material things, such as cars and country houses. Fanon refers to this middle-class as the "bourgeois dictatorship." He argues that they are not real bourgeois in the true sense of the word, but rather a "sort of little greedy caste, avid and voracious, with the mind of a huckster, only too glad to accept the dividends that the former colonial power hands out to it."[15]

According to Fanon, the reason that this middle-class is corrupt is because it has a permanent wish to identify with former colonizers. Consequently, this middle-class adopts with enthusiasm the ways of thinking characteristic of the former colonizers. The results are that this new middle-class is incapable of generating great ideas to manage and develop the economy, for it remembers what it has read in European textbooks.

The logic that underlies Fanon's analysis is that post-colonial governments and the black middle-class betray the revolution because, among other things, they want to be white or to occupy the position formerly occupied by the colonizer. For example, he writes that before independence the "look that the native turns on the settler's town is a look of lust, a look of envy; it expresses his dreams of possessions—all manner of possession: to sit at the settler's table, to sleep in the settler's bed, with his wife if possible."[16]

History teaches us (for example, see *A People's History of the United States: 1492 to Present*, by Howard Zinn[17]) that when people are oppressed, they always rebel sooner or later. Furthermore, they do not rebel because of lust or envy or because they want to sleep with the oppressor's wife, but because they believe in justice, equity, and freedom. And, in most cases, the revolution is betrayed because of the combination of issues such as the lack of vision regarding the new institutions we want for a democratic society and a mixture of internal and external forces. Internal forces refers to sections of society that might be resistant towards the new regime due to their own selfish interests, while external forces refers to the global economy and global political climate, such as the Cold War. To view post-colonial politics from this standpoint is more revealing and enables us not only to explain but to predict political and social phenomena. A theory based on flawed assumptions that compel us to focus on lust, envy, and desires to be white forces us to chase after psychological reductionist dead ends.

On National Culture

Fanon's basic premise in this chapter is that because of colonialism and the cultural hegemony that goes with colonialism, native intellectuals respond by rejecting Western culture and embracing pre-colonial history and a way of life. To escape from the hegemony of the Western culture, Fanon argues that the native intellectual feels the need to turn backward toward his unknown roots. As a result, the native intellectual sets a high value on the African customs and traditions. "The sari becomes sacred, and shoes that come from Paris or Italy are left off in favour of pampooties, while suddenly the language of the ruling power is felt to burn your lips."[18]

Fanon writes that the native intellectual goes through three different phases to arrive at this level. The first phase is when the native intellectual assimilates the culture of the occupying power and all his or her sources of inspiration are European. The second phase is characterized by the disturbance of the native intellectual. In this phase the native intellectual decides to remember who and what he is. The third phase Fanon calls a fighting phase. In this phase the native intellectual turns himself to be an awakener of the people; "hence comes a fighting literature, a revolutionary literature, and a national literature."[19] However, at the moment when the native intellectual is trying to create a cultural work "he fails to realise" that he is utilizing techniques and language which are borrowed from the colonizer, writes Fanon.

The appreciation of certain Western ideas and the fact that certain post-colonial writers are influenced by Western writers and write in European languages should not be presented as a failure to create an authentic post-colonial cultural work, as Fanon presents it. To write in an African language or to quote only African writers does not necessarily translate into originality. A progressive post-colonial vision on culture[20] ought not to be opposed to diverse cultures (including Western cultures) and their influences thereof or to reduce diverse cultures to a least common denominator. The point, however, should be to enjoy their benefits while transcending prior debits. As Albert points out, the only real cultural salvation lies in eliminating racist institutions, dispelling colonialist ideologies and changing the colonial environment within which historical communities relate so that they might maintain and celebrate difference without violating solidarity. A radical post-colonial theory ought to encourage individuals to choose cultural communities they prefer rather than have elders or others of any description define their choice for them.[21]

Talking About Race in the Post-Colony

Some South African writers, such as Neville Alexander, argue that South Africans should struggle for "the dream of a raceless" society. Alexander explains that a raceless society or non-racialism means the non-existence of race as a biological entity to begin with, and the "constructedness" of race as a social category and therefore the potential to deconstruct race as a social category.[22]

In his book *Why Race Matters in South Africa*, Michael MacDonald argues that non-racialism should be the ultimate goal in any society, and that non-racialism consists of three objectives, namely, overcoming racism, eradicating official racialism, and propounding universal citizenship. Strengthening his argument, MacDonald writes that racialism, generally, usually derives from and abets racism.[23]

The common thread running through the above arguments is that the post-apartheid South Africa ought to mean an obliteration of racial and cultural differences. It is my contention that the presence of racial differences and racial hierarchies throughout South African society no more means we should eliminate racial and cultural diversity than the existence of overt or covert gender or sexual hierarchies means we should eliminate diversity in those realms.[24] It would seem that by subscribing to the notion of "non-racialism," thinkers who comment on South African social issues confuse cultural differences and racial differences with cultural and racial oppression.

Class and Race Analysis

The dominant theme that characterizes the socioeconomic debate is that South Africa is moving away from racial apartheid to class apartheid. Patrick Bond, a political economist based at the University of KwaZulu-Natal, captured the views of many when he penned an essay entitled "From Racial to Class Apartheid: South Africa's Frustrating Decade of Freedom."[25] In that essay, Bond's premise is that South Africa has witnessed the replacement of racial apartheid with what is increasingly referred to as class apartheid.

Echoing Bond, Devan Pillay, a South African sociologist at the University of the Witwatersrand, contends that the primary political question of our time has to be the class question—the question of poverty and socioeconomic inequality. In their book *Class, Race and Inequality in South Africa,* Jeremy Seekings and Nicoli Nattrass argue along similar lines.[26] They write that at the end of apartheid the primary basis of inequality shifted from race to class. "By the end of the apartheid era, South African households were rich or poor according primarily to the number and earnings of wage earners, and earnings in turn depended overwhelmingly on education and skill. Privileges could be reproduced on the basis of class rather than race."[27]

What Seekings and Nattrass are clearly oblivious to is the fact that due to the cumulative effects of longstanding racial discrimination and oppression, which result in direct barriers to black capital formation; the white households are far more likely to inherit or otherwise benefit from family wealth than black households.[28] Looked at from this angle, one is able to explain the socioeconomic developments in post-apartheid South Africa more adequately than the empty claim that South Africa is moving away from race to class apartheid.

What is remarkable, however, is that there seems to be a confusion regarding how a market-based economy operates. According to Albert,[29] a market-based economy will use the existing expectations of community members, such as the racist expectations that whites are superior and more competent than blacks, to enforce, and, where possible, to enlarge its own economic hierarchies of exploitation. Available evidence in post-apartheid South Africa supports this claim.

For example, according to research done by the Human Sciences Research Council (HSRC), the increased government assertiveness with regard to Black Economic

Empowerment (BEE) since 2000 has propelled an increasing number of companies, large and small, into scrambling to find black partners.

> Hence Ernst & Young, for instance, record that compared with 132 black empowerment deals valued at R23.1 billion in 1999, 126 valued at R28 billion were made in 2000, 101 at R25 billion in 2001, 104 at R12 billion in 2002, and 189 at R42 billion in 2003.... However, although these figures are not unimpressive, black control on the Johannesburg Securities Exchange (JSE) amounted to not more than four per cent at the end of 2004, even though the stock market had boomed with a 50 per cent increase in market capitalisation to R2.500 billion.[30]

Simply put, this means that, Black Economic Empowerment (BEE) notwithstanding, black control of the economy is still insignificant. So, to posit an argument that the central political question of our time has to be the class question, is, at best, to overstate the case, and, at worst, to be recklessly dogmatic.

Affirmative Action

It has become an indisputable fact that apartheid left behind a legacy of inequality. However, what has proved to be a source of dispute is how we go about rectifying the status quo. According to the Polity website, the state of affairs is characterized by a disparity in the distribution of jobs, occupations, and incomes, and this is due to the effects of discrimination against black people.[31]

To rectify the situation, the South African government has introduced the Employment Equity Act to address some of these issues. The act is based on the assumption that through affirmative action programs society is able to address the imbalances of the past and create equality in employment.

Critics have responded by labeling programs such as affirmative action as "reverse racism." For example, Neville Alexander has pointed out that:

> the acknowledgement of superficial differences should not become, even potentially, a lever for marginalisation or exclusion of any individual or group of people. This is the essence of a non-racial approach to the promotion of national unity and social integration and cohesion. As against this insight, almost every actual AA [affirmative action] measure tends to undermine such integration and cohesion.[32]

According to Alexander, affirmative action programs unavoidably perpetuate racial identities and that is disastrous.

Seekings and Nattrass argue that institutionalized racism against people of color in South Africa ended in the 1970s. They write that in the 1970s the racial barriers began to be less restrictive and, therefore, less oppressive, in large part because new employment opportunities opened up for "better-educated African workers."[33]

However, a study done by the HSRC refutes the myth that institutionalized racism is a thing of the past. The study shows that white males continue to dominate management and empowering positions in business, social, and cultural institutions. According to the study, opportunities for whites are abundant, and it is easier for whites to get credit, start a business, find a job, and make more money in their lifetime than it is for the average black person.

PART TWO: LIBERATORY POLITICS IN PRACTICE

Background to the Study

South Africa became a democratic country in 1994, after almost 350 years of colonialism and state regulated racism (normally referred to as apartheid). For over three centuries white settlers unleashed the worst form of institutionalized violence, oppressed and enslaved indigenous people, while putting themselves in a position to accumulate wealth. According to Professor Sampic Terreblanche, this was achieved in three different ways. Firstly, the white settlers created a political and economic power structure that placed them in a privileged position vis-à-vis the indigenous black people. Secondly, the white settlers deprived black people of land; and, thirdly, the white settlers turned black people into slaves. What that history has achieved is the impoverishment of black people, and what that history left behind is the legacy of racial hierarchy based on white supremacy, authoritarianism, and the widespread gender oppression that manifests itself as violence against women.[34]

It has been pointed out by many political commentators that the African National Congress (ANC) has done little to change the structural unequal distribution of wealth and resources in post-apartheid South Africa. One of the reasons for this is because during the negotiations between the apartheid government and the ANC in 1994, the Transitional Executive Council (TEC)[35] accepted an $850 million loan from the IMF to "help tide the country over balance of payments difficulties," according to Terreblanche.[36] And, before the IMF could grant the loan to South Africa, the future government (which was to consist of the Apartheid government and the ANC) needed to sign a secret protocol on economic policies of the country. Terreblanche writes that in the "Statement on Economic Policies" agreed upon with the IMF, the TEC committed itself to a neoliberal, export-oriented economic policy, and a redistribution through growth strategy. The TEC-IMF statement reads as follows:

> Monetary policy has carried much of the burden of SA's adjustment during the 1990s. An easing of [the strict] monetary policy would have risked a further undermining of [international] confidence and a resurgence of inflation. To redress social backlogs, SA's economic policies must be driven by the objective of durable [economic] growth in which all can share equitably. This will require political stability and a package of macroeconomic and structural policies that address the problems of high unemployment and weak investment, respect financial restraints, and promote [international] confidence in the country's economic management. There is widespread understanding that increases in

the government deficit would jeopardize the economic future of the country [and that] given the importance of maintaining a competitive tax structure [fiscal policy] will emphasise expenditure containment rather than rising taxes. It is [also] recognized that unless social needs are addressed in a responsible manner socio-political stability would be difficult to sustain. Trade and industrial liberalization will be an important part of the restructuring of the economy.[37]

Terreblanche argues that as soon as the ANC's leaders agreed to the statement above, they were trapped in the web of the domestic corporate sector and the international financial establishment, represented by the IMF and World Bank. The consequences of this agreement are the unequal distribution of wealth and resources in post-apartheid South Africa. Poverty has intensified, racism has become subtler but remains as institutionalized as ever, and workers are losing their jobs en masse.

Last year, on May 18, 2006, the Congress of South African Trade Unions (CO-SATU) took to the streets to show their unhappiness about the loss of more than 100,000 jobs over the past three years, according to the UN news agency IRIN.[38] The Human Sciences Research Council (HSRC) reports that South Africa's unemployment rate has steadily increased from 1,912,471 in 1990 to 4,789,582 in 2002.[39] To put this in a context, one has to bear in mind that South Africa has a population of about 46 million; the majority of those unemployed are black—a legacy of the apartheid regime, which today is maintained by neoliberal policies.

The HSRC study reveals that unemployment continues to be linked to race in South Africa. A survey of 2,672 university graduates who obtained their first degrees between 1990 and 1998 revealed that 70 percent of white graduates found employment immediately, compared to 43 percent Africans who experienced periods of unemployment.

Moreover, millions of people still do not have access to basic services. Research done by the HSRC shows that about 11.5 million people did not have basic access services to safe water in 2003, and that about 18.1 million people do not have adequate sanitation.[40] I must emphasise the fact that these statistics refer mostly to people of color.

Whites, on the other hand, dominate ownership of businesses, social, and cultural institutions. Whites control about 80 percent of the arable land in South Africa. Opportunities for whites continue to be abundant, irrespective of income or educational status, according to research done by the HSRC.[41]

Another group that is benefiting from this state of affairs is the black elite. The BEE is a government-led initiative to create a class of black capitalists and has served as a catalyst in the creation of this class. Consequently, a number of business companies in South Africa have made it a point to have black partners. However, it must be pointed out that this black elite is very small and, compared to white capital, this black elite has no economic power. As already mentioned in this essay, black control on the Johannesburg Securities Exchange (JSE) amounted to not more than 4 percent at the end of 2004, even though the stock market had boomed by 50 percent at the end of 2004.

With this historical background, one wants to highlight the fact that not much decolonization has taken place in South Africa. Further, post-apartheid South Africa serves as a good example to show that it is not enough to be against injustice and oppression; rather, in addition, one must have a concrete proposal for a different and liberatory society. Such a proposal ought to be based on sound economic assumptions and revolutionary values. Pan-Africanism has failed us, so has black nationalism and black Marxism. What is needed is a proposal that takes into account the best of all three theories, but at the same time goes further than that by presenting a vision of what a better society ought to look like.

I propose participatory economics for such a project. Parecon is characterized by the following: social ownership, participatory planning allocation, council structure, balanced job complexes, remuneration for effort and sacrifice and participatory self-management with no class differentiation.[42]

Through parecon I believe a decolonized society is possible. Let me show you how by dissecting the different components of parecon.

Social Ownership

Albert argues that private ownership of the means of production exists when private individuals own the buildings, equipment, tools, technologies, land, and resources with which we produce goods and services. Further, having a few members of the society own these means of production and decide on their use, and, in addition, to dispose over the output and profits they generate has meant that this privileged group has always had more wealth and more economic power than other people in society. Looked at from this point of view, we can boldly state that private ownership of the means of production lead to inequality, the haves and the have-nots, the owners and non-owners.

So, owing to over three centuries of colonialism and almost five decades of apartheid's oppressive policies, the haves and the owners in South Africa have always been and continue being white, while, on the other hand, the have-nots and non-owners are blacks. When statistics show that black control on the Johannesburg Securities Exchange (JSE) amounted to not more than 4 percent at the end of 2004, even though the stock market had boomed by 50 percent at the end of 2004, it proves the validity of my statement that owners in South Africa continue being white. This racialized ownership of the means of production perpetuates the inequality and the racial hierarchy in South Africa. Private ownership of the means of production is the main contributor to the increasing inequality in post-apartheid South Africa. Moreover, the owners sustain this state of inequality by extracting maximum labor from the workers as cheaply as possible, thereby maximizing their profits, while simultaneously working to maintain the conditions that allow the haves and the owners to appropriate profits.[43]

Parecon would aim to preclude such a status quo. In a pareconish society we would remove the ownership of the means of production from the economic picture.

> We can think of this as deciding that no one owns the means of production. Or we can think of it as deciding that everyone owns a factional share of every single item of means of production equivalent to what every other person owns of that item. Or we can think of it as deciding that society owns all means of production but that it has no say over any of the means of production nor any claim on their output on that account.[44]

An economy designed in such a way would facilitate the equal distribution of wealth and resources in society. Also, as Albert points out, this would mean that there will be no individual or institution that can claim an income different from what the rest of the economy warrants for that particular person or institution.

Council Structure

In an economy workers create the social product, while consumers enjoy the benefits of the social product. In a pareconish society, Albert argues that for workers to do their jobs responsibly and in an empowering way, workers ought to consider what they would like to contribute to the social product, both by their own efforts and in association with those they work with.[45] In addition, workers ought to address how to combine their efforts and the resources and tools they have access to, to generate worthy outputs that other people will benefit from. Most importantly, workers ought to be directly in touch with the dynamics of production and with its implications for themselves and others.

The same logic applies to consumers. Consumers ought to consider what they would like to have from the social product, either as individuals or in collective association with neighbors for example. They ought to address what to ask for to advance their lives as best they can in line with the impact their choices will have on the people producing their outputs.[46]

To achieve the above, workers could form "workers' councils" and consumers could establish "consumers' councils." Albert argues that this would lead to a situation whereby a workplace is governed by a workers' council in which each worker has the same overall decision-making rights and responsibilities as every other worker.

The same applies to consumers' councils. It is important to highlight that each neighborhood consumer council would belong in turn to a federation of neighborhood councils. The rational behind these consumer councils is to accommodate the fact that different kinds of consumption affect different groups of people in different ways, explains Albert.

To reach decisions, councils use either a one-person-one-vote majority rule or a consensus decision-making procedure. The councils have an oversight as to when to use which decision-making mechanism to achieve maximum participation by members.

> Moreover, in addition to all these councils and federations of councils, parecon will have various "facilitation boards" or agencies that facilitate information exchange and processing for collective consumption proposals and for large-scale investment projects, workers requests for changing places of employment, and individuals and families seeking to find membership in living units and neighborhoods, among other functions. Finally, at every level of the economy there will also be facilitation boards to help units revise proposals and search out the least disruptive ways of modifying plans in response to unforeseen circumstances."[47]

In the South African context, councils would not only help eliminate the corporate hierarchy but would destroy the racial and gender hierarchy that characterizes the South African society. As has been pointed out in this essay, research conducted by HSRC has shown that the fact of the matter is that whites still dominate ownership and management positions in business, social, and cultural institutions. The councils could serve as a force to oppose this white domination and institutionalized racism.

Regarding consumption, the cultural institutions in South Africa would, for example, because of demographics, reflect strong African cultural values and not Western values as is the case at the moment. However, because the cultural institutions are managed and controlled by whites, the cultural production and cultural values that are promoted by these institutions are Western values, standards, and aesthetics. The targeted audience for these cultural productions are whites, mainly because whites in South Africa have a strong buying power. In a participatory economy where the concept of "buying power" is irrelevant and basically nonexistent, cultural productions produced by these institutions would be determined by consumers' councils. In these councils every person has the same overall decision-making rights and responsibilities; money does not enter into the equation.

Balanced Job Complexes

In a pareconish society, corporate divisions of labor would be a thing of the past; workplaces will be run on the basis of balanced job complexes instead. This means that every single person in society will have a chance to do an unpleasant and disempowering task for some time each day or week, and then for some other time everyone in society will have a chance to work at pleasant and empowering tasks. The point that Albert wants to get across here is that, overall, people should not do either rote and unpleasant work or conceptual and empowering work all the time. This is what creates class divisions in society, after all.

In a society like South Africa, a workplace organized on the values of balanced job complexes would mean that systematic biases or institutionalized racism and sexism are addressed effectively and institutionally. As I have argued above, research shows that 83 percent of those trained for operational occupation in South Africa are black Africans compared to 4.9 percent of whites. Further, 71 percent of those trained for managerial and professional positions are whites, compared to 16 percent of blacks. This institutional practice that facilitates white domination is based on the racist assumption that whites are generally more competent and superior to blacks.

Balanced job complexes would terminate this practice by making sure that there are no jobs in the economy that are systematically reserved for a certain group of people. Depending on what sector people fit into, everyone will have their own share of rote and unpleasant work, as well as their share of conceptual and empowering work. Balanced job complexes will not only terminate institutionalized racism and sexism but will also guard against the creation of a coordinator class. A coordinator class consists of teachers, academics, social workers, health workers, industrial engineers, and a host of types of bureaucrats. Albert and Hahnel argue that the function of this class is to "serve the people" and yet also to continually preserve the conditions which give rise to the need for such services in the first place.[48]

Decolonization in Africa has succeeded in producing such a class; with flying colors too. Fanon is referring to the coordinator class when he, for example, writes that for the post-colonial middle-class, nationalization of the economy simply means the transfer into native hands of those unfair advantages which are a legacy of the colonial period. Fanon adds that this coordinator class is quite content with the role of the Western bourgeoisie's business agent, and it will play its part without any complexes in a most dignified manner. Fanon's only mistake is to want to attribute the creation of a coordinate class to a supposedly rampant black inferiority complex instead of subjecting the emergence of such a class into a structural and ideological critique.

Self-management

Decolonized Africa did not usher in a different and better way of organizing a workplace. Instead workplaces are still characterized by the same hierarchical and authoritarian structure of the old colonial order. In post-apartheid South Africa, the workplace consists of managers who transform job roles according to the dictates of market competition.[49]

Even in other parts of Africa, where after decolonization post-colonial governments experimented with different versions of socialism (for example, Julius Nyerere's Tanzania), the process was basically carried out in a top-down approach, and it was a state-driven project. Such an approach can only facilitate an environment where technical and critical decisions are made by "experts" who belong to the coordinator class. And that, as Albert points out, can lead to an increase in the fragmentation of work, and in turn bloat managerial prerogatives and in the end substitute experts' goals for those of the people. Once such a process is in motion, Albert argues that it is not long before a burgeoning managerial class of "coordinators" begins to increase their influence on society as a whole and to search for ways to preserve their own power.

So, the rational behind self-management is to subvert authoritarianism and the creation of a new oppressive class (i.e. coordinator class); the goal being to encourage workers to take initiative in workplace decisions. In a participatory society, the economy will be designed in such a manner that "each actor in the economy should influence economic outcomes in proportion to how those outcomes affect him or her."[50] In a workplace, for example, self-management will be achieved by means of workers' councils, and in society at large, self-management could be achieved through consumers' councils and neighborhood councils. As I have argued in this essay, workers' councils are there for workers to consider what they would like to contribute to the social product. And consumers' councils serve as a forum for consumers to discuss and debate what they would like to have from the social product.

Remuneration for Effort and Sacrifice

In a participatory society, Albert argues that those people who are able to work would be remunerated for the effort or sacrifice they expend in contributing to the social product, and those people who are not able to work would be remunerated at some appropriate level based on social averages and special needs. This means that no one should have claims on output on the basis of owning some means of production, nor should anyone have claims on output on the basis of bargaining power. Albert adds that no one in a participatory society will have claims on output on the basis that they put a larger sum into the social product than others by using some special genetic endowment or talent, or due to having some highly productive learned skill, better tools, or more productive workmates, or because they happen to produce things that are more highly valued.

To reward someone based on the notion that they own the means of production is inequitable and unjust. For example, most of those who own means of production in South Africa do so due to white privilege, and because black people in South Africa were oppressed as a group and were not allowed to own property for over three centuries. The same white privilege has put white people in this country in a better bargaining position than other cultural groups; and so to use a bargaining position as a determining factor as to how people should be rewarded in the economy is not equitable.

In post-apartheid South Africa, whites do not only own means of production, they are better trained and are better educated than most South Africans. To deal with such a situation based on our parecon values, Albert explains that although differences in contribution to output will derive from differences in talent, training, education, tools, and luck, if we define effort as personal sacrifice for the sake of the social endeavor, only effort merits compensation. Effort can take many forms; it may be longer work hours, unpleasant and disempowering work, or dangerous and unhealthy work.[51]

Based on this logic, in a participatory society, for a person to receive higher or lower remuneration, that particular person would have worked more or less hours or at a higher or lower intensity of effort. Workers would receive an "evaluation report" to indicate hours worked at a balanced job complex and the intensity of work performed, and this will yield an "effort rating in the form of a percentage multiplier."[52] In addition, the evaluation report will be utilized as a tool to determine workers' income to be used for consumption expenditure. So, based on the parecon logic, Albert explains that those doing the most onerous, harmful work would be the highest paid; and those doing the most pleasant and intrinsically uplifting work would be the lowest paid.

Participatory Planning Allocation

Allocation is the process whereby an economy determines the amounts to be produced and the relative exchange rates of all inputs and outputs.[53] Albert explains that the economy chooses from a nearly infinite list of every conceivable product that might be produced in a year with every conceivable combination of patterns of labor and resource use, "plus every conceivable apportionment of the product, the single final list of what all the various economic actors actually produce and consume."[54]

Unlike market-based economies, allocation in a participatory economy will be guided and informed by people's wishes and choices. For example, workplace councils will influence decision making regarding production; and the consumers and neighborhood councils will influence decision making relating to consumption. Albert points out that for these councils to make intelligent and informed decisions that are in tune with parecon values, they need to have access to reliable information regarding production and consumption patterns of the society they inhabit.

> Suppose we keep records of the production and consumption that took place in the just completed year. Then with each year we will have information about last year's plan. Suppose the prices used to calculate social costs, benefits, and income last year are also recorded. Then each year we will have a set of final prices from last year to use to begin this year's estimates. By storing last year's full plan in a central computer, access to relevant information, including indicative prices, could be made available to all actors in the planning process. Additionally, by accessing such information, each unit can easily see what its own proposals were in each round of the prior year's planning process.[55]

With this kind of information available, Albert explains that the councils will then receive information from facilitation boards estimating this year's probable changes in prices and income in light of existing knowledge of past investment decisions and changes in the labor force. Albert adds that the councils will also receive information regarding long-term investment projects already agreed to in previous plans. Further, councils will have to take into consideration any increases in average income and improvements in the quality of average work complexes that are projected for the coming year.

Access to this kind of information will make the councils function more effectively. This is because the availability of such information will compel councils to develop a proposal, for example, for the coming year, not only enumerating what they want to consume or produce, but also providing qualitative information about their reasons.[56] "This proposal enters the mix with all others, feedback arrives, and revisions are made, round by round, until a final version is reached."[57]

The advantages of a participatory economy are that instead of the state or the elite making decisions regarding production and consumption, workers' councils and neighborhood councils will decide what is good for society. To bring it close to home, instead of white capital and the coordinator class deciding what is good for the economy, ordinary South Africans will decide which direction the economy should take.

Findings

The first part of this essay dealt with the conceptual flaws and inadequacies that hinder post-colonial writers and activists from fighting for a better and liberatory society. My point of departure is that a post-colonial theory ought to provide us with concepts and tools to describe and explain what constitutes an anti-classist, anti-racist, and anti-sexist society. The findings of the literature review on Fanon show that: (1) Fanon's assumptions regarding what decolonization entails, (2) Fanon's views on what inspires the natives to violently rebel against a colonial regime, and (3) Fanon's explanation on why post colonial governments betray the revolution and the decolonization agenda are completely unfounded. Fanon's theoretical explanation on the above-mentioned issues does not help us fully understand the post-colonial reality.

The findings of the literature review on the issue of race show that for white liberals to argue that South Africa has witnessed the replacement of racial apartheid with what is increasingly referred to as class apartheid is to overstate the case.

bell hooks explains the attitude of white liberals differently.

> White critics who passively absorb white supremacist thinking, and therefore never notice or look at black people on the streets, at their jobs, who render us invisible with their gaze in all areas of daily life, are not likely to produce liberatory theory that will challenge racist domination, or to promote a breakdown in traditional ways of seeing and thinking about reality."[58]

It is these findings that compelled me to search for a more liberatory politics. As I have argued in this essay, a political theory that advocates for a participatory society makes sense, for it relates sensibly to our situation and our aspirations. Parecon does not encourage single-issue activism, nor does parecon devalue other people's experiences and oppressions by prioritizing a certain ideological perspective over the other. Through parecon I believe we can achieve a truly decolonized Africa.

Conclusion

The motivation to write this essay is underpinned by the belief that different political schools of thought (such as Pan-Africanism, black nationalism and black Marxism) that Africans have always used to carry out decolonization projects have failed us, and that a much more revolutionary, far-reaching political theory ought to be explored if we are serious about decolonization.

The thinking that went into this essay is influenced and shaped by the logic that to have a growth-oriented attitude about one's ideas, rather than a stability-oriented attitude is healthy and is the antithesis of sectarianism.[59] And, if we wish to overcome sectarianism, we need to be self-critical and to strive for clarity and seek truth as best we can.

(Endnotes)

1   Mikhail Bakunin, "Who am I?" in *No Gods No Masters: An Anthology of Anarchism*, Book One, ed. D. Guérin (AK Press, 1998): 126–28

2   Ibid.

3   Frantz Fanon *The Wretched of the Earth* (Penguin Books, 1990)

4   Ibid.: 28

5   Michael Albert *Thought Dreams: Radical Theory for the 21st Century* (Arbeiter Ring Publishing, 2004)

6   Ibid.

7   Ibid.

8   Ibid.

9   Fanon *The Wretched of the Earth*: 74

10   K. Owusu-Bempah and D. Howitt, *Psychology Beyond Western Perspectives* (British Psychological Society Books, 2000)

11   William E. Cross *Shades of Black: Diversity in African-American Identity* (Temple University Press, 1991)

12   Ibid.: 117

13   Albert *Thought Dreams*

14   Frantz Fanon *The Wretched of the Earth*: 122

15   Ibid.: 141

16   Ibid.: 30

17   Howard Zinn *A People's History of the United States: 1492 to Present* (HarperCollins, 2001)

18   Fanon *The Wretched of the Earth*: 178

19   Ibid.: 179

20   Michael Albert *Realizing Hope: Life Beyond Capitalism* (Fernwood Publishing, 2006)

21   Ibid.

22   Neville Alexander "Language and Culture in a Postcolonial State" (2006) *Pambazuka News* website: www.pambazuka.org/en/category/comment/38360 (accessed on December 5, 2006)

23   Michael MacDonald *Why Race Matters in South Africa* (University of Kwazulu-Natal Press, 2006)

24   Albert *Realizing Hope*

25   Patrick Bond "From Racial To Class Apartheid: South Africa's Frustrating Decade Of Freedom" *Monthly Review* Vol 55. (2006) website www.monthlyreview.org/0304bond.htm (accessed December 11, 2006)

26   Jeremy Seekings and Nicoli Nattrass *Class, Race and Inequality in South Africa* (University of Kwazulu-Natal Press, 2006)

27   Ibid.: 300

28   Tim Wise *Affirmative Action: Preference in Black and White* (Routledge, 2005)
29   Albert *Realizing Hope*
30   S. Buhlungu., J. Daniel, R. Southall, and J. Lutchman, eds. *State of the Nation: South Africa 2005–2006* (HSRC Press, 2006): 178
31   www.polity.org.za offers free access to South African legislation, policy documents and daily political news.
32   Neville Alexander Affirmative Action and the Perpetuation of Racial Identities in Post-Apartheid South Africa (2006) Human Sciences Research Council website: www.hsrc.ac.za/research/programmes/DG/events/20060511NevilleAlexander.pdf (accessed on December 8, 2006)
33   Seekings, and Nattrass, *Class, Race and Inequality in South Africa*
34   Sampie Terreblanche *A History of Inequality in South Africa: 1652–2002* (University of Natal Press, 2002)
35   The TEC consisted of all the parties involved in the Kempton Park negotiations.
36   Terreblanche *A History of Inequality in South Africa: 1652–2002*: 96
37   Ibid.: 96
38   "South African Workers Take to the Streets" *IRIN* website: www.irinnews.org/report.asp?ReportID=53450&SelectRegion=Southern_Africa&SelectCountry=SOUTH_AFRICA (accessed May 21, 2006)
39   *Human Sciences Research Council* website: www.hsrc.ac.za
40   Ibid.
41   Ibid.
42   Michael Albert *ParEcon: Life After Capitalism* (Verso, 2003)
43   Ibid.
44   Ibid.: 90
45   Ibid.
46   Ibid.
47   Ibid.: 128
48   Michael Albert and Robin Hahnel *Unorthodox Marxism: An Essay on Capitalism, Socialism and Revolution* (South End Press, 1978)
49   Albert *ParEcon*
50   Ibid.: 40
51   Ibid.
52   Ibid.
53   Ibid.
54   Ibid.: 122
55   Ibid.: 129
56   Ibid.
57   Ibid.: 130
58   bell hooks *Yearning: Race, Gender, and Cultural Politics* (South End Press, 1990): 25
59   Albert *Thought Dreams*

Chapter 12

LOCAL PLANNING: THE KERALA EXPERIMENT

Richard W. Franke

IN 1996 INDIA'S KERALA State embarked on a remarkable experiment in local planning.[1] At the time it was known as the "People's Campaign for the Ninth Plan." "The Ninth Plan" referred to India's Ninth Five-Year Plan in which each state within the national federation draws up its own annual plan. The "People's" part referred to Kerala's decision to devolve 35 percent of its state development budget down from a centralized bureaucracy to local communities where local people could determine and implement their own priorities.[2] Later known as the People's Plan Campaign (PPC), Kerala's experiment radically improved delivery of public services, brought about greater caste and ethnic equality, facilitated the entry of women into public life at a much greater pace, and enhanced democratic practice. By the third year the Campaign began to generate local employment utilizing and improving upon the famous Grameen Bank micro credit idea to bring households above the poverty level.[3] Following the 2001 electoral defeat of the Left Democratic Front (LDF) that had initiated the PPC, the Congress Party Ministry undercut many features of the project but local planning survived and is now being stimulated again by the LDF ministry elected in 2006. In this brief overview I propose to summarize the historical roots of the PPC, the main elements and outcomes, and some of the most important failures or shortcomings.

Historical Background

Kerala's People's Plan Campaign was not inspired by parecon theories or writings but grew instead out of Kerala's general Left history. Starting in the late 19th century as opposition to the caste system, the Left movement grew alongside and within the Indian independence movement and the trade union movement of the 1920s and '30s, as well as the land reform movement of the peasants. A key moment in the growth of the Left movement in Kerala was the 1957 election victory of the Communist Party of India in the state assembly elections. The 1957 Communist Ministry advanced many programs for the poorest sections of society. In the following decades several Left coalition ministries have been elected, including the LDF Ministry, in power from 1996 to 2001 and the present LDF Ministry, elected in 2006. After many reforms and programs to redistribute wealth—which gave Kerala among the best health and education indicators in India—progressive activists by the 1990s came to the conclusion that the energy and creativity of local democracy might be tools to advance a development agenda independent of corporate-dominated globalization. Their agenda had to be consistent with both Marxist goals of egalitarianism and Gandhian ideas of local autonomy and maximum self-sufficiency within the constraints of the international capitalist system. Already in the 1980s an LDF Ministry had experimented with local initiatives in cooperative farming, environmental projects, local planning assemblies, and elected District Councils to try to decentralize the bureaucratic state government and bring political power to more local levels. The PPC was an enormous "going to scale" of these local experiments.[4]

The Campaign Begins

The PPC unfolded as a sequence of assemblies, seminars, task forces, local council meetings, implementation and monitoring committees, and the like. The first stage was to hold local assemblies in each of Kerala's 14,149 village wards and urban neighborhoods. Each assembly had 1,500 to 2,000 voting age members (age sixteen and above). In the first year average attendance was 159 persons or an estimated 11 percent of voters. Attendance increased somewhat in the second and third years but fell off slightly in the fourth and fifth years.

The local assemblies were held on Sunday afternoons to make it easier for workers to attend. Schools were the main venue—every Kerala village and urban neighborhood has several—and they facilitated the structure of the meetings. Politicians were banned from taking more than thirty minutes for speeches and the main business was to break down into small groups in individual classrooms to focus on particular areas for planning, such as agriculture, safe drinking water, animal husbandry, improving the status of women and former untouchable caste members, industry, health services, and the like. These discussion groups were intended to bring out the felt needs of the people attending. The small groups reported back to the plenary session later in the day.

The local assemblies were guided by facilitators trained in a massive education program in which more than 100,000 people learned how to run meetings, how to ask questions to keep the discussions as focused as possible, and how to encourage the maximum number of people to participate. In later stages, these "resource persons" received training in how to help local councils draft project reports, estimate budgets, and hire contractors where appropriate. The training program was a key element of the major successes achieved by the PPC.

At the end of the local assemblies small teams were elected to take on the next phase: data gathering. Each team had to have at least one male and one female. Over the next several weeks these teams visited local government offices to collect information, carried out "transect walks" where they would draw a line on a map of the community and walk through as many different ecological and social areas as possible, and make notes. The data gathering led to the next stage—writing a local community self-report. These reports run from seventy-five to more than two-hundred pages.[5]

The self-study reports were the basis for the development seminar, attended at the all village level—about ten wards per village or urban neighborhood—where task forces were elected to begin to draft project proposals based on the felt needs expressed in the first round of local assemblies. The task forces worked for several more weeks before presenting a list of projects to the elected village and urban councils. The elected representatives made the final priorities: in the first year of the PPC 150,000 projects emerged from the local communities of which about 68,000 were implemented. A key feature at the last stage of planning was that about 4,000 retired engineers, doctors, and other experts volunteered to assist at no pay in making technical evaluations needed in many of the projects.

From the Bottom Up

In terms of parecon theory, an interesting aspect of the PPC is the relations that emerged among the various levels of government. In Kerala local communities are grouped into "blocks," sets of two to thirteen communities recognized by the Indian national government for delivery of certain project funds. The 152 blocks group into taluks or sub-districts and into fourteen districts. With the PPC came the idea that the higher levels of government exist to serve and support the lower levels—a fairly revolutionary concept in some ways. In recent development theory this idea has become known as the "principle of subsidiarity"—"decisions should be made at the lowest level of government authority competent to deal with them," leading to the consequence that "decisions should constantly move closer to the people most affected by them."[6] In the Kerala PPC this worked out in practice as each lower level sent up its plans to a higher level, the higher level assembly attempted to iron out inconsistencies, fill in gaps, and thus make the local plans more effective. This created the possibility of making public services function more effectively by assigning each level responsibilities most appropriate to it. Several local communities for example improved the supply of medicines at the local Primary Health Center (PHC). This made it possible for the taluk level hospitals to spend more of their allotments on fixing up the surgery rooms or adding MRI machines or outpatient public health projects requiring greater resources than a village or urban neighborhood could provide.[7]

Some communities pushed the limits of local power through creative and unexpected projects. One village constructed a bridge to facilitate foot and bicycle traffic over a major river where people had been demanding the Public Works Department do it for years.[8] One town developed an innovative suicide prevention program while another linked up with a team of local scientists to create one of the most promising biological mosquito control projects anywhere internationally.[9] Several communities developed highly efficient techniques for social auditing by which decisions about beneficiaries were made publicly, thus helping to prevent corruption and favoritism. One village created an innovative "labor bank" system for regularizing employment of farm laborers and for smoothing out work patterns over the farming year.[10] In an example of higher levels of government serving the lower levels, the Kerala State Planning Board organized numerous seminars and regional meetings where activists could learn from each others' experiences. This process culminated in May of 2000 with the International Conference on Democratic Decentralization, where over seven hundred local activists and elected representatives shared presentations on their communities' problems and achievements. The proceedings were published in six volumes in Malayalam, the language of Kerala. Some materials are also available in English.[11]

From Public Services to Cooperative Employment

The first few years of the PPC focused on training facilitators, mobilizing popular participation, and improving the delivery of public services via the government development budget that was being devolved. By the third year of the Campaign local activists were putting together Neighborhood Groups (NHGs) of about forty households. These groups evolved from meetings to discuss local problems to rotating credit associations—called "thrift collection" in Kerala—to nuclei from which small-scale micro-credit cooperative businesses could be launched. Using the thrift funds as startup capital, local cooperative banks would issue credit to groups of ten to twenty households, usually represented by an adult female, to manufacture soap, school supplies, umbrellas, some electrical equipment, and processed foods. According to the current LDF Minister for Local Self-Government Institutions, Paloli Mohammed Kutty, as of 2006, across Kerala 3.8 million households (possibly 40 percent of all households—RWF) belonged to 179,000 neighborhood associations.[12] Many of these NHGs have grown into production cooperatives that are bringing thousands of households above the poverty line. The logic of organizing the co-ops through adult women is that women are usually the least employed so that their co-op income has the greatest strategic impact on the household's income. Increased women's empowerment is an anticipated by-product of the program but no evidence appears to be available to indicate whether this is occurring. Recent research indicates that the Kerala unemployment rate has dropped from 19 percent to 9 percent.[13] It seems likely that the micro-credit business that emerged from the PPC has played a large role in this dramatic improvement.[14]

Why Cooperatives?

Why use local participatory democracy to create institutions that generate local private businesses owned by their workers? Kerala's local democracy advocates have never spelled out a formal theoretical explication of their strategy but we can make some educated guesses. Firstly, cooperatives are inherently more egalitarian than conventional private firms and therefore hold out more promise of development with social justice. Simply improving government services to assist regular capitalist development runs the risk of reproducing inequality and intensified accumulation on the part of a few. Secondly, cooperatives are a historic feature of Kerala's long history of Leftwing activism—people are familiar with them as goals to be achieved. Thirdly, cooperatives by their nature create an ethic of solidarity that can be used to amplify their effects throughout the community. While there is no guarantee co-ops will see their role in the community as similar to the role of each worker in the co-op, when co-ops grow up together as part of a local planning process, inter-co-op cooperation can be attempted. This has occurred especially in one part of Kerala where an ambitious local-regional plan is being built up from the local communities to integrate cooperatives producing coconut, coconut products, fish, vegetables, recycling, coconut fabric (coir) spinning and mat making, soap production, and several other undertakings to generate a mostly egalitarian and environmentally sustainable regional economy where local resources, local labor, and local consumer markets will automatically provide some resistance against the predations of multinational corporate globalization.[15]

Shortcomings and Failures

Kerala's remarkable achievements in launching a process of local participatory planning should not blind us to many weaknesses in the project. From the outset in 1996 many on the Left were skeptical of the revolutionary credentials of such a program and some activists played less of a role than they might have. Physicians, engineers and many other technically needed persons sat on the sidelines or even worked to undermine the new program. Organizers discovered too late that many local communities were not sufficiently versed in cost-benefit analysis or simple budgeting skills to draft effective project proposals. All kinds of glitches and delays occurred, some of them with serious consequences, such as the mistaken decision by many communities to purchase animals on the open market at the same time for distribution to poor families. This drove up the price of the animals and created disillusionment among many activists. Most importantly, by the second and third years many middle-class persons came to view the entire PPC as exclusively a poor people's activity. They withdrew from the local assemblies, taking their opinions and their skills with them. Many of them may have provided the vote shift that pushed the LDF government from power in the 2001 elections.

The 2006 LDF comeback, however, has brought new energy to local democratic planning. While not being carried out in campaign mode, the new project is attempting to build on the successes and avoid the failures of its original run.

(Endnotes)

1   Kerala State, located in southwest India, had a 2007 population of 32 million.
2   The other 65 percent was kept for large scale projects such as port dredging and major electrification.
3   Detailed accounts of the PPC and its aftermath can be found in T. M. Thomas Isaac and Richard W. Franke *Local Democracy and Development: The Kerala People's Campaign for Decentralized Planning* (Rowman and Littlefield, 2002, also Leftword Books, 2000); Joy Elamon, Richard W. Franke, and B. Ekbal "Decentralization of Health Services: The Kerala People's Campaign" *International Journal of Health Services* (2004): 34 (4):681–708; Srikumar Chattopadhyay and Richard W. Franke *Striving for Sustainability: Environmental Stress and Democratic Initiatives in*

Kerala (Concept Publishing Company, 2006). Additional materials and links can be found on my website: http://chss.montclair.edu/anthro/franke.html

4   For the theoretical origins and local experiment examples see Isaac and Franke, chapter 2. For local initiatives coming out of the PPC, see Chattopadhyay and Franke, chapter 10.

5   Details in Isaac and Franke, chapter 3.

6   John Cavanagh and Jerry Mander, ed. *Alternatives to Economic Globalization: A Better World Is Possible* (Berrett-Koehler, 2004): 149

7   Details and examples in Elamon, Franke, and Ekbal. See note 3 above for full references.

8   Richard W. Franke and Barbara H. Chasin "Power to the (Malayalee) People" *Z Magazine* (February 1998): 11(2):16–20

9   "The Chapparappadavu People's Bridge" in Isaac and Franke, chapter 10; the Koyilandy Mosquito Control Project in Elamon, Franke, and Ekbal and online, website: http://chss.montclair.edu/anthro/Koyilandi.htm

10   Isaac and Franke, chapter 10

11   For information in Malayalam and English, go to: http://chss.montclair.edu/anthro/frankemayconference2000.htm

12   www.kerala.gov.in/1year_img/lsgi.pdf. See also: www.keralaplanningboard.org/html/Economic%20Review%202006/Chap/Chapter14.pdf especially page 364 for previous year's figures.

13   www.hindu.com/2007/09/18/stories/2007091850030100.htm

14   www.keralaplanningboard.org/html/Economic%20Review%202006/Chap/Chapter14.pdf especially page 362 et seq.

15   Details in Chattopadhyay and Franke, chapter 10.

Chapter 13

PARTICIPATORY BALKANS

Exchanges between Andrej Grubacic and Michael Albert

PART 1: CIVIL SOCIETY OR PARTICIPATORY SOCIETY?

Andrej Grubacic interviewed by Michael Albert (August, 2003)

Albert: To start, can you tell us something about the context of organizing in the Balkans?

Grubacic: There is a term flooding the progressive press all around the Balkans, lurking like a phantom over the editor's desk. It is present in all "critical analyses" and has become unavoidable in the discourse of the so-called non-government organizations. "Civil society" is the term. It just refers to non-governmental elements presumably working on behalf of the social good. It seems that the term has gone beyond civility and become royalty in political journalism in the Balkans.

In the West, too, it is virtually impossible to get away from this term. You encounter it even where you least expect. "Why wouldn't we ally Davos and Porto Alegre?" asked Philip Watts, Shell President, in a serious tone of voice at the gathering of the World Economic Forum in New York. The very fact that at that year's Porto Alegre Forum there were three French candidates for president, eight government members with Prime Minister Jospin, and two hundred mayors of major world cities, speaks of the fact that global resistance to neoliberalism has become a "planetary reality." However, it also warns of probably the greatest challenge so far posed to the subversiveness of the movement itself: in the name of the "civil society."

Editor's note: The following chapter is comprised of two interviews conducted four years apart. Part one, Andrej Grubacic interviewed by Michael Albert, is from August 2003 and remains a good contextual bridge to part two, a shorter more recent interview from August 2007, where Andrej interviews Michael. This latter interview. is a brief excerpt from a larger piece prepared for Z Magazine Balkans, a new print magazine produced by "Freedom Fight Collective" for Balkan audiences, modeled on Z Magazine U.S., utilizing content from it as well as local content bearing more directly on the Balkans. This second interview was conducted at the request of workers in a pharmaceutical factory, "Jugoremedija," in Zrenjanin (Serbia) for an issue of Z Magazine Balkans focusing on participatory economics. The workers are running the plant, having taken it over, and are looking for information and ideas about how to rearrange their workplace to escape the ills of both capitalism and the market socialism they experienced in Yugoslavia.

But you ask about the Balkans. Here the comedy of "listening and repenting," of civil society rhetoric and practice, are at full swing. What is it all about?

The capitalist discourse is changing its bullying approach (denying it out loud) in a metamorphosis which leaves one breathless. The rhetorical fireworks include the phrases "mutual agreement," "transparency," "ethics," and my favorite: "closeness." In order to have the current system appear in the new velvety outfit, it requires part-ners—those denying it. Therein begins the comedy of civil society, the noise and the well-tempered rage, the new mythology of the "citizen-mate" which in the strategy of the authorities has the aim of simply integrating the deniers.

Albert: Can you give some examples?

Grubacic: Such "partnership for social peace" in the Balkans stands in the service of maintaining the "social monologue." Are you criticizing the neoliberal economic model of Serbian Ministers? You will be asked to state your point of view. Are you surprised at the fact of Romania signing of the neo-colonial agreement with the U.S.? The Minister of the Defense will welcome you and listen to you carefully. Are you worried because of the poverty in Croatia? Come to the conference on "reduction of poverty" organized by the government.

Renewing the system by criticizing it, readiness to co-opt those denying it, pater-nalism in the guise of participation—all these aspects of social control are as old as the system itself.

According to the writing of Luc Boltansky, the sociologist, the denial which capi-talism was faced with in the seventies has brought about the creation of a "new spirit of capitalism aimed at appeasing critique by acknowledging its appropriateness, or to simply avoid it by not even responding to it."

Social control by way of civil society offers an interaction of different modes of domination. Authorities can direct fictitious conflicts in which they let the artificial op-ponents of their own choice specify social difficulties that they then together, through dialogues—do not solve, or even do partly solve—but at no serious loss for the system. When the system is in question, of course, the elites oppose the opposition and ad-vocate change only in a limited manner that will not endanger the system. From this stems the leaning of "civil society" towards different variants of reformist thought that tolerates the denial of some of the aspects of the system, but does not tolerate denying the principle of the system's existence. In other words, "civil society" strives to change the rules of the game a bit here and there, but due to its being integrated, keeps par-ticipating in the game submissively.

Albert: So you are implying that going beyond civil society and reformist organizing, which assumes system maintenance, is one thing that needs to happen. What do you have in mind for that?

Grubacic: The concept of civil society ought to be abandoned for the sake of the vision of another society that does not rest on class, religious, or ethnic discrimination. We need a participatory society committed to authentic "politics from below."

In order to get closer to such a society, it is necessary to "step out of the game," abandon the system, renounce abstract "social-schmertz," and opt for "social conflict," for breaking up with traditional social-political communication and organization. Such a "conflict" would imply getting beyond endless reliance on typical political parties, hierarchical trade unions, bureaucratized non-governmental organizations, and following a path toward new models of association.

It is time, here in the Balkans, for a "horizontal social dialogue." Every vertical social dialogue that history has shown us has turned into a monologue in which workers first "stay without a say, and then without a pay."

In contrast we need to seek a horizontal social dialogue conducted among all participants in the social-economic processes—all workers, including those who are going to lose their jobs, unemployed workers who have already lost them, refugees and "displaced persons" who have nothing to lose, Romas who have never had anything, students who cannot afford to go to the university, farmers, social movement activists, women, and many more.

Albert: Where does this horizontal dialogue go?

Grubacic: It could immediately encompass the "minimum common plan," a social right that would include: request for minimum income, refutation of privatization as a model, and developing strategies subordinating profits to preserving non-renewable resources and the real environment, but it could also seek longer term goals for a whole new economy. Instead of advocating a productivistic cult of privatization, a horizontal dialogue would likely lead toward advocating solidarity and participatory economic relations, including a different transition which emphasizes collective initiative and real democracy, and which, in its calculations, takes into account the price of the suffering and dignity and everything else more precious than profits.

Albert: You say you seek democracy, real democracy. What do you have in mind?

Grubacic: I think that for the Balkans it is the perfect time for social movements to try to re-invent—even beyond democracy—self-management, or participatory management, as I prefer to call it. The "Yugoslav experience" shouldn't be a discouragement here. In Yugoslavia there was no private ownership of productive assets, true, but there was a market system which dramatically limited economic options and a corporate division of labor that put a ruling coordinator class above workers in power and income. Those were the roots of our economic evil.

So, we haven't had, in actual reality—in so-called socialist Yugoslavia—real self-management, but only a rhetorical reference to it. We had a phenomenon that Milovan Djilas had called a "New Class" in the polity, which is true enough for the state, but to get beyond Djilas, who was identifying only to a political bureaucracy, we need to see that we also had a ruling coordinator class arising from our economy's structure. There cannot be participatory management in a situation where the economy uses markets and corporate divisions of labor, whatever the state may look like, bureaucratic or not.

Albert: Do you think putting forward an economic vision that advocates participatory planning to replace markets, and balanced job complexes to replace the corporate division of labor, and that favors what I guess you might call participatory management to replace authoritarian decisionmaking, could be beneficial in the Balkans?

Grubacic: The prospect for that kind of model, the one we call participatory economics, in today's Balkans is great. An anti-authoritarian, Left libertarian economic system that accomplishes economic activity to meet needs and fulfill potentials while propelling solidarity, diversity, equity, and participatory management, with positive implications as well for other parts of life and society's key domains such as polity and kinship and culture, gives us a promise of a true classlessness and a powerful alternative both to the neoliberal models now favored in the Balkans, and to the authoritarian systems I like to call coordinator economies that previously existed in this part of Eastern Europe, including in my own Yugoslavia.

You are right that I would not use the term self-management in the Balkans. This is because I think that a fight over labels is a waste of time. We have to be more tactical than to cloud our meaning by misleading labels. If I speak about socialism and self-management in Post-Yugoslavia, people will look at me like I am a supporter of Tito or a member of Slobodan Milosevic's "socialist" party. They won't hear anything beyond that wrong association. I don't think that we have time for that kind of confusion. It hurts communication as much as if I were to try to speak to folks in Belgrade in Japanese. In fact, it is worse.

The Balkans, or the greatest part of this region, in any event, is far and away the poorest part of Europe. The most frequent word here is strike. And I don't think that we have a right to waste time in endless confused discussions about what class is a real revolutionary agent, or about what socialism really stands for. I am happy saying I am for participatory management, meaning just what you mean by self-management, to communicate my commitments in a way that can be heard without bias. And I am happy saying I am for parecon rather than for socialism, for the same reason. Being for socialism here means to people that you are for oppression. It would not open the door to horizontal dialogue. But saying you are for a new type of economy, and describing its features, may help open that door.

Albert: But would people in the Balkans relate to the claim that market socialism was really market coordinatorism and that for that reason it doesn't demonstrate that there is no better future beyond capitalism?

Grubacic: I don't think that there is widespread insight of this sort, at least not yet. But there is no impediment that prevents it. And at least some activists, and activist scholars, are trying to convey this claim.

Albert: Do you think people would find the idea of balanced job complexes a corrective to what they have known in workplaces—or would they see it as an ultra Left excess that would have horrible implications?

Grubacic: I spend a lot of time talking to workers, inside and outside of the state controlled unions. My strong impression is that they are very much in favor of this participatory model, as soon as they hear about it, and often really implicitly on their own. The same holds for grassroots activists. And, as far as my discussions about parecon as a new model of economic organization, people seem very enthusiastic. Of course, there are also people who see this as an "ultra Left excess" or just the old ways in disguise. For example, I have been involved in a public debate recently with one of the authors of the neoliberal reforms in my country. The guy was screaming "neo-communism!," "neo-communism!" all the way through this debate. That is what he is being paid to do. But I don't think that this new class of intellectual commissars in the Balkan countries should be our audience, and in contrast working people are very receptive.

Balanced job complexes, as I understand the idea, means a situation where each job is a mix of tasks and responsibilities, such that the overall quality of life and especially the overall empowerment effects of the work are comparable for all. It is, in my opinion, very hard to disagree with a vision of society that gets rid of a hierarchy between managers and workers, lawyers and assembly line workers. How can one oppose keeping the functions, but having them fairly shared?

Among working people and activists working for social justice, I encounter overwhelmingly positive reactions. A vision of participatory society where each person's mix of tasks and responsibilities accords with their abilities and also conveys a fair share of rote and tedious and interesting and empowering conditions and responsibilities, seems to people precisely in tune with their hopes. And so does participatory management—people having a proportionate say in the decisions that affect their lives.

Albert: What about remunerating effort and sacrifice only? Do you think people would fear that doing this would reduce their prospects for riches or disrupt production, or do you think they would anticipate that remunerating only effort and sacrifice would enhance justice and their incomes as well?

Grubacic: The feedback I have gotten has been very interesting. Yes, for many Leftist economists—I remember my debate with one very fine old man, and a great economist, Branko Horvat—rewarding only the effort and sacrifice that people expend in their work is very controversial. But I fail to see, I have to admit, why is it so difficult for some anti-capitalists, even if they have suffered the harmful socialization of becoming famous economists, to recognize the inherent injustice in getting more income by virtue of being more productive due to having better skills or greater inborn talent, or due to having better tools, not to mention due to having more power or owning more property.

Being entitled to more consumption only by virtue of giving more effort and enduring more sacrifice is morally appropriate and it also—it seems to me—provides proper incentives due to rewarding only what we can affect, and not what we can't. It seems that people to whom I have been talking about these issues in my country—workers, peasants, movement activists—are far more receptive to this idea than my colleagues who teach and even than "anti-capitalist" intellectuals in general. But I guess that is no surprise.

Albert: Being from the U.S. we don't encounter some of the trends of thought that exist in Europe. You are advocating participatory economics and related approaches for politics, gender, etc., for the Balkans. But I am wondering if other Left approaches are finding more response there, even among the audiences you are working with—say, for example, ideas coming out of the work of Michael Hardt and Antonion Negri and the people advocating such focuses as Empire and the Multitude. Are these views gaining support in the Balkans? Do you think they are making a positive contribution? Do you see a relation to the pareconish ideas, or are the two viewpoints contrary?

Grubacic: Yes, Hardt and Negri's book,[1] which is very interesting, so the people who have understood it are telling me, is a popular read among Lefty intellectuals. I am not sure if it is really gaining any support. It is very hard to communicate what they are trying to say: they cultivate a style that excludes the vast majority of potential readers, leaving most of even the highly educated in a state of confusion. Reading a book which is describing something called "Empire" which has supposedly superseded nation states, in a country occupied by U.S. military forces is, I suppose, a strange experience for most of the readers. But I don't want to say that this book is not useful. I think it is of value to Marxist intellectuals in a country where "Marxism" was an official state ideology. For them, I suppose, it is challenging. But I doubt that it will have any significant influence in this part of Europe. I could be wrong, of course.

Traditional Marxist analyses of capitalist societies centered on the polarization between two classes and two alone: the capitalist class and the proletariat. Both pareconish analyses, and the one of Hardt and Negri, present a very different model, one which is meant to describe the class dynamic specific to modern times.

Hardt and Negri are recognizing the central dynamic in the emergence of an entity called "the multitude." I am not sure anyone really knows what this means, but, broadly, the idea seems to be that the working class has lost its privileged position as the revolutionary agent, and, instead, now there is something called the multitude, which includes housewives, farmers, students, and so on. I am not sure what is new in that, but something that does seem different is to minimize differences among constituencies. We are all just going to be in the multitude. Differences between men and women, gays and straights, different types of workers and also workers and managers, and so on, all fade into the background and get much less attention than before, it seems.

Pareconish analyses present a model, at least regarding the economy, of a three-way polarization between the capitalist class, the working class, and the coordinator class. They also put into sharp focus differences having to do with gender, sexuality, race, etc., identifying institutions that lead to these different positions and trying to understand different needs, agendas, etc. Pareconish efforts also seek, like Hardt's and Negri's, to have people become revolutionaries—and I guess pareconish activists could call those who arrive at such commitments a multitude, once it is that large in size, but they wouldn't ignore that how different people become committed depends on their position in society, nor would they minimize that some folks are on average less likely to move Leftward than others, and may even have contrary interests. I would argue that the later analysis is more useful.

In fact, keeping on the class part, with any Leftist analysis that fails to comprehend the coordinator class as an actor that can take the lead in defining a new economy, there is a good chance of it leading to a dictatorship not of the proletariat but of the coordinator class (of technocrats, government and party bureaucrats, professional ideologues, managers)—just as happened in Yugoslavia or the U.S.S.R.

The antagonisms which exist between the coordinator class seeking its own agenda and the working class seeking its own agenda cannot be wished away in the name of the "multitude." To get rid of the conflict one must have a movement that self-consciously forges new structures that eliminate class divisions rather than putting the more educated and powerful class from our society into a ruling position in the movement and then in tomorrow's society. To be able to forge an alliance between those in the coordinator class who want real justice and the working class—to be able to build a strong movement for real classlessness we need to recognize the antagonisms, not make believe they aren't there. I think the pareconish view can help with that, both by identifying the problems, and by the classless vision and methods it offers. The approach based on the idea of the multitude seems instead to move back in the old directions.

Albert: Finally, what about anarchist trends in the Balkans? Are they moving toward economic aims and goals like those we have been discussing, or do they have other aims in mind? Do they have a political vision for the region and more broadly? Do you think the Balkan's anarchist trends should find pareconish commitments positive, or that they should have strong criticisms of them?

Grubacic: Anarchism, as a political philosophy, is going through a veritable explosion in the Balkans in recent years. Anarchist, or anarchist-inspired, collectives are growing everywhere; anarchist principles—autonomy, voluntary association, self-organization, mutual aid, direct democracy—have become the basis for organizing within a good number of the collectives in the Balkans.

But I would be very cautious with regard to the "political vision" offered by anarchists in the Balkans. Serious reflection on vision remains a "blind spot" of anarchism around here as, I guess, pretty much everywhere else. Hopefully that will change.

And that is one of the reasons why I think that anarchist trends in the Balkans should recognize participatory economics as an anarchist economic vision which generates participation, classlessness, and participatory management: the hallmark goals of anarchism. Parecon is in accord with all the most important themes of traditional anarchism (freedom, justice, solidarity, participation, equity), but contributes even more to what I like to refer to as "modern anarchism," through its provision of specific positive economic institutions not advocated by traditional anarchists, such is balanced job complexes and participatory planning. What we anarchists need to do is add a political vision to go with it.

PART 2: PARECON AS A NEW PATH FOR THE BALKANS?

Andrej Grubacic interviews Michael Albert (August 2007)

Grubacic: Isn't your aim, advocating and seeking to attain a participatory economy, what we have already had to endure here, in the Balkans, under the name of "socialism"?

Albert: No. Socialism has come in two shapes, either with markets or with central planning. You had the former in Yugoslavia, but the latter also existed, of course, for example in the Soviet Union. This system that has called itself socialism has also included remunerating labor for its output and for its bargaining power. And it has included the familiar corporate division of labor in which about 20 percent of the workforce, whom I call the coordinator class, had a monopoly on the empowering tasks and the rest were stuck doing only rote and obedient labor. As a result of these institutional commitments, socialism, as you and others have known it, was not a classless economy, but an economy in which about 20 percent ruled over the workers below. There have also been other flaws, including political, cultural, social—but the basic problem with what has been called socialist economics has been that it has eliminated one boss—the owning class or capitalist class—only to enshrine another boss, whom I call the coordinator class.

Grubacic: So how exactly is this new system different from Yugoslav self-management?

Albert: Yugoslav self-management had markets, the old corporate division of labor, and remuneration for bargaining power and output. In place of these, parecon has participatory planning, which is a kind of cooperative, horizontal, negotiation of inputs and outputs; balanced job complexes in which each worker gets a combination of responsibilities so their overall work load is empowering comparative to what other workers enjoy; and remuneration for how long people work, how hard people work, and the onerousness of the conditions under which people work.

These are not minor but are instead centrally important differences. They yield very different motivations, in turn generating very different outcomes. The core institutions of Yugoslav self-management, with the exception of doing away with private ownership of workplaces, are rejected by parecon for being class biased and antithetical to equity, solidarity, and self-management. In their place parecon adopts classless institutions favoring real self-management, solidarity, equity, diversity, efficiency, etc.

Grubacic: Do you think that working people in Serbia, who used to live under state socialism, and now live in transitional capitalism, would be able to find parecon attractive and persuasive?

Albert: I can't see why not. Would working people in Serbia like to control their own destiny? Would they like a fair share, a truly fair share, of the social product? Would they like to have no rulers above, and no obedient passive people below? Would they like an economy that treats the environment—and people, too—with respect and with dignity? I can understand why Serb citizens might be skeptical that an economy can deliver such benefits—but once a compelling case is made that parecon can do just that, even coming out of the disastrous experiences you have endured, I don't see why advocacy wouldn't follow.

The ills of market socialism that people in Serbia have experienced and rejected are what induced the design and advocacy of parecon. It is precisely because the market system was so flawed that a new vision was needed and created. Your distaste for that old system should not reduce interest in parecon but should instead foster it.

(Endnotes)

1   Michael Hardt and Antonio Negri *Empire* (Harvard University Press, 2000)

Chapter 14

THE ORGANIZATION OF SAC AND ITS COMPANIES

Anders Sandström

SAC'S ORGANIZATION TODAY

SAC, THE CENTRAL ORGANIZATION of the Workers of Sweden (Sveriges Arbetares Centralorganisation), is a union based on libertarian socialist values with approximately 8,000 members. One of its basic ideas expressed in its statutes is decentralized decision making, meaning that those affected by a decision should be the ones that make the decision. Another basic idea expressed in the statutes is that the organization of SAC today should reflect the way that we want the future society to work. The union work is done by members in workplace-based sections that federate into syndicates for different industries in geographical areas. Political and common work is done in local units and districts. Tasks of the central entities, the "central committee," and "executive committee" deal with overarching, strategic, and common issues, and to function as judge between different local entities during the period between the congresses, which are held every fourth year. Representatives in these central entities are elected by members and are expected to report to and from the local entities on an ongoing basis. There are also a number of paid employees for centrally performed tasks that are elected by congress or referendum, such as editor of the member magazine *Syndikalisten*, bookkeeper, and a number of union ombudsmen. Some of the larger local entities also have paid employees.

Besides union activities SAC is also owner of three companies. These companies:

(a) handle real estate on Sveavägen 98, which rents out a number of offices to different businesses besides SAC.

(b) produce the weekly paper *Arbetaren* (The Worker) which is one of the last Left-oriented papers in Sweden with a nationwide audience.

(c) administer a printing company whose customers nowadays are mostly external.

Finally, SAC is also associated with an unemployment office that administers the payments of unemployment payments to SAC members and directly associated members.

PROBLEMS REGARDING WORK ORGANIZATION IN SAC

The role of employer and business owner creates, for obvious reasons, certain confusion within a radical and libertarian socialist union such as SAC, which defines its task to always stand up for employees against employers and to fight to jettison the capitalist system. This confusion gives rise to at least two questions that have been debated within SAC for a long period:

(1) Should SAC use paid employees or voluntary workers in performing the union work?

(2) Should SAC keep the capitalist-run companies?

Paid Personnel vs. Voluntary Workers

Lately certain parts of SAC have seriously questioned SAC's practice of paying people to do work and the congress has decided to minimize the number of ombudsmen and other paid administrative personnel even though this potentially decreases members' capacity to successfully fight employers at their workplaces. As far as I understand four reasons have been given for this decision:

(1) Paid employees develop their own agenda and their own interests such as maximizing their salaries and their own influence and power which per definition is not in the interest of the other members.

(2) Employed experts become specialists and this inhibits other members' activity. By avoiding experts other members should be forced to activate themselves.

(3) It is cheaper to use voluntary workers than paid employees.

(4) Voluntary work is per definition "better" in a moral sense than paid work.

The Companies

The companies (maybe with exception of the weekly paper *Arbetaren*) exist in a capitalist market environment and are basically run as any other capitalist company regarding remuneration, decision making, and work division. As owner, SAC has taken a relatively passive position and delegated the major decisions to the companies, which means managers in charge of the different companies. The underlying assumption for this position is that there is no alternative to capitalist organization if you are to exist in a capitalist market. SAC has for a long time rightly questioned its role, as capitalists and business owners, but since the assumption is that there exists no alternative to capitalist organization the only thing to do, it seems is to sell the companies. Furthermore it is argued, SAC has no need for the services that the companies provide anymore, which has not been the case historically. By selling the companies SAC also wants to get rid of the risk that is associated with working in a capitalist market. On the other hand, some parts of SAC have shown interest in keeping the companies, referring to their potential profit-making capacity that could be used to lower the member fees.

The Need of Vision and Strategy

Considering the above described confusion, the need for a clearly stated vision becomes obvious. It is only with the help of vision and strategy that is commonly understood and agreed upon that the confusion and strife that exist can be dealt with in a productive manner. If you have a vision, an idea of where you are headed, you can work out strategies for how to get there and judge different options with regard to what degree they move us forward in the right direction. Clearly stated vision is also important for recruiting members, since it gives an answer to the question, "What do we want instead of capitalism?" Within SAC today there are clearly stated strategies for short- and middle-term union-work, but a clearly understood vision for the long term, toward an alternative society, is missing. Since most potential members, and SAC itself, see SAC as something different from a reformist union interested only in maximizing short-term wages and working conditions, but rather a union that questions underlying institutions, the creation of long-term vision is indispensable. According to the "Declaration of Principles," SAC works for an alternative to today's capitalist society for a future libertarian socialist society. To be successful in this work it is crucial that SAC can describe its vision in a way that is deemed to be realistic and trustworthy. Certain basic values for a future society are expressed already in the "Declaration of Principles," but apart from that SAC has been reluctant, as the rest of the libertarian Left, to describe more far-reaching visions.

Michael Albert and Robin Hahnel have created a model for a libertarian socialist society which to me is the most interesting model proposed within the Left for many years. The model, participatory economics, is based on values such as solidarity, equity, diversity, and self-management. The model is founded on four institutions: a network of workplace-based and consumer-based councils within which all decision making takes place, balanced job complexes that allocate different work tasks in a way that balances empowerment, remuneration in accordance to effort and sacrifice, and finally a participatory allocation model that differs from both market allocation and central planning. The model has also been briefly touched on in *Arbetaren* and the member magazine *Syndikalisten*. There are libertarian socialist organizations around the globe that have implemented the model in their daily work. Parecon is without doubt very interesting for an organization such as SAC with regard to the organization of SAC's work and the companies it owns, and it should work extremely well as a guiding vision for the organization since parecon is in accordance to the values expressed in the "Declaration of Principles." The positive effects of successful implementation of parecon principles in the SAC organization, with regard to credibility and experience, cannot be overestimated.

The Value of "Living as You Preach"

For an organization that wants to abolish the existing society and create a fair and more just alternative, it is extremely important to live the way you preach. If you express a value or vision that you believe in, and at the same time don't act in accordance to it, you come across as a hypocrite or someone that doesn't believe in what you are preaching. If this is the case, you cannot expect potential members to join. On the other hand, if through your own actions you can show that your vision and strategy is realistic and is working successfully, it creates a very powerful force behind your arguments. The value of "living as you preach" cannot be overestimated.

The Power of the Central Entities

Central decision-making entities in a libertarian socialist organization are problematic. The potential power concentration in these instances is much more problematic than the potential power concentration with paid employees such as ombudsmen with limited decision-making power. Formally and theoretically the issues handled by these central entities and the decisions taken by them should reflect the will of the local entities. This supposedly happens through interaction between representatives and the local entities that representatives act on behalf of. This does not happen in real life today. I think there are very few members today that feel they have real influence over decisions taken by AU (Arbetsutskottet, working committee) and CK (Centralkommitten, central committee) or that are even aware of what decisions are made and on what grounds. The AU and CK of today function in principal, in some aspects (at best), as representative democracies where members elect representatives and go into a passive state until it's time for the next election. This situation is not acceptable for a libertarian socialist organization and is way more problematic than having paid employees doing constructive work. Power should rest with the local entities, and the representatives in the central parts of the organization have to take their assignments and responsibility toward the local parts seriously. The interaction with the local entities and their influence is fundamentally important.

The Companies

Job division, decision making, and remuneration in the companies, with few exceptions (maybe remuneration and certain decision making in *Arbetaren*), are organized in accordance to capitalist principles and values. SAC's argument for accepting this has been that there is no alternative. "You have to adjust to the market. An implementation of libertarian socialist values and ways of organizing work would lead to a loss of customers and revenue and finally to bankruptcy," it is said. By interpreting the situation this way SAC sends out very strange signals: "We believe we have an alternative way of organizing companies and society but we do not believe it would work in our own companies." Why should potential members believe in our values if SAC doesn't believe in them? Parts of SAC are aware of this problem but feel the solution is to sell the companies, not to introduce libertarian socialist values in the businesses.

There is enormous potential in organizing the businesses in accordance to our own values. The positive "marketing effect" among serious Leftist circles would be huge. SAC would possibly take the lead in a far-reaching project, on a grassroots level, within large parts of the Left, in creating alternative organized companies based on socialist values. Obviously, such a project would be time consuming, and demand hard work and sacrifices, both economical and other, but the potential positive effects would justify all of this.

WHAT WOULD AN IMPLEMENTATION OF PARECON MEAN FOR SAC?

The Relation to Paid Work

It is, according to me, a misunderstanding that paying a person for work means that this person per definition develops an agenda that is in opposition to all other members. This could happen, of course, but this would most likely be explained by the work assignments in question and not employment per se. A paid person can have work assignments that include few or no tasks that strengthen empowerment (for example cleaning toilets) or she/he could have many empowering tasks (for example business controller). What needs to be avoided from a socialist point of view are work assignments that include decision making, that are standing and not motivated, and feature control over decisions that affect other members/employees, not paid personnel itself.

Nor are there any reasons for excluding specialized knowledge or experts per se, so long as these experts don't make decisions that affect other members/employees without giving them influence in accordance to the degree they are affected. Experts can be very useful, even crucial. Few argue that brain surgeons should not be experts. Once again, unmotivated influence and control over decisions that affect other people should be avoided, not experts and specialized knowledge per se.

Remuneration

The principles for remuneration have to be adjusted. According to parecon, work should be remunerated for effort and sacrifice and not bargaining power or productivity that is explained by better tools or talents that are inherited. A starting point could be an equal remuneration per hour decided as an average of all members' wages. This remuneration could then be adjusted by a ranking system among the employees in question.

Central Instances

Central entities and their work have to be organized in a manner that minimizes power concentration. Delegates have to be active within their local entities and local entities have to have the power to withdraw any representative from power.

The Companies

Adjustment of activities in the companies to parecon principles would introduce big challenges, but the potential gains of credibility, experience, and so on would definitely justify the project, especially if the alternative is to sell the companies. The most striking changes in the daily work compared with today's routines would be:

(1) Introduction of decision-making councils

(2) Remuneration in accordance with effort and sacrifice, which would basically mean the same pay for every worked hour with an adjustment for especially demanding or boring tasks

(3) Introduction of balanced job complexes where every job consists of a set of tasks that are comparable to every other job with regard to influence and empowerment

These changes would mean big adjustments for many people, and many would think that the implications are too controversial. Hesitation, and maybe even resistance from some, would probably be considerable, and there would be need for lots of discussion and education, but if the alternative is to give up the companies, it should be possible to create enough support within SAC to succeed. SAC would have to be prepared to set aside resources in different firms in order to make it happen, but, once again, the potential effects of a successful implementation of parecon principles cannot be overestimated.

Chapter 15

PROJECT FOR A PARTICIPATORY SOCIETY– UNITED KINGDOM

Mark Evans interviewed by U.K. Watch[1]

U.K.W: What is Project for a Participatory Society-U.K.? How did it come about?

Evans: Project for a Participatory Society is a U.K.-based initiative started in 2006 set up to facilitate the coming together of U.K.-based social justice activists who, along with others in different parts of the world, are interested in developing and organizing around participatory vision and strategy.

When I say "started in 2006," I mean this was when a conscious commitment to set something up was made. Since the initial conception there was a lot of work to be done trying to make the idea real. We have made slow but steady progress over the past year or so putting the basics for the organization into place.

After making the initial commitment the first thing that needed to be done was to establish "Our Basic Organizing Framework."[2] This document lays out our purpose, our values, our internal culture, and our structure—without which no serious organization can take place. This document was then sent to various people who have been working on participatory vision and strategy for feedback.

U.K.W: PPS-U.K. seems to take its principle inspiration from the writings of Michael Albert and Robin Hahnel, in particular the theory of "complementary holism" first put forward in Liberating Theory.[3] *What is it about their approach you find so useful? How has their work informed the founding of PPS-U.K.?*

Evans: Like a lot of people out there I feel very unhappy with the way in which society is organized and managed. I wanted to try and do something about this, and so, over many years, I got involved in various campaigns with different organizations. This was a real learning experience—mostly in the negative sense of how not to do things. I soon became aware of the shortfalls of single-issue campaign work and the difficulties of working in traditional coalitions, and perhaps most of all of the dogmatic culture of the old Left, which seems to lead to stagnation and factions (interestingly, the opposite of what they claim to be about).

This dissatisfaction with existing options led me to search for a conceptual framework for organizing that addressed these problems. It seemed to me that a failure to find, develop, and implement a new radical-progressive organizing framework would condemn the Left to a future of continued decline. That framework turned out to be what is referred to as "complimentary holism," which, as you say, was first put forward in *Liberating Theory*.

This framework is relatively easily to understand, which is important if you are interested in working toward a participatory society—as I am. It was developed from both practical and theoretical understandings of Left history. I should also say that it is more than just a framework for organizing—it is also proposed as a means of understanding historical continuity and changes as well as contemporary social dynamics.

It identifies four social spheres that make up society: kinship, community, economics, and politics. One of the basic insights presented in *Liberating Theory* is that none of these spheres should be seen as more important than the other. Typically, the various constituencies that make up the Left take the opposite position, organizing as though only one sphere is of prime concern. For example anarchists tend to prioritize the political sphere over the other three; feminists tend to prioritize kinship; Nationalists tend to prioritize the community sphere, and Marxists tend to prioritize the economic sphere. This is what is called a monist theory and whilst all four constituents may feel that they have a genuine commitment to solidarity, it is not hard to see how this approach leads to factions within the movement.

A slightly more sophisticated approach comes with what is called a pluralistic approach, where an anarcho-syndicalist prioritizes both the political and economic spheres or where a socialist-feminist prioritizes economic and kinship spheres. However this approach still prioritizes some spheres over others, which again leads to tensions within the movement.

In line with the framework proposed in *Liberating Theory*, PPS-U.K. organizes around all four social spheres in a conscious effort to overcome these problems and hopefully to contribute to building a much healthier culture of solidarity within the Left and therefore a much more effective movement.

U.K.W: Can you tell us about the projects PPS-U.K. is involved in?

Evans: First of all, projects and other activities are initiated and run by PPS-U.K. activists—there is no leadership spoon-feeding activists' campaign ideas or delegating tasks. Activists who initiate and/or participate in projects and other activities that go under the "banner" of PPS-U.K. must respect and operate within "Our Basic Organizing Framework."

At present we have five projects posted on the site. "Solidarity Works" is a simple but important project that provides links to organizations that PPS-U.K. activists want to express a feeling of solidarity with and encourage others to work with.

"Intellectual Self-defense" is an online resource that introduces the notion of a "propaganda-managed democracy." This project includes a recommended-reading list plus links to appropriate organizations. "Project for a Participatory Trade Union Movement" facilitates the coming together of trade union activists who want to join forces to advocate and organize for a participatory economy. "Project for a Participatory Credit Union" has been set up to investigate the possibility of establishing a credit union as a means of creating a financing system to fund parecon businesses. We are also looking at organizing a PPS-U.K. Forum which will include talks and debates on participatory vision and strategy, project development sessions, courses on intellectual self-defense, and media-production workshops.

U.K.W: PPS-U.K. advocates the development of relatively detailed blueprints for models of a future society—for instance the participatory economics model. Is there danger in developing such definite aims? Are diverse movements able to agree on such specific aims? Moreover, is there a danger that people living within a debilitating social reality that undermines rationality and compassion will come to advocate goals that will perpetuate the various maladies of contemporary society?

Evans: Many people on the Left become concerned about the development of vision and some people become very hostile toward any attempts at proposing what the social justice movement might adopt as its long-term objectives. While I think the concern is entirely valid I think the hostility is unwarranted. The concern is valid for the obvious reason that we might get our vision wrong and therefore, in this sense, there is a very real danger. But this danger is not specific to the development of vision. It is also true of strategy and every other activity we get involved in. Recognizing this danger should not lead us to abandon our efforts but should instead lead us to be more careful about what we advocate and how we organize.

Furthermore, some people seem to think developing vision is somehow undemocratic and elitist. I don't understand this at all—what they are basically saying is that if, for example, someone has an idea for an alternative to the corporate division of labor, or markets, then they are not allowed to discuss it. It is a very strange position. You can't help but ask, Who's being undemocratic?

There are two basic ways forward. One is to organize using broad principles as guidance. The other is to consider possible alternative institutional features. Despite concerns of developing more detailed alternative institutions, as with parecon, the problem with the broad principles approach is that it is hard to inspire people with such vague notions as freedom and justice alone. I think given the history of the Left (which hardly inspires confidence), and in today's world of spin (which renders words like freedom and democracy virtually meaningless), people require more than vague notions. They need compelling vision that is discussed and agreed upon—but always open to further refinement.

Whether people can agree on such specific aims, only time will tell. But it is worth mentioning that we don't really have that much to choose from. Take the economic sphere for instance—what are the actual options for the anti-capitalist movement? What are our options for an alternative to private ownership? To top-down management? To the corporate division of labor? To markets? To rewarding ownership? As it turns out, our basic options are quite limited. I feel quite confident that if we clearly identify our basic options and simply ask which of these options best reflects our values then a lot of agreement can be reached. If we can get this far then I think we are more than half way to building a popular movement. It is a lot of hard work, but pretty straightforward.

As for "people living in debilitating social realities that undermine rationality," in my experience most people are not as irrational as the Left generally seems to think. Most people make perfectly rational choices given their circumstances and based on the information they have. Personally, I think that people know things are not right. They know that they are being lied to. They know that they are being exploited. The point is that they do not see an alternative. This is why developing compelling vision is so important. Yes we live in a debilitating social reality, but one that principally undermines hope.

(Endnotes)

1   *U.K. Watch*, www.ukwatch.net
2   *PPS-U.K.*, www.ppsuk.org.uk/index.php?option=com_content&task=view&id=6&Itemid=2
3   Michael Albert, Leslie Cagan, Noam Chomsky, Robin Hahnel, Mel King, Lydia Sargent, and Holly Sklar *Liberating Theory* (South End Press, 1986). See the introduction to this book for a brief overview of complimentary holism.

Chapter 16

FASINPAT (FACTORY WITHOUT A BOSS): AN ARGENTINE EXPERIENCE IN SELF-MANAGEMENT

Marie Trigona

We are proposing a major change in how a factory is run. We have built new social relations in the factory. We have built alliances with universities, unions, and unemployed worker organizations. Zanon is not an isolated experience or crazy idea, it is a concrete experience that a group of workers have put into action. Many people talk about Zanon as a laboratory for experimenting with workers' dreams. After five years, this is no longer a laboratory: we are demonstrating an economic alternative to what the capitalist model proposes.
— Alejandro Quiroga, a Zanon worker

ARGENTINA'S WORKER-RUN FACTORIES ARE setting an example for workers around the world that employees can run a business even better without a boss or owner. The new phenomenon of employees taking over their workplace began in 2000 and heightened as Argentina faced its worst economic crisis ever in 2001. Nationwide, thousands of factories have closed and millions of jobs have been lost in recent years. The example points to the struggle ahead on the path toward an emancipatory society free from exploitation and oppression, like the vision of participatory society offered in this book.

As the largest recuperated factory in Argentina, and occupied since 2001, the Zanon ceramics plant in the Patagonian province of Neuquén now employs 470 workers. Along with some 180 recuperated enterprises up and running, providing jobs for more than 10,000 Argentine workers, the Zanon experience has re-defined the basis of production: without workers, bosses are unable to run a business; without bosses, workers can do it better. While these experiences are forced to co-exist within the capitalist market, they are forming new visions for a new working culture.

In 2001 Zanon's owners decided to close its doors and fire the workers without paying months of back pay or indemnity. Leading up to the massive layoffs and plants closure, workers went on strike in 2000. The owner, Luis Zanon, with over 75 million dollars in debt to public and private creditors, fired en masse most of the workers and closed the factory in 2001—a bosses' lockout. In October 2001, workers declared the plant under worker control. The workers camped outside the factory for four months, pamphleteering and partially blocking a highway leading to the capital city, Neuquén. While the workers were camping outside the factory, a court ruled that the employees could sell off remaining stock. After the stock ran out, on March 2, 2002, the workers' assembly voted to start up production without a boss.

Legality vs. Legitimacy

The plant functioned for almost four years without any legal standing whatsoever.

By taking over an abandoned businesses and running it without any legality the workers questioned the very logic of private property. The workers put into question what is legitimate: the workers' right to defend their jobs or an owner's right to private property acquired at the expense of public subsidies and exploitation of workers? Using direct political action and breaking the logic of private property has been a key tactic in gaining legal status for many of the recuperated enterprises that follow the slogan Occupy, Resist, and Produce. When asked why community members should defend Zanon, Raul Kellerman, who has worked at the factory for over twenty-five years, answered, "because the factory belongs to the people and we defend jobs."

Since the worker takeover the long-term demand at Zanon has been for national expropriation under worker control. However, the workers have fought a parallel battle in federal court for legal recognition of the FASINPAT ("Factory Without a Boss") cooperative. They have carried out innumerable political actions to pressure the courts to recognize the cooperative.

As part of self-management, workers have had to organize themselves to defend their factory. Self-defense against violent attacks has been the backbone of radicalization and production at Zanon. The government's response has been violent, using different tactics to evict the factory workers. The government has tried to evict them five times using police operatives. On April 8, 2003, during the most recent eviction attempt, over 5,000 community members from Neuquén came out to defend the factory. In addition, workers have faced physical attacks and threats. In March 2005 a group of four individuals kidnapped and attacked the wife of an employee at Zanon. They forced her into a green Ford Falcon—a model of car security operatives used to kidnap activists during the dictatorship—sending a chilling reminder of the military's. human rights abuses. They tortured her and cut her face, hands, arms, and breasts. On all occasions, the workers' collective responded that they are willing to use their legitimate right to defend themselves and their factory by any means necessary.

In October 2005, FASINPAT won a legal dispute, pressuring federal courts to recognize it as a legal entity that has the right to run the cooperative for one year. As the October 2006 expiration date neared, the worker assembly voted to step up actions and community efforts in 2006. On October 20, 2006, the workers won a long-standing legal battle for federal recognition of FASINPAT for three years.

Argentina's working class has celebrated the Zanon workers' temporary victory. With legal status FASINPAT can concentrate on planning production, improving working conditions, and developing community projects. As part of this celebration, the cooperative has invited other workers to visit Zanon to learn that they, too, can function without a boss or owner. The workers' assembly has resolved that it is now in a position to teach others from its five years of learning from self-management.

Worker Self-Management

The phrase "self-management," derived from the Spanish concept of "auto-gestión," means that a community or group makes its own decisions, especially those kinds of decisions that fit into processes of planning and management. Zanon workers are putting into action systems of organization in a business in which the workers participate in all of the decisions. Worker self-management in Argentina is helping plant the seeds so that future generations can reverse the logic of capitalism by producing for communities, not for profits, and empowering workers, not exploiting them. Zanon has formed part of the movement of recuperated enterprises that are putting into practice democratic alternatives and worker self-determination.

Argentina's employee-run businesses are very diverse, each with specific legal standing and forms of organizing production. In almost all cases workers took over businesses that had been abandoned or closed by their owners in the midst of Argentina's financial meltdown in 2001. The owners usually ceased production, stopped paying wages, and went bankrupt. The workers' decision to take over their plant was a decision made out of necessity not necessarily out of ideology. The clear worry of how to safeguard workers' jobs motivated the act of taking over a factory and making it produce without a boss or owner.

Growing unemployment, capital flight, and industry break-up served as the backdrop for factory takeovers. Argentines lived through the nation's worst economic crisis ever in December 2001. Unemployment hit record levels—over 20 percent unemployed and 40 percent of the population unable to find adequate employment. Argentina, one of Latin America's industrial giants, struggled to feed its population between 2001 and 2002, with 53 percent of the population living below the poverty line. In 2006 unemployment stood at 12.5 percent, with over 5.2 million people unable to find adequate paid work to meet monthly needs.

Creating New Social Relations Under Self-Management

As soon as the workers began to produce without an owner or boss, relationships inside the Zanon factory were re-invented, breaking with hierarchical organization, alienation, and exploitation. Prior to the workers' occupation, production inside Zanon was set to maximize the company's profits, reducing salaries to the minimum possible levels, cutting corners on worker safety measures, and pressuring workers. This made it possible to keep high production levels while having the least amount of workers on the factory line.

This changed drastically through the workers' union organizing and factory take-over where relations inside the plant were socialized and a new culture of camaraderie formed. Maté (a traditional tea-like drink) and the *comedor* (the factory's lunch room) became keystones in building new social relations. One of the assembly's first decrees was to permit workers to drink maté while working on the production lines. Maté is a pillar in Argentine culture; the hot drink is prepared and shared in a social setting among a group of people. Workers comment that drinking maté hasn't slowed down their work rhythm, on the contrary the drink has served to bring fellow workers closer and discuss problems in the factory in a comfortable setting.

Conditions previous to the workers' occupation led to an average of twenty-five to thirty accidents per month and one fatality per year. In the years of Zanon's production, fourteen workers died inside the factory. Since Zanon's occupation by its workers accidents inside the factory have been reduced to a minimum, with only several minor accidents. "With the owner, you worry and are pressured. Without a boss you work better, you take on more responsibility with consciousness," one worker comments.

Organization and Syndicalism

Former management kept the workers alienated, enforcing a rule that employees from each production line had to wear a specific colored uniform. Workers from the blue line were unable to speak with workers wearing a beige uniform, etc. Employees were unable to chat freely in the lunch room, changing rooms, or factory entrance. Alien-ation served as a method of control, preventing workers from organizing union repre-sentation independent from company interests.

Carlos Villamonte participated in the efforts to win the rank-and-file union seat, organizing secretly in the late nineties. "It was very difficult to win back the inter-nal union at the factory because we had to do it clandestinely. The company had a very repressive system. They couldn't see you in another sector, talk with fellow workers, or even use the bathroom freely. Many times we had to communicate by passing notes under the tables in the cafeteria or walk through each sector making secret times and places to meet. We found ways to evade the boss' and bureaucratic union's control." One such way was forming a ceramists' soccer team. Between prac-tices, games, and tournaments, workers were able to strategize how to win shop-floor union representation.

The struggle at Zanon didn't start with the 2001 factory takeover. A shop-floor movement won union representation elections inside the factory in late 1998, ousting the old union delegate tied to the bureaucracy and the employers. In 2000, delegates from the rank-and-file movement won the provincial-wide elections of the Neuquén Ceramists Union by a 3-to-1 margin. Recently, the Neuquén Ceramists Union as-sembly voted in favor of a new union statute reinventing the democratic principles and guidelines for the union.

Many workers note that efforts to win the rank-and-file union seat, organizing secretly in the late nineties helped them build the organization necessary to take over the factory under worker self-management. Omar Villablanca stressed the importance of union organizing during a talk with labor organizers from Greater Buenos Aires in 2006. "Zanon is what it is today because the workers recuperated the factory's internal trade union. If we hadn't won back the union, Zanon wouldn't be functioning under worker control. The Zanon workers learned from the lessons of the internal union and listening to workers from other factories."

The death of Daniel Ferras, a twenty-two-year-old line worker, led to a major union conflict in 2000. The company didn't have a nurse or ambulance on hand and Ferras died from lack of emergency medical attention. The workers held an eight-day work stoppage and forced the company to provide an ambulance on sight. Shortly after the factory takeover, workers printed a ceramic in memoriam of Ferras, a fellow companero who died from exploitative conditions inside the plant. The ceramics hang in several parts of the factory, reminding workers of the doom they were able to escape through direct action and workers' organization.

In his essay *Workers' Liberation and Institutions of Self-Management,*[1] Tom Wetzel suggests that, "if we are to create a society in which the people can directly control their lives, where workers run the industries where they work, the process of self-management must emerge in self-management of mass organizations of working people." The Zanon workers' experience of fighting for control of a mass union prior to the worker takeover at the plant helped create a precedent of collectively self-managing a struggle within capitalist society, and helped to develop in people a sense of their power to run things. In this case, the sense of self-managing a union struggle led to autogestión of a massive factory.

The Neuquén ceramist union assembly continues to be a central organizing tool for the FASINPAT collective, although the regional ceramics union is made up of workers from three other companies that continue to work with a boss and capitalist model. The Neuquén Ceramists Union last year voted in favor of a new statute, which Zanon's newspaper, *Nuestra Lucha,* considers to have revolutionized the union. Under the new statute, union delegates and rank-and-file workers are paid the same wage, the general assembly is the ruling organ, and affiliation is voluntary, as are the dues paid.

Democratic Social Relations

Carlos Saavedra, a Zanon worker with over ten years' laboring on one of the glazing lines, says that every worker in the plant has equal standing. "For the workers the decisions should be decided by the assembly as the only authority in the factory. It shouldn't be like the old administrative system with managers, unionists, or one delegate who decides what is to be done." At Zanon every worker is paid the same wage, with the exception of a small pay difference based on seniority, but seniority based on who withstood the old boss, firings, stand-off, and occupation.

The workers at Zanon have had the most political approach to hiring workers. Today, the plant employs 473 workers, more than 230 of whom were hired after the plant came under worker control. When Zanon began to produce under worker control they hired former Zanon workers who had been fired. Later they began to divide the job openings for grassroots activists working with the unemployed (piquetero) worker organizations.

Workers at Zanon have developed a coordinator system to organize production and basic functioning. Each production line forms a commission. Each commission votes on a coordinator that rotates regularly. The coordinator of the sector informs on issues, news, and conflicts within his or her sector to an assembly of coordinators. The coordinator then reports back to his or her commission news from other sectors. The workers hold weekly assemblies per shift. The factory also holds a general assembly, during which production is halted, each month.

Every month the bookkeeping coordinator gives an extensive report on the income and expenditures at the plant. During the assemblies workers decide how profits should be used. One month, the assembly voted on a pay bonus for workers as the production quota goal for June 2006 went above expectations. Workers also voted in favor of hiring fifteen new workers. Who will get the job is decided on criteria based on family needs, political commitment to the struggle, and technical experience. One participant also brought up the possibility of workers rotating to explore other areas of worker management.

While the factory has adapted democratic practices, many workers have found that smaller meetings have been more effective for workers to address specific concerns or volunteer ideas.

Gender Relations

Women at Zanon created a Women's Commission (Comision de Mujeres de Zanon) in 2004 after a national congress on gender and equality in the coastal city of Mar del Plata. They have begun to print a newsletter, which is distributed to all 470 workers. In a recent newsletter, the Commission interviewed Rivera, who gave testimony of her history as a working-class woman. "It's great that the women at Zanon are organizing and doing something for ourselves."

The objective of the Women's Commission is for the women at the factory to build their own space to meet and discuss prejudice they face in a sexist society. Many of the FASINPAT women have triple roles as working women, mothers, and activists, with particular challenges women must face. Many of the workers have said that the Women's Commission has served as a space to discuss the challenges women face in their workplace even when there isn't a boss.

The Commission also functions as a group providing solutions to different problems that come up in the factory, whether related to politics or production. One issue the workers' assembly has still to resolve is the need for daycare for children, not only for mothers but for the majority of workers who are fathers as well. The Women's Commission has organized specific activities like giving away decorative ceramic calendars in the city center, meeting with other women from social movements, and coordinating activities like a talk on domestic violence in the factory for November 25: International Day for the Elimination of Violence Against Women.

Re-learning Production

Under worker control, no management or professional stayed at the factory. The workers not only had to re-learn the process of production but also other traditionally administrative areas like sales, bookkeeping, and production planning. Workers at Zanon regularly work with lawyers, accountants, and other professionals whom they trust, but the professionals don't make decisions. The worker assembly votes on technical decisions. Professionals have provided specific skills training for workers at Zanon. However, for many of the recuperated enterprises there is a deficit of trustworthy professionals.

In June 2006 the plant produced over 410,000 square meters of ceramic tile, a record for the factory since the take over in 2001. "Quality control is the responsibility of all the workers," said the plant's production coordinator, Francisco Murillo who has worked at Zanon for fifteen years. The factory has competed successfully within the domestic market, which is growing. Zanon ceramics plant is one of Latin America's largest and most modern tile factories. While the former owner Luis Zanon exported over 80 percent of the factory's production, the FASINPAT cooperative has marketed high quality and low price products to markets locally and nationally.

Over time industrial buyers realized that Zanon workers had developed a high quality and low price product, in a market where most producers exported the majority of production. Many workers say the legal status of the cooperative has allowed them to catch an edge on the market by getting rid of middlemen. Currently, the FASINPAT cooperative is invoicing all sales, purchases, and payments with legal status. Unusual for industrial plants, Zanon features a showroom where locals can buy ceramics directly from the plant at a discount.

Capacitación—Empowerment

Autogestión implies that manual and intellectual production is divided equally to benefit all collective members. In the factory, the assembly is attempting to implement a rotating system for manual tasks as well as tasks that involve conceptualization. In the midst of running a business and fighting legal battles, long-term production planning and training often becomes last priority. However, with production in full-steam and growing, the Zanon collective is slowly taking steps toward developing training programs. It is a political decision to make training and education accessible to all workers.

Some workers from the FASINPAT collective are working on several education initiatives, including a library. The assembly will vote on a project to build a library inside the factory for the 473 Zanon workers. Literature will include technical training books, history books, and other literature. The library may also serve as a meeting space for study groups where workers can develop writing, reading, and public speaking skills. A number of workers have pushed to develop training programs and production planning along with Neuquén's public Comahue University. Currently, FASINPAT has collaborative relationships with Engineering and Economics schools at the National Public University of Buenos Aires and Comahue University.

The dream for Jorge Bermudez, an engineer supervisor at the factory, is for every worker at FASINPAT to have the opportunity to study. "The most exciting thing would be for all the compañeros to have the opportunity to rotate in all of the job posts in the factory, get an education, and train themselves in a technical profession." He added that workers assume responsibility to improve their factory, not for personal benefit. "One of the advantages of worker control and equal salaries is that workers who take on job responsibility chose to do so to learn something new, rather than pursuing hierarchy and a higher salary."

The Zanon collective has faced challenges to increase political participation of all workers in decision making and street actions. In some cases, new workers and even some old timers have been reluctant to participate in political activities while off the time clock. Orientation is especially important so that new workers understand where they are working, the history of worker self-management, and the importance of workers controlling their own destinies. Education and orientation would facilitate accountability and solidarity.

Education initiatives could help to assuage fears and reluctance to participate in decision making at the plant. Sharing knowledge and developing skills would help to avoid dependency on particular people so that all workers can become effective agents of social change.

Communication

The plant has taken numerous precautions to ensure that every aspect of the plant's functioning is run by workers, especially communication. The workers' assembly quickly voted to form a press commission, made up of a small group of workers who do press work and have numerous tasks—ranging from informing local and national media of political actions in defense of worker control at the Zanon ceramics factory to developing community projects and informing the workers' collective of news at the plant. The press commission has transformed from a small group producing press releases and pamphlets to a highly skilled political branch at the plant, producing radio programs, newspapers, a website, and videos.

Nuestra Lucha, Zanon's newspaper focusing on working-class struggles, began publishing in 2002. The newspaper, which printed 8,000 copies monthly, was an important motivator in coordinating workers' struggles nationwide. The newspaper stopped publishing in 2006 due to a drop in circulation and disorganization. However, the FASINPAT press commission has taken on numerous new projects directed to the community and workers.

FASINPAT hosts two weekly radio programs on local community radio stations. The programs have a regular audience who tune in to an hour-long program featuring news from the Zanon plant, local news from social movements, interviews, live calls from listeners, and rock music. The press commission has made great efforts to start up a video program, so that workers can film and edit their own stories without having to rely on outsiders to produce documentaries. Grupo Alavío, a direct action and video collective, has helped facilitate regular video workshops at the plant. Several workers have produced short commercial spots for a local TV station to promote the rock concerts the plant regularly hosts. Workers from the plant filmed Rata Blanca's performance, a massive concert held in the plant's stock lot, which over 15,000 people attended. The workers' assembly voted to copy over five hundred DVD's of the Rata Blanca video to be distributed among workers and within the community.

Most important, the press commission has helped coordinate communication within the factory. Newsletters circulate among the collective informing workers of the plant's current legal challenges, news from the production lines, financial news, and updates from coordinators. However, communication could be improved. During assemblies some workers have disputed the need to put resources (monetary and human) into expanding the press commission. Learning communication skills like filming and writing has been a fundamental part of transforming the FASINPAT experience. In many cases, watching videos in groups or creating an effective media campaign has been instrumental in creating a new working-class subjectivity.

Producing for the Community

Besides producing ceramics, the factory has committed itself to projects like donating ceramics to community centers, building homes for working-class families, hosting student field trips, and printing ceramic alphabets for schools. During an interview with Omar VillaBlanca, he was interrupted by a phone call from a public school teacher coordinating a visit to the factory. "One of our slogans is that we have opened our doors to the community. We bring the school children to visit to find out for themselves what a factory in production looks like and so they know they can build another kind of society," he said. In the press office at the factory, the walls are lined with thank you posters hand-made by grade school students. For many students visiting Zanon is a curious and moving experience. VillaBlanca said that the students usually ask a long list of questions. "The first question they ask is, 'Why isn't there a boss?'" The school visits have served as an outreach tool because most of the students talk about their visit with their families at the dinner table.

Zanon workers in 2006 inaugurated a home they built for a family who had lost theirs in a fire. Workers cried at the inauguration from the emotion of providing solutions for a working-class family in dire need. The neighborhood only has one luxury, a church. There are no paved streets, gas lines, or health clinics. The FASINPAT assembly voted to build the home, concluding that workers must resolve their own problems autonomously from the state, political parties, or institutions because the government doesn't want to resolve inequity.

Zanon has held rock concerts and theater productions open to the community. The massive concerts have been very effective in generating support for the recuperated enterprises. The concerts have received major news attention from media outlets reluctant to publish news about the recuperated enterprises. In September 2006, more than 15,000 fans and supporters attended the concert mentioned above, featuring heavy metal veterans Rata Blanca in Zanon's stock lot. The 473 workers from the worker-controlled factory organized the entire event—building the massive stage, putting up posters, and selling the low-cost tickets.

One of the keys to Zanon's success has been the insertion of the workers' struggle into the community. According to VillaBlanca the workers have a lot more at risk than a factory. "First all the jobs are at risk, secondly the community work we've developed wouldn't be possible. Also we'd lose an experience developed over five years that has become very valuable for workers nationally and internationally."

At the factory's entrance, a group of art students have constructed a mural made of broken ceramics. The mural tells of the history of the struggle inside Zanon. It begins with men and women around a large pot cooking above a fire. During the months outside the factory neighbors, students, and workers from the piquetero movement demonstrated solidarity—giving funds and groceries for the workers' campaign. The prisoners from the jail behind the factory donated their food rations to the workers. Social organizations such as Mothers of Plaza de Mayo have acted in solidarity, some of the women who are seventy-years old have declared that they too will defend the factory with their lives.

Zanon has formed a broad mutual solidarity network among local community groups, workers in struggle, and recuperated enterprises nationally and internationally. Unlike the worker-run factories in Buenos Aires and other metropolitan Mecca's, the small size of Neuquén has favored Zanon's networking capability. In addition, social movements in the province have grown in the past years since Argentina's 2001 economic crisis. Students, teachers, public workers, unemployed workers, and indigenous communities protesting have faced increasing hostility from the Popular Movement of Neuquén (MPN), Neuquén's ruling right-wing party. Zanon has been a pain in the government's backside. Neuquén's provincial governor, Jorge Sobich, has attempted to evict the factory numerous times, but community support backfired his plans.

Ties with Occupied Factories

The Zanon co operative, formally named FASINPAT, functions as an autonomous entity but also forms part of the Ceramists Union in Neuquén. Zanon is the only recuperated factory demanding national expropriation of their ceramics plant under worker control. FASINPAT does not form part of the recuperated enterprises largest grouping, MNER (National Movement of Recuperated Enterprises). Over forty worker-run businesses—among them BAUEN Hotel, Chilavert printing factory, Pismanta Hotel and Spa, La Foresta meatpacking plant, Maderera Cordoba woodshop, and Zanello tractor manufacturer—belong to MNER. The Peronist MNER, led by Eduardo Marua, has been very effective in creating legal tactics for the occupied factories. Zanon regularly coordinates activities with recuperated enterprises belonging to MNER.

BAUEN Hotel, Chilavert, and Zanon have worked together in a coalition for a national expropriation law. The government has offered short-term solutions, giving temporary legal ownership to workers who have recuperated their workplace. This legal permit is usually granted for anywhere between two to five years. A definitive expropriation law for factories producing under worker control would provide legal security for jobs and allow workers to dedicate their energy to improving factory production and community projects.

On a local level, BAUEN Hotel has become a prime example of coalition building and development of a broad mutual support network. In the midst of legal struggles and successfully running a prominent hotel, the cooperative's members haven't forgotten their roots. BAUEN, a nineteen-story worker run hotel, has become a political center for worker organizations, including Zanon. The floor is covered with beautiful high-quality porcelain tile, a trade between worker controlled Zanon ceramics factory and BAUEN. Regularly, Zanon workers and other social activists put on activities and stay at the hotel while visiting Buenos Aires.

International Solidarity

Many Zanon workers have had the opportunity to travel abroad and share their experience. Workers in Italy, Germany, and Spain experimenting in worker cooperative models have eagerly met with workers from Zanon to exchange information and strategies. Unions and social organizations in Europe have offered solidarity to keep FASINPAT up and running. In March 2006, Spain's General Labor Confederation (CGT), the anarcho-syndicalist union, donated a bus to the factory to transport workers.

Representatives from worker-controlled factories and businesses from Argentina, Uruguay, Venezuela, and Brazil organized the First Latin American Congress on Recuperated Enterprises October 28 and 29, 2005, in Caracas to build coordinated strategies against government attacks and dog-eat-dog markets. Venezuelan President Hugo Chávez inaugurated the event with more than 1,000 self-managed workers present who are putting into practice the slogan Occupy, Resist, and Produce. The Congress served as an initiative to build an economic and mutual support network among the some three hundred businesses and factories currently run by worker self-management in Latin America.

The agreements between recuperated enterprises have had the most concrete impact. Even in the case of Venezuela, Latin America's recuperated factories have had to learn that workers can't rely on the state to move a business forward. The occupied factories and enterprises are proving that they are organizing to develop strategies in defense of Latin American workers susceptible to factory closures and poor working conditions.

Challenges for Autonomy and Autogestión

Workers at Zanon have maintained their autonomous vision while having to rely on the state for legalization and also producing within the capitalist model. The experience is so strong because the workers put into practice models for autonomy and self-management before using the terminology. They experimented with those ideas out of necessity, but their past experience in union organizing and alliances to working-class organizations helped build the path toward autogestión. At Zanon there is a strong working-class identity, that's to say they identify with working-class liberation struggles. They recognize the social conflict with capitalists, with a perspective of emancipation for the working class. "Zanon represents a triumph for the working class and represents the possibility of organizing society in another way: without bosses and the pressure of having to serve somebody that takes all the money and leaves the rest destitute," says one worker.

The workers at Zanon are putting into practice direct action for workers' liberation that goes beyond demanding small gains for workers' rights. They are proposing something revolutionary: get rid of the bosses and allow workers to organize themselves democratically. This logic is intolerable for the state.

Zanon has successfully overcome state challenges posed such as legal battles and violent attacks. While doing so, the FASINPAT collective has turned into a major mobilizing factor in the Neuquén province. The local government has faced highly organized groups with broad bases of mutual support that Zanon has helped to build and sustain. Worker self-management in Neuquén has also helped build popular power among local social movements.

Beyond legal attacks, Argentina's recuperated enterprises have had to strategize to overcome market challenges, with no capital support from the state. Due to lack of infrastructure and outdated technology, many of the worker-run cooperatives have little chance of surviving competition in the capitalist market. Zanon had an edge in this area due to its size and the advanced technology inside the plant. Workers at Zanon have historically been highly skilled in the ceramics trade, making it easier for the worker collective to resolve technical issues like maintenance and ensuring a high quality product. The plant also features a tool and die shop, making it possible for workers to produce replacements parts in house and by-passing importing parts.

The best way for the recuperated enterprises to survive is to create an alternative market for products produced inside the recuperated enterprises. Bartering products manufactured by worker-run enterprises among a network of recuperated workplaces and local organizations would guarantee that a percentage of production becomes profitable for the community and workers. Creating an extensive bartering market could be one way to by-pass the capitalist market and directly benefit the community.

Almost all ceramics produced at Zanon are destined for the capitalist market. The assembly has also discussed the need to produce other products for the benefit of the community, even though ceramic tiles are used to build homes, schools, and hospitals. For now, the FASINPAT collective is focusing on using profits generated from the market to fund community projects.

Other autonomous solutions include generating funding independent from the state to help new recuperated enterprises get started. There is an urgent need to open new recuperated enterprises. A movement of recuperated enterprises could pull together a collective fund specifically for getting new recuperated enterprises started. This would be a solid motivation for workers to take over their workplace, knowing that they have support.

New Subjectivity and Working Culture

Along with defending jobs, recuperated enterprises are also creating a new culture and subjectivity. Worker self-management creates a sense of pride, self-worth, and control over one's destiny. Worker self-management has helped many workers around the world realize that they have the ability to build tools for liberation and fight against exploitive conditions. Zanon workers often say that taking over their work place and production has changed their views of the world and themselves as part of the working class. They know that they don't need a boss to run a factory or society.

Whenever the workers took over the plant, the factory or workplace became a physical space for liberation. A new working culture is being built in many of these spaces. Building cultural centers and holding concerts have been important strategies for the working class to recuperate its culture of dignity and freedom. In front of a crowd of 10,000 people, Raul Godoy, Zanon's union delegate, greeted spectators and celebrated that the concert was being held without bosses or police at the factory. Through self-managing cultural events, Zanon workers have sent a message that the working class is capable of creating its own culture and art.

The factory takeover has been used for over a century as a tool for working-class liberation. In many historical struggles, the factory takeover was simply used to make demands heard rather than taking over production. The Argentine working class has been devastated from thirty years of intense neoliberal policies. In order to implement the current economic order a military dictatorship had to disappear 30,000 labor activists and students during the 1976–1983 military dictatorship. In a moment when the Argentine working class is recently recuperating from the blows against labor laws and privatization, Zanon is proposing a model radically different from the capitalist model. Zanon is putting into practice a production model based on equality, direct democracy, and solidarity. FASINPAT is creating new working-class subjectivity for the working class worldwide.

The state has been directly threatened by the experience at Zanon. The process of transforming working-class subjectivity is difficult to reverse; hence the state and capitalism push to prevent workers from building their own culture of dignity and freedom. FASINPAT has set an example for workers all around the world, a glimpse of how society could be organized after capitalism. What's keeping these experiences of worker takeovers from multiplying? This is the biggest challenge for workers at Zanon, the spread of autogestión outside the factory.

Despite political and market challenges, Argentina's recuperated enterprises represent the development of one of the most advanced strategies in defense of the working class and resistance against capitalism and neoliberalism. Worker-run businesses have battled for laws to protect workers' jobs and opened legal doors for other recuperated enterprises. Many of the recuperated factories have built an extensive international solidarity network among Latin America's some three-hundred recuperated enterprises in Argentina, Venezuela, Brazil, and Uruguay.

Argentina's recuperated factory movement has created jobs, formed a broad network of mutual support among the worker-run workplaces, and generated community projects. FASINPAT's experience in worker self-management and organization have directly challenged capitalist structures by questioning private property, taking back workers' knowledge, and organizing production for objectives other than profits. Rosa Rivera, a worker at Zanon for fifteen years, explains that Zanon is not only a struggle for the 473 workers inside the factory, but a struggle for the community and social revolution. "If factories are shut down and abandoned, workers have the right to occupy it, put it to work, and defend it with their lives."

(Endnotes)

1   Tom Wetzel "Workers' liberation and institutions of self-management" www.zcommunications.org/znet/viewArticle/4332 (accessed February 27, 2006)

Chapter 17

VENEZUELA'S PATH

Michael Albert

GOING TO VENEZUELA? THERE are beautiful waterfalls and mountains. There is rich surf, sand, and sun. But nowadays the biggest attraction is revolution.

In October 2005 I spent a week in Caracas. That's not much information to work with, but for what it's worth, here's what I found and felt.

Toward a New Political System

My first and arguably most personally surprising encounter with the Bolivarian Revolution was at the Ministry for Popular Participation, which was created in accord, I was told, with Chávez's desire "that the people should take power."

I asked the officials we interviewed, "What does that mean, 'that the people should take power'"? After noting thousands of years of "empires obstructing people from participating in politics," all culminating in "the North American empire," the official said the "U.S. has had two hundred years of representative government, but in your system people turn over control to others." Instead, in Venezuela, "we humbly are proposing a system where people hold power in a participatory and protagonist democracy. We want a new kind of democracy to attain a new kind of society."

On the wall was a diagram of their aims. It had lots of little circles, then other larger ones in another layer, and so on. The idea, they said, "was to establish numerous local grassroots assemblies or councils of citizens where people could directly express themselves." These local councils would be the foundational components of "a new system of participatory democracy."

The bottom layer of the vision focuses on communities with "common habits and customs," the officials said. "We define them as comprising 200 to 400 families, or 1000 to 2000 people each." One could of course imagine sub-units within each local unit as well, but that wasn't immediately on their agenda, nor was it in their diagram. The local units would in turn send "elected spokespersons" to units another layer up. Units in this second layer would "encompass a broader geographic region," and then from there "spokespeople would be elected to another layer, and so on," creating a network covering "parishes, municipalities, states, and the whole society."

The participation officials, explaining their diagram and their goal, said the smallest units were meant to become "the decision-making core of the new Venezuelan polity." Chávez and this ministry hoped to have, they said, "3,000 local assemblies in place by the new year." Their goal was to have "enough in place, throughout the country, in four or five years, to account for 26 million Venezuelans."

They didn't want "a dictatorship of the proletariat or of any other kind," they said. Strikingly, they also said they didn't want "what Che died for, though they wanted to learn from that." They wanted to build something new, from the bottom.

I asked, "What happens if the local assemblies want some new policy, and the ministers, legislature, or Chávez don't want it?" "No matter," they said, "the assemblies, once they are in place and operating, rule."

But, I said, "you don't want an assembly of one hundred families making a decision for the whole country, surely." "Correct," came the answer, "the local assemblies can only make final decisions bearing just on their own area."

"Suppose one assembly decides it wants some change bearing on crime that has to do with federal courts or police or whatever, extending beyond that community?" I asked. "What happens? When does the law or policy change?"

"On every level there should be a response" came the reply. "On the lowest level assemblies would do whatever they can within their community. But crime goes beyond a community, and requires going to the next higher levels where the issues would have to be confronted, too. On the municipal level they might change ordinances, etc., to also respond. And it could go higher, then."

Okay, I asked, "Suppose one local assembly wants a younger voting age. They bring it to the next higher level and members there are excited about it too. Does it go up to a legislature and does the legislature have any choice?"

I was told the local unit would—through its spokespeople—send the proposal to the next layer of the popular democratic structures. "Had they decided something bearing only on their local neighborhood, which is all that is happening now, such as the age required for local votes, it would simply be enacted, under their supervision, for them, without having to be discussed more widely." But if their desire stretched wider, as a general new voting law for national elections would, "their proposal would go up, as far as is relevant. Then the proposal would go back to the base of all assemblies for all to consider."

These Bolivarians, entrusted by Chávez's administration with building a new, parallel polity, didn't want any more representative decision making than absolutely necessary. They wanted the proposal from one assembly to go up not so that it could be decided by representatives, but so that it could be discussed by spokespeople and then be brought back to other local assemblies by their spokespeople, eventually to all of them, to be decided at large. "If support came," I was told, "then the goal is that it would yield a new voting age, whether Chávez or mayors or the legislature or anyone else wanted the change or not."

I said surely there must be many elected or just appointed mayors, governors, or bureaucrats who would obstruct this vision, not wanting their power reduced or that of the populace increased. Yes, I was told, "many bureaucrats have held positions for twenty or thirty years and about sixty percent of them are putting breaks on the proposal."

"Even among ministers in the Chávez administration," I asked, "do some resent that they would go from having power to just obeying the public? Cuba's *poder popular* began with many of the ideals you express," I noted, "but never got to the point where the national power was participatory. Do you believe that the Chávez government will help the assembly system reach its full development, or that after a while the assembly system will have to push against the government to get full power?"

The answer was "only the organized population can decide. We are on a path to invent a new democracy. We have gone forward from what we had before. There are no guarantees, but we are trying to go further." There was no need, however, the officials said, to remove or otherwise forcefully conflict with the old structures. Rather, the new system would be built alongside what now exists and would prove its worth over time, in parallel. Many in the old would come around, others wouldn't. But either way, in time the old forms would be replaced by the impressive reality of the new forms' success, not by fiat or by force.

"How will Chávez's initiative encourage people to create these local assemblies?" I wondered. The whole assembly structure was a project in development, the officials said, and there were diverse ideas about how to make it happen. Here was the most striking and instructive one I heard "We Bolivarians have a program for citizens in barrios to gain ownership of their current dwellings. They need only petition to do so, but they have to do that in groups of two hundred families or more for the petition to be accepted." In that case, the dwellers get their homes and the community of families hopefully becomes a grassroots assembly.

I asked, "Do you find that the government has to prod the people to participate?" The officials replied, "The people are taking initiative, but it is very important that the government supports them." People taking power involves "a new way of thinking and a new culture," the officials said. "The president and we are working hard to make participatory democracy happen, but we all have limitations in our heads to overcome, as well as old structures." This was a recurring theme. In Venezuela, while there have been coups and thus struggle against capital and also external imperialism, at the moment the struggle seems to be more against the imprint of the past on even poor people's habits and beliefs.

"How many people," I asked, "already support this program?" "The full picture of assemblies is very new, just about to be announced," they said, "but the general goal of people's power, maybe about a quarter understand and strongly support, with more soon." They emphasized they didn't want a system "that gives power to another person." They didn't "want representative democracy." The people elect, in the Venezuelan model, "spokespeople, not representatives." What will be proposed in one unit will get to the other units by going up via elected spokespeople, and then back down to the base, through other spokespeople, for further discussion and decision. What will be decided at lowest levels will be binding. "The country has 335 municipalities," they noted. About 255 are with the president."

Discussions about police and courts are also proceeding, I was told, but I didn't get to talk with people working on that dimension of change and apparently it was, as yet, not nearly as far along. These officials told me that the "socialism we are trying to construct incorporates understanding the history of past efforts in Russia, Cuba, etc., but it is not about state run enterprises or a dictatorship. We have to create our own model to reduce the work week, to defend nature, and to create social justice for both the collective and the individual. If it continues, capitalism will put an end to the planet. We have to find a way for everybody to have a better standard of living but also preserve the planet. A virtuous individual thinks about the community. That is what we are looking for."

Additional Examples

Regarding health, though I didn't get to talk to any government officials directly involved with the program, or to any doctors dispensing medicine, it was clear that again the government hadn't simply taken over the old structures and as yet had no inclination to do so. Instead, in cooperation with Cuba, which sent 20,000 doctors, the government had set up new clinics all over the country, dispensing health care locally in barrios, bringing to the poor their first local health care. We were told these clinics serve people's needs, operate pretty democratically, and have doctors who earn typical workers pay and often less. The people love the clinics, and the Chávista health officials, I would bet, look for the old structures to bend and break under the competitive pressure of the new ones, but without having been directly coerced.

We visited barrios, which were gigantic stretches of hillside covered with small shack-like homes, and we saw intermittently the newly constructed small but clean medical clinics the Cuban doctors worked from. Compared to nothing, which was the correct comparison, it was a huge improvement and helps explain Chávez's support from the barrio communities. We also heard about a plan for eye care, even offering free eye operations of diverse kinds, 500,000 operations over ten years, to poor U.S. citizens. The Venezuelans would provide the transportation. The Cubans would do the surgery. Having eye problems myself, I listened closely, smiling at the thought.

The same general pattern was true of a project aimed at raising literacy throughout Venezuela. With the same logic and methodology, this project also proceeded by not fighting with the old, but instead existing alongside it. In under two years, Chávez reports and apparently UNESCO verifies, Venezuela has eliminated illiteracy.

Indeed, this same pattern is being employed, we saw, even for higher education. The government didn't take over the national universities, private or public. Instead, after the oil industry strike failed during the last coup attempt, when almost a third of the industry's managers and other technical workers were fired for having participated in trying to bring down the government, many of the prior oil administration buildings were no longer needed. Obviously the bureaucratic waste and fraud had been enormous. A group of these liberated buildings were transformed into the new Bolivarian University.

Workers' councils ruled the new university. The government minister of education became its rector. In time, he overrode the council, determining instead that there would be only meetings of smaller groups, and that he would only interact with representatives from those. This characteristic pattern of a central planner interacting with a workplace and demanding a chain of command in it and in that way interfering with direct self-management was disturbing. The Bolivarian revolution is juggling many tendencies with roots in many aspects of social life. But the pedagogy of the new university is, I learned by interviewing a professor there, very innovative, emphasizing serving diverse communities by students having to do projects at the grassroots, having to relate their studies to social conditions and needs, and having grading being a shared task for students, faculty, and community residents.

In an interview with Justin Podur, the then university rector put it this way: "We will prove that you can have quality and equity in education. We will form holistic professionals who are citizens. They will learn ethics, social responsibility, respect for a Latin American and Caribbean identity, solidarity, respect. The professional produced by this institution will work for the transformation of society. She will be a critical thinker who can stimulate others and generate questions. Our curriculum is based on 'axes' of education. Any plan or program of study—say an engineering or teaching professional program—is your 'professional axis.' But you also have a cultural axis, a political axis, ethical axis, aesthetics axis, a social-community interaction axis where you work directly with sectors of society outside of the university from the start."

Bolivarian University has about 7,000 students, we were told, and about 700 staff of whom 250 are non-faculty but only 120 are full-time professors. Some faculty resist the new pedagogy as too flexible. Some see it as too community oriented. In meetings there are radicals and reactionaries. Some faculty resist the trend toward providing classes for non-teaching staff. Some resist having steadily more equitable pay relations among all employees. Some resist the drive to bring the school's resources out into the country, setting up missions beyond Caracas, promoting higher education while reaching out educationally to Venezuela's rural areas for the first time.

Looked at in the large, Bolivarian University competes with the rest of the system of higher education by offering an evolving, but already dramatically different, experience. The minister heading Bolivarian University might not be optimal in terms of workers self-management, but we were told he does talk frequently and forcefully about proving that the new approaches are better and replacing the old ways via having people see the benefits of change. The students at Bolivarian University, not surprisingly, are mostly poor, which is the opposite of the old system. Ties between the school and local co-ops, which are in turn constructed with uniform wages and council self-management, are continually extended, building a kind of parallel world to what has gone before.

Considering still another key domain of social life, media, the emerging pattern continued. A look at the daily newspapers showed that of the first twenty five articles, reading from the first page forward, fully twenty were broad attacks on or highly critical of Chávez. The rest were on entirely other topics. And this was typical, day after day, I was told. The papers are privately held corporations, not surprisingly hostile toward Chávez's inclinations. Chávez doesn't restrict them, however, much less nationalize or otherwise take them over. The same situation holds for key TV stations. Regarding the TV stations, however, and I bet something like this will also happen with print before too long, the government has a strategy.

VIVE TV is a new station created, like Bolivarian University, by the Chávez government. We visited and enjoyed touring its facilities. The widest salary difference, from the head of the company to people who cleaned up, was three-to-one, but the new payment policy, being steadily if slowly enforced, was to attain equal hourly pay for all by periodically raising wages of those at the bottom until they reached parity.

VIVE has roughly three hundred employees. Their equipment wasn't like CBS, but it was certainly excellent and far reaching in its potential. The new VIVE website presents their shows, archived, for the world to see. The station's governing body is, of course, a workers' assembly. Workers at VIVE lacking skills are encouraged to take courses, including in film production and other topics, given right on the premises, and those facilities are also used to teach citizens from Caracas and more widely how to film in their own locales.

Indeed, the station's mandate was to provide a voice for the people. Its shows, we were told, routinely present citizens speaking their mind, including voices from well outside Caracas, which was a first for Venezuela. To that end, VIVE undertakes lots of community training, distributing cameras to local citizens as well, so people around the country can send in footage and even finished, edited material for national display.

In some respects VIVE is like a local community cable station in the U.S., except that it is national and the élan is far, far higher, and the desire to incorporate the seeds of the future in the present structure is far, far more explicit and radical, with the employees seeing themselves as presenting to the country and world a new kind of media that, they hope, will be a model picked up elsewhere as well.

VIVE takes no ads, "to avoid being controlled." There is actually, on the shows, much criticism of the government, since the shows convey grassroots opinions. But this criticism, unlike that on mainstream private stations, is honest and heartfelt, not manufactured. Rather than trying to create dissension, it is constructive.

Along with VIVE and a national public station directly under government control, there is also a new federal law which imposes on private stations that 25 percent of their shows must be produced by independent producers, not by the stations themselves. This is a kind of service requirement, but, interestingly, it is VIVE who trains many of these contracting producers. Here again is evidence of a kind of multi-pronged, legal, almost stealth-like incursion on old ways, both within the new institutions that are creating new approaches even against recalcitrant attitudes and habits, and also via the new institutions challenging the old ones, by a contrast effect or by outright competition, and injecting ideas into them through the independent producers as well. Venezuela has also embarked on a continental station, to broadcast news and the voices of the poor throughout Latin America, but we didn't have a chance to visit so as to comment on that.

Regarding the economy, Venezuela starts out with huge advantages compared to other third world countries. The oil industry is nationalized and is the centerpiece of the society's economy. Moreover the oil industry provides a gigantic flow of revenues, unlike what any other dissident country has ever enjoyed while trying to chart a new path for itself. Likewise, oil not only provokes U.S. interest, it also provides considerable defense against U.S. intervention.

We were told by an oil industry official, however, that there are still many transnational firms who contract for various aspects of oil business in Venezuela. The government's reaction, he said, was not to challenge them, much less expropriate them, but to form new co-ops doing the same functions, intended to out compete the transnationals. These new co-ops are worker self-managed. They usually are seeking equal wages and even in the least egalitarian ones the ratio is at most three-to-one. In addition, a minimum social wage is guaranteed. An idea slowly being implemented is to federate the co-ops, facilitating their interacting and exchanging via social rather than market norms. The vision, it seemed to me, is that in time contracts will go almost exclusively to the co-ops so that the transnationals will simply leave, of their own accord, no confrontation needed.

I asked if officials thought using competing on the market as the strategy to drive out transnationals risked entrenching market mentalities, but the question wasn't really understood. Similarly, my asking whether officials were worried that utilizing as a key strategy market competition would impose on self-management old-style aims and means, greatly reducing its latitude for change and perhaps even causing it to give way to new hierarchies, also didn't resonate. There is immense opposition to capitalism and its private ownership. There is major opposition to large disparities in income. There is considerable opposition to gaps in job types yielding passivity versus domination. But only a few people seem to be hostile to markets per se.

One of the few who seem to reject markets, however, is Chávez himself. How else can we explain his approach to international economics, which not only predictably rejects the IMF, WTO, World Bank, and particularly the FTAA, but is beginning to hammer out an alternative based on mutual aid and, in effect, violating market exchange rates to instead undertake transactions in light of true and full social costs and benefits, and with a commitment to sharing gains from exchanges not just equally, but more advantageously for the poorer participants? This certainly seems to be the logic of the wide array of agreements into which Venezuela is entering, with not only Cuba, but many neighboring countries, as well as specific occupied factories throughout Latin America, for example, providing oil at amazingly low rates and beneficial terms, often in exchange for goods, not payments. This is quite like Cuba's historic sending of aid and items to poorer countries at cut rates, but the scale is tremendously increased, and where Cuba primarily offered people, as in doctors, Venezuela is doing this with resources and economic products, more directly subverting specifically market logic.

Returning to my exchange with the oil official, when I asked about CITGO—the oil industry owned by Venezuela operating in the U.S.—moving toward having a workers' council to self-manage it, moving toward equal wages, and changing its division of labor, not only on behalf of those working at CITGO but as a demonstration inside the U.S. for other U.S. workers of the potential of self-management and equity, the official was very excited, even wanting to immediately call others to talk about this idea. Later discussion of the related possibility of Venezuela making inroads, via CITGO or otherwise, into media and information dispersal in the U.S., instead of information incursions always occurring only in the reverse direction, caused still more excitement.

We were told by the oil ministry officials and also by trade unionists and others how in Venezuela, like in Argentina, there was a movement, just getting up to speed, to "recuperate" failing or failed workplaces. The difference was that while in Argentina this occurs against the inclinations of government, in Venezuela the government welcomes and even propels it. Indeed, the government has now assembled a list of seven hundred such plants and is urging workers to occupy and operate them on their own. Another difference, however, is that in Venezuela the method of decision making adopted for the recuperated plants is called co-management and involves both a workers' council and government representatives. The upside of this is that the government is often to the Left of the local workforce in the affected workplace, helping to educate and prod it. The downside is that the centralizing inclination of the government and the participatory inclination of real self-management are in opposition. We saw both these tendencies in the Bolivarian University, with the government minister pushing radical pedagogy on sometimes contrary faculty, but also reducing the influence of the workers' council. In fact, however, it seemed for the moment, in any case, the government was so over stretched that if there are widespread recuperations, government involvement will be slight and workers will in practice be left to self-manage.

Beyond a factory recuperation movement in Venezuela, the government also creates new co-ops from scratch. These are also co-managed, at least in theory, and also tend to seek equitable remuneration, etc. These co-ops have often been small and local, everything from little dress shops to small construction projects, but plans exist for creating new firms to produce computers, mine resources, run an airline, etc.

As I understood what I heard, the co-ops are expected to out-compete old capitalist firms—a very reasonable expectation given that the co-ops have lower overhead (due to reduced management pay rates, reduced numbers of managers, and altered job roles), and that co-op workers have an inclination to produce more consistently and energetically under the new social relations. The danger of the co-op strategy, however, is that operating via market norms and methods and specifically trying to out-compete old firms in market-defined contests may entrench in them a managerial bureaucracy and a competitive rather than social orientation, leading more toward what is called market socialism, which in my view is a system that still has a ruling managerial or coordinator class, and that operates in light of competitive prices and surplus seeking, instead of the approach pushing them toward what the most radical Venezuelans clearly desire, which is a classless, participatory, and self-managing economy in which people are socially motivated and are well off and efficient, operating in light of full social implications seeking both personal and collective well-being.

In capitalist firms, still dominant in economic sectors other than oil, there is a change in mood as well. Workers identify more with the state and feel it is an ally, providing by its initiatives, in the words of a trade union leader, "a more promising moment for change." This has led to workers in capitalist firms "challenging old union norms and methods" and feeling uncomfortable being "stuck in old relations while others are building new co-ops." This trade union leader estimated that "80 percent of Venezuela's workers firmly support Chávez." She also said this is why the better unions are thinking about pushing for self-management even against capitalist owners. She said "while at first occupying failing firms was just self defense" seeking to protect "jobs and union freedoms," more recently more radical unions are seeking "more consistent strategies to win co-management or self-management."

She told us that "five or six years ago the typical Venezuelan worker would not exhibit any class consciousness, but now the Bolivarian revolution was awakening class consciousness not only in workers, but in all people." I asked what would happen if "workers in a successful capitalist firm, knowing friends in co-ops or recuperated firms who enjoyed controlling their conditions and having equitable incomes, struck against their owners and petitioned the government to take over the firm and make it self-managed." She talked about how arrangements would likely be made providing the private owners "credits and investments if they would undertake co-management with the workers." I wondered why businesspeople "would make such a stupid deal when it was clearly just a first step toward their disappearing. Why would they do it, even with short term benefits?" I also asked again about "workers wanting to take over a really successful firm, not giving the owners anything, but just taking over? Why weren't workers all over Venezuela seeking that? And what would happen if they did?"

The trade union leader replied that "of course the businesspeople are not stupid, but they believe we are." She talked about unions spreading "the revolutionary virus into the workers" and I asked again, How come it didn't spread quickly, all on its own?

She blamed "old union leaders, afraid of taking new steps." But she also said that "just two years ago no one would have believed a worker-managed factory was possible but now there are over twenty, with over seven hundred under study for occupation to get them back to work." She pointed out the need to do all this "along with raising consciousness of people." She said, "going too fast, without people wanting it, wouldn't work." And she noted that the businesspeople are "still trying to manipulate and buy off the workers, and especially the leaders."

I also asked this trade union leader, who was explicitly responsible for international relations, about links with movements and unions in the U.S. She reported Venezuelan Chávista unions having links to the "AFL-CIO in California, some grassroots unions, and the anti-war movement," but not with the national AFL-CIO because they are still giving money to those imposing old bureaucracy and fomenting coups."

I asked her what proportion of the paid workforce was female and she replied, "about 50 percent." I asked about women's salaries compared to men's and she said there was no difference for the same jobs, but "women didn't get as good jobs as men." I asked if things were better in the occupied factories, and she said, "As far as I can tell things are somewhat better, yes, but not ideal." She said, "The double duty of women is the biggest obstacle to their deeper involvement in union work." I asked if the Bolivarian movement was trying to address this and she said "The new constitution says domestic work has to be acknowledged as work for social security purposes," but I asked about men and women doing it more equally and she said that that "was progressing very, very slowly. At the grassroots level lots of women participate, despite double or even triple work, but our men are very macho, and regrettably many women spoil them by doing all household work." She said her situation was unusual because she got lots of help at home.

Overview

From my trip it seemed to me that…

(1) The Bolivarian movement, and in particular President Hugo Chávez, is pushing the population Leftward. Even more, the Bolivarian movement, and particularly President Hugo Chávez, is seeking to replace old capitalist forms with new forms that they call anti-capitalist, participatory, socialist, and Bolivarian, among other labels. They are not directly and forcefully challenging and taking over or removing old structures. They are operating legally in the interstices of society to nurture new forms into existence and to then show by contrast and via socially acceptable competition that Venezuela's old forms are inferior, expecting that in time the new forms will legally win out over the old. But as to what these new forms are, there is far more clarity concerning political norms and structures than economic ones. One would like to see a national exploration, debate, and consciousness-raising campaign aimed at clarifying and advocating the ultimate goals of the revolution, and at making knowledge of

its goals and continuous critique and enrichment of them a national possession, not a possession only of some leaders.

(2) The Bolivarians' unusual transitional approach has as its vanguard aspect that the Bolivarian leadership is ideologically and programmatically far ahead of its populace and trying to get that populace to move further and faster than it is alone inclined to. It has as its anarchist aspect, however, that the movement is being nourished, even if by a national president, mostly from the bottom up. It seeks to exist in parallel and to become prevalent without violence and even without confrontation. It seeks to embody the seeds of the future in the present to avoid generating a new domination. It is trying to win adherents by evidence, not force.

(3) The centrality of a single leader, at least that it is Hugo Chávez, seems to be a highly unexpected benefit. Chávez, so far, has not just been congenial and inspiring, audacious and courageous, willing to step outside every box and implement program after program, experimenting and learning, but has also shown remarkable restraint in utilizing the accoutrements of central power and has even been a key source of anti-authoritarian influence. At the same time, it is also true that the centrality of a single leader, Hugo Chávez, though perhaps unavoidable, is also a debit. The leader could turn bad, or could disappear, and at this point either turn of events would be calamitous. A related problem is the lack of a serious opposition on the Left. Revolution benefits from disagreement, debate, and diversity, but those attributes have trouble arising amidst a siege mentality. One wonders who will succeed Chávez, and how the people will succeed the leaders, unless there is massive popular education in leadership and the revolution's aims.

(4) Finally, the idea of out-competing the old system with a new one created in parallel is very cleverly beneficial in that it avoids undue premature conflict that might bring down holy hell on the Bolivarian project even as it also draws on strengths and sidesteps weaknesses. But the idea of out-competing the old system with a new one created in parallel is also at least in one respect detrimental because it risks ingraining competitive qualities and methods and buttressing bureaucratic and classist structures, and because it may ignore some recalcitrant features from the past that need early dramatic attention lest they later drag down the whole project.

My overall impression was that the Bolivarian revolution is still vague. It doesn't have clearly enunciated feminist politics, anti-racist politics, or even anti-capitalist politics, though in all three cases the inclinations are incredibly humane and radical and are moving rapidly forward toward enunciating full aims and proposing immediate program in that light. Chávez appears to be a remarkable detonator of insights, himself moving Leftward at a great pace. The Bolivarian revolution is most ideologically clear, which is ironic and a powerful testimony on his behalf, given Chávez's military background, regarding political democracy and political participation where it seems to be already committed to a well conceived, compelling, and innovative institutional vision that outstrips what any other revolutionary project since the Spanish anarchists has held forth.

The future is not certain. The Bolivarian revolution could still stall in social democracy. Co-management and not self-management could lead that way. It could still stumble or even rush into typical old style "socialist" channels. Its market strategies and lack of clarity about class divisions based on divisions of labor, not property, push that way. There is always a danger of authoritarianism when a government is prodding a populace, of course. But the Bolivarian revolution could also, however, provide a remarkable model, both of a better world and of a very original way to arrive at that better world. Which of these results, or of others, happens is largely going to be up to Chávez, the Bolivarian movements, and the Venezuelan people, though mass external support, not least to restrain U.S. aggressive inclinations before they can corrupt or destroy the experiment, are also profoundly needed.

I left Venezuela inspired and very hopeful. Venezuela looks to me like Uncle Sam's worst nightmare. I was humbled by Bolivarian ingenuity and steadfastness and by my own continued citizenship in the world's most rogue and brutal nation, against which I and other radicals have had such limited organizing success. Hopefully my country can follow Venezuela's lead rather than crushing its aspirations. Hopefully, citizens in the U.S. can make that happen. Officials won't, of course.

PART IV

Looking Backward, Looking Forward:

History's Lessons for the Future

Chapter 18

WORKERS' POWER AND THE RUSSIAN REVOLUTION

Tom Wetzel

I WAS ATTRACTED TO radical politics in the late 1960s and early '70s, when I was in my twenties. Most people who were drawn to serious revolutionary politics back then ended up in Leninist organizations of some sort, if only for a time. Third World revolutions were one influence. Various Marxist-Leninist parties had come to power based on guerrilla struggles in places like China and Cuba, and this augmented the claim of Leninism that it was "successful" in charting a way to a post-capitalist future.

But it seemed obvious to me that workers did not have power over production in the various communist countries. They're subordinated to a managerial hierarchy. Thus, I reasoned, workers must be a subjugated and exploited class in those countries.

A work I found particularly helpful in the seventies was Maurice Brinton's *The Bolsheviks and Workers' Control*.[1] This clear-headed and well-researched little book was an indispensable source of arguments to explode the myth of the Bolshevik party building "proletarian power" in Russia. AK Press has reissued this booklet as part of an anthology, *For Workers' Power*.[2] Brinton was the main writer for the London libertarian socialist group Solidarity. This anthology collects in one place many of Brinton's writings, including "The Irrational in Politics," and "Paris: May 1968." In this review I'll mainly focus on the Russian revolution.

Brinton believes that the working class cannot have power in society, cannot liberate itself from its condition as a subjugated and exploited class, unless it gains direct management power over production. He believes that the working class must also gain control over the whole structure of society to ensure its liberation. He rejects the idea that the working class could have power in society if it is subjugated in production. This is the heart of Brinton's argument.

People sometimes say that "workers' councils" were the organizational means for workers fighting for and attaining power in the Russian revolution.[3] But there were two different types of mass organization supported by workers in the Russian revolution that could be called "workers' councils": the soviets ("soviet" is Russian for council) and the factory committees. Let's look at each.

The Petrograd soviet was formed during the tumultuous events in February 1917 that led to the abdication of the czar. A group of radical and liberal intellectuals formed the soviet top-down when they constituted themselves as the "Executive Committee of the Petrograd Soviet" on February 27, 1917. They then sent out a call for election of delegates.[4] Moreover, soviet assemblies were not where the real decisions were made. The executive made the real decisions in the backrooms. Some decisions were submitted to the assembled delegates for ratification, some were not. The soviet assembly tended to be just an open meeting, where anyone could speak. Soviets formed in other Russian cities were similar.

The factory committees, unlike the soviets, were initiated directly by Russian workers themselves, and these organizations became the main vehicle of self-organization of workers in the revolution. These committees were typically made up of elected worker delegates. The most important decisions were made in general assemblies of the rank and file.

On May 30, 1917, there was a meeting of over four hundred representatives of factory committees in the Petrograd area. They described the situation they faced:

> From the beginning of the revolution the administrative staffs of the factories have relinquished their posts. The workmen of the factories have become the masters. To keep the factories going, the workers' committees have had to take the management into their own hands. In the first days of the revolution, in February and March, the workmen left the factories and went into the streets.... Later, the workmen returned to their work. They found that many factories had been deserted. The managers, engineers, generals, mechanics, foremen had reason to believe that the workmen would wreak their vengeance on them, and they had disappeared. The workmen had to begin work with no administrative staff to guide them. They had to elect committees which gradually re-established a normal system of work. The committees had to find the necessary raw materials, and ... take upon themselves all kinds of unexpected and unaccustomed duties.[5]

The factory committees were described as "fighting organizations, elected on the basis of the widest democracy and with collective leadership," with the aim of creating "the organization of thorough control by labor over production and distribution."

Russian workers found that neither the soviets nor the industrial unions could be used by them to solve their immediate economic problems or help to coordinate activities between different workplaces. The soviets were tightly controlled by their executive and were taken up with fighting the government over political issues such as continued Russian involvement in the world war.

The industrial unions weren't much help either. Unions had been illegal under czarism. The unions had been formed top-down by the political parties and continued to be largely an appendage of the parties. Throughout most of 1917, most unions were controlled by the Mensheviks. Although union membership rose from 100,000 to over a million during 1917, this was largely an effect of the growth of the factory committees. Radical workers tended to join industrial unions as a matter of principle, not because unions had a real presence in workplaces. Bill Shatov, an American IWW member who returned to his native Russia, described the Russian unions as "living corpses."

By September 1917 the Bolsheviks had gained majorities in the key Russian soviets. About half the delegates in the Petrograd soviet represented personnel in the Russian military. With troops loyal to the soviets, Bolshevik control of the soviets enabled them to capture state power at the end of October.

The new governmental structure vested authority in the Russian parliament—the 350-member Central Executive Committee of the All-Russian Congress of Soviets. As in other parliamentary systems, the government was formed as an executive committee, or cabinet of ministers, of the parliament. This executive was the Council of People's Commissars (Sovnarkom). Lenin, as chair of this committee, was premier or head of the government.[6] The local and regional soviets, which were little more than rubber stamps for their party-controlled executives anyway, came to function as an "electoral college" (in the American sense) for the indirect election of the parliament. The soviet structure provided legitimacy for the new Bolshevik government, based on widespread support for the soviets among Russian workers and military personnel in 1917. But the indirect system of election and tight centralization meant it could not be effectively controlled by rank-and-file workers or used by them to initiate and control decisions.

By October 1917 a complex situation existed in Russian industry. "In practice the implementation of workers' control took on a variety of forms in different parts of Russia," Brinton writes. "These were partly determined by local conditions but primarily by the degree of resistance shown by different sections of the employing class. In some places the employers were expropriated forthwith, 'from below.' In other instances they were merely submitted to a supervisory type of 'control,' exercised by the factory committees."[7]

This "supervisor control" included, for example, the right to veto management hiring decisions, to prevent employment of strikebreakers. After the coming to power of the Bolshevik Party, the situation would become even more complex with some enterprises "nationalized from above by decree of the Central Government."

At the end of 1917 Lenin did not favor immediate nationalization of the economy. Brinton believes that Lenin opposed expropriation of the capitalists "because of his underestimation of the technological and administrative maturity of the proletariat." Lenin envisioned that the "dual power" situation of "supervisory control" which existed in many privately owned enterprises would continue for some time. The right of the factory committees to engage in this supervisory control was legalized in November 1917 by Lenin's decree on "workers' control." Lenin was not advocating that workers take over management of production or expropriate capitalists on their own initiative.

During 1917 many Russian workers envisioned a division of labor where the factory committees would take over the running of the economy while the soviets would become the new polity or governmental structure.[8] The Bolsheviks encouraged the factory committee movement to restrict its ambitions to "the economy." The "workers party" would take political power.

Limiting their aspiration for power to the economy would prove to be the undoing of the Russian factory committee movement. Direct management of production may be necessary for worker power in society, but it is not sufficient. Workers need also to control the polity—the institutions for making the basic rules in society and enforcing them. If they don't, they won't be able to defend their power in production.

Russian workers assumed that the Bolshevik seizure of state power through the soviets would support their aspirations for economic control. The creation of the new Bolshevik government in October thus spurred a new burst of activity by the factory committee movement. Although Lenin's "workers' control" decree only legalized the degree of control the factory committees had already achieved, it encouraged workers to go farther because now they believed their efforts would gain official sanction. Workers didn't put too much stock in the boundary Lenin drew between control and management. Moreover, Lenin's idea that the situation of "dual power" in the factories could be maintained indefinitely was unrealistic. Kritzman, a "Left" Communist, criticized the workers' control decree:

"Employers would not be inclined to run their businesses with the sole aim of teaching the workers how to manage them. Conversely, the workers felt only hatred for the capitalists and saw no reason why they should voluntarily remain exploited."

"The spontaneous inclination of the workers to organize factory committees," wrote historian E. H. Carr, "was inevitably encouraged by a revolution which led the workers to believe that the productive machinery of the country belonged to them and could be operated by them at their own discretion and to their own advantage. What had begun to happen before the October revolution now happened more frequently and more openly; and for the moment nothing would have dammed the tide of revolt."[9]

Out of this upsurge of activity came the first attempt by the factory committee movement to form its own national organization, independent of the trade unions and political parties. In December the Central Soviet of Factory Committees of the Petrograd Area published the Practical Manual for the Implementation of Workers' Control of Industry. The manual proposed that "workers' control could rapidly be extended into 'workers' management'". The manual also announced the intention of forming the factory committees into regional federations and a national federation.

Isaac Deutscher explains what then happened:

The Factory Committees attempted to form their own national organization, which was to secure their virtual economic dictatorship. The Bolsheviks now called upon the trade unions to render a special service to the nascent Soviet State and to discipline the Factory Committees. The unions came out firmly against the attempt of the Factory Committees to form a national organization of their own. They prevented the convocation of the planned All-Russian

Congress of Factory Committees and demanded total subordination on the part of the Committees.[10]

However, the Bolshevik Party had only just taken state power—and their grip on power would become even more tenuous with the onset of the Russian civil war in May 1918. This resulted in a compromise in which the party committed itself to trade union control of the economy.

This helped the party leadership to gain the cooperation of the party's trade union cadres in suppressing the drive of the factory committee movement for direct worker management. The trade union control concept would be encapsulated in Point 5 of the program adopted at the 1919 Communist Party congress:

> The organizational apparatus of socialized industry must be based primarily on the trade unions ... Participating already in accordance with the laws of the Soviet Republic and established practice in all local and central organs of industrial administration, the trade unions must proceed to the actual concentration in their own hands of all the administration of the entire economy, as a single economic unit.

The first step in supplanting the workers' drive for economic self-management with central planning from above was the decree on December 5, 1917, setting up the Supreme Economic Council (Vesenka), under the direct authority of Sovnarkom. Vesenka was made up of Bolshevik trade union officials, Bolshevik Party stalwarts, and "experts" appointed from above by the government. Vesenka was assigned the task of creating "a plan for the organization of the economic life of the country" and was to "direct to a uniform end" the activities of all existing economic authorities. Here we have the beginnings of a central planning apparatus assuming managerial functions.

The fate of the factory committee movement was fought out at the first All-Russian Congress of Trade Unions in January 1918. Here the Bolsheviks put forward their plan to subordinate the factory committees to hierarchical union control. The main Russian political tendency with a vision for direct workers' management were the anarcho-syndicalists. At the congress, the twenty five anarcho-syndicalist delegates, representing Don Basin miners, Moscow railway workers, and other workers, made a desperate effort to defend the factory committee movement and its drive for direct workers' management. They proposed "that the organization of production, transport and distribution be immediately transferred to the hands of the toiling people themselves, and not to the state or some civil service machine made up of one kind or another of class enemy." G. P. Maximov, a prominent anarcho-syndicalist, distinguished between horizontal coordination and hierarchical control of the economy, "The aim of the proletariat was to coordinate all activity ... to create a center, but not a center of decrees and ordinances but a center of regulation, of guidance—and only through such a center to organize the industrial life of the country."

However, the Bolsheviks got the decision they wanted. The majority of delegates, and Mensheviks, and Social Revolutionary Party supporters at the congress also voted for subordination of the factory committees to the trade unions.

With control over government, armed forces, the trade union apparatus, and majorities on many of the factory committees, the Bolshevik Party was able to tame the factory committee movement. Any factory committee that didn't go along could be isolated; a factory could be denied resources it needed.

"Bolshevik propaganda in later years," Brinton notes, would harp on the theme that the factory committees "were not a suitable means for organizing production on a national scale."[11] Deutscher, for example, says "almost from their creation, the Factory Committees … aspired to have the … final say on all matters affecting their factory, its output, its stocks of raw materials, its conditions of work, etc. and paid little or no attention to the needs of industry as a whole."[12]

The Leninist argument makes a false assumption: either uncoordinated autonomy of each individual factory, or a central planning apparatus to create a plan and then issue orders through a hierarchy. Leninists "dismiss workers' self-management with derogatory comments about 'socialism in one factory,'"[13] says Brinton, "or with profundities like 'you can't have groups of workers doing whatever they like, without taking into account the requirements of the economy as a whole.'"[14] But there is a third alternative: A system of horizontal, self-managed planning and coordination. Why can't workers and consumers themselves create the plan?

Through their own experience the Russian workers themselves had come to realize the need for coordination and planning of the economy on a broader scale. This was the point to the proposals for regional and national federations of factory committees, and the convening of a national factory committee congress.

The consumer cooperatives in the Russian revolution grew to 12 million members. When workers took over factories in 1917, they sometimes developed links with these organizations for distribution of the products of their factory. This relationship could have been systematized to provide consumer input to some sort of grassroots-controlled, participatory planning system.

The proposal for union management of the economy, endorsed by the Communist Party congress in 1919, was never implemented. In exchange for their efforts to suppress the independent initiative of factory committees, Communist Party trade union cadres had been appointed to various government and management bodies, but this was combined with government appointment of managers and control from above. As early as November 9, 1917, the Central Soviet of Employees that had taken over the postal system during the revolution was abolished. The new minister in charge decreed: "No … committees for the administration of the department of Posts and Telegraphs can usurp the functions belonging to the central power and to me as People's Commissar."

By 1921 worker discontent was widespread and strikes broke out in Petrograd and Moscow. The immediate danger posed by foreign embargo and civil war had ended and now the trade union base of the party was pushing for a greater say in the running of the economy. This debate would come to a head at the Communist Party congress in March 1921. The Workers Opposition charged that the party leaders had failed to carry out the promises in the 1919 program, and had "reduced to almost nil the influence of the working class." With "the Party and economic authorities having been swamped by bourgeois technicians," they argued that the solution was union management of the economy. They thus proposed to invoke an All-Russian Producers Congress to elect the management of the national economy, with various industrial unions electing the management boards of their respective industries.

Lenin denounced the push for union management as a "syndicalist deviation." "It destroyed the need for the Party. If the trade unions, nine-tenths of whose members are non-Party workers, appoint the managers of industry, what is the use of the Party?," Lenin asked. Here we see Lenin's view of the party as managers, implementing their program through a top-down hierarchy. He assumes that the workers themselves are somehow incapable of running the economy, that the party intelligentsia must be in charge.

Trotsky denounced the Workers Opposition for raising "dangerous slogans":

> They have made a fetish of democratic principles. They have placed the workers' right to elect representatives above the Party. As if the Party were not entitled to assert its dictatorship even if that dictatorship clashed with the passing moods of the workers' democracy.

The party congress ended not only with the defeat of the Workers Opposition but with the party banning internal dissent. The officers of the Russian metalworkers union were leaders of the Workers Opposition. When the party fraction in the union refused to go along with party orders to kick them out of office, the party-state leaders imposed a trusteeship (as the AFL-CIO would say). The union's elected officers were replaced with party appointees. This was not the first time this tactic had been employed. In 1920, Trotsky, as Commissar of Transport, had broken the railway workers union by appointing new leaders.

Shortly after the 1921 party congress Bogdanov and his Workers Truth group (of Bolshevik origin) were to declare the revolution had led to "a complete defeat for the working class."

Probably the most important condition that made victory difficult for the workers revolution in Russia was the fact that the working class in Russia was a small minority of the population, no more than 10 percent. Russia in 1917 was still semi-feudal. The vast majority of the population were peasants whose concern in the revolution was mainly to expropriate the big landlords and gain control of their small farms. Peasants produced largely for their own consumption; productivity was low. The poverty, disorganization, and illiteracy of the Russian peasantry prevented them from imposing their own solution on Russian society. In Russia there didn't exist the sort of widespread worker unionism in agriculture that enabled the Spanish agricultural workers to play an important role in the Spanish revolution in 1936.

Did the minority status of the working-class doom it to defeat? G. P. Maximov, who was an agronomist, had hoped that czarist war industry could be converted to the manufacture of tractors, electrical generating equipment, and other things to exchange with the peasantry for their products. He hoped that a strategy of investing in the agricultural economy would encourage collective organizational methods, a collectivist outlook, and increased productivity in the peasant communities. This was Maximov's libertarian socialist path for Russian agriculture.[15]

Even if the Bolsheviks had wanted to pursue this peace conversion strategy, the onset of the Russian civil war in May 1918 would have gotten in the way. Virtually the whole of Russian industry was converted into a supply organization for the Red Army. The cities produced virtually nothing that could be traded to the peasants for their products. So, the Bolsheviks resorted to forced requisitions, seizing agricultural products at the point of a gun. This strategy was not very effective. The peasants resisted and the cities starved. The urban population of Russia was reduced by at least half during the civil war. Workers moved in with their country cousins. At least they wouldn't starve in the countryside.

Lenin's solution to the growing peasant discontent was the New Economic Policy, enacted in 1921. This policy encouraged capitalist development and free trade in agricultural products. Eventually it was Stalin who "solved" the problem of low agricultural productivity through forced collectivization and mechanization. This allowed much of the rural population to be moved to work in urban industry. The state hierarchy could then capture the efficiency gains from agricultural investment to build up Russian industry.

Bolshevik apologists usually point to various "conjunctural" factors to explain the defeat of the workers revolution in Russia—foreign invasion and civil war, failure of the revolution in Germany and other European countries, and so on. But neither these factors nor the minority status of the working class in Russia are sufficient to explain why the Russian workers' revolution was defeated in the peculiar way it was. Worker revolutions have at times been defeated by a violent reaction that saves the property system of the capitalist class, as in Italy in the twenties, Spain in the thirties, and Chile in the seventies.

But the capitalist class was expropriated in Russia, and a new economic system emerged, based on public ownership and subordination of the economy to central planning, not market governance.

A new class emerged as the rulers of this economic system. Unlike the capitalist class they were hired labor, employees of the state. Brinton refers to this class as "the bureaucracy." But there are "bureaucracies" in all kinds of organizations. A class, however, is distinguished by its particular role in social production.

I think it is helpful here to look at the sort of hierarchy that was being developed in capitalist industry in the U.S. in the early 20th century. The emergence of large corporations gave capitalists sufficient resources to systematically re-design jobs and the production process to their advantage, destroying the skill and autonomy of workers that had been inherited from the artisan tradition. "Efficiency experts" like Frederick Taylor advocated concentration of conceptualization and decision making in the hands of a managerial control hierarchy, removing it from the shop floor. The point to Taylorism was to shift the balance of power on the shop floor to the advantage of management. This attempt to gain greater control over what workers do was justified to the owners in terms of the ability of the firm to ensure long-term profitability, but it also empowers a new class. The period between the 1890s and 1920s saw the emergence of a new class of professional managers, engineers, and other expert advisors to management. These were the cadres who made up the new control hierarchies in the corporations and the state. As hired employees, the power of this techno-managerial or coordinator class[16] is not based on ownership of capital assets, but on concentration of expertise and decision-making authority.

The coordinator class was only in its early stages of development in the Russian economy in the early 20th century. In the actual situation the Bolshevik party intelligentsia were thrown into the breach, along with technicians and managers inherited from the capitalist regime. The Russian revolution showed it was possible to use the state to build an economy where the coordinator class was the ruling class. Bolshevik ideology and program are an essential part of the explanation for the emergence of this new class system.

Brinton makes a convincing case that neither Lenin nor Trotsky ever believed in, or advocated, workers' management of production. After the Bolshevik takeover in October, 1917 Lenin's "whole practice," Brinton notes, "was to denounce attempts at workers' management as 'premature,' 'utopian,' 'anarchist,' 'harmful,'" and so on.[17]

Much of the debate within the Communist Party in 1920–21 was over "one-man management." As early as April 1918 Lenin wrote: "Unquestioning submission to a single will is absolutely necessary for the success of labor processes that are based on large-scale machine industry … today the revolution demands, in the interests of socialism, that the masses unquestioningly obey the single will of the leaders of the labor process."

But the "one-man management" debate was somewhat misleading since the real issue is not whether there is a committee or one person in charge but the relationship of the mass of workers to the authority of management. Would they possess this authority themselves or not?

Nonetheless, the logic of central planning does favor having one person in charge. If plans are crafted by an elite group of planners and then implemented as a set of orders that must be carried out by the workforce, the planning apparatus will want to have the ability to enforce their orders. And this is easier if there is just one person who is answerable to those above rather than a whole collective.

The Bolshevik leaders assumed that the sort of hierarchical structures in industry evolved by capitalism were class-neutral. They maintained that the managerial hierarchy could be wielded in the interests of the working class as long as the "workers' party" controlled the state that owned the economy.

This idea was not unique to Bolshevism but was common among social-democratic Marxists prior to World War I. For example, in *The Common Sense of Socialism*, published in 1911, John Spargo, a member of the American Socialist Party, argues that control of the state by the labor-based socialist political party is sufficient to ensure working-class control of a state-owned economy.[18] In Brinton's view, the commitment to the persistence of hierarchy—the division of society into those who give orders and those who are expected to obey them—is as rooted in social-democracy as it is in Leninism.

When Marx drew up the statutes of the first International Workers Association in 1864, he included Flora Tristan's slogan: "The emancipation of the working class must be the work of the workers themselves." Brinton's analysis of the Russian revolution shows how the Bolsheviks failed to take this principle seriously. Brinton agrees with Marx that the class struggle is a process that drives social change, and that through this process the working class can liberate itself. The fact that workers must work not to fulfill their own aims, but are forced to act as instruments for the aims of others—our situation in capitalist society—is what Marx called "alienated labor." Brinton believes this condition of "alienation" is pervasive in existing society, not just in work. Liberation presupposes that this condition be replaced by self-determination in production and all aspects of life. In order to work out a path to liberation, Marx believed it was necessary to be realistic, to "see through" all phony ideology, like the rhetoric in bourgeois liberalism about "freedom" and "democracy."

The emphasis upon self-activity, class struggle, and realism about society are the good side of Marx, the part that Brinton retains in his own thinking. But in the Marxist political tradition this is combined with hierarchical aspects. Why? In Marx's theory of "historical materialism," social formations become vulnerable to instability and replacement when they "fetter the development of the productive forces." Marx assumes that a drive for ever-increasing productive output is a trans-historical force that is the gauge of social progress. If Taylorism and the development of hierarchy in industry are the particular way that capitalism increases productive output, these must be "progressive," some Marxists infer. "We must raise the question of applying much of what is scientific and progressive in the Taylor system," Lenin wrote in 1918. Lenin thus supported the adoption of Taylor's piecework schemes. "The Soviet Republic … must organize in Russia the study and teaching of the Taylor system." The fallacy in this argument is the assumption that productive effectiveness could not be achieved through the development of the skill and knowledge of workers, under workers' self-management.

In Marx's analysis of capitalism the division between labor and capital takes center stage. Because the working class does not own the means of production, we must sell our time to employers. The class power of the owners enables them to rip off the working class, accumulating surplus value as private capital.

But there is another systematic rip-off of the working class that becomes entrenched once capitalism reaches its mature corporate form. The logic of capitalist development then systematically under-develops worker potentials, as expertise and decision making are accumulated as the possession of another class, the coordinator class. But Marxism doesn't "see" this class.

This failure makes Marxism self-contradictory. The hierarchical dimension of Marxism converts it into a coordinator class ideology, a program for the continued subordination of the working class. The concept of the "vanguard party" as managers of the movement for social change, concentrating expertise and decision making in their hands; the idea that "proletarian power" consists in a particular party leadership controlling a state, implementing its program top-down through the state hierarchy; control of the economy by a central planning apparatus—these things don't empower the working class.

Hierarchies of the state, like similar hierarchies in private corporations, are based on concentration of professional expertise and decision-making power into the hands of a coordinatorist elite. A statist strategic orientation that thinks in terms of a party leadership capturing a state and then implementing its program top-down through the state hierarchy is a strategy that empowers the coordinator class. This contradicts the liberatory and egalitarian rhetoric that socialism traditionally appeals to in attempts to motivate activists.

I'm not arguing that the empowerment of the working class would not presuppose the taking of political power. The working class can't liberate itself from subordination to dominating classes if it doesn't take over both the running of industry and the governing of the society. This presupposes that it controls the polity—the structure through which the basic rules in society are made and enforced. But a hierarchical state is not the only possible form of polity. We can also envision a self-managed polity, based on institutions of grassroots democracy. The point is that it must be the mass of the people themselves who "take power," through mass democratic institutions that the people create and directly control.[19]

(Endnotes)

1   Maurice Brinton *The Bolsheviks and Workers' Control* (Black & Red 1975)
2   Maurice Brinton *For Workers' Power*, ed. David Goodway (AK Press, 2004)
3   For example, Alan Maass of the International Socialist Organization writes, "the October revolution of 1917 won power for the workers' councils, or soviets, establishing the basic institution of a socialist society." Maass therefore identifies "the basic institution of a socialist society" not with a particular economic institution or workers' direct management of industry but with the Soviet polity, that is, a state controlled by the Bolshevik Party. "Maass reply to Michael Albert" ZNet website: www.zmag.org/isoreply1maass.htm

4   Oscar Anweiler, Les Soviets en Rusie, 1905–1921, cited in Peter Rachleff "Soviets and Factory Committees in the Russian Revolution" Lib.com, website, http://libcom.org/library/soviets-factory-committees-russian-revolution-peter-rachleff

5   Paul Avrich *The Russian Anarchists* (Princeton University Press, 1967): 140–141. John Reed provides descriptions of some worker takeovers in the article cited in note 6.

6   John Reed "The Structure of the Soviet System" *Liberation* (July, 1918), reprinted in *Socialist Viewpoint* (Sept. 15, 2002)

7   Brinton, *For Workers' Power*

8   Rachleff "Soviets and Factory Committees in the Russian Revolution"

9   E. H. Carr *The Bolshevik Revolution Vol. II* (Macmillan, 1952): 69, cited in Rachleff.

10   Brinton: 320

11   Ibid.

12   Ibid.

13   Ibid.

14   Ibid.

15   G. P. Maximov *Constructive Anarchism*

16   "Coordinator Class" is the term that Michael Albert and Robin Hahnel use for this class. Albert and Hahnel "A Ticket to Ride: More Locations on the Class Map," in *Between Labor and Capital*, ed. Pat Walker (South End Press, 1979)

17   Brinton, *For Workers' Power*

18   John Spargo *The Common Sense of Socialism* (Charles H. Kerr & Company, 1911)

19   For alternative political vision and complimentary analysis, see Stephen R. Shalom's contribution in chapter 2 of this book, "Parpolity: A Political System for a Good Society."

Chapter 19

THE SPANISH ANARCHISTS, THROUGH
A PARTICIPATORY LENS

Dave Markland

THE SPANISH REVOLUTION. AMONG today's anarchists and radical activists, those three words alone have the power to conjure visions of triumph and heroism. Maybe you picture a group of enthusiastic CNT militia members crammed onto the back of a truck repainted black and red, fists raised in solidarity with their well-wishers who line the streets of Barcelona; some think of George Orwell, shot through the neck while fighting the fascists on the Aragon front; others think of Ernest Hemingway, pissed drunk at a cafe in Madrid, slurring through some rant about hunting or booze; or maybe you emotionally sing the strains of the anarchist battle hymn "Las Barricadas." (Embarrassingly, my version always ends up sounding like the "Imperial March" from *Star Wars*.)

We all know the story (roughly, anyway): Franco, Morocco, July 19, CNT militias, the POUM (pronounced "poom"), Stalin, the UGT, the PSUC (aptly pronounced "pee-suck"), Durruti, the International Brigades, and the Falangists (usually pronounced "fascists"). Yet this list covers only the military and political aspects of the struggle. Behind the lines, in Republican-held zones, blossomed the social revolution: agrarian collectives and syndicalized industry. This, too, is fairly well-known amongst anarchists, as is the fate of these admirable accomplishments. (Here, phrases like "communist treachery" and "Stalinist counter-revolutionaries" are useful.)

But what were these collectives and self-managed factories actually like? How was work organized and carried out? How was consumption organized? More to the point: What can the experiences of the Spanish comrades teach us about goals, vision, tactics, and strategies? That is, before we adopt pages from the anarchist playbook, we would do well to critically examine the substance of those plays as well as their outcomes.

Editor's note: This essay is the basis of a talk given by Dave at a Vancouver Parecon Collective event commemorating the 70th anniversary of the Spanish Revolution in July 2006. The event was hosted by the local anarchist book store, Spartacus Books, and accompanied by two movies, Land and Freedom *by Ken Loach, and the first ever English screening of* Nosotros somos asi *("This is How We Are"), a musical starring children playing on several revolutionary themes, produced by the CNT during the 1937 civil war.*

No doubt many readers are familiar with the question of anarchist participation in the Republican government. Another well-worn argument concerns military tactics and strategy, as well as wider concerns about hierarchical discipline and militarization of the militias. These will be set aside to pursue the narrower issue of the economic accomplishments of the revolution.[1]

And we shall see, not surprisingly, that these revolutionaries deserve credit and unbridled respect for the incredible advancements they made in libertarian economic organization. However, we shall also see that some of their actions and institutions need to be rejected—and in fact they have been rejected by many anti-authoritarian activists who have come since. Indeed, entire movements (like the women's movement) have emerged to address injustices of a type to which the Spanish Revolution was not immune. The purpose of the present essay is to help illuminate those troublesome features of the Spanish accomplishments. In so doing, I rely on a set of insights and analyses which will be familiar to anyone acquainted with participatory economics (parecon), which I think can be fairly described as a modern anarchist economic vision. To expropriate a line from the bard: I have come to praise anarchism, not to bury it. Thus, we shall begin with a short description of the revolutionary economy, followed by a discussion of various lessons which can be drawn from the Spanish experience.[2]

Agrarian Collectives

The workers' committees which arose locally throughout Spain, and which took up arms to defeat the right-wing revolt, soon found themselves the only organized social actors in large parts of Republican Spain. Wealthy landowners having fled or been killed, the committees held general assemblies in villages in order to redistribute land. At these meetings the anarchists generally advocated for collectivization and many of their neighbors responded with enthusiasm. Families who did not want to join the collectives, called individualists, were each allotted family-sized plots which they worked without hired help. (Collectivists generally respected these dissidents and hoped the positive example of the collective would win them over; often that was indeed the case.) Meanwhile, collectivists pooled their personal possessions—such as money, work, animals, and tools—and set to work on the liberated land in crews of five to ten workers. Work assignments were decided by a council of elected delegates and work days were the same duration for everyone (usually eight or nine hours).

Initially, these newly formed collectives abolished money and in its place consumption was reorganized according to the long-held vision of anarchist communism. This can be described as "to each according to their need," or perhaps more accurately "take what you feel you need." In any case, the demands of the Civil War soon revealed this approach to be irresponsible. Consequently, in an effort to provide more supplies for the militias (and also to stop instances of cheating) a rationing system was typically introduced. This centered around a uniform daily wage denominated in pesetas (which were not redeemable for the official peseta of Republican Spain). Adjustments were made according to a worker's family size. For example, an unmarried collectivist might get ten pesetas a day; a married couple seventeen pesetas, plus four pesetas per child. Additional measures were taken to ensure that those villagers who were unable to work received credits also. All of these guaranteed wages were earmarked in advance for several types of consumer products. Thus, every week families received a week's worth of grocery credits, a week's worth of clothing credits, a week's worth of credits for wine, etc. Credits could be saved from week to week if necessary to purchase a valuable item, though they were not transferable to other types of goods or to other people. In this way, individual differences in consumption desires were accommodated, though this was decidedly limited in scope as there were scarcely twenty different items to be bought in most places, owing to a long-standing lack of economic development.

Many villages had some level of light industry—olive presses, flour mills, bakeries, sandal factories, construction, and so on. These operations were frequently integrated with the collective, with all workers therein receiving equal consumption rights. With the village economy integrated in this way, both production and consumption were socialized. Elected (and recallable) councils dealt with finding outlets for the village's surplus goods as well as purchasing things the collective required but which were not produced locally. In addition, these councils took care of rationalizing existing workplaces while also establishing new industries if needed. Amazingly, all this was done while organizing supplies to be sent to the militias at the front.

So, we have seen that the anarchist collectives eventually rejected the model of anarchist communism, expressed in the slogan "From each according to their abilities, to each according to their needs." Each worker took on an equal share of the work to be done, and there were, in effect, punishments if one did not perform one's duties. These ranged from social disapproval to expulsion. And, as we have also seen, consumption was more or less equally allotted. While this system was austere (and the pressing needs of the war certainly justified that), it wasn't unfair. Fairness was ensured through the each collective's council, where collective members could voice their differing needs and preferences or explain unique circumstances which might justify adjustments to work load or consumption.

Syndicalized Industry

Meanwhile, in the more industrialized areas of Republican Spain, like Barcelona, revolutionaries faced a different set of circumstances. Capitalist owners of industry were expropriated and workers' councils established self-management in many anarchist-influenced workplaces. However, it was immediately clear that use of the official Spanish currency could not be abolished, as it was essential to the highly commerce-oriented role of industry. The official currency was still in use in large parts of Republican Spain, where the revolution hadn't taken hold (the Basque region, for example).

These areas, as well as foreign countries, constituted much of the market for industrial production.

Despite this obstacle that hampered the advancement of the economic revolution, tremendous strides were made in the advancement of workers' control of industry. Elected and recallable workers' committees took over the functioning of vast swaths of industry. The full value of their labor accrued to the workers along with decisions over investment, marketing, and planning. And, initial steps were taken toward integrating the rural collectives with urban industries. This step was necessitated by the Republican government's deliberate withholding of raw materials and currency—an attack which focused on those factories which did not produce badly needed weapons. Thus, in response, the desperate industrial workers' committees intensified their efforts to barter their products for those of the rural agricultural collectives, thus sidestepping the market.

Vision

While the spirit of spontaneity was strong in the Spanish anarchist movement, there was an underlying commitment to preparation and planning which long preceded the revolution's successes. The years before the revolution saw a virtual cottage industry of anarchist vision, whose stand-out text was Diego Abad de Santillan's *After the Revolution*.[3] Gaston Leval comments: "The new form of organization had already been clearly thought out by our comrades when they were engaged in underground propaganda during the Republic."[4] And, if planning and pre-figuring was normal, anarchists were not shy about modifying and changing their goals as circumstances required. Leval, again: "If the pragmatic methods to which they had to have recourse may appear to be insufficient, and sometimes unsound ... the development tending to eliminate these contradictions was taking place rapidly ... and progress was being rapidly made towards unifying and decisive improvements."[5] Developments and innovations were unfolding well into the period of collectivization and anarchists did not hold back in sharing their insights and solutions: "In July 1937, 1000 members of the Levante Collectives had been sent to Castile to help and to advise their less experienced comrades. As a result... great strides were made in a minimum of time."[6] All this points to the self-critical, pragmatic aspect of the movement, as well as the importance placed on insights derived from anarchist vision: "The need to control and to foresee events was understood from the first day."[7]

Solidarity

Virtually all contemporary observers were struck by the ability of the anarchists to harness and propel the tremendous outpouring of solidarity and sacrifice exhibited by the workers. Throughout revolutionary Spain, common people made great efforts with their bodies and minds, motivated by nothing more than a desire to see the revolution carried through. Certainly some of this solidarity stems precisely from the threat of the re-emergence of a totalitarian state should the war be lost. However, it is clear that the accomplishments of the revolution spurred efforts of such great enthusiasm that propaganda was often thought to be redundant.

Balancing

In considering the divvying of work it is obvious that rural collectivists made efforts to balance the onerousness of jobs, thus not overtaxing people's enthusiasm. That is, solidarity was not over-exploited so as to make the most enthusiastic people work the most disdained jobs. Instead, efforts were made to share the more difficult tasks. In Mas de las Matas, peasant labor crews were organized into work groups which aimed to balance time on easily worked land with time spent working in more difficult conditions.[8] Meanwhile, in syndicalized industry, there was further concern for countering capitalist tendencies toward the de-skilling of workers; thus Leval reports on plans among Barcelona's industrial workers to send workers to technical schools "so that they do not continue to be, as has been the case hitherto, simple mindless cogs in a machine."[9]

Democratic Economic Planning

Once collectives had been established and federated with the goal of integrating their economies, possibilities for large-scale economic planning arose. This was accomplished through workers' councils and regional committees. Typically, elected (and recallable) administrative commissionaires made decisions on production and consumption. These decisions could be made on a local level if the affected population was localized, or it could be at a higher-level council such as Valencia's regional council deciding to build a new juice factory to meet demand summed at a regional level.[10] The extent and nature of this planning procedure was well illustrated in Castellon de la Plana, a large town of 50,000: "Every month the technical and administrative council presented the general assembly of the Syndicate with a report which was examined and discussed if necessary, and finally approved or turned down by a majority. Modifications were introduced when this majority thought it of use."[11]

Economic Rationality

Collectives faced pressures on all sides: many of the able-bodied were with the militia, plus these localities were attempting to provision those same fighters. All this created an urgent need to get the most production out of existing inputs of labor, physical plants, and raw materials. Consequently, great strides were made in rationalizing and taking advantage of economies of scale. Throughout the reports on agricultural collectives, redundant workplaces are eliminated. In one locale, four bakeries operated where there had been six before the revolution.[12] In Aragon, the labor force was integrated above the local level, so that neighboring collectives would borrow and lend members as needs arose. Leval reveals the extent of this integration: When farming villages were approached by representatives from revolutionary areas outside Aragon, "the reply they got was, 'Comrade, what we have here does not belong to us; you must get in touch with the secretariat of the regional Federation in Madrid' ... for it was understood that respecting decisions taken ensured the success of the whole enterprise."[13]

We have thus far seen that the Spanish anarchists had vision. They had dynamic goals, flexible strategy, and sought useful methods of analysis. They also fostered tremendous enthusiasm and solidarity. And they wisely re-organized their workforce and resources for maximum efficiency while instituting some level of democratic economic planning which included production, consumption, and even, to some degree, investment planning. But, from the writings available to us, it is clear that certain problems arose alongside the new revolutionary institutions. Some of these were noticed, and remarked upon, by the anarchists themselves. Other problems, it seems, did not overly trouble many participants.

Anarchist observers of the Spanish collectives give scant attention to certain types of procedural questions which many of today's anarchists no doubt take for granted. There is, for instance, no indication that any collective was concerned about the possibility that women may not be properly heard at meetings, though concern was certainly voiced about the need for the collectives' assemblies to hear the views of (male) individualists who were not members of the collective. (It would, of course, be wrong to take this lack of evidence as proof that there was no concern for women's participation. However, the lack of recorded discussion itself strongly indicates that such issues were not given the same importance as they typically are given today.)

Gender, Kinship, and Morality

Modern students of the revolution are immediately struck with Spanish anarchism's outdated response to the gender question. While the revolution certainly ignited feminist struggle (which was completely ignored by Leval and other male observers), certain facts give an indication of how significant the obstacles were for women. For instance, women's wages in the revolutionary agrarian collectives were typically equal to half or three-quarters of the wages of their male comrades—a fact that is reported (repeatedly) without comment by Leval and other observers. Neither is there any mention of kinship institutions coming under scrutiny at collective meetings. In fact, the revolutionary economy of the villages was predicated on traditional families, as consumption was organized along the basic unit of the household. Unmarried women were for the most part expected to remain living with their parents as adults, and the economy reflected this and other traditional expectations. Augustin Souchy writes of the village of Beceite: "The gong sounds ... to remind the women to prepare the midday meal."[14]

The sexual revolution that often accompanies massive progressive social upheaval is strangely absent in accounts of revolutionary Spain, particularly in rural areas. Indeed, in the town of Rubi, there was said to be an active effort to prevent sexual liberation among young people.[15] This is perhaps less surprising in light of the fact that anarchists in many rural areas had been viewed as moral leaders in their communities since well before the revolution. In contrast to traditional economic and religious elites who led debased and debauched lives, anarchists had often advocated, and practiced, abstention around such sinful subjects as sex, booze, and coffee. Indeed, Leval's comment about the town of Andorra generalizes: "Work was the major occupation ... There was no place in the rules for the demand for personal freedom or for the autonomy of the individual."[16] I shall leave it to the reader to decide the proper attitude toward sexual liberation (not to mention caffeine), but suffice it to say that anarchists (and others) have long been at work attempting to overcome whatever shortcomings the Spanish comrades exhibited on this subject.

Market Behavior

The attitude of Spanish anarchists toward markets is perhaps best described as ambiguous. On one level, it seems that Spanish anarchists had a long-standing aversion to markets. Gerald Brenan notes this opposition among pre-revolutionary anarchists, citing their "condemnation of cooperatives, friendly societies and strike funds 'as tending to increase egoism in the workers.'"[17] Similarly, several months into the revolution, the workers of Valencia "realized that a partial collectivization would degenerate over time into a kind of bourgeois co-operativism."[18]

Yet, working against this was the fact that anarchists had a serious commitment to both village autonomy and worker/peasant control of the full value of the products of their labor. The result was that collectives sent all of their surplus goods to the cantonal capital where elected councils were responsible for bartering those goods with surplus goods from other collectives. Leval relates: "The profits from the sale of various commodities provided the municipal Council with the resources needed for other communal tasks."[19] José Peirats' observations are germane: "Once the economic necessities of the collective itself were covered, the surplus was sold or bartered on the external market, directly or by way of confederal organizations."[20] "Barter was not rigorously regulated. In some places items were valued in terms of July 19th prices: in others, according to current prices in the free market. Among the Aragonese collectives there was not much control over what was exchanged."[21]

While it is evident that various councils did engage in planning, it is clear that once products had left the locality, they were exchanged with an eye toward maximizing returns. While it is true that profits thus derived were often sent to the front or shared with less profitable collectives, this was not enough to overcome several negative effects of markets. And these negative effects were by no means unrecognized by the collectivists. Souchy reports on a dispute involving two collectives in Aragon, where one collective refused to pay the pre-revolutionary rate for the electricity supplied by a neighboring collective. The electricity-producing collective insisted on the old rate, which entailed payment for workers' wages, plus profit on top of that. Unable to resolve the issue otherwise, the matter was taken to court.

Spanish anarchists thus sought, but did not achieve, the elimination of the market. This failure occurred partly because total collectivization was not possible, but also partly because the anarchists lacked the theoretical tools to readily identify the aspects of markets which undermine efforts at self-management, equality, and solidarity. Thus the challenge for anarchists forming economic vision is to conceptualize the economy so as to highlight what needs to be created or abolished. Of course, parecon is one answer to this challenge.

Red Bureacracy / Co-ordinator Problems

Attitudes toward gender issues aside, it is the Spanish revolutionaries' response to bureaucratic tendencies which is most surprising. Compared to today's anarchists, the Spanish anarchists had a considerable blind spot in regard to hierarchies arising from concentration of work skills, the role of experts, and the like. A few examples should illustrate:

- In Rubi: "The member with the highest professional experience was nominated as the technical councillor, with the task of supervising and guiding all the work on the various sites. And accountancy was put in the hands of the specialist deemed the most able."[22]

- In Alicante's syndicalized construction industry, "it was from among the employers that the site managers were selected." These former employers "had a greater sense of duty than that of the average worker, accustomed to being given orders and not to taking responsibilities." Perhaps it's not surprising that in this syndicate "it was not possible to put into operation at one stroke the absolute equality of wages."[23]

- In the industrial centre of Alcoy: "A comrade whose ability for this kind of work was recognized was put at the head of the sales section. He supervised work in his section..." "The personnel of the whole industry was divided into specialties: manual workers, designers, and technicians."[24]

- In Granollers: "The economic section of the commune set up a 'technical bureau' consisting of three experts, and which in agreement with the syndical Economic Council, steered the work of the industrial undertakings." This was the same town where technicians "considered themselves a class apart," according to Leval.[25]

- Two comrades (one CNT, one UGT) "were in charge of the general secretariat" in Graus and were "also entrusted with propaganda."[26]

While there are some indications that for certain economic roles it was felt unwise for just one person to fill them (that of an "eminent doctor," for example[27]), the anarchists' response was typically to rotate the role in question. Otherwise, filling it with a reliable anarchist was evidently the back-up plan. (Thus, Souchy writes, "the Chief of Police was the well-known anarchist Eroles."[28]) Yet another solution (this one out of the parecon playbook) would be to work to eliminate all undesirable roles by redrawing their constituent tasks and spreading those tasks into balanced job complexes.

This blind spot concerning bureaucracy has its echoes down to the present and is well illustrated in the memoirs of Sam Dolgoff,[29] the late anarchist militant and author. Dolgoff approvingly cites Spanish militia leader Buenaventura Durruti's own investigations into the alleged formation of a bureaucracy within the CNT's administrative offices. Durruti's findings are reported by his biographer:

> The national headquarters of the CNT were not centralized. All the people working in the national headquarters and in the organization were employed, not by the National Committee, but were elected by and accountable to the plant assemblies. They were paid not by the National Committee, but by enterprises in which they were employed.

Dolgoff comments:

> Both Augustin Souchy, who administered the Foreign Information Bureau of the CNT, and one of his coworkers, Abe Bluestein, of New York, told [m]e that everyone working in the National Headquarters from responsible officials to porters and maintenance workers were paid the same equal wages. Durruti and others who investigated were convinced that there was no bureaucracy in the CNT anywhere.[30]

At risk of belaboring a point, it is doubtful that many of today's anarchists would view such traditional work roles ("responsible officials" and "porters") as evidence of victory over bureaucratic tendencies. That this attitude existed among the Spanish comrades is perhaps understandable given that the Russian Revolution, which offers a litany of lessons about bureaucracy, was at the time very poorly understood in Spain, to say nothing of elsewhere. (However, Dolgoff, it should be noted, was writing in the 1980s.)

In closing, it bears repeating that the Spanish Revolution, as the high-water mark of libertarian organization, provides a host of lessons for today's anti-authoritarians. And, as we have seen, sifting through the Spanish experience for useful insights is in fact part of a long-standing anarchist tradition. So too is the promotion of anarchist vision. It is my hope that this essay can help stimulate both of those trends.

(Endnotes)

1   The author wishes to thank Tom Wetzel for his comments on an earlier version of this essay. Any errors of fact or interpretation, however, are solely the author's responsibility.

2   A note on sources: Primary documents (i.e. firsthand accounts) concerning the structure and dynamics of the Spanish collectives and syndicates are frustratingly small in number, though much of what there is has been translated into English. In all practicality, the works of Gaston Leval, Augustin Souchy, and José Peirats represent all that is currently available for examining the revolution's economic aspects in any detail. Leval's work is rich in detail and the most readily available.

3   Diego Abad de Santillan *After the Revolution* (Greenberg, 1937)

4   Gaston Leval *Collectives in Spain* (Freedom Press, 1945): 145
5   Ibid.: 198
6   Ibid.: 183
7   Ibid.: 193
8   Ibid.: 138
9   Ibid.: 262
10 Ibid.: 156
11 Ibid.: 303
12 Ibid.: 94
13 Ibid.: 186
14 Augustin Souchy *With the Peasants of Aragon* (published originally in Spain, 1937) www.anar-chosyndicalism.net
15 Leval, *Collectives in Spain*: 299
16 Ibid.: 125
17 Gerald Brenan *The Spanish Labyrinth* (Cambridge University Press, 1976): 178
18 Jose Peirats *Anarchists in the Spanish Revolution* (Freedom Press, 1990): 125
19 Leval, *Collectives in Spain*: 288
20 Peirats, Ibid.: 141
21 Ibid.: 143
22 Leval, *Collectives in Spain*: 297
23 Ibid.: 307–08
24 Ibid.: 234–35
25 Ibid.: 287
26 Ibid.: 97
27 Ibid.: 272
28 Souchy
29 Sam Dolgoff *Fragments: A Memoir* (Refract Publications, 1986)
30 Ibid.

Chapter 20

WINNOWING WHEAT FROM CHAFF: SOCIAL DEMOCRACY AND LIBERTARIAN SOCIALISM IN THE 20th CENTURY

Robin Hahnel

Social Democracy: Giving Credit Where Credit Is Due

I MEAN IT AS a great compliment when I say that capitalism functions poorly indeed without social democrats. The "golden age of capitalism" was due more to the influence social democrats exerted over capitalism than any other single cause. Only when social democratic policies have been ascendant has capitalism proved able to avoid major crises and distribute the benefits of rising productivity widely enough to sustain rapid rates of economic growth and create a middle class. Political democracy in the 20th century also received more nurturing from social democratic parties than from any other single source. However, despite their important accomplishments, crucial compromises social democrats made with capitalism bear a major responsibility for the failure of the economics of equitable cooperation to make greater headway against the economics of competition and greed in the 20th century.

Of all political tendencies critical of capitalism, social democrats have participated in reform campaigns and electoral democracy most effectively. Sometimes social democratic parties won elections and formed governments that carried out major economic reforms. Other times reforms that began as planks in platforms of social democratic parties out of power were implemented by rival parties decades later. Some of the major reforms social democrats deserve a great deal of credit for include old age insurance, universal health care coverage, welfare for those unable to work or find work, financial regulation, stabilization of the business cycle through fiscal and monetary policies, incomes policies to combat cost-push inflation while reducing income inequalities, and long-run, comprehensive planning policies to promote growth and development. Wherever and whenever social democrats were politically stronger, reforms were more numerous and went deeper. Social democrats were strongest in Sweden from the mid-1950s to the mid-1970s where social democratic reforms achieved their apogee. Social democracy in Germany was strongest under Helmut Schmidt and Willy Brandt in the 1970s. The high point for social democratic reforms in the United States occurred prior to World War II during the New Deal of President Franklin Delano Roosevelt. The high point in France and Great Britain occurred immediately after World War

II when a united front government in France and Labor Party government in Great Britain each ruled briefly. Lyndon Johnson's "war on poverty" in the mid-1960s and Francois Mitterrand's first year in power in 1981 proved to be short-lived resurgences of social democratic agendas in their respective countries.

Failures of Social Democracy: The Benefits of Hindsight

I do not pretend to offer a comprehensive critique of social democracy. In this essay[1] I do not even address what I consider to be the greatest failing of 20th century social democracy—its failure to oppose Western imperialism and support Third World movements for national liberation. I only consider the economic ideology and programs of social democracy, and review only the work of two authors whom I consider particularly insightful. Michael Harrington and Magnus Ryner are peerless students of social democratic history whose support for their cause did not prevent either of them from writing critically. As the leading social democrat in the United States from the 1960s until his untimely death in 1989, Michael Harrington combined insider knowledge with a critical detachment derived from viewing powerful European social democratic parties from the perspective of a small party in the United States that could not have been farther from the halls of power itself. In *The Next Left: The History of the Future*,[2] and in *Socialism: Past and Future*,[3] Harrington provides a sympathetic, but critical, evaluation of social democracy. In "Neo-liberal Globalization and The Crisis of Swedish Social Democracy,"[4] and in *Capitalist Restructuring, Globalization and the Third Way: Lessons from the Swedish Model*,[5] Magnus Ryner provides an insightful, up-to-date analysis of the "Swedish model." Harrington and Ryner both try to explain why social democratic reforms were not more successful in their heyday, lost momentum in the 1970s, and were rolled back over the last two decades. I will emphasize where I think we must go beyond their criticisms.

What IS the Alternative to Capitalism? As the 20th century progressed, social democrats' answer to this crucial question became increasingly more vague, ambiguous, and self-contradictory. In the early part of the century they dealt in rhetorical flourishes counterposing democratic direction of the economy to rule by profit seeking capitalists, but in Harrington's words, social democrats "were woefully imprecise about what it meant, much less as to how to put it into practice."[6] Harrington concludes that for the first half of the 20th century social democrats:

> attempted, with notable lack of success, to figure out what they meant by socialism, and remained inexcusably confused about its content. Was there a socialist substitute for capitalist markets, either a plan or a new kind of market? Even if one could solve the political difficulties and achieve a sudden and decisive socialist take over, that would simply postpone all the other problems to the next morning—as happened, catastrophically, with the Bolsheviks after the Revolution.[7]

I could not agree more with Harrington on this point. I am convinced that until progressives clarify how the economics of equitable cooperation can work, convincingly and concretely, we are unlikely to avoid the fate that befell 20th century social democrats.

Harrington went on to point out that after World War II social democrats gave up on their search for an answer to the question that eluded them, and instead embraced a concrete answer to a different question: "John Maynard Keynes miraculously provided the answer that Marx had neglected: socialization was the socialist administration of an expanding capitalist economy whose surplus was then partly directed to the work of justice and freedom."[8] While Keynesian policies humanized capitalism significantly, unfortunately that was all they did, or ever can do. Harrington tells us that when the "Keynesian era came to an end sometime in the seventies, the socialists were once more thrown into confusion."[9] By then, however, social democrats had long forgotten the original question whose answer had always alluded them: Exactly how does the economics of equitable cooperation work?

Unfortunately, even social democrats like Harrington who recognized the above problem contributed nothing to its solution. In an entire chapter on "Market and Plan," Harrington fails to remove any of the vagueness from social democratic rhetoric about how equitable cooperation could actually function. He tells us "only under socialism and democratic planning will it be possible for markets to serve the common good as Adam Smith thought they did under capitalism."[10] But he provides no compelling reasons for why this would be the case. He sits squarely on the fence, contributing nothing to the debate over the existence of an alternative to markets and command planning. "Alec Nove argues either there is a centralized and authoritarian plan for the allocation of resources or there must be markets. Nove, I think, overstates this counter position. Ernest Mandel projects a vision of democratic planning, but I am not sure it is feasible."[11] Harrington concludes his chapter in a paroxysm of ambiguity and double talk surrounding reiteration of the obvious:

> Markets are obviously not acceptable to socialists if they are seen as automatic and infallible mechanisms for making decisions behind the backs of those who are affected by them. But within the context of a plan, markets could, for the first time, be an instrument for truly maximizing the freedom of choice of individuals and communities. I would not, however, use the phrase 'market socialism' to designate this process. What is critical is the use of markets to implement democratically planned goals in the most effective way. That, it must be said, involves a danger: that the means will turn into ends. There is no guarantee that this will not happen short of a people genuinely committed to solidaristic values and mobilized against the threat inherent even in the planned employment of the market mechanism. The aim, then, is a socialism that makes markets a tool of its nonmarket purposes.[12]

What Harrington completely fails to address in his confusion is whether or not when people interact through markets this subverts their commitment to Harrington's vaunted "nonmarket purposes." If participation in markets systematically undermines the "solidaristic values" of even those most "mobilized against the threat inherent in the market mechanism," then why would Harrington believe that "means" will not "turn into ends"? What is particularly galling about this abject failure of intellectual leadership regarding plan versus market is that it effectively endorses the unofficial policy of social democracy in favor of market socialism while avoiding responsibility for renouncing the idea of a system of democratic planning. Harrington tells us that "putting market mechanisms at the service of social priorities rather than in command of the economy is an area in which democratic socialists have contributions to make,"[13] and reminds us that social democrats in the Swedish Labor Federation (LO) were taming the labor market through a labor market board and incomes policy as early as 1950. This is all well and good. But the question remains: Is the phrase "democratic planning" to mean something more than political intervention in particular markets in particular ways. After reading an entire chapter on the subject, readers of Harrington's book remain as clueless about his answer to this fundamental question as they were before beginning.

Coping With a Fractured Working Class: Harrington's second explanation for the failure of social democracy is that the homogeneous, majoritarian working class prophesied by Marx never materialized. Instead the working class "divided on the basis of skill, gender, religion, and the like, and in the post–World War II period, when the shift toward the professionals and the service sector became blatantly evident, the socialists were forced to confront the fact that their historic ideal had been shorn of its supposed agency."[14] While social democrats may have been slow to give up on the myth of a homogeneous working-class, they were quicker to adapt than most communists and libertarian socialists who continued to labor far longer under the illusion of a growing working class majority who would eventually identify primarily in class terms. So I am less inclined than Harrington to chastise social democrats for coming to grips slowly with the fact that a majoritarian movement for the economics of equitable cooperation would have to be built not only from segments of the working class who saw themselves as different and with interests at odds with one another, but from non-class "agents of history" as well. However, I am more critical than Harrington of how social democrats chose to adapt to something that came as a surprise to all Leftists. As explained below, I believe social democratic union leaders and politicians too often found it convenient to prioritize more privileged sectors of an increasingly diverse working class at the expense of less privileged ones, and embraced theories that rationalized their behavior by obfuscating the meaning of economic justice.

The Pitfalls of Gradualism: I think Harrington's third reason for social democratic failures is critical. He points out that even when social democrats realized they were "stuck with gradualism and all its attendant problems," and responded in the only sensible way—to "have socialists permeate the society from top to bottom"—unfortunately they "overlooked one of capitalism's most surprising characteristics: its ability to co-opt reforms, and even radical changes, of the opponents of the system."[15] Harrington clearly understands the problem well. He points out:

> Capitalists themselves were, in the main, not shrewd enough to maneuver in this way. The American corporate rich fought Roosevelt's functional equivalent of social democracy with a passionate scorn for the 'traitor to his class' who was President. Yet these same reactionaries benefited from the changes that the New Deal introduced far more than did the workers and the poor who actively struggled for them. The structures of capitalist society successfully assimilated the socialist reforms even if the capitalists did not want that to happen.[16]

But while Harrington goes to great lengths to search for what New Leftists called "non-reformist reforms," he has little to say about the only real way to confront the problem that capitalism will co-opt reforms and co-opt reformers as well: create institutions of equitable cooperation for people to live in even while they are engaged in the lengthy process of fighting for reforms and convincing the victims of capitalism to jettison the economics of competition and greed entirely. It is not enough to complain, as Harrington tells us Karl Kautsky did in a letter after World War I, "that it had become impossible to get anyone in the movement to do anything as a volunteer," or to agree with Robert Michels who demonstrated in his famous study of German social democracy how "outcast revolutionaries had turned into staffers."[17] There is only so long activists will volunteer while others secure positions in the movement that allow them to wield more power and secure economic livelihoods for themselves that are more commodious than most of those whom they lead. Social democracy insufficiently inoculated its members against the virus of capitalist values, and failed to ensure that leaders lived up to the values they preached. More important social democratic practice provided too little institutional support for members who wanted to live in ways that "keep the dream alive," even while most around them competed individualistically in the capitalist market place. Below I offer suggestions about how this problem can be better addressed, but I do not think the answer lies in searching for reforms that are somehow less "reformist" than most reforms social democrats pursued in the 20th century. Reforms ARE reformist. They do make capitalism less harmful while leaving capitalism in tact. It does no good to think we can resolve this dilemma by finding some kind of "non-reformist reform." Instead, the answer lies in how we fight for the only kind of reforms there are, and in providing people who reject capitalist values practical ways to personally live according to human values—and insisting that those who would lead the movement for equitable cooperation do so as well.

Harrington's last two reasons why social democracy did not fare better are important historically, but there was no way social democrats could have avoided them in the 20th century, just as there will be no way for us to avoid them in the century ahead. Therefore, lessons must take the form of how to mitigate predictable damage from circumstances we cannot prevent.

The Pitfalls of "Lemon" Socialism: Harrington complains:

In ordinary times, when the system was working on its own terms, the socialists never had the political power to make decisive changes and were thus fated to make marginal adjustments of a basically unfair structure. In the extraordinary times when the socialists did come to power, after wars or in the midst of economic crises, they had a broader mandate, but never a support for revolution, and they inherited almost insoluble problems from their capitalist predecessors."[18]

A popular joke in Peru in the mid 1980s captured this dilemma perfectly. For more than sixty years the Peruvian military assassinated and arrested leaders of the Peruvian social democratic party, APRA, and prevented APRA from taking power after it won elections on several occasions. According to the joke, the cruelest punishment the Peruvian military ever meted out to APRA was to finally allow the party to take power after winning elections in 1985. The oligarchy had so badly mismanaged the economy that neither they nor the military wanted to take responsibility for the economic crisis that was unavoidable. The jokesters proved to be remarkably prescient. In twelve months the approval ratings for President Alan Garcia dropped from 60 to 15 percent, and it took more than a decade for APRA to recover its position as a significant political force after his disastrous term in office ended.

This problem is also referred to as "lemon socialism." When social democrats were able to nationalize companies, or industries, it was usually because they were in terrible shape. Consequently they often performed badly as public enterprises simply because they were going to perform badly in any case. After World War II this was a problem for the Labor government in Great Britain and for the popular front government in France. Harrington comments that Francois Mitterrand's Socialist Party failed to realize in 1981 "how run down the industrial plant had been allowed to become," and quotes from a 1984 retrospective on the Mitterrand victory in *The Economist* that concluded: "The Socialists thought they would nationalize a phalanx of rich industrial concerns that could be used to boost output, jobs, and national wealth. Instead, with one or two exceptions, the state had acquired, at high cost, a collection of debt-ridden, wheezing remnants of the go-go years of Gaullist giantism."[19] On a smaller scale this problem plagued steel companies in Pittsburgh, Pennsylvania, and Youngstown, Ohio, that were taken over in the 1980s in employee buy outs with support from local governments anxious to preserve their tax base. Of course it is always more advantageous to take over winners than losers for public and employee management. But we will no doubt find ourselves faced with less attractive options in the future, just as social democrats were in the past. What lessons are to be learned?

There may be circumstances so unfavorable that they are literally programmed for failure, in which case we must be patient enough to refrain from taking over only to preside over a disaster. However, rather than turn away from opportunities because they are risky, I think wisdom will more often take the form of negotiating for a larger mandate. After all, with a large enough mandate we believe there is no social problem we cannot tackle successfully! Problems arise when one takes over a lemon with insufficient financial resources, or takes over a government with an insufficient voting majority in the legislature, or with debilitating constraints imposed by the military or by hostile financial interests. My own reading of 20th century social democratic history leads me to the conclusion that tougher negotiations over how much leeway our opponents permit us when we take over a situation our opponents do not want to take responsibility for themselves, and a greater willingness to turn down the job if we are not given the tools necessary to do it, will often serve us well. But these are always tough calls, and there will no doubt be disagreements among those fighting to replace the economics of competition and greed with equitable cooperation over this kind of tough call in the century ahead, just as there were in the past.

Global Capital Markets: The Nine Hundred Pound Gorilla: Finally, Harrington tells us social democrats were "utterly unprepared for the internationalization of politics and economics that has been one of the decisive trends of the twentieth century."[20] In particular Harrington blames the failure of the socialist government of Francois Mitterrand in France in the early 1980s primarily on hostile global capital markets. "The failure of the bold plans of the Mitterrand government in 1981–82 were caused, above all, by an open economy that had to bow to the discipline of capitalist world markets rather than follow a program that had been democratically voted by the French people."[21] The extent to which social democratic reforms in a single country can be vetoed by global financial markets in the neoliberal era is of great importance to consider carefully.

A mushrooming pool of liquid global wealth—created by record profits due to stagnant wages, downsizing, mega mergers, and rapid technical innovation in computers and telecommunications—is now more free to move in and out of national economies at will than at any time in history. A trend away from prudent restraints on international capital flows built into the Bretton Woods system, toward full blown "capital liberalization," began with the unregulated Eurodollar market in the 1960s and culminated in a successful neoliberal crusade to remove any and all restrictions on capital mobility in the context of a global credit system with minimal monitoring and regulation, no lender of last resort, and serious regional rivalries that obstruct timely interventions. Neoliberal global managers have literally created the financial equivalent of the proverbial nine hundred pound gorilla: Where does the nine hundred pound gorilla—global liquid wealth—sit? Wherever it wants! And when a derivative tickles, and savvy investors—who realize they are functioning in a highly leveraged, largely unregulated credit system—rush to pull out before others do, currencies, stock markets, banking systems, and formerly productive economies can all collapse in their wake. What this does, of course, is give international investors a powerful veto over any government policies they deem unfriendly to their interests. If neoliberal global capitalism could trump Mitterrand's program in an advanced economy like France that was not facing international bankruptcy in the early 1980s, and forced the most powerful of all social democrats in Sweden to abandon their reforms in the late 1980s and early 1990s, what hope is there for social democratic programs that attempt to spur equitable growth in bankrupt third world economies facing even more powerful global financial markets and an even more implacable IMF in the early 21st century? Both Harrington and Ryner provide useful insights based on 20th century social democratic experiences that I will add to, more than disagree with.

In chapter 6 of *The Next Left*, Harrington provides a detailed analysis of the failure of the Mitterrand Socialist government in France in the early 1980s that is extremely instructive. He begins: "President Mitterrand and the French socialists received an absolute majority in 1981 and proceeded faithfully to carry out a program that had been carefully worked out over a decade. Within a year they were forced to sound retreat, and by the spring of 1983 they had effectively reversed almost every priority of their original plan. Had a movement that had boldly promised a 'rupture with capitalism' on the road to power become more capitalist than the capitalists once in power?"[22] Harrington admits that "rupture with capitalism" rhetoric was partly hype, but points out that "practically every campaign promise was redeemed during the first year," in which the Mitterrand government "honored the clenched fist of working-class history and the poetic rose of May 1968."[23] The program was, indeed, every bit as "audacious" as one could have hoped for. It consisted not only of Left Keynesian policies to stimulate equitable growth, but aggressive nationalizations and a "new model of consumption," i.e. "a qualitative rather than merely a quantitative change."[24] It is worth taking a close look at what happened precisely because unlike many other 20th century social democratic governments, on taking office the Mitterrand government did not immediately back off from bold campaign promises.

The French socialists immediately increased the buying power for the least-paid workers through dramatic increases in the minimum wage and a "solidaristic wage policy" giving the greatest wage increases "to those at the bottom of the occupational structure."[25] To increase demand for labor the government increased hiring in the public sector and increased government spending on social programs. To decrease the supply of labor and shift use of society's social surplus from more consumption to more leisure the government sponsored programs for early retirement at age sixty, increased annual paid vacation from four to five weeks, and tried to reduce the work week from forty to thirty-five hours. All this is hard to fault. Unfortunately the last program fell victim to political machinations within the Left over whether or not it would be reduced hours for the same pay, i.e. a real wage increase, or reduced hours for less pay, i.e. "work sharing." The communist-led federation of unions and the more traditional business unions opposed any reduction in pay. The Catholic Democratic Confederation of Labor supported work sharing as did the government's Minister of Labor, arguing that real wages had already been increased in other ways and that work sharing benefited the least advantaged—the unemployed—and encouraged leisure over consumerism. The end result was thirty nine hours for thirty nine hours of pay, i.e. an insignificant work sharing that left nobody satisfied and everyone bitter.

Proclaiming themselves different from social democrats elsewhere in Europe who had long since abandoned nationalization, the French socialists went through with an impressive list of nationalizations they had promised during the election campaign. Again the courage displayed by the nationalizations is hard to fault. However, besides the fact that many of the companies they took over were much weaker than they realized, two other problems limited benefits from the nationalizations. Harrington tells us: "At the cabinet meeting at which the decision was made to go ahead with the nationalizations, there was a fateful debate that pitted Michel Rocard, Jacques Delors, and Robert Badinter against most of the rest of the ministers and, the decisive factor, against the president. There is no need, Rocard and Delors argued, for Paris to pay for one-hundred percent of an enterprise that is targeted for government ownership. Fifty percent is quite enough—and much less expensive. But Mitterrand went ahead with one-hundred percent buy outs."[26] Harrington points out that the consequences were not dissimilar to corporate takeovers with borrowed money in the United States—"the acquired company had to be starved for cash in order to finance its own acquisition."[27] The second problem, how the newly nationalized companies were managed, was caused, in part, by the first. Harrington quotes from a letter sent to the new administrators which said: "You will seek, first of all, economic efficiency through a constant bettering of productivity. The normal criteria of the management of industrial enterprises will apply to your group. The different activities should realize results that will assure the development of the enterprise and guarantee that the profitability of the invested capital will be normal."[28] In other words, the new managers were given marching orders no different than those stockholders would send to a CEO they had just hired! Harrington goes on to tell us: "Alain Gomez, a founder of the Marxist Left wing of the Socialist party, CERES, and a new official in the public sector, was even blunter: 'My job is to get surplus value.'"[29]

The problem is, of course, that if capitalists are paid the full present discounted value for their assets, and if nationalized enterprises are managed no differently than private enterprises, the only thing that will change is who employees and taxpayers will resent. Instead of resenting greedy capitalists they will resent the "socialist" government, the "socialist" ministers, and their new "socialist" bosses. Like Harrington, I can understand this is easier to see from the outside free from budgetary and managerial pressures, but it is true nonetheless. Moreover, the government's efforts to promote decentralization and worker participation were no more successful in state enterprises than in the private sector. Harrington tells us: "Although the Auroux laws were unquestionably progressive, they fell far, far short of the ideal of self-managed socialism. In essence, the workers were given the right to speak up on issues affecting their industry—which was a gain—but they got no power to make decisions. One of the consequences of genuine worker control is that productivity goes up. But given the extremely limited nature of the workers' new rights—and the mood of moroseness that settled over the society not too long after the euphoria of May 1981—that pragmatic bonus from living up to an ideal was not forthcoming."[30] Unfortunately the administrators of newly nationalized enterprises who received the letter quoted above were no more inclined than their counterparts in the private sector to accede power to make decisions to their employees from whom they were busy extracting "surplus value."

Finally, the government launched strong expansionary fiscal and monetary policies to provide plenty of demand for goods and services so the private sector would produce up to the economy's full potential and employ the entire labor force. Again, there is nothing to find fault with here. Everyone deserves an opportunity to perform socially useful work and be fairly compensated for doing so. However, there is only so much any progressive government can do about this as long as most employment opportunities are still with private employers. Mitterrand deserves praise for doing the most effective thing any government in an economy that is still capitalist can do in this regard: ignore the inevitable warnings and threats from business and financial circles and their mainstream economist lackeys preaching fiscal "responsibility" and monetary restraint, and unleash strong expansionary fiscal and monetary policy.

Unfortunately this is where the Mitterrand government had its worst luck and discovered just how powerful global financial markets can be. They were unlucky when OECD projections in June 1981 of a strong global recovery proved completely wrong. They were unlucky that French trade had shifted toward the Third World over the previous decade where the global slump was most severe. They were unlucky that "the Socialist stimulus created new jobs in West Germany, Japan, and the United States, as much as, or more than, in France."[31] More to the point, they were unlucky there were conservative governments in Washington, London, and Bonn since while Reagan, Thatcher, and Kohl all helped each other juggle expansions at crucial political junctures, they could not have been more pleased when capital flight and growing trade and budget deficits brought the French socialist program to a grinding halt. But mostly, Harrington tells us they were unlucky "because France could not afford to run a relatively large internal (government) deficit and an external (balance of trade) deficit at the same time."[32] The only government fortunate enough to be able to do that, Harrington pointed out, is the United States government, as the Reagan administration proved with its military Keynesianism accompanied by tax cuts for the rich during exactly the same years when international financial markets prevented France from running such smaller budget and trade deficits as a percentage of its GDP. However, with the benefit of hindsight it is apparent the Mitterrand government did not handle an admittedly difficult situation as well as it might have.

Harrington points out that trying to avoid devaluing the franc was a mistake. Whether it was because the advice to devalue came from Mitterrand's "arch inter party rival, Michel Rocard," or due to false pride—"one does not devalue the money of a country that has just given you a vote of confidence"—matters little. Of course hindsight is twenty-twenty, particularly regarding currency devaluations. Nonetheless, devaluation would have reduced the balance of payments deficit, thereby buying the government more time for its program. But the most important lesson is one Harrington shied away from, just as the African National Congress government in South Africa and the Lula Worker Party government in Brazil have shied away from it more recently. There are only three options: (1) Don't stimulate the domestic economy in the first place because you are not willing to stand the inevitable heat in your kitchen. (2) Stimulate, but back off as soon as new international investment boycotts your economy, domestic wealth takes flight, financial markets drive interest rates on government debt through the ceiling, and the value of your currency drops like a stone. Or (3) stimulate, but be prepared to counter the heat international capital markets will bring by (a) implementing strong measures restricting imports and capital flight, (b) replacing declines in international and private investment with increased government investment, and (c) telling creditors you will default unless they agree to rollovers and concessions. Option three is the economic equivalent in the neoliberal era of not only playing hardball with international creditors, but going to financial war if need be. As daunting as option three is, it is important to remember that the Mitterrand government in France proved that option two does not work. As Harrington admitted, "within less than two years the Socialists were engaged in administering a regime of 'rigor,' otherwise known as capitalist austerity."[33] Moreover, option two almost always leads to even worse austerity measures than option one because regaining credibility with global financial markets is usually more difficult than not losing it in the first place. Option two also creates more political damage because voters understandably hold the reformers responsible for the pain caused by the austerity program reformers preside over. On the other hand, the ANC government in South Africa and the Lula government in Brazil have proved that option one inevitably undermines support from the social sectors that bring progressive governments to power in the first place. If you make no serious attempt to fulfill campaign promises, you inevitably alienate those who voted you into office.

So what lessons can we learn from Harrington's retrospective? Unlike some Left critics, I do not believe that social democracy's success in taming capitalism was responsible for the failure to replace capitalism in the 20th century. Had social democratic parties been less successful at reducing capitalist irrationality and injustice, I believe 20th century capitalism would simply have been more crises ridden and inhumane than it was. Had Herbert Hoover presided over the Great Depression instead of Franklin Delano Roosevelt, I believe the depression would only have been deeper and caused more unnecessary suffering. Without New Deal reforms to build on, I believe socialists' chances of replacing capitalism in the U.S. in the years before World War II would have been even slimmer than they were. Without social security, unemployment insurance, and a minimum wage, and without the example of more robust social democratic reforms in Sweden during the 1960s and 1970s, I believe even fewer people today would believe that equitable cooperation is possible. Broadly speaking, I believe the road to equitable cooperation lies through more and more successful equitable cooperation, not through less.

"Crises" that sometimes trigger the overthrow of structures of privilege are crises of legitimacy, crises of public confidence in ruling elites, or ideological crises that free people from the myths that make them unwitting accomplices in their own oppression. Cracks in the ideological hegemony that undergirds the status quo are the catalysts of social change precisely because they allow people to see that a better world is possible. More suffering in and of itself does not lead people to revolt. Becoming convinced that suffering can be prevented is what motivates people to take risks and stand up for change. Since winning reforms rather than standing by and pointing accusatory fingers at deteriorating conditions is what convinces people that suffering is unnecessary, in my opinion the problem with social democratic reforms was not that they were too successful, but that they were not successful enough.

Nor do I believe that more competition and greed teaches people how to cooperate more equitably. Quite the opposite, the more people practice competition and greed the more difficult it is for them to develop the trust and social skills necessary for equitable cooperation. And the more competition and greed is tolerated the stronger becomes the capitalist enabling myth that people are capable of no better. Unfortunately social democrats eventually accepted the necessity of a system based on competition and greed. Michael Harrington formulates the "great social democratic compromise" accurately enough: social democrats "settled for a situation in which they would regulate and tax capitalism but not challenge it in any fundamental way."[34] But I don't think Harrington fully appreciated the full consequences of the compromise. It is one thing to say: We are committed to democracy above all else. Therefore we promise that as long as a majority of the population does not want to replace capitalism we have no intentions of trying to do so. It is quite another thing to say: Despite our best efforts we have failed to convince a majority of the population that capitalism is fundamentally incompatible with economic justice and democracy. Therefore we will cease to challenge the legitimacy of the capitalist system and confine our efforts to reforming it. The first position is one I believe must guide the movement for equitable cooperation in the century ahead. Unfortunately the second proposition was the compromise accepted by the leadership of social democratic parties, and eventually by all who remained members.

The first proposition does not promise to refrain from voting capitalism out when the majority is ready to do so. Nor does it promise to refrain from taking effective action against capitalists and their supporters should they try to thwart the will of a majority if and when the majority decides they wish to dispense with capitalism in favor of a new system of equitable cooperation. It does not promise to refrain from explaining how private enterprise and markets subvert economic justice and democracy no matter how many believe otherwise. It does not promise to refrain from campaigning in favor of replacing capitalism with something different even when polls indicate that a majority still favors capitalism. It is a simple, unwavering promise to always respect and abide by the will of the majority. The second proposition, on the other hand, bars social democrats from continuing to argue that private enterprise and markets are incompatible with economic justice and democracy. It bars social democrats from campaigning for the replacement of capitalism with a system more compatible with economic justice and democracy. The second proposition implies that if capitalism precludes certain outcomes, then social democrats must cease to lobby on behalf of such outcomes. Therefore the second proposition implies either: (1) social democrats were historically wrong, and economic justice and democracy are fully compatible with capitalism, or (2) while social democrats can continue to fight for some aspects of economic justice and democracy they can no longer support full economic justice and democracy. In effect the second proposition buys political legitimacy within capitalism for social democratic parties in exchange for accepting the legitimacy of a system based on competition and greed. So in my view the problem was not that social democrats fought, often successfully, for reforms to mitigate the effects of competition and greed. The problem was that they ceased to keep fighting for further reforms when their initial reforms fell short of achieving economic justice and democracy because they agreed to accept a system of competition and greed even though the system obstructed the economic justice and democracy they had pledged to fight for.

But eventually the damage went deeper. To his credit Harrington admits that by mid century social democrats he describes as "bewildered and half-exhausted" no longer had any "precise sense of what socialism means" and no longer "challenged capitalism in any fundamental way." By accepting the economics of competition and greed the "social democratic compromise" led social democrats to lose sight of what economic democracy and economic justice are as well.

By the end of the 20th century social democrats no longer agreed among themselves about what economic democracy meant. Moreover, they no longer debated these disagreements vigorously, preferring not to engage in divisive debates they convinced themselves were irrelevant to the immediate tasks that confronted them. Consequently, many social democrats no longer understood why leaving economic decisions in the hands of private employers who survived the rigors of market competition was not an acceptable way to capture expertise. Many no longer understood why "consumer and producer sovereignty" provided by markets was not, by and large, sufficient means of securing economic democracy. Many social democrats no longer understood why joint labor-management advisory committees in capitalist firms were usually fig leafs rather than meaningful vehicles for self-management. By century's end, the debate among social democrats over plan versus market was merely a debate about situations where markets were relatively more efficient and circumstances when efficiency required more "planning" in the form of policy interventions of one kind or another in the market system. Why markets violate economic democracy, and how planning by bureaucrats and corporations can obstruct economic self-management for workers and consumers were no longer issues addressed by social democratic parties by the 1980s.

Similarly, by century's end social democrats no longer knew what economic justice was. Were workers exploited only when they were paid less than their marginal revenue products? If who deserves what is to be decided according to the value of contributions, why do owners of machines and land that increase the amount it is possible to produce not deserve compensation commensurate with those contributions? Unable to answer these questions, social democrats increasingly avoided them. Social democratic union leaders fell into the trap of justifying wage demands on the basis of labor productivity. By doing so they lost track of the fundamental Marxist truth that profits are nothing more than tribute extracted by those who own the means of production, but do no work themselves, from those who do all the work. Moreover, having accepted the morality of reward according to the value of contribution, it was a short step to concentrating on winning wage increases for employees with more human capital and abandoning workers with less human capital. According to a contribution-based theory of economic justice, who is more exploited is determined by whose wage is farthest below their marginal revenue product. No matter how much lower the wages of some workers are than the wages of other workers, if the difference between the marginal revenue product and wage of high-wage workers is greater than the difference between the marginal revenue product and wage of low-wage workers, it would be the workers with higher wages, not those with lower wages, who are more exploited. So social democratic leaders could justify abandoning the worst off sectors of the working class and prioritizing the interests of high wage sectors on (false) grounds that workers with higher wages were often "more exploited." Had they remained clear about what economic justice really means—reward according to effort or sacrifice—it would also have remained clear that workers with lower wages are not only worse off, they are also more exploited. But losing their moral compass provided a convenient excuse for social democratic union leaders and politicians since those with less human capital are often harder to organize, harder to win wage increases for, harder to collect dues from, harder to solicit campaign contributions from, and harder to motivate to get out and vote. In short, accepting reward according to contribution provided a ready-made excuse for a shift in priorities toward a constituency that could increase social democratic political power within capitalism more easily.

In sum, accepting capitalism in a strategic compromise turned into accepting the ideology that justifies capitalism as well. While the effect of strategic concessions on electoral results was always hotly debated, the effects of theoretical and moral concessions were less debated in social democratic circles. In my opinion, however, it was the theoretical and moral concessions that were primarily responsible for slowing social democratic reform momentum and finally rendering social democracy powerless to fight back against right wing campaigns that rolled back reforms with remarkable speed and ease at century's end.

The Decline of the Swedish Model: Magnus Ryner introduces his insightful discussion of the crisis of Swedish social democracy as follows:

> The overall theme of my argument is that it is important to neither reduce the crisis of social democracy to a set of external constraints totally outside the control of social democratic actors, nor to argue that nothing fundamental in the structural environment has changed, and that the crisis is simply an effect of a betrayal of ideas by social democratic elites. The former approach ignores actual tactical and strategic failures of actors, fails to appreciate alternative options and strategies that might have been pursued and that might provide lessons also for the future. The latter approach ignores the profound structural change that has taken place, and that has redefined the terms of social democratic politics.[35]

Not only is this a realistic and useful way to look at the issue, Ryner provides insightful particulars to flesh out the picture. He does not exaggerate when he says "the transformation of international monetary institutions and global financial markets, the emergence of the Eurodollar and other offshore markets, the flexible exchange rate system, mounting government debt, and the growing asymmetries between creditor and debtor nations has made high finance the pivotal agent in the allocation of economic resources."[36] And he fingers the crucial difference between "the 'double screen' of Bretton Woods that ensured the capacity of states to manage aggregate demand and to mitigate market-generated social disruptions," and the neoliberal transformation that "deliberately reshapes state-market boundaries so as to maximize the exposure of states to international capital markets and discipline social actors to conform to market constraints and criteria."[37] As far as I'm concerned Ryner could have dispensed with questionable theories like "Taylorist production norms reaching their sociotechnological frontiers," "the end of Fordism," and "flexible specialization replacing economies of scale" others have written much about in explaining why Sweden's social democrats faced more difficult circumstances at the end of the 20th century than they had in mid century. Multinational corporations' success in getting the rules of the international economy rewritten in their favor, and in favor of financial capital in particular, is sufficient to explain why it became more difficult for Swedish unions and the Swedish government to wrestle part of the social surplus away from Swedish and multinational corporations for those who actually produced it. But not only do all social democrats bear some of the blame for permitting the rules of the international economy to be rewritten in ways that were detrimental to the interests of their traditional constituencies, Swedish social democrats played into the hands of Swedish capitalists allowing them to regain their dominant position in the Swedish economy.

Failure to Wage Class War: Ryner tells us "one should not underestimate the sense of weakness in business circles" in 1970 when Swedish capital faced "the profit squeeze, increased employers' contributions to finance social consumption, juridification of the labor process, and an outright challenge to private ownership of the means of production."[38] But instead of pushing for a new social compromise that won employees greater participation as the Meidner plan called for, and instead of increasing the role of the state in accumulation and investment, Swedish social democrats concentrated on preserving the status quo and their distributive gains in face of a worsening international economic situation. In other words, when they had the chance, Swedish social democrats balked at taking that next reformist step no social democrats ever dared take in the 20th century, which would also have permanently weakened the power of Swedish capitalists.

What went little noticed at the time was that by frightening Swedish capitalists but leaving them breathing room, the social democrats allowed the Skandinaviska Enskilda Ganken/Wallenberg group, who had only reluctantly accepted the social democratic compromise in the first place, to take over the Swedish Employers Association (SAF) from the Handelsbank group which had supported the "Swedish model." The shift in power became clear to all when "Asean's Curt Nicolin was appointed executive director of the SAF in 1978, an event described as a 'culture shock' by senior officials of the organization."[39] Under new "hyper-liberal leadership" Ryner tells us the SAF "assumed a position of total non-accommodation in the public commission responsible to iron out a compromise on wage earner funds, attempts to overcome difference with the Swedish Labor Confederation (LO) on wage levels and collective savings were abandoned, and by January of 1992 the SAF had unilaterally exited from all corporatist forms of bargaining."[40] In short, frightened Swedish capitalists embraced new internal leadership willing to battle not only against social democratic programs but social democratic ideology as well. Taking advantage of neoliberal international conditions that strengthened their cause, and a retreat offered by moderate proponents of "the third way" within the Swedish social democratic party, the SAF went on to roll back the "Swedish model" in the late 1990s.

The Third Way: A Trojan Horse: Ryner argues convincingly that despite external shocks to an overly specialized and vulnerable Swedish export sector, and despite the increasingly hostile neoliberal international environment, Swedish social democrats still had options they failed to pursue that could have changed the outcome. Moderate "third way" social democrats called for a retreat in face of more difficult economic and political conditions, while the more progressive wing of the Swedish Social Democratic Party (SAP) called for an expansion of economic democracy. Ryner provides an invaluable description of how "third way" policies paved the road to economic failure and political defeat that all who are attracted to such policies would do well to heed. This lesson is so important I quote Ryner at length:

> The economic policy of the SAP 1982–90, coined "the third way" (between Thatcherism and Keynesianism), presupposed that "supply-side" selective labor market policy measures and a coordinated restraint in collective bargaining would be sufficient measures to contain unemployment and inflation. The policy ultimately faltered because long-term GDP and productivity growth were not realized, and the implicit incomes policy failed. A basic fallacy of the policy was the premise that increased private profits and investments would regenerate

GDP and productivity growth. Apart from the success of pharmaceuticals, there was little growth in new dynamic sectors and enterprises. Instead the strategy benefited existing firms, which had a "golden decade" despite the lackluster performance of Sweden's economy.[41]

The government deregulated capital and money markets in 1985, and this was followed by a formal deregulation of foreign exchange markets in 1989. Moreover, the strategy in managing the public debt changed. Together with a vow not to devalue again, the government declared it would no longer borrow abroad directly to finance the debt or cover balance of payments deficits, but would rather only borrow on the domestic market. This meant that in order to maintain balance of payments, the Swedish interest rate would have to increase to a level where private agents would hold bonds or other debts in Swedish krona, despite the devaluation risk. In other words, the Ministry of Finance and the Central Bank deliberately sought to use global financial markets for disciplinary purposes on unions (LO and TCO) and social service agencies in wage and budget bargaining. The LO and TCO did not consent to their marginalization, and continued to demand support for solidaristic wage policy and did not heed the "moral suasion" of incomes policy since there no longer was a coherent common moral framework. It led to what became known as the "War of the Roses" between the Ministry of Finance on the one hand and the unions and social service cadres on the other.[42]

It should be noted that these policy changes were not subjected to debate and approval in any party congresses or in the electoral arena. Only the Central Bank and the Ministry of Finance were effectively involved. Concurrently, just as these policies were implemented, the "third way" was still presented to party ranks and in the electoral arena as a reformist socialist response to the crisis in opposition to neo-liberalism.[43]

These "third way" economic failures Ryner describes so well also led to electoral defeat. "It was in the context of the 'extraordinary measures' of a wage freeze and a temporary ban on strikes that the electoral support of the SAP plummeted to a historical low, ultimately leading to a humiliating electoral defeat in 1991."[44] But more importantly Ryner explains how "third way" politics led to a rightward shift in the entire Swedish political spectrum.

The SAF began to assume the role of an aspiring hegemonic party, attempting to shape intellectual and popular discourse and the terrain of contestability in civil society in a market friendly direction. Although this strategy has fallen short of realizing a Thatcherite national-popular hegemony in Sweden, it has nevertheless been quite a success. It ensured the defeat of wage earner funds in the electoral arena. More broadly, it has made neo-liberal ideas popular in the middle-class strata, which is reflected in the successes of the Moderaterna (the neoconservative party) and the rightward shift of the liberal Folkpariet on economic issues. The subsequent shift in the substance of academic discourse in economics also took place in the context of strategic business funding of economic research.[45]

Is "Economic Democracy" Still Possible?: Rear guard measures clearly failed to save the Swedish Model, and it should now be apparent to all that "third way" politics functioned as a Trojan horse for the economics of competition and greed inside the walls of the Swedish Social Democratic Party. But was there a viable alternative that could have produced better results? Ryner admits conditions were unfavorable, and there is no way to know for sure. But he goes to great lengths to point out ways in which moving the reform agenda forward—increasing what Swedish social democrats call "economic democracy" rather than unleashing market forces—might have had more success.

Ryner argues that continued expansion of social welfare programs that were the hallmark of the Swedish Model in its heyday eventually required increases in productivity. But he points out that the Left within the SAP consistently offered proposals aimed at these objectives. In other words, contrary to complaints from neoliberals abroad, Swedish conservatives, and third wavers inside the SAP that the Swedish Left was only about redistribution, the LO, social service agency cadre, and their progressive intellectual allies inside the SAP did have a coherent program to stimulate productivity, investment, and growth. In other words, they were neither short-sighted nor exclusively about redistribution.

The LO launched an offensive for "industrial democracy" in the early 1970s which led to the Codetermination Act, the Work Environment Act, and Legislation of Employment Protection. But all attempts to build on these beginnings came to naught. In 1976 the LO endorsed the "Meidner Plan" to expand worker participation and gradually give them partial ownership of the firms where they worked. On numerous subsequent occasions the LO proposed ways to increase "collective savings and investment" through excess profit taxes and wage earner funds (The fourth AP fund, the Waldenstrom Report, and the LO wage earner fund proposal of 1981.) Unfortunately "the LO never managed to convince the rest of the social democratic movement that it was worth the electoral risks to mobilize around the issue."[46] In their excellent chapter on what they call the Swedish "Middle Way,"[47] Charles Sackrey and Geoffrey Schneider describe what reformers hoped would be the effect of wage earner funds: "The funds were intended to be used to buy up shares of companies, so workers could gradually gain a voice in all business decisions. Once labor leaders became owners, they would sit on corporate boards and directly influence corporate decision making. Laborers could then keep firms from moving overseas, or downsizing workers unnecessarily. The funds would also inject Swedish firms with new capital for investment." But of course, this is not the kind of program for investment and growth that Swedish capitalists were interested in. More to the point, advocates of "the third way" in SAP did not buy it. As we saw, they preferred instead to put their faith in private savings and investment, and in market discipline and financial liberalization to promote investment and growth. It is widely acknowledged that increasing participation increases worker productivity. Unfortunately there is no telling to what extent this might have happened in Sweden because it was never tried.

The second plank in an alternative response to the crisis of Swedish social democracy would have been to strengthen government control over credit, rather than loosen it. Gregg Olsen provides a mind-numbing description of the disaster unleashed by "third way" social democrats who succumbed to the croonings of neoliberal financial reformers instead of heeding the warnings of Keynes and the old guard leadership of SAP.

> The Swedish credit market was rapidly deregulated throughout the 1980s. By the end of the decade, Sweden's long standing system of controls over foreign investment and exchange and the financial sector were effectively eliminated. Finance houses proliferated during this period, and money flooded into office buildings and real estate. However, the speculative boom ended in short order. The Swedish credit system foundered by the end of 1991, forcing the government to divert tax revenues to bail out several of its major banks at a cost of 3% of GDP.[48]

Along with retaining strong controls over domestic credit, Swedish social democrats would also have had to adopt strong measures to prevent capital flight and prevent international finance from exercising *de facto* veto power over Swedish social democratic policies. But unlike underdeveloped economies where it is more important to achieve a net inflow of investment, as a highly developed economy Sweden faced the less daunting task of merely preventing a net capital outflow. With sufficient controls on Swedish capital flight, Swedish social democrats could have withstood a virtual boycott by international investors. It is not unreasonable to believe that once having done so, international investors would have eventually reentered profitable Swedish markets on terms acceptable to social democratic governments.

There is no telling if Swedish social democrats could have mobilized enough popular support to sustain an alternative program along these lines. Ryner provides compelling evidence that there was strong support for such policies among workers and beneficiaries of Sweden's social programs. Quoting surveys, Ryner tells us "there is a profound divide between the increasingly neoliberal paradigm of Swedish elites and the continued welfarist 'common sense' of the Swedish people."[49] So according to Ryner support for a program to deepen "economic democracy" was lacking in the SAP leadership and its economic advisors rather than in the SAP base. Nor is there any way to know if the SAP had mobilized support behind such a program whether international conditions would have permitted Sweden to move from a Left Keynesian welfare state toward deeper and more productive "economic democracy." What is now known is that the "third way" was a huge step back toward the economics of competition and greed, and the vast majority of the Swedish people are worse off for it.

Libertarian Socialism: Not Always a "Basket Case"

Libertarian socialists were by far the worst underachievers among 20th century anti-capitalists. Even so, I count myself a libertarian socialist, and believe "we" have the most to offer those fighting to replace the economics of competition and greed with the economics of equitable cooperation in the century ahead. After 1939 libertarian socialism became almost invisible as a political force on the Left for twenty-five years. The eclipse was so complete that most progressives today are unaware that libertarian socialism was ever more than an intellectual footnote on the Left—an early warning against the totalitarian dangers of communism. But this was not always the case. Early in the 20th century libertarian socialism was as powerful a force as social democracy and communism. The Libertarian International—founded at the Congress of Saint-Imier a few days after the split between Marxists and libertarians at the Congress of the Socialist International held in the Hague in 1872—competed successfully against social democrats and communists alike for the loyalty of anti-capitalist activists, revolutionaries, workers, unions, and political parties for over fifty years. Libertarian socialists played a major role in the Russian revolutions of 1905 and 1917. Libertarian socialists played a dominant role in the Mexican Revolution of 1911. Libertarian socialists competed with some success against social democrats for influence inside the British Fabian society, later to become the British Labor Party. Before and after World War I libertarian socialists competed against social democrats and communists in Germany, and were more influential than both in the low countries, France, and Italy. In uprisings that failed to overthrow capitalism in Europe in the aftermath of World War I, revolutionaries allied with the Bolsheviks in the new Communist International were more active in Germany, but anarchists allied with the Libertarian International were more influential in rebellions that lasted longer in Italy. And twenty years after World War I was over, libertarian socialists were still strong enough to spearhead the largest and most successful revolution against capitalism to ever take place in any industrial economy—the social revolution that swept across Republican Spain in 1936 and 1937.

After their defeat in Spain, libertarian socialists vanished for a quarter century. When libertarian socialist themes reappeared in the 1960s in the New Left it took on very different forms and never again resembled the movement that played such an important role in the first third of the century. More recently the vacuum left by the demise of communism and decline of social democracy in the 1990s has given rise to a resurgence of interest in libertarian socialist thought on the Left. But if all that comes of this "rethinking" is that tiny anarchist groups replace tiny communist sects on the far Left of the political spectrum, little will be accomplished.

Libertarian Socialist Insights: Twentieth century libertarian socialists were right about capitalism. They saw it as a system based on competition and greed, disenfranchising and exploiting producers while manipulating consumers. They objected to capitalism first and foremost on moral grounds and believed in organizing people to overthrow capitalism irrespective of whether or not capitalism contained the seeds of its own destruction. Libertarian socialists were also right about communism, or more properly Marxism-Leninism, and central planning. They believed that communism merely substituted rule by commissars for rule by capitalists, no matter what differences there were between centrally planned, public enterprise economies and private enterprise, market economies. The history of 20th century capitalism and communism has vindicated libertarian socialists in these regards. However, the lynchpin of all libertarian socialist thinking is the conviction that workers and consumers are quite capable of managing themselves and their own division of labor efficiently and equitably. That, of course, is why libertarian socialists believe people can do very well, not only without capitalist employers to boss them and market competition to drive them, but also without communist overseers and bureaucrats from the central planning ministry to tell them what to produce. I believe libertarian socialists are correct in this belief. But I do not think the intellectual case for how this can be done is as obvious as 20th century libertarian socialists claimed, or how to do it is as simple and non-problematic as libertarian socialists pretended. On the contrary, I think much more careful thinking needs to be done about exactly how to organize equitable cooperation so that injustice and elite rule do not reappear, and so people do not despair that their time and energies are being wasted. In any case, if history is going to vindicate libertarian socialism regarding the feasibility of economic self-rule by ordinary workers and consumers it will have to be 21st century history—because the history of the twentieth century certainly did not.

What was responsible for the organizational successes of libertarian socialists early in the 20th century and their singular lack of success in the second half of the century? I think careful investigation by future historians will reveal that behind every success lay decades of agitation and organization building where the message of libertarian socialism resonated strongly with large segments of the population, who, for one reason or another, were largely unaffected by rival messages about what people could and should do. I believe the notion that popular uprisings with real possibilities of consolidating self-rule occur spontaneously will be dispelled by careful historical examination. I also suspect investigation will confirm that the lack of success of libertarian socialists in the second half of the century was largely due to their inability to participate effectively in reform organizing during an era when this was the only way to reach significant numbers of people. The brief analyses below of libertarian socialist successes in building mass movements in Russia and Spain early in the century, compared to later failures, is intended only to outline a *prima facie* case for this hypothesis. If I say enough to stimulate others to investigate more thoroughly I will consider my meager efforts successful.

Libertarian Socialism in the Russian Revolution: The Narodniki, the Left Social Revolutionary Party, and various anarchist groups had been agitating for land reform and leading the opposition to Czarist tyranny in Russia for more than half a century before these Russian libertarian socialists were politically powerful enough to play a prominent role in the Russian Revolutions of 1905 and 1917. The ideological hegemony of the Czar and the Russian landed aristocracy was in eclipse, and the best efforts of powerful officials like Prime Minister Stolypyn to promote capitalism in the Russian countryside were mostly unsuccessful, as bourgeois ideology made little headway with Russian landlords and peasants alike. Instead, Narodniki and anarchist intellectuals became the teachers of Russian peasants creating countless clandestine and legal organizations over fifty years. The rural "soviets" that formed the spearhead for revolution and land reform in Russia were not the creations of Mensheviks or Bolsheviks—who were virtually unknown in the Russian countryside prior to 1917—but the fruit of decades of organizing by different groups of rural Russian libertarian socialists. Nor did the rural soviets spontaneously appear from the untutored consciousness of the exploited peasant "masses" without organizational precedent. Rural soviets only appeared suddenly and acted decisively because the idea of radical land reform had been nurtured for decades in most Russian villages by Narodniki, anarchists, and cadre from the Left Social Revolutionary Party, and because village committees with battle tested leadership already existed to form the backbone of the rural soviets. The message of rural libertarian socialists resonated strongly with land starved Russian peasants: Eliminate the landed aristocracy—who do nothing but collect exorbitant rents from peasant tenants already responsible for organizing as well as carrying out production—so village assemblies can distribute land to the tillers and reclaim the traditional mir as common land to be managed, once again, collectively by the village. In other words, libertarian socialists rooted for generations in the Russian countryside, organized peasants to do exactly what they wanted to do and came to believe they were capable of doing once they eliminated the parasites who prevented them from becoming masters of their fate.

In Russian cities anarchists enjoyed great success even though there was stiffer competition for the loyalty of workers from other anti-capitalist groups. First, the fact that much of Russian industry was foreign owned reduced the appeal of foreign employers to their Russian employees in general. Second, the fact that much of the Russian proletariat was newly arrived from the countryside and maintained ties with their native villages gave anarchists an advantage over Mensheviks and Bolsheviks, since many workers were more familiar and trusting of anarchists to begin with. Finally, anarchists' preference for clandestine, revolutionary factory committees over reformist unions turned out not to work to their disadvantage in recruiting supporters in Czarist Russia. For the most part the Czarist government banned unions and factory committees alike, meeting out the same punishment to activists in both kinds of organization if caught—assassination, imprisonment, or exile to Siberia. So if anything, the willingness of Mensheviks and Bolsheviks to organize through more reformist organizations like unions where they had to reveal themselves to negotiate with employers worked to their competitive disadvantage and to the advantage of the more secretive anarchists. Anarchist influence among Russian workers was so dominant that when Bolshevik cadre showed up in factories in order not to be ignored they had to preach the same message as the anarchist cadre who were already there: Owners be gone! The factory committee is ready to take over. How it was that Russian anarchists and Left Social Revolutionaries found themselves banned, assassinated, arrested, deported to Siberia, and thoroughly political defeated after building a significant popular following and playing crucial roles in both the February and October Revolutions, is an important question to address. But it is a different story and irrelevant to my purpose here, which is only to explore the basis for the considerable organizational successes of libertarian socialists in Russia prior to 1919.

Libertarian Socialism in the Spanish Revolution: For the same reason we need not explore why Spanish anarchists found themselves on the losing end of revolutionary history after building an even larger following and playing an even greater role in the Spanish Revolution of 1936–37. Our question is how and why Spanish anarchists were able to build a mass following and establish themselves as a powerful political force in the first place. Just as traditions of grassroots economic self-management like the mir long preceded the arrival of anarchist agitators in Russian villages, there were strong traditions of economic self-management in various parts of Spain dating back to the 15th century or earlier. Drawing on primary research by T. F. Glick,[50] and A. Maass and R. L. Anderson,[51] Elnor Ostrom brought the centuries-old practice of collective self-management of irrigation systems in Valencia (Turia River), Alicante (Monnegre River), and Murcia and Orihuela (Segura River) to the attention of modern scholars studying democratic self-management of common property resources in her award winning book *Governing the Commons*.[52] Reading from historical accounts of the Spanish Civil war we discover that this region of Spain, the Levant, was one of the hotbeds of rural anarchist collectives. In *The Anarchist Collectives: Workers Self-management in the Spanish Revolution 1936–1939*[53] (Free Life, 1974), Sam Dolgoff quotes Gaston Leval, who provided a firsthand study of the collectives:

> The regional federation of Levant, organized by our comrades of the CNT, was an agrarian federation embracing 5 provinces with a total population of 1,650,000 at the outbreak of the Civil War, with 78% of the most fertile land in Spain. It is in the Levant where, thanks to the creative spirit of our comrades, the most and best developed collectives were organized. (The number of collectives grew from 340 in 1937 to 900 at the end of 1938, and 40% of the total population of these provinces lived in collectives.) These achievements will not surprise those acquainted with the social history of the region. Since 1870 the libertarian peasants were among the most determined and persistent militants. While at certain times the movement in the cities (particularly Valencia) was altogether suppressed, the movement remained alive in the countryside. The peasants carried on. For them the Revolution was not confined only to fighting on the barricades. For them the Revolution meant taking possession of the land and building libertarian communism. In the Levant, the collectives were

almost always organized by the peasant syndicates on the grass roots level. But they remained as autonomous organizations. The syndicates constituted the necessary intermediary connection between the "individualists" and the collectives. Mixed commissions did the purchasing for the collectives as well as for the individual farmers (machines, fertilizers, insecticides, seeds, etc.). They used the same trucks and wagons. This practical demonstration of solidarity brought many formerly recalcitrant "individualists" into the collectives. This method of organization served a double function: it encompassed everything that could be usefully coordinated, and, thanks to the syndicates, succeeded in spreading the spirit of the collectives among new layers of the population rendered receptive to our influence.[54]

What Leval describes above is remarkable. The movement was popular and massive, but hardly spontaneous since it had been thoroughly prepared by anarchist agitation and organization building for sixty years. Moreover, thanks to Ostrom we know this libertarian socialist movement that was more than fifty years in the making was itself built on the social achievements of hundreds of years of democratic management of river irrigation systems in the region. The anarchist collectives were voluntary, yet comprised 40 percent of the population. Relations of solidarity with autonomy between collectives and more reformist, all-inclusive syndicates permitted both efficient economic coordination and friendly political relations between "individualist" and "collectivist" peasants. In other parts of his account Leval tells us that the federation of collectives sponsored large scale improvements to irrigation systems and programs on animal husbandry and plant cross-breeding. The collectives established schools in every village, reducing the rate of illiteracy from 70 percent to below 10 percent in a little over two years, and the federation of collectives ran a school for accounting and book keeping in Valencia, as well as the "University of Moncada," which the regional federation of the Levant placed at the disposal of the Spanish National Federation of Peasants. In sum, we have quite a remarkable example of energetic and efficient economic and cultural self-management occurring despite disruptions from the Civil War and suppression from a hostile government of social democrats and communists centered in Valencia. But "remarkable" should not be confused with "spontaneous."

When we look at other regions even more famous for their revolutionary accomplishments like Aragon, Catalonia, and the city of Barcelona, we find a similar pattern: sixty years of libertarian socialist agitation and institution building on top of democratic, collectivist experiences and practices, in some cases dating back centuries. In *The Spanish Labyrinth*, Gerald Brenan—by no means an anarchist sympathizer—provides the following description of Port de la Selva in Catalonia before the Civil War based on investigations by J. Langdon Davies and Joaquin Costa:

> The village was run by a fishermen's co-operative. They owned the nets, the boats, the curing factory, the store house, the refrigerating plant, all the shops, the transport lorries, the olive groves and the oil refinery, the café, the theater, and the assembly rooms. They had developed the posito, or municipal credit

fund possessed by every village in Spain, into an insurance against death, accident, and loss of boats. They coined their own money. What is interesting is to see how naturally these co-operatives have fitted into the Spanish scene. For Port de la Selva is one of the old fishermen's communes of Catalonia which have existed from time immemorial. Here then we have a modern productive co-operative grafted on to an ancient communal organization and functioning perfectly.[55]

Far from presuming the masses would spontaneously organize their own self-rule, Spanish libertarian socialists devoted a great deal of time and energy to discussing exactly how the new society should be reorganized and how and by whom different kinds of decisions should be made. Dolgoff tells us "the intense preoccupation of the Spanish anarchists with libertarian reconstruction of society has been called an 'obsession' and not altogether without reason. At their Saragossa Congress in May, 1936 there were lengthy resolutions on 'The Establishment of Communes, Their Function and Structure,' 'Plan of Economic Organization,' 'Coordination and Exchange,' 'Economic Conception of the Revolution,' 'Federation of Industrial and Agricultural Associations,' 'Art, Culture and Education,' and sessions on relations with non-libertarian individuals and groupings, crime, delinquency, equality of sexes, and individual rights."[56] But what is even more telling about the topics taken up at the Saragossa Congress is that the resolutions debated, refined, and approved there had been worked on by every congress of the Spanish section of the Libertarian International beginning in 1870. In other words, policies put into effect by the agrarian collectives and socialized industries during the Spanish Revolution had been debated by tens of thousands of delegates in dozens of major congresses dating back over thirty years.

Moreover, Dolgoff tells us "the resolutions mentioned above were more than just show pieces; they were widely discussed. In a largely illiterate country, tremendous quantities of literature on social revolution were disseminated and read many times over. There were tens of thousands of books, pamphlets, and tracts, vast and daring cultural and popular educational experiments (the Ferrer schools) that reached into almost every village and hamlet throughout Spain."[57] According to Brenan, "by 1918 more than fifty towns in Andalusia alone had libertarian newspapers of their own."[58] And based on statistics derived from Gaston Leval's *Espagne Libertaire*, Dolgoff reports that in Barcelona the CNT published a daily, *Solidaridad Obrera*, with a circulation of 30,000. *Tierra y Libertad* (a magazine) of Barcelona reached a circulation of 20,000; *Vida Obrera* of Giron, *El Productor* of Seville, and *Accion y Cultura* of Saragossa had large circulations. The magazines *La Revista Blanca*, *Tiempos Nuevos*, and *Estudios* reached circulations of 5,000, 15,000, and 75,000 respectively. In Dolgoff's words, "by 1934 the anarchist press blanketed Spain."[59]

The revolutionary Barcelona that George Orwell made famous in his eyewitness account in the first chapter of *Homage to Catalonia*[60] clearly did not appear spontaneously. But not only was the intellectual and organizational groundwork for the Spanish Revolution painstakingly laid over six decades; not only was the anarchist led confederation of labor, the CNT, the oldest and largest organization of workers in Spain with a million and a half members by 1934; the popular impression that revolutionary Spain was inefficient and undisciplined, and that anarchists were sectarian, divisive, and bear much of the responsibility for the defeat of the Spanish Republic by Franco's fascist-backed military, is almost entirely unsubstantiated. Noam Chomsky, citing sources friendly and unfriendly to anarchists alike in *Objectivity and Liberal Scholarship*,[61] demonstrates that industrial and agricultural production and deliveries were strongest in anarchist areas, and that military courage and discipline of anarchist troops was unparalleled. In case after case Chomsky refutes accusations made at the time by their communist and social democratic rivals that it was anarchists who engaged in sectarian politics, showing that available evidence indicates that exactly the opposite occurred. Chomsky also demonstrates in case after case that the presumption of liberal scholars writing after the fact that the libertarian revolution that swept over much of Spain was dysfunctional was almost entirely lacking in credible evidence.

The Demise of Libertarian Socialism

Libertarian socialism never recovered from its defeat in Spain. After World War II social democrats and communists dominated Left politics in Western and Third World societies alike for over forty years. Lacking a comprehensive history of libertarian socialism we are at a disadvantage in trying to learn what contributed to its demise in the middle third of the century. No doubt many factors contributed—not the least of which was that both social democrats and communists achieved state power in various countries allowing them to provide ideological, material, political, diplomatic, and even military aid for allied parties elsewhere, while no libertarian socialist group enjoyed help from any outside source. But what strikes me is that ingredients crucial to libertarian socialist successes early in the century were absent later in the century: (1) Nowhere did they exercise significant influence or enjoy a substantial following in the labor movement, as unions and their federations became dominated by social democrats, communists, or business unionists. (2) Their message that reforms were doomed and worker takeovers were the only answer fell on deaf ears. In the "golden age of capitalism" reformist unions were winning significant wage increases, and takeovers by individual groups of workers from employers fully backed by the power of the state seemed particularly unrealistic and suicidal. (3) As Taylorism de-skilled ordinary workers and concentrated productive knowledge in the hands of supervisory staff, worker self-management became less appealing to industrial workers than to their predecessors with living memories of craft and guild controlled production, and instead had only esoteric appeal to small groups of intellectuals and students. (4) Only where Third World national liberation movements came to power did realistic possibilities of organizing non-capitalist economies present themselves, but this invariably occurred where communist influence and the Soviet model held sway. Always unwilling to engage in electoral politics, fixated on organizing workers "at the point of production" but unable to make any headway in convincing them to reject capitalism *en toto*, libertarian socialists were left with no connections to any significant segment of the body politic. It was not until the rise of the New Left in the late 1960s that libertarian socialists were able to do more than provide a Left critique of totalitarian socialism—that was completely drowned out by the conservative critique of communism backed by the full force of the Western intellectual establishment—and a radical critique of capitalism—that was at odds with more elaborate Marxist treatments that enjoyed hegemony in anti-capitalist circles.

The New Left: The rise of the New Left in the 1960s led to a revival of libertarian socialist themes but not libertarian socialism itself. New Left activists were largely unaware of their own parentage which had become all but invisible over the previous thirty years. Many New Left leaders reinvented libertarian socialist wheels without being aware of their intellectual antecedents. Grassroots democracy, control over one's community and work life, solidarity combined with autonomy, and rejection of materialism became powerful New Left themes whose allure may even have been increased by the vagueness and lack of intellectual rigor with which they were expressed.

The popularity of the New Left—of which I am a proud product—derived from the power of themes that had long been libertarian socialist staples in modern capitalist societies where the gap between the hollow rhetoric of justice and democracy for all and the hard reality of discrimination and oligarchic rule was becoming ever more apparent. The popularity of the New Left also derived from the intellectual and moral bankruptcy of both social democratic and communist parties in Western democracies. Blinded by fear of communism, and unwilling to risk their fragile status in the political mainstream of Western societies, social democrats were unreliable allies against imperialism and more likely to exaggerate the accomplishments of Western capitalism compared to communism than to criticize its systematic failings. Communists in Western societies, on the other hand, were doomed to political oblivion by their betrayal of democracy that manifested itself in the excuses they offered for totalitarian regimes abroad and in their own undemocratic practices. But nowhere did the New Left succeed in establishing a coherent intellectual analysis and program. Nowhere did the New Left create organizational vehicles to participate successfully in electoral politics. Nowhere did the New Left succeed in maintaining the libertarian, anti-materialist, cultural revolution that accompanied its emergence in the 1960s. And nowhere did the New Left establish a solid and lasting base in any significant segment of the body politic. Instead, most of the relatively privileged participants in the New Left drifted back into their original life trajectories in mainstream society, while a minority went on to pursue their radicalism in the mainstream labor movement or in one of the new social movements that grew in the 1970s and 1980s—the feminist and gay liberation movements, the environmental movement, and solidarity movements associated with particular Third World liberation struggles.

New Social Movements: While new social movements have each made invaluable contributions, they accelerated the trend begun in the New Left away from developing a comprehensive libertarian socialist theory and practice. Progressive activism became more compartmentalized, more practical, and more reform oriented. Theoretical discussion receded further into discussions of "core values" that were often not clearly spelled out, allowing people to conveniently assume they agreed even when phrases like economic justice, economic democracy, and sustainable development meant quite different things to different interpreters. Activists in the 1970s and 1980s with libertarian socialist values did not further develop their theoretical critique of capitalism. Instead, confusion about why capitalism was unacceptable and what was wrong with both mainstream and Marxist analyses of capitalism increased. They did not deepen their understanding of how an economics of equitable cooperation guided by democratic planning rather than markets or central planning could operate. Instead their answers to the question "What do you want instead of capitalism?" became even more self-contradictory and confused. Finally, most of them did not learn how to throw themselves into reform campaigns without abandoning their anti-capitalism and commitment to economic self-rule. Instead many New Leftists leap frogged right over social democrats they once regarded as stogy and overly cautious, to flaunt the flag of pragmatism they had scorned in their "idealistic youth." Very few retained any commitment to the libertarian socialist "big picture." Most who moved on to work in the labor movement, the women's movement, the gay rights movement, the environmental movement, or in Third World solidarity movements renounced "big picture politics" altogether, and focused instead on writing grants and press releases, fundraising from foundations and through bulk mail solicitations, lobbying local, state, and national officials, running shelters and petition campaigns, contract negotiation, and learning to use the internet to publicize campaigns and create alternative media outlets. Whatever knowledge was required by a particular campaign, whatever skills were needed by a particular organization became the almost exclusive focus of intellectual inquiry. Only a very few former New Leftists, usually hidden away along with old Left die-hards in Left caucuses of organizations in the social movements, continued to adhere to libertarian socialist politics. For the most part the revival of interest in anarchism and libertarian socialism in general that has taken place in the past decade has come from a new generation of young activists, as unfamiliar with the New Left as they are with the old Left, looking for democratic, fair, and sustainable alternatives to neoliberal, global capitalism.

New social movement activism has more to its credit than reform victories and successful efforts to minimize roll backs—which are important enough. For one, by brute force, i.e. by building large, lasting movements on a par with the labor movement, as much as through intellectual discourse, they have shattered the hold of economistic theories and bankrupt political strategies based on them that handicapped progressive activists for most of the 20th century. The women's and gay rights movements have revolutionized thinking about gender relations and created a mind set that makes explanations that insist on tracing the roots of gender oppression to economic dynamics unacceptable to a majority of women and gay activists. Failure to treat gender oppression and patriarchy as central to the project of human liberation will never again be tolerated by a large constituency necessary for its achievement. Similarly, the anti-racist movement will no longer accept treating racism as nothing more than a ruling class trick to divide the working class, and will never again limit its goals to demanding only minimal civil rights. The various ways that whole communities who were once conquered or enslaved continue to be oppressed by other communities will have to be dealt with as a central part of social reconstruction rather than as secondary or derivative issues. Nor will the anti-imperialist movement any longer put up with explanations in purely economic terms that ignore the important roles that national chauvinism, jingoism, racism, sexism, authoritarianism, and militarism all play in imperial politics. The environmental movement has wisely conditioned its supporters to always question whether any theoretical framework fully incorporates all the implications of human dependence on the biosphere, and made sure they will never take claims on face value that any economic system can be trusted to preserve and restore the natural environment. The women's, gay, civil rights, peace, and environmental movements are forces to be reckoned with and are here to stay. While the labor movement rightly insists that class exploitation is very much still with us and on the rise, never again will labor or Leftist leaders be able to successfully insist that the class struggle must always take precedence over other struggles, or that classes are the only important agents of progressive social change.

The new social movements have created a promising new starting point for social change activism in the 21st century. Oppressed communities and genders as well as classes are now recognized as important agents of historical change. Transformations of oppressive community and gender relations as well as economic relations are now accepted as high priority goals. And the need for dramatic rethinking about the very meaning of human progress in light of environmental constraints is now taken for granted by the majority of progressive-minded people. Since much of traditional libertarian socialist theory was plagued by economism and lacking in environmental awareness, the theoretical analyses by those active in new social movements provide a welcome theoretical corrective. Since libertarian socialist practice focused almost exclusively on class issues, the existence of multiple social movements provides a corrective social environment as well.

I have suggested that in large part because of their hostility to reformist organizations libertarian socialists in the middle of the 20th century became isolated from large movements fighting against their oppressors. Moreover, their insistence that little could be accomplished until capitalism was overthrown despite the fact that sensible people came to realize that capitalism was going to be with us for quite some time, only served to keep them isolated. New social movements have spread awareness that there is always much to be accomplished in different spheres of social life, and that no single revolutionary break is going to be the be-all and end-all for those working for social reconstruction. Hopefully the power of the new social movements will help libertarian socialists to see this as well, and having learned that the forces shaping history are different in important ways from what they long believed, libertarian socialists will adjust their strategy and practice accordingly. If not, I think libertarian socialists will ignore the lessons new social movements teach at their own peril.

Libertarian Socialists and Capitalist Reform: I suspect that 20th century libertarian socialists were always too "purist" and reluctant to enter into reform campaigns. I suspect they were always too quick to assume that reformist unions and cooperatives were largely ineffectual. They believed electoral politics was pointless because they assumed capitalists would never tolerate interference in their control over government policy. Too often they believed lobbying the government for policy reforms favorable to workers was useless since the state was the executive committee of the capitalist class. And finally, they feared that failing to overthrow capitalism once only mislead workers into thinking things can get better. But one of the great lessons of the 20th century is there is considerable room for maneuver within capitalism, and that reforms can make a great deal of difference in how the majority fares. So it turns out that 20th century libertarian socialists greatly underestimated the possibility of improvement through reform. Moreover, I suspect that libertarian socialists who did participate in reform campaigns often did so less than wholeheartedly because they were convinced that little could be accomplished. Armed with a ready made theoretical explanation for the failure of reforms, libertarian socialists were programmed to give up too easily, and I suspect they often abandoned campaigns prematurely. I suspect their negative attitude about reform work also put them at a competitive disadvantage in leadership battles within reform organizations *visa vis* their social democratic rivals who arrived with unshakable faith that meaningful reforms were possible—and a sneaking suspicion that anything beyond reform was a pipe dream.

While always a handicap, I believe early in the century libertarian socialists sometimes got away with their misguided policy on reforms within capitalism for peculiar historical reasons. I suspect they were able to build large mass organizations of their own because sometimes there were no alternative reform organizations for people to choose from. When this happened, libertarian socialists could become the dominant ideological force within large organizations, as we saw in both pre-Revolutionary Russia and Spain. Libertarian socialists did not consider these to be reformist organizations because they were led by dedicated revolutionaries, namely themselves, and because they were staunchly anti-capitalist, since their memberships routinely approved anti-capitalist resolutions introduced by their libertarian socialist members. But I believe these organizations attracted large numbers of members because they met crucial needs within capitalism no other organizations addressed. In this respect the organizations were reform organizations, they were just hard to recognize as such because they routinely rubber stamped revolutionary proclamations. In other words, my hypothesis is this: Libertarian socialists early in the century owed their successes in large part to their wholehearted participation in reform campaigns and organizations. They were able to trick themselves into doing effective reform work because these campaigns and organizations took on revolutionary trappings that were largely irrelevant to the majority of participants they attracted, but which allowed libertarian socialists to participate without violating their ideological pledge to eschew the politics of reform. As a result, early in the century libertarian socialists were often able to reach large numbers of people and participate in enduring, mass organizations despite their official policy of boycotting organizations dedicated solely to achieving reforms within capitalism. But by mid century a plethora of reform organizations and campaigns had filled this vacuum, at least in most advanced democratic capitalist economies, and that is where large numbers of people struggling to improve their lives through collective action have been found ever since. Consequently, ever since World War II libertarian socialists' longtime policy of turning up their noses at reform work has doomed them to isolation.

Beside the mistaken belief that meaningful reforms within capitalism were impossible, other factors influenced libertarian socialists to shy away from reform organizing. Many fell victim to false theories of capitalist crisis. If capitalist development was inevitably killing the goose that laid the golden eggs by substituting capital, i.e. dead labor, for living labor, when profits in the long run come only from exploiting living labor, then capitalism could be relied on to dig its own grave. If by keeping wages depressed capitalists witlessly created crises of over production leading to ever more severe depressions, what was the point in fighting for higher wages or lobbying governments to stimulate demand through expansionary fiscal and monetary policies? Believing in misguided theories of capitalist crisis such as these led some libertarian socialists to conclude it was better to concentrate on criticizing the immorality of profit income altogether and agitate for an uprising to replace capitalism with a libertarian socialist economy when the next crisis arrived. But faith in false theories of capitalist crisis proved debilitating for two reasons. Most obviously, strategy premised on crises that do not occur is like waiting for Godot, and unlikely to prove effective. Secondly, people don't appreciate those who give them up for dead and fail to extend a helping hand. If my misery can be even slightly alleviated, I will judge those around me according to how hard and effectively they work to do so. The idea that bystanders are waiting for me to be further abused, even hoping I might be if this stimulates me to revolt, is hardly ingratiating.

I think libertarian socialists were also loath to dirty their hands in reform campaigns and participate in institutions like unions and legislatures because they considered them to be breeding grounds where anti-capitalists eventually betray the cause. In this regard they were not wrong. The anti-capitalist movement has long suffered from a steady hemorrhage of former members who are worn down and corrupted by the roles they play in various reform institutions and who eventually "sell out." But the question is how libertarian socialists should respond to this very real danger. Unfortunately they usually decided to avoid becoming corrupted by not participating in reform campaigns and organizations. Why risk being corrupted like social democratic union officials or elected politicians? Better to stay intellectually pure and committed to the libertarian socialist vision of a wholly new economy while waiting for capitalism to crumble. The main task of libertarian socialists then becomes to prevent authoritarian socialist groups from seizing and fortifying the state to fill the vacuum created by the collapse of capitalism and capitalist class rule. Many libertarian socialists convinced themselves that if the danger of usurpation by a self-appointed vanguard could be avoided, with minimal encouragement workers and citizens would quickly learn how to manage their own economic and political affairs free, at last, from authoritarian power of all kinds. But of course, none of this proved to be true.

The Myth of Non-Reformist Reforms: What many libertarian socialists failed to realize was that any transition to a democratic and equitable economy has no choice but to pass through reform campaigns, organizations, and institutions however tainted and corrupting they may be. The New Left tried to exorcise the dilemma that reform work is necessary but corrupting with the concept of non-reformist reforms. According to this theory social democrats erred in embracing reformist reforms while early libertarian socialists erred in rejecting reforms altogether. According to New Left theoreticians the solution was for activists to work on non-reformist reforms, i.e. reforms that improved people's lives while undermining the material, social, or ideological underpinnings of the capitalist system. There is nothing wrong with the notion of winning reforms while undermining capitalism. As a matter of fact, that is a concise description of precisely what we should be about! What was misleading was the notion that there are *particular* reforms that are like silver bullets and accomplish this because of something special about the nature of those reforms themselves.

There is no such thing as a non-reformist reform. Social democrats and libertarian socialists did not err because they somehow failed to find and campaign for this miraculous kind of reform. Nor would New Leftists prove successful where others had failed because New Leftists found a special kind of reform different from those social democrats pursued and libertarian socialists rejected. Some reforms improve peoples' lives more, and some less. Some reforms are easier to win, and some are harder to win. Some reforms are easier to defend, and some are less so. And of course, different reforms benefit different groups of people. Those are ways reforms, themselves, differ. On the other hand, there are also crucial differences in how reforms are fought for. Reforms can be fought for by reformers preaching the virtues of capitalism. Or reforms can be fought for by anti-capitalists pointing out that only by replacing capitalism will it be possible to fully achieve what reformers want. Reforms can be fought for while leaving institutions of repression intact. Or a reform struggle can at least weaken repressive institutions, if not destroy them. Reforms can be fought for by hierarchical organizations that reinforce authoritarian, racist, and sexist dynamics and thereby weaken the overall movement for progressive social change. Or reforms can be fought for by democratic organizations that uproot counterproductive patterns of behavior and empower people to become masters and mistresses of their fates. Reforms can be fought for in ways that leave no new organizations or institutions in their aftermath. Or reforms can be fought for in ways that create new organizations and institutions that fortify progressive forces in the next battle. Reforms can be fought for through alliances that obstruct possibilities for further gains. Or the alliances forged to win a reform can establish the basis for winning more reforms. Reforms can be fought for in ways that provide tempting possibilities for participants, and particularly leaders, to take unfair personal advantage of group success. Or they can be fought for in ways that minimize the likelihood of corrupting influences. Finally, reform organizing can be the entire program of organizations and movements. Or, recognizing that reform organizing within capitalism is prone to weaken the personal and political resolve of participants to pursue a full system of equitable cooperation, reform work can be combined with other kinds of activities, programs, and institutions that rejuvenate the battle weary and prevent burn out and sell out.

In sum, any reform can be fought for in ways that diminish the chances of further gains and limit progressive change in other areas, or fought for in ways that make further progress more likely and facilitate other progressive changes as well. But if reforms are successful they will make capitalism less harmful to some extent. There is no way around this, and even if there were such a thing as a non-reformist reform, it would not change this fact. However, the fact that every reform success makes capitalism less harmful does not mean successful reforms necessarily prolong the life of capitalism—although it might, and this is something anti-capitalists must simply learn to accept. But if winning a reform further empowers the reformers, and whets their appetite for more democracy, more economic justice, and more environmental protection than capitalism can provide, it can hasten the fall of capitalism.

In any case, it turns out we are a more cautious and social species than most 20th century libertarian socialists realized. And it turns out that capitalism is far more resilient than libertarian socialists expected. More than a half century of libertarian socialist failures belie the myth that it is possible for social revolutionaries committed to democracy to eschew reform work without becoming socially isolated. Avoidance of participation in reform work is simply not a viable option and only guarantees defeat for any who opt out. Moreover, no miraculous non-reformist reform is going to come riding to our rescue. Though most 20th century libertarian socialists failed to realize it, their only hope was to throw themselves wholeheartedly into reform struggles while searching for ways to minimize the corrupting pressures that inevitably are brought to bear on their members as a result. While admittedly a caricature, the image of libertarian socialists in the latter part of the last century shunning "tainted" reform organizations and campaigns to knock on working-class strangers' doors seeking to enlist them directly into "the anti-capitalist revolution" gives an idea of how I think they went wrong on this crucial issue.

The Myth of Spontaneous Revolt: After World War II some libertarian socialists lapsed into a naïve belief in spontaneous anti-capitalist revolts, and an unwarranted faith that once having risen, workers would quickly leap frog to smoothly functioning systems of equitable cooperation. If I am correct, this was very much at odds with their own historical experience earlier in the century where decades of successful agitating and organizing on a mass scale invariably proved necessary. Nonetheless, isolated libertarian socialists in mid-century sometimes convinced themselves that exemplary actions on their part could lead "the masses" to reject the cautionary advice of corrupt officials in reformist organizations, and spark a spontaneous worker uprising to replace capitalism with libertarian socialism. However, there is a world of difference between believing that capitalism is dysfunctional and that ordinary people can figure this out, and believing people will spontaneously decide they want to replace capitalism stimulated by agitation and "exemplary action" alone. There is also a world of difference between believing a majoritarian movement can overthrow capitalism, and believing such a movement will suddenly arise like a phoenix without the aid of a myriad of imperfect social institutions through which millions of people have struggled for decades to better their lives. And there is a world of difference between believing that workers and consumers can coordinate their economic endeavors equitably and efficiently, and believing participation in the economics of competition and greed under capitalism will prepare them to do so. Finally, it is one thing to think workers and consumers can engage in participatory planning and self-management, and quite another to believe they can do so without prior deliberation over appropriate procedures, and without a great deal of practical experience in economic self-governance. Libertarian socialists in the latter part of the 20th century all too often confused these differences.

Finally, libertarian socialists were misled by the myth that the grinding of the gears of capitalism would generate revolutionary consciousness in the working class. They underestimated the extent to which capitalism instead teaches people to accept the desirability and inevitability of the economics of competition and greed. Unfortunately capitalism does not nurture the seeds of its own replacement in the way 20th century libertarian socialists hoped it would. Instead capitalism fosters commercial values, teaches people they are incapable of behaving except out of greed or fear, and teaches that only market competition can harness human egotism to socially useful purposes. Capitalism teaches people to accommodate and make their peace with capitalism because it is inevitable. In the later part of the 20th century libertarian socialists ignored this feature of capitalism to their detriment. Unlike their predecessors early in the century, they underestimated the importance of creating practical examples of equitable cooperation no matter how imperfect and impermanent. They forgot it was necessary to create institutions for workers that served as "schools" to teach the habits of equitable cooperation, and failed to realize the longer capitalism endures the more important this task becomes. They did not understand that beside dispelling myths about capitalism's supposed virtues and criticizing its commercial values, they had to create opportunities for people to learn and practice efficient, democratic and cooperative behavior patterns in accord with human values, precisely because this kind of behavior and these values are not rewarded by market competition. As pre-capitalist cultures of cooperation like the Russian mir and Spanish common property irrigation systems receded in the collective memory, new cultures of cooperation swimming against the capitalist tide became more, not less important, to create and nurture.

What to Avoid

We need look no further than to the history of 20th century social democracy to see how fighting for reforms can make a movement reformist. Social democrats began the 20th century determined to replace capitalism with socialism—which they understood to be a system of equitable cooperation based on democratic planning by workers, consumers, and citizens. Long before the century was over social democratic parties and movements throughout the world had renounced the necessity of replacing private enterprise and markets with fundamentally different economic institutions, and pledged themselves only to pursue reforms geared toward making a system based on competition and greed, which they accepted as inevitable, more humane. As a result social democrats were doomed to grapple with two dilemmas: (1) What to do when leaving the system intact makes it impossible to further promote economic justice and democracy, much less environmental sustainability. (2) What to do when further reforms destabilize a system one has agreed to accept while the system constantly threatens to undermine hard-won gains. Social democrats struggled unsuccessfully with these dilemmas, all too often abandoning important components of economic justice and democracy and denouncing political tendencies to their Left whose programs they considered politically or economically destabilizing.

We need look no further than to the history of 20th century libertarian socialism to see how failing to embrace reform struggles can isolate a movement and make it irrelevant. The principle failure of libertarian socialists during the 20th century was their inability to understand the necessity and importance of reform organizing. When it turned out that anti-capitalist uprisings were few and far between, and libertarian socialists proved incapable of sustaining the few that did occur early in the 20th century, their reticence to throw themselves into reform campaigns, and ineptness when they did, doomed libertarian socialists to more than a half century of decline after their devastating defeat during the Spanish Civil War of 1936–39. What too many libertarian socialists failed to realize was that any transition to a democratic and equitable economy has no choice but to pass through reform campaigns, organizations, and institutions however tainted and corrupting they may be.

Combine Reform Work with Experiments in Equitable Cooperation

If the answer does not lie in finding a special kind of reform, how are we to prevent reform work from weakening our rejection of capitalism and sabotaging our efforts to eventually replace it with a system of equitable cooperation? Besides working for reforms in ways that lead to demands for further progress, and besides working in ways that strengthen progressive movements and progressive voices within movements, I believe the answer lies in combining reform work with building what I call imperfect experiments in equitable cooperation.[62]

Before we will be able to replace competition and greed with equitable cooperation, before we can replace private enterprise and markets with worker and consumer councils and participatory planning, we will have to devise intermediate means to prevent backsliding and regenerate forward momentum. For the foreseeable future most of this must be done by combining reform work with work to establish and expand imperfect experiments in equitable cooperation. Both kinds of work are necessary. Neither strategy is effective by itself.

Reforms alone cannot achieve equitable cooperation because as long as the institutions of private enterprise and markets are left in place to reinforce antisocial behavior based on greed and fear, progress toward equitable cooperation will be limited, and the danger of retrogression will be ever present. Moreover, reform campaigns undermine their leaders' commitment to full economic justice and democracy in a number of ways, and do little to demonstrate that equitable cooperation is possible, or establish new norms and expectations. On the other hand, concentrating exclusively on organizing alternative economic institutions within capitalist economies also cannot be successful. First and foremost, exclusive focus on building alternatives to capitalism is too isolating. Until the non-capitalist sector is large, the livelihoods of most people will depend on winning reforms in the capitalist sector, and therefore that is where most people will become engaged. But concentrating exclusively on experiments in equitable cooperation will also not work because the rules of capitalism put alternative institutions at a disadvantage compared to capitalist firms they must compete against, and because market forces drive non-capitalist institutions to abandon cooperative principles. Unlike liberated territories created by national liberation movements in third-world countries, in the advanced economies we will have to build our experiments in equitable cooperation inside our capitalist economies. So our experiments will always be fully exposed to competitive pressures and the culture of capitalism. Maintaining cooperative principles in alternative experiments under these conditions requires high levels of political commitment, which it is reasonable to expect from activists committed to building a "new world," but not reasonable to expect from everyone. Therefore, concentrating exclusively on reforms, or focusing only on building alternatives within capitalism are both roads that lead to dead ends. Only in combination will reform campaigns and imperfect experiments in equitable cooperation successfully challenge the economics of competition and greed in the decades ahead.

Since both reform work and building alternatives within capitalism are necessary, neither is inherently more crucial nor strategic than the other. Campaigns to
reform capitalism and building alternative institutions within capitalism are both integral parts of a successful strategy to accomplish in this century what we failed to
accomplish in the past century—namely, making this century capitalism's last! Unfortunately, saying we need stronger reform movements and stronger experiments in
equitable cooperation does not do justice to the magnitude of the tasks. Particularly
in the United States, we are going to need a lot more of both before we even reach a
point where a professional odds maker would even bother to give odds on our chances
of success. While capitalism spins effective enabling myths to spell bind its victims,
the Left has too often spun consoling myths about mysterious forces that cause capitalist crises that will come to our rescue even if our organizational and political power
remains pathetically weak. There is no substitute for strong organizations and political
power, and there are no easy ways to build either. Over the next two decades most of
the heavy lifting will have to be done inside various progressive reform movements
because that is where the victims of capitalism will be found, and that's where they
have every right to expect us to be working our butts off to make capitalism less destructive. But even now it is crucial to build living experiments in equitable cooperation to prove to ourselves as well as to others that equitable cooperation is possible.
Expanding and integrating experiments in equitable cooperation to offer opportunities to more and more people whose experiences in reform movements convince them
they want to live by cooperative not competitive principles will become ever more
important as time goes on.

Reform Campaigns and Reform Movements

Unless anti-capitalists throw themselves heart and soul into reform movements we will
continue to be marginalized. At least for the foreseeable future most victims of capitalism will seek redress through various reform campaigns fighting to ameliorate the
damage capitalism causes, and these victims have every right to consider us AWOL
if we do not work to make reform campaigns as successful as possible. Moreover, we
must work enthusiastically in reform movements knowing full well that we will usually not rise to leadership positions in these movements because our beliefs will not
be supported by a majority of those who are attracted to these movements for many
years to come. Working in reform campaigns and reform movements means working
with others who still accept capitalism. Most who are initially attracted to reform
campaigns will be neither anti-capitalist nor advocates of replacing capitalism with
a wholly new system of equitable cooperation. And most of the leadership of reform
campaigns and movements will be even more likely to defend capitalism as a system,
and argue that correcting a particular abuse is all that is required. But we must never
allow others to decide how we work in reform movements, or permit others to dictate
our politics. We *do* know something most others at this point do not—that capitalism
must eventually be replaced altogether with a system of equitable cooperation.

Taming Finance: Because the financial sector is particularly dysfunctional due to so-called neoliberal "reforms" pushed through over the past two decades by the financial sector and sympathetic politicians in both the Republican and Democratic parties—with an assist from mainstream economists—there is a very large margin for improvement in the performance of both the domestic and international financial sectors. Anti-reforms like the repeal of the Glass-Steagall regulatory system in the U.S. in 1999 and various measures that go under the label of "international capital liberalization" orchestrated by the U.S. Department of Treasury and the IMF, have eliminated minimal protections and safeguards imposed by legislation and international practices dating back to the New Deal and the Bretton Woods Conference. Not since the roaring twenties have national economies and the global economy been as subject to the destructive effects of financial bubbles and crashes as we are today. Consequently, there is a great deal that can be accomplished to improve the lives of capitalism's victims through financial reform, both domestic and international. Moreover, many of these reforms are not a radical departure from past policies.

While reforms that should be relatively easy to sell can make substantial improvements, unfortunately campaigns for financial reform are particularly difficult for popular progressive forces to work in effectively. Unlike "peace, not war," financial reform is more technically complicated, and therefore harder to educate and mobilize ordinary citizens around. Unlike campaigns against polluters that can often be fought locally, to a great extent financial reform must proceed at the national and international levels through organizations and coalitions that are many steps removed from local constituencies and invariably led by people who are no friends of the economics of equitable cooperation. These are important liabilities to bear in mind for groups deciding whether or not to prioritize this kind of reform work. There are some exceptions. Anti-red lining and community reinvestment campaigns can be fought at the local level. The Financial Markets Center even has a campaign to increase the influence of ordinary citizens over monetary policy by exploiting provisions in the enabling act that created the Federal Reserve Bank for representation of community groups on local boards of the Federal Reserve Bank. But unfortunately, taming domestic and international finance is largely an activity that will appear esoteric and distant to most citizen activists, as much as it affords attractive opportunities to point out how badly the capitalist financial sector miss serves the ordinary public.

Full Employment Macro Policies: There is no reason aggregate demand cannot be managed through fiscal and monetary policies to keep actual production close to potential GDP and cyclical unemployment to a minimum. Moreover, forcing governments to engage in effective stabilization policies not only makes the economy more efficient, but strengthens the broad movement struggling for equitable cooperation in other ways as well.

Wage increases and improvements in working conditions are easier to win in a full employment economy. Affirmative action programs designed to redress racial and gender discrimination are easier to win when the economic pie is growing rather than stagnant or shrinking. Union organizing drives are more likely to be successful when labor markets are tight than when unemployment rates are high. The reason employers obstruct efforts to pursue full employment macro policies—it diminishes their bargaining power—is precisely the reason those fighting for equitable cooperation should campaign for it. For all these reasons it is crucial to win reforms that move us even closer to "full employment capitalism" than the Scandinavians achieved during the 1960s and 1970s. But it is important not to overestimate what this will accomplish. Even if everyone had a job, they would not have a job they could support a family on, much less one that paid them fairly for their sacrifices. Low-wage jobs flipping burgers at MacDonald's are a poor substitute for better-paid jobs producing farm machinery. Even if everyone had a job, they would not have personally rewarding, socially useful work since most jobs in capitalism are more personally distasteful than necessary, and much work in capitalism is socially useless. Jobs in telemarketing or temp services without benefits are poor substitutes for jobs with benefits teaching reasonably sized classes or cleaning up polluted rivers. A full employment economy through military Keynesianism and tax cuts for the wealthy is hardly the kind of full employment program progressives should support.

So when we fight for full employment stabilization policies we should never forget to point out that what every citizen deserves is a socially useful job with fair compensation. We should never tire of pointing out that while capitalism is incapable of delivering on this, it is just as possible as it is sensible. We must also work to expand opportunities for socially useful, self-managed work for which people are compensated fairly by increasing the number of jobs in worker owned and managed cooperatives so more and more people have an alternative to working for capitalists.

Tax Reform: Progressive taxes, i.e. taxes that require those with higher income or wealth to pay a higher percentage of their income or wealth in taxes, can reduce income and wealth inequality. There are a number of organizations with tax reform proposals that would replace regressive taxes with more progressive ones and make progressive taxes even more progressive. Citizens for Tax Justice (www.ctj.org) and United for a Fair Economy (www.ufenet.org) not only provide useful critiques of right wing tax initiatives, but present excellent progressive alternatives for tax reform as well. Unfortunately, we have been "progressing" rapidly in reverse in the United States over the past twenty-five years as the wealthy have used their growing influence with politicians they fund to shift the tax burden off themselves, where it belongs, onto the less fortunate, where it does not.

Besides making the tax system more progressive, we need to tax bad behavior not good behavior. Efficiency requires taxing pollution emissions an amount equal to the damage suffered by the victims of the pollution. Moreover, if governments did this they would raise a great deal of revenue. But even if the tax is collected from the firms who pollute, the cost of the tax will be distributed between the firms who pollute and the consumers of the products they produce. Studies of pollution tax incidence—who ultimately bears what part of a tax on pollution—have concluded that lower income people would bear a great deal of the burden of many pollution, or "green taxes." In other words, many pollution taxes would be highly regressive and therefore aggravate economic injustice. On the other hand, the federal, state, and local governments in the U.S. already collect many taxes that are even more regressive than pollution taxes would be. In 1998 highly regressive social security taxes were the second greatest source of U.S. federal tax revenues, responsible for more than a third of all federal revenues. If every dollar collected in new federal pollution taxes were paired with a dollar reduction in social security taxes we would substitute taxes on "bad behavior"—pollution—for taxes on "good behavior"—productive work—and make the federal tax system more progressive as well. At the state and local level there are even more regressive taxes to choose from that could be replaced with state and local green taxes making state and local taxes less regressive than the are currently. Redefining Progress (www. redefiningprogress.org) is one organization promoting sensible proposals for combining green taxes with reductions in more regressive taxes to achieve "accurate prices" that reflect environmental costs while making the tax system more, not less fair.

Living Wages: Contrary to popular opinion, raising the minimum wage not only promotes economic justice but makes the economy more efficient in the long run as well. In other words, it is good economics in every sense. Similarly, living wage campaigns in a number of American cities have been important initiatives to make U.S. capitalism more equitable and efficient over the past ten years. Particularly where unions are weak and represent a small fraction of the labor force, minimum and living wage programs are important programs to steer capitalism toward the high road to growth.

As of June 2004 the number of cities that had passed living wage ordinances had risen to 121 and included New York, Los Angeles, Chicago, Boston, Baltimore, Detroit, Denver, Minneapolis, St. Paul, Buffalo, Pittsburg, Cleveland, St. Louis, and Miami. The Living Wage Resource Center posts up-to-date information on the status of living wage campaigns on their website: www.livingwagecampaign.org. United Students Against Sweatshops has made available on their website, www.usasnet.org, data on a number of campus living wage campaigns in which they were involved, including campaigns at the University of California at San Diego, Valdosta State University in Georgia, Stanford University, Swarthmore College, and the University of Tennessee at Knoxville. As union power has diminished in the United States, living wage campaigns have become increasingly important ways for progressive communities to protect their working members against declining living standards.

Single-Payer Health Care: The U.S. health care system is in shambles. From both a medical and financial perspective it has been a mushrooming disaster for well over two decades. In all reform campaigns there is always tension between those who want to hold out for more far reaching, significant changes and those who preach the practical necessity of a more incrementalist approach. Usually the debate reduces to how much better a far reaching solution is compared to how much more likely incremental changes are to be won. The struggle for health care reform in the United States over the past two decades is a rare case where the incremental approach is actually less practical than fighting for significant reform because there is simply no way to extend adequate coverage to all and control escalating costs through the private insurance industry. Other than expanding Medicare coverage—for example, to cover those between fifty-five and sixty-four-years old—there is no way to even begin to set things right until we have universal coverage and single payer health insurance in place. At the national level HR676, the Expanded and Improved Medicare for All Bill, introduced by Congressman John Conyers Jr. in 2003, is clearly the reform worth working for.

Only a single-payer, government insurance program can provide universal coverage while containing costs by eliminated the considerable administrative expenses of private insurance "cherry picking." Only a single-payer program can eliminate the paper work and confusion associated with administering multiple insurance plans—all of which are worse deals than provided through single-payer systems in every other industrialized country in the world. A single-payer system is best suited to use monopsony power to control drug prices and hospital fees. And only a system separated from the workplace and employers' choices about providing insurance can end the strife caused when some companies in an industry who do provide healthcare benefits to their employees must compete against other companies who do not. The fact is that providing health care through employer benefit plans, private insurance, and managed care organizations for profit is so inefficient that incremental reforms that leave those institutions in control of the health care system simply cannot succeed. Instead, there is a much better deal for health care recipients, health care professionals, taxpayers, and the business community as a whole—single-payer, government insurance.

While there is a great deal to discuss about how best to run a health care system so it is effective, fair, responsive and efficient, there is no way a system in the hands of insurers and managed care organizations trying to maximize profits in a market environment is going to deliver anything other than the mess we have—43 million uninsured Americans and counting, along with spiraling costs bankrupting families and businesses alike. In this reform struggle settling for anything less than universal, single-payer coverage is not only immoral, it is impractical as well. Once coverage is complete and a single-payer is controlling costs, progressives can move on to what we do best—make suggestions about how to make health care services more user friendly and equitable through regulation of private providers and democratization of public providers—until a fully public, patient-friendly, well-care system is finally achieved.

Community Development Initiatives: When employers, banks and developers withdraw from areas they consider less profitable than other alternatives, abandoned communities are left without jobs, adequate housing, or a tax base sufficient to provide basic social services. According to the logic of capitalism, when this occurs people should not waste time whining about their fates, but get with the program and move to where the action is. Capitalism tells people they should abandon the neighborhoods they grew up in before they are blighted and move to the suburbs. Capitalism tells people to leave their family and community roots in the rust belt and migrate to the sun belt. According to the logic of capitalism any who fail to move in time are losers and deserve what they get. Community development initiatives are testimony to peoples' unwillingness or inability to follow capitalism's advice.

Many poverty stricken areas in the United States still have community economic development projects. Many others have had community development programs cut back or abandoned. Community development corporations (CDCs), community development banks (CDBs), and community land trusts (CLTs) can all be useful parts of reform efforts to revitalize blighted urban neighborhoods and combat urban unemployment, and should be revived and expanded. These projects also afford excellent opportunities for collaboration between economic reformers and organizations fighting against racism and for minority control over their own communities. Whenever the private economy fails to provide some useful good or service we should demand that the government step in to rectify matters. So when the financial sector fails to provide credit on reasonable terms for rebuilding poor neighborhoods in our cities, we should call for both regulation and intervention. We should insist that the government prevent redlining and require adequate reinvestment of savings from poor communities back into those communities by private banks. But we should also call on the government to create public, or semi-public, financial institutions whose mandate is to finance renovation of deteriorated housing stock in city ghettos and help local businesses provide employment opportunities. Particularly when the boards of community development corporations and banks are dominated by strong community organizations, they are a better way to tackle market failures that create urban ghettos than free enterprise zones which buy little development at the cost of large tax breaks for businesses while weakening existing community organizations.

Community development projects reject the Faustian choice between economic abandonment and gentrification by trying instead to catalyze redevelopment that benefits current residents. Community development projects do this either by changing incentives to re-attract capitalist activity or by substituting non-capitalist means of employment and housing for the capitalist activity that departed. Community development initiatives that emphasize the latter course are important areas where people are busy meeting needs capitalism leaves unfulfilled. Community land trusts (CLTs) can play an important role in breaking several destructive aspects of capitalist housing markets. Over a hundred CLTs have been formed in communities in the U.S. in response to disinvestment and gentrification. The CLT acquires land for community use and takes it permanently off the market. A CLT may rehab existing buildings, build new houses or apartment buildings, or use the land in any other way the community wishes. Residents may own the buildings, but the CLT retains ownership of the land.

More institutional space exists in existing community development projects than progressives presently make good use of. When working in these projects progressives need to reaffirm the right of people to remain in historical communities of their choice, irrespective of the logic of profitability. We need to point out the inefficiency and waste inherent in abandoning perfectly good economic and social infrastructure in existing communities to build socially costly and environmentally damaging new infrastructure in new communities elsewhere. We need to point out the socially destructive effects of speculative real estate bubbles. We need to press for strategies based on non-capitalist employment and housing since this provides more worker, resident, and community security and control than relying on newly courted private capital. And where non-capitalist institutions are not possible or insufficient, progressives should work to maximize community control over employers and developers who benefit from incentives offered by community development initiatives.

Anti-sprawl Initiatives: The flip side of capitalist abandonment of poor, inner city neighborhoods, is environmentally destructive growth, or "sprawl" in outlying areas. But while it is more profitable for developers to spread new homes for upper and middle class families indiscriminately over farm land, this is not what is best for either people or the environment. It is an environmental disaster because it needlessly replaces more green space with concrete and asphalt than necessary. It is a fiscal disaster because for every new dollar in local taxes collected from new residents, because they are spread over a large area lacking in existing services, it costs local governments roughly a dollar and a half to provide new residents with the streets, schools, libraries, and utilities they are entitled to. And it has a disastrous effect on people's life styles as the "rural character of life" in outlying areas is destroyed for older residents, and those moving into bedroom communities spend more and more of their time on gridlocked roads commuting to work and driving to schools and strip malls at considerable distance from their homes. Nor does sprawl even address the nation's most pressing housing need—a scandalous shortfall of "affordable" housing.

Instead what is called for is "in growth" and "smart growth." New housing should be built in old, abandoned neighborhoods whose infrastructures are renovated, and concentrated in new areas that are environmentally less sensitive. Instead of construction patterns dictated by market forces and developers' bottom lines, what is called for is development planning through appropriate changes in zoning, combined with impact fees that distribute costs equitably. Instead of allowing developers to only build the kind of housing they find most profitable, they must be required to build a certain percentage of low-cost units in exchange for permits to build high-cost units. Instead of abandoning farms and green space to the ravishes of market forces, what is needed are preservation trusts, easements, and transfer development rights programs to preserve green space without doing it at farmers' expense.

The battle to replace sprawl with smart growth is a battle to replace the disastrous effects of market forces on local communities with democratic planning by the residents of those communities themselves. It requires democratic determination of community priorities. It requires challenging conservative defenses of individual property rights no matter how damaging to community interests. It requires clever strategies to win farmer approval for down zoning agricultural land so it cannot be developed, by giving farmers transfer development rights and requiring developers to purchase them in order to build in areas designated for concentrated development. It requires withholding construction permits for high income housing unless accompanied by a sufficient number of affordable units. It requires building coalitions of environmentalists, longtime residents, farmers, and those in need of affordable housing with a package of policies that serve their needs and shields them from shouldering a disproportionate share of the costs of in growth and smart growth, and politically isolating and defeating developers, banks, and wealthy newcomers who favor gentrification and sprawl because it serves their interests. It requires running in growth and smart growth candidates for local offices who spurn contributions from developers for their election campaigns, and who laugh at developer bluffs to boycott localities who insist on protecting community interests.

Of course the slogan "smart growth" can be misappropriated by clever developers, just as "sustainable development" has been misappropriated by clever corporations seeking to disguise their environmentally destructive growth objectives. What matters are the policies, not the labels put on them for salesmanship. And what matters are whose interests are served by those policies, and which groups and organizations dominate a coalition for smart growth. But anti-sprawl campaigns, campaigns for slow growth, in growth, and smart growth, and campaigns to protect disappearing "green space" that are already going on in every major metropolitan area and its surrounding communities afford progressives important organizing opportunities.

The Labor Movement: There is no substitute for a strong labor movement. Elaine Bernard, Executive Director of the Harvard Trade Union Program, argues it is essential to move beyond "bread and butter" unionism: "It is becoming increasingly clear in today's political environment that unions need to do both. Unions, like any organization, will not survive if they do not serve the needs of their members. But unions will not survive and grow, if they only serve the needs of their members. The experience of organized labor in the U.S. demonstrates that simply delivering for their own members is not sufficient in the long run." Jobs with Justice (www.jwj.org) is one organization that learned this lesson well. Founded in 1987, Jobs with Justice had organized coalition chapters in over forty cities by 2003 with impressive records of active support for a variety of labor causes. According to its mission statement, Jobs with Justice exists "to improve working people's standard of living, fight for job security, and protect workers' right to organize. A core belief of Jobs with Justice is that in order to be successful, workers' rights struggles have to be part of a larger campaign for economic and social justice. To that end, Jobs with Justice has created a network of local coalitions that connect labor, faith-based, community, and student organizations to work together on workplace and community social justice campaigns." For those who are not fortunate enough to be represented by a union where they work, Jobs with Justice is an organization open to individual as well as organizational membership providing excellent opportunities for people seeking to build the labor movement.

Unions must return to their mission of being the hammer for economic justice in capitalism. There is no good reason unions can't do a better job of educating their membership about economic justice. What union today teaches its members that nobody deserves to be paid more than them, unless someone works harder and makes greater personal sacrifices than they do? What union teaches its members that as long as wages are determined by the law of supply and demand in the market place, unions can only slightly and temporarily reduce the degree of economic injustice? Yet every union can teach these lessons, and grow larger and stronger by doing so.

All too often unions are even less democratic than mainstream politics. This is a disgrace for a movement that purports to stand for greater political and economic democracy. Prosecuting attorneys appointed by politicians in the pockets of corporations cannot be trusted to police unions against fraud and corruption. That is one reason progressives must lead reform movements of members to clean up their own unions and tell the government attorneys and judges to butt out. But that is only the beginning of what is necessary to make unions democratic. Electoral systems that stack the deck even more in favor of incumbent union officials than the deck is stacked in favor of incumbent U.S. Congress people are an outrage. Yet this is what those who we expect to effectively promote industrial democracy have come up with for themselves. As in the case of economic justice, unions must practice what they preach about democracy.

Until unions increase the percentage of the labor force they represent in the United States, what unions can hope to accomplish will remain severely restricted. Progressives working in unions must obviously press for a dramatic reallocation of union resources and energy toward organizing new workers. Union power will not increase until unions reallocate resources from legislative and political affairs, and from support for contract negotiation, to organizing the unorganized. These are difficult choices for unions. For the most part lobbying legislatures, get out the vote campaigns for lesser evil candidates, and support for contract negotiation does serve workers' interests. But union dollars spent on these activities are, on average, far less productive than union dollars spent on organizing drives. In this area the AFL-CIO Organizing Institute has turned over more than one new leaf since the late 1990s, and is busy providing valuable practical training for a new generation of union organizers. For young people aspiring to become labor activists, right now the Organizing Institute (www.aflcio.org/aboutunions/oi) is an excellent place to start. Among the national unions, the Service Employees International Union (SEIU) is setting the best example in organizing drives, and has recently challenged the AFL-CIO to make organizing Wal-Mart the number one priority of the union movement.

There are two traditional models for Leftists going to work in the labor movement—join the union establishment, or remain a rank-and-file activist. In the first case a person convinces herself that more can be accomplished by working within the union than against it. She runs for local union office, and tries to proceed up the union ladder in order to promote policies she regards as more effective more widely. The danger with this strategy lies in succumbing to pressure to tow the union line even when it is wrong, i.e. becoming a union bureaucrat. In the case where a labor activist steadfastly remains a rank-and-file worker in the factory, she avoids the corrupting temptations associated with union office and retains her independence to criticize union policy and union officials as well as capitalist employers. But in the 20th century most who pursued this model found it necessary to join a revolutionary sect which provided the psychological and social support necessary to sustain a life of Left activism fighting against capitalist exploiters and sell-out union officials alike—all on behalf of fellow rank-and-file workers who were often less than appreciative. One danger in this approach lies in ceding power over issues essential to the labor movement to less principled and talented competitors who covet positions in the union hierarchy. The other danger is becoming isolated from one's fellow workers who do not share one's passion for discussing articles from the latest issue of a revolutionary newspaper.

There are unavoidable dilemmas associated with working either inside or outside any reformist organization, and deciding whether to accept or reject a compromise deal any reformist organization negotiates. Whether to work inside or outside unions, and whether to support or reject contracts, are not exceptions to the rule but merely cases in point. Unfortunately, the traditional models for Leftist work in the labor movement exaggerate these dilemmas unnecessarily. Labor activists can begin to enjoy the fruits of living the economics of equitable cooperation even while capitalism denies people that opportunity in general by joining experiments in equitable cooperation. If activists who believe they can be more effective working as union officials commit to equitable living communities they will be less susceptible to the lure of perks from union office, less fearful of losing office and returning to the shop floor, and therefore more inclined to buck the union line when it is called for. Moreover, their primary peer group—others living in their equitable living communities—will consist of people who respect and honor others because of their principled behavior rather than their wealth and power.

The Anticorporate Movement: The best thing about Ralph Nader's campaign for president in 2000 was that he never tired of talking about the biggest problem in the world today: unchecked corporate power run amok. Nader is a master at explaining how corporations deceive consumers and manipulate the political system. The best thing about the movement for corporate responsibility is that its campaigns publicize particularly egregious cases of corporate abuse, and provide people who become outraged something concrete to do about it. Corporate power and ideological hegemony has never been greater in the United States than it is today—even surpassing the power of the great "trusts" during the era of the "Robber Barons" over a century ago. Moreover, multinational corporations in general, and U.S. corporations in particular, have never held greater sway over the global economy than they do today. Exposing corporate abuse and fighting corporate power describes a great deal of what those fighting to replace competition and greed with equitable cooperation must do for the foreseeable future. Whereas the labor movement and unions fight corporate power primarily as it adversely affects employees, and the consumer movement seeks to protect consumers from corporate abuse, the anticorporate movement opposes corporate abuse principally from the perspective of citizens. We need to build all three movements to bring corporate power to bay.

The Consumer Movement: There are a host of organizations in the United States today that seek to protect consumer interests and force government agencies like the Food and Drug Administration to protect consumers from corporate abuses. Three of the most important are the Consumer Federation of America (CFA), the network of Public Interest Research Groups (PIRGs), and Center for the New American Dream (CNAD). Of course CFA, PIRGs, and CNAD do not run their campaigns to highlight anti-capitalist lessons. Nor do they tell consumers the only way they can really exert control over what they consume is to have consumer councils and federations who run their own R&D operations and play a powerful role in a participatory planning process. But when anti-capitalist activists committed to a full system of equitable cooperation work in the consumer movement we can draw those lessons. The dilemmas anti-capitalist activists face when working inside or outside reform organizations in the consumer movement are the same as those faced by activists working inside or outside reform organizations in the labor movement, and the anticorporate movement, and the best ways to deal with those dilemmas are similar as well.

The Poor People's Movement: Unfortunately, by the end of the 20th century all of the progressive economic reform movements discussed above had become, to some degree, middle class movements. I say this not to condemn them, but because I believe this is an important "fact" activists need to recognize in order to deal with the problems it implies. Which is why a movement representing the interests of poor Americans is an absolute necessity, and should receive the highest priority from activists committed to economic justice. Moreover, it is critical to take whatever measures are necessary to guarantee that the leadership of this movement reflects its base.

In the late 1960s and early 1970s the National Welfare Rights Organization, NWRO, was the prototype organization in a poor people's movement. But since so-called "welfare reform" replaced federal welfare programs (Aid to Families with Dependent Children, AFDC) with underfunded state workfare programs (Temporary Assistance to Needy Families, TANF) in 1996, local grassroots organizations like

Community Voices Heard (New York City), the Contact Center (Cincinnati), Oregon Action, the Kensington Welfare Rights Union (KWRU, Philadelphia), and the Georgia Citizens Hunger Coalition have taken center stage in efforts to fight against cutbacks. The demise of NWRO and the fragmentation of the welfare rights movement after 1996 has left the Association of Community Organizations for Reform Now, better known as ACORN, as the largest organization in what is a very beleaguered poor people's movement today.

Social justice activists need to prioritize work in national organizations like ACORN as well as local organizations like those above over the next decades to rebuild and expand the poor people's movement. We need to support their campaigns because presently they are the most effective ways to improve the situation for America's most desperate families. We need to support their claim that all who work should be paid not only a living wage with benefits, but a wage commensurate with the sacrifices they make, and that childcare is socially valuable work that deserves compensation like any other. We especially need to support efforts to develop and retain indigenous leadership in poor people's organizations and integrate activists into communities supporting equitable lifestyles. Instead of complaining that other progressive economic movements are "too white" and "too middle class," we need to work to build the poor people's movement into the most dynamic progressive economic movement of all, and make sure that other progressive economic movements support the campaigns of the poor people's movement more fully and consistently than they do at present.

The Movement for Global Justice: It is more important to build what is popularly known as the anti-globalization movement correctly than to have the "correct" analysis or the "correct" set of demands. Organizing opposition to corporate sponsored globalization "from the bottom up" is the right approach. Organizing all constituencies negatively affected to fight for their own interests while they learn why their own success necessarily hinges on the successes of other constituencies against whom global corporations will constantly pit them is the right approach. Working closely with third world organizations in the campaign against the global "race to the bottom" is the right approach. Adopting the "Lilliput strategy," where each constituency struggles to tie its own string to contain the "Gulliver" of global capital knowing (correctly) how weak and vulnerable its own string is without the added strength of tens of thousands of other strings, is the right approach.

At this point it is also critical for the radical wing of the anti-globalization movement not to become isolated from the reform wing. What frightened corporate globalizers most about the demonstration against the World Trade Organization in Seattle in 1999 was not its size but its composition. There were fewer than 50,000 participants in the permitted rallies, and no more than 10,000 activists who engaged in civil disobedience. I have been to dozens of larger demonstrations over the past thirty years that had far less impact. But the specter of people from mainstream environmental organizations dressed as sea turtles marching together with middle-aged white men from the United Steelworkers, Teamsters, and Longshoremen's unions, as well as with elected officials from small cities and towns—all joining in the chants and songs led by amazing groups of lesbian and anarchist cheerleaders—was a scary sight to the pro-globalization establishment. But only if the constituencies of mainstream labor, environmental, and civic organizations remain active in the movement, and only if the radical message that a better world is possible continues to infect them can the anti-globalization movement grow enough in size and depth to finally force policy change as well as influence the tenor of public debate. This requires tolerance and patience. This requires respecting others who do not agree with everything we stand for. This requires remembering that we all need each other. Without the organizational skills, dedication, creativity, and courage of radical anti-globalization activists, reformist organizations would not have been nearly as successful as they have been in slowing the globalization juggernaut. Without large numbers of participants at demonstrations, and support from reformist organizations the radical wing of the anti-globalization movement will become isolated and vulnerable to ever-more-violent repression. In the aftermath of anti-globalization demonstrations in Quebec, Cancun, Windsor, Miami, and Savannah, the danger is that the reform and radical wings of the movement are drifting toward a counterproductive division of labor, where the radical wing only demonstrates and the reformist wing only lobbies. We need to remember that is just how the neoliberal globalizers like to see us, not the specter that frightened them in Seattle nine years ago.

How to Work for Reforms

In an era of increasing corporate power, much of our energies must be devoted to reform campaigns. But we must make clear that the reason we work in reform campaigns is that we believe everyone should control their own economic destiny, and everyone should receive economic benefits commensurate with their effort and sacrifice. It is also important for activists working in reform campaigns to make clear that victories can only be partial and temporary as long as economic power is unequally dispersed and economic decisions are based on private gain and market competition. Otherwise, reform efforts give way to disillusionment, and weaken, rather than strengthen the movement for progressive economic change when victories prove partial and erode over time. Not only must activists working for reforms explain why those reforms will be temporary as long as capitalism survives, they must also take time in their reform work to explain concretely how victories can be fuller and more permanent if capitalism is replaced by a system designed to promote equitable economic cooperation in the first place.

Working in reform movements does not mean we must abandon, or play down our politics. When we work in the labor movement we must teach not only that profit income is unfair, but that the salaries of highly paid professionals are unfair as well when they are paid many times more than ordinary workers while making fewer personal sacrifices. And we must be clear that workers in less developed countries deserve incomes commensurate with their efforts, just as workers in the United States do. In other words, when we work in the labor movement we must insist that the labor movement live up to its billing and become the hammer for justice in capitalism. When we work in the anticorporate movement we must never tire of emphasizing that corporations and their unprecedented power are the major problem in the world today. We must make clear that every concession corporations make is because it is rung out of them by activists who convince them that the anticorporate movement will inflict greater losses on their bottom line if they persist in their antisocial and environmentally destructive behavior than if they accede to our demands. When we promote programs like pollution taxes that modify incentives for private corporations in the market system, we must also make clear that production for profit and market forces are the worst enemies of the environment, and that the environment will never be adequately protected until those economic institutions are replaced. Even while we work to protect consumers from price gouging and defective products we must make clear how the market system inefficiently promotes excessive individual consumption at the expense of social consumption and leisure. And finally, even while antiglobalization activists work to stop the spread of corporate-sponsored, neoliberal globalization, we must explain how a different kind of globalization from below can improve people's lives rather than destroy their livelihoods.

Until these economic reform movements have attracted more supporters, until all these reform movements have become more politically powerful, until all these reform movements are more clear about what they are fighting for and how to go about it, the goal of replacing capitalism with a system of equitable cooperation will remain far beyond our reach. But while nothing can be accomplished unless these reform movements have been greatly strengthened, and activists must therefore prioritize this task, it is not the only work that needs to be tackled. Strong economic reform movements are necessary—and in the United States not one of the above movements is nearly strong enough at present. But strong economic reform movements are not enough. Twenty-first century activists must also nurture, build, and begin to connect a variety of creative living experiments in equitable cooperation within capitalism if we want to avoid the fate of our 20th century social democratic predecessors.

Build Experiments in Equitable Cooperation

The culture of capitalism is firmly rooted among citizens of the advanced economies. Most employees, not just employers, believe that hierarchy and competition are necessary for the economy to run effectively, and that those who contribute more should receive more irrespective of sacrifice. And why should people not believe this? Even if you feel you haven't gotten a fair shake, or that people born with a silver spoon in their mouth don't deserve what they get, few are likely to reject a major linchpin of capitalist culture all on their own. We should not fool ourselves that capitalism teaches people about its failings, or shows them how to live non-capitalistically—quite the opposite. The only sense in which capitalism serves as midwife for its heir is by forcing people to learn to think and live non-capitalistically in order to meet needs it leaves unfulfilled. It falls to progressives to learn and teach others how to do this. And there can be no mistake about it, this is a monumental task. But where can the culture of equitable cooperation grow in modern capitalism? A variety of existing experiments in equitable cooperation need to be strengthened, new kinds of experiments must be created, and ways to link experiments together must be found—to offer an increasingly attractive alterative to capitalism. Failure to find ways within advanced capitalist economies to build and sustain non-capitalist networks capable of accommodating the growing numbers who will be drawn to the economics of equitable cooperation can prove just as damaging to our cause as failure to wage successful economic reform campaigns and build mass economic reform movements.

Local Currency Systems: Activists working in local currency systems like Ithaca Hours and Time Dollars make valid criticisms of the capitalist monetary system and financial markets. They are correct to point out that local regions often remain in recession even when the national economy picks up, and that national and global financial markets often siphon savings out of poor communities to invest it elsewhere where it is less needed. Advocates for local currencies are also right when they sense that we can arrange a division of labor among ourselves that is more fair than the one capitalism arranges for us. On the other hand, local currency activists sometimes espouse crackpot theories about money, and become overly enthusiastic about what their local currency system can, and cannot accomplish. While local currencies can bring modest improvements, other reforms are frequently more effective. And while the spirit of anti-capitalist independence generated by local currency activists can be empowering, the focus on a new kind of money and market exchange as the antidote to capitalism is unfortunate. Local currency systems are useful to the extent that they reduce local unemployment, reward people for their labor more fairly than capitalist labor markets, and help people understand that they can—and should—manage their own division of labor equitably. Local currency systems are counterproductive when participants deceive themselves about how much can be accomplished and see nothing wrong with allowing the laws of supply and demand to determine the terms of their labor exchanges.

Producer Cooperatives: Roughly 10 million Americans are worker-owners in more than 10,000 employee-owned companies with assets of over $400 billion. The National Cooperative Business Association (www.ncba.coop) has served as a trade association for producer cooperatives in all sectors of the American economy since 1916. However, NCBA does not promote worker ownership as an alternative to capitalism. Grassroots Economic Organizing (GEO), founded in 1988, actively promotes worker-ownership as an alternative to capitalism and has a radical perspective, as its mission statement makes clear: "GEO's mission is to build a nation, and worldwide movement for a cooperative, social economy based on democratic and responsible production, conscientious consumption, and use of capital to further social and economic justice."

Activists who work tirelessly to promote the growth of worker-ownership in capitalism should not expect their efforts to succeed in replacing capitalism incrementally. The vision of reversing who hires whom—instead of capital hiring labor, labor hires capital—by slowly expanding the employee-owned sector of modern capitalist economies is a utopian pipe dream. The deck is stacked against worker-owned firms, making it very difficult for them to survive, particularly in modern capitalist economies dominated by large multinational firms. And when forced to compete against capitalist firms in a market environment, even the most idealistic worker-owners find it difficult to retain their commitment to decision making according to human values. In short, incrementally increasing the number of worker-owned firms is not a feasible transition strategy from the economics of competition and greed to the economics of equitable cooperation.

However, this is not to say that creating employee-owned firms cannot be an important part of a feasible transition strategy. If we are to succeed in the century ahead, building, expanding, and improving imperfect experiments in equitable cooperation within capitalism must occur at the same time that capitalism is being rendered less harmful through various reform campaigns. Worker-owned firms are one kind of partial experiment in equitable cooperation. They afford workers important opportunities to participate in economic decision making unavailable to them in capitalist firms. They train workers to make decisions collectively, together with their co-workers. When they compete successfully against capitalist firms, worker-owned firms challenge the myth that workers cannot govern themselves effectively, and therefore require bosses to decide what they should do and compel them to do it. So the more worker-owned firms there are, and the more successful they are, the stronger the movement for equitable cooperation will become. But until worker-owned firms establish truly equitable systems of compensation, until producer cooperatives coordinate their activities democratically and equitably with other producer and consumer cooperatives, until worker-owned firms plan production priorities together with organizations representing consumers, until worker-owned firms embrace constraints on their use of the natural environment placed on them by organizations of citizens, they are only partial and imperfect experiments in equitable cooperation. So while they can play an important role in a transition to a self-managed system of equitable cooperation, expanding employee ownership in capitalism is no panacea.

Consumer Cooperatives: Nobody knows how many consumer cooperatives there are in the United States. A survey in the early 1990s counted more than 40,000 and consumer cooperatives have expanded rapidly since then. The problem is not so much lack of consumer cooperatives, but (1) failure to cultivate cooperative principles and practices within the consumer co-operatives that already exist, and (2) failure to develop cooperative relations between producer and consumer cooperatives, leaving individual cooperatives to interact instead with capitalist firms and each other through the marketplace.

Progressives need to help sustain and expand self-management practices and develop more equitable wage structures in consumer cooperatives. We need to devise more creative procedures to help members participate in consumer cooperatives without heavy burdens on their time. We need to develop ways to take advantage of the energy of dedicated staff without the staff usurping member control over cooperative policy. Activists working in consumer cooperatives are already hard at work on these tasks, and are already sharing ideas and experiences with one another through organizations of consumer cooperatives and internet discussion forums. The Co-operative Grocers Information Network, CGIN (www.cgin.coop) maintains a discussion group for the National Cooperative Grocers Association, NCGA (www.ncga.coop). There is an active discussion group facilitated by Co-op Net (www.co-opnet.coop). And both the University of Wisconsin Center for Cooperatives, UWCC (www.uwcc.wisc.edu) and the International Co-operative Alliance (www.coop.org) provide educational materials on cooperative principles and sponsor information exchanges by topic areas. However, there is a great deal more educational work to be done inside consumer cooperatives by those who understand how pressure from the bottom line can undermine cooperative principles.

Linking Producer and Consumer Cooperatives: Members of producer and consumer cooperatives also need to learn and teach one another how the competitive market environment limits the capacities of their cooperatives to meet their stated goals. Activists in producer cooperatives need to teach their fellow workers how market relations limit their ability to transform the work process in desirable ways. Activists in consumer cooperatives need to teach their fellow members how market relations limit their ability to secure high quality, safe, environmentally friendly products. And activists in all cooperatives need to explain how market relations prevent them from developing democratic and equitable relations between cooperatives and undermine economic democracy and justice within their organizations as well.

Once the difference between market and cooperative principles is more clearly understood by more cooperative members, progressives need to try to link cooperatives together in new ways. The first step is to try and help producer and consumer cooperatives buy and sell more from each other, and less from capitalist firms. This would cut down on ways in which relationships with capitalist suppliers and buyers undermine cooperative principles. There is now a major effort underway to link Community Supported Agriculture (CSA) with local food co-ops. Local Harvest, an organization supporting CSA, sponsors a program to link local farmers with food co-ops in nearby urban areas (www.localharvest.org/food-coops/).

A second step could be to establish something like an "eBay" on the internet exclusively for producer and consumer cooperatives. Once cooperatives are trading with other cooperatives through a cooperative eBay, those exchanges could be transformed from purely commercial transactions toward a system of equitable interrelations. Just as the "fair trade movement" has recently introduced a moral element into international trade, this would bring the "cooperative market" more in line with the core principles of equitable cooperation. After "fair trade" between cooperatives became a familiar norm, cooperatives participating in the co-operative eBay market could move toward replacing fair trade exchanges with a rudimentary form of participatory planning, which would facilitate even fairer relationships and allow for greater economic democracy.

Egalitarian and Sustainable Intentional Communities: Besides religious communities like the Amish, the Mennonites, the Hutterites, and the Bruderhoff, who all live outside the capitalist mainstream to varying degrees, there are close to a thousand secular "intentional communities" in the United States where individuals and families live in ways that are self-consciously different from capitalist lifestyles. Some of these communities concentrate on living in ways that are environmentally sustainable, including pioneering new environmentally friendly technologies. Others are primarily concerned with building egalitarian relationships. Many intentional communities try to do both, and practice democratic decision making in various forms as well.

The Fellowship for Intentional Community dates back to 1948, but was revitalized in the 1980s, and incorporated as a non-profit organization in 1986. The FIC today serves as both a membership organization for over two hundred communities, and as a clearinghouse for information on more than seven hundred communities appearing in the FIC encyclopedic publication, *Communities Directory: A Guide to Intentional Communities and Cooperative Living*. A directory of "eco-villages," with links to each one, can be found at www.ecobusinesslinks.com/sustainable_communities.htm. In 1976 more than a dozen communities focused primarily on changing people's relations with one another formed the Federation of Egalitarian Communities (FEC) to promote egalitarian life styles. Communities in the FEC cooperate on publications, conferences, and recruitment, engage in labor exchanges and skill sharing, and provide joint healthcare coverage. The FEC now has members and affiliate communities spread across North America, ranging in size and emphasis from small agricultural homesteads to village-like communities with over a hundred members, to urban group houses. The stated aim of these "egalitarian communities" is "not only to help each other, but to help more people discover the advantages of a communal alternative and to promote the evolution of a more egalitarian world." Each of the communities in the federation: (1) holds its land, labor, income, and other resources in common, (2) assumes responsibility for the needs of its members, receiving the products of their labor and distributing these and all other goods equally, or according to need, (3) practices non-violence, (4) uses a form of decision making in which members have an equal opportunity to participate, either through consensus, direct vote or right of appeal or overrule, (5) works to establish the equality of all people and does not permit discrimination on the basis of race, class, creed, ethnic origin, age, sex, or sexual orientation, (6) acts to conserve natural resources for present and future generations while striving to continually improve ecological awareness and practice, and (7) creates processes for group communication and participation and provides an environment that supports people's development. The FEC has accumulated a library of information they call "systems and structures" available without charge to any who are interested, containing advice on topics as varied as children, conflict resolution, economic planning and budgeting, and taxes.

The number of intentional communities in the United States committed to living in environmentally sustainable and egalitarian ways is truly impressive, as is the longevity and size of some of the communities. Unfortunately, these communities are virtually unknown to most Americans, including most who think of themselves as part of the Left. While their lack of visibility in the mainstream is understandable, the disconnect between Left activists and those living in intentional communities is surprising since many who live in intentional communities participate faithfully, year in and year out, in various environmental, anti-war, and social justice campaigns. But for the most part, Left activists and theoreticians ignore the existence of these experiments in equitable cooperation as both valuable sources of information about how well our visions of alternatives to capitalism work in practice, and as opportunities to practice what they preach themselves. Overcoming this unfortunate "disconnect" is an important priority.

Collectives Practicing Participatory Economics: Last but not least, there are a handful of collectives who are not only owned and managed entirely by their members, but organized self-consciously according to the principles of participatory economics. (See Part 5 of this book, "Theory and Practice: Institutions and Movement Building.") These collectives balance jobs for empowerment and desirability, reward members according to effort, promote participatory economic goals, seek to relate to other progressive organizations on a cooperative rather than commercial basis, and explicitly agitate for replacing capitalism with a participatory economy. South End Press in Boston was the first self-conscious attempt to organize a workplace according to the principles of participatory economics, www.southendpress.org. The A-Zone in Winnipeg was the first network of collectives operating according to participatory economic principles. The collectives in the network include a bookstore and restaurant, Mondragón Bookstore & Coffee House, www.a-zone.org/mondragon, a publishing house, Arbeiter Ring, www.arbeiterring.com, a recording company, the G-7 Welcoming Committee, www.g7welcomingcommittee.com, and a bicycle shop and courier service, Natural Cycle. The Vancouver Participatory Economics Collective does educational work promoting participatory economics and participatory budgeting throughout British Columbia (http://vanparecon.resist.ca.). And the Blue Space collective in East Sussex, England, offers adventure travel services around the globe www.thebluespace.com/index.shtml.

It is important not to put any particular experiment in equitable cooperation on a pedestal and blind oneself to its limitations. It is also important not to focus exclusively on the limitations of a particular experiment and fail to recognize important ways in which it advances the cause of equitable cooperation. But it is most important not to underestimate the value of living experiments in equitable cooperation in general. The glass will always be part full and part empty. All real world experiments in equitable cooperation in capitalist economies will not only be imperfect because human efforts are always imperfect; more important, they will be imperfect because they must survive within a capitalist economy and are subject to the serious limitations and pressures this entails. Of course it is important to evaluate how successfully any particular experiment advances the cause of equitable cooperation and resists pressures emanating from the capitalist economy to compromise principles of economic justice and democracy. But there is little point in either pretending experiments are flawless or vilifying those struggling to create something better. What is called for is to nurture and improve experiments that already exist, to build new ones that can reach out to people who continue to live in their traditional communities, and to eventually link experiments in cooperation together to form a visible alternative to capitalism in its midst.

Live Within the Movement: Finally, we need to begin to think differently about what "the movement" is and how it functions. By "the movement" I mean the community of progressive activists devoted to winning fundamental social change, which in the case of the economy means replacing capitalism with a system of equitable cooperation. But whereas in the past anti-capitalist activists identified primarily as members of particular radical political organizations, i.e. organizations defined by a particular political ideology and strategic program, I suspect in the future activists will more often be identified by their work in particular reform struggles and by how they express their willingness to live according to the principles of equitable cooperation. In other words, I suspect movement activists will increasingly come to have two different organizational reference points, instead of a single, all embracing political sect, pre-party, party, or group. Which reform struggle or anti-capitalist educational project I work on, and what organization or caucus I belong to when doing that work, will be one point of reference. How I choose to live according to the principles of cooperation, and which experiment(s) in equitable cooperation I belong to will be my second point of reference as a movement activist. Of course there will continue to be differences of opinion among activists about the best way to pursue both tasks—anti-capitalist reform work and living according to cooperative principles. And since movement activists are human too, different "preferences" will enter into activist choices of how and where they work. But I detect a change toward dual allegiances instead of single allegiances among movement activists, and I think this is a fortuitous trend. I think activists who orient and work with a dual orientation and allegiances will be not only more effective, they will be able to sustain themselves longer as activists and enjoy themselves more in the process. Since I have long been of the opinion that it is activists and organizers who make the world go round, anything that improves their effectiveness and enhances their numbers in my opinion greatly improves our chances of success.

In any case, movement activists need to preach what they practice. We must not only fight along side others for reforms that make capitalism more equitable and democratic and less environmentally destructive, we must prove by personal example that it is possible for people to live in ways that are more democratic, equitable, and sustainable than anything capitalism permits. We must commit to live according to the principles we espouse. We must go beyond arguing theoretically that equitable cooperation is possible and desirable, and begin to show by concrete example that participatory economic decision-making and reward accord to sacrifice do not breed laziness or stifle initiative. We must demonstrate that environmentally friendly lifestyles are enjoyable, and that after economic security is assured, sacrificing excessive income for more leisure improves the quality of life. Quite simply, we must show that people will want to choose equitable cooperation when given the chance. When we begin to do this the difference between those who are committed to the cause of equitable cooperation and those who seek only limited reforms of capitalism will no longer be that the former espouse more militant strategies and tactics during reform campaigns than the latter. The measure of dedication to the cause of equitable cooperation will be willingness to enter into arrangements with others as they become available that better express the cooperative principles we espouse.

Participation by activists is also crucial to the success of non-capitalist experiments. Experiments must not only compete successfully to survive, they must also reject competitive principles and remain faithful to cooperative principles to be successful experiments in equitable cooperation. As an examination of experiments like the Mondragon cooperatives in Spain reveals, this is not easy, and requires a high level of political awareness and commitment by participants. Whereas religious convictions can provide the necessary ingredient in church-based intentional communities, political convictions about the superiority of cooperation to competition are necessary for the success of secular intentional communities. Without the presence of committed activists who share this conviction, experiments are less likely to succeed.

Remuneration based on effort, decision-making power in proportion to the degree one is affected, making use of expertise while preventing experts from usurping power cannot be demonstrated as viable and desirable within the workings of capitalism. The fact that capitalism makes economic justice and democracy impossible is the reason it must be replaced! But sensible people do not endorse new ideas until they are sure they work. Especially in light of the history of failed alternatives to capitalism that is part of the legacy of the 20th century, the progressive economic movement must respect people's skepticism. This means testing the principles of equitable cooperation and proving that they do work in living experiments in equitable cooperation. Since these experiments cannot succeed without committed activists, and since activists often find it difficult to sustain their commitment to the struggle without the kind of social support these experiments provide, it is important for activists not only to prioritize their work in reform struggles, but also to prioritize finding where and how to live with other like-minded people according to cooperative principles. That is how to "keep hope alive," and how the principles of economic justice and economic democracy can successfully challenge the hegemony of "might makes right."

Standing Fast

The next century will prove no easy road for social activists and organizers—in any of the movements in any of the spheres of social life. Unfortunately for those of us working for progressive economic change, capitalism does not dig its own grave. Instead it charges us dearly for the shovels it sells us to dig our own graves. Only when enough of us come to our senses and put our shovels to better use will the increasing human misery and environmental destruction that marked the end of the century that should have been capitalism's last give way to a sustainable economy of equitable cooperation. Unfortunately, "coming to our senses" is easier said than done. It will come to pass only after more sweat and tears have flowed in more reform campaigns than we can yet imagine. It will require countless lives devoted to building experiments in equitable cooperation that swim against the current in the increasingly global cauldron of competition and greed. Fortunately, pouring sweat and tears into the cause of justice and democracy are at the center of the human spirit and make our lives fuller.

(Endnotes)

1   Prepared for the Political Economy Seminar at the University of Massachusetts at Amherst on March 8, 2005
2   Michael Harrington *The Next Left: The History of the Future* (Henry Holt & Co., 1986)
3   Michael Harrington *Socialism: Past and Future* (Little, Brown & Co., 1989)
4   Magnus Ryner "Neo-liberal Globalization and The Crisis of Swedish Social Democracy" in *Economic and Industrial Democracy20* (SAGE, February 1999)
5   Magnus Ryner *Capitalist Restructuring, Globalization and the Third Way: Lessons from the Swedish Model* (Routledge, 2002)
6   Harrington *Socialism: Past and Future*: 20–21
7   Ibid.: 20, 21, 24
8   Ibid.: 21
9   Ibid.
10   Ibid.: 219
11   Ibid.: 242
12   Ibid.: 247
13   Ibid.: 233
14   Ibid.: 21–22
15   Ibid.: 24
16   Ibid.: 25
17   Ibid.: 21
18   Ibid.: 25
19   Ibid.: 123
20   Ibid.: 25

21   Ibid.: 27
22   Harrington *The Next Left: The History of the Future*: 116–17
23   Ibid.: 119
24   Ibid.: 119
25   Ibid.: 127
26   Ibid.: 136–37
27   Ibid.: 137
28   Ibid.: 136–37
29   Ibid.: 136
30   Ibid.: 137
31   Ibid.: 133
32   Ibid.: 117
33   Harrington *Socialism: Past and Future*: 20
34   Ibid.: 105
35   Ryner "Neo-liberal Globalization and The Crisis of Swedish Social Democracy"
36   Ibid.: 42
37   Ibid.: 43–44
38   Ibid.: 58
39   Ibid.: 59
40   Ibid.
41   Ibid.: 60
42   Ibid.: 62
43   Ibid.: 63
44   Ibid.
45   Ibid.: 59
46   Ibid.: 57
47   Geoffrey Schneider, Janet Knoedler, and Charles Sackrey *Introduction to Political Economy*, 4th
      edition (Economic Affairs Bureau , Inc., 2005)
48   Gregg Olsen "Half Empty or Half Full?" *Canadian Review of Sociology and Anthropology* (May
      1999): 241
49   Ryner "Neo-liberal Globalization and The Crisis of Swedish Social Democracy": 39
50   T. F. Glick *Irrigation and Society in Medieval Valencia* (Harvard University Press, 1970)
51   A. Maass and R. L. Anderson *And the Desert Shall Rejoice: Conflict, Growth and Justice in Arid
      Environments* (R.E. Krieger, 1986)
52   Ostrom E.L. *Governing the Commons* (Cambridge University Press, 1990)
53   Sam Dolgoff *The Anarchist Collectives: Workers Self-management in the Spanish Revolution 1936–
      1939* (Free Life, 1974)
54   Ibid.: 143–44
55   Gerald Brenan *The Spanish Labyrinth: An Account of the Social and Political Background of the
      Spanish Civil War* (Cambridge University Press, 1950): 227–338
56   Sam Dolgoff *The Anarchist Collectives: Workers Self-management in the Spanish Revolution 1936–
      1939*: 27
57   Ibid.
58   Brenan *The Spanish Labyrinth*: 179
59   Dolgoff *The Anarchist Collectives: Workers Self-management in the Spanish Revolution 1936–1939*:
      28
60   George Orwell *Homage to Catalonia* (Beacon Press, 1955)
61   Noam Chomsky *Objectivity and Liberal Scholarship* (Black & Red, April 1997)
62   Others call this "prefigurative organizing." However, many who favor prefigurative organizing
      mean adopting practices within cadre organizations or even reform organizations that "prefig-
      ure" the values and norms of the new society. While "prefigurative organizing" is useful in these
      settings as well, when I say "experiments in equitable cooperation" I am talking about creating a
      whole new network of social institutions that prefigure what life in the new society can be like
      that are *in addition to* traditional cadre and reform organizations.

PART V

Theory and Practice: Institutions and Movement Building

Chapter 21

THE MAKING OF SOUTH END PRESS AND Z

Lydia Sargent

IT'S 1975 AND YOU'VE spent years marching and demonstrating against the U.S. war in Vietnam and you have no intention of participating in "the system" that waged that war, but you need to earn some money, so what do you do? Well, you do what any 1960s–70s white middle class activist does. You head to graduate school, in my case to get certified to teach sports ("phys-ed" to you, "human movement" in the 1960s-inspired curriculum). The last thing you're thinking of doing is creating a radical, self-sustaining media institution, in this case book publishing. So when my partner proposed starting a press to publish books that would reflect the politics, analysis, and critique of the 1960s New Left, I thought it was (a) impossible; (b) going to be sexist and I would end up cleaning the office and doing the typing, feminist consciousness not withstanding; (c) not for me, my skills lay elsewhere, in theater; and (d) I knew nothing about publishing books and neither did he.

Well, that's not entirely true. What prompted the idea in the first place was the experience he had trying to get his first book, *What Is to Be Undone?*,[1] published. The book critiqued existing "isms"—Marxism, anarchism, socialism, etc.—and posited a "totalist" theory. As most of the existing "Left" presses were either orthodox, single issue, or social democratic/liberal, *What Is to Be Undone?* was rejected many times before being accepted at a small Boston publisher named Porter Sargent (no relation). To speed up the publishing process, we offered to typeset and layout the book ourselves. Of course, we knew nothing about using a phototypesetter and weren't the best typists, but what the heck? We used the phototypesetter generously loaned to us by the Boston Community School, which had been started by a friend from the anti-war movement. As it was occupied in the daytime, we produced *What Is to Be Undone?*, working overnight for about three weeks. Once we delivered the finished book to the publisher, we expected it to be released within a month and on the front shelves of bookstores. Shows how much we knew. The book seemed to take forever to come out, appeared in hardly any bookstores, and received no reviews worth mentioning.

Getting back to South End Press (SEP), our experience with *What Is to Be Undone?* made clear that the broad, radical politics we had been part of and the lessons we had learned were not going to reach a mainstream audience or even a widening New Left audience. But seeing the need for a book publishing collective is different from actually doing it, especially when we were talking about having to raise around

$150,000 over the next three years. On the other hand, we had stopped a war, hadn't we? Surely we could sell 3,000 to 5,000 copies of each book—the figure we were told was the average lifetime sales of a trade paperback.

So, somewhat reluctantly, in 1976–77, I joined with seven others in bi-monthly planning meetings for what became South End Press.[2] I was willing to do this because I was assured that it would be: (a) possible; (b) something I could do very well—an actor/gym teacher was just what was needed; (c) it would be nonsexist as it would not recreate the hierarchical division of labor of the profit-driven corporations we had been criticizing; and (d) so what if we didn't know anything about publishing? We could learn. How hard could it be?

During this pre-planning period we consulted mainstream publishing resource material, such as Literary Marketplace,[3] which lists distributors; printers; warehousing, mailing, and distribution services; and we visited alternative publishers. On a trip to Monthly Review[4]—Left publishers of a monthly journal and numerous invaluable political books in New York City—the structure of their operation made us even more determined to create an alternative model. At that time, three white males ran the show. Well educated white females did most of the editing. A black female acted as receptionist. Latinos packaged and shipped the material from MR's warehouse. Other Left publishers were similarly arranged, with hierarchical (usually sexist, classist, and racist) divisions of labor and decision-making. To us this was not very "alternative." The structure of Left media institutions affects the mind-sets and priorities of their staff. Plus, if Left institutions are set up with oppressive corporate divisions of labor and decision making structures, isn't our New Left critique of existing institutions somewhat hypocritical?

As we approached our intended startup date, we tried to raise funds to no avail. Finally, we found someone who was willing to finance the purchase of a building where we could live and work. Initially, the press would pay room and board, but no salaries. This seemed a good solution to our money/fundraising problem. Most of us were able to get by with very little money in those days, so all we would need, once we moved into the building, was some part-time work of some sort. In addition, the building would serve as an insurance policy in the event the project failed, as the original investor could recoup some of her money from the sale of the building.

By the summer of 1977, six of the initial planners had moved into the five-story townhouse we'd purchased in the South End of Boston, a diverse community at the time, home to much organizing around low-income housing—later the area became gentrified and property values soared. Of those original six members, four had recently been grad students in economics at UMass-Amherst (Michael Albert, John Schall, Pat Walker, and Juliet Schor), one was a teacher and member of a contra dance band (Mary Lea), and one (me) was involved in theater, substitute teaching, and raising three children.

During the next few months, we opened a bank account; purchased typesetting, layout, and office equipment; located a printer and a warehouse; taught ourselves how to produce books; and incorporated as "The Institute for Social and Cultural Change, d/b/a South End Press," a non-profit, tax exempt institution. Besides reflecting our politics, the non-profit status would allow people to deduct donations to SEP from their taxes and would enable SEP to get the very important bulk rate permit, with which we could mail promotional pieces for three cents each (at the time).

Also in those preplanning months we discussed how to give the project a radical activist feel. After all, book publishing sounds like any other business. One way (besides our structure) was to define ourselves as activists who publish books, rather than career publishers. This meant that not only would we, as individual staff members, stay involved with existing activist organizations and movements, we planned to create and distribute other media projects such as a journal, newspaper, cultural magazine, school, radio show, speakers' bureau, and distribution/sales collective (the Internet didn't exist then).

The startup tasks went fairly smoothly and the building held an air of excitement, almost like a movement office—writers visited and stayed overnight in the bedrooms upstairs; we even offered a room to an exiled Leftist from Brazil.

In those early days the main contentious decision was over what to call the press. Finally, we reached an impasse over our two top choices, "HOB" (for Heart of the Beast) Press or "Seventh Wave" Press. So we decided to name the project after the area of Boston we were living in, hence South End Press.

We met every morning with the sun streaming through the bay window on the second floor of our new home on Pembroke Street. Two of us (both women) went to the bank closing, presided over by a woman banker (a rarity in 1976). Just to shake things up, we handed her a cigar after the "signing" and we all lit up.

Because we lived upstairs, those morning meetings were often held post-shower, wet hair and all. At those meetings we hammered out a mission statement that would reflect our politics:

> We are concerned with the totality of oppressions in the United States, especially those based on race, sex, class. We see the need to understand how these oppressions are perpetuated through our economic and political system, and in our culture, ideology, and consciousness. Although our main focus is the U.S., we are concerned with exploitation in other countries and opposition to it. We see these struggles as fundamentally linked with our own. As activist publishers we hope our books will help further the socialist, feminist, anti-racist movement in this country. And we want to assist in the development of visions and strategies for a future society.

We laid out the general principles for a democratic workplace. They were:

• Availability of all information relevant to decisions to all project participants

- No hiring and firing other than by agreement of the whole project according to well understood guidelines

- Disbursement of the capacity to fundraise

- Participatory democracy in decision making, including one person/one vote on overarching decisions; self-management of one's own circumstances; autonomy within "departments" based on yearly, collectively decided policy mandates; consensus on accepting new staff members

- Salary equalization, with provisos for assistance to those with dependents, special needs, or pegged to extreme effort

- Equality of work assignments for empowerment (referred to years later as balanced job complexes)

To "institutionalize" the principles stated above, we divided work into three main categories: editorial/book production, business, and "shit work." This meant everyone would be responsible for deciding on and "coordinating" books—from the time they came in through the publishing and promotion phase. In addition to book production, each staff member would also do one of the jobs in the business areas, which we divided into promotion (catalogues, ads), fulfillment (warehousing, distribution, customer service), and finances/fundraising.

In the beginning we rotated the business jobs every three months so that people could learn about the entire operation very quickly; later we changed to a yearly rotation (with variations for individual needs). Other jobs, like phone answering, chairing meetings, opening mail, cataloguing incoming manuscripts, and cleaning the office were rotated on a monthly or weekly basis. The result of this arrangement of tasks would be, we hoped, that everyone would have a relatively balanced job complex that would promote a democratic work experience, empower them in meetings, and avoid institutionalizing hierarchies and inequalities.

During the summer of 1977, we had also begun soliciting manuscripts through our contacts in various existing movements or through friends from our prior political work. We had set January 1978 for the release of our first books, so in the fall of 1977, we announced ourselves to the progressive community of activists, academics, and writers by producing and mailing a brochure describing our politics, structure and process, editorial policy, and promotion and distribution plans. We also prepared and mailed our first book catalog.

We released *Theater for the 98%* in January 1978. Six to ten books came out every year after that.[5] We almost went bankrupt in 1978, 1979, 1980, 1981, 1982, 1983, 1984, 1985, etc. Somehow we managed to hang in and raise just enough money to avert various crises. We struggled to get our books into stores as distribution was extremely controlled. We urged faculty (who often had limited budgets and already-assigned texts) to adopt our books for their college and high school courses. We begged for reviews and were most often turned down by mainstream and Left media.

We attended movement events, professional conferences, and industry book fairs to promote our catalog.

One of many high points was the 1979 release of the two-volume *Political Economy of Human Rights*,[6] by Noam Chomsky and Edward S. Herman. A reviewer, George Scialabba, raved about the volumes (*The Washington Connection* and *After the Cataclysm*) in *The Village Voice*. After that review appeared, orders came pouring in and bookstore buyers, formerly reluctant to meet with us, came rushing out from backroom offices to greet us with open arms. These books were followed by two others that attracted similar attention: bell hooks's *Ain't I A Woman*[7] and *No Nukes*,[8] a collection edited by Anna Gyorgy. The former became a huge seller and is still used in college courses to this day. *No Nukes*, as fate would have it, came out a few months before the disaster at Three Mile Island. The book was designed as a handbook for the growing anti-nuke movement of the late 1970s and early 1980s. It sold an incredible (for us) 26,000 copies in its first five months as we packed up box after box and shipped them to anti-nuke groups around the country. In a way it was a quintessential book for an activist publishing collective as it directly served an existing movement.

During that time, I helped produce over 150 books and countless catalogues, flyers, ads, and newsletters. I attended book fairs in Chicago, Atlanta, the UK, Germany, and Nicaragua. I went on publishing trips to Poland and Cuba. I took two sales trips a year to bookstores in Boston, New York, Philadelphia, and Washington. I also edited a collection of essays, wrote and/or directed three plays a year (as a sideline activity), and sent three kids off to college. And, oh yes, around 1982 or so, we all started getting paid. Some staff moved out of the building, others stayed (and paid rent). Eventually, we purchased a new building in the same area and became a work collective only. By the time I left in mid-1987 all of the founding staff had moved on to other pursuits.

Over the ten years I worked at South End Press we pretty much stuck to the original set up, but made changes to meet the needs of new staff members. If rotation or other tactics weren't working, we modified them—as long as they didn't contradict our principles. If inequalities arose informally (dominating meetings, ability to articulate arguments, quick learners, etc.), we addressed these in meetings, on a case-by-case basis, as they affected the overall power dynamics.

Looking back, I wonder how we made it. There were many tense interpersonal moments—mostly over work style, the nonhierarchical process, and issues between men and women—rarely over political/editorial issues. Striving for equality (and democracy) with a staff of six white people with advanced college degrees, many of whom eventually wanted to be doing something else, had its problems. Nonetheless, we were determined not to recreate the hierarchies and oppressions of corporate/capitalist workplaces. In fact, it was that experiment in workplace democracy that made the experience an exciting adventure in applying our political values in our day-to-day work. It was also a clear challenge to the establishment and it's what annoyed potential "socially conscious" (yet still capitalist) grant givers and wealthy funders the most.

I think there were several key reasons for South End's success (SEP is thirty at this writing). First, we started with a clear mission statement. We knew our purpose and principles—that is, we were a collective of activists who published books that reflected a broad new Left politics. Our mission and democratic workplace principles were described in a "founding" brochure for future collective staff members to refer to and a shorter version appeared on the copyright page of each book. No matter how bad the financial situation became or what the internal problems were, our goal was to get the books into as many hands as possible and, in so doing, to "assist in activist struggles for radical social change." Our editorial decisions were informed by our political mission and by what we thought would be a contribution to the Left, broadly defined, i.e., what we then referred to as "totalist" politics (recognizing the importance of race, gender, and class both in analyzing existing institutions and envisioning a better future).

Second, we paid careful attention to the budget, with yearly estimates of numbers of books we would produce and what we thought we could sell. We had seen "movement" operations fold due to financial mismanagement. To avoid a debacle in this area we got advice from movement accountants and were creative and aggressive about asking for money. Of course, we overestimated how much we would sell and underestimated the monopolization of distribution as it affected income. But we usually knew when a crisis was coming and could head it off with appeals to readers and others. Thankfully they always came through.

Third, we ignored the numerous derogatory comments about collectives—that they are not suited to a publishing "business" as they are flaky and inefficient; that all they do is have meetings and try to achieve "consensus." This did not compel us to "sellout" and compromise our principles. This criticism seemed to suggest that meetings themselves were the problem, but, to us, bad and unnecessary meetings were the problem. So we learned how to have good meetings and be competent chair-people (a job that was rotated). In the beginning, of course, we needed daily meetings as there was a lot to discuss and decide. The entire collective was involved in every decision, including what cleanser to use to clean the bathrooms and the font size and space between the lines (leading) in every book. We were nervous about the project and meetings gave us a sense of security and support.

Later we delegated autonomy to book coordinators and within business areas. We were able to do this because every year we held an annual retreat in mid-June. Well, it was a retreat to the extent that we closed the office and "retreated" to a rented house by the sea for four days of meetings. The first day we'd discuss the state of the world as it might inform our editorial decisions. The next day we discussed the press itself and internal policies and finances. The following days were spent on reorganizing people's job complexes and creating a budget. The resulting yearly budget and editorial mandates informed decisions for individuals and departments for that year. This allowed us to function with just two collective meetings a month—editorial and business. These meetings had an assigned chair, a note taker, a time limit, and a prepared agenda. An editorial meeting, for instance, would cover (1) assigning incoming manuscripts to coordinators and readers (2) reporting on books under consideration and (3) making final decisions on books that were being recommended (or not).

We were also able to be "efficient" by making adjustments in our voting procedure. We mainly used one person/one vote, majority rules, with attention to a strong minority. This system worked extremely well. We didn't want trying to achieve consensus to hold up producing books; we also wanted to know what kinds of disagreements there were in the group. Utilizing a strong minority was a good check on decisions, as well. If a few people felt strongly enough to hold up a decision and argue their case, then perhaps we were making a hasty decision. As it turned out, the strong minority reversed many decisions and promoted some of the best discussions.

Fourth, we established a careful hiring process to accomplish two main goals: (1) improve staff diversity and (2) avoid debilitating staff interactions. As we never wanted to have to "fire" anyone (to my knowledge only one staff member has ever been "fired"), we set up a careful interview process, followed by an eight-month apprenticeship (this varied over the years). Apprentices were paid the same as everyone else (once we started paying people) and could vote after four months. Votes on new staff members were consensus, as we felt that if even one person was uncomfortable with a prospective hire, the collective would suffer.

Fifth, we had fun, told jokes, and gave ourselves occasional "percs." We tried to balance long hours and no pay (in the beginning) with these percs. For instance, those who had rotated to "fulfillment," a business job involving inventory and customer service issues, would do the most odious part of the job on Fridays and then go to a local bar after work. Or we'd combine hunting for office supplies with a lunch in Harvard Square. In addition, we rotated trips to book fairs and offered a six-month paid sabbatical.

Collective members also stayed active. Some were in bands, others did political theater, others were teaching, and still others belonged to various activist organizations. We were also able to hate capitalism, patriarchy, racism, homophobia, environmental degradation, and still enjoy sports, movies, TV, music, mystery novels, and, yes, even shopping. This enabled us to stay involved for the long haul.

Sixth, we kept up with technological changes, which were immense. In the first few years we produced books and promotional material by typing them from a typewritten manuscript into a photo-typesetter where, once a line had justified, it couldn't be corrected. The copy was produced on a cylinder of film paper, which was then sent through a developer and came out in rolls of continuous text, page wide. Often the film failed to develop correctly and hours of work would be lost. Once the film was developed it was cut into page length strips that were then waxed and laid out on letter size paper. This copy was eventually sent to the printer after numerous one-line, one-word, or entire page corrections were laid in. We managed to get very fast at this process, but it still had nightmare qualities and often you would hear people in the layout room screaming in frustration.

This process was followed by typing submitted manuscripts onto a computer, which was attached through a wire to the phototypesetter. The copy was then sent through the wire to the typesetter after numerous codes were entered. The book would then go through the same process as before. This was followed by a majority of writers submitting books on computer discs, thereby eliminating the typing process. By 1987, entire books were being submitted on discs and were then "laid out" on the computer using a desktop publishing program. (This technology made it possible to start Z *Magazine* with a staff of two people.)

Seventh, we were able to pay salaries with benefits.

Working at SEP for ten years was one of the most important times in my life and it was difficult to leave, but the press was finally financially stable with an experienced staff. It seemed time to address our early mission of expanding into other media.

Starting Z *Magazine*

In 1987 Michael Albert, an SEP cofounder, took his six-month paid sabbatical, after which he decided not to return to the press. When the idea of starting a magazine was raised, I said publishing a 112-page magazine is: (a) impossible; (b) not where my skills lay, I'm a book publisher now; and (c) I didn't know anything about magazine publishing and neither did he. But, hey, we had stopped a war. We'd started a radical book publishing project, so what the heck?

We proceeded to ignore all those who said we couldn't possibly publish a monthly magazine for less than a guarantee of $1 or $2 million over the next three years. We proceeded to take our initial bank account of $35,000 and set up a home office near SEP. We applied for non-profit status and a second-class postage permit, created a mission statement, and applied the SEP workplace principles to a staff of two (not so easy), later a staff of three as Eric Sargent joined us in 1989.

And, instead of a huge phototypesetter, developer, and so on, we purchased two computers, a large printer, and a desktop publishing and graphics package. This technology made it possible to produce a magazine and maintain a subscriber database with our tiny staff. In the beginning we still laid in the graphics on light tables and received the articles on computer discs. After 1993, we received all the articles and most of the graphics by email. The entire magazine was produced on the computer and then mailed to the printer. (By 2006, both the magazine and the subscription list were emailed to the printer.)

Meanwhile, finding a name turned out to be a lot easier than the marathon debate around what to call SEP. During a planning meeting with some political activists and writers, we asked their advice on what to call the new magazine. Various names were suggested and then someone said, "Why not call it Z?"[9] Everyone looked dubious until the person said, "After the movie Z."[10] It took ten seconds to realize it was perfect.

The movie had been very popular among progressives when it came out in the U.S. in the late 1960s. The movie was directed by Costa Gavras and told the story of repression and resistance in Greece in the 1960s. The film opens with the (reactionary) chief of police in Athens lecturing his cohorts on the "mildew of the mind that menaces our ideological security." He speaks of the infiltration of malignant germs that appear as "isms" or "spots on the sun." He attributes the increase in sunspots to the advent of hippies and peaceniks in the United States and elsewhere. He calls on the police and military to "spray the young sprouts early" in the schools, universities, factories, and farms to restore national faith in God and King.

By the end of the movie, Comrade Z (a leader of the opposition) has been assassinated and his killers, including the chief of police, indicted. Yet, instead of the expected positive outcome, the prosecutor of Comrade Z's killers dies mysteriously and a military junta takes over. As the final credits roll, a list of things banned by the junta appears on screen. These include: peace movements, long hair on men, Sophocles, Tolstoy, Aeschylus, Chekhov, Mark Twain, the bar association, sociology, Becket, the International Encyclopedia, the free press, modern and popular music, new math, and the letter Z.

Inspired by the letter Z that is scrawled on the sidewalk at the end of the movie, in the spirit of resistance, we launched Z as a magazine "dedicated to resisting injustice, defending against repression, and creating liberty." During the five months of planning, we sent out a prospectus to various potential funders and received almost no money. We were clearly on our own. We signed up over twenty-five writers to contribute regular columns, features, and shorts on such areas as foreign and domestic policy, Black America, Native America, psychology, ecology, media, economics, gender, sexuality, education, and so on. Some writers were to appear every month, others every other month, and still others were on a quarterly schedule.

In the fall of 1987, with a planned deadline of January 1988 for the release of the first issue, we mailed a thirty two-page brochure—describing the magazine's purpose and listing all the writers we had signed on—to thousands of people in order to solicit subscribers. From that mailing we got enough subscribers and money to continue. If that mailing had failed, Z would not exist.

We started work on the first issue in mid-November. As the contracted articles came in, we realized we had lots of text and very few graphics. Just as we were despairing over this lack, a large package arrived from a cartoonist named Matt Wuerker. He had apparently seen our brochure. We couldn't believe our luck and put almost every one of Matt's cartoons in the first issue.[11]

Then, having conquered the graphics problem and having learned how to use our desktop publishing program, the magazine was ready to send to the printer, complete with cover. A letter arrives from a lawyer prohibiting the use of the name Z *Magazine* as it was the name of a TV magazine for Channel Z in Los Angeles. Since we had already prepared the magazine, we quickly inserted an ETA next to the Z on the cover, spelling ZETA, the Greek letter for Z (appropriate, considering the movie of that name took place in Greece). Two years later the TV magazine folded and we dropped the ETA.

We mailed the first issue to around 4,000 subscribers as well as (free) to thousands of others, many of whom subsequently subscribed. As our size was pretty much determined by the number of mailings we could send out and the number of reliable lists we could use, and the amount of money to pay for these mailings, our circulation only reached around 26,000 at its height—around 8,000 to stores, the rest to subscribers. That was, of course, before the Internet.

Over the next twenty years, things ran relatively smoothly. Our initial contracted writers met their schedules (later magazine contributors were almost entirely freelance). We had ten illustrators drawing graphics to order. We paid writers, cartoonists, and staff. We made every deadline. Needless to say, we almost went bankrupt in 1988, 89, 90, 91, 92, 93, and so on. In 1992 the financial situation was so dire that we cut the magazine from 112 to 64 pages and managed to raise enough money to keep going, while continuing to raise around $50,000 each year after that. We moved the production office from Boston to Cape Cod, Massachusetts, so we could enjoy the sun and sea now that we were in our late forties and early fifties.

In 1994, feeling the passage of time, we felt we should share some of what we learned, both about radical politics and about the projects we had started. To do that, we came up with the idea for Z Media Institute (ZMI), a nine-day summer school to teach media analysis and skills, radical politics, and the principles and practice of a democratic workplace. Since 1994 over 700 activists have been to ZMI (as of this writing in April 2007). In the course of the nine days, various faculty (most of them from New England) come for a day or two. Classes are held in living rooms, kitchens, community halls, an abandoned fire station, and on porches overlooking Nantucket sound. Students stay at local motels and dine at the Marine Biology dining hall. Classes taught include: Mainstream Media Analysis, Research and Reporting, Desktop Publishing, Foreign Policy, Economic Vision, and eighteen others. ZMI concludes with a mock graduation where students present, in dramatic form, details of the media/activist projects they have created during the nine days.

In 1998 we started Z Video Productions to bring live lectures, classes, etc. to people in video format. Also in 1998 our *Z Magazine* website, after going through various permutations, became ZNet.[12] With the expansion of the Internet we were able, through ZNet, to start a Z Sustainer Program that has provided the funds to keep going without resorting to regular crisis fundraising appeals. In 2002 *Z Magazine* became available online as well as in print.

The work of all these projects was carried out by a staff of three until 2003 and 2004, when we added two staff people.

With ZMI you could say we had come full circle, as the inspiration for starting it was to teach people what we had learned about structure and process at South End

Press; to encourage others to start long-lasting radical institutions around a similar mission; and apply similar principles to their projects.

During the thirty years I have been involved in alternative media, I have witnessed the tremendous control of not only what gets published, but also what gets to have "impact" on the public consciousness. I have seen the activism of the 1960s and 1970s (it lasted well into the late '70s) slowly lose visibility in the U.S. through the Reagan/ Bush/Clinton years to be rekindled in 1999 or so with the Seattle anti-capitalist glo-balization movement and the World Social Forum. I've seen independent magazines, bookstores, and distributors go out of business.

And I have seen the tremendous growth of the Internet, which has allowed us to meet, discuss, and make our politics and critique available online to hundreds of thousands around the world.

As for me, I'm still hard at work, producing the magazine, videos, and theater performances. Since the magazine is almost (not really) financially stable, it must be about time for a new project. In fact, just the other day, the idea of starting a radio production company that would create shows for the Internet and for Ipod down-loading came up. My first reaction was that it was: (a) impossible; (b) not where my skills lay, I'm a magazine publisher now; and (c) we don't know anything about radio production. In other words, when do we start?

(Endnotes)

1   Michael Albert *What Is To Be Undone: A Modern Revolutionary Discussion Of Classical Left Ide-ologies* (Porter Sargent, 1974)
2   South End Press, website: www.southendpress.org
3   Literary Marketplace, website: www.literarymarketplace.com
4   Monthly Review, web site: www.monthlyreview.org
5   Maxine Klein Theater for the 98% (South End Press, 1978)
6   Noam Chomsky and Edward S. Herman *Political Economy of Human Rights* (South End Press, 1979)
7   bell hooks *Ain't I A Woman* (South End Press, 1981)
8   Anna Gyorgy *No Nukes* (South End Press, 1979)
9   See Z Communications website for an overview of all Z operations: *Z Magazine*, ZNet, Z Video, and Z Media Institute: www.zcommunications.org.
10   Costa Gavras *Z* (1969), based on the novel of the same title, authored by Vassilis Vassilikos (1967, reprinted by Ballantine Books, 1969)
11   Matt Wuerker's cartoons and graphics can be found here: www.cartoonistgroup.com/proper-ties/Wuerker/search_2.php.

Chapter 22

PARECON AND WORKERS' SELF-MANAGEMENT: REFLECTIONS ON WINNIPEG'S MONDRAGÓN BOOKSTORE & COFFEE HOUSE COLLECTIVE

Paul Burrows

I. INTRODUCTION

FROM WHAT I UNDERSTAND, this panel is meant to address the question of work after capitalism, to outline a vision of what work might look like in a desirable non-capitalist economy, as well as discuss strategies for getting from here to there that are achievable. My plan is to give as brief an overview of the topic as possible, to highlight the main areas as I see them, stimulate some brainwaves, and then get right into open discussion as quickly as possible.

I assume people already know the nature of the problems we face, and that something needs to be done to change society and the world, to alter the basic structures of power and inequality that have become so dominant, and so obscene. I am not going to stand up here and insult people's intelligence by telling them "capitalism is bad." The Left, or at least the Anglo-American Left (of which I am a part), has been pre-occupied with this for decades, and has done a reasonably good job of it. Unfortunately, in my opinion, the Left has become so good at *observing*, *documenting*, and *critiquing* social ills that it has become more like a witness, and less like activists engaged in day-to-day struggles as it ought to be. It has forgotten about vision, forgotten about alternatives, and forgotten that a movement cannot inspire, motivate, and grow without positive—and achievable—examples to point to. Most of all, it seems to me, we should not tell people *anything*, unless our own movements, our own alternatives, our own institutions embody the values we profess to hold.

So, with this in mind, I'd like to talk mostly about alternative visions of work, and end with a discussion of transition. Inevitably, my vision of a desirable post-capitalist economy, and vision of alternative forms of work, owes much to a legacy of radical theory informed by libertarian Marxist, feminist, anarchist, Green, and other currents. Particularly helpful and inspiring, in terms of thinking about class and work, has been

Editor's note: This chapter is based on a talk given at the Life After Capitalism Conference, World Social Forum III, Porto Alegre, Brazil, January 23–28, 2003.

the "participatory economic" model developed by Michael Albert and Robin Hahnel. But this vision is not strictly theoretical. Much of my perspective is informed by my *actual experience* working in a nonhierarchical, collective, worker-run bookstore and restaurant in Winnipeg, Canada, between 1996 and 2001. So I would like to think that the vision of work after capitalism that I want to discuss has lessons and applications for the real world today. Even though my perspective is informed primarily by work and activism from inside the "belly of the beast" (or, more accurately for describing Canada, inside the "belly of the lap-dog of the beast"), I would like to believe that it has broader relevance. I would like to believe that it has relevance for those of us working in a range of institutions today, both mainstream and alternative, whether we live in the so-called "advanced" capitalist countries, or the so-called "developing" world. Its relevance, if any, is NOT as a blueprint for replication, but as a case study for discussion and learning and refinement.

A good deal of what is called "visionary" thinking about the nature of work after capitalism operates at a high level of generality. When asked about how work might differ, or how a just economy might operate, many progressive people will say something about direct democracy, and insist that democracy (to be meaningful) must extend beyond the political realm into the economic realm. They insist that there will be collective control over resources and social spending, rather than what we have under capitalism: a state-corporate alliance that runs the economy top down, makes all fundamental production and allocation decisions, and systematically transfers public wealth into private hands. Some Leftists will suggest that socially necessary work that is also rote or dangerous will be largely eliminated by technological advances and automation, leaving humanity with a lot more free time, and work that is, by definition, more creative and fulfilling. (Others imagine that the *disappearance* of technology will lead to the same thing.) And in terms of work itself, with respect to both decision making and divisions of labor, many progressive people will advocate some kind of workplace democracy and self-management, suggesting that a just economy will redefine the meaning of "work" and "job" in ways that enhance diversity and equality.

A good example of this is Marx's famous assertion in *The German Ideology*[1] that traditional divisions of labor will disappear, and individuals under "communism" will have the opportunity "to hunt in the morning, fish in the afternoon, rear cattle in the evening, [and] criticize after dinner." Apart from being a vegetarian's nightmare, Marx's vision of work after capitalism, and his hope that work will be varied and more egalitarian (a mix of creative and rote tasks), is nice, but vague. Unfortunately, few Left theorists have felt the need to elaborate, and most have followed Marx's lead (even the anarchists, by and large) in terms of concentrating on institutional analysis and critique of capitalism, rather than developing their vision of a non-capitalist economy.

The problem with these existing "visions" (or more accurately, "glimpses") of a desirable economy and work is NOT that the values and sentiments expressed are bad, but that Left vision tends to stop there. It is less a vision of the future than a series of hopeful assertions which touch on the KINDS of things we would like to see, and give clues as to the kinds of values we hold, but do not offer much in the way of practical details or actual institutions. We are still left with more questions than answers, and unable to answer ordinary people who might justifiably be skeptical. Is it feasible? Does it "deliver the goods" without sacrificing the values we want to uphold? How much will people work? At what kinds of jobs? What will be the basis for remuneration? What will be my standard of living? How will social spending be conducted? Will there be trade? What about research and development? What about artistic pursuits? What about ecological concerns? How will conflicts be resolved in the workplace? What will my work day, or work week, look like? What will be decided in meetings, and conversely, how much room will there be for my own initiatives, creativity, and autonomy on the job? Are there any historical examples of what you're talking about? And so on. Each question leads to two others, and while the vagueness, generality, and ambiguity of Left "vision" can make for good polemic, it becomes less satisfactory when one begins to scratch the surface.

Some activists suggest that this is all we can hope for, or that this is all we *should* attempt to outline. They think that to elaborate a more detailed model is arrogant or authoritarian or simply utopian. According to this objection, either we can't speculate about future details because only actual practice will reveal them. Or we *ought not to* devise alternative models because we don't want to impose our pre-conceptions and ideas on the future. We don't want to be "vanguardist" about imposing a particular vision or model on a larger movement.

While concerns about rigidity and vanguardism are important, I don't think they follow from model building and visionary thinking per se. First of all, I think people need vision, and concrete real world examples of that vision in practice, to inspire hope. It is not enough to be motivated by a critique of the status quo, by outrage, by the purely negative. We also need a sense that desirable alternatives are possible, we also need the hope of something better; we need to be driven as much by positive values and examples.

But just as important, I think that different visions of a non-capitalist future directly affect the strategies we adopt today (and vice versa). In other words, the programs and strategies we adopt TODAY, the structures of the movements and institutions we build TODAY, affect the direction we want to take, and *inevitably* shape our vision of a desirable future economy. If we are good little materialists, we should be able to acknowledge this. The harder part is seeing the reverse: how our different visions of a desirable future economy might affect or shape our movements or institutions, and strategies, in the present. The harder part is seeing how differences over long-term economic vision might also reflect substantive differences over values, over what is wrong with capitalism, over what is fair, and over how people should work together.

Having said all this, it might seem strange that I'm not going to outline any alternative economic model in depth. The basics of the participatory economic model have already been fleshed out, focusing particularly on balanced job complexes, and the values and arguments behind them. This model is detailed in numerous books and articles available online (www.parecon.org). In my opinion, the important thing about the parecon model, and what makes it different from anything else out there, is that it not only asks what we want an economy to achieve—what values we want it to satisfy—using clear and accessible language for laypersons like myself. But it also systematically outlines institutions to fulfill the production, consumption, and allocation requirements of any economy. The model rejects both markets and central planning in favor of "participatory planning," a third way that is not only based on workers' self-management and collective ownership of the means of production, but also satisfies my own anarchist concerns about power, hierarchy, and freedom. More important for today's discussion, the literature on the model also goes into detail about work, division of labor, and decision making at the workplace level, using a range of enterprises (from book publishing to more complex institutions like airports) as examples. Anyone interested in economic democracy, or a liberatory socialist or anarchist vision, should *at least* be aware of this stuff.

What I would like to do here is discuss the *application* of these ideas in terms of day-to-day practice, drawing on my personal experience with workplace democracy at Mondragón Bookstore & Coffee House in Winnipeg. (The business is named after the Basque Mondragón cooperative network, but, as will become apparent, the two have almost no similarity in terms of actual internal structure.) I'll start by giving a quick overview of Mondragón's workplace, the type of enterprise, as well as the internal structure, divisions of labor, and decision making. Then, I'd like to discuss some differences between the theory and practice of parecon, the complexities that arise whenever real people try to work together, the pros and cons of this specific workplace, the successes and failures, the way the institution has evolved over time, and the constraints of operating as an island in the midst of capitalism. I'd like to end by talking about the political relevance of such institutions, their place in the larger anticapitalist struggle worldwide, the lessons that can be learned (from this, and other "experiments" such as the Basque system, Kerala,[2] and so on), and discuss the transition to a full participatory economy.

II. OVERVIEW OF MONDRAGÓN

Mondragón is a joint political bookstore and full vegetarian (vegan) restaurant. It's also a community space, both in terms of being a "hang out" for activists, as well as being a space for public events, speakers, panels, social evenings, and so on. Since opening in 1996, Mondragón (and the larger "Autonomous Zone" building of which it is a part) has become a focal point for activism in Winnipeg, and has contributed to a larger community and culture of resistance in the city. Its existence and example has also inspired activists in other cities, across Canada and the United States, who have written wanting advice and information about starting up their own projects.

This is "what" Mondragón is, not "how" it operates. The politics of the business are reflected in numerous ways: in the choice of books it carries, the type of food, the criteria for selecting suppliers and products (for example, fair trade principles, organics, veganism, ecological concerns, and the labor conditions used to produce the inputs or goods that are needed), as well as the relationship with the larger community and activism, and of course, the internal structure of the business. Sometimes the different values and choices conflict with one another or with the "bottom line" of the business, and it is the collective as a whole that decides (often after excruciating meetings or debates) how to resolve such problems without sacrificing fundamental principles or overall economic viability.

In terms of internal structure, job responsibilities at Mondragón are varied and often intellectually interesting, but also sometimes physically and emotionally demanding. Each collective member is part waiter, cook, dishwasher, business manager, book buyer, bookseller, personnel administrator, cashier, events coordinator, and janitor. The restaurant component of the business is more labor-intensive than the bookstore, and so fully three-quarters (or more) of each worker-member's labor time is devoted to this side of the business—where the tasks are more physical, and pace is often more hectic.

While each worker has some specialized business area responsibilities (such as committee work, which generally requires greater training and continuity), all critical tasks are supposed to rotate over time. In this way, collective members share responsibility for tasks that are creative and empowering on the one hand, and rote or menial on the other—whether this is organizational "management," inventory and ordering, accounts payable, bookkeeping, food preparation, planning events and speakers, or running errands and performing miscellaneous chores and cleaning. Being a worker-run collective also requires time and energy spent on solving problems or completing tasks that do not fall under pre-existing job descriptions. There is *no finite task* list for each person. The "job" does not end, necessarily, with one's scheduled shift. As equal partners or co-managers, workers often volunteer to do, or are expected to do, "whatever it takes" to keep the doors open, to keep the business running smoothly, to deal with emergencies or crises, and to enhance both the financial viability and work environment of the business.

Most of the day-to-day tasks performed at Mondragón are assigned to a particular shift, while the particular person filling each shift varies over time. Certain tasks are associated with bookstore shifts, others with cafe shifts, certain tasks are required by morning (opening) shifts and others only by closing shifts. There are also special shifts for food orders and menu development, as well as for bookkeeping and accounts payable. On any given day, job tasks (and even length of time spent working) are *not equal.* But over the course of a three or four week period, each worker receives a roughly balanced set of shifts and committee work, designed to provide *rough* equity in terms of overall desirability and empowerment for each person. This is the *theory* at least—and what it means to have "balanced job complexes."

In terms of decision making, one of the goals of Mondragón is to create a work environment in which each worker-member can carry out their tasks without managerial supervision, and each is taught the necessary skills to make any day-to-day business decisions that might be required. Part of the reason behind this is to avoid a workplace characterized by unequal knowledge and divisions of labor, in which a single individual is considered indispensable, or might argue for special privileges on the basis of some monopoly on information or skills. In positive terms, this has to do with creating a workplace that empowers its members, fosters solidarity, and puts democracy and equality into practice.

The collective as a whole establishes and implements all business and personnel policies, specifies hiring goals and firing criteria, approves all job and committee parameters, interviews all new applicants, and conducts all worker-member evaluations. While a good deal of individual maturity and responsibility is expected (or at least hoped for!) from coworkers in terms of resolving grievances, the collective as a whole is also ultimately responsible for mediating and resolving major disputes and interpersonal conflicts. Ultimately, the basic goal of the workplace with respect to decision making is to give each worker a good deal of latitude for self-management of their own work circumstances, but *within* the constraint of meeting collectively agreed upon priorities, tasks, and policies that affect the group as a whole. The idea is to develop a system that balances individual and collective needs in a way that is both fair and efficient.

Members of the collective are expected—as part of their "job complex"—to attend all regular general meetings in order to discuss and assign new or unusual job tasks, formulate and debate Mondragón policies, listen to committee or personal reports, discuss finances, evaluate the equity or efficacy of existing job complexes, propose changes to the internal structure or division of labor, as well as raise and resolve possible grievances. The time, length, and frequency of such meetings is determined by the collective, the needs of the business, possible crises, individual inclination, as well as the need for an informed and empowered staff to handle all contingencies. (You'll note that these don't necessarily coincide.) When Mondragón first opened its doors, and no one had a clue how to operate a business (much less an egalitarian one), we held meetings every single day after the business closed, debating everything from the most mundane (like the "proper" way to wash lettuce!), to the philosophical. Today, the collective meets once every second week for general meetings, although during moments of hiring, firing, or otherwise crisis situations, everyone is expected to participate in extra or emergency meetings. Finally, "participation" at such meetings doesn't mean simple attendance. It means being attentive, as well as willing to articulate and argue for one's opinions, when these are relevant to the day's agenda, or the well-being of the workers and the business as a whole.

III. PARECON THEORY VS. PRACTICE

That gives you a rough idea of the nature of the business, as well as its internal structure, and some of the principles and goals behind it. But how does this translate into day-to-day practice? How does the theory mesh with the reality? What happens when real people, with different historical, class, gender, or cultural experiences (or privileges or biases or baggage) attempt to work together as equals? What have been the successes and failures of the business? How has it evolved over time, in an attempt to address some of the problems?

First, it should be pointed out that there is a big difference between the participatory economic model and a single workplace—and so the dynamics at work in our one little business, operating within and underneath capitalism, are completely different than what they would be in a full parecon economy. For one, Mondragón has no relationship to many of the other proposed institutions outlined in the full model—from consumer and neighborhood councils, to participatory allocation institutions—because they simply do not exist yet. At least, not in Winnipeg. The Mondragón experience is limited to one domain—namely, production—and even within this domain it incorporates only two major components advanced by the model: 1) remuneration based on effort, and 2) balanced job complexes (or "BJC's" for short). Furthermore, in the model, BJC's are not meant to be limited to one enterprise or workplace. Their effectiveness in terms of fostering greater equity, empowerment, and diversity throughout the economy is predicated on their being extended *across enterprises*, not just within them. For all these reasons, there are serious limits as to what the Mondragón example can even say about parecon theory. In other words, our successes and failures may or may not imply *anything* about the strengths or weaknesses of the model.

Having said this, I'd like to discuss the relationship (if any) between parecon theory and practice by focusing on a few key areas: 1) balanced job complexes; 2) skills, training, and empowerment; 3) remuneration on the basis of effort; 4) decision making, nonhierarchy, and self-management; and 5) conflict resolution. There is a good deal of overlap in each area, and problems in one often relate to problems in another, or have similar explanations. However, in each case, I'll note some of the achievements and limitations as I see them, and suggest some possible explanations and solutions for the latter.

Balanced Job Complexes

Balanced job complexes within a single enterprise or workplace means that each worker has a roughly comparable set of jobs and job types in terms of their overall desirability and empowerment effects.

This might not *seem* like a controversial goal, it might even sound attractive to everyone here, but it needs to be stressed because Left and progressive organizations, businesses, political parties, and movements almost *universally fail* to challenge traditional divisions of labor—falling back far too easily, comfortably, uncritically on sexist, classist and hierarchical divisions. (Why that is, is a matter to be discussed elsewhere.)

Where the Left *has* historically recognized the inequities and problems associated with the separation of intellectual and manual labor, and between those who make the policies and decisions and those who carry them out, the solutions proposed to "overcome" the disparities have been few and *not* far reaching. When they've actually thought about it, there are about three ways Leftists have traditionally proposed to deal with unequal divisions of labor:

• Pay people more for doing shitty work.

• Don't worry about those kinds of inequalities, because at least under socialism (or so it is alleged) workers will have the right to vote for, and recall, their managers. (This is what is often, unimaginatively, held up as the definition, and thus limit, of "economic democracy.")

• Attempt to rectify the imbalance by rotating jobs now and then, or by having those in privileged positions "dirty their hands" once in a while. (Thus, you have Maoist party cadres being sent to countryside to work with peasants, or you have Che Guevara cutting sugar cane. In each case, they return to their managerial or coordinator role, their greater privilege and status, their greater decision-making power, once the "exchange" is done—presumably with a newfound respect for the "ordinary" worker.)

At any rate, not one of these "solutions" is satisfactory from a *working class*, and indeed libertarian socialist or anarchist perspective. Balanced job complexes *are* consistent with those perspectives, but they require a shift in the way we have been taught to think about, and define, *jobs*.

In any workplace, some tasks will be more intellectually stimulating, creative, and empowering, and others will be dull, repetitive, rote, dangerous, and less desirable. One thing I want to note is that these two sets are not mutually exclusive: some empowering tasks are also boring as hell; some physical and menial tasks are, in turn, therapeutic or creative or rewarding in their own way. So, what is considered desirable or less desirable work is much more complicated than a simple "rote versus empowering" or "mental versus manual" dichotomy.

At any rate, leaving aside for the moment what constitutes desirable or undesirable work, if the *undesirable* tasks are necessary for the operation of the business, then basic fairness dictates that the burden should be divided equally. More creative and rewarding and desirable tasks *can be* (but need not be) divided on the basis of *preference*, so long as each person's overall job package is roughly comparable in terms of empowerment effects, and so long as there is a general agreement amongst the workers themselves about the equity and fairness of the different job packages. Parecon theory insists that work *must* be organized according to BJC's, not only because it is simply unfair to do otherwise but also because the *absence* of BJC's would have serious implications for workplace democracy and participatory decision making. It simply doesn't matter if everyone in a given workplace has a formal and equal right to vote! If some people have jobs that are empowering, and others that are exclusively deadening or menial, the former will *necessarily* dominate all conceptualization of policy options, all proposals for structural change, all discussion at meetings, and all decisions which affect the business and workers as a whole. The latter will listen, and perhaps debate proposals made by others, and even vote if such is required—but the very nature of their work package will limit their knowledge and skills, and thus their ability to participate effectively as equal partners in the workplace.

It is clear that there are numerous ways to actually implement balanced job complexes, and that there is a good deal of room for individual workplaces and collectives to experiment—without sacrificing core values. Variation based on type of industry, size of workplace, number of people involved, and genuine differences in personal preferences and strategies is not only inevitable, but also desirable.

At Mondragón, job complexes have changed over the last six years, and continue to change, to satisfy the needs of the collective at the time, as well as to make them more balanced if and when inequities have been perceived. "Job complexes" are thus works in progress. The simple fact that workers can propose changes to, *and alter*, their own work circumstances in ways they feel will improve the work itself, or increase fairness and efficiency, or make jobs more enjoyable and the business more viable, is testament to the existence of a meaningful level of workplace democracy. In my opinion, this alone is an important achievement—given that many workplaces that call themselves "cooperatives" are very resistant to actual workers' control, adopting lesser forms of participation which may "allow" for feedback or some kind of representation, and restricted voting rights, but fall far short of self-management.

But in practice it has been incredibly difficult to achieve that elusive, pure, and equitable "balanced job complex"—particularly in areas that require greater levels of skill and training. For one thing, learning the range of skills required by both sides of the business (from cooking and baking, to computer software, to bookstore orders, to data entry procedures and accounts payable) necessarily means longer, perhaps even ongoing, training. In and of itself, this would not be a problem if it weren't for worker turnover and the loss of skills and knowledge and "historical memory" that this entails. For another, it has been much more difficult to motivate people to push themselves to learn new skills, or to take on unfamiliar tasks, than one might expect. Even when there are *no institutional obstacles* blocking access to certain types of work (whether these are the so-called "managerial" or "administrative" tasks, or otherwise creative and empowering types of work), and even when the work itself is not overly complex (as in our case), it can be extremely difficult to get people to take the initiative to train themselves, or take advantage of existing training mechanisms.

One explanation for this is that Mondragón lacks a clear, effective, consistent training system (discussed in more detail later on). But in my experience, unless a "job complex" is very specific, and unless it becomes impossible to avoid certain types of tasks (and impossible to avoid the training required to do them), people tend to gravitate toward the kinds of work and tasks that they either enjoy or already know how to do. It is often easier to do the familiar, even if sometimes it is repetitive or boring. It is not that learning new kinds of work, training and self-training, requires greater concentration per se. Part of the problem lies with the absence of a training system. Part of it is due to the fact that we are not used to work situations in which individuals are supposed to "police themselves," and in which individuals are allowed, encouraged, and expected to train themselves on "company time." And part of it rests with the individual person, whose political sensibilities do not necessarily override their own laziness.

So, while *most* tasks required by the business are shared evenly, and while every worker does have a job complex that includes elements of cooking, cashier work, dishwashing, cleaning, book orders, not to mention participation at meetings, there are continuous problems with balancing some of the so-called "managerial" roles. Particularly difficult to balance has been work related to the following:

- Conceptualization of *structural* alternatives to address problems or omissions (rather than simply noting problems and raising grievances); Holding co-workers accountable (which we have discovered is a *really* rote task that no one wants to do)

- Representation of the business or its politics (from writing pamphlets or other collective literature, to conducting interviews and workshops, as well as public speaking related to the business or activism more broadly)

- General trouble-shooting or problem-solving required by the business on a day-to-day basis

Informal hierarchies and inequities in the division of labor are more difficult to address, and sometimes *more difficult to even see*, than formal ones. Some of these have to do with inevitable differences between experienced and new workers, and worker turnover usually means losing someone with key skills and "institutional memory," and starting from scratch with someone new. Some of these inequities have to do with people becoming too comfortable in their roles, or with a "natural" gravitation towards one's preferences. And some have to do with feeling (rightly or wrongly) that inequities in balancing are too difficult to change, or that even articulating them will lead to personal conflicts. In practice, some people prefer to remain silent about grievances or perceived inequities, for fear of jeopardizing relationships or friendships with co-workers, or because they feel that the *potential* conflict with a coworker will create a more negative work environment than the continuation of the inequity or grievance itself.

The point is that structures designed to equalize skills and knowledge do not automatically do so, and even people who agree that this *should* be a goal may find, in practice, that their own preferences or comfort collides with their politics. There is no single answer for overcoming disparities in job complexes, and for rectifying formal or informal hierarchies as they arise. As always, a combination of structural fine-tuning and holding individual coworkers accountable needs to be considered. Rather than blaming all the inequities or problems within their workplace on either some "hegemonic" structure beyond their control or on individuals who are assumed to be usurping power or neglecting responsibilities, workers' collectives need to be open to self-criticism and proposals that take into account both kinds of responsibility. There is a reciprocal relationship between workplace structure and individual behavior, and even if it is personally gratifying to blame one or the other for our problems, it is not necessarily productive in terms of addressing real people and correcting real inequities.

Even when there are no institutional obstacles blocking access to certain types of work—and even when there is a genuine openness to discussing problems, to listening to alternatives, and to implementing structural or policy changes to address inequities—the goal of achieving fully balanced job complexes is much easier said than done. Ultimately, a "pure" balanced job complex is perhaps best viewed as an endless horizon, toward which we are always moving, always refining our practices, but never quite reaching.

Skills, Training, and Empowerment

Closely related to the achievement of balanced job complexes is the question of skills, training, and empowerment. People simply cannot have balanced job complexes if they do not have the training and skills required to perform *any or all* of the empowering or creative tasks in their workplace. Of course, there is a big difference between training conducted by individuals for and within a single workplace, and training conducted by an entire workforce across an entire economy. In a large, established participatory economy, individuals will likely be able to train and work in areas according to broad preferences, so long as their overall job package is roughly comparable (in terms of desirability and empowerment) to the social average. As such, people will more likely train for long-term work in *primary* areas they enjoy, which may in some sense be considered a career or vocation, balanced by work in other secondary or tertiary areas which they may dislike but which rounds out their overall job complex. As such, "turnover" in a participatory economy will likely be less prevalent, and motivated by different factors, than turnover in a capitalist economy.

Within capitalism individuals are forced by economic necessity to find whatever work is available, and often choose to apply for work on the basis of *minimizing un-*

desirable work circumstances, especially if they feel they cannot find employment that satisfies their actual interests or preferences. Problems of training, skill acquisition, empowerment, and worker turnover—even within workplaces employing parecon principles—must be understood in this restricted context. Balanced job complexes within a particular business increase diversity of the tasks performed, and can thus reduce repetition and boredom, but they *do not* change the fundamental nature of the work required. At Mondragón, for example, regardless of how equitable the internal division of labor, the majority of work is still by definition retail, service-oriented work. More, it has been difficult to generate sufficient revenues to keep the doors open, let alone raise wages beyond the bare (legal) minimum, or develop a comprehensive worker benefits package. As such, and even though Mondragón has a degree of job security unheard of in the current neoliberal climate, it has nevertheless been difficult to attract and keep workers in any long-term sense. Turnover has been comparable to, perhaps even better than, industry norms, but still far more of a problem than was originally expected. Few people (and activists are no exception) envision or aspire to a life of full-time, retail, restaurant work—even if that workplace advocates, or puts into practice, many of their deeply held political principles.

For both the founders of Mondragón, and subsequent long-term, committed collective members who have worked and remain there, this has been a hard truth to come to accept. There is a mistaken assumption (but maybe understandable hope) that anyone who shares the basic vision and politics of a project will remain committed to it for some significant time period: two years, five years, maybe ten. (Certainly we never expected some people to leave after only two weeks, two months, or six months, given the rigorous nature of our hiring process!) At Mondragón we assumed (correctly) that training was a heavy investment in workers, and would be ongoing. But we also hoped that it would pay off in the long-term, because *people would remain.* We underestimated the extent of turnover, and the different motivations and desires of even the most politically conscious people for wanting to work at Mondragón in the first place, and then in some cases for wanting to quit. Most of all, we underestimated the significance of the loss of historical, institutional, collective memory and skills that turnover necessarily entails, particularly if the person leaving has been a long-term, committed collective member.

Parecon theory never suggests that training during any period of transition will be easy, that people's politics will automatically translate into long-term commitment (or that it *should*), or that turnover will be a non-issue. But balanced job complexes, almost by definition, require greater training of each person in a given workplace than training each person to do a *category* of work ranked by desirability and empowerment (i.e., the norm for capitalism). The parecon model suggests that "the mutually enforcing benefits of knowing more about each type of work, the enrichment that comes from having diverse responsibilities and the increase in morale that accompanies understanding the whole ... will more than offset these additional training costs."[3]

These costs may not be a problem in a full-blown participatory economy, but they are perhaps more of a problem for parecon-inspired businesses operating within capitalism than one might expect. Turnover makes this kind of broad, balanced training even *harder on parecon-inspired businesses* than regular capitalist ones (which either don't need to bother, or which pass on the expense of training to the individual worker—and then call it "ambition.") The kind of investment in worker skills development that BJC's require may be much less efficient in this transitional context (in terms of cost and long-term benefit) than one would hope—at least until or unless the workplace is able to address the problem of turnover.

This is by no means an argument for abandoning such training or avoiding balanced job complexes. But it needs to be acknowledged as one more in a long line of financial constraints imposed on alternative businesses, and that it is a *political* and *collective* choice to ignore the added costs, in favor of other values or workplace goals. (This political choice to assume extra financial burdens—which no capitalist business would *voluntarily* entertain—is a common experience among alternative, progressive businesses and institutions, and goes well beyond training for balanced job complexes. For example, spending more for fair trade, organic, union-made, or non-sweatshop goods consumed by the business *could* translate directly into lower net revenues, and thus lower overall wages. But in any case, it is a collective decision, taking into account qualitative information beyond the market cost, which workers must impose on themselves during any period of transition.)

Beyond the question of added costs, and the problem of turnover, training in any nonhierarchical workplace has other dimensions and difficulties. Mondragón has tried to formalize its training process, and incorporate things like checklists and training "buddies" for new workers, but in practice training has remained fairly *ad hoc*, and often left to individual initiative. The absence of a clear, consistent, transparent training system has been a big problem, but doing the work to establish a system that will help facilitate training *in the future*, and in fact doing *any kind* of conceptualizing and system building routinely gets put on the back burner. Sometimes, though not always, this is for understandable reasons. People are stressed about immediate work *in the present* (getting a produce order in on time, getting the doors open on time, helping the customer who's standing right there, and so on). New and veteran collective members are expected to take initiative in terms of their own training, and veteran members can be impatient when it comes to training new people—at least, if they are simultaneously doing their own work in a retail or restaurant context, and the pace is fast. Impatience can lead to veteran workers doing work for newer workers—rather than showing them how to do it themselves—simply because it is quicker, or there are deadlines, or they are tired and want to go home. Making the time and effort to arrange proper training workshops for those who need or want them, or for putting together training guidebooks for ongoing reference, has been a constant battle.

As with the achievement of balanced job complexes, training difficulties in a non-hierarchical workplace reflect a constant tension between individual initiative and collective responsibility, between individual self-motivation and peer review and oversight. Mondragón has by no means come close to solving these problems. Recognizing the shortcomings, and recognizing the importance of establishing a formal, clear, and comprehensive training system, is the easy part.

Remuneration on the Basis of Effort

Before discussing remuneration, and the problems of evaluating effort in practice, I would like to address the concern of some activists that payment for labor necessarily corrupts it. While I recognize the importance of volunteer work on a range of issues, I think that making it a principle, or worse, a litmus test for what constitutes "untainted" labor, is a mistake and an obstacle to building self-sustaining and growing infrastructure for the Left. Income is not the same thing as money, money is not the same thing as capitalism, and consumption is not the same thing as excess. Yet many activists have a tendency to conflate these things, and believe that the only way to transcend the corruption, greed, privilege, and excess of capitalism is to remove oneself completely from the so-called "money economy."

However, having an income is simply another way of saying you have a right to consume a portion of the social pie. There is nothing inherently evil about this. Everyone needs to eat, acquire new clothes, stay warm in winter, have access to health care or day care, and so on—and even beyond the basic biological requirements, we have other social and intellectual needs. We want to learn, read books, enjoy or make music, drink beer, watch movies, maybe even travel to other parts of the world (heaven forbid!). The question is *not* "to consume or not to consume," as we are told by some advocates of "Buy Nothing Day," but rather under what conditions, who decides what is produced, what are the social and ecological implications, and what should be the basis for rewarding work and setting income?

There is a whole range of things that an economy, or workplace, could reward. We could pay people on the basis of job type or job performed, on the basis of ownership rights or investment, on the basis of gender, age, or ethnicity, on the basis of some perceived talent, some level of education or training or seniority attained, or on the basis of some quantitative output. All of these are used to some extent under capitalism and markets, although actual income is affected (upward or downward) by the relative bargaining power of workers, managers, and owners—sometimes called "class war." But it seems clear to me that not one of these criteria for pay has any moral basis whatsoever.

What are the alternatives? Can we imagine an economy in which the sole basis for receiving income and benefits is desire or need? Sounds wonderful, but could reward really be divorced from effort and obligation, from work itself? Short of sci-fi fantasies about pure automation, in which every human need is provided for by robots and "replicators," and presumably, in which the robots repair themselves, I doubt it. Not even Star Trek entertains this possibility, which in my opinion would be undesirable even if technically feasible. Marx was more realistic: "From each according to his ability, to each according to his need." Even though he argues that reward should be based on need, he ties this directly to ability, and by implication to work and sacrifice. It is a very powerful sentiment, even if its meaning and application are open to different interpretations.

The parecon model proposes that we ought to reward people *equal pay for equal effort*, in part because effort is one of the few things affecting performance over which people have exclusive control. This is not the same thing as rewarding people on the basis of needs alone, although in any just society (parecon included), there would have to be provisions or exceptions based on need (for dependents, sick and injured, and others who may be unable to work at socially average job complexes, or unable to work at all). Leaving aside for the moment the question of quantifying and evaluating effort (and who or what is best situated to do it), it seems clear to me that remuneration on the basis of effort satisfies our desires not just for equity, but also for efficiency. (Traditional capitalist norms satisfy neither principle, despite the rhetoric about "equal opportunity" and "market efficiency.") Payment on the basis of effort would allow some variations in total pay based on differential effort, and it would allow a more fair and flexible trade-off between income (or consumption rights) on the one hand, and leisure time on the other.

Parecon theory assumes that individual workers will be motivated to work, in part because they will have a direct say over setting work norms and priorities, and in part because people will share the basic politics and values underlying the entire social and economic order. It also assumes that they will be motivated because their income will be directly tied to something they can actually control (i.e., personal effort). If they work more or harder, they'll get more. If they work less, they'll get less. Finally, it assumes that motivation will also come from being held accountable by one's own co-workers, through a mechanism of peer review and effort ratings (which will be more or less formal depending on the particular workplace and workers' councils).

In a period of transition, where isolated workplaces attempt to implement parecon-inspired norms in the midst of capitalism, each and every one of these factors can and does influence worker motivation, but there are added complexities and constraints. People may share the politics, values, and vision of the workplace, but there are always different levels of commitment, and different understandings as to what constitutes the acceptable "average" effort for the workplace or the "minimum" work expectations. Clarity and communication related to job responsibilities and expectations is obviously critical. But even beyond establishing clear norms and expectations regarding average effort, the role of peer review and effort rating is more problematic in a transition period than perhaps suggested by the model.

Alternative workplaces operating within capitalism are almost by definition marginal. Most struggle merely to survive with their principles intact, and paying workers a minimum "living wage"—while far from what we aspire to—is nevertheless a victory in the current context. (Many valuable community institutions cannot afford to pay *anyone*.) Evaluation of effort, and adjustments (up or down) to a worker's already marginal income, is quite a different matter from the situation in a full participatory economy. The stakes are much higher. The consequences of being assessed negatively are potentially serious, threatening one's ability to pay rent or buy groceries, and one's coworkers *know* this. Furthermore, it is quite common for people working in alternative, progressive situations (including collective workplaces) to be friends—and to develop bonds far beyond the basic, everyday empathy one might feel for a coworker. Finally, people committed to building parecon-based institutions are more often than not committed opponents of authority and hierarchy, who instinctively (or politically) despise the notion of monitoring, evaluating, or "policing" one's coworkers and comrades. Even if they understand, in theory, that there is no better mechanism or body able to do so, and believe that it is important to have "checks" against "free riders," in practice, they find the task reprehensible.

All of these things make the evaluation and rating of coworkers' effort much more problematic in practice. Even if they think the theory makes sense, most people *do not want to do it* in practice—at least, not in any systematic or precise manner. At best, people consider it a "rote" task to hold others accountable or to monitor their coworkers. At worst, they find that attempting precision in the realm of peer review is socially or politically offensive (some mistakenly call it "authoritarian"), but in any case, they feel it is not at all conducive to a harmonious work environment. I have serious doubts that many workers' collectives *would* choose to implement an effort rating system with the degree of formality and precision suggested (albeit as one extreme) by the model. This does not mean that anything goes. At Mondragón, formal peer review and negative repercussions arise, but only as a consequence of *major* work deficiencies, and consistent *patterns* of unacceptable behavior or job shirking. In "normal" situations, if Mondragón is any indication, there will likely *be* differences in effort and remuneration that are unfair. Some people will work harder than others, without getting extra pay or acknowledgment. Some people will occasionally shirk duties and "get away with it," with or without their coworkers' knowledge. But I think most people, in practice, are willing to accept a little imperfection, perhaps even a lot, if it means the overall work environment is more welcoming and supportive and relations with one's coworkers remain good.

Another added complexity of remunerating on the basis of effort, specifically during periods of transition, is what happens *outside* the otherwise balanced, collective, pareconish island. Differences in workers' class and cultural backgrounds, gender, levels of education, individual inclinations and histories, and a myriad of other factors (including luck in the genetic "lottery"), all can play a role in determining what each worker needs to do in order to survive. They all can play a role in shaping what each worker sees as his or her options. If two people work in a parecon workplace, and *internally* relate to one another as equals, and *internally* both receive the same rate of pay, but outside come from very different class backgrounds, then there will be inevitably different pressures upon them. They may perceive different options available for them to pursue, and different constraints upon them, and due to outside income differentials, there will be *power* differentials that can be brought to bear inside the workplace.

For example, if one worker is a landed immigrant with no money, no secondary education, and few skilled employment opportunities outside the parecon collective, while the other worker has investments that earn her a steady income regardless of labor, then paying these two workers equal pay for equal effort *inside* the collective environment is, well, nice. But it obscures very real class differences, and makes overall remuneration on the basis of effort problematic, if not impossible.

If one worker can put in a relaxing work week of twenty hours, and then spend their remaining time doing other forms of activism, going to meetings, reading Howard Zinn, playing guitar, or even doing some high-paying, empowering contract work on the side—but the other worker has to work full-time and still pick up a second job—then, for starters, there is no actual economic equality, and remuneration on the basis of effort is an agreed-upon myth. It is a kind of laboratory experiment that "succeeds" inside the parecon workplace but that fails to account for many real-world variables. More, the differential power that can be brought to bear inside the otherwise equal collective workplace should be apparent. One worker has a power that comes from the ability to *refuse* work. They also have a power that comes from being less tired and deadened by overwork. They have more time to read, and think, and debate, and will have a greater inclination and ability to conceptualize policy options or propose alternative structures for the parecon workplace—not due to some innate capacity that the other worker lacks, but due to their different life and work circumstances. They can also pretend that when *they* volunteer to do work, above and beyond the average expected for the workplace, or above and beyond what they expect to get paid for, then it means their overall effort is greater, and that they are somehow more "committed" to the workplace or politics or principles.

The other worker actually works harder. But much of their effort takes the form of necessary work *outside* the participatory collective environment, and is therefore not considered relevant to the calculus. Amazingly, not many Leftists consider it relevant to the calculus, even ones who agree with the values and aims of parecon. Why, they ask, should our workplace reward someone for work they do elsewhere? Or, the flip side of this, why should our workplace penalize someone for the greater income they make elsewhere—even if that income derives from the "luck" of birth or class privilege? My point in all this is not that it *should not* be relevant. But few activists, socialists, anarchists, and even pareconists think it is something that can be addressed today, right now, within and beyond our own institutions. No workers' collective, trying to survive in the midst of capitalism, is likely to acknowledge outside effort in the form of actual compensation. Few individuals are willing to work for less or no pay, voluntarily, to offset their own privilege. (I'm not talking about the occasional pro bono work here; I'm talking about altering one's day-to-day work circumstances.) Leftists are really good at acknowledging the fact of such disparities; we even spend a lot of time complaining or moralizing about them. We insist they will not exist in the future economy we aspire to create. But we either do not know how to deal with such class (and related effort) disparities in the present, or we do not think they *can* be addressed, or that they even *ought* to be addressed (again, conveniently, "in the present").

The latter belief is the hardest to overcome, and speaks to one of the main problems of transition from capitalism to a participatory economy; namely, our seemingly endless capacity to rationalize material self-interest and even class privilege as something "deserved." I am in no way suggesting that material interest is a problem per se. A good economy will need to satisfy material and many other kinds of human needs. Something else is at work. Even Leftists, who in theory aspire to a future egalitarian economy and classless society, almost universally insist that any income they earn today (whether it is the result of inheritance, or the result of a high status, cushy job, or the result of royalties from some book they have written or music they have made, or some other idea or institution that happens to do well in the market, parecon-inspired or otherwise) is something *they have* earned and deserve, or if not earned, is nevertheless something that they alone have the legal and moral right to "dispose of." They put in the work, they underwent the training or education, they came up with the idea, they made the initial sacrifices (financial or labor), and therefore they deserve to reap the market benefits—or so the argument goes. Often, this rationalization is even expressed in the language of workers' rights, as in the slogan "labor is entitled to all it creates." Left professors call themselves "intellectual workers," obscuring the fact that they are part of a managerial, coordinator class below true capitalists but far above and beyond the experience of ordinary workers. They insist upon the right to dispose of their six-digit salary as something "earned" through years of hard work, and the idea of redistributing some of this income to progressive individuals or institutions is seen as their own personal "charity," an example of their "generosity," rather than a "correction" of systematic market mis-valuation of prices and labor.

But regardless of the example, this insistence that whatever one "earns" under the market is "deserved," has more to do with reproducing capitalist values, work relations and principles of remuneration, than subverting them. It obscures the fact that most workers under capitalism deserve *more* income than the market allocates, while a good deal of what generates high income (investments, ownership, royalties, relatively desirable and empowering careers) deserve a lot *less* remuneration, or in some cases, none at all.

How do we begin to address such disparities, and move toward a parecon future, if Leftists themselves won't question the privileges they sometimes attain under capitalism? How can we talk about rewarding work on the basis of effort and sacrifice in a single parecon workplace, without discussing measures to overcome class and work disparities that exist between individual workers *outside* the collective, and without simultaneously trying to overcome market-induced disparities between different professions and parecon institutions themselves? I do not attempt, or have time, to address these problems here in any depth, though I see them as fundamental to any discussion of transition to parecon. But it seems clear to me that some kind of conscious redistribution (or parecon-inspired allocation), running counter to our own (exclusively) individual self-interest and counter to market imperatives, needs to take place. Individuals and institutions of relative privilege under the market—either in terms of income, or work circumstances, or both—need to shift income to those who are worse off, to those whose labor is undervalued by the market, or to those who expend greater effort and make greater sacrifices to produce the things we value. This is what we claim to aspire to, for the entire economy, down the road. But we need to begin thinking of ways to correct the terrible mis-valuations of the market within, and between, our own alternative institutions today. We need to begin to question our own personal privileges, and think of ways to redistribute income in ways that are fair and will help strengthen or expand the network of alternative institutions that exists right now. It is not about "charity" work. It is not about "donating" to whichever radical organization one feels affinity toward, and thereby easing one's conscience. It is about coming up with our own criteria for correcting the mis-allocation of resources and mis-valuation of labor that occurs under capitalism—right now. Until we resolve some of these disparities, any attempt to pay people for equal effort within a single workplace will necessarily be partial under capitalism.

Finally, problems with motivating workers, problems with productivity and accountability, problems with workers taking initiative and setting their own standards and pace of work, have led some of Mondragón's own collective members to question the effectiveness of rewarding work on the basis of effort. They see areas of work that are consistently neglected, they see disparities in terms of the labor that different co-workers are willing to conduct, they see critical tasks getting performed poorly or not at all, they see some people treating the workplace like they are full partners (keeping the "big picture" in mind, doing "extra" tasks, trouble-shooting as needed), while others often act like employees (shirking duties, foot-dragging, remaining silent about business direction and political vision—except insofar as it might affect their immediate work circumstances). In my opinion, these are all serious problems that any collective needs to face and resolve. But they are *not* a consequence of attempting to reward people for effort—as opposed to rewarding people for something seemingly more tangible, such as productivity and desired outcomes. In my opinion, these problems arise in part because Mondragón has failed to actually implement the principle—*not because the principle fails.* Mondragón, strictly speaking, does not reward people on the basis of effort. It tries to approximate such a principle. It pays people equal pay for equal hours shifted and, over time, the kind of work performed by each worker is roughly balanced with every other worker. But Mondragón leaves some tasks to individuals (who often perform unequal non-shifted "volunteer" work), and more important, workers' relative efforts on and off shift are *not* weighed and evaluated in any strict sense. Poor performance or under-average effort is *not* penalized, unless it becomes a systematic pattern and problem that others become unwilling to further tolerate. (Occasionally, people mark themselves off a certain number of paid hours, on a kind of honor system, if they feel they have worked significantly less hard than expected while on shift. Or they will request extra paid hours to accomplish some task necessary for the business. But this is fairly informal and rare.) Paying people equal pay for equal effort would involve holding one's coworkers accountable for, say, getting things done at agreed-upon times. It would involve more systematic judgment and evaluation of effort on and off shift, than actually happens at Mondragón, precisely because many are reluctant to do it. And it would probably involve acknowledging, and attempting to mitigate or correct, some of the class and income disparities among collective members which operate *outside* the workplace.

Decision Making, Nonhierarchy, and Self-management

The participatory economic model is based on the assumption that workers, when given the chance, not only have the *capacity* to govern their own work circumstances, to make the necessary business decisions that affect their lives, to participate in collective meetings and decision-making processes, and to exercise effective self-management—but they will be *inspired* to do so. Working with one's coworkers, as equals, in a nonhierarchical environment, in which the benefits and burdens of work are shared equally, is not only possible, but more desirable. According to this view, workers will thrive under such circumstances, take initiatives, and teach themselves and others the skills necessary to enjoy a creative, empowering, and harmonious work environment. It is also often assumed, or hoped, that workers will likely be *more* motivated, and *more* productive than under capitalism, where their true interests are subverted, their creative energies curbed, and the very nature and purpose of their work is often pointless, dehumanizing, and directed toward the profits of the few.

In practice, however, such assumptions and hopes are often difficult to sustain—and people who have had extensive involvement and experience working in collective institutions are well aware of the gap between hope and reality, between what might be possible in a new economy and what seems to occur in our own experiments. No, I am *not* suggesting that Ayn Rand was right about "human nature," and that workers need managers to keep them in line. But the difference in behavior, attitude, participation, effort, politics, and commitment between individuals involved in alternative workplaces and collectives—operating right now within capitalism—is often more disappointing than one would hope. How much of this has to do with structural problems or failures of vision in the particular workplace, how much has to do with individuals, how much has to do with problems of hiring in the first place, or inadequacies of training, or lack of clarity of job descriptions or expectations, or how much has to do with the many constraints of operating under capitalism, and the personal baggage we bring from our otherwise hierarchical backgrounds and lives is not easy to determine. But for whatever reason, building a workplace without formal and informal hierarchies, in which workers manage their own affairs, take their own initiatives, set their own collective norms regarding pace and work expectations, in which empowering and rote tasks are balanced, and in which workers effectively participate as equals in the overall decision-making process of the business—is much easier said than done. Explaining why different people respond to opportunities to build, or work within, such a workplace in such radically different ways seems almost impossible. But arguably, it is critical to overcoming many of the problems such institutions face, and critical to any strategy of transition to a participatory economy.

At Mondragón there were often jokes between collective members—indicative of a kind of unofficial "understanding" that things were *not* equal in practice—about the gap between "partners" and "staff." A lot of bitterness arose from the sense by some that others were not "committed" enough to the workplace or politics, or were simply lazy. The flip side to this was the sense by some that others (typically more veteran members) act like managers, or won't relinquish certain tasks, or wield disproportionate influence over decision making, policies, and work circumstances. These perceptions, and in some cases realities, are hard things to change, even when they're recognized as problems which need to be addressed.

One example of this relates specifically to participation at meetings. Just because there are no formal barriers preventing participation does not mean the particular workplace or collective is conducive to it, does not mean people are welcoming of disagreement and debate, and does not mean people are respectful toward their coworkers when they do express opinions or make suggestions. Just because there are no formal barriers barring participation, and even if one's coworkers are generally respectful during discussion, does not mean there are not all kinds of class, gender, and cultural factors at work which shape people's levels of comfort and influence their ability or confidence to participate in meetings, to articulate their views, and so on. Of course, there are things that a workers' collective can do to try to compensate for such things, and to try to make meetings more welcoming, and participation more widespread. There are *always* ways to better approximate the goal of having decision making input in proportion to the degree one is affected. But the best structure, and most welcoming environment for meetings, does not automatically eliminate some people's fears of speaking in front of groups, their reluctance to defend a minority or unpopular position, or their worries about personal conflicts with coworkers or friends.

I still believe that the goals of nonhierarchy and effective self-management are achievable, desirable, and realistic, even in the midst of capitalism. To believe otherwise is an argument for either corporate or Leninist structures on the one hand, or total apathy on the other. (Unfortunately, many of the people who become frustrated or disillusioned by their experience with this or that collective workplace or organization become advocates of traditional corporate business structures, ownership relations, and hierarchy, or they drop out of activism altogether—or both.) But we will not achieve our goals by obscuring the difficulties and problems that arise in our own alternative institutions, by glossing over the limitations and failures of our collective experiences. The literature on parecon does not address the issue of transition in any serious depth. It assumes that the transition will be difficult, that there will be a lot of baggage to deal with, and it assumes that reactionary resistance to (and violence directed against) our efforts will grow in proportion to our own successes, in proportion to elite perceptions that we constitute a "threat." The real difficulty, it seems to me, is this: How do we be honest (and sometimes brutal) in our self-criticism, so that we can learn from our own successes and mistakes, so that we can continue to revise our theories and strategies in light of new experience—and *still* paint a picture of our collective experiences that inspires hope, generates interest, and more importantly, motivates new people to incorporate parecon values and principles into their own lives and work circumstances? It's not just about the *language* we use to describe our vision and alternative examples, though language and representation is also important. The examples themselves must *be attractive*—materially, politically, socially—in order to generate excitement, inspire hope, motivate new people, and keep existing supporters from getting disillusioned or burned out.

Conflict Resolution

Parecon aspires to an economy and type of workplace which "promotes social ties and empathy rather than having an anti-social effect."[4] But the model says very little about a critical component of any workplace, which relates directly to solidarity, as well as nonhierarchical decision making and self-management—namely, interpersonal conflicts. In *Parecon: Life After Capitalism*, Albert states "Of course there are disagreements and personality clashes. But surely these are more manageable once demeaning hierarchy has been eliminated."[5] Albert's faith in the ability of sensible, mature people to raise and resolve grievances, as equals, is reflected in such statements, and perhaps more tellingly reflected in the *absence* of any systematic treatment of grievances and conflict resolution in the model. But, in my opinion, it is not at all obvious that interpersonal conflicts between coworkers will be "more manageable" without hierarchy. My experience at Mondragón, in many ways, suggests the opposite. Obviously, there are critical differences between a participatory economy, and a parecon-inspired workplace struggling within capitalism. Mondragón has eliminated formal hierarchy in terms of its decision making and division of labor, but it still needs to address many informal ones. But regardless of the facts, it is important to point out that conflicts and personality clashes do not *need to be* "more manageable" in order to defend a parecon vision—so long as they are not debilitating, so long as people are not constantly miserable, and so long as they do not sacrifice the other values and goals we want.

In my experience, interpersonal conflicts within egalitarian collectives are vastly more prevalent and difficult to address than most people think or hope. Apart from our complete lack of business experience and knowledge when Mondragón first started up, I would argue that the nature and long-term threat of interpersonal conflicts was one of the things we most underestimated, were most surprised by, and were least prepared to deal with. Why that is, and how different things might be between our present difficulties under capitalism and a long-established parecon, is not intuitively obvious. No doubt there are forces which shape and constrain conflict resolution under capitalism, including within our own alternative institutions, which may be absent in a future participatory economy. For starters, none of us has been raised, right now, to deal with one another as equals. We need to acknowledge that there are actually skills and training involved to deal with one another openly, with respect, to cut through the baggage of our classist, racist, sexist socialization, to transcend the harmful elements of our own pride and egos, and so on. Acknowledging this is not the same thing as resolving it.

But certain manifestations of interpersonal conflicts may also be suppressed under traditional corporate, top-down structures, or channeled into various antisocial aspirations and behaviors, and most people's voices and opinions are silenced. This is hardly meant as a defense of hierarchy as a means of conflict resolution. I am merely suggesting that when we eliminate hierarchies within the workplace, we unleash a whole lot of forces which we have not been prepared or socialized to handle, and that conflicts during such periods of transition are not only inevitable, but possibly *exacerbated* by our own inexperience.

Will such conflicts and our ability to handle them be different under a fully developed parecon? No question. Material pressures and sources of stress will be qualitatively different. We will have been raised, not just in our workplaces, but presumably also in our families, schools, communities, relationships with friends and neighbors, and in our larger affiliations with society or nation or "world community" (however defined), to interact with one another in qualitatively different ways. We will have been trained to be equals, instead of givers or takers of orders. The literature on parecon never suggests that conflicts will disappear. But I doubt very much that they will be as easily "managed," even after capitalism, as Albert and Hahnel seem to suggest. I think that interpersonal conflicts may become much larger parts of our daily lives and work than we currently experience. (Other things, which currently preoccupy our minds and consume our energies, may disappear or become much less time-consuming.) I think they will be qualitatively different, in both source and resolution, but not necessarily less time-consuming or "more manageable." Certainly today, under capitalism, trying to build our own alternatives that foster different values and social relations, it is hard to underestimate the prevalence, importance, and dangers of such conflicts, let alone envision a society in which they are negligible or easily "managed."

The important point in all this, in my opinion, relates to a discussion of language and representation when it comes to parecon vision and practice. There is an inherent tension between wanting to generate "excitement" and interest in parecon values and vision, and wanting to present a picture which minimizes problems, or exaggerates the ease with which they will be resolved. In my own speaking and writing about parecon, and talking about the experiences of Mondragón as a kind of "case study," this has always been an issue. Whether we're talking about the ease with which job complexes can be balanced, or asserting our faith in workers to manage their own affairs, set their own pace, take initiatives, and motivate themselves, or whether we're talking about the relative ease and maturity with which workers will raise grievances and resolve personal conflicts—we *want* things to be easier than they are. But presenting a picture that is less than accurate, or that implies that things will be easier, more manageable, less stress-free in our own alternative workplaces, can contribute to the very disillusionment, burnout, and personal conflicts we want to avoid. This is by no means the *only* source of bitterness and disagreement inside our own institutions, it is not the only factor contributing to turnover, but it is certainly one way that we contribute to our own unrealistic expectations. There will *always* be room for improvement, there will *always* be stressful, difficult, draining, personal conflicts, and we will often handle them less well than we should. Unrealistic expectations about a "conflict-free" (or easily managed) work environment, or unrealistic expectations about a "harmonious family" of activists, happily marching toward egalitarian "paradise," are simply a fast road to burnout and despair.

IV. CONSTRAINTS OF CAPITALISM

Not all of the problems at Mondragón can be attributed to the fact that it is a small "alternative" island in the midst of a capitalist ocean. Mondragón has its own share of structural problems, its own failures of vision, and one can rarely *over*estimate the potential for interpersonal conflicts to destroy otherwise positive projects and alternatives. None of us have been socialized to deal with one another as equals. Having spent our entire lives learning to give or take orders, and to submit to a hierarchy (in the family, school, workplace, state, and often through religion), the difficulty of learning to resolve conflicts openly, as equals, should never be underestimated. And we all, inevitably, bring lots of baggage from the hierarchical, competitive, sexist, homophobic, ageist, classist, and racist institutions that together make up the air we breathe. So yes, things will be difficult, and we should expect that there will always be room for improvement of our own internal structures and practices, social relations, room for self-criticism, and so on.

But certainly the constraints of operating within capitalism are huge. The market inevitably mis-values certain industries and services, certain kinds of labor, not to mention mis-values, and attempts to ridicule, undermine, co-opt, or crush any kind of dissent, organization, movement, or individual that seeks to abolish capitalism. These constraints take many forms, but are perhaps most strongly felt by alternative businesses in terms of the "bottom line." In alternative institutions within a market system, there's an inevitable conflict between politics, values, and integrity on the one hand, and the "bottom line" on the other. At Mondragón, this can be seen in the choices made about suppliers and various inputs required by the business. Where does the coffee come from? Is the produce organic? Where, and under what labor conditions, were the Che Guevara or Propagandhi t-shirts made? It can cost more to avoid pesticides in your food, to avoid items made in sweatshops, and to support products and cooperatives made by union labor or cooperative labor, or to support "fair trade" principles, and so on. Sometimes the ethical thing *does not* cost more under capitalism, but these are parameters that no regular business or corporation is likely to accept, and ones which can help to keep alternative and Left movements and businesses financially marginal.

Regardless of one's goals, businesses within capitalism are forced to compete, not simply with mainstream or corporate versions in the same industry, but often also with other alternative institutions. A principal example of this relating to Mondragón's experience in the book-selling industry is the deliberate undercutting of prices on certain titles and authors by the corporate bookstores in Winnipeg, in a deliberate attempt to undermine and squeeze out the competition (namely, us). It is also reflected in the occasional scouting out of the competition, and the stocking of certain "alternative" titles by the big-box stores, which they would not otherwise order or highlight.

Another constraint has to do with "economies of scale" that favor big businesses or corporations in pretty much every type of industry. At Mondragón, large-scale corporate buying power in both the book-selling and food industries was—and remains—a significant advantage that mainstream business holds over small-scale business (whether it is a small family-owned business or farm, or an alternative worker-run business). This might seem obvious, but it is the kind of thing that contributes to the marginalization or eventual destruction of alternative institutions, not to mention increased concentration and monopolization in industries. It is also something that otherwise progressive and Left people often forget when they (sometimes unfairly) expect alternative institutions to mimic corporate ones in terms of prices or services. In the bookselling industry, large corporate chains can demand and exact larger discounts from publishers and distributors simply by virtue of their buying power. This is one critical way that corporations can undercut alternative store prices, and eventually force competition out of business. Small bookstores often have to take lesser discounts (and either mark-up retail prices to reflect industry standards, or take lower profit margins to remain "competitive"), or they have to forfeit their "right of return" (i.e., to return unsold titles) in order to get the same discounts as corporate giants. This is just one more in a long line of financial constraints which complicate any evaluation of parecon in practice.

Competition between different alternative, already marginal bookstores within a particular city can be just as pronounced, as can competition in terms of online website development and sales. While it makes sense for each city to have at least one progressive bookstore outlet, it is doubtful that any but the largest cities can sustain multiple alternative bookstores under capitalism, and less doubtful that a single country or continent can sustain online book sales from dozens—let alone hundreds—of online Left and progressive alternatives, competing amongst themselves to be a kind of "dissident" amazon.com. And yet this is precisely what the market pushes alternative bookstores and other businesses to do. Regardless of our other intentions and possible commitment to parecon values, we still want to maximize *our* revenues, we still want to pay our bills, we still want to increase workers' wages and benefits as an end in and of themselves. Regardless of its complete and utter inefficiency, we might still ship special-order books clear across the continent (or planet) because our "online store" could be easier to find than an actual progressive store in the buyer's own hometown! It is in our immediate financial interest to ship books from Winnipeg to some buyer in Glasgow, charging them extra for postage and handling, even though there are probably a number of decent anarchist bookstores in Scotland. So in the realm of online book sales, this means that whatever we gain, others tend to lose. The forces at work are such that individual self-interest tends to collide with solidarity and collective interests, and even in some cases, the interests of the customer—not out of necessity or "human nature" but by virtue of market imperatives.

Revenue generation through the provision of a needed service or alternative product, or to cover wages for workers, can take on a logic of its own—such that work can become all-consuming, revenue generation can become more important than political or economic vision, and alternative institutions must struggle to avoid becoming completely parochial or irrelevant. Parecon institutions may have important advantages and "checks" in this regard over "progressive" institutions which adopt hierarchical structures of decision making, labor, remuneration, and so on. But they are by no means immune.

Another constraint of capitalism on this type of work has to do with the limitations on the *diversity* of balanced jobs complexes. At best, BJC's will be confined to single enterprises, or a small set of enterprises in a particular city. The types of work available will be narrower, and the diversity of the tasks able to be performed will obviously be diminished from what would be available under a full participatory economy. This will inevitably have implications for burnout and turn-over in the workplace—making these much more prevalent during any period of transition than the model suggests will be the case in the future. Nothing about the internal structure of the work at Mondragón changes the fact that it remains a service-oriented retail workplace, and that most people do not envision working in such an industry for their entire lives.

One could go on and on about such constraints. The main thing to keep in mind is that they complicate any discussion of parecon theory versus practice, and make tentative any lessons that we might draw from the experiences of, say, Mondragón, or South End Press, or G-7 Welcoming Committee Records, or ZNet/ZMag. All our examples of alternative parecon institutions are shaped by the constraints of capitalism, and the limits of our own vision, and sorting out the causes of our successes and failures, and revising our own vision and practice, will go on forever. At least, I hope so.

V. POLITICAL RELEVANCE AND TRANSITION

I would like to end by talking about political relevance and some questions of transition to a full participatory economy, and in effect, a new post-capitalist society.

But before I do this I want to talk a little about the relationship (commonalities and differences) between what I have been talking about—building alternative institutions, examples of alternative workplaces, and some lessons we can draw—and other points of potential struggle, such as traditional labor unionism, mass civil society movements, and even electoral politics.

First thing's first: cooperatives are a *type* of labor, not separate from it. Both the labor movement as it is typically understood and the cooperative/collectivist tradition are worker strategies to mitigate the brutality of the market system. In this entire discussion, I have *not* been trying to suggest one road over the other. Both are strategies, with their own flaws and advantages. Both have sought to do three things historically:

• Fight for immediate material gains in order to mitigate the exploitation and brutality of the economic system and increase workers' bargaining power (sometimes dismissed as "bread and butter" issues);

• Raise consciousness about the systemic imperatives of capitalism and markets (which *require* an under-class), in an attempt to build a mass movement, and press for larger social and political gains (not just for ourselves, but in solidarity with others at home and abroad); and

• Leave the next generation more skilled and empowered, better able to fight for further gains, and ultimately: create a self-sustaining and growing network of institutions, widening the sphere of social and economic life under community control, and fostering a "new worker" with the practical skills, knowledge and experience to be able to govern their own lives and work.

At their *worst* moments, both labor and cooperative movements have fought for the first of these three (sometimes poorly, but even sometimes with remarkable success), *while ignoring the world beyond* their immediate borders, or accepting the basic framework of inequity as "inevitable."

Now obviously, neither the labor nor cooperative movements are homogenous, and there are vast differences, organizationally, nationally, globally, and historically, within each tradition. At their best, both traditions fight for all of these things. I am in no way suggesting that a parecon-inspired collectivist approach is better or more relevant than radical unionism, than fighting for gains within an existing capitalist business. This is absolutely necessary too. No one will win lasting, systemic changes, "revolution," unless we open up multiple fronts simultaneously. Nor am I suggesting by focusing on labor and work that political and electoral campaigns are useless—although I have yet to find a political party in my own country of Canada that didn't make me vomit! At any rate, winning lasting, systemic changes in any one domain of social life will not happen unless we challenge the structures of power in every domain.

But just as important as it is to not be dogmatic by insisting upon some "primary" front or vehicle of social and revolutionary change, I think it also needs to be pointed out that the values and norms I've been talking about for work and workplaces apply equally to other kinds of institutions, and to our larger "civil society," community, and solidarity movements themselves. For example, if you think the most important thing to be focused on right now is preventing the war on Iraq, or highlighting and mitigating human rights abuses in Palestine (or Turkey, or Colombia, or elsewhere), or challenging U.S. imperialism and corporate globalization more generally, then I think there are still important lessons regarding work and hierarchy to bring to these struggles and to apply to the organizations we work within to advance them.

But, one might ask: Given the horrendous state of domestic and world affairs, and the sheer scale of injustice and oppression that exists, shouldn't our priority be to expose, document, and mitigate atrocities right now—rather than wasting time (or talents) fussing about internal structure, balancing job tasks, or nit-picking about who does what? Isn't it more important to act now?

While I agree with the ethical imperative to act, I think the assumption that equity and job balancing leads to wasted energy, time, or a misuse of talents is simply unfounded. There are a lot of assumptions wrapped up in this, not all of them entirely related to one another. First of all, almost no one uses every hour of their day doing the single most important thing they *could be* doing from an ethical or progressive political standpoint. We socialize, drink beer, dance, take naps, have sex, play games, make music, go to movies, sit in the sun, or just think in quiet solitude. To do otherwise, to be a puritan or martyr without time for human interaction, creativity, or play, is neither realistic nor desirable—even if it is technically feasible. Therefore, to cut back on *some* of our leisure time, to spend *one less* evening at the pub this month, and instead to put some thought into conceptualizing fair and equitable work circumstances, is hardly to turn one's back on activism.

Second, the claim that skills or talents in some area (such as public speaking or writing articles about repression and resistance) will be under-utilized by requiring such people to perform less skilled or less desirable work (like going to planning meetings, or putting up posters), does not withstand even mild scrutiny. It is no different from saying that to abolish racist or sexist divisions of labor (and unequal pay) in the workplace, or inside our movement organizations, would be inefficient, because the "scarce talents" of, say, white men would be under-utilized. The "wasted talent" argument assumes that key talents are present in only small fractions of the population, or assumes that training others to the same level would be too costly. The implicit assumption is that while it is inefficient for skilled orators or journalists to waste time in organizing meetings, or worry about office cleaning, booking rooms for events, fund-raising, or other mundane tasks associated with activism—it is apparently *not* inefficient for others to do so. (As noted earlier, I am in no way suggesting by this that differential knowledge, skills, capacities, and training are irrelevant, or that real differences do not exist. I am merely saying that we cannot use this as a perpetual justification for maintaining class hierarchies and cushy job privileges within our own workplaces and movement organizations.) We need to construct workplaces and broader movements in which the stated policies, structures, and goals include training and empowerment to offset inequalities—rather than accepting them as "unfortunate" inevitabilities.

These are not the only arguments against the "wasted time" and "wasted talent" objections. But, ultimately, I think the insights of parecon, and the lessons of those workplaces attempting to incorporate them into their daily practice, are equally valuable for our movement organizations—regardless of their particular focus. In short, anywhere that there are decisions that need to be made, and work that needs to be done, the questions of internal structure, division of labor, hierarchy, participation, and conflict resolution are central.

Finally, while I have talked a little about the constraints of capitalism on building alternative workplaces and how this complicates any discussion of parecon theory in practice, there are lots of important areas related to transition that have been left out. I have not said anything, for example, about the different constraints upon such alternative institutions, depending on one's country, including its particular history of struggle, and reactionary or repressive obstacles. I also have not had time to discuss some important cooperative/collective experiences around the world, in relation to parecon, including the Basque Mondragón network in Spain, similar networks in Italy, various cooperative experiments in Africa (like the Oodi Weavers), or India's Kerala. Each of these incorporates many of the same values and goals of parecon, and each has its own successes and failures, and many lessons to teach.

So, in terms of political relevance, I think that talking about work after capitalism *need not be* an academic exercise, and building alternative institutions today *need not be* parochial, reactionary, or what is often dismissed as "reformist." It is *up to us* to decide if they remain that way. And it is *up to us* to decide if our alternative institutions and movement's welcome new people, raise awareness, and further *revolutionary* goals. Not only do we not *need* to wait for the (capital "R") Revolution, but we can not wait for it. If everyone does that, there simply will not be one. And if there actually was one—a situation in which the institutions of capitalist power were disabled or dismantled by some popular movement—nobody would have a clue about what to do next, or the skills necessary to do it.

Part of the motivation behind building participatory businesses and organizations today is that we simply want to live in ways consistent with our principles, with dignity, and in solidarity with others, and yes, we want to mitigate the brutality of capitalism, even as we sit in its shadow. But equally important is that we need to learn the skills necessary to govern ourselves, to organize key areas of production, to establish networks of communication and distribution, and to build a culture of resistance and cooperation—all of which will leave us better prepared to fill the political and economic vacuum left by a revolution, and to head off the rise of vanguards, skilled orators, technocrats, "new democrats," Leninists, what-have-you, claiming to rule in "the people's interest."

So, in terms of transition to a full participatory economy, building a network of alternative institutions today is one approach,[6] one front of many—but in my opinion, it is a necessary one. Unfortunately, it is one front on which the Left has often done poorly, at least in terms of building alternatives that actually incorporate *into the work structures* the values that Leftists profess to hold. But the lessons of existing alternative workplaces in Canada and around the world—both parecon-inspired ones, and other "fellow travelers"—are simple. Work *can be organized* without hierarchy, and still be organized, still be efficient, still get the job done. Workers *can* democratically control their own workplaces, set production goals, decide what is an acceptable average effort and pace, and determine their own wages, without running a business into the ground (as Ayn Rand and so-called "coordinator class" managerial advocates everywhere suggest), and we *can* do this without turning our backs on "activism" as it is typically understood.

We need to be realistic about the pace of social change, but we also need to be building *self-sustaining* and *growing* alternative networks right now. And we need to be doing it in a way that will leave the next generation of activists better equipped to press their demands, intensify or widen the struggle, and assume an even greater degree of control over their own lives and work. It is absolutely unrealistic to think that an egalitarian, participatory, feminist, socialist, anarchist, or any other "paradise" can be created in a day, or for that matter *ever*, and unrealistic expectations are a fast road to burnout and despair. But equally paralyzing is the belief that everything is hopeless, or all our efforts are trivial, or everything short of some sweeping revolution is "reformist." We need to strike a balance between hope and reality if we want our efforts to be truly sustainable. And we need real, positive examples to point to, which embody the principles we hold and incorporate aspects of the vision we aspire to. So, I'll end by borrowing a phrase from an unnamed sweatshop corporation: "Just do it!"

(Endnotes)

1   Karl Marx *The German Ideology* (1845–1846), website: www.marxists.org/archive/marx/works/1845/german-ideology

2   See Chapter 12 of this book for an overview of the Kerala example by Richard W. Franke.

3   Michael Albert and Robin Hahnel *Looking Forward: Participatory Economics for the Twenty First Century* (South End Press, 1991): 35

4   Michael Albert *Parecon: Life After Capitalism* (Verso, 2003): 23

5   Ibid.: 196

6   See Brian Dominick's contribution in Part 6 of this book.

Chapter 23

THE NEWSTANDARD:
A PARECON WORKPLACE IS POSSIBLE

Jessica Azulay

A PARECON WORKPLACE IS possible. I have experienced one, and now I believe we can overcome capitalism.

The hierarchical workplace is an insidious institution. It is a powerful mechanism through which capitalism imposes and normalizes some of its most vicious values: It thrives on competition. It encourages authoritarianism and subservience. It rewards workers for their race, gender, education, output, age, conformity, and their ability to "work the system." It is dangerous for individual empowerment and democracy, yet it is embraced even by most social-change organizations. It must be subverted.

The theory of participatory economics provides a framework for creating a new kind of workplace in present-day market economies. It shows us how to organize our work around a different set of values: equity, solidarity, democracy, and diversity.

Unlike some facets of the parecon vision, which may seem lofty and futuristic, the workplace model can to a great extent be immediately implemented. I say this with confidence because I have done it.

For four years, I, along with several coworkers, labored in a parecon-based workplace to produce a daily, online news publication called *The NewStandard. TNS* as we called it, was 100 percent reader-funded and not-for-profit. It upheld the highest ethical standards in the news industry and focused on the perspectives of people most affected by current events and government and corporate policy.

Our particular project was a less-than-ideal laboratory for parecon. At its peak, when there were six of us, we worked from four different locations, which made communication challenging. We worked grueling hours to meet daily publishing deadlines, leaving little time and energy for other aspects of our organization. And the funding pressures of the news and alternative-media industries kept our publication on the financial brink.

Yet we found even this to be a rich environment in which to stave off hierarchy. Using the parecon fundamentals—balanced job complexes, participatory decision making, and payment for effort and sacrifice—we were able to experiment, invent, and reinvent until we found ways of operating that were increasingly efficient and fair.

The workplace structure we created for ourselves was unlike any other parecon-based organization we have ever heard of. Parecon's emphasis on diversity, self-management and solidarity allowed each of us to participate in the development of our organization and to help it work for each and all of us. So here is how this exciting economic vision was put into practice by Megan Tady, Shreema Mehta, Catherine Komp, Brian Dominick, Brendan Coyne, Michelle Chen, Simone Baribeau and myself.

Jill of All Trades

There are many ways to implement balanced job complexes. Some groups have rotated tasks, giving everyone a turn at each to-do. I know of at least one organization that tried to assign an empowerment ranking to each chore. At *TNS*, we didn't have the time to get very scientific about it and we also needed each staffer to work on things she was good at.

We divided our work into four categories: managerial, content, administrative, and something we called "conmin." Had we all been working in the same physical space, there would have been a janitorial category, but since we each worked from home, the messiness of our respective workplaces was not a collective concern.

The managerial category covered work related to decision making. It included attending collective meetings, participating in email discussions, serving on decision making committees, and other forms of coordination and management that involved policy-related decision making.

The content category included tasks associated with creating and publishing: reporting, editing, website development, etc. Since this work became the public face of our organization and required a high skill level, we considered it very empowering.

Administrative work included most of the behind-the-scenes tasks: bookkeeping, answering email, providing technical support to website users, opening the snail mail, answering the phone, cutting and pasting website text or computer code, taking meeting notes, etc.

Finally, the conmin category was something we created to encompass tasks that were less desirable than most content work, but more empowering than most administrative work. This was not one of our original categories, but we created it out of necessity to acknowledge that some tasks carry empowerment with them, but are nonetheless tedious. This category included activities like writing text for our fundraising drives, fact checking, and putting together our member newsletter.

When we divided up the work, we tried to make sure that each staffer was assigned roughly the same number of hours of each kind of work. It didn't always come out equal, but we tried to address inequities by rotating tasks when possible and assigning new or temporary tasks according to who was low on certain types of work. We also audited ourselves periodically by keeping track of who spent how much time on what.

Some aspects of our jobs were very similar. For instance, participation in collective meetings and email discussions were part of everyone's balanced job complex. We also took turns acting as facilitator and note taker at meetings.

The rest of our workdays were fairly specialized. My own balanced job complex during the last year of publication consisted mostly of editing work (content) and an occasional writing assignment (content). I was also the main fact-checker (conmin), the article coordinator (managerial), and the bookkeeper (administrative). And I posted content to the website most mornings (administrative).

Brian Dominick's job complex included website development (content), copy editing (content), and writing/editing short news bulletins (content). He also posted content to the website (administrative), answered the mail and phones (administrative), performed website upkeep (administrative), and provided technical support (administrative). And he coordinated our In Other News section (managerial).

Another coworker, Megan Tady, spent most of her time writing articles (content) as well as doing some editing (content). She was a member of the fundraising/promotion and accountability committees (both a mix of managerial and conmin). And she managed all member email (administrative). Most of the other "managing reporters" like Megan had similar job complexes.

Organized Anarchy

At *TNS* it wasn't that no one was in charge; everyone was in charge. But we did not make decisions in isolation, which would have lead to chaos. Instead, we developed a sophisticated structure to facilitate quick group decisions, self-management and accountability. This was based on a formal policy we called the Participatory Decision-Making Process.

The goal of the decision-making process was to engage all participants in order to account for diverse views and opinions and arrive at the most widely agreeable or acceptable outcomes. The greater the impact a decision would have on the organization, the more agreement it needed.

We arrived at decisions using a variety of democratic methods, including consensus and voting. When a decision had a large impact on our organization, we required consensus, which to us meant that everyone actively accepted the decision. We also limited the circumstances in which members could block consensus to those in which a member felt a decision constituted a radical departure from the mission or core values of the organization or the decision would pose a moral dilemma unacceptable to the blocker.

When impact on the organization was smaller and removed from the realm of morality and core values, we employed a voting method. Sometimes we used simple majority (four out of six votes, for instance), and sometimes we required a super majority (five out of six votes).

Regardless of which method was used, a formal discussion process always preceded a decision so that staffers could weigh in, ask questions, modify proposals, or express dissent. Dissent was always recorded in our meeting notes, even when dissenters eventually accepted an outcome.

To better comply with the principles of parecon, we also sometimes used other, more unorthodox methods, in conjunction with consensus or voting.

One such method was called "proportional input." We used this to account for the disparate impact a decision might have on one or more staff members. When using a voting method, like simple or super majority, individual staffers were assigned additional votes based on how much the decision would impact them.

When using proportional input with consensus, a person who stood to be disproportionately affected by a decision could block consensus, even if the decision posed no departure from the organizational mission and presented no moral dilemma.

Another unorthodox method we used was called "proportional outcome." This method was designed to increase the diversity of our decision-making outcomes. For instance, we used proportional outcome to decide which of several possible new features to implement on our website. We each ranked the possibilities from favorite to least favorite, added up the scores assigned to each item and then used the items with the top three scores.

Proportional-output voting was invaluable in cases where we were seeking the "best" solutions, rather than trying to determine right and wrong ways of moving forward. We often used this method when deciding how much to buy or how much to spend on something. Instead of trying to gain majority support for a specific number, we would each propose a number, average the proposals and use that average as our final decision.

This Participatory Decision-Making Process probably sounds complicated, but over time it became pretty intuitive. For most day-to-day decisions we reached unanimity very easily, even when a voting procedure could have been used. Most of us found it easy to reach compromises and stay relatively unattached to our own preferences because no one wanted to sit in meetings longer than necessary. Staffers had to agree to the decision-making process before joining, and experienced staffers helped newer collective members navigate the process until they were comfortable with it.

Speaking of meetings, we did have a lot of them. We held short morning meetings (about twenty minutes) most weekdays to decide which stories *TNS* would pursue. These meetings took place at the same time every morning and were conducted over a free conference-calling system. Other day-to-day decisions were made over email, instant message, or an occasional emergency conference call.

Decisions that could not be made with these methods or that needed longer discussion were saved for our weekly meetings, which were also held by conference call. These lasted about one to two hours. Facilitation for these meetings rotated among all staff members. The facilitator was also in charge of putting an agenda together and sending it out to all collective members ahead of time. Note taking for these meetings also rotated.

We also held board meetings a few times a year. For these, everyone traveled to one location for a "retreat," which involved a series of meetings over two or three days.

Whenever possible, we saved major organizational decisions for these face-to-face discussions. The task of creating the agenda for these retreats rotated among staff as well.

Before you think the *TNS* workplace was utopian, let me assure you that we did have problems. Sometimes people habitually missed their deadlines. Sometimes staffers violated our policies. Sometimes they abused power. Eventually, we realized that we needed a way to hold each other accountable for such transgressions.

The main goals of our accountability process, developed over several months, were (1) to provide a fair and quick way to address problematic behavior, (2) to focus on restitution instead of punishment, (3) to provide staff members with support or resources they needed to change their behavior, (4) to allow transgressing staff members to own up to their mistakes and self-manage their remedies.

Any staff member could ask for an accountability meeting about another staffer. At the meeting, the problematic behavior would be described in detail and the negative impacts on individuals or the organization would be listed. Staffers would then decide if the violation was mild, medium, or severe. Severity of violations would determine which remedies staffers would have at their disposal.

For mild violations, staffers could ask the violator to write an "owning up letter" to the rest of the collective in which she would describe her own problematic behavior and apologize for it. For medium violations, there were several options, including asking the transgressor to come up with her own plan for restitution, prescribing a course of restitution (like extra work to make up for the extra work she caused someone else), corrective instruction (like re-reading the journalist handbook or read a tutorial about the specific area she messed up with).

For situations in which decision-making power or other forms of empowerment were abused, the collective might temporarily shift the transgressor's balanced job complex to include more rote work and less content or management work.

For the most severe violations, the collective could decide to take away decision making power specific to the offense. The collective could also decide to downgrade a staffer's status from full collective member back to trial collective member. This was a severe step that would strip the transgressor of blocking power for six months at the end of which all other collective members would have to reach consensus to restore full membership.

Payment for Effort and Sacrifice

All full-time staff members at *The NewStandard* were paid the same salary, regardless of seniority. Though we started off having to receive pay in the form of promised "sweat equity," by the end we were paying $21,600 per year, a living wage in most of the cities from which we worked. We also provided health insurance and eleven days paid vacation.

Our sick-day policy was a little less traditional. We wanted to recognize that some people get sick more often or have more family emergencies than others through no fault of their own. So we gave each collective member three personal days that they could use in the event of sickness or personal emergency. And then we created a collective "pot" in which we put four days for each staffer. (For instance, when there were six of us, there were twenty four days in the pot at the beginning of each year.) Anyone could use days in the pot if they ran out of personal days. But if the pot had ever run out of days (which it never did), anyone who used more than four from the pot might have to start paying days back. This just meant that some of the days they took would revert from paid to unpaid days.

The result of this policy was that people had a disincentive to take more days than they needed because they knew that leaving days in the pot would help other collective members. Staffers also knew that if they took more than seven days, they might have to pay some of them back if the pot ran out. This policy helped foster solidarity among the staff as well as accommodate a diversity of needs.

Aside from employing a full-time staff, *TNS* also paid several dozen freelance journalists over the years. We knew that coming up with a system for paying reporters based on their effort and sacrifice would be difficult, but we tried anyway. I think we got pretty close.

We made a list of the different kinds of work entailed in writing news articles and then we assigned a dollar value to each. For instance, conducting a full interview with a source was worth twenty dollars, while reading a document (like a court transcript or a scientific study) was valued at ten dollars. Calling a source for comment chalked up five dollars. There was a base fee for all articles on top of which fees for these specific types of work were added.

We set up an online system so that, after publication of an article, a journalist could log on through our website and fill out an invoice. She would list all the interviews conducted, calls for comment made, documents read, etc. She could also note any extra effort that went into the article. For instance, sometimes journalists had to read documents that were hundreds of pages long or sometimes sources were particularly difficult to interview. When she was done, her editor would review the invoice and adjust amounts accordingly. The editor could also add bonuses for clean copy (which saved others labor time), a quick turnaround (which implied sacrifice) or other extra efforts.

The Capitalist Intersection

Many people think that our nonprofit, reader-driven funding model killed *TNS*. I think it would be more accurate to say that capitalism killed *TNS*. Our funding strategy, which was to ask readers to donate a small amount each month, proved successful in many ways. Per reader, we raised an extraordinary amount of money, much more than we could have if we had tried selling our readers' eyeballs to advertisers.

Our main funding problem was that we never gained enough readers. I believe that is because our news-making model incorporated gobs of hard work and ethics, and we were competing in a greed-driven marketplace that generally rewards exactly the opposite.

Aside from funding, the toughest challenge our collective faced was hiring. The U.S. education system and capitalist economy do not prepare people for working in a parecon workplace. We needed people who were skilled journalists, but willing to work for low pay while putting in the extra effort our high standards required. We also needed people who were ready and able to take on the challenges involved in managing a struggling nonprofit organization, but who were willing to share that power collectively.

We found that many skilled journalists did not always have the desire to manage an organization or enthusiasm for collective decision making. And people with enthusiasm for our workplace values often lacked the reporting or editing skills we required. On top of that, almost everyone qualified for the job could find better pay elsewhere.

For those of us who did end up working at *TNS*, it was life changing. Those who had never even heard of parecon before joining our collective quickly adapted to it and became devotees. The very things that made hiring hard made working on *TNS* rewarding. Each of us was able to learn and grow in many different directions at once and develop diverse aspects of our professional lives. Although our adventure did not last forever, the four-year experience that we created for ourselves and the example that we provided to those who came into contact with us still reverberates.

We discovered the parecon workplace to be an inspirational institution. I believe it could be a powerful mechanism through which a movement for radical economic change could facilitate and normalize its most vital values: equity, solidarity, self-management and diversity. It encourages individual empowerment and democracy, yet it is rejected by most social-change institutions. They see it not as a threat to capitalism, but as a threat to their internal status quo. But, if we must become now what we wish to see in a better society, resistance to true workplace equity and democracy must give way, and nonhierarchical workplaces must be implemented.

Chapter 24

VANCOUVER PARECON COLLECTIVE: FOUR YEARS OF ORGANIZING

Marla Renn

IT HAS BEEN OVER four years since the Vancouver Parecon Collective came into existence. It was sometime in September 2003 that a few of us Vancouver *pareconistas* stumbled upon one another. Since then we have created a project far exceeding any of our expectations and have opened doors for future possibilities that are exciting, intimidating, inspiring, and hopeful. Here, we want to review some of our achievements, failures, and ongoing challenges. We also share some of our aspirations for the near future. We do this with the hopes of encouraging others to learn from our experiences and pursue similar adventures.

After meeting each other we discovered that we all shared a very strong interest in economic justice. But not the kind of economic justice claimed in the myths and lies extolling the virtues of capitalism, with its privately owned productive property, competition, markets, corporate hierarchies, class rule, and inequitable remuneration schemes. Nor were we interested in the kind of economic justice heralded by promoters of authoritarian models of communism characterized by central planning, state owned productive property, and a small elite of coordinators who plan the overall economic course of society. No, we found our commitment to economic justice articulated in Robin Hahnel and Michael Albert's vision of participatory economics.

Beyond discovering our similar commitments to social and economic justice we also had the luck of good timing. Before the first meeting even occurred, one of us was asked to give a parecon presentation to university students. We quickly mobilized to create leaflets, a website, and a mailing list. We recorded the talk with hopes of disseminating the audio; a tactic that over time has led us to make our work available as a resource on the website, as well as channel it through a variety of media outlets such as radio and Lefty publications. That first talk had a very impressive turn out and established a familiar tradition of hosting and participating in events filled with insightful discussion from a wide diversity of perspectives. We emerged from the evening with a sense of inspiring success. It affirmed our belief that people were interested in a model of economic justice that transcended both the failures of capitalism and central planning.

We quickly began organizing regular monthly meetings in order to outreach to those interested in learning more. We have concentrated on being accessible and welcoming in order to encourage participation. Our meetings are advertised as opportunities for organizing and brainstorming new and ongoing projects, activities, and events, or simply to meet and ask questions of the collective. Those interested but unable to attend are invited to forward their ideas or comments via email, as well as suggest another time or meeting location which would accommodate their participation.

Our collective has grown and fluctuated. We were, are, and have been teachers, students, social service workers, computer programmers, journalists, anti-war activists, mothers, political party representatives, vegetarians, vegans, and carnivores.

Our second workshop, "Participatory Economics: A Just Alternative to Capitalism & Communism," was held at the University of British Columbia (UBC). And only a few months later we gave another workshop for "Critical U," a Simon Fraser University (SFU) program aimed at giving people access to university curriculum, outside the university, on the east side of Vancouver. In April 2004 Global Justice TV broadcast our UBC presentation on televisions across British Columbia's lower mainland. Not just once, but three times!

As we closed the door on our first year of organizing and looked forward to the future, our goals, focus, and efforts crystallized further. The foundation of our organizing continued to be education and advocacy based, and toward those ends there were several areas of activity we concentrated on and expanded over the coming three years.

In May of 2004, the Vancouver Area Anti-Capitalist Convergence asked the Vancouver Parecon Collective to present a workshop on "Alternative Economic Models." We presented various models of capitalist, socialist, and democratically planned economies—specifically parecon. Our purpose was to orient Vancouver's anti-capitalist movement toward thinking about what alternatives are available. We also explored the desirability and feasibility of these different economic models, and how we might get there. The result was our talk "Parecon & Other Alternatives to Capitalism."

Around this time we asked Noam Chomsky to comment for us about the importance of organizing for a participatory economy. We thought we would use it on our website and other promotional material. To our surprise, Noam kindly generated a comment in which he said:

> A great many activists and concerned people ask, quite rightly, what alternative form of social organization can be imagined that might overcome the grave flaws—often real crimes—of contemporary society in more far-reaching ways than short-term reform. Parecon is the most serious effort I know to provide a very detailed possible answer to some of these questions, crucial ones, based on serious thought and careful analysis.

This comment obviously exceeded any of our expectations. We are very grateful to Noam for this.

Perhaps one of the most difficult events to organize was our showing of the documentary film *The Corporation*. This was supposed to be a fundraiser for a local anarchist book store, Spartacus Books, which had been destroyed by fire. We also hoped to raise money for another parecon project, *The NewStandard*. For this event we had *The Corporation*'s co-director Bart Simpson present to introduce the film. After the film we held a workshop on parecon. The whole event went off without a hitch, with one substantial exception. Organizationally, it was a success. We put an enormous amount of effort into the event and it went very smoothly. However, financially it was a total failure. We put close to a $1000 dollars into it and made only $150 dollars back. Collective bummer. That did not stop us from enjoying the rest of the day out for lunch and at the beach. Despite the financial failure there was a strong sense of accomplishment in our experience organizing the event. We decided we would not keep the money we raised, that it would be better to give it to the groups we were fundraising for. In the end we felt it was a success.

Another notable event was the "Post-Market" flea market and discussion group, a two-day gathering organized by "Counter Publics," a group of local activist artists. They invited us to hold an info table at their flea market for the first day. The flea market offered an opportunity to interact in new ways via barter and exchange. Participants could trade goods and services for any other goods and services, the only rule being that participants could not use money. One of us traded a copy of *Looking Forward: Participatory Economics for the Twenty-First Century*[1] for a bottle of juice. We didn't dare calculate whether the indicative prices embodied in our swap made this an equal exchange. Such are the limitations to barter, and we were thirsty.

For the event's second day we participated in a discussion weaving through the topics of parecon, the open source software movement, and surrealism. It was here that we were able to fully elaborate on the benefits of a full system of democratic planning as compared to markets or barter systems. We also discussed art in a parecon and possible implications of the open source movement for the anti-capitalist movement.

Tabling events has become a common and effective outreach tool in our ongoing organizing efforts. Our first year, we tabled the first four opening nights for the film *The Corporation*, reaching literally thousands. We have repeatedly attended Vancouver's "Under the Volcano" festival of art and social change, and Vancouver's May Day fair, discovering that these have always been good places for us to mix, mingle, and meet new and like minded people. In June 2006, our collective was invited to table at the East Vancouver car-free street festival, a fun-filled day for 35,000 people. This was a memorable event owing to our creative use of free lemonade and colorful balloons, featuring our own handwritten messages to get our message out and entice visitors. Some of the balloon slogans included, "Economic Justice not Tyranny!," "Equity... Self-management... Solidarity... Diversity... Participatory Economy!," "Self-management is fun!," "Abolish markets for democratic planning!," and "Solidarity makes me happy!" It was nice to see many children holding balloons espousing the virtues of parecon. As is common when tabling events we looked for opportunities to engage in conversations about economic systems, capitalism, its ills, how a society with a participatory economy would operate, and what benefits it would offer. We have observed that a collective post-event recap, analysis, and back pat often highlights many key insights of effective presentation and interaction as well as providing ample opportunity to learn from each other. Over time, this final part of the process has become a respected and anticipated tradition.

A major focus in our education and advocacy work has been our attempts to generate more audio and print media content exploring all aspects of participatory economics for our website and other outlets. We have written, published, and produced commentary, interviews, workshops, reviews, and essays on a wide variety of parecon related focuses. From *Parecon: The Unofficial Economics of Star Trek*[2] to a look at the possible future of architecture in a parecon,[3] and a reexamination of the Spanish Revolution through a participatory lens.[4] Member interviews have featured many of the familiar contributors to parecon commentary and analysis. Our list of usual suspects includes Stephen R. Shalom, on the political vision accompanying a society organized on the principles of parecon,[5] Robin Hahnel on parecon and the concerns of environmentalism[6] and of peace,[7] and Michael Albert on movement strategy.[8] Interviews have also targeted a broader base of anti-capitalists, radical Leftists, and the alternative visions of those not already associated with parecon—such as one member's interview with the band International Noise Conspiracy,[9] discussing the effect of capitalism on art and music and the challenges faced in advancing social change. We have taken care to also include content from other parecon collectives or other economic justice initiatives. Our education initiatives in themselves also represent attempts to spread familiarity and serious consideration of parecon within communities that we as collective members respect and are engaged with.

Our focus on education and advocacy has led us to develop our website as a resource to be used by others, therefore all of the pamphlets, presentations, and workshops we have developed are accessible there. The site hosts blogs, forums, and listserves. And we have also included photos of our events celebrating our efforts and accomplishments. One of the ways our collective has attempted to democratize and bring equity to the uneven distribution of specialized skills has been to develop a wiki website.[10] A wiki has the advantage of allowing those unfamiliar with website building and computer coding to contribute to the addition and manipulation of the site's content, design, and maintenance in an easy and accessible fashion. This transition has allowed our collective to more equally spread around the tasks and skills associated with the website.

We have discovered that a focus on content building has allowed us to champion the production of content by members that would normally not attempt such endeavors, and it has also made apparent the need for us to develop and facilitate skill-sharing workshops within the collective. It remains a challenge for our collective to balance the glory and acknowledgment that some receive for making use of disproportionately valued and already developed skill sets, with the alienation, pressure, and the desire to focus on less visible projects that others experience.

In April 2006, our collective was invited to present two workshops by two different collective members for the "Canada 22: Envisioning Post-Neo-liberalism"[11] conference. Our workshops addressed two questions: "What will the world look like after neoliberalism?" And "What social and political structures and events will take us beyond neoliberalism?" This event was followed soon after by the World Peace Forum which Vancouver hosted in June 2006. Our collective facilitated a talk by Robin Hahnel under the WPF theme of "Economy of Peace." His talk was entitled "War, Peace, and Parecon,"[12] and it was a very successful event judging by the full room, and the great diversity of thoughtful questions and engagement that he received. It was also very exciting and rewarding for our collective to have the opportunity to sit down with Robin afterward and discuss some of the challenges our collective faces, as well as matters related to vision and strategy. Another notable success was our celebration of the seventieth anniversary of the Spanish Revolution, in part because it allowed us to extend an invitation to a new audience largely consisting of the local anarchist community.

In April 2007 we participated in the "Philosopher's Café," a local university initiative to bring philosophical consideration to current issues. Presenting a talk on economic vision, we introduced the ideas of parecon and a lengthy discussion followed. This again was a great success and once again sparked new organizing ideas, contacts, and communication with interested folks. During this month we were also invited to present an introduction of parecon to a university-level political-science class. This invitation prompted us to collectively revisit and rework our introductory presentation. The process that followed was a frustrating challenge to our individual understanding and articulation skills, but the result was a greater capacity for each of us to advocate for our participatory vision in different ways to people from diverse backgrounds and concerns and to support each other in doing so.

We have hosted many social gatherings that commonly take advantage of superb (and free) local beaches and parks. These informal meet-and-greets often include a brief introduction to parecon as well as a facilitated discussion that is commonly related to a current economic issue, such as the latest neoliberal trade pact. Our members have noted the ability of parecon ideas to foster an accessible analysis of the principles and activities of the capitalist economy. Organizing events that make connections to the latest disasters of our capitalist economy, and its effects on our communities, has allowed us to collectively refine and communicate the relevance of viewing our current challenges through a participatory lens.

One of the benefits that parecon theory offers is an ability to present the principles of economic organization to people who either do not see the importance and connection to the pressing social, cultural, kinship, and political issues that we currently face, or to those who feel alienated and intimated by the nature of such conversations.

Our female members have often commented that they have traditionally related to the "economy" as something that experts or people who at least seem qualified (most often men) and are capable of having conversations about. For groups such as women, who hold less power and privilege in our society, economics embodies terminology and logic that is elusive, confusing, and intimidating. This is not a coincidence. In fact, parecon not only offers an alternative vision but also a framework through which to understand, reconstruct, and make explicit the logic and operational structure of capitalist and centrally planned economies. Parecon makes sense of the results and casualties of these traditional economic systems, including the alienation many feel from participating in its design and operation. It also provides sophisticated tools for social organization, insights that anticipate the reliance on or unintentional reproduction of hierarchies where processes are not put in place to directly dismantle the socialized values of our competitive patriarchal, racist, and classist society. By making very clear the disastrous consequences of such a poorly designed system, parecon also sheds light on why it is so important to envision an alternative. The insights offered by parecon help make economic conversations and analysis available to those traditionally alienated from understanding it and engaging in projects to create an alternative. Therefore, we have found that some of the best explanations and introductions that are offered by members of our collective come from those least familiar with the framework of economics.

A major challenge that we face is the great amount of interest exhibited by those whom we present to or interact with compared to the small numbers participating in the collective on an ongoing and consistent basis. This has meant that, at times, aspects of our work have come to a grinding halt or there have been prolonged hiatuses from our organizing efforts. Picking up, losing, and picking back up steam, over and over again, has been an underlying plot of our organizing. We are all volunteering our time and energy to parecon organizing. The organizing is dispersed among what our own time and commitments allow us to do. This means that, even though we may try to share our work equitably, sometimes our efforts are scattered and even dissipate around certain projects. In this context we are constantly fighting against institutional pressures, capitalist and other, in order for us to make our project sustainable and able to grow.

It was after three years of organizing together, experiencing various levels of success and failure in our efforts to share the work equitably, and ensure that as a collective we embodied the same guiding principles of parecon, that we decided it was time to stop and reflect in order to move forward empowered. And so, the idea for the first Vancouver Parecon Collective weekend retreat was born. We began by first identifying all of the tasks that the collective performs throughout its various projects. Soon we followed by classifying all of the empowering and disempowering attributes of each task. But we quickly discovered we had to first define empowerment. We eventually arrived at "the degree of decision-making power and glory that a particular task is made up of."

While elaborating on the attributes of each task, we stumbled over the category of "internal development." Previously, we had listed "mentoring" as a task, attempting to describe the work that is done when new members come in: to make them feel comfortable, be informed, pass on skills, and generally orient them. But we found that by labeling it "mentorship" we were imbuing the role with a hierarchal one-way relationship (I give—you take, I speak and bestow knowledge—you listen; and so forth). We decided that the foundation of the task was really skill sharing, and so we were able to let go of the compulsion to sneak in an unfair power-relation or two.

The next step brought us to rating each of the task categories on the empowerment scale so that we would be prepared to equitably and transparently establish a process for rotating them according to an equal amount of empowering and rote work. While rating the tasks we struggled to focus on empowerment as expressed by our definition, which forced us to acknowledge that the empowerment ratings would be derailed if they were to reflect the accumulation of skills that are transferable into capturing private profits (or a better job, title, lover, car, dog, and so forth). We were able to move forward and avoid the trap of thinking of empowerment as a gain to be coveted and enjoyed independently, rather than one that would generate our capacities to work collectively and foster the development of participatory institutions. Our mapping out of the organization and structure of our work did everything that participatory structures are capable of—challenging assumptions, creating new realities and insights, and making sure that everyone leaves having been heard. It also left us as a collective standing in solidarity, demonstrating our commitment to learn and grow through being vulnerable, honest, and critically thoughtful with ourselves and each other.

We continue to be enthusiastic in fostering new interest in participatory economics as a reliable and concrete alternative, especially for those already organizing around the ills of capitalism. But our initiatives have also highlighted the challenge of advocating for parecon within activist communities that are often well informed about the disastrous consequences of capitalism, but traditionally respond by organizing around an adherence to a specific political ideology.

Four years into our organizing, a central problem that has arisen for our collective is to whom do we target our efforts to communicate parecon as a viable economic alternative. Some of our members are actively involved in the city's activist scene, regularly interacting with and contributing to other organizations such as those within the peace and women's movement. As individuals we naturally extol the virtues of parecon where opportunities present themselves, and raise questions about internal organization and vision, but we do so knowing that we run the risk of subversively attacking the organizational vision or sectarian principles of others, or of behaving like the vanguard for the "participatory path." Reaching into existing activist communities, and sharing participatory principles that effectively transcend the tradition of debilitating hierarchies within organizing, is nevertheless still an attractive initiative for our collective, although we struggle with how exactly to do that. Currently one idea that we are brainstorming around is organizing an activist workshop conference focused on effective organizing.

Collective members have often observed that some of our most eager and active participants have come from backgrounds that include very little involvement with the activist community. Perhaps this is owing to a genuine commitment to the outcome of an equitable and just society along with a lack of adherence to a particular political ideology, but we do find that there is a level of understanding and acceptance of parecon that often surpasses those who position themselves at the cutting edge of social movements. We have and continue to present parecon as a desirable post-capitalist economy within activist circles. So, for these reasons we have considered our education and advocacy efforts would be most efficiently used by targeting those not often directly engaged in battles for social justice. Some of the current ideas we are considering involve doing speaking engagements or film screenings in smaller towns, at community centers, among workers in specific fields such as waitresses and caregiving providers, and facilitating consciousness raising groups amongst specific populations such as women.

Finally, we are challenged by questioning what can or should we do beyond our original mandate of parecon education and advocacy. It has occurred to many of us that, although we are convinced of the importance of such work, we often feel left wanting to do more and questioning what else we could do.

One way we have tried to overcome some of these barriers is to develop a "One Year Plan" which looks forward, mapping out the coming twelve months. However, the process of looking forward is harder than reviewing our past. It demands much more creativity and, in the process, a reevaluation and realignment of our commitments. Below are some of our ideas for the coming year:

- Continue to present introductions to parecon and facilitate discussions on economic issues within university, college, and high school classrooms as well as other community environments we have not accessed yet

- Begin a women's economic reading and consciousness-raising group

- Sponsor an exploration of participatory economics and its related structures of participatory politics, kinship, and culture within an art exhibition

- Collaborate with and provide solidarity to those involved in organizing around trade agreements and the effects they have on our communities

- Make our collective organizing efforts financially sustainable allowing growth. This would mean developing some kind of membership and donation base for our website operations.

• Continue to generate regular parecon content for our website, mostly from Vancouver Parecon Collective members, but also from other diverse writers, activists, organizers, and theorists. In addition this would include generating regular content, applying editorial practices, skills, tasks, and deadlines, just to name a few things we would have to do on top of what we already do as volunteers.

• Create proposal's for participatory budgeting locally in Vancouver, provincially in British Columbia, and also nationally for Canada. We hope to stimulate efforts between diverse activists, community groups, Left think tanks, and policy institutes to create a "shadow participatory budget" which will demonstrate its effectiveness at empowering workers and consumers. This would be used to critique official budgets and push for a series of non-reformist reforms and participatory policy proposals. The outcome would hopefully be to galvanize mass movements and political will power.

• Initiate the development of a Canadian National Parecon Organization. This is something that we think is definitely feasible since Canada already has a rich history and practice of experimentation in parecon institutions. The folks in Winnipeg are the main source of this experimentation. They have the Mondragón Bookstore & Coffeehouse, G7 Welcoming Committee Records, and Arbeiter Ring Publishing house. This is motivated by a recurring desire among us in the Vancouver Parecon Collective to establish networks of cooperation and solidarity among all parecon organizations, enterprises, and individuals. The purpose would be to create an effective parecon advocacy group. Our experience in Vancouver tells us that there is interest in parecon across the country. Some kind of national structure could facilitate interaction and organizing for parecon groups across Canada, becoming an effective tool for advocacy. However, many issues arise, not least of which is a consideration of whether this is a wise pursuit.

• Our efforts to date have been very exciting and, again, more than many of us have expected over the past four years. However, there are still areas we think are very important, but have been unable to make very much progress in. These efforts have been overwhelmed by the enormity of redirecting our energies from everyday commitments in our lives. Instead, and this is reaffirming, we seem to be making progress on many other fronts. One of which is the battle to make parecon a visible alternative economic system that people can then choose from. Locally we have made very impressive progress. Globally, we hope to act as an inspiration and perhaps one model for how others can organize for a participatory economy.

(Endnotes)

1   Michael Albert and Robin Hahnel *Looking Forward: Participatory Economics for the Twenty First Century* (South End Press, 1991)
2   Matt Grinder "Parecon: The Unofficial Economics of Star Trek" Vancouver Parecon website: http://vanparecon.resist.ca/StarTrekEcon/index.html

3   Chris Spannos "Architecture of the New Society" *Z Magazine*: www.zcommunications.org/zmag/viewArticle/14075

4   Dave Markland "The Spanish Anarchists, Through a Participatory Lens" Vancouver Parecon website: www.vanparecon.org/index.php/The_Spanish_Anarchists%2C_Through_a_Participatory_Lens. See Part 5 of this book for a revised and updated version of this essay.

5   Stephen R. Shalom interviewed by Matt Grinder "ParPolity: Political Vision for the Good Society" Vancouver Parecon website: www.vanparecon.org/index.php/ParPolity:_Political_Vision_for_the_Good_Society. See also Part 1 of this book for related vision.

6   Robin Hahnel interviewed by Chris Spannos "Participatory Economics and the Environment" Vancouver Parecon, website: http://www.vanparecon.org/index.php/Participatory_Economics_%26_the_Environment_%28part_1%29 See part one of this book for a substantially revised and updated interview with Robin on this topic.

7   Robin Hahnel interviewed by Marla Renn "A Participatory Peace" Vancouver Parecon website: www.vanparecon.org/index.php/A_Participatory_Peace

8   Michael Albert transcribed by Dave Markland "On Movement Strategy" Vancouver Parecon website: www.vanparecon.org/index.php/Interview_on_movement_strategy

9   Dennis Lyxzen interviewed by Chris Spannos "International Noise Conspiracy Interview" Vancouver Parecon website: http://www.vanparecon.org/index.php/The_International_Noise_Conspiracy_Interview

10   Vancouver Parecon website: www.vanparecon.org/index.php/Main_Page

11   Text and audio available at the Vancouver Parecon website: www.vanparecon.org/index.php/Main_Page

12   Transcription available of talk on the Vancouver Parecon website: www.vanparecon.org/index.php/World_Peace_Forum_talk

Chapter 25

CAPES: THE CHICAGO AREA PARTICIPATORY ECONOMICS SOCIETY

Matt McBride, Lloyd Philbrook, and Mitchell Szczepanczyk

CHICAGO HAS BECOME A hotbed for organizing and educational efforts toward a participatory economy. One such grassroots initiative is the Chicago Area Participatory Economics Society (CAPES).

The Beginnings

One Friday evening in September 2004, two Chicago software developers, Jon Osborne and Mitchell Szczepanczyk, met at a coffeehouse in downtown Chicago. They had met through the website Meetup.com, which helps users start and organize discussion groups on almost any topic in practically any city or community in the U.S. This meeting was themed to the theoretical model of participatory economics, which gained increasing popularity after the 2003 publication of Michael Albert's book *Parecon: Life After Capitalism*.[1]

It was at that meet-up that we decided a new name for the group, separate from Meetup.com, and dedicated to work on and around parecon. The suggested name was the Chicago Area Participatory Economics Society, abbreviated CAPES. We liked the name, and CAPES was thus born.

The first task would be to get more people involved, and Meetup.com had attracted a handful of interested potential *pareconistas*. CAPES continued to meet once a month along the lines of its first meeting—in an informal setting and continuing to use Meetup.com as a mechanism for organizing and outreach. In the coming months through May 2005 CAPES would grow from two members to five to include Lloyd Philbrook, Matt McBride, Dylan Clayton among its early members.

The first actions CAPES took on included efforts to widen awareness of parecon. In April 2005, CAPES members rehearsed a four-person presentation of the parecon model and gave an adapted version of the Power-point presentation created by the Vancouver Parecon Collective at the 2005 Chicago Social Forum. In addition, Jon Osborne, using his computer expertise, was working to build a computerized simulation of the model, based on the mathematical formalisms in the book *The Political Economy of Participatory Economics*.[2]

Around this time, CAPES opted to disassociate itself from Meetup.com—both for reasons of cost and since there was now a core group of active organizers and interested participants in the Chicago area. By then CAPES had its own website, developed by Lloyd Philbrook (online at www.chicagoparecon.org).

The Chicago School of Participatory Economics

With increasing momentum, CAPES members opted to organize another presentation. A natural choice of locale was the University of Chicago, whose Department of Economics bears more than a degree of fame (more Nobel Prizes than any other such department on Earth) and infamy (UC Economics is stridently pro-market, and was key for developing and promoting the market-uber-alles philosophy of neoliberalism).

The CAPES forum proposal sounded audacious: Organize a forum about participatory economics on neoliberalism's spawning grounds—indeed, in the very building (the Social Science Research Building at the University of Chicago) where the Department of Economics used to call home. The forum was actually doable. The schedule for the main lecture hall in the building is handled not by any department, but by a separate office in the building. While the Department of Economics might have disagreed with the parecon model, the office readily reserved room SS112 for the event on October 18, 2005.

The forum was dubbed "The Chicago School of Participatory Economics" (a pun on the influential Chicago School of Economics), and parecon co-inventor Robin Hahnel came to Chicago to participate. The event generated some publicity on campus and in Chicago (some 30 people attended). Audio of the event is online at our website.

Additional Efforts

The main success stemming from the Chicago School of Participatory Economics was that it increased the number of people who got involved in CAPES. Among them was Chicago activist Sean Reynolds, whose involvement was pivotal in the organizing of a number of additional CAPES-related events, including:

> • A bilingual Spanish-English presentation about parecon held in March 2006 in Chicago's predominantly Hispanic Pilsen neighborhood

> • Presentation about parecon at the 2006 Chicago Social Forum and at the 2007 Midwest Social Forum in Milwaukee

> • An extended discussion with the 49th Street Underground, an anti-capitalist discussion group from Chicago's south side

> • Frequent distribution of bilingual English-Spanish mini-flyers at assorted Chicago-area progressive events, films, and community markets

Beyond the Capitalist Horizon

In early 2006, CAPES had opened negotiations for a presentation about parecon with the Open University of the Left (OUL), a Chicago group that organizes weekly presentations on topics of interest to political activists. Unfortunately, those negotiations (for assorted logistical reasons) did not quickly lead to a presentation. By October 2006, OUL changed the event from a presentation to a debate, in order to make the event "more interesting." OUL invited David Schweickart, a philosophy professor at Loyola University of Chicago and noted critic of parecon, for a debate at OUL against CAPES about parecon and economic vision.

This led to a debate within CAPES as to whether or not CAPES should participate. Schweickart, although he was and is an ardent Leftist, had gained notoriety in parecon circles for his critique of parecon, summarized in an essay entitled "Nonsense on Stilts."[3] Schweickart was also the inventor of his own economic model, dubbed "Economic Democracy"—a variant of market socialism.

Schweickart's critique presented debating tactics and an understanding of the model that, in the eyes of many *pareconistas*, were considered questionable at best. Still, OUL members refused to consider an alternate proposal or proposals because of the length of time the negotiations took, so the final choice was: take it or leave it. Debate or nothing. In the end, CAPES members voted to pursue the debate, feeling that another presentation of the model was better than none, despite whatever may follow.

A format for the debate was then agreed upon among CAPES, OUL, and Schweickart. Mitchell Szczepanczyk, the CAPES representative for this debate, would present parecon in thirty minutes. Schweickart would have thirty minutes to respond to the model and present his own. The debate took place February 10, 2007, at the Chicago offices of *In These Times* magazine, and dubbed "Beyond the Capitalist Horizon."

By all accounts, the event was hugely successful. As Szczepanczyk noted in the ZNet blogs:

> The event certainly drew a crowd. The room where the event took place was completely filled—about sixty people attended where a robust audience is often twenty. And it was a far more, shall I say, diverse audience than one would find in similar wonky presentations...

> During my presentation, a small number of people scattered throughout the audience would noticeably laugh (but not laugh out loud, thank goodness). This was, as you can imagine, pretty distracting, but maybe the most difficult thing I had to handle all day ... There was not a single time in the entire event where I was left unable to give a response, whereas David was rhetorically trapped at least twice...

However, despite the pretty serious disagreements and serious questions that arose, I should say the event was also very civil, among all participants. I think it was understood that, differences aside, we've got to get to work on figuring out something better. And what was extraordinary about this event was that it was a very real step, however small, in proceeding in that direction.[4]

CAPES: Structural Issues

One of the most pressing issues we face as a group is our structure. How do you structure a group that is volunteer based, seeks a participatory structure absent of illegitimate authority or hierarchy, and have it effectively accomplish the work it seeks to achieve? Participatory economics offers a model for workplace structure, much of which we can apply to our own group, though we can not use remuneration for effort and sacrifice or effort ratings because we are not accountable to each other in a workplace; there is no obligation to do any work at all beyond the word of the members that they will do the work.

So how do we structure it? Certainly every group is different and ought to be structured differently in many respects. Most importantly for CAPES, we do not want to embody traits that undermine the values that make up participatory economics. And up to this point we have not run into too many problems. But CAPES is relatively small in size. What happens when we grow larger, to twenty five or fifty people? With groups of larger size it becomes harder to involve more people in meaningful ways. Suppose we have an upcoming presentation, how do we decide who participates? Should anyone who wants to participate be a participant? What if the number of people who want to participate is twenty? Is that too many participants? If so, how do we decide who participates?

One possible way is to create several working groups: writing group, tech group, presentation group, and so forth, rotating people in and out of each group over time. Then you have more focused groups that work on specific tasks like organizing presentations or designing and maintaining a website. The people within the working group would have more say or control over the content, though the work produced would then be subject to approval or modification by everyone else. But there are some potential problems within this setup. What if someone rotates into a group that they don't want to be in or are just not productive in? If I don't know very much about computers or technology and I do not have the desire to learn that much about it, then my rotation into the tech group might not be very productive for the rest of the group. Should I switch to a different group?

Obviously people are more skilled at certain tasks or possess more of a liking for them, but over time will that keep them in those groups for longer, or indefinitely? How would this affect empowerment, control, or diversity within the group? I suspect this is not a huge issue, but it could develop into one over time.

What happens when we then throw money into the mix? We may not like it, but raising enough money to keep a group afloat is a constant struggle for any Leftist organization. CAPES so far has operated without taking in donations or monies aside from what the members of the group have contributed. But we do not have very many expenses at this point. We do not have to pay for rent, and whatever equipment we need we already possess, borrow, or buy and then return. But what happens when we do start to take in money or work off a budget? Should we use our own money, splitting costs equally, like a membership of sorts? What if someone cannot afford to contribute? Should they have less control within the group? If someone in the group contributes much more money than others in the group should they have more control over how that money is used? I assume most people who work around participatory economics would answer that contributing more money should not give you more control. But it is easy to imagine how this could become a problem.

The issues of group size and money may actually be much easier to figure out than the issues that surround the amount of work or effort someone contributes and how much control that affords. Currently, there are people in CAPES who put in much more time and effort into the group than others. While this does not seem to be a problem in relation to control at this time, how do we guard against it for the future? We do not want a virtual leader or boss to emerge because they do more work or have more knowledge of how the group operates. If CAPES were a workplace and we agree with Participatory Economics' value that we remunerate someone more for more effort and sacrifice, we could remunerate accordingly those who put in more effort and sacrifice. But because it is not a workplace we face the possibility of those who put in more work feeling as though they are being taken advantage of or that they are entitled to more control. And, in the other direction, those who put in less work feel like they are not involved in the group and leave the group because of those feelings. This also affects any new members who join and may not have very much knowledge of Participatory Economics. We want to welcome them and have them contribute as much as possible.

Some of the questions raised here may be obvious to answer or may not present problems at all. But we cannot assume that they will not. Groups that do work around participatory economics have, in some ways, more at stake than other groups on the Left when it comes to matters of structure. If we fail to get it right within our groups, then we can not expect anyone to take us seriously when we talk about structuring workplaces in the present economy to be self-managed, efficient, diverse, solidaristic, and equitable, much less replacing the entire economy with one that embodies these values. Other parecon groups and advocates out there will tell you what they think, what works well for them and what has not, and we will do the same.

CAPES, Parecon, and the Future

We hope that CAPES can continue and expand its work. The way for CAPES to approach the future might be like that of seeing it through the lens of something like a chess game. In chess, you have an expressed goal (win the game by capturing your opponent's king), you have one or more strategies to achieve that goal (things like positioning or relative chess piece value), and you have specific tactics to carry out those strategies (like trapping pieces or attacking two different pieces at once).

A similar situation can be drawn regarding Participatory Economics. The goal here is to replace capitalism with a participatory economy, preferably within a specific and hopefully reasonable time frame. What strategies might we employ to move toward this goal?

Right now, it would seem that one major strategy is to help spread the word about Participatory Economics. It is hard to organize people without letting them know what they are organizing toward. To a great extent, this is what CAPES has been doing already—by presenting the model to various audiences large and small across Chicago and the Midwest. This strategy of outreach would involve a serious media and creative component—which is where the specific realm of tactics then comes into play. Such tactics include the following:

- Refine the presentations that CAPES has already done to make parecon easier to present

- Create other presentations that might depict parts of a participatory economy—in film, videos, works of printed speculative fiction, role playing games, radio games, an appropriately themed blog or series of blogs as other games

- Join with other activist initiatives across Chicago to demonstrate how parecon can be a positive resource for current struggles already underway, using the struggles at hand as "teachable moments"

Once knowledge about parecon is sufficiently widespread, with enough of an audience and base of support, then perhaps another strategy can begin: channeling that base of support into tangible efforts to build alternative institutions. Tactics toward this end can include the following:

- Building new initiatives—perhaps as nonprofit businesses, perhaps as sustainable volunteer efforts—which can implement pareconish institutions in the current economy

- Encouraging sympathetic and like-minded individuals within current capitalist institutions to push pareconish norms and institutions within capitalist institutions

At some point, a much wider and stronger backlash against this pareconish movement is bound to transpire. Of course, the violence of the state will be deployed as part of this backlash, just as it has been against past opposition movements.

For example, if we look at only the economic aspects of this backlash, advocates of the status quo would use the inertia of the present system to help wait out rival efforts for a different economy or even a reform like higher wages. In this go-around, it may be harder to play the waiting game where the economic rival in this case can offer tangible and credible reasons for its support. Therefore, the backlash may respond with tangible concessions of its own: higher wages, greater workers' rights, greater visibility, etc.

Then again, the neoliberal agenda has not considered offering concessions in its arsenal of tactics. So, in the absence of substantive arguments that the backlash can deploy in return, the bulk of this backlash may materialize as the biggest smear campaign in the history of public relations—and that is saying something. It might be prudent to begin to think about how to respond back, or at least how to weather this future storm.

Such matters are quite a ways down the road, but like in chess, it is sometimes good to think about your endgame right as you are pondering your opening moves. What you do or do not do in the beginning can affect the outcome in the end.

(Endnotes)

1   Michael Albert *Parecon: Life After Capitalism* (Verso, 2003)
2   Michael Albert and Robin Hahnel *The Political Economy of Participatory Economics* (Princeton University Press, 1991)
3   David Schweickart "Nonsense on Stilts" ZNet, website: www.zcommunications.org/znet/view-Article/4340
4   ZNet blogs: http://blogs.zmag.org

Chapter 26

DOING VISION:
THE AUSTIN PROJECT FOR A PARTICIPATORY SOCIETY

Marcus Denton

RECENT YEARS HAVE WITNESSED a quiet but hopeful advance within the Left to prioritize issues of vision and strategy. To many, including myself, our traditional marginalization of these issues has not only been frustrating but is a major reason for the absence of a mass movement capable of winning a new society. In contrast, a slowly but steadily increasing number of people have been learning about and advocating a set of participatory visions informed by a holistic theory of society and social change.[1] Most visible among these is parecon, but also includes Participatory Politics (ParPolity), Polyculturalism, and Kinship vision, among others.[2] Most inspiring have been the increasing efforts to organize around these visions, with some even launching experiments to implement them in the present.

Still, with notable exceptions, most of those believing in the vision of a participatory society have had few avenues to work toward developing, promoting, and organizing such a vision. It was in this context that the Austin Project for a Participatory Society formed in January 2007.

Beginnings

The idea for the Austin Project occurred to me as a way to incorporate several previous ideas of mine, such as a book discussion group or a Z meet-up group. The goal was to find and build a community of people who shared a basic Left perspective that was radical, institutionally focused, broad in its perspective, inclusive in its makeup, and concerned with matters of vision and strategy. Beyond being a mechanism to advance participatory society, an internally healthy and supportive community of this sort seemed vital if I was to actively rejoin the Left after largely dropping out for more than a year, and with the accumulated residue from seven years of activism amidst Leftist dysfunction, judgment, and sectarianism still fresh on my mind.

Three visionary efforts were particularly inspirational in APPS's formation. As the name suggests, the International Project for a Participatory Society (IPPS), born during the Z Sessions on Vision and Strategy in June 2006, was very promising to me and appeared to be a potentially significant step forward for the prioritization, development, and promotion of vision on the Left. Also important were the Vancouver Parecon Collective and the Chicago Area Participatory Economics Society, which provided valuable models of groups organizing around parecon. Similar to their approach, I imagined the Austin Project as a way to organize locally, but consistent with IPPS and the totalist social theory shaping it, with an expanded focus that would include vision for all realms of social life.

Our initial biweekly meetings centered primarily on issues related to the group's identity, such as whether we should formally endorse parecon or any ideological framework, and where we should concentrate our efforts: whether on educational pursuits or on organizing pareconish projects; directed inward toward the group or in outreach toward the Left; focused on vision and theory or on strategy and practice.

Since members of the group had different levels of familiarity with issues of vision and strategy and particularly the theories, values, and institutions behind parecon and other social visions, early on we began a book discussion group to explore these topics. This has also served as an undemanding way to attract new members to the group and has been valuable as we have begun looking at ways to organize around participatory vision. The books we have chosen have alternated between those focused on theory and case studies. Included in the former category have been Michael Albert's *The Trajectory of Change: Activist Strategies for Social Transformation*[3] and *Moving Forward: Program for a Participatory Economy*,[4] as well as Cynthia Kaufman's *Ideas for Action: Relevant Theory for Radical Change*.[5] Our practice-oriented books have included Theda Skocpol's *Diminished Democracy: From Membership to Management in American Civic Life*,[6] Marina Sitrin's *Horizontalism: Voices of Popular Power in Argentina*,[7] and *La Lega: The Making of a Successful Cooperative Network*, by Piero Ammirato.[8]

The APPS mission statement also gives some insight into our approach thus far. After several rounds—or iterations, for the pareconistas out there—of feedback and editing, we adopted the following:

> The Austin Project for a Participatory Society develops and promotes vision for society based on the values of equality, solidarity, diversity, and self-management. We extend these visions—as well as strategies for implementing them—to all areas of our lives, including work, family, culture, politics, and activism. We have been inspired in this work by the model of Participatory Economics and present it as a vision that exemplifies our values.

Several points are worth noting. As the mission statement suggests, APPS does not view the world through any single Leftist framework or find any one realm of social life to be *a priori* the most fundamental and important, and therefore focuses on each in its own right and with an eye toward the possible influences that diverse oppressions commonly exert. And yet, readers familiar with this approach may notice the absence of the usual descriptors—economy, polity, kinship sphere, and community/cultural realm. This choice to use common, more personal language is consistent with our group makeup and our desire to appeal broadly, including to those without extensive political experience. It also reflects our willingness to modify parts of the participatory framework as circumstances and evidence require. This is also seen in our decision not to endorse participatory economics but rather to "present it as a vision that exemplifies our values," leaving space for continuing critique and adaptation. Finally, our inclusion of activism as an area of focus signifies our belief that the work of vision includes analyzing and building the kind of movement that can be successful in winning fundamental changes—strategy—as well as our intent to apply internally the values we espouse, as evidenced by our rotation of facilitation and note-taking duties, our use of self-management in group decision making, and our concern with being a comfortable, sustainable activist space.

Moving Forward

To date, the primary APPS activity has been our book discussion group, which, in addition to serving as an educational tool, has helped anchor the group while we worked to establish ourselves. Recently we began moving beyond this, pursuing ways to engage and act on these ideas more broadly. In thinking about the means by which the Project can pursue issues of vision and strategy and work toward a participatory society, I have found it helpful to divide our efforts conceptually into five overlapping functions: education, promotion, development, solidarity, and organizing.

The group's educational component has helped members develop shared understandings and explore in more depth parecon and other social visions, historical and contemporary social movements, alternative modes of social organization, and complementary holism as a general social theory, among other topics. In addition to the book group, we are hoping to screen relevant videos such as the Z Sessions on Vision and Strategy[9] and other IPPS and parecon-related material, as well as to host public talks exploring these issues. A local solidarity activist's discussion of the Zapatista movement is one example of the latter. We have also aimed to create a space where local activists can step back and think through longer-term issues of vision and strategy as they apply in their own organizing efforts, something not usually possible in the midst of a campaign. Our panel featuring representatives from local groups who attended the U.S. Social Forum illustrates this.

The second of the Project's functions—promotion—is directed at increasing the priority of vision and strategy on the Left as well as increasing support for parecon as an alternative to capitalism. In addition to hosting speakers and screening DVDs, we hope to prepare and deliver our own talks to area activist groups, colleges and universities, and at public events. Another idea is to conduct a series of motivated interviews with local activists and organizations to learn about their priorities, methods, obstacles, and successes, as well as to push them to define and reflect on their long-term goals and efforts to achieve them.

Reaching further, we have considered sending a series of parecon care packages to prominent individuals and groups both here and abroad. Each care package could include a letter from APPS, parecon articles and books, and even a DVD (not to mention some playing cards, their favorite magazine, and some GORP). While it is possible that the impact of these would be negligible, one can also imagine the importance an acknowledgment or even endorsement by groups such as Argentina's National Movement of Recuperated Enterprises (MNER), Venezuela's National Workers' Union (UNT), or the Zapatistas would have for our collective efforts. What would happen if Hugo Chavez held up *Parecon: Life After Capitalism*[10] at the UN? Could Jon Stewart make parecon relevant overnight? Could parecon and a three-class analysis make the Wobblies relevant overnight? The thought of Rage Against the Machine or System of a Down dropping some pareconish lyrics brings a smile to my face.

While advancing parecon is important, we also understand the need to critique and develop vision for the other main realms of society—the kinship sphere, community/cultural sphere, polity, international relations, and ecology—in order to replace patriarchy, white supremacy, authoritarianism, and imperialism. One idea to accomplish this is to dedicate a month of activities to each realm of society in order to learn about their respective functions, institutions, and governing oppressions and to envision alternative institutions that can meet people's needs and fulfill their potentials. In addition to using speakers, film screenings, book discussions, and other events, APPS members could work together to produce original assessments of previously proposed alternatives and develop proposals and presentations of our own. We also intend for the group's website to eventually be an interactive space to critique and develop vision.

Moving more actively into building a participatory society, the Austin Project also envisions providing support for existing participatory projects and campaigns as well as creating our own. The former task might involve financially supporting and publicizing pareconish businesses—*The NewStandard*, a non-corporate online newspaper being a prime though sadly overdue example—as well as assisting other groups' projects and organizing around participatory society. We have also discussed establishing our own worker-owned business and starting a community-directed organization to channel grants into worker cooperatives. Other possibilities include establishing a Participatory Credit Union and building a self-sustaining network of local worker, housing, and consumer co-ops. These efforts to create new participatory institutions and to fight for pareconish values within existing institutions underlie our belief that such experiments are necessary to provide hope that another world is possible, practical experience to get there, and, through their demonstration effect, momentum for a movement that can win.

From Project to Movement

While APPS' future seems promising, even more exciting is the idea that similar efforts could begin to spread nationally and even internationally. This is not a distant possibility: we have been in touch with individuals considering starting their own PPS chapters in Houston, Texas; Lafayette and New Orleans, Louisiana; and Amherst,

Massachusetts. And in a development that is both hopeful yet underscores our lack of coordination, we recently learned of UK-PPS, a sister participatory group formed in January 2006.[11] Though needing time to develop, such efforts could very well envisage an emerging participatory movement.

What would such a movement look like? It is not difficult to imagine a growing national network of local PPS chapters coinciding with an increase in pareconish experiments and organizing and the increasing incorporation of participatory vision and strategy by existing Leftist organizations and campaigns. A broadening of participatory vision in the kinship, cultural, political, and international spheres would inspire organizing in these areas as well.

Moreover, these developments could be self-propelling. As a loose PPS network evolved into an increasingly coordinated yet self-managing national and international organization, resources would exist to launch larger and broader undertakings and organizing campaigns. As local projects expanded they would compel and inspire increasing solidarity from local—and for exemplary endeavors and pivotal struggles—national participatory activists. And as autonomous organizations increasingly oriented their immediate campaigns around a vision of a participatory society, they could both offer and expect real solidarity from diverse movements sharing the same goal, a possible framework for a movement of movements. Conceivably, a participatory movement that organized through new institutions such as non-corporate media and community assemblies could see these become the infrastructure of a new participatory society.

Whether these imaginings turn out to be wildly over-ambitious remains to be seen. It is clear, however, that any movement capable of creating the changes we long for will be the result of ordinary yet exceptional people acting self-consciously in ordinary and exceptional ways. One of the great strengths—and joys—of the Austin Project for a Participatory Society has been just such participation; members have put forward effective facilitation procedures, produced original handouts, contributed meeting space, ordered books, pitched in for chips and salsa, initiated new projects, and offered ongoing, perceptive feedback, to name only a few examples.

Where do such people come from? While it is possible that we have lucked out due to Austin's progressive political climate or to happenstance, a more likely explanation comes from the nature of the group's focus on positive vision, appreciation for all sides of social life, and self-reflective character. Whereas much of the political Left seems to be tinged with varying degrees of negativity, we generally attract a more hopeful crowd. The mood at our meetings is light, yet thoughtful. We are at once introspective and visionary, looking in and looking out—at our world, our movement, and ourselves.

As with any young organization, APPS faces its share of obstacles. To be honest, I doubted being able to even get the group off the ground, and there have been issues to work through since—among them how we can consistently maintain our momentum, and how to continue to grow and remain open without losing our character and identity. What makes these concerns manageable is the existence of genuine, concerned individuals seeking to understand and build a better world. And fortunately for the movement, that includes just about everybody.

(Endnotes)

1   Complementary holism / totalist social theory is outlined in several works, including Liberating Theory (South End Press, 1986), Michael Albert's *Thought Dreams: Radical Theory for the 21st Century* (Arbeiter Ring Publishing, 2004), and "Radical Theory for a Participatory Society" (March 17, 2007) by Chris Spannos, ZNet, website: www.zcommunications.org/znet/viewArticle/1819

2   See Part 1 of this book, "Defining Spheres of a Participatory Society."

3   Michael Albert *The Trajectory of Change: Activist Strategies for Social Transformation* (South End Press, 2002)

4   Michael Albert *Moving Forward: Program for a Participatory Economy* (AK Press, 2000)

5   Cynthia Kaufman *Ideas for Action: Relevant Theory for Radical Change* (South End Press, 2003)

6   Theda Skocpol *Diminished Democracy: From Membership to Management in American Civic Life* (University of Oklahoma Press, 2003)

7   Marina Sitrin *Horizontalism: Voices of Popular Power in Argentina* (AK Press, 2006)

8   Piero Ammirato *La Lega: The Making of a Successful Cooperative Network* (Dartmouth Publishing Group, 1996)

9   Z Video Productions website: www.zcommunications.org/zvideo/main

10 Michael Albert *Parecon: Life After Capitalism* (Verso, 2003)

11 See the contribution by Mark Evans in Part 3 of this book, where he outlines PPS-U.K.

PART

VI

Moving Toward a Participatory Society

Chapter 27

PRAXIS MAKES PERFECT:
THE NEW YOUTH ORGANIZING

Madeline Gardner and Joshua Kahn Russell

"Vision without action is a daydream. Action without vision is a nightmare."

—Japanese proverb

YOUNG PEOPLE HAVE ALWAYS played a crucial role in revolutionary change. Young people are creative, passionate, idealistic, brilliant, and fearless.

We are both youth organizers. We have worked in movements for racial, economic, and environmental justice since high school. We've been part of struggles for gender equality and indigenous rights. We are currently focusing our energy on engaging majority-white anti-authoritarian sections of the Left, and trying to build another kind of politics: one that takes seriously the issue of race and oppression in our movements, one that is strategic, one that is horizontal, bottom-up, serious, and committed to winning a participatory society.

Strategy is a central thread in our work. Strategy means we make a plan to win concrete changes that work toward building a movement that will win our vision of society. To do that, we integrate the concept of praxis into everything we do. Praxis is the cycle of theory, action, and evaluation/revision (which then modifies your theory and starts the cycle over again). With praxis, each action, whether it is how we go about coalition building, our outreach plan, or how we run a meeting, holds lessons that will deepen our theory of how change is made. So we develop explicit theories about what will work and why, and constantly re-work them by taking time to learn from our practical experience. Praxis is a commitment to continued learning and openness.

Praxis may seem like an obvious concept. *Of course* we should evaluate each action we take and try to learn from it. Yet our generation faces some deep and often unexamined assumptions that leave young activists to constantly reinvent the wheel. The result is that people look for *formulas*—often in the anti-authoritarian youth culture we first came to politics in, that means "franchise activism"—things like food not bombs, critical mass, expressive protest, etc. It is not that those tactics are *bad*, it is that they are *contextual* and often not part of an escalating plan to make tangible systemic changes that affect large numbers of people. Sometimes formulas work, and sometimes they don't. The search for formulas has been the logic behind the worst sectarianism and dogmatic authoritarian Left, and produced front groups that continue to co-opt and subvert movements today. In the past, the formulaic impulse translated into the problematic idea that revolution was a hard science. In youth culture today, it often translates into romanticizing a narrow definition of "direct action" for its own sake, confusing an even narrower definition of "militancy" for radicalism, mistaking subculture for social movement, and taking certain simplistic and absolutist notions around "leadership" and "decentralization" as gospel.

Without a culture of praxis and strategy, social change becomes mysterious and looks arbitrary—it seems like magic. Often form becomes more important than function—concrete tangible changes are no longer the goal, but the act of protest in itself is the point.

In response to these often stagnant cycles, a new youth activism has been bubbling under the surface and is just beginning to flourish. This activism is directly confronting the cynicism with which our generation was raised. Our generation knows change is *necessary*, but we have been raised to be skeptical of anyone saying that it is actually *possible*. All it takes is to see that campaigns *can* be won, collective power *can* be built, and that cynicism melts away.

In the last few years we have seen the birth of a host of inspiring organizations that have been breathing life into young activism. These groups are cutting and pasting from diverse organizing models. They are forging something new by drawing the best from decentralized anarchist networks, socialist party–building, feminist consciousness-raising circles, community base–building organizations, Zapatista caracoles, and many others.

Learning from these models and building a movement more successful than ever before is the challenge of our generation.

Young folks today have more questions than answers, to be sure. But the questions themselves reveal a new line of thinking in our organizing. Some of the most pressing ones for movement building are:

- How do we communicate radical ideas to millions of people?

- What does it mean to organize in ways that are accountable to those most impacted by the issue at hand?

- How do we avoid marginalization? How do we channel youth rebellion into a force that extends beyond subculture?

- What does anti-authoritarian leadership look like?

- How do we facilitate participation by people with varying levels of commitment, capacity, time, experience, and analysis?

- How do we meaningfully account for the way race has historically divided (and continues to divide) social movements?

- How do we make our movement more fun, nurturing, and accessible than ever?

In searching for answers to questions like these, the two of us have been engaged in projects that are putting forth new models of youth organizing. Below are three quick examples of many groups we work in and have been helping build.

(1) Beyond the Choir is an organization dedicated to strategy, training, and analysis. It focuses on helping to create a greater culture of strategy with local grassroots groups working on a variety of issues. Beyond the Choir publishes articles and pamphlets, and is made up of trainers who do workshops with groups across the country. Beyond the Choir's work draws on lessons from past social movements, works to translate social movement theory into accessible language, and is a vehicle to engage in peer-mentorship and leadership development for movement building.

(2) The "new" Students for a Democratic Society (SDS) is a mass-based multi-issue organization that has gained thousands of members and hundreds of chapters within its first year and a half of existence. SDSers across the country are working on national issues including anti-war and just immigration policy. Recently a number of chapters have also won local campaigns for living wages for campus custodial workers, and forced corrupt university presidents to resign. SDS is 100 percent run by students and young people. SDS is pulling from multiple traditions; a wide spectrum of the political Left is represented in its ranks. Ideologues range from anarchist to Leninist, but most SDSers see themselves as unaffiliated radicals. SDS is in a process of growth and learning, and is struggling to find ways to embody its core principle of participatory democracy. There are competing visions for SDS, and the rich debates around organizing and structure have themselves helped shape a new generation of radicals. It is the first time in recent U.S. history that such a large group of (mostly) self-defined anti-authoritarians have participated in building a mass organization that challenges the limits of loose network models.

(3) The new youth network being built by the Rainforest Action Network (RAN) is another example of mixing models—RAN is in the early stages of developing a system of chapters uncommon for nonprofits of its size. Unlike the standard non-profit model of building small clones of itself on campuses and in communities, RAN chapters are semi-autonomous and self-directed. They are developing ways to collaborate with large institutions to participate in international campaigns and leverage nonprofit resources to do grassroots work.

In our experiences helping to build these organizations and networks, we have attempted to distill a set of organizing concepts useful to young activists today. The concepts below were first articulated in an SDS organizational vision document we co-drafted with fellow SDSers Kelly Lenora Lee, Michael Gould-Wartofsky, Kateri Woestman, and Nick Martin.

Our intention for the document was that, unlike a vision for the society we want to win, these could form a vision for the kind of organization we want to become. Rather than a laundry list of things we are for or against, these concepts serve as organizational building blocks that both challenge dominant assumptions and offer us tools with which to do our organizing.

Included below are the revised and edited concepts in that vision document that are both relevant to, and emblematic of, our new generation of youth and student organizing. While they were initially drafted for SDS, we find the excerpts below to be relevant to a much broader audience on the Left.

We Want to Win.

We really believe we can create a more just society. It is possible, and we can do it—therefore we have a responsibility to do it. Our activism is not simply a matter of "fighting the good fight," or some jaded push toward insularity or purism, but is instead grounded in the day-to-day reality of what it takes to build a movement that can win concrete objectives and ultimately transform society.

We are In It For the Long-haul.

Realizing that we can win, we think about what it means to be involved in long-haul struggle, and what it really means to do this for our whole lives. We believe there is more to a movement than taking to the streets for a day. We are building our power over the long haul. This helps give perspective on our collective goals and how we achieve them. We think about how we want the movement—and our organization—to look in five years, in ten years, in twenty years. We think about what we need to do now to get there. We will keep our eyes on the prize.

We are Organizers.

Activists are people who take action to make change in society. Organizers are activists who additionally work to bring many other people into movements. They help build organizations and spaces that engage and activate new people. As organizers, we try to meet people where they are, listen to their concerns, and help to amplify their voices. As organizers, we constantly reach out to new people and build alliances whereever we can. As organizers, we strive to see the big picture—not simply our own viewpoint and agenda. We collectively take responsibility for the direction of our organizations and groups.

We Must be Relevant.

Our actions will be relevant to a context, a community, a target, and a movement. We believe change will be made by many, many people working collectively, not by an elite "vanguard" or a crew of professional activists. Real change is made by mass movements, and we see our organization as part of a mass movement for social change. We will therefore organize around issues that provide tangible, concrete gains to meet real needs in our campuses and communities.

In order to be relevant and build power, our organization must grow. We have to continually grow in numbers and chapters, as well as in our capacity and the depth and sophistication of our organizing. We will continually reach beyond existing circles, building our base and expanding our scope. We will not allow ourselves to become activist cliques, nor allow our movement to be limited to one culture or subculture.

We seek to be an organization that students and youth from all walks of life can see themselves joining. We seek to build an organization with which groups and communities in struggle can ally themselves. We strive to be inclusive and accessible.

A large majority of young people in our society are ready for change. We will appeal to the positive values already commonly held in our society and demonstrate how they are antithetical to the way our current system operates.

To build the movement, it is crucial that we maintain humble and open-minded attitudes. Elitist attitudes discourage new voices and ideas. We take seriously the way activist language, attitudes, and subcultures have been alienating and intimidating and kept us marginal. We can be ourselves while being mindful and attentive to the needs of others in their communities, respectfully, without putting appearances above and beyond the goals of changing the world.

We Believe in Mentorship and Leadership Development.

We want organizations and movements that create the space for new folks to learn organizing and activist skills. Mentorship must occur intergenerationally between youth and movement elders and veterans, as well as internally among our members of various experience levels. We view every new member of our group as a peer-mentor, someone to learn from, as well as encourage and teach.

Mentorship is also about leadership development. We reject leadership that centers on charismatic individuals whom others blindly follow. Instead, we strive to create a space where everyone can develop the skills and analysis to be an empowered change maker. We believe in collective leadership. We will strive for leadership development that pushes everyone up. We can all be leaders in a way that the different talents, skills and experience we each bring will be used for the good of the group. If we are all leaders, we must each take responsibility for our choices and think about the group as a whole, not just ourselves. It is on us to develop each other's leadership—to see the potential in one another and encourage it. We will build one another up and support one another in becoming leaders and taking on responsibilities.

We Will Learn From the Past. We Will Reinvent Our Movement.

Younger generations, without realizing it, often re-invent ways of organizing and thinking about change that have been tried before. However, we know we don't have to do that. We can ground ourselves in a real sense of our organizing history, valuing the lessons of the movements that have come before us. We are committed to a process of asking questions about past social movements and organizations. We will ask why and how the movements of the past have succeeded or failed. We will study each situation so that we are ready to build a stronger movement than ever before. To this we will add our creativity and unique insights. If we hope to win, our generation must engage in a process of reinvention, on its own terms.

We are Building Toward Collective Liberation.

Oppressed people are at the forefront of movements for liberation. We understand that our work must target structures of domination in order to build powerful diverse movements for change. We realize that lines of power cut deep in our society, and we must be grounded in the work of combating systems of white supremacy, patriarchy, capitalism, imperialism, heterosexism, transphobia, and the many other forms of oppression thoughtfully and strategically.

We realize that having a verbal commitment to this work is not enough. We must be *doing* this work. We will make personal commitments to learning how oppression operates and how we can transform it. We are committed to leveraging whatever resources we as students and individuals have, thoughtfully, respectfully, and transparently, for the benefit of the larger movements we participate in.

We are committed to listening to, learning from, and amplifying the voices of oppressed communities and their allies. On our campuses, we will prioritize worker rights, gender justice, affirmative action, defense of Ethnic, Women's, Queer, and African/a Studies Departments, and other issues relevant to oppressed members of our community.

We know that peoples not traditionally recognized as part of the student movement have always been and still are organizing, at the forefront. We recognize that activism and knowledge are not the sole province of peoples of certain colors, languages, nationalities, or genders, and that our movement must equally and accountably nurture and connect the struggles of all. We will not let ourselves be limited by standards and scripts of activism and action that do not account for the experiences of peoples engaged in a variety of struggles. We recognize the diverse and significant ways in which ordinary people resist and combat oppression daily. We recognize and support acts of resistance that empower people, whether or not such acts fit nicely into an activist mold.

We Will be Accountable and Rooted in Solidarity.

Our work must be grounded in strong human relationships. We seek to build relationships on solidarity and trust, will stand together and recognize others' struggles as our own. Our organization will not simply proclaim itself "in solidarity," but actively *practice* solidarity with communities, workers, oppressed peoples, and all allied movements in struggle.

We will build strong movements where we live that can both combat oppression at home as well as have the capacity to offer meaningful support to other movements and communities. Our solidarity will be locally rooted and nationally/globally linked. It will be solidarity across borders, and solidarity against borders. Our solidarity will be horizontal, shared from below. In order to win, we must be able to rely on each other's solidarity.

We will also strive to be an *accountable* movement, one that recognizes, respects, and responds to the collective agency of those struggling for liberation. We affirm our commitment to make our organizing actively accountable to the communities it occurs in and to people organizing from within these communities. We respect the experience of, recognize the leadership of, and actively support the struggles of those directly affected.

We Will be Strategic

Our actions will be strategic, fitted to a collective purpose, a direction, and a need. Strategy is a lens with which we approach our organizing. We will have a clear sense of our goals, and evaluate how our actions move us toward them. We will always act with respect to the community and context in which we find ourselves. We will always think about how to build our organization, develop new allies, and support other movements.

Strategic action is not a "line"—not a mandated set of rules, but a shared orientation. Therefore, strategic action looks different in different places. Our strategy will guide our tactics—not the other way around. Tactics are like a toolbox. If you are building a house, you need different tools at different times—sometimes you need a hammer, other times you need a screwdriver. But you need those tools to be part of a strategy if you want to build the house. More than any tactic for its own sake, we are committed to strategic action to win our goals.

We Will Practice Participatory Democracy.

We believe all of our members have a right to meaningful participation in decision making in the organization. People have a right to participate in decisions proportionate to the degree they are affected by them. Everyone is encouraged to access channels to decision making and those who do access them will be held accountable, wherever possible, to the rest of the organization.

Having good, well-facilitated processes ensures that all voices get heard. We are committed to setting up our organization in a way that those with limited time constraints and resources can all participate. We understand that if our movement is limited only to people who have time for endless meetings, it is not participatory at all. If a space does not nurture diverse voices, it is not democratic. When process becomes a free-for-all it ceases to be participatory—democracy does not mean everyone must speak to every issue in order to make a decision. Accountable delegation is democratic. Recallable delegates are democratic. Roles and responsibilities are democratic.

Participatory democracy is *horizontal* and *organized*.

Our Culture...

Beyond our shared vision and principles we share a certain culture in our organization. A culture can't be written down on paper and agreed to at a convention. It must be made every day, every time we interact with one another.

The culture we build in our group will greatly influence our ability to retain membership, increase commitment, and foster healthy debate between us. If we really do want to win a new society, and thus really are committed to long-haul struggle, our movements and organizations must support us as whole people. They must be fun, nurturing, accepting, and positive. We can't martyr ourselves to the cause and in return get only endless meetings.

Instead, we commit to supporting each other in our work for personal and collective transformation. We will see one another as allies, even when we disagree, and will work to find common ground. We are on the same team. This does not mean shirking away from important debates, or minimizing divisions—dissent and disagreement is what democracy thrives on. But it does mean we will give each other the benefit of the doubt. We will not fall into listserv-demonizing, holier-than-thou posturing, or self-righteous condemnation. We will hold one another accountable to the larger community we are working in.

If we are going to change the world together, we must work to build trust in one another. That can be difficult, but we are up to the task. We recognize that radicalization is a process. We know we all come into the movement at varying levels of political understanding and experience. We will support each other's processes. We will move forward together.

Conclusion

There is a new wave of energy and activity washing over our social movements right now. Students and young people can play a pivotal role in the push to build a participatory society. By grounding ourselves in our situation and thinking strategically, we begin to approach organizing by answering the question posed by Paulo Freire: "What can we do today, so that tomorrow we can do what we are unable to do today?" Today we can do a whole lot. Tomorrow we will be able to do a lot more. We're ready to build. Will you join with us?

Chapter 28

AUTONOMOUS POLITICS AND ITS PROBLEMS: THINKING THE PASSAGE FROM SOCIAL TO POLITICAL

Ezequiel Adamovsky

PART ONE: TWO HYPOTHESES ON A NEW STRATEGY FOR AN AUTONOMOUS POLITICS

MY AIM IN THIS article is to present some hypotheses on issues of strategy for anti-capitalist emancipatory movements. The idea is to rethink the conditions for an effective politics, with the capacity to radically change the society we live in. Even if I will not have the space to analyze concrete cases, these reflections are not a purely "theoretical" endeavor, but spring from the observation of a series of movements I had the chance to be part of—the movement of neighbors' assemblies in Argentina, some processes of the World Social Forum, and other global networks—or that I followed closely in the past years—the *piquetero* (unemployed) movement, also in Argentina, and the Zapatistas in Mexico.

From the viewpoint of strategy, current emancipatory movements can be said to be in two opposite situations (somewhat schematically). The first one is that in which they manage to mobilize a great deal of social energy in favor of a political project, but they do that in a way that makes them fall into the traps of "heteronomous politics." By "heteronomous" I refer to the political mechanisms by means of which all that social energy ends up being channeled in a way that benefits the interests of the ruling class or, at least, minimize the radical potential of that popular mobilization. This is, for example, the fate of Brazil's PT under Lula, and also of some social movements (for example certain sections of the feminist movement) that turned into single-issue lobby organizations with no connection to any broader radical movement.

The second situation is that of those movements and collectives that reject any contact with the state and with heteronomous politics in general (parties, lobbies, elections, etc.) only to find themselves reduced to small identity-groups with little chances to have a real impact in terms of radical change. This is the case, for example, of some of the unemployed movements in Argentina, but also of many anti-capitalist

Editor's note: This paper was prepared for the June 1–7, 2006, Z Sessions on Vision and Strategy, held in Woods Hole, Massachusetts. The session brought together activists from around the world to share ideas and experiences regarding social vision and strategy.

small collectives throughout the world. The cost of their political "purity" is the inability to connect with larger sections of society.

To be sure, this is just a schematic picture: there are many experiments in new strategic paths that may escape those two dead-end situations (the most visible example being that of the Zapatistas and their "Sixth Declaration"). The reflections I present here are aimed at contributing to those explorations.

Hypothesis One: On the difficulty of the Left when it comes to thinking power (or, what truth can be discerned in peoples' support for the Right).

Let us face this awkward question: Why is it that, being the Left, a better option for humankind, we almost never succeed in getting the support of the people? Moreover, why is it that people often vote for obviously pro-capitalist options—sometimes even very Right-wing candidates—instead? Let us avoid simplistic and patronizing answers such as "the people don't understand...," "the pervasive power of the media...," and so on. These sorts of explanations give us an implicit sense of superiority that we do not deserve—nor do they help us, politically speaking. Of course, the system has a formidable power to control culture so to counter radical appeals. But we cannot look for an answer just there.

Leaving aside circumstantial factors, the perennial appeal of the Right lies in that it presents itself (and to some extent really is) a force of order. But why would order be so appealing for those who do not belong to the ruling class? We live in a type of society that rests upon (and strengthens) a constitutive, paradoxical tension. Each day we become more "de-collectivized," that is, more atomized, increasingly isolated individuals without strong bonds with each other. But, at the same time, never in the history of humankind was there such interdependence when it comes to producing social life. Today, the division of labor is so deep that each minute, even without realizing it, each of us is relying on the labor of millions of people from all over the world. In the capitalist system, paradoxically enough, the institutions that enable and organize such a high level of social cooperation are the very same that separate us from the other, and make us isolated individuals without responsibility with regards to other people. Yes, I am talking about the market and the (its) state. Buying and consuming products and voting for candidates in an election, involve no answerability. These are actions performed by isolated individuals in solitude.

Such is our current interdependence that (global) society requires, like never before, that each person does not behave as he or she is not supposed to behave. Yes, we have the freedom to dress like a clown if we want to, but we can't do anything that may affect the "normal" course of society. Because, today, a small group of people, or even one person, has a bigger chance than ever to affect that normal course if they/he wants to. Like never before, a single person has the chance to affect the lives of millions and to cause chaos. Why is this the case today more than in the past? Let us consider an example: if a peasant in 17th century France decided not to farm his land, he would not be putting his neighbors' lives in jeopardy, but only his own. Imagine that he was angry or mad, and set out to impede his neighbors to harvest. In that case, the community would deal with him very soon; in the worst scenario, he might affect one or two of his neighbors. Fast forward to any country in the 21st century. If the three operators of the subway security system decide not to work (or to mess with the system just for fun), or if this important guy from the stock exchange lies about the prospects of AOL, they would be affecting the lives and labors of thousands of people, without those people even knowing the reason for the accident they had, or the loss of their jobs. The paradox is that the ever increasing individualism and lack of answerability before the other makes it more likely than ever before that there will be people who will be ready to cause trouble or harm other peoples' lives and interests, even without good reasons. Ask the students of Columbine about that. Our mutual dependence in some respects paradoxically contrasts with our subjectivity of isolated, non-answerable individuals.

As people who live in this constitutive tension, we all feel to some extent the anxiety for continuity of social order and of our own lives, in view of the vulnerability of both. We unconsciously know that we depend on other individuals doing the right thing; but we don't know who they are, or how to communicate with them. They are close but alien at the same time. This is the same anxiety that popular movies enact once and again in hundreds of films whose narrative structure and themes are almost the same. A person or a small group of people puts society or other peoples' lives in jeopardy—be it because of evilness, criminal orientation, madness, strange political reasons, you name it—until some powerful intervention restores order—a caring father, Superman, the police, the president, Charles Bronson, etc. As a movie-goer we come out with our anxiety sedated, but that comfort only lasts for some minutes...

Just like those films, the political appeal of right-wing calls to order comes from society's anxiety for the ever-increasing possibility of catastrophic disorder. From the viewpoint of an isolated individual, it makes no difference if disorder is produced by another individual for random reasons, or by a progressive collective that does it as part of a political action. It does not matter if it is a criminal, a madman, a union striking, or an anti-capitalist group doing direct action: whenever there is fear of catastrophic disorder and of the dissolution of social bonds, right-wing calls to order find a fertile soil.

There is no point in complaining about that situation: that fear is part of the society we live in. And it is not a matter of attitude: popular support for right-wing options is not due to "lack of political education"—something that could be remedied by simply telling the people what to think in a more persuasive way. There is no "error" in popular support for the Right: if there are reasons to believe that social life is in danger (and there usually are), the choice for more (right-wing) "order" is a perfectly rational option in the absence of other feasible and more desirable options.

What I am trying to argue is that there is a valuable truth to be learnt in the perennial appeal of the calls for more "order." It is time that we consider that, perhaps, what we (the radical Left) are offering is not perceived as a feasible or better option simply because, well, it isn't. The Left has indeed the best diagnosis of what's wrong with society. We now also have a fairly decent offer of visions of what a better society would look like.[1] But what about the question of how to get there? When it comes to that, we either have the option of traditional Leninist parties taking power (sorry, neither desirable nor better for me), or vague and sometimes utterly non-realistic generalizations.

In any case, we invite people to destroy the current social order (which is obviously necessary) so we can then build something better. Our political culture so far has been more about destroying, criticizing, and attacking the present for the sake of the future than about building and creating new and effective forms of cooperation and solidarity here and now. As we live in the future and despise the present, and as we do not bother to explain how we will protect peoples' lives from catastrophic social disorder while we try to build a new society, it is normal that the people perceive (rightly) that ours are nothing but vague, unreliable promises.

For reasons I will not have the space to explain here, the tradition of the Left has inherited serious impediments when it comes to thinking about social order and, therefore, to relating to society as a whole. In general, the Left cannot think power as immanent with respect to social life. We tend to think of it as an external thing, a sort of parasite that colonizes society "from without." In turn, we tend to think of society as a cooperative whole that exists before and independently from that external entity. Hence the Marxist idea that the state, the laws, etc. are nothing but the "superstructure" of a society that is defined primarily in the economic realm. Hence also the attitude of some anarchists, who tend to consider all rules (with the exception of those freely and individually accepted) as something purely external and oppressive, while believing that the state could be simply destroyed with no cost for a society that—they think—is already "complete" and exists below the state's domination. Hence also the distinction that some autonomists propose between power as "power-over" (the capacity to command) and power as "power-to-do" (the capacity to do), as if it was a struggle between two independent and clearly distinguishable "sides"—one evil, the other good.

What matters for our purposes here is to understand that from all three cases mentioned above, it follows a strategic viewpoint (and also a certain "militant culture") that is based in an attitude of pure hostility and rejection of social order, the laws, and all institutions. While some Marxists reject that order for the sake of the new order to be created after the Revolution, some anarchists and autonomists do so in the belief that society already possesses an "order" of its own ready to flourish as soon as we get rid of the political-legal-institutional burden.

Maybe in the past it made sense to think of social change as, first and foremost, a work of destruction of the social order—I do not want to discuss this now. In any case, the situation today makes that strategic choice completely nonviable. Because nowadays there isn't any society "beneath" the state and the market. Of course, there are many social connections and forms of cooperation that happen beyond them. But the main social bonds that organize and produce social life today are structured by means of the market and the (its) state. The market-state has already transformed social life in such a way that there is no "society" outside of them. What would be left if we could make the state and the market cease to function right now by some magical twist? Certainly not a liberated humankind, but catastrophic chaos: more or less weak groupings of de-collectivized individuals here and there, and the end of social life.

From this it follows that, if we adopt a political strategy for radical change that is completely "external" with regard to the market and the state, we would be choosing a strategy that is also, and by the same token, "external" with regard to society. In other words, any emancipatory politics that explicitly (in its program) or implicitly (in its "militant culture" or "attitude") presents itself as a purely destructive endeavor (or that offers only vague promises of reconstruction of social order after the destruction of the current one) will never manage to attract larger numbers of adherents. This is due to the fact that the others perceive (correctly) that that sort of politics puts the current social life in jeopardy, with little to offer instead. We are asking the people to trust us and jump into the abyss, but the people know (and they are right) that the complexity of our society is such that it cannot take that risk. In conclusion, the people do not trust the Left, and they have very good reasons not to.

I would like to argue that we need to rethink strategy, taking into account this fundamental truth: the rules and institutions that enable and organize oppression are, at the same time, the rules and institutions that enable and organize social life as such. They are immanent and constitutive of society. Of course we can have other non-oppressive rules and institutions. But for the time being, the market-state has become the spinal column of the one and only social life we have. In view of this, we cannot continue to offer a political option aimed at simply destroying the current social order. On the contrary, we need to present a strategy (and a "militant culture" or "attitude" according to it) that makes explicit the path by which we plan to replace the market and the state with other forms of management of social life. While struggling against the current order, we need to create and develop, at the same time, institutions of a new type that are able to deal with the complexity of society's common tasks on the appropriate scale.

In conclusion, no emancipatory politics has a chance to succeed if it has a strategy that, implicitly or explicitly, remains external to the issue of the alternative (but actual and concrete) management of social life. There is no autonomous politics or autonomy without taking responsibility for the overall management of the really existing society. In other words, there is no future for any strategy that refuses to think of the creation of alternative forms of management here and now, or that resolves that problem either by means of an authoritarian device (such as the traditional Leninist Left) or by escapes to utopian daydreaming and magical thinking (such as "primitivism," the reliance in angelic and altruistic "New Men" or in abstract schemes of direct democracy, and so forth). To avoid any misunderstanding: I am not suggesting that we anti-capitalists should find and get involved in a nicer way of managing capitalism (that would be the traditionally "reformist" or social-democratic option). What I am trying to argue is that we need to create and develop our own political devices able to manage the current society (thus avoiding the danger of catastrophic dissolution of all social order) while we walk toward a new world free of capitalism.

Hypothesis Two: On the necessity of an "interface" that enables the passage from social to political.

I shall argue that if we are to present a new political strategy that is both destructive and creative at the same time, we need to collectively explore and design an autonomous "interface" that enables us to link our social movements to the political plane of the global management of society. I do not mean by this to endorse the prejudice of the traditional Left, according to which social self-organizing is just fine, but the "real" politics starts only in the realm of party and state politics. When I refer to the "passage from social to political" I do not imply any higher value to the latter. On the contrary, I believe that autonomous politics needs to be firmly anchored in processes of social self-organization, but it also needs to expand so to "colonize" the political-institutional plane. Let me explain what an "interface" would be.

In capitalist society, power structures itself in two fundamental planes, the general social plane (bio-political), and the political plane properly speaking (the state). I call the social plane "bio-political" because, as Foucault has shown, power has penetrated there, in our own lives and daily relationships, so deeply that it has transformed them according to its image and likeness. Market and class relations have shaped us in such a way that we reproduce by ourselves the capitalist power relations. Each and every one of us is an agent who produces capitalism. In other words, power not only dominates us from without, but also from within social life. Yet, in capitalist society that bio-political plane of power is not enough to ensure the reproduction of the system. It also needs a plane that I call simply "political": the state, laws, and institutions. That political plane makes sure that bio-political power relations continue to function properly: it corrects deviations, punishes infractions, decides where to channel social cooperation, deals with larger scale tasks that the system needs, and monitors everything. In other words, the political plane deals with the global management of society; in a capitalist kind of society, it does so under the form of the state.

In current capitalist societies, the social (bio-political) plane and the state (political plane) are not disconnected. On the contrary, there is an "interface" that links them: the representative institutions, political parties, elections, etc. Through these mechanisms (usually called "democracy") the system gets a minimum of legitimacy so that the global management of society can take place. In other words, it is this "elective" interface that ensures that society as a whole accepts that a particular body of authorities makes all the important decisions that everybody else must then accept. Needless to say, this is a heteronomous interface, for it builds legitimacy not for the co-operative whole that we call society, but only for the benefit of the ruling class. The heteronomous interface channels the political energy of society in a way that it impedes society to make its own decisions and to be autonomous (that is, self-managed).

I would like to argue that the new generation of emancipatory movements that is emerging has already done some amazing experiments in the bio-political realm, but is facing great difficulties when it comes to the political plane. There are numerous movements and collectives throughout the world that are practicing forms of struggle and organization that challenge oppression and capitalist domination. Their bio-politics creates—even if in small scale, local territories—human relations of a new type, horizontal, collective, bringing about solidarity and autonomy instead of competition and oppression. However, we still have not found the way to transport those values so that they also become the core of a new strategy for the political plane. As we have argued before, this is indispensable for changing the world. In other words, we still need to develop an interface of a new type, an autonomous interface that allows us to articulate forms of political cooperation in a higher scale, thus connecting our movements, collectives, and struggles with the political plane where the global management of society takes place. We have rejected the other models of interfaces that the traditional Left offered, namely, the parties—be it electoral or vanguardist—and the enlightened leaders, for we understood that they were nothing but a (slightly) different form of heteronomous interface. Indeed, is was an interface that, instead of colonizing the political plane with our values and ways of life, operated the other way around, by bringing the hierarchical, competitive values of the elite to our movements. So the rejection was healthy and necessary. But we still have to explore and design our own autonomous interface. Without resolving this question, I am afraid that our movements shall never establish stronger ties with society as a whole, and will remain in a state of constant vulnerability. (The experience of the Zapatistas' "Other Campaign" will perhaps bring important developments in this respect.)

PART TWO: THE AUTONOMOUS INTERFACE AS AN INSTITUTION OF A NEW TYPE

What would an autonomous interface look like? What kind of new political organization, different from parties, would allow us to articulate vast sections of the emancipatory movement in a large scale? How should it be if it also has to be able to deal with the global management of society, becoming a strategic instrument for the abolition of the state and the market? These are questions that the social movements are beginning to ask themselves and that only they can resolve. The following ideas are aimed at contributing to this debate.

Thesis One: On the need of an ethics of equality

Since there is no point in thinking of rules and institutions for abstract human beings without taking into account their customs and values (that is, their specific culture), let us begin with a thesis on a new emancipatory culture.

One of the most serious tragedies of the Left tradition has been (and still is) its refusal to consider the ethical dimension of political struggle. In general, in both practice and theory, the typical attitude of the Left regarding ethics—that is, the principles that must orient us toward good actions by distinguishing these from the bad actions—is to consider it as a merely "epistemological" issue. In other words, political actions are considered "good" if they correspond with a "truth" that we know beforehand. The issue of the ethically good/bad is thus shrunk into the problem of the correct/incorrect political "line" to be followed. In this way, the Left often ends up implicitly rejecting any ethics of care for the other (and I mean here the concrete other, our fellow beings); instead, the Left replaces it by a commitment to a certain ideology-truth that alleges it represents an "abstract" other ("Humankind"). The concrete effects of this absence of ethics can be seen in our concrete practice, in countless cases in which otherwise good-hearted activists manipulate and inflict violence upon others in the name of "the truth." (No wonder, then, that common people tend to keep as far as possible from those activists).

This nonethical attitude is not bad due just to its lack of ethics, but also because it is often an unconsciously elitist behavior that impedes true cooperation among equals. If you think you own the truth, then you will not "waste" your time listening to the others, nor will you be ready to negotiate consensus. That is why a real emancipatory politics needs to be based on a firm and radical ethics of equality and of responsibility before (and to care for) the concrete other. We still have a long way to go in this sense if we are to create, divulge, and embody a new ethics. Luckily, many movements are already walking along this path. The Zapatista slogan "we walk at the pace of the slowest" is nothing but the inversion of the relation between truth and ethics that we are proposing here.

Thesis Two: Horizontality needs institutions (badly)

Our institutions of a new type need to be "anticipatory," that is, they must embody in their own shape and form the values of the society we are striving to build.

One of our main problems when it comes to getting new institutions lies in two wrong (but deeply rooted) beliefs:

> (1) that organizational structures and rules per se conspire against horizontality and against the openness of our movements, and

(2) that any kind of division of labor, specialization, and delegation of functions brings about a new hierarchy. Luckily, social movements in many corners have started to question these beliefs.

Any person who has participated in a nonhierarchical kind of organization, even a small one, knows that, in the absence of mechanisms that protect plurality and foster participation, "horizontality" soon becomes a fertile soil for the survival of the fittest. Any such person also knows how frustrating and limiting it is to have organizations in which each and every one are always forced to gather in assemblies to make decisions on every single issue of a movement—from general political strategy to fixing a leaking roof. The "tyranny of structurelessness," as Jo Freeman used to say, exhausts our movements, subverts their principles, and makes them absurdly inefficient.

Contrary to the usual belief, autonomous and horizontal organizations are more in need of institutions than hierarchical ones; for these can always rely on the will of the leader to resolve conflicts, assign tasks, etc. I would like to argue that we need to develop institutions of a new type. By institutions I do not mean a bureaucratic hierarchy, but simply a set of democratic agreements on ways of functioning that are formally established, and are endowed with the necessary organizational infrastructure to enforce them if needed. This includes:

(a) a reasonable division of labor, which is indispensable if we are to have a higher scale of cooperation. If everybody is responsible for everything, then noone is accountable for anything. We need clear rules as to which decisions are to be taken by the collective as a whole, and which ones are to be decided by individuals or smaller groups. This division of labor, needless to say, has to be in agreement with our values: tasks and responsibilities have to be distributed in a way that we all have a relatively equal share of empowering, and repetitive, tedious, duties.

b) "weak" forms of delegation and representation. We are right in that representatives often end up "replacing" the rank-and-file and accumulating power to the expense of the rest. But it does not follow from this that we can have large-scale cooperation without any form of delegation. The belief that we can do with simply calling an assembly and practicing (abstract) direct democracy whenever something needs to be decided or done is nothing but magical thinking. We need to develop forms of representation and delegation that make sure that no group of people becomes a special body of decision makers detached from the rest. We need to move from strong leaders to soft "facilitators" who put all their capacity and knowledge at the service of organizing collective deliberation and decision-making processes. For this— again in this case—we need clear rules and procedures.

c) a clear delimitation between the rights of the collective and its majorities, and those to be kept by individuals and minorities. The belief, according to which a collective organization needs to "transcend" the diverging needs/interests of its members, is authoritarian and most harmful. Individuals/minorities cannot, and should not, "dissolve" in the collective. We need to accept the fact that in any human collective there always remains an irresolvable tension between the will and needs of the person and those of the collective. Instead of denying or trying to suppress that tension, an organization of a new type needs to acknowledge it as a legitimate fact and behave accordingly. In other words, we need to reach collective agreements on the limits between individual (or minority) rights and collective imperatives. And we need institutions to protect the former from the latter, and to defend the decision of the collective from unduly individual behavior.

d) a fair and transparent conflict-management code of procedure, to resolve the inevitable internal conflicts in ways that do not lead to divisionism and to the end of cooperation.

Thesis Three: A political organization that "mimics" our bio-political forms

Forms of political organization tend to establish a "mimetic" relation with regard to bio-political forms. They crystallize normative and institutional mechanisms that, so to speak, "copy" or "imitate," certain forms that are immanent to society's self-organization. This does not mean that they are "neutral"; on the contrary, the shape that political organizations acquire may direct social cooperation in a sense that either strengthens heteronomy (power-over) or, inversely, favors autonomy (power-to-do). The political-institutional-legal organization of capitalism is a good example of the first situation: its pyramidal form both mimics and strengthens the basic vertical and centralized relationships of domination. It does not necessarily destroy other decentralized or egalitarian forms of cooperation, but rather places them within a hierarchical framework.

The good society of the future will surely "invert" this current relationship between horizontal and vertical forms in a way that the former, if they are inevitable, can be used for the benefit of the latter. Parecon and the contributions that other authors have presented in this book provide excellent examples of such types of institutional models. The following exploration on strategy and political organizing have been to a great extent inspired by these models.

Our organizations of a new type can be better thought of as an "imitation" of the way cooperative, bio-political networks function. Let me explain myself by using the example of the Internet. The Internet's technical frame and its network-like structure have provided unexpected opportunities for the expansion of social cooperation to a scale that we had never imagined before. The existence of vast "intelligent communities" on the Internet, created spontaneously by users themselves, has been well documented. These communities are nonhierarchical and decentralized, and yet they manage to learn and act collectively, without the need of someone shouting orders. These communities have achieved impressive levels of cooperation.

However, the Internet also displays opposite tendencies toward the concentration of information and of exchanges. I am not referring to the fact that certain governments and corporations still control important technical aspects of the Web, but to phenomena of emergence of "centers of power" as part of the very life of cyberspace. In theory, in an open network any given point can connect with any other in a free, unmediated way. And yet we all use websites and search engines such as Google, which both facilitate connectivity—therefore expanding our possibilities for cooperation and our power-to-do—and centralize the traffic. Sites like Google thus play an ambivalent role: on one hand they "parasite" the Web, but on the other they are part of the very architecture of it. For the time being, the negative effects of the centralization of traffic are not very noticeable. But, potentially, that centralization can easily be transformed—and is already being transformed—in a form of power-over and a hierarchicalization of the contacts within the Web. Take for example the recent agreements between the Chinese government with Google and Yahoo! to censor and control the Chinese cybernauts. Take also the possibility to pay Google in order to appear prominently in searches. These examples show how easily the most important sites can restrict and/or channel connectivity.

What to do then with Google-like sites? They help us find each other, but the very use we give them puts in corporate hands a great power that can easily be used against us. What is to be done? Let me answer with a joke. The strategy of the traditional Left would be that the party has to "take over Google," eliminate their owners, destroy any rival (such as Yahoo!), and then "put Google at the service of the working class." We all know the authoritarian and ineffective consequences of such politics. What would be, instead, the strategy of a naive libertarian? He or she would probably argue that we need to destroy Google, Yahoo!, etc., and make sure that no other big sites emerge, so no one can centralize the traffic. But the result of this would be the virtual destruction of the potential of the Internet, and of the experiences of cooperation that the Web enables. We would still, in theory, be able to communicate with each other. But in practice it would be extremely difficult to find each other. In absence of better options, and in view of the virtual collapse of the possibilities of cooperation, we would all end up surrendering to the first would-be businessman that offers us a new Google.

What would be the strategy of an autonomous politics of the kind we are trying to describe in this text, when it comes to resolve the (rather silly) example that we are discussing? It would probably start by identifying the main crossroads of the Web of cooperation that the Internet articulates, and the loci of power and centralization (such as Google) that the very life of the Web produces. Having identified the immanent tendencies that might give birth to forms of power-over, the strategy of an autonomous politics would be to create an organizational alternative that helps us perform the tasks that Google performs in favor of our power-to-do. It would do so by surrounding any necessary concentration of traffic with an institutional framework that makes sure that that concentration will not subvert emancipatory values present in the "daily (bio-political) life" of the Web. This strategy is about creating a political-institutional device (that is, one that transcends the possibilities of the Web's own bio-political plane) that protects the network from its own centralizing, hierarchical tendencies. An autonomous strategy would not protect the Web by denying those tendencies, but by acknowledging them and giving them a subordinate place within an "intelligent" institutional framework that keeps them under control. The thesis on the "mimetic" nature of the institutions of a new type with regard to the bio-political forms refers to such kinds of "intelligent" institutional operations.

Imagining an Organizational Model of a New Type

Mutatis mutandis, the example of the problems of the Internet may be applied to emancipatory movements as a whole. We have today a loose network of social movements connected on the global level. As part of the very life of that network, there are also loci of centralization and (some) power comparable to Google. The World Social Forum, the "intergalactic" initiatives of the Zapatistas, some NGOs, and even some national governments have helped to expand the connectivity of that network and, therefore, the possibilities to strengthen its cooperating capacities. But that concentration is also potentially dangerous for the movements, for they may easily become a door for the return of heteronomous politics.

How do we think of autonomous strategy in this context? Who would do it, and how? The hypothesis of an "autonomous interface" is about answering these questions. It goes without saying that any strategy has to be developed in and for concrete situations. The following thoughts do not intend to be a model or a recipe, but only an imaginative exercise aimed at expanding our horizons.

We have already argued that an organization of a new type that may perform the task of an autonomous interface has to have an anticipatory design (that is, it has to agree with our fundamental values) and also have the capacity to "colonize" the current state structures in order to neutralize, replace, or put them within a different institutional framework, so that we can walk along the path of emancipation. In practical terms, this means that the fundamental virtue of a new type of organization lies in its capacity to articulate non-oppressive, solid forms of social cooperation on a large scale. Even when all this may sound new, the tradition of emancipatory struggles has already experimented with forms similar to the "autonomous interface" we are talking about. The most famous example would be that of the Soviets during the 1905 and 1917 revolutions in Russia. As an autonomous creation of the workers, the Soviets emerged firstly as bodies for the coordination of the strike movement. But during the course of the revolution, and without "planning" it in advance, they started to perform tasks of "dual power" or, to say it in the terminology we have been using here, of "global management of society." The Soviets were the meeting of the "deputies" that each factory or collective appointed, in a number relative to their size. In 1917 they offered open and multiple spaces for the encounter and horizontal deliberation of a variety of social groupings—workers, but also soldiers, peasants, ethnic minorities, etc.—with diverse political inclinations. Unlike political parties, which demanded exclusive membership and competed with one another, the Soviet was a space of political cooperation open to everybody. During the revolution they dealt with issues such as the provision of food for cities, public transport, and defense against the Germans, etc. Their prestige before the masses came from both aspects: they "represented" the whole of the revolutionary movement in an anticipatory way, and they also offered a real alternative of political management.

The Soviet "interface" had different strategies toward power in 1917: they initially "collaborated" with the Provisional government but without being part of it; then there were the times of "coalition," when the Soviet decided to appoint some of the ministers of the government; then, in October, they finally decided to get rid of the state altogether and replacing it with a wholly new government of their own "peoples' commissars." During that process the dynamic of Soviet self-organizing had multiplied themselves; hundreds of new Soviets emerged throughout the country, which came together in the All-Russian Congress of the Soviets.

True, the experience of the Soviets was soon to collapse under the Bolshevik leadership, for reasons I won't have the chance to discuss here.[2] What matters for our purposes is the historical example of an autonomous interface that was able to articulate the cooperation between those groups and sectors who were in favor of the revolution, and also, at the same time, to take care of the global management of society.

How to imagine a comparable interface, but adapted to our times? Let us imagine an organization designed to be, like the Soviets, an open space, that is, an arena for the deliberation of all groups committed to social change (within certain limits, of course). In other words, it would be an organization that does not establish "what to do" beforehand, but offers its members the space to decide it collectively. Let us imagine that this organization emerges by defining itself as a plural space of coordination of anti-capitalist, anti-racist, and anti-sexist movements; let us call it the Assembly of the Social Movement (ASM).

The ASM is conformed by one spokesperson for each of the collectives accepted as members (the individuals who may want to participate first need to group in collectives). Like the Soviets, the Assembly itself decides whether to accept, or not, new collective members. One of the criteria for inclusion of new members would be to have the highest possible multiplicity by having collectives representative of different social groups (workers, women, students, indigenous people, lesbians and gays, etc.) and also of different types of organizations (small collectives, large unions, NGOs, movements, campaigns, parties, etc.). Unlike the Soviets, larger member-organizations would not have the right to have more spokespersons, but the right to have more "votes" in proportion to their relative importance to the ASM as a whole. For example, the spokesperson of a small collective of political artists would have the right to cast two votes, while the spokesperson of a big metal workers union would have the right to cast two hundred votes. The "voting capacity" would be assigned by the Assembly to each member according to a series of criteria defined beforehand (of course, democratically decided). Thus, the ASM would be able to acknowledge differences in size, previous trajectory, strategic value, etc. according to an equation that also makes sure that no single groups gets the capacity to unilaterally condition the decision-making process. The ASM would try to decide by consensus or, at least, qualified majority for important matters. If voting was necessary, each member-organization would have the chance to use its "voting capacity" the way it prefers. Thus, for example, the metal workers union may decide to cast all of its 200 votes in favor of, say, this direct action against the government that is being discussed. However, if the union was internally divided on this matter, they may also decide to "represent" their minority opinion in the ASM also, by casting 120 votes for the direct action and 80 against it. In this way, the way the ASM functions would not "force" the homogenization of the opinions of its members (which usually brings about divisionism).

Important decisions would always remain in the hands of member-organizations. Each of them would decide freely the style of their spokespersons. Some may prefer to delegate in them the capacity to make all decisions, while others would prefer them to be representatives only in a weaker sense. In any case, the ASM would implement decision-making mechanisms that allow each organization to have the time to discuss the issues beforehand, and then give their spokesperson an explicit mandate on how to vote. By means of electronic methods, member-organizations would also have the chance to express their views and cast votes from afar if they can't be present for any reason, or if they want to follow the debates and make a decision in "real time."

The ASM's decisions would not compromise the autonomy of any member; the ASM would not claim to be the exclusive representative of all struggles, nor would it demand exclusive membership. There may exist several organizations like the ASM operating at the same time, with some overlapping members, without that being a problem. It would be in the interest of all to cooperate with any organization that represents a valid struggle.

The ASM would not have "authorities" in the strong sense of the word (that is, leaders). Instead, it would appoint task-groups of facilitators to deal with different functions, for example:

(1) To receive and evaluate petitions of new membership and recommend the ASM whether to accept them or not, and with how much "voting capacity"

(2) To deal with fundraising and finances

(3) To act as press spokespersons

(4) To visit other organization and to invite them to join ASM

(5) To act as representatives of the whole ASM before other political organizations

(6) To be in charge of conflict management in the case of conflicts between member-organizations.

(7) To organize a school of emancipatory politics.

(8) To make tactical decisions in urgent situations when the ASM cannot respond on time.

(9) To have a partial veto-power on decisions that seriously contradict the fundamental principles of ASM.

(10) To run specific campaigns decided by the ASM (anti-war, anti-WTO, etc.).

(11) Etc.

The post of facilitators would have a limited duration, and they would rotate between different member-organizations so as to avoid accumulation of power of some at the expense of others, and the typical struggles of power between leaders.

What would such an organization be good for? Depending on the political context, it could serve different goals. Let us imagine a context in which the ASM is only starting to organize. It only has a small number of member-organizations, and therefore has little social impact. In such context, the ASM would be a sort of "political cooperative." Each member would contribute with some of its resources—contacts, experience, funds, etc.—for common goals (for example, to organize a demonstration, to protect the members from state repression, to campaign against the IMF, etc.). This cooperative work would, in turn, help strengthen links between social movements in the network.

Let us now imagine a more favorable context. In view of the evidence that the ASM has been working for some time, and that it has helped to articulate forms of cooperation useful for all and in accordance with the emancipatory values it claims to represent, several organizations have decided to join. The ASM has grown, and it now gathers a good deal of organizations of all types; its voice is already audible in society as a whole, and many people listen to their messages with interest. In this context, the "political cooperative" may be useful to mobilize its resources so as to have direct impact on state policies. The ASM may, for example, threaten the government with strikes and direct actions if it decides to sign a new free-trade treaty. If convenient, the ASM may call for an electoral boycott for the next elections. Alternatively, the ASM may decide it would be more useful to have their own candidates run for the legislative elections. According to its main tenets, those candidates would only be spokespersons for the ASM, without the right to decide anything by themselves, and without the right to be re-elected for a second term. If some of those candidates were elected, the "political cooperative" would then be useful to mobilize forces for electoral purposes, and then for distributing the political "benefits" (that is, certain influence in state politics) among all member-organizations. As the candidates would run not as individuals or representatives of particular organizations, but as spokespersons of the

ASM, political "accumulation" would be in favor of the ASM as a whole. Moreover, in view of the great capacity for cooperation thus displayed by the ASM, and in view also that the ASM makes sure that its candidates do not become a caste of professional politicians, its prestige would surely grow in the eyes of society as a whole.

Let us now imagine an even more favorable context. The ASM already has a long experience of work in common. It has grown and has several thousands of member-organizations. It has perfected its decision-making procedures and its internal division of tasks. It has contributed to the spread of a new militant culture and ethics. It has a proficient method to deal with internal conflicts and to make sure that no person or organization accumulates power to the expense of the rest. Its debates and political positions are followed with great attention by the whole of society. The strategy of electoral boycott has been effective, and the government and all parties are losing all credibility. Or, alternatively, the strategy to "colonize" parts of the state with its own people has been successful, and the ASM now controls vast sections of the Legislative power, and some of the Executive power. In either case, the state has lost credibility and a vast social movement is demanding some radical changes. There is disobedience, strikes, and direct action everywhere. In this case, the "political cooperative" may be used to prepare the next strategic step by proposing itself as an alternative means (at least transitional) for the global management of society. The strategy here may vary: the ASM may decide to continue to "colonize" the electoral positions that state politics offer, thus taking over more and more sections of the state until it controls most of it. Or, alternatively, the ASM may promote an insurrectional strategy. Or a combination of both.

Needless to say, this was just an imaginary exercise only aimed at providing an example of an "autonomous interface" at work. In this hypothetical case the ASM has worked both as a tool for the cooperation of emancipatory movements and also as an institution able to take care of the management of society here and now. Its strategy consisted in, first, developing an institutional model that "mimics" the multiple shapes that structure our cooperating networks (that is, an open and plural space, but also endowed with clear rules) with an "anticipatory" character (it is horizontal and autonomous; it expands our power-to-do without concentrating power-over). Secondly, the ASM developed an intelligent strategy by "reading" the configuration of the main links of cooperation in the current society. Thus, the ASM identified the crossroads in which the power-over has an ambivalent role (that is, those tasks performed by the state that are to some extent useful or necessary) and offered a better, autonomous alternative. In this way, ASM's strategy was not purely destructive. Unlike political parties—including the Leninist ones—which "colonize" social movements with the forms and values of heteronomous politics, the ASM provides an interface between our movements and the state that ended up "colonizing" the state with the forms and values of the movements. It does so either by occupying state positions, by draining their power, or by destroying them when necessary.

Once again, this does not intend to be the model of a perfect political machine. The ASM does not require "angelic" beings. Of course, there would be internal struggles for power and conflicts of all kinds. Such an institution would not resolve and eliminate for good the intrinsic distance between the social and political. Emancipatory politics would continue to be, as it is today, a difficult, daily task with no guaranties, aimed at expanding day by day our autonomy. The benefits of such an institution is that all those struggles, conflicts, and tensions would be at the same time acknowledged and ruled, so that they do not inevitably destroy the possibilities of cooperation.

Even if this was a purely imaginary exercise with many limitations, I hope it may contribute to expanding our horizon of possibilities when it comes to answering the crucial question of an emancipatory strategy: What is to be done?

(Endnotes)

1   See Parts 1 and 2 of this book, "Defining Spheres of a Participatory Society" and "Revolutionizing Everyday Life."
2   See related contributions by Tom Wetzel and Robin Hahnel in Part 4 of this book.

Chapter 29

U.S. SOCIAL FORUM:
VISION AND STRATEGY PROPOSAL

Z Staff and Marcus Denton

THE PEOPLES' MOVEMENT ASSEMBLY has been described as a "coming together" of all the movements, networks, alliances, and organizations to articulate: "What we want, What we are for, and Our next steps," and as a "means of connecting the first U.S. Social Forum and the proposed second USSF in 2010."

Consistent with this focus on vision and strategy, we propose:

That the U.S. Social Forum put out a call/entreaty that each organization, coalition, project, and movement that intends to participate in the second 2010 U.S. Social Forum and be a contributor to, and part of, an emerging movement of movements for a new equitable, just, and participatory U.S. society, prioritize developing proposals and presentations for vision and strategy to win that new world, particularly emphasizing economy, culture/community, gender/sexuality/kinship, polity, ecology, and international relations, rooted in present conditions and possibilities, but very explicitly aimed toward a future revolution in the United States.

Editor's note: This proposal was presented at the 2007 U.S. Social Forum Peoples' Movement Assembly. It was drafted by Marcus Denton and the Z staff for the International Project for a Participatory Society and presented by Marcus at the assembly.

Chapter 30

WHICH WAY FOR THE NEW LEFT?: SOCIAL THEORY, VISION, AND STRATEGY FOR A REVOLUTIONARY YOUTH AND STUDENT MOVEMENT

Pat Korte and Brian Kelly

OUR GENERATION

"We've all been raised on television to believe that one day we'd all be millionaires, and movie gods, and rock stars. But we won't. And we're slowly learning that fact. And we're very, very pissed off..."

—Tyler Durden, *Fight Club*

GROWING UP WE SAW the failed reforms of the Soviet Union. They were hailed by leaders of government and business as the "triumph of capitalism" and the final "defeat of communism." In school it was used as clear evidence for why the capitalist system is the final and ideal stage of human history. Their words and deeds implicitly claimed, over and over, that there was no alternative to capitalism, authoritarianism, patriarchy, racism, and imperialism. But the more we learned, the more it became clear to us that what the entire world was telling us—the media, government, corporations, and our families—was simply untrue. Systematic lies became the norms of our lives. Hopelessness and cynicism became the defining attitudes of our generation.

It was difficult for many of us to understand why our friends and schoolmates weren't enraged by the world they endured. To our shouts of "Another world is possible!" and "Resistance is unstoppable!," came even louder shouts of "Grow up!," "Get a life!," and "Deal with reality!" It seemed incomprehensible that such logical people—people who we agreed with on so many other things—could fail to see what was right in front of them. How could such levels of apathy exist alongside such chaos?

Obviously we were doing something wrong. It wasn't that what we were telling them wasn't compelling or logical. The problem was that they already knew everything we were saying. What we were telling them was too logical. They didn't want to hear that capitalism destroys our fullest potentials or that U.S. imperialism has killed tens of millions of people. Instead they wanted to have some semblance of a decent human existence. Ignoring the horrific problems was a prerequisite for such an existence.

Pessimism, lack of hope, and cynicism are perhaps the greatest hurdles to social change that exist today. These hurdles demand development of a visionary and strategic youth and student movement, and revolutionary youth and student organization. If we are serious about engaging with the skepticism of our entire generation, then we must be able to answer the question "What do you want?"—answering it in a way that makes sense and is desirable. Developing a vision of what a participatory society might look like, and then using that vision as a flexible and evolving compass for our organizing, will help to lead us on a path to fundamental social transformation.

The Revolutionary Potential of Youth

Social movements have always needed young people. As youth, we must not underestimate our own power and ability to bring about real social change. We also must not underestimate our ability to be the spark that will set off an explosion of transformation throughout all society.

History has shown, from the Civil Rights Movement to the Black Power Movement, from divestment and disarmament campaigns to Third World Solidarity campaigns, from movements against sweatshops to movements against corporate globalization, from the anti-war movement during the Vietnam War, to the current anti-war movement during the so-called "War on Terror," that young people and students have not only been on the front lines of these struggles, but have played crucial roles in shaping their direction.

Clearly, students have the power to rock the boat. But, imagine how much more the campus Left could accomplish if it had well-developed social vision through which to interpret events, clearly defined vision of alternative values and institutions for a future society, and shared and easily employed strategy for social revolution. Below, we have outlined what we believe is missing from student organizations on the Left currently and historically. We hope the ideas presented here will serve to inspire a new campus Left that wants not only to derail the killing train, but also to play its role in starting the fire that will spread through every corner of the globe.

The revolutionary potential of youth must be harnessed in a productive manner. We believe that to win a new world, we need millions of people—tens of millions of people. Our efforts to help build that mass movement must be rooted in serious long-term goals. Winning in the long-term is not primarily about the daily tactical battles (i.e. winning a street fight against the police, occupying a building for a given number of hours, or having a certain number of people arrested in a non-violent civil disobedience, etc.), it is primarily about bringing new people into the movement, solidifying their commitments, and building a movement which is welcoming, loving, and supportive. Our long-term success must be judged by the ability of our movements to retain existing members and recruit masses of new members. Our movements must be judged by their ability to grow.

Our predecessors had, as their calling, the job of "naming the system." They called that system capitalism, patriarchy, white supremacy, authoritarianism, imperialism, and environmental devastation. Our job is no longer to name the system. Past generations have already done that, eloquently. Instead, our job is to uproot and abolish these oppressive institutions by building a mass revolutionary movement, by exploring, expanding, and promoting vision for a participatory society which can inspire and guide our actions, and by developing and implementing radical alternatives to the current order. Their job was to "name the system." Our job is to "name the visionary alternatives" to that system—and to usher in a new society.

The world is decaying and we have the opportunity to change the course of history.

You Say You Want a Revolution?

Revolution is an uncommon word in many circles of the U.S. Left. Its avoidance stems from fear of having potential radicals associate revolution with violence and chaos, the belief that revolution is far beyond our reach, and the subconscious feeling that we really can't win. All this must change. If we believe in fundamental social transformation, then we must be honest with ourselves and with those around us. Moreover, with flexible social theory to interpret the world in which we live, widely shared vision of what social relations and institutions could look like in the future, and realistic strategy for radical change, we really can win a good society.

We want fundamental transformation in the spheres of political, economic, kinship, community, cultural, ecological, and international life. The name for this type of change is revolution. Revolutionaries are those who organize to bring about such changes. Though we seek to win reforms that improve the day-to-day conditions of people and simultaneously weaken the power of oppressive institutions, our long-term commitment to revolution makes these reforms non-reformist.

THE ROLE OF REVOLUTIONARY YOUTH AND STUDENT ORGANIZATIONS

Building Dual Power

What is dual power? Dual power is the ability of popular movements to present a serious challenge to the system's claim of ownership and control over the world. It is the organized effort of the Left to create a serious threat for the system and provide a viable alternative for the system's citizens. By building and strengthening self-managing institutions that prefigure a participatory society and compete with oppressive institutions for power and support of the people, we arouse radical consciousness among the public, encourage people to want still more changes in society, and demonstrate the viability of alternatives to present systems of domination.

Why a Revolutionary Student Organization?

Universities, like corporations, communities, families, and governments, are social institutions. They are built around a particular set of values. The people who are a part of them have certain prescribed roles. Universities themselves have specific institutional features. Like all other institutions, they can be replaced with participatory alternatives which carry out the same institutional functions with different values and goals in mind.

The primary function of our universities is to maintain the hegemony of the current ruling order. The U.S. school system is carefully divided into various "tiers." Public K–12 school is designed to "weed out" individuals who refuse to follow orders or actively rebel against those in power. Entrance to college is heavily regulated through standardized testing, high school GPA's, high tuition rates, college application fees, and reactionary recruitment policies. Finally, the few who do make it to college suffer outrageous debt, attacks on academic freedom and free expression, authoritarian security policies, and a narrow curriculum that is explicitly designed to maintain the status quo.

Young people and students clearly have a self-interest and strategic position in the struggle for radical change.

It is this revolutionary potential combined with the planned and oppressive nature of the system that necessitates revolutionary student organization. As young progressives living within the U.S., we stand face-to-face with the largest and most intentionally planned system of domination that has ever existed. To ensure success in dismantling that system, we must be equally intentional in our political work.

The primary goal of an organizer is to help build the movement—both quantitatively and qualitatively. We must increase our movement in numbers while at the same time increasing the level of analysis, strategic insights, visionary goals, and commitment to radical change in members of the movement. Student organizers must position themselves to direct attention toward the fundamental flaws in our society's basic institutions—and to organize to change them.

A revolutionary student organization provides an intentional place where young people can develop vision for a participatory society, debate day-to-day political questions, learn and hone their organizing skills, plan and wage strategic and high-stakes non-reformist campaigns, and widen the discussion on revolutionary strategy and dual power. It is the job of such organizations to provide a supportive and loving community that can sustain the long-term participation of its members while helping to develop their fullest potential.

Non-reformist Reforms in Education

The university system has become increasingly less accessible to young people in the U.S. Winning reforms that make education more democratic, liberatory, accessible, and affordable all have potential to build a movement than can help lead to a participatory society. Our vision helps to guide the daily work we do in ways that help us build better movements. It forces us to take leaps that can make our reforms non-reformist.

When calling into question the lack of self-management and the corporate division of labor—the divide between workers, faculty, and administrators—we can also provide alternatives that can help lead us to a system of participatory education and economics. Balanced job complexes can be demanded as an alternative to the unequal division of labor between staff and faculty. Students, staff, and teachers can demand the university be brought under their direct control. When talking about racism, sexism, and classism, demands can be made around creating or strengthening Black, ethnic, women, labor, and queer studies programs. These demands can help lead to a better society if framed and organized in such a way that they lead to a stronger movement and put us on a path to future (and eventually revolutionary) gains.

Liberating Theory

Revolutionaries need ways of interpreting history, current events, and predicting future possibilities. To accomplish these tasks, we must build a flexible conceptual framework through which we can analyze and understand society.

As an alternative to the reductionist social theories of the past, we offer a totalist social theory. The conceptual framework of totalist social theory does not prioritize the dominance of any primary social spheres over the others. Instead, it seeks to understand the various interactions and interrelations among different primary spheres. Though society is composed of many parts that appear to be independent at times, various spheres of social life always interact to form an entwined whole. The parts which compose the entwined whole interrelate to help define one another. We abstract various parts from the whole to further understand the internal dynamics of each sphere and the interrelations between spheres.

Society is comprised of four primary spheres, all of which are set within an international and ecological context, and each of which has a set of defining functions:

- *The Political Sphere*: Primary functions include legislation, adjudication, and collective implementation.

- *The Economic Sphere*: Primary functions include production, consumption, and allocation of the material means of life.

- *The Kinship Sphere*: Primary functions include procreation, nurturance, socialization, gender, sexuality, and organization of daily home life.

- *The Community and Cultural Sphere*: Primary functions include development of collectively shared historical identities, religion, spirituality, linguistic relations, lifestyles, and social celebrations.

Within each sphere there are two components. The first component is the Human Center, the collection of people living within a society. Each person has needs, desires, personalities, characteristics, skills, capacities, and consciousness. The second component is the Institutional Boundary, all of society's social institutions that come together to form interconnected roles, relationships, and commonly held expectations and patterns of behavior that produce and reproduce societal outcomes. Though these institutions come together to help shape who we are as individuals, our human consciousness empowers us with the capacity to transform society's institutional boundary.

VISION FOR A PARTICIPATORY SOCIETY

"If we don't stand for something, we may fall for anything."
—Malcolm X

To overcome the cynicism and hopelessness that currently define our generation, we need a flexible and widely shared radical social vision to provide people with hope and inspiration. To build alternative institutions that prefigure a participatory society, we must have a clear vision of what a future society will look like so that its defining features can be incorporated into our organizational structures. If we don't have ideas for how social life could be organized in the future, we obviously cannot embody the seeds of the future in the present. We also cannot develop effective strategies to get from the dominant institutions of the present to the revolutionary institutions of the future if we haven't outlined the defining features of future social institutions. We want to abolish institutions that produce and perpetuate oppression, but to make the jump from resistance to revolution, we must outline the goals of our revolution.

Participatory Politics

As an alternative to both Leninist-style dictatorship and representative democracy, we offer a polity in which every citizen plays a crucial role in the political process, with each individual having a say proportionate to the degree which they are affected by outcomes. A federation of nested councils will replace the authoritarian state and be used to efficiently organize political life while fostering maximum participation. In addition to society providing all citizens with adequate time to participate in the political process, all individuals will have equal access to empowering opportunities, to a diverse range of single-issue and multi-issue organizations with varying social agendas, and a media system that is under direct democratic control of the people and serves to foster greater participation and to better inform the decisions of the public by presenting a diverse range of ideas and opinions, as well as the views of competing groups.

Participatory Economics

Instead of capitalism, we offer an economic system built on values of solidarity, equity, diversity, self-management, and efficiency. To replace markets or central planning, Participatory Economics utilizes federations of workers' and consumers' councils in which each individual has a say in decisions proportionate to the degree they are affected by the outcomes. Allocation of goods and services will be accomplished through a social, iterative planning procedure called Participatory Planning. Through this planning process, workers and consumers will collectively develop, propose, revise, and implement a coherent economic plan. Social ownership of the means of production will replace private ownership. To ensure equity, workers will be remunerated according to effort and sacrifice, and in some cases according to need. To break down the corporate division of labor and prevent the rise of a coordinator class, job complexes will be balanced to ensure a relative level of empowerment, confidence, knowledge, and quality of life among all members of society by requiring each worker to complete a mix of both rote and empowering tasks.

Feminist Kinship

Feminist kinship relations seek to free people from oppressive definitions that have been socially imposed and to abolish all sexual divisions of labor and the sexist and heterosexist demarcation of individuals according to gender and sexuality. Society must be respectful of an individual's nature, inclinations, and choices and all people must be provided with the means to pursue the lives they want regardless of their gender, sexual orientation, or age. Feminist kinship relations are dependent on the liberation of women, queers, youth, the elderly, transgender, and inter-sex individuals.

To extend liberation into daily home life, a participatory society aims to provide the means for traditional couples, single parents, lesbian, gay, bisexual, transgender, inter-sex, and queer parents, communal parenting, and multiple parenting arrangements to develop and flourish. Within the home and the community, the task of raising children must be elevated in status, highly personalized interaction between children and adults should be encouraged, and responsibilities for these interactions must be distributed equitably throughout society without segregating tasks by gender. A participatory society would provide parents with access to high quality day-care, flexible work hours, and parental leave options allowing them to play a more active role in the lives of their children.

The liberation of women and society requires reproductive freedom. Society must provide all with the right to family planning without fear of sterilization or economic deprivation, the right to have children through unhindered access to birth control and abortion, and the right to sexual education and healthcare that provides every citizen with information and resources to live a healthy and fulfilling sexual life.

In a participatory society the full exploration of human sexuality would be accepted and encouraged. A participatory society would encourage the exercise of and experimentation with different forms of sexuality by consenting partners.

Intercommunalism

We will not be reborn into a perfect society after a revolution, and our society's long and brutal history of conquest, colonization, genocide, and slavery will not be transcended easily. To begin the step-by-step process of building a new historical legacy and set of behavioral expectations between communities, a participatory society would construct intercommunalist institutions to provide communities with the means to assure the preservation of their diverse cultural traditions and to allow for their continual development. Under intercommunalism, all material and psychological privileges that are currently granted to a section of the population at the expense of the dignity and standards of living for oppressed communities, as well as the division of communities into subservient positions according to culture, ethnicity, nationality, and religion, will be abolished.

The multiplicity of cultural communities and the historical contributions of different communities must be respected, valued, and preserved by guaranteeing each sufficient material and communicative means to reproduce, self-define, develop their own cultural traditions, and represent their culture to all other communities. Through construction of intercommunalist relations and institutions that guarantee each community the means necessary to carry on and develop their traditions, a participatory society assists eliminating negative inter-community relations and encourages positive interaction between communities that can enhance the internal characteristics of each.

In a participatory society, individuals should be free to choose the cultural communities they prefer and members of every community shall have the right of dissent and to leave. Intervention shall not be permitted except to preserve this right for all. Those outside a community should be free to criticize cultural practices that they believe violate acceptable social norms.

An Unfinished Project

The above visions for how a participatory society would affect political, economic, kinship, community, and cultural life are far from complete and require significant expansion. In addition to the above alternatives for each of the four primary spheres of social life, a participatory society would revolutionize international relations, ecology, education, art, journalism, sports, and other areas of life. It is our hope that revolutionaries in the U.S. in general, and youth and student radicals in particular, answer the call to transcending the theories, visions, and strategies of the past and break on through to the revolutionary future, a future that belongs to us all.

"Paths of Victory"
Trails of troubles,
Roads of battles,
Paths of victory,
We shall walk.

—Bob Dylan

We can win. Not only must we come to realize that the institutions of capitalism, patriarchy, authoritarianism, racism, and imperialism will be overcome through the conscious revolutionary action of the people, but we must be passionate about doing so. Our movements require radicals who have not only a clearly defined social theory, analysis of present systems of domination and oppression, visions for future values and institutions, and strategies for revolution. We must also be excited about seeking the changes we wish to see in the world.

Chapter 31

DID YOU JUST SAY CLASS?

John J. Cronan Jr.

WE SEEM TO FACE a serious class crisis within our movements and organizations that has taken two forms: 1) the issue of class has fallen off the list of priorities, and 2) those who do spend adequate attention to it have the wrong class analysis, rendering it useless. As a member of Students for a Democratic Society (SDS), I see that we are not immune to this problem; therefore this essay seeks to briefly tackle and address these problems, beginning with the latter. The traditional Left's two-class analysis will be scrapped in favor of introducing a third class—the coordinator class; and after identifying this new class, I will discuss the ramification it has on our movements and organizations, drawing especially from SDS experiences. It should be noted that class is going to be examined in a more simplistic nature than it should; however, keep in mind that this author believes that class can never been defined as an individual oppression separate from other oppressions that stem from community and cultural, kinship, and authority relations. Rather, each is actively entwined with the others; what is sometimes called a "totalist" approach, or "complimentary holism."

What is Class?

Class is defined as a group of people that have shared interests, circumstances, and powers by virtue of their on-going position in the functioning of the economy; though income may be a factor due to a class's increased bargaining power, it is not as essential as the liberal notion of class makes it out to be. Furthermore, a class must be able to, at least potentially, develop a consciousness that gives it the ability and will to act autonomously. The position of a class results in it forming its own psychology and culture distinct from other classes. Moreover, it can be said that class can be defined by its role in social production. Now, the controversial question is, What positions and roles are the basis for determining a class?

The traditional Left's answer to this question is that class antagonism is solely based on the relationship to the means of production. A small group of people, capitalists, own the means of production, and workers are those people who must sell their labor for a wage to the capitalists, because they do not own the means of production.

Editor's note: This is a version of an essay originally appearing in pamphlet form at the 2007 SDS National Convention.

Based on this definition of class, we can agree that capitalists and workers both, indeed, constitute two classes. The capitalist class has shared interests in maximizing profits and increasing control over the production process—at the detriment of the workers—and to facilitate this they organize business organizations, political parties, clubs, etc. Capitalists also develop a culture and mentality of greed and superiority, as well as, in many cases, thinking of workers as mere statistics and instruments of their wealth.

Workers, on the other hand, have an interest in extracting the highest wages possible for the least amount of work, the exact opposite of capitalists. To pursue this workers form unions, sporting clubs, political parties, and other workplace organizations. The fact that workers *must* sell their labor, even if they do not want to do the work, results in an alienation from one's labor. And given their economic position, workers are obviously going to pursue and live within different cultural conditions. This is the basis of the traditional Left's class analysis and the root of its conception of class struggle (Of course, there are more nuanced analyses, but these features remain at the core of most of them).

The Coordinator Class

This analysis held by the Left—Marxists, independent socialists, and anarchists alike—is wrong, however. Though we do accept that the relationship to the means of production is a criterion for class division, it is not the only one. It is not only theoretically wrong but historical examples prove otherwise also. There is a third class that lies in between workers and owners, labor and capital—the coordinator class—that rises from the division of labor, giving coordinators relative monopoly over empowering knowledge and skills, and as a result considerable say over their own jobs and the jobs of workers below them. These are the waged and/or salaried high-level managers, engineers, doctors, lawyers, and other professionals.

Coordinators defend their skill, knowledge, and authority against workers below them, and fight to gain more wealth, autonomy, and bargaining power from the capitalists above them. They see capitalists as obnoxious impediments to reason and believe that their technocratic solutions to economic and social production are superior. Conversely, coordinators occupy economic positions that generate feelings of self-worth and capability, and, in turn, view workers paternalistically with a great sense of elitism, often adopting conceptions as "workers are intellectually incapable or psychologically ill-equipped to administer their own lives without our compassionate aid." They also form their own organizations to protect their class status—professional associations like the American Medical Association, for doctors, and the American Bar Association, for lawyers—or, even, create organizations to help them ascend to the position of new ruling class, which we have seen done under the guise of a "vanguard" party. The latter point, that the coordinator class could have the desire and ability to become a new ruling class, is key to solidifying it as a class. It also allows us to better understand the so-called "socialist" or "communist" revolutions of the past, where in fact they were "coordinatorist." In other words, the coordinator class can be explicitly anti-capitalist but not be for working-class self-management.

As we can see, coordinators have their own shared interests, circumstances, power, psychology, culture, and ability to become a new ruling class; therefore they fit our definition of a class.

Another Look at the Working Class

In addition to recognizing a whole other class, the existence and definition of the coordinator class can help us better define the working class. Now, instead of not owning the means of production and merely working for a wage being sole criteria for the working class, we can say that the working class is comprised of wage or salaried workers who do mostly rote, onerous, and disempowering tasks, and have their work defined for them by coordinators or capitalists, because they have been systematically denied access to the skills, knowledge, time and energy, and decision-making power to have it otherwise. Subsequently, in the United States and nearly all other industrialized countries, the class breakdown goes like this: 1–5 percent capitalist, 15–20 percent coordinator, and 75–80 percent working class (keeping in mind that there are various strata within the each class, but right now we are just trying to get a basic understanding of a three-class outlook).

Class, Students, and Young Adults

Using a three-class analysis, we can also better understand where college students and young adults fall on the whole class map—something that will be important to grasp with the growing student movement and the need for working-class students to have a self-managed role within them. Classism definitely exists within student and young adult movements, but if some are not workers and some are obviously not capitalists, or children of capitalist, then what are they? The class identity of a college student largely depends on their family background and their expected job placement once they get out. If a student is working class by upbringing and working class by job or likely job, they should still be considered and will most likely identify with the working class. If a student is coordinator class by upbringing and coordinator class by job or likely job, then they are still part of the coordinator class. The student or young adult, graduate or not, will stay in that class slot until their own circumstances overcome it. Let me give two examples.

First, say there is a coordinator class student working a low-wage service job while in school. They would not all of a sudden be lumped into the working class. They still have the familial ties and experiences, culture and psychology, of a coordinator-class upbringing that will greatly distinguish them from a working-class student, whether that student has a job at the moment or not.

Second, say there is a coordinator-class student who has recently graduated but has been completely cut off from their parents, either by choice or not, and is forced to get a working-class job. Again, it does not make them working class because they do not lose their background; however, over time, if they continue to be in a working-class slot, they may come to identify, rightfully, as working class—but not immediately or in the near future.

As a result of this analysis, I hope that students will rightfully identify as working class when appropriate and create forums where they can discuss concerns with others who have the same prior experiences, life situations, and probable futures, based on their class, such as we have done in SDS through caucuses; and I hope that coordinator-class students will not wrongfully take up space in these forums because they lack a class analysis that understands that not all wage laborers are working class; and conversely, that many students *are* working class.

Coordinator Class and Organizing

I believe that the failure of most activists and organizers, especially those that would consider themselves revolutionaries, to embrace the concept of the coordinator class is highly detrimental and will hurt in the long run if not remedied. We see already in the major anti-war coalitions—you know who they are—that a coordinator class has taken control of them, whether intentionally or not. Even though they all claim to be fighting to end a war and to having internal democracy, nothing could be further from the truth. The fact that groups on the "Left" suffer from this problem comes as no surprise to anyone who understands the dynamics of the coordinator class. Moreover, even proclaimed "anti-authoritarian" groups and collectives have fallen victim to coordinator-class control. Besides the fact that some organizations' structure is even somewhat top down on paper and that others are supposedly not, let me give an example of how a class of ruling elites could rise in a situation where voting was done by one person, one vote—even in an organization dedicated to participatory democracy like SDS.

Say there are ten people who are part of an SDS chapter, anywhere in the country, and each person is guaranteed an equal vote on all the issues concerning them. However, at the same time, only three people were doing empowering work like taking care of the chapter's finances, writing all of the press releases, and speaking at all of the events. The other seven just hand out flyers, attend events, paint banners, etc. When it comes time to vote on issues, the seven people not doing the empowering work technically have the ability to out vote the three doing the empowering work, on paper at least. However, 99 percent of the time this will never happen because the seven people will not know enough about what the hell is going on to make an informed decision, or not feel confident enough to speak definitively and challenge the word of the other three; and even more likely, they might be too worn out from doing rote and onerous tasks to even show up to the meeting. This will happen because the corporate division of labor still exists and those with the most initial knowledge, experience, and skills will occupy these positions, thereby the structure that allows for the coordinator class to rise is still intact. (Again, this is merely focused on class as a whole. Race, cultural, kinship, and other oppressions and factors are also at play.)

So what do we do to remedy this class division within our own movements and organizations, including the new SDS? First, we need to recognize there is a problem—so far, that has not been easy. Second, we need to incorporate the idea of "balanced job complexes" into our movements. Basically, we rearrange the tasks that make up jobs and institutional positions, so that there is a relatively equal amount of empowering and disempowering tasks. For example, speakers at events and those who write press releases should be rotated, as well as each time pairing a more experienced member with someone less experienced. This way, the latter can learn and not feel on their own, and next time they will be the experienced one paired with a less experienced person, and so on. This should be done wherever possible, and in cases where delegation of tasks and/or authority might be needed for periods of time, those positions should have term limits, frequent rotation, immediate recall, and clearly set guidelines for responsibilities. Also, to tackle the problem, in general, of unequal development, study groups and other such activities should be held within chapters, so that people can gain the knowledge and skills needed to bridge any gaps. Third, we need to recognize the need for and right to form strictly working-class organizations, allowing them their right to self-management, just as we now recognize the necessity and right of people of color, woman-identified, queers, and other oppressed groups to do so. Finally, we need to actively combat classism within our movements and address it head on.

Classism

The problem of coordinator-class domination not only violates participatory democratic decision making within movement institutions; it is also a problem because working class people are not idiots, contrary to coordinators' beliefs, and will be weary to join coordinator-class-dominated movements and organizations. Why? Because they tend to be classist. Would a person of color want to join a racist movement and/or organization? Probably not, and we have seen the ramifications of this also. In fact, working class people tend to have more visceral reactions toward coordinators because most of them have never actually met a real capitalist before. The coordinators are the ones who hassle them at work, discipline them at school, and betray them in their unions.

Classism can take many forms structurally by the mere fact that a movement and/or organization has coordinator leadership/majority membership, but it can appear structurally also in the form of extremely long meetings, and no money to fund working-class people's transportation to important events. Then there are the actual interactions between working-class people and coordinators. We have seen both kinds of classism within SDS and we have been consciously combating it, but more attention definitely needs to be paid.

Here is a list of the "Top 10 Mistakes of Middle-Class Activists in Mixed-Class Groups," from the Class Matters website (www.classmatters.org). What they refer to as the Professional Middle-Class is quite similar to what I call the coordinator class (however, in the end, our class analyses and specifications are different).

1. Overlook necessity

2. Overlook intelligence

3. Romanticize working-class people

4. Impose inessential weirdnesses

5. Hide who they really are

6. Think they know it all

7. Think they know nothing

8. Focus on education more than organizing

9. Focus on goals and tasks more than people

10. Take over

I would also like to show some examples of what they call "inessential weirdness":

Herbal tea and no coffee at an event

Waving hands in the air instead of applauding

Holding hands or chanting at a meeting

Elaborate, ritualized consensus decision-making processes

Nudity at rallies

Property destruction at rallies

Speaking in acronyms or jargon

Serving tofu as the only main dish at a coalition event

Sitting on the floor; providing no chairs, only cushions

Unwashed hair or clothing

Bandana facemasks

If you would like a more in-depth look at inessential weirdness, go to www.class-matters.org. However, you might get the idea.

Finally, there is the issue of working-class culture being looked down upon by the Left (more so, amongst what you could call the white Left). Working people are looked down upon for eating at McDonald's, but it is fine for people on the Left to eat at vegan restaurants, where the workers are no less exploited. They are looked down upon for watching sports, even though they get some fulfillment out of it and it allows them to talk to their peers at work or at school the next day. Oh, but wait! It is fine to watch certain sports, like golf and tennis. They are looked down upon for reading the *New York Post*, while the Left reads what they themselves call the lying, war mongering *New York Times*; meanwhile, the working-class person is reading the only section of the paper that tells the truth, the sports page. These are generalizations somewhat, but speak up if it does not resonate with you. The list could go on...

The Road Ahead

I have presented the traditional Left's two-class analysis and shown that it comes far short of being sufficient in developing a framework for class analysis and struggle. In its place, I have argued that a third class, the coordinator class, should be recognized as a class between labor and capital. This new class arises not from the relationship to the means of production but from the division of labor. Additionally, I showed how our movements are coordinator-class dominated and classist, and I presented some possible solutions. I could be wrong, but I think the proof is in the pudding. Take what I have said to a working class person and see how much resistance you get. Then, do the same with someone who would fall under what I recognize as the coordinator class. I am willing to bet that there will be many more coordinators denying that they exist than working class people saying coordinators do not exist. My purpose, however, is not to be right out of spite but, instead, to bring the issue of class back to the forefront, side by side with issues of race, gender, authority, and others. I hope what I have offered can at the least fuel growing discussion on the topic, and at best convince a few people. Either way, my ultimate goal is classlessness and SDS, being an active agent in this struggle, and recognizing the coordinator class is the first step toward achieving it.

Chapter 32

FROM HERE TO PARECON: THOUGHTS ON STRATEGY FOR ECONOMIC REVOLUTION

Brian Dominick

IN TEACHING OR DISCUSSING parecon, inevitably, and quite rightly, we are expected to present options and ideas for activists to mobilize around in the present. Indeed, we all face economic problems in our day-to-day lives—as consumers, as workers, as activists, as citizens. To the extent we can act in accordance with our values, we should; this alone promotes participatory economics by prompting us to apply parecon's concepts to our "daily routines," in some cases altering those routines.

Unfortunately, however, what we do as individuals has slight impact on society, and no impact on social structures. It is also constricted by the dominant economic system: market capitalism. So the implementation of parecon, by its very definition consisting of radical social changes, cannot be brought about by behavioral changes alone, be they on the part of one individual or even a popular movement.

More important will be attention to, and alteration of, economic institutions at all levels, from home to neighborhood to workplace to industry to society at large.

To make matters more complicated, Participatory Economics is by definition a *system* that can only be brought about and maintained by a *society* that is simultaneously undergoing various other social transformations. Changes need to take place in cultural, kinship, and political relationships and institutions as well as economic ones. Unless dramatic changes are made in the ways we relate to each other as individuals; as families and friends; as cultures, races, ethnicities; in the ways we organize our moral affairs and our relationships with other societies—failing such a holistic revolution, the task of establishing a participatory economy will be Sisyphean; failures in other spheres can undo economic progress.

The demand for economic self-management relates directly to questions of democracy—questions we aren't even able to deal with in our political affairs, never mind production and allocation of goods and services. We have yet to successfully grapple with pressing issues of cultural tolerance, much less diversity, so why should we expect those values to translate into our workplaces and consumption practices?

At the same time, radical changes in our economic lives must come about in order for active transformations in the spheres of kinship, culture, and politics to occur.

Those are the prospects with which we are faced, and by now the implication should be rather obvious. We are talking about a broad, holistic revolution in the most thorough sense of that word.

Still, accepting that, we do not have to accept the connotations typically associated with the idea of revolution. The social changes briefly outlined are both intricate and sweeping; however radical they may be, changes must come about as a process—most likely a long one. As we expect of processes, there will be stages to this one, on all fronts: personal, economic, interpersonal, cultural, and political.

For our purposes, because we will be discussing some specific ideas here, my presentation will be restricted to strategy and tactics for engaging the process of economic change. Suffice it to say, economic change must occur in the context of broader social reforms and revolution.

Concepts of Change

The method by which we develop an understanding of society (and of social change) is basic, but that doesn't mean the process is simple. We do it in steps, but each step is rather complicated. Let's look at this method as it applies to economic change.

(1) We have articulated our shared values, as we understand them (solidarity, self-management, equity, diversity);

(2) We have assessed the present economic system and determined it is wholly inconsistent with our stated values;

(3) We have developed a vision of an alternative economic system that is not only acceptable in that it fulfills our values, but is also practical—that system, or some variation on it, will likely work if we can implement it.

While certainly the discussion is not finished, and the ideas thus far presented as "the parecon vision" are amenable to further conclusions, the ground we really haven't covered sufficiently regards how we proceed from here, and how we arrive at our long-term objective of a full-scale parecon. How do we, as activists not just visionaries, begin to work toward the achievement of a participatory economy? At this point, we need to:

(1) develop a strategic framework: general methods by which we will establish our visionary goals—the path to be followed in the time ahead;

(2) set strategic goals: specific points along the path outlined in our strategic framework

(3) formulate tactics: specific actions and projects meant to achieve our strategic goals

There are basically two fronts on which we need to struggle for social change in any sphere, including economics. The first is the objective front: we have to change conditions in society—social structures, organizations, institutions, relationships—so they yield optimal results consistent with our values and vision. Second is the subjective front: our individual and "collective" understandings of the world around us, our beliefs, our convictions, our behaviors, etc.

It might seem that this second front should be listed first, but in truth neither front precedes the other—not in priority, not in movement chronology. Subjective progress is as dependent on changes in social structures as those structural changes are dependent on altering people's mindsets. We are back to looking at strategy in terms of steps instead of fell swoops. We change some minds (already accomplished); we build some institutions (already underway) and an increasingly cohesive movement; that movement helps change more minds; those minds resist oppressive institutions and help develop liberatory ones. The process continues until we have changed a "critical mass" of institutions and minds. At that point, the institutions we've already built are seen as the pioneer projects of a new society, prompting us to force whatever remains to fall in line or be rendered obsolete.

There are three separate, though not necessarily distinct, ways we will go about changing our economy from its current set of mostly oppressive, antisocial, and counterproductive institutions. First, many existing institutions will be transformed from their current structures into liberatory alternatives. But we will also need to dismantle some existing institutions, as well as create many alternative institutions virtually from scratch. It isn't as though every aspect of our present economy is in some way amenable to social metamorphosis from within or without.

When it comes to developing revolutionary strategy, it is critical to expect the course of history to be at least as much a determining factor as an affected result of social change strategy. Any strategic movement must be able to adapt as circumstances change, and it cannot be expected to manipulate history to any useful degree of accuracy by the mere force of its own will. As important as a coherent vision and a relatively clear path are to building revolutionary social movements, the utter unpredictability of the future requires great flexibility of tactics in addition to some leeway in terms of vision. The only aspect of our movement that cannot change is its basis in unwavering principle; our core values remain constant throughout.

Role of the Polity

In working toward implementation of a radical economic vision, perhaps the greatest outside factor that could sway our strategic goals is politics. We need to consider the types of political changes that will be necessary for setting a participatory economy into motion. More, we need to consider what roles a polity (i.e. government) might play in facilitating or inhibiting parecon.

Some advocates of parecon assume the government will need to help establish a participatory economy. How else, they wonder, could such a vast transformation take place? The question becomes more complicated when we wonder if that polity will be a progressive incarnation of our current form of government (in the U.S., a republican democracy), or whether it will be some revolutionized form (such as a direct or delegate democracy brought about by full-scale insurrection).

Surely central national governments have the power necessary to revolutionize economics. Whether the government itself is revolutionary, or whether it is relatively traditional, a sea change of political attitudes could enable radical changes in an economy. If Venezuelan president Hugo Chávez so wished, he might be able to make not just sweeping reforms but truly revolutionary structural changes to his country's economy. His government could even mandate some form of Participatory Economy to replace Venezuela's current mixed capitalist system. So it is not entirely inconceivable that, were fiercely progressive or radical governments to take power in the Global North, one such country's economy could undergo massive economic overhaul, perhaps even including major elements of a parecon-type economy.

Yet the more important question is not whether a government could theoretically establish a parecon, but whether it is desirable to create a parecon using a top-down approach. The answer for anyone who supports the principles of parecon is certainly yes, it would be desirable for a contemporary government to mandate that its economy embody elements of, or even yield entirely to, a Participatory Economy, abandoning market capitalism in whole or in part. Capitalism is just that bad, and parecon is simply that inherently good. Even if badly implemented, parecon trumps capitalism any day, given the rampant, systematic ravages of markets and private ownership and their resultant suffering.

Nevertheless, the likelihood that a non-revolutionary polity would ever mandate a parecon is too remote to take seriously. Even in the case of Venezuela possibly converting to a participatory economy by decree, most societies will never be so lucky as to find a truly benevolent dictator at their helm. Driven as they are by capitalism, modern governments are structurally opposed to resisting, let alone smashing, capitalist institutions, infrastructure, and agendas, aberrations excepted.

It is conceivable that a Parecon Party could be formed in some Northern nation and that it could run for offices local and national. A massive grassroots movement would be required to establish the party's name, given that corporate and small-business operators would be less likely to fund such a threat than they have Green parties or other progressive political movements. In an electoral system dominated by capital, that makes parecon-by-ballot a likely non-starter.

So what of a revolutionary government? It is probably safe to assume that the establishment of a Participatory Economy on any real scale, along with the abolition of conflicting market institutions, will only come about as part of a larger movement for radical social changes. We are unlikely to see a movement for social ownership of wealth, job complexes balanced economy-wide, an intricate system of democratic allocation planning, and other major elements of a parecon vision without attendant demands for direct, participatory political democracy, a new system for dealing with crime and conflict, and myriad other structural features of the polity.

We can probably assume that a movement for parecon would only happen in concert with demands of political transformation. But what of a movement for political revolution? It is highly unlikely that dramatic reforms of a political system like that of the United States could be carried out using the rules of that system. A new form of government will not be legislated into existence. Instead, the current system would have to be overturned, new constitutions written, and new political structures enacted—all by bodies other than the current legislatures and executives.[1]

But would a transition to more-direct democracy necessarily facilitate transition to a Participatory Economy? The real question is, Would we want even a revolutionary government—one controlled far more directly by the people themselves—to manipulate the building blocks of the next economy? After all, if a Participatory Economy is meant to eventually be largely separate from and independent of government, how sensible would it be to let the government revolutionize the economy?

Because it makes virtually no sense to actually direct the establishment of a participatory, grassroots democratic economy from the top-down or center-out, the most sensible role for a government in the establishment of a Participatory Economy is that of interference runner. A grassroots social movement needs to develop the alternative economic institutions and system, through creation and transformation of economic institutions. The government needs to protect that movement from reactionary political and economic forces. For instance, progressive elements of whatever political system exists at a given phase will need to keep government bureaucracies and agents from destroying parecon-building institutions and movements. They might also need to create special protections to allow for parecon institutions to be fostered and implemented amidst a rabidly pro-market economy. In its most active role, the government might be called on to subsidize parecon experiments on various scales.

But the primary impetus and leadership of a movement to form a Participatory Economy must remain at the grassroots: inside the communities and workplaces, the regions and industries, that will do the real work of running the economy. Just as parecon is a libertarian economy, the movement to create it must be primarily extragovernmental.

Parecon in the Marketplace

Without a doubt, the greatest factor inhibiting the development of parecon institutions in today's economy in North America and nearly everywhere else is their existence within markets. Truly progressive firms that operate in a manner respectful of workers, the environment, and society at large must compete with firms that have no such allegiances. With few exceptions, the modern market discourages consideration of any such factors.

The second greatest impediment at this phase is access to capital. Unconventional workplaces are frightening to lenders and investors. Firms that tout their adherence to values other than profit maximization tend not to attract much financial support.

Related to the problem of markets, not only is it difficult to compete in the consumer market with companies that lack humane standards for labor, the environment, and other factors, but what about the labor market? A democratic workplace requires extraordinary workers. Due largely to the sheer inadequacy of conventional education at all levels, coupled with the veritable absence of diverse job descriptions in the modern workplace, it is difficult to find people who have talents and skills in a broad range of workplace duties. People with management skills tend not to know much about day-to-day activities. Meanwhile, those who are good at getting things done and used to following orders have rarely been empowered to help chart the path of a company. Finding these "renaissance workers," as it were, can be very costly. And since every secretary, technician, and janitor in a parecon is also a manager, if a parecon firm is to be competitive in the labor market, it must pay accordingly.

It does not matter that none of the above are as things should be. Establishing parecon businesses in contemporary society is nothing if not an exercise in contrasting today's insane economic realities with the beautiful ideals (and potential) of a radical alternative. But it is precisely those absurdities that likewise demonstrate the accidental ingeniousness of capitalism. A clearly superior alternative finds it nearly impossible to take root within the institutional confines of the current system.

None of this is to suggest it is not worth trying to establish parecon workplaces in today's economy. Indeed, aside from being potential building blocks of a new economy, they are perhaps the greatest propaganda tool at our disposal. Those of us who have experienced them tend to believe there is no better way to convince someone that parecon can work than by implementing one of its greatest features—the democratic workplace—in the midst of such countervailing pressures as the capitalist market. Well, there is one better way to convince them: actually employ them. Working in a collective atmosphere where solidarity and diversity are cherished tends to be habit-forming, and people who have worked in such conditions tend to want to replicate them when they move on.

But the path of creating parecon workplaces or transforming existing firms into democratically operated, worker-controlled businesses is only one element of inspiring and facilitating economy-wide transformation. As tempting as it might be to work exclusively on the micro level, building and converting workplaces until everyone in society works a balanced job complex and engages in participatory planning will not a parecon make.

Grassroots Dual Power

Whether or not a polity is to direct the establishment of a participatory economy, the real work of transforming old and establishing new economic institutions will be done at much lower levels. It is at the grassroots level where real learning about what works and does not work well in a parecon will take place. A government might be able to mandate the creation of workers' councils and consumers' councils and iteration boards and so forth. It might even print up and distribute fancy handbooks for doing so. But no central authority can be expected to possess the expertise, the flexibility or the attention to circumstantial detail of grassroots organizers. As much as that may be obvious, it should also be self-evident that the more experience such ground-level organizers have with the practice of parecon, the better off any coordinated attempt to transform the economy will be.

And what if there is no government to mandate from on high the complete revolutionization of the economy? What if a revolutionary government is unable to go that far, or a conventional government is uninterested in even trying? There is no need to wait around for the polity to sponsor a parecon initiative, especially since workers and consumers will be expected to do the heavy lifting either way.

The strategic approach known as "dual power" suggests that the way forward is to create institutions of the new society "in the shell of the old" establishment. In the case of economic transformation, this means building, maintaining, and defending alternative institutions such as cooperative businesses, workers' councils, consumers' unions, and so forth, and eventually forming networks of such entities to create a stronger and larger-scale foundation.

Dual-power strategy also refers to the need to both create these alternatives and do away with the contemporary capitalist institutions and services they replace. Even in capitalism, the system obviously serves real needs, to some extent, of nearly everyone in society. Be it a five-star restaurant, a fast-food joint, a grocery store, a soup kitchen or a dumpster, capitalism and its byproducts fulfill our most basic need for food. The same can be said of clothing, shelter, and even health care. Though not everyone gets what they need, let alone what they want—nearly everyone in the U.S. and other industrialized nations gets enough to scrape by.

Where there are outstanding needs—and there are today countless of these for far too many people—a dual-power economy should seek to fill them. Foremost, it should provide goods and services to the unemployed and the working poor. In so doing, the dual-power economy earns their allegiance and, hopefully, their democratic participation. The only way for this to come about is if working-class and poor people lead the formation of dual-power institutions, ensuring they are maximally attractive to their intended constituencies.

Radical organizers need to conceive and present the alternative economy as a movement to which one belongs, not an outside entity that acts on us each as alienated workers and consumers. The dual-power economy is a union of people who participate as consumers and workers, but as in parecon vision, they democratically engage in directing the economy. The unemployed are given the opportunity to work, if not for pay then for access to resources and the betterment of society (which is, of course, exactly what everyone works for in a Participatory Economy). Everyone else is given roles in a social movement explicitly intent on securing the power of working people and the rights of consumers to determine their own economic lives.

There are two categories of organizations formed in a dual power: alternative institutions (AIs) and counter institutions (XIs). The former provide basic goods and services to people in need. Meanwhile, XIs resist the intrusions of capitalists and the state and even go on the offensive, leveraging their every asset—from popular power to underground tactical approaches—in service to the movement.

Alternative Institutions

The most important alternative institution in any dual-power economy will be the credit union. Cooperatively owned and democratically managed, credit unions can act as movement banks. They offer individuals and organizations a place to invest their savings while ensuring those same funds are put to good use in the form of loans for movement groups and low-income people. The senses of solidarity and ownership a radical credit union can instill are without equal.

A staff of a cooperative credit union can self-organize as a participatory economics collective. Just as important, the credit union should specialize in helping others form and fund parecon ventures. Organizations that offer balanced job complexes and democratic empowerment need to also provide personal development opportunities to their participants. Credit unions can offer critical training to those who would start or become involved in a parecon business.

Truly alternative economic institutions are breeding grounds for the kinds of personal changes that will be necessary to make social revolution. They provide not only material needs but invaluable social space for personal transformation. Engagement in a parecon collective fosters commitment to broader economic changes. Not only does the participant see that another workplace is possible and learn valuable workplace and analytic skills, but the contradictions of capitalism take on a radically different form when viewed from within a participatory economics business.

Aside from acting as vital incubators for the economic actors of the future, alternative economic institutions should fulfill real needs of the communities they serve. Across any society, different communities have needs that vary in priority. Likewise, different people will reflect varying inclinations in terms of the types of needs they wish to help fulfill. So a broad range of institutions can and should develop in places throughout society. Where housing shortages and costs are extraordinarily harsh, housing cooperatives might be the most important type of alternative economic institution one could work to establish.

But social priority is not the only factor in determining what a particular activist might engage in. In the end, the most sustainable activism is that which we are good at and find enjoyable or fulfilling. Few people find organizing homeless shelters or housing cooperatives to be fun, but it is challenging, and the rewards of course extend well beyond monetary gain. Nevertheless, society's needs are not limited to the most immediate physical needs. Anything that has distinct social value and is currently provided by hierarchically organized capitalist or governmental institutions is ripe for replacement.

Ideally, a local dual-power economy will seek not only to fulfill a range of material needs, but to provide them for a range of local constituents. While the most obvious forms of dual-power economic activity might be the provision of food to the hungriest or shelter to the homeless, lending a helping hand to people in less-desperate circumstances will be invaluable. Poor people in highly industrialized economies will not be able make revolution without the sympathies and eventual alignment of those with more means.

Renters should be the natural allies of the homeless. Working parents often have as much trouble adequately nourishing their families as indigent people encounter finding their next meal. Institutions that seek innovative ways to fulfill the related needs of people who might not otherwise find themselves in cahoots can create situations of solidarity that will cross class lines to form interdependence.

Working people who find themselves frequenting fast-food chains to put food on the table would benefit greatly from alternative sources of prepared food that subsidize the meals of poor people self-organized to provide them. Indeed, that relationship exists today, in the form of McDonald's and its ilk, except for a few key differences. First, existing fast-food chains offer few healthy options and draw their ingredients from extra-regional sources. Second, executives and investors siphon profits that could be used for better pay or cheaper food. Third, fast-food joints extract capital from the community. And finally, restaurant workers are typically alienated from the products of their labor, and patrons of such establishments are similarly alienated from those who toil over their meals—this when bonds of solidarity and understanding could be formed so easily at various points of transaction.

The successful alternative institution is not only structured as a nonhierarchical collective, it also makes explicit efforts to connect to the community and broader movement as well as find a place of interdependence in the dual-power economy.

Examples of such consumer-producer relationships abound, but rarely are they identified as revolutionary or even social-movement undertakings. Take the example of community-supported agriculture (CSA) projects. At the beginning of a growing season, community members buy seasonal shares in a nearby farm in exchange for a proportion of that year's harvest, however bountiful or weak it may be that year. This provides farmers with vital up-front capital, reducing their need to deal with banks and such. It also helps alleviate the hardship of a poor harvest. In the best examples, shareholders visit or even work some hours on the farm, breaking the standard barriers of alienation to some extent.

But how often do shareholders, farm workers, or even the organizers of such arrangements see their CSA project as a movement endeavor? How can such a great institution even be a movement endeavor without more-explicit connections to a broader movement for social change? CSAs are a great example of a project that seeks some form of the consumer-producer ties of a democratically planned socialist economy, yet most participants do not see them as a means to achieve such an alternative economic system. It is as if participants are content with the arrangement, which is after all necessitated by the callous nature of market capitalism.

But the CSA need not be considered the pinnacle achievement in alternative economic relationships. Nor need it be seen as a settlement that helps dwindling small farms eek out a meager existence in the shadow of a corporatizing industry. CSAs can instead be tied to movements for economic change that see innovative consumer-producer relationships as a strategic goal on the path to abolishing capitalism and markets in favor of parecon. And this would be more than an abstract realization—the allegiance instilled by such a revolutionary perspective can inspire and support an expansion of the CSA itself as well as solidarity between the CSA and other AIs that self-identify as movement projects. Not insignificantly, the CSA can then obtain the protection and assistance of counter-institutional movement organizations.

Other forms of alternative institutions that a dual-power movement will need to form are less conventional. If we wish to someday establish consumer councils, the workplace cannot be the only site in which we practice the principles of parecon. Neighborhood organizations can serve as consumers' unions. Such institutions could raise and spend money on public goods (such as daycare, laundry, recreational facilities, neighborhood security); pool buying power to purchase everyday items at wholesale prices in order to save members' money; or pressure municipal institutions to shift budget priorities away from elite interests in favor of local needs.

In tandem with counter institutions (or perhaps coexisting as AIs and XIs), neighborhood organizations can apply pressure for needed reforms to local government policies as well as the structure and priority of local businesses. Additionally, they can seek ties between consumers and the workers' councils and unions of local parecon and mainstream firms and establish explicitly movement-oriented objectives and strategy. Ideally organized neighborhood councils could network municipality-wide to form a shadow government, leveraging their power where possible while building democratic infrastructure capable of assuming popular control over municipal operations in the event of insurrectionary change.

Counter Institutions

As discussed in the section on markets, alternative institutions have a difficult time surviving in capitalism. The problem is that the costs of doing business will tend to be higher for organizations that consider the well-being of workers, society, and the environment. In order to offset this disadvantage, counter institutions are needed to handicap capitalist competitors or offer certain advantages to parecon alternative institutions.

AIs' main advantage will always be that they are part of a movement. Individual and institutional members of that movement will thereby have some incentive to choose the parecon alternative over its capitalist competitor. But good intentions can go just so far.

In many cases, cost will still be a factor. If you pay less than your competitors or you charge more, you'll have trouble finding reliable workers, a growing pool of customers, or both.

Counter institutions are rooted in the broader social movement. They are in touch with alternative institutions, but usually they are not officially associated with them. They can be relatively covert, so long as they remain accountable to and in communication with the broader movement. Counter institutions derive their support from those movements, so they are only as strong as the amount of trust broader movements are willing to vest them with.

Counter institutions' work in the economic sphere is critical. They can place pressure on capitalists to reform, and they can help raise their costs of competition. XIs can raise labor costs, force PR nightmares, spoil brand recognition through propaganda, decrease sales through pickets and boycotts, even engage in property damage or other escalated acts.

XIs are also more attractive to donors than most parecon firms will be. While giving a dollar to a cooperative business helps that business spend another dollar, the impact of funds donated to XIs can go much further, since their primary activity is not economic exchange but movement building, not least through leveraging their power.

Not only is it hard to form and maintain an alternative institution from scratch, it is difficult to transform an existing business into a cooperatively owned, democratic workplace. Here counter institutions are also an integral tool. We might not realize it given how docile today's labor movement has become in North America, but unions are a form of counter institution. Their main purpose is to represent workers in opposition to management. They defend workers and sometimes even go on the offensive for workers, demanding fundamental changes like profit sharing or even greater control over the workplace.

In several countries, including the U.S., workers have taken over companies' means of production and gone into business for themselves as cooperatives. While the resultant organization is typically an alternative institution, a counter institution was often needed to drive off prior owners, capitalist speculators, and other forces that would have interfered with the workers' assumption of control.

In reality, counter institutions will need to be highly flexible, able to respond to the changing needs of the constituency they serve. They will need to find ways to remain connected to the broader dual-power movement without compromising—instead protecting—alternative institutions that serve those communities more literally, with goods and services. Imagine local, regional, and even national federations of counter-institutions that include protest groups, propaganda outfits, and underground cells. Such federations democratically conspire over targets and tactics, always with immediate and long-term strategic trajectories and goals in mind.

From Here to Revolution

It is premature to lay out a clear path between present-day circumstances and our eventual parecon vision. History has a way of changing objective circumstances, and lessons learned along the way will prove invaluable. Even widespread popular support for total economic transformation—itself a long way off—would be no guarantee of a successful transition, let alone a smooth one.

Lucky for us, the path to parecon is almost certainly one of relative social progress. Even if current movements fail to establish a participatory socialist economy in one uninterrupted series of strides, each of those strides would leave people better off. Beginning with reforms and leading to radical changes on a mass scale, improvements are an inevitable byproduct of grassroots movements for revolutionary economic change. If an elite cadre tries to seize (or otherwise obtain) state power and wield economic changes with wide brushstrokes, the perils of vanguardism leave wide open the possibility for changes in the wrong direction, as we have seen historically time and again. An incremental approach that engages grassroots movements in a participatory manner carries almost none of this risk.

The early building blocks of a participatory economy are indistinguishable from those of a progressively reformed economy. The creation of alternative institutions that not only fulfill vital needs but are structured for democracy, equity, diversity, and solidarity do not require universal devotion to economic revolution. They're good ideas with or without lofty long-term aims. Consumers' co-ops, community credit unions, worker collectives, neighborhood and consumer councils—these all tend to make capitalism less terrible for those they affect. Present-day examples of such institutions typically serve the needs of privileged classes to the extent they are disconnected from active social movements. But there is nothing inherent in the idea of these institutions that makes them elite friendly; rooted in social movements, they can serve a wholly different constituency.

Some will argue that making capitalism less horrible without abolishing it altogether is dangerous. Our goal is not, after all, to make a fundamentally bad economic system more palatable, thus prolonging the inevitable revolution. But we have more reasons than the immediate problems caused by markets, hierarchy, and private ownership to be concerned with. Ameliorating such horrors will not suffice. Market capitalism happens to be inherently incapable of reversing the trend toward worldwide, human-induced climate change. Since only planned economics can stave off the worst eventualities of global warming (given that markets will remain all but blind to the devastation until they themselves are virtually melting down), the need for truly revolutionary change will press more and more as time goes on.

Besides this, the privilege to oppose an ever softening of the impact of capitalism reflects exactly the attitude we need to be fighting. If we set out to create a perfect economy, we are guaranteed disappointment in our lifetimes. If our near-term goal is to create circumstances that workers and consumers find more empowering, less alienating, more sustainable, less disenfranchising, and so forth—then we cannot go completely wrong. If we can achieve all of this while maintaining explicitly radical objectives and never losing track of our critique of capitalism as a chronic, if not apocalyptic, detraction from social health and ecological sustainability, we stand a significant chance of committing revolution.

It is in our strategic goals and projects that we will be able to plant the seeds of revolutionary economic change. The use of counter institutions will mark the difference between an alternative-economy movement that can be accommodated or co-opted and a revolutionary movement that can tear down all that is bad in a contemporary economy.

With XIs targeting competitors and defending AIs, movement roots take hold and the alternative economy has a chance. This is done by organizing boycotts, pickets, smear campaigns, and the like, targeting institutions that compete with local parecon firms or that resist concerted efforts by workers to leverage more power internally.

XIs must further agitate for political changes that create space for alternative institutions to network with one another and begin replacing market and political forces with democratic planning.

As the dual-power economy develops into a real threat—first as a good, anti-capitalist example, and later as actual competition for consumers, workers, resources, etc.—reactionary forces will undoubtedly seek to squash it. But if alternative institutions are rooted in social movements, they may be strong enough to resist such intrusions. AIs will be better off to the extent XIs have obtained political clout by forcing politicians and government institutions to protect them rather than harass them.

It will not be the case that we simply replace the old economy with a new one by mere evolution, any more than we can expect it to happen by legislation or decree. Long before even a majority of economic institutions are aligned with the dual-power economy and reflect parecon structures and aims, critical mass will be perceived by one side or the other—probably both. At this juncture, the next step forward will be insurrection.

For this reason, it will be integral to have a great majority of the population somewhat sympathetic to or, ideally, somewhat reliant upon the dual-power economy. That means most people are either in a movement-aligned union, or shop at a movement-aligned AI, or benefit from a movement-oriented neighborhood council, or have some other tangible connection to the movement economy. Not everyone has to live a completely alternative lifestyle, but people must be threatened with a sense of real material loss, and a loss of great hope, if the state or other reactionary actors move to crush a burgeoning movement to revolutionize the economy.

Alternative currencies may prove to be a critical factor in expressing alignment with the dual-power economy. By keeping economic power local and out of the hands of capitalists, advocates of parecon can define and demonstrate their actual reach using a currency valued in accordance with parecon principles. While money has no place in a true parecon, units of exchange can be developed to convey time spent working at a balanced job complex or otherwise interacting with the alternative economy. Anyone with such currency in their wallet would think twice about watching a rising new economy get crushed.

At the historic moment of insurrection, the desired next step will be for the movement to leap forward, toppling capitalist institutions and at the very least rendering impotent the political forces that protect them. Revolution is not a game of capture the flag; there is no key—literal or figurative—to social control. But if governments and economic systems draw their authority from the passive or active allegiance of the populations they control, a radical shift in that allegiance is the closest thing to a flag our movement can procure.

Markets cannot be instantly replaced by participatory planning, but the coordination of workers' and consumers' councils, coupled with the creation of democratic allocation systems, can occur precisely to the extent that markets are disqualified and rendered obsolete. All of the grassroots planning and practice that has occurred up to that point, then, can be applied to organizing alternatives to markets on larger scales and in new economic areas or industries.

To be less abstract about insurrection, one can imagine the very real destruction of stock exchanges, offsetting one of capitalism's greatest assets. Because corporate investments are of zero value to protagonists of a participatory economy, what little incidental value they have thus far served to working people (the maintenance of pensions, for instance) can be appropriated and the rest done away with. Stocks held by investors can be transferred directly to workers. This may sound fantastic, but there is no realistic reason a movement with the technical power and political clout to seize control of stock exchanges cannot do precisely this. And since most people in industrialized nations own little or no stock, the idea of transferring real ownership will be that much more appealing.

Replacing competition with cooperation, as well as reducing redundant labor and management, become possible and necessary during insurrection. Having shed capitalist ownership, firms competing in the same industry now have massive incentive to consolidate. Managers would have the choice of sharing their power democratically or jumping ship. In industries that serve real economic needs, engineers and workers would finally have reason to do their best work, and an influx of workers deemed superfluous elsewhere in the organization, industry, or economy will offer nearly immediate relief. Solidarity can finally replace competition within and between workplaces, and concepts such as planned obsolescence and vacuous marketing can give way to needs-based planning. Workers can move more freely from field to field, and those who need or desire further or diversified education can find it offered to them by allocation institutions (formerly government bodies) under newly popularized control.

Economic institutions and industries that now operate antisocially can be abolished, freeing up workers to engage in industries that provide relevant goods and services. Banks and insurers begin the process of transformation into socially valuable institutions geared toward providing resources on an equitable basis, starting with new opportunities for the traditionally disenfranchised. Real-estate developers no longer have any reason to show up to work. Military contractors find their gates blockaded—by dissident elements in what remains of the military.

Likewise, movements on all levels demand direct control of governments' budgeting power. If democratic shadow councils have been organized, at the point of insurrection they can take the reins held by indirectly democratic legislative bodies. Those who answer to such bodies will have new governors: the constituencies they are already supposed to serve. The first order of business would of course be to empower government workers to collectively manage their own workplaces, helping to ensure their cooperation and make the transition that much smoother.

If a public-works supervisor shows up to work one day and a delegate from the council that is now exercising real control of municipal government is waiting with a new list of priorities, he or she might still be disinclined to follow those orders. But if the first order of business on that list is to equalize pay for everyone in that organization, and to implement worker control, that supervisor's reluctance may well be moot. After all, it is his or her erstwhile underlings that wield practical control of the institution and its operations.

It is probably not worth speculating beyond the phase of insurrection—that is, between insurrection and final establishment of a permanent participatory economy. There is no way to know precisely how these eventualities will be brought about, much less how they will yield truly stable economic institutions and relations. We cannot predict their details, their timing, or their precise order. We certainly cannot expect the transition—from private to social ownership, from modified markets to participatory planning—to be anything but messy. Mistakes and oversights will cause suffering, but a revolutionary movement can correct such problems, and will actually be inclined to do so, unlike capitalism and its present-day political champions. The movement will involve violence by both sides, since one side is disciplined to favor and depend on coercion and the other will be forced to use whatever tactics can authentically achieve the immediate objectives of protecting the revolution and blazing a path through reactionary obstacles.

All we can predict for certain is that if modern movements make concerted efforts toward midterm goals of reforming capitalist forces and establishing radical alternatives, we can improve society and build a foundation for farther-reaching action. Oh, and we can also predict that without making changes along these lines, capitalism will continue to dehumanize us, markets will continue to ravage our well-being and environment. If we don't act toward replacing our current economy with a radical alternative, future generations will have to work that much harder, suffer that much longer, and hate us that much more as they take it upon themselves to do what our parents' generation should have begun.

(Endnotes)

1   See Part 1, Chapter 2, of this book for Stephen R. Shalom's "ParPolity" political vision for a participatory society. It should be noted here that Shalom's presentation is limited to what the political system of a future society may look like and does not discuss transitional strategy, as is the focus of Brian Dominick's presentation in this chapter.

Chapter 33

BUILDING A PARECONISH MOVEMENT

Michael Albert

I WOULD LIKE TO offer ten claims about the vision and strategy of participatory economics and participatory society. I believe each claim is true. I also believe each claim is important enough that projects, organizations, and movements seeking a better world ought to embrace and or adapt the ten claims to help inspire and orient our efforts. My priority in this presentation is not to address all possible claims even about pareconish movement building, much less about movement building in its entirety. Nor is my priority to recount all reasons for advocating the few claims that I offer or to address all possible doubts people may have. Instead I hope to advocate for these claims and elicit in reply reasons people may have for rejecting any of them so as to inspire people to explore and act on the collective reactions, perhaps coming to some shared agreement or at least clarity about disagreement.

CLAIM 1: *We need shared institutional vision to inspire hope, incorporate the seeds of the future in the present, and inform program so it will take us to where we want to wind up. We must create such vision.*

We know that the idea that "there is no alternative," Margaret Thatcher's TINA, cements reaction. The justification for Claim 1 is that, first, uprooting this cynical view requires a convincing case for an alternative. Second, however, having transcended cynicism, we cannot incorporate seeds of an unknown future in our present endeavors. To prefigure a desired future, we need to know its main features via having shared vision. Finally, third, even with hope and guidance in our organizational efforts, we cannot contour our demands and methods to lead where we want to arrive if we don't know where that is. Strategy has to pay attention to existing relations lest it exceed or fall short of possibilities. But strategy also has to pay attention to sought vision, lest it run in circles or, worse, lead away from a desirable destination.

No one who rejects the need for developing and sharing vision rebuts these simple arguments. Instead, opponents of the importance of vision emphasize that a proposed vision could congeal inflexibly and thereby exclude new insights. They also argue that a shared vision could fuel sectarianism, could overextend into details that aren't know-

---

Editor's note: This paper was prepared for the June 1–7, 2006, Z Sessions on Vision and Strategy, held in Woods Hole, Massachusetts. The session brought together activists from around the world to share ideas and experiences regarding social vision and strategy.

able, could become frivolous and divert attention from more important concerns, and could be monopolized as a bludgeon to aggrandize power.

Such worries shouldn't be dismissed. The critics of vision are right that these possibilities do constitute a real danger. But the correct implication is not to reject shared vision. The correct implication is to hold vision flexibly, to welcome constructive criticism and seek continual innovation, and to focus on essentials and not overextend. It is to share results widely, openly, and without elite jargon or posturing.

Finally, the fact that a non-elitist, flexible vision may be difficult to achieve is no more an argument against having vision than the fact that sharing participatory political organizations, militant struggles, worthy winnable demands, and effective tactics, all in ways that are not sectarian or elitist, is difficult implies that we can do without these also necessary components of making change.

CLAIM 2: *Classlessness ought to be part of our economic goal. We must end the rule of the capitalist class over labor. We must also end the rule of the coordinator class over labor.*

To have classes means to have groups that by their position in the economy have different access to income and influence, including benefiting at one another's expense. Attaining classlessness, instead, means establishing an economy in which everyone by their economic position is equally able to participate, utilize capacities, and accrue income.

We cannot eliminate the distinction between those who own means of production and those who do not own means of production unless no one owns means of production, or, conversely, and what amounts to the same thing, unless everyone owns all means of production equally. That much is an obvious tenet of advocating a new classless economy transcending capitalism. All socialists, for example, accept this insight.

But class division can also arise due to a division of labor that affords some producers, whom I call the coordinator class, far greater influence and income than other producers, whom I call the working class. Claim 2 focuses on this latter point, which many socialists do not accept.

A modern capitalist economy has owners whom we call capitalists. It also has people who have no structurally built-in economic power other than owning their own ability to do work. These people must sell that ability, and are called workers. The controversial/important thing about Claim 2 is that it notices that capitalism also has a third class, the coordinator class, who, though they sell their ability to do work like workers, unlike workers also have great power and standing built into their position in the economic division of labor. These coordinator-class members, such as lawyers, doctors, engineers, managers, accountants, elite professors, and so on, do for their labor largely empowering tasks. By their position in the economy they accrue information, skills, confidence, energy, and access to means of influencing daily outcomes. They largely control their own tasks and define, design, determine, control, or constrain the tasks of workers below. They utilize their empowering conditions to enhance their position most often at the expense of workers below and, as well, also in conflict with capitalists above.

Capitalism is by this pareconish account a three-class system. Seeking classlessness therefore means not just eliminating capitalist rule, but also avoiding settling for coordinator-class rule in its place. "Out with the old boss, in with the new boss" does not end having bosses. To eliminate private ownership but retain the distinction between the coordinator class and working class ensures, by the structure of the coordinator/worker relationship, that the coordinator class will rule the working class. This type of change can end capitalism, and has done so, on occasion, historically, but this type of change will not attain classlessness, and it has not done so, not even on so much as one occasion, historically.

Claim 2 says our aims must take us beyond what have been called market socialism and centrally planned socialism (which systems have in fact been market coordinatorism and centrally planned coordinatorism, called such for elevating the coordinator class to ruling status). That is, our movements and projects must be not only anti-capitalist, they must be pro-classlessness. They must prioritize both eliminating the monopoly of capitalists on productive property and also the monopoly of coordinators on empowering work.

CLAIM 3: *Beyond classlessness, for the economy, we also ought to seek positive economic values including equity, solidarity, diversity, self-management, ecological balance, and efficiency in utilizing assets to meet needs and develop potentials.*

To be against something bad—such as class division and class rule—is very desirable, of course. But rejecting bad features does not generate clear standards for positive goals. To transcend mere dissent and become constructive, we need positive values that we can measure new institutions against. Claim 3 is about positive values.

Economics affects how much we each get from what we all produce. We want equitable outcomes, and what's equitable is that each person who is able to work receives back from society in proportion to what they expend, at a cost to themselves, in production. We should be remunerated, that is, for the duration, intensity, and, when it varies from person to person, the onerousness of our socially valued work. This remunerative norm is a matter of preference, of course, not proof, but it is consistent with the most morally enlightened Left thought. More, remunerating effort and sacrifice is also economically sound. It provides appropriate incentives to elicit what each individual has the ability to in fact withhold or provide: his or her socially valuable time, intensity, and willingness to endure hardship. Our first value is equity.

Economics affects relations among people. Anyone who isn't pathological would presumably prefer to have people concerned with and caring about one another in a cooperative social partnership—rather than seeking to fleece one another in an antisocial competitive shoot out. Our second value is solidarity.

Economics affects our range of available options. We are limited beings who have neither time nor means to each do everything. We are also social beings who can enjoy vicariously what others do that we cannot. And, finally, we are thinking and pragmatic beings who can benefit from avoiding overdependence on narrow options that leave us stranded if some of those limited options are flawed. Homogeneity of options delimits possibilities and risks overdependence on flawed scenarios. Diversity of options enriches possibilities and protects against errors. Our third value is diversity.

Economics affects how much say we each have over what is produced, in what quantities, by what methods, with what apportionment of people to tasks, and with what product allotted to people. Economic decisions determine outcomes that in turn affect us. For that matter, the act of decision making itself also affects us by influencing our mood, our sense of involvement and efficacy, and our sense of personal worth.

Save in exceptional cases, there is no moral or operational reason any one person should have excessive say compared to how much they are affected, nor is there any moral or operational reason for any one person to have insufficient say compared to how much they are affected. One decision-making norm can apply to all people equally, exceptional cases aside, yet can also respect the variation of specific operational needs from case to case. By this pattern of thought we arrive at a fourth value, self-management. We should each have a say in decisions in proportion as those decisions affect us. Means of developing, discussing, debating, tallying, and acting on preferences are context dependent. No single approach such as majority vote, two thirds vote, consensus, and various methods of information dissemination and deliberation will optimally suit all cases. What will suit all cases, however, is the overarching self-management norm by which we choose among possible means of decision making in each instance.

Economics affects relations to our natural surroundings. An economy should not compel us to destroy our natural habitat, leaving ourselves a decrepit environment to endure. But nor should an economy compel us to so protect the natural habitat that we are left no means with which to fulfill ourselves in its embrace. What an economy should do instead is reveal the full and true social costs and benefits of contending choices, including accounting for their impact on ecology, and convey to workers and consumers control over what choices to finally implement. In that way we can cooperatively care for both our environment and ourselves, in relative proportions that we freely choose. Our fifth value is therefore ecological balance, understood in this broad manner of incorporating ecological information and attentiveness in economic calculation and decision making.

Economics, finally, of course, also affects the social output we have available for people to enjoy. That is indeed the reason economies exist. If an economy abides all the above proposed values, but wastes our energy and resources by producing output that fails to meet needs and develop potentials, or by producing harmful byproducts that offset the benefits of intended products, or by splurging what is valuable in inefficient methods and as a result wasting assets needlessly, it diminishes our prospects. Even as an economy operates in accordance with equity, solidarity, diversity, self-management, and ecological balance, it should also efficiently utilize available natural, social, and personal assets without undo waste or misdirection of purpose.

These values together require classlessness, but they go beyond simply seeking classlessness, to provide positive guidelines for institutional choices. Claim 3 is therefore that, other things equal, in any economy more equity, solidarity, diversity, self-management, ecological balance, and productive efficiency is good—and less of any or all of these qualities is bad. Economic institutions should by their operations as well as their outcomes advance these qualities, not violate or obliterate them.

CLAIM 4: *While economics is profoundly important, which is why we seek to build a pareconish movement, we do not live by economics alone and economics alone is not profoundly important. A pareconish agenda for movement building must address other central sides of social life consistently with parecon's economic structure but also respectful of equally prioritized agendas to revolutionize those other sides of life.*

A new and better world will include new and better economics, yes, but also new and better relations of kin and family; religion, race, and culture; law, adjudication, and collective action; ecological arrangement; international relations; and also of more specific parts of life in these and other dimensions as well, such as science, art, education, health, and so on.

We therefore need social vision that can help us explore our options, inspire commitment, rebut cynicism, and guide practice not only for economics, but for kin relations and socializing, cultural and community relations, legislative and juridical relations, ecology, and international relations.

More, just as our economic vision and strategies provide a context that feminist vision and strategy, cultural vision and strategy, political vision and strategy, ecological vision and strategy, and internationalist vision and strategy must abide and augment, so too, in reverse, feminist, cultural, political, ecological, and internationalist vision and strategy provide a context that pareconish economic vision and strategy must abide and augment.

In every case, new arrangements in one realm will have to fit compatibly with new arrangements in other realms. Worthy movements for a new world must combine vision and strategy across spheres of social life. They should not prioritize one area of focus above the rest since that would be both morally bankrupt and strategically suicidal.

It follows that, insofar as we develop a pareconish vision and strategy for economic life, to be worthy it must incorporate not only the seeds of the future economy but also the seeds of the future vision we share for other defining parts of life. The same urgency and standards that we apply to economy we must apply equally to other domains, fulfilling the need for compatible activism.

CLAIM 5: *Seeking classlessness as in Claim 2, as well as the positive values of Claim 3, as well as accommodating economy to gains in other spheres of social life and vice versa as in*

Claim 4, compels us to reject private ownership of productive property, corporate divisions of labor, top down decision making, markets, and central planning.

Without belaboring the obvious, each of these institutional possibilities, ubiquitous in the world around us, intrinsically violates one or more (and usually all) of the values set forth above. For example, noting even just the most obvious violations, private ownership produces capitalist class rule over coordinators and workers. It obliterates equity by remunerating property and power. It obliterates self-management by vesting primary power in the hands of owners.

Corporate divisions of labor produce coordinator class rule over workers. They disempower some and aggrandize power to others, as does top-down decision making.

Markets obscure true social costs and benefits of all items that involve positive or negative effects that extend beyond immediate buyers and sellers. They lead to incredible misallocation of assets, particularly ecological, not to mention orienting output to maximizing surpluses rather than human well-being. Markets also impose antisocial behavior so that, perversely, nice guys finish last, and produce class division between coordinators and workers because firms must compete by cutting costs and because to cut costs firms will free an elite from the implications of their cost-cutting choices so that they may grow callous to the immediate human implications of their choices.

Central planning also intrinsically violates self-management and imposes coordinator-class rule to ensure obedience. Central planning typically aggrandizes the ruling coordinator class at the expense of workers below, including centralizing control in ways that yield ecological imbalance.

For all these economic institutions, the propensity to produce class division in turn homogenizes options within classes, which violates diversity and creates a war of class against class which violates solidarity.

Beyond economics, capitalist relations also aggravate hierarchies of power, status, and wealth generated by other spheres of social life, for example aggravating and exploiting sexual, gender, racial, and political hierarchies born of extra-economic relations. Capitalism likewise produces ecological imbalance and even violates ecological sustainability. It produces as well a competitive rat race that, writ large, internationally unleashes colonialism, imperialism, neocolonialism, empire, unimaginably extreme destitution, and war.

The logic of Claim 5, therefore, is that, if we are serious about classlessness, economic equity, solidarity, diversity, self-management, ecological balance, and socially oriented efficiency, as well as about broader positive aspirations for race, gender, political power, ecology, and peace, we must reject typical economic institutions as violating our values. We must seek alternatives.

CLAIM 6: *Seeking the classlessness advocated in Claim 2, and the proposed positive values advocated in Claim 3, and the broader social aims hinted at in Claim 4 but still to be elaborated more fully, and rejecting the capitalist and coordinator institutions dismissed in Claim*

5, leaves us needing to advocate new economic institutions, including the defining core structures of participatory economics. These are self-managing workers' and consumers' councils; remuneration for duration, intensity, and onerousness of socially valued work; balanced job complexes; and participatory planning.

For workers and consumers to influence decisions in proportion as they are affected by those decisions requires venues through which they can express and tally their preferences. We call these venues self-managing councils and they are the first centrally defining institutional component of participatory economics.

Equity requires equitable remuneration under workers' and consumers' own auspices and in accord with accurate valuations. It is parecon's second defining institutional component and has two primary purposes. On the one hand, ethically, workers are remunerated in compensation for the cost of their participation in time, intensity of effort, and harshness of conditions. On the other hand, economically, remunerated work must be socially useful to garner income, which ensures that workers and firms have incentives consistent with eliciting fulfilling output.

Self-managed decisions require confident preparation, relevant capacity, and appropriate participation. Self-managed decisions therefore require parecon's third defining institutional feature—balanced job complexes—in which each actor has a fair share of empowering work so that no sector of actors monopolizes empowering work while others are left disempowered and unable to even arrive at, much less manifest, a will of their own. Balanced job complexes eliminate the monopoly on empowering labor that differentiates coordinators from workers. Balanced job complexes ensure that all workers are enabled by their work conditions to participate in self-management.

All the economic values of Claim 3 plus classlessness from Claim 2 together imply that allocation should be accomplished in accord with the freely expressed will of self-managing workers and consumers and that it should be undertaken not to competitively aggrandize a ruling class against its subordinates, but by cooperative and informed negotiation in which all people's wills are proportionately actualized and in which operations, mindsets, and structures further the logic of self-managing councils, balanced job complexes, and equitable remuneration, rather than violating each. All this implies the fourth and last centrally defining institutional feature of participatory economics—participatory planning—which is the horizontal cooperative negotiation of economic inputs and outputs throughout the economy.

Insofar as workers' and consumers' self-managing councils; plus equitable remuneration for duration, intensity, and onerousness of socially valued work; plus balanced job complexes; plus participatory planning treat all actors identically economically, they also counter any possible hierarchies among actors generated outside the economy, and insofar as they properly value ecological effects and convey decision-making power to those affected, and insofar as writ large, internationally, they progressively eliminate inequality of wealth and power between nations, these institutions are also well oriented to accommodate and even augment aims for other spheres of social life, though this determination can only be fully evaluated when vision and strategy for those other domains exist in sufficient detail to permit evaluation of mutual compatibility.

CLAIM 7: *Requirements for our own projects, organizations, and movements ought to include patiently incorporating the seeds of the future in the present, including self-managed decision making, balanced job complexes, equitable remuneration, and cooperative negotiated planning, as well as central features of other dimensions of the new world we seek.*

Creating institutions in the present that incorporate seeds of the future makes sense as an experiment to learn, as a model to inspire, as a way to do the best possible work now, and for current fulfillment, for consistency, and to begin developing tomorrow's infrastructure today.

Of course we need to keep in mind that we cannot have perfect future structures now, both because of surrounding pressures that militate against libratory features now and also because of our own emotional and behavioral baggage. But the fact that we need a sense of proportion about what future seeds we can experimentally harvest now is not the same as calling for entirely rejecting immediate harvesting. Just as movements should foreshadow a future that is feminist, culturally diverse, and also politically free and just, lest they are internally compromised in their values, incapable of inspiring diverse constituencies or even prone to alienate them, incapable of overcoming cynicism, and weak in their comprehension even of current flaws and potentials, so too should movements, for the same reasons, foreshadow a future that is classless, including incorporating council organization, balanced job complexes, equitable remuneration, and self-management.

Put strategically, constructing movements that embody coordinator-class assumptions, mannerisms, and aspirations would violate our aims and cripple our prospects just as horrifically as constructing movements that embody sexist, racist, or authoritarian assumptions, mannerisms, and aspirations would cripple our prospects. Just as we do regarding visions for gender, race, and culture, politics, ecology, and international relations, we should incorporate as best we can in our current economic projects, organizations, and movements economic relations we desire for the future. Our movements should not slavishly reproduce the features of a class-divided economy any more than they should slavishly reproduce the features of racist, sexist, or authoritarian structures. They should instead patiently and carefully adopt the features of classlessness.

CLAIM 8: *Seeking participatory economic institutions requires that we not only create in the present pareconish institutions as described by Claim 7 as well as in fuller descriptions elsewhere, but that we also fight for changes in capitalist institutions. Demands made against existing institutions ought to enhance people's lives, advance the likelihood of further successful struggle, and advance the consciousness and organizational capacity to pursue those further aims. These aims provide the yardsticks for measuring success.*

As valuable as experiments in creating pareconish (or gender, race, or politically inspired) organizations in the present are, to only prioritize the creation of forward-oriented experiments in our present activism would consign those who work in existing institutions to peripheral observer status as well as callously ignore pressing needs of the moment. The path to a better future includes creating experiments in its image in the present, yes, but it also includes a long march through existing institutions, battling for changes there that improve people's lives today even as they auger and prepare for more changes tomorrow.

Changes in existing institutions that do not replace them down to their defining core features are reforms, but the effort to win reforms need not accept that only reform is possible. On the contrary, efforts to win reforms can presume that we seek desired modest economic changes not only for the immediate gains they will engender but also as part of a process to win a new economy. Efforts to win reforms can choose demands, language, organization, and methods, all in accord not only with winning sought-after short-term gains that improve people's lives in the present, but also with increasing the inclination and capacity of people to seek still more victories in the future, up to winning a new economic order. Rather than presuming system maintenance, battles around income, decision making, allocation, and other facets of economic life should be undertaken to enlarge future-oriented desires and capacities. The rhetoric should advance comprehension of ultimate values. The organization should embody visionary norms and persist to fight anew. This should hold for economics as for other spheres of life, and vice versa. Win changes now not only to enjoy the benefits but also to win more changes later. This is a non-reformist approach to winning reforms.

CLAIM 9: *At some point in the future vast movements will have features such as those noted above as well as many others, and will on the basis of their merits become vehicles toward winning, as well as themselves helping to compose, the infrastructure of a new world. This will not happen, however, until people self-consciously make it happen.*

This claim is a truism, but it is also arguably the most powerful point of all. Change will not come via an unfolding inevitable tendency in current relations that sweeps us, uncomprehending, into a better future. Changes will come, instead, only via self-conscious actions by huge numbers of people bringing to bear their creativity and energy in a largely unified and coherent manner that will have internal difference and debate, of course, but that will also have overarching shared aims and steadfast purpose.

If we travel well into the future in our minds' eyes, and we imagine looking back into the past, we will see a relatively brief period, at some point, during which people in one nation or another, or in many at once, form projects, organizations, and movements that thereafter persist to become centrally important vehicles for fighting for, constructing, and even finally merging into, a new world.

Whether we look forward, or imagine looking back, we can reasonably ask what attributes such a lasting project, organization, or movement would incorporate. We can also reasonably act on our answers, once we feel we have them more or less in hand, to try to create such vehicles of change. Then, in light of lessons, we can adapt our insights. Might we get these efforts all wrong? Yes, we might. But if we don't try, then we have no chance of getting them right. And if we do get them wrong, we can take lessons from our mistakes, and try again.

The implication seems to be that building worthy vehicles not just of opposition but for self-conscious creation of a new world must become our agenda. We should act without exaggerated images of instant success, of course, but we should also refuse to succumb to cynical or excessively patient delay.

CLAIM 10: *When a capable and caring group agrees on Claims 1 through 9, it becomes incumbent on them to collectively seek wider agreement from a still-larger group, and to solidify their inspiring intellectual unity into a more practical organizational and program-matic unity, in accord with all the claims. If not now, when?*

CONTRIBUTOR BIOS

Ezequiel Adamovsky is a historian and anti-capitalist activist. Apart from his academic publications, he has written extensively on issues of globalization, anti-capitalism, and Leftist politics. He has recently published the books *Anti-capitalism for Beginners: The New Generation of Emancipatory Movements* (2003) and *Beyond Old Left: Six Essays for a New Anti-Capitalism* (2007).

Michael Albert is a leading critic on political economy, U.S. foreign policy, and mass media. A veteran writer and activist, he currently works with *Z Magazine* and ZNet, both of which he cofounded. He has coauthored, with Robin Hahnel, many books on participatory economics. *Realizing Hope* (2006) and *Remembering Tomorrow* (2007), a memoir, are his latest books. He lives in Woods Hole, Massachusetts.

Jessica Azulay is a writer and activist based in Syracuse, NY. She cofounded *The New-Standard* in 2003 and was a member of its collective until it shut down in 2007. Jessica is available to help groups wishing to start up pareconish workplaces. Get in touch with her at jessica@disconnection.org.

Paul Burrows, a Winnipeg-based social justice activist and organizer since the late-1980s, has cofounded a number of worker-run collectives and activist institutions in Winnipeg, including the Old Market Autonomous Zone (A-Zone), Mondragón Bookstore & Coffee House, the Canada-Palestine Support Network, and, more recently, the Rudolf Rocker Cultural Centre. Information about all these projects can be found on the A-Zone website at: www.a-zone.org.

Noam Chomsky is one of the foremost political dissidents in the U.S. He is author of numerous bestselling political works, including *Failed States* (2006) and *What We Say Goes* (2007). A professor of linguistics and philosophy at MIT, Chomsky is widely credited with having revolutionized modern linguistics. He lives outside Boston, Massachusetts.

John J. Cronan Jr. lives in New York City, where he is restaurant worker and recent graduate of Pace University. He is also an organizer with Students for a Democratic Society (SDS) as well as the Industrial Workers of the World (IWW) Food and Allied Workers Union I.U. 460/640.

Marcus Denton founded the Austin Project for a Participatory Society in 2007. A 2003 graduate of the Z Media Institute, he teaches at a class- and race-segregated inner city high school in Austin, Texas.

Brian Dominick has been organizing collectives in central New York and elsewhere for nearly fifteen years. He was a cofounder of PeoplesNetWorks, the parecon organization that published *The NewStandard* from 2003 to 2007.

Barbara Ehrenreich is the author of many books, including *Nickel and Dimed* (2001), *Bait and Switch: The (Futile) Pursuit of the American Dream* (2006), and, most recently, *Dancing in the Streets: A History of Collective Joy* (2007).

Mark Evans works in a hospital as a health care assistant and lives in Birmingham, U.K. He has been active within the trade union movement undertaking a variety of roles. Over the last year he has spent most of his spare time helping set up a new organization called Project for a Participatory Society—United Kingdom (PPS-UK).

Richard W. Franke is Professor and Chair of Anthropology at Montclair State University in New Jersey. He received his Ph.D. in anthropology from Harvard University in 1972. His most recent works on Kerala include *Local Democracy and Development: The Kerala People's Campaign* *for Decentralized Planning* (2002, coauthored with Thomas Isaac) and *Striving for Sustainability: Environmental Stress and Democratic Initiatives in Kerala* (2006 coauthored with Srikumar Chattopadhyay).

Jerry Fresia received his Ph.D. in political science from the University of Massachusetts in 1982. He also has studied art and painted his entire life. In 1989, he moved to San Francisco, where he organized alternative and independent outdoor exhibitions for visual and performing artists. Currently, he lives on Lake Como, Italy, where he and his wife host painting workshops.

Madeline Gardner has done a breadth of local work from indigenous rights to anti-war walkouts to defending equal access to higher education. Nationally she has conducted listening projects and organized mass direct actions and convergences around the IMF/WB. Madeline is cofounder, author, and trainer with Beyond the Choir. She is 25 years old and a member of SDS at the University of Minnesota.

Andrej Grubacic is an anarchist propagandist, and anarchist historian, from the Balkans. He works with Z Balkans, GlobalBalkans, and ZNet. He is a member of the Post-Yugoslav anarchist collective "Freedom Fight."

Robin Hahnel has taught political economy at American University for over thirty years and is currently a visiting professor of economics at Lewis and Clark College. He has coauthored, along with Michael Albert, numerous books on participatory economics. His most recent book is *Economic Justice and Democracy: From Competition to Cooperation* (2005).

Brian Kelly, age twenty, is a political organizer with Students for a Democratic Society (SDS), the newly reformed national student organization. Since 2006 he has helped to build SDS as a powerful, radical student organization rooted in vision, strategy, and long-haul struggle. He is a

student at Pace University in New York City and currently lives in Brooklyn.

Pat Korte is an organizer with, and a founder of, this century's Students for a Democratic Society (SDS). He is an undergraduate at Eugene Lang College at the New School in New York City. Since high school, Pat has been active in anti-imperialist, student power, and labor struggles. He is nineteen-years-old and lives in Brooklyn.

Mandisi Majavu is with the Africa Project for Participatory Society (www.apps. org.za). He is a postgraduate student at the University of Cape Town, South Africa. He can be reached at majavums@gmail. com.

Dave Markland is a social service worker and occasional writer/researcher. A member of the Vancouver Participatory Economics Collective and organizer with StopWar.ca, he lives in Vancouver with his partner, Marla.

Cynthia Peters is a writer, activist, and mother of two. She has contributed essays on organizing, gender and sexuality, the politics of parenting, and movement building to numerous books and periodicals, especially *Z Magazine* and ZNet. For her day job, she edits *The Change Agent*—a social justice magazine for adult learners and adult educators.

Justin Podur is a writer and editor at ZNet. He is based in Toronto and has reported from Haiti, Colombia, Venezuela, Israel/Palestine, and on race/culture issues in North America.

Nikos Raptis was born in Athens, Greece, in 1930. He is a retired civil engineer. He has been writing on social matters for the last forty years. He has also translated works by Noam Chomsky and Michael Albert.

Marla Renn lives in Vancouver, where she is an anti-war organizer and a member of the Vancouver Parecon Collective. She is passionate about community building and education. Marla is currently an aspiring stilt-walker and clown.

Joshua Kahn Russell is a twenty-three-year-old trainer and organizer with Students for a Democratic Society and Rainforest Action Network. Josh was a cofounder of the Activist Resource Center and the Radical Student Alliance at Brandeis University. Recently, he has helped coordinate a barrage of activist training camps, convergences, and events, including the U.S. Social Forum 2007. Josh currently lives in Oakland, CA.

Anders Sandström is active in the Swedish syndicalist union SAC, the Central Organisation of the Workers of Sweden. After working ten years in the business world as a financial manager and business controller, he quit, changed sides, and joined SAC in 2002 with the intention to work for a different type of society. He has been working in several different positions within the organization and in the SAC-owned businesses since then.

Lydia Sargent cofounded South End Press (where she was collective member for ten years). She also cofounded *Z Magazine* (where she has worked since 1987). She is editor of *Playbook* (1986) and *Women and Revolution* (1981), and contributes editorials, features, and a regular "Hotel Satire" column to Z. Active in theater for 30 years, Lydia has written, adapted, directed, and performed numerous political satires, including a three-part play mystery series about a collective of revolutionary women setting up a kind of participatory society, *The Long Sigh, Vanish Like A Summer Trantrum*, and *The Second Street Hotel*.

Stephen R. Shalom teaches political science at William Paterson University in New Jersey. He writes for *Z Magazine* and ZNet and is on the editorial boards of *Critical Asian Studies* and *New Politics*. Among his books are *Socialist Visions* (ed.,

1983) and *Which Side Are You On? An Introduction to Politics* (2003).

Chris Spannos is an activist, organizer, and anti-capitalist. He is a full-time staff member with Z. He resides in Woods Hole, Massachusetts. In addition to editing this collection, Chris is also editing *Hope, Reason, & Revolution* (2009).

Marie Trigona has reported from Argentina for numerous media outlets around the world. A writer, radio producer, and film maker, her work focuses on labor struggles, social movements, and human rights in Latin America. Her writing has appeared in publications including *Z Magazine*, ZNet, *NACLA, Monthly Review*, and many others. She collaborates with video and direct-action collective Grupo Alavío (www.agoratv.org).

Tom Wetzel is a native of Los Angeles, where he received a Ph.D. in philosophy at UCLA. He has worked as a gas station attendant and typesetter, taught philosophy at several colleges, and currently works as a technical writer in the computer industry. He has been involved in union organizing and affordable housing activism. He is a member of the board of directors of the San Francisco Community Land Trust and is working on a book, entitled, *Workers' Liberation and Self-management*.

Matt McBride, Lloyd Philbrook, and **Mitchell Szczepanczyk** are residents of Chicago and are longtime members of CAPES, the Chicago Area Participatory Economics Society. Matt works in the food service industry, Lloyd works as a computer consultant, and Mitchell works as a software developer.

INDEX

Symbols

49th Street Underground 324

A

A-Zone 258, 278
Diego Abad de Santillan 197
Abstract Expressionists 78
Ezequiel Adamovsky 10
affirmative action 118
AFL-CIO 188, 249
AFL-CIO Organizing Institute 248
African National Congress 119, 214
Aid to Families with Dependent Children 250
Michael Albert 4, 5, 9, 10, 44, 56–73,
    113–114, 117, 121–122, 124–126,
    151, 265, 271, 276, 316, 331. See
    also Parecon: Life After Capitalism;
    See also Realizing Hope: Life Beyond
    Capitalism
Alcoholics Anonymous 36
Christopher Alexander 90
Neville Alexander 116, 118
All-Russian Congress of Soviets 184, 186, 358.
    See also Russian Revolution
American Bar Association 374
American Medical Association 374
American Popular Revolutionary Alliance
    (APRA) 209
American Socialist Party 191
American Society of Civil Engineers 91, 93
    Hurricane Katrina External Review Panel
    91
Amish 257
Piero Ammirato 331
anarchism/anarchists 4, 14, 223, 224, 225–228,
    231, 349, 374
    influence with Russian workers 226
    in the Balkans 142–143
    themes of traditional anarchism/libertarian
    socialism 143, 224
R. L. Anderson 226
AOL 348
apartheid 112–113, 117, 118–121, 124–126
Arbeiter Ring 258, 321
Arbetaren 145, 146, 147, 148. See also Central
    Organization of the Workers of
    Sweden
architecture 3
Rita Arditti 94
Argentinian self-management 155–168
    Bauen Hotel 165
    Chilavert printing 165

La Foresta 165
Maderera Cordoba 165
Pismanta Hotel and Spa 165
Zanello 165
Zanon 155–167
    changed social relations 157–158,
    159–160, 167
    harassment of workers 156
    Women's Commission 160–161
Association of Community Organizations for
    Reform Now (ACORN) 251
Austin Project for a Participatory Society 10,
    330–335
Autonomous Communities 27, 31
Jessica Azulay 10

B

Robert Badinter 212
Michael Bakunin 11, 14, 112
balanced job complexes 15, 18, 71, 79,
    123–124, 140, 150, 281–285, 307, 368,
    370, 385, 402. See also participatory
    economics
Balkans 136–144
Simone Baribeau 307
Edward Bellamy 58
Jorge Bermudez 162
Elaine Bernard 247
Between Labor and Capital. See also Barbara
    Ehrenreich, John Ehrenreich
Beyond the Choir 340
Janet Biehl 68
Jacob Bigelow 88
bioregionalism 68
Black Economic Empowerment 118, 120
black nationalism 112
black power 21
Black Power Movement 365
Abe Bluestein 202
Blue Space collective 258
Carl Boggs 57
Bolivarian University 173, 174, 176
Bolsheviks 25, 184, 185, 187, 190, 205, 223,
    225, 358
Luc Boltansky 137
Patrick Bond 117
Murray Bookchin 68, 69
Boston Community School 264
Willy Brandt 204
Gerald Brenan 200, 227
Bretton Woods system 210, 218–222, 241
Maurice Brinton 182, 184, 187, 191
Charles Bronson 348
Bruderhoff 257
Buddhist Economics 68
Paul Burrows 10

Buy Nothing Day 288

C

Leslie Cagan 4
Canadian National Parecon Organization 321
capitalism 3, 14, 15, 20, 58, 59–60, 69, 72, 84,
    95, 97, 137, 144, 157, 168, 172, 175,
    191, 192, 204, 229, 380
  adaptation of and recuperation by 204,
    207–208, 236, 237
  and attempts at reform 206, 208, 215, 239.
    See also Keynesian economics; Kerala
    experiment; Grameen Bank; social
    democracy
    anticorporate movement 249–250
    campaigns and movements 240–252
    community development and anti-sprawl
      246–249
    consumer movement 250
    full employment 242
    global justice movement 251–252
    labor movement 247–248
    living wage capaign 243
    poor people's movement 250–251
    single-payer health care 243–244
    taming financial markets 241
    tax reform 242–243
  and social-democratic policy 204, 210–213,
    216, 217
  attempts to abolish 223. See also participato-
    ry economics
  defining features of 71, 223, 276
  work after capitalism 275–278. See also par-
    ticipatory economics; See also balanced
    job complexes; See also self-manage-
    ment
Patrick Carnes 40
E. H. Carr 185
Catholic Democratic Confederation of Labor
    211
Center for Socialist Study, Research, and Edu-
    cation (CERES) 212
Center for the New American Dream 250
Central Organization of the Workers of Swe-
    den 145–150
central planning 19, 69, 143, 224, 401
Ronald A. Chadderton 91
Hugo Chávez 165, 178, 179, 333, 383
Anton Chekhov 272
Michelle Chen 307
Chicago Area Participatory Economics Society
    10, 323–329, 331
Chicago Social Forum 323
Noam Chomsky 4, 9, 229, 268, 314
CITGO 176
Citizens for Tax Justice 242

Civil Rights Movement 365
class 3, 14, 95, 142, 207, 351, 373–379,
    397–398. See also coordinator class
  class struggle 4, 7, 191
  contemporary lack of analysis 5
  two-class analysis 11
  working-class identity 166
Class Matters 378
Dylan Clayton 323
Co-operative Grocers Information Network
    256
National Cooperative Grocers Association 256
Co-op Net 256
Columbine massacre 348
Comahue University 162
communism 72, 224
  Communist Party of India 130
community 8, 49
community-supported agriculture (CSA)
    388–389
community development banks 245
Community development corporations 245
Community land trust 84–87, 245
Community Supported Agriculture 256
Community Voices Heard 251
complimentary and holistic approach 8, 151,
    373
Congress of Saint-Imier 223
Congress of South African Trade Unions 120
consumers' councils 15, 17, 71, 122, 123, 125,
    370, 385, 402. See also participatory
    economics
Consumer Federation of America 250
Contact Center 251
John Conyers Jr. 244
coordinator class 5, 125, 139, 142, 143, 177,
    192, 374–376, 397–398
  development during Russian revolution 190
corporate division of labor 98, 139, 143, 368,
    401
The Corporation 314–315
Joaquin Costa 227
Council of People's Commissars 184. See
    also Russian Revolution
court system 31
Brendan Coyne 307
William Cross 114
Michel Crozier 109
culture 3, 8, 49

D

Herman Daly 68
J. Langdon Davies 227
decision making 399
  Consensus 29
  majority rule 30

protecting minority rights 30–31
decolonization 113
Jacques Delors 212
Marcus Denton 10
Isaac Deutscher 185, 187
Paul DiMaggio 80
Direct democracy 27
diversity 3
Milovan Djilas 138
Sam Dolgoff 202, 226, 228
Brian Dominick 10, 307
dual power 357, 366, 386, 389
Dudley Street Neighbors 86
Buenaventura Durruti 194, 202
Bob Dylan 372

E

eBay 256–257
eco-socialism 68
ecology 3
economy/economics 3
  Left economic vision 56
education 3, 106–108
Barbara Ehrenreich 5, 9
John Ehrenreich 5
Employment Equity Act (South Africa) 118
equitable cooperation 239–240
  experiments in 253–260
    consumer cooperatives 255–256
    experimenting with parecon 258–259
    intentional communities 257–258
    local currencies 254
    producer cooperatives 254–255
ethnicity 49
Expanded and Improved Medicare for All
    Bill 244

F

Fabian society 223
Falangists 194
Frantz Fanon 113–116, 124–125, 127–128
  Wretched of the Earth 113, 114
Joshua Farley 68
Federal Reserve Bank 241
Federation of Egalitarian Communities 257
Fellowship for Intentional Community 257
feminism 4, 21. See also kinship
Daniel Ferras 159
Ferrer schools 228
Fight Club 364
Financial Markets Center 241
First International
  split between libertarian and authoritarian
    socialists 223
Nancy Folbre 44
Food and Drug Administration 250

Fordism 218
Michel Foucault 351
Francisco Franco 194
Richard Franke 9
Freedom Fight Collective 136
Jo Freeman 354
Free Trade Area of the Americas 175
Paulo Freire 345
Jerry Fresia 9
Erich Fromm 32

G

G-7 Welcoming Committee 258, 321
Alan Garcia 209
Madeline Gardner 10
Costa Gavras 272
gender 3, 46–47, 232, 370
  gender oppression 232
General Labor Confederation (CGT), Spain
    165
General Union of Workers (UGT) 194
gentrification 84
Georgia Citizens Hunger Coalition 251
T. F. Glick 226
Global Justice TV 314
Raul Godoy 167
Alain Gomez 212
Google 356, 357
Michael Gould-Wartofsky 340
Grameen Bank 130
Grassroots Economic Organizing 254
Great Depression 214
Greenpeace 71, 73
Green Party 71, 383
Andrej Grubacic 9
Grupo Alavío 163
Che Guevara 170
Anna Gyorgy 268

H

Robin Hahnel 4, 5, 9, 14, 20, 44, 124–125,
    151, 276, 316, 324
  Economic Justice and Democracy 57
  personal views regarding the environment
    58–60
Michael Hardt 141
Michael Harrington 205–215
Harvard University 106
Harvard Trade Union Program 247
Paul Hawken 68
Howard Hawkins 57, 68
Ernest Hemingway 194
Edward S. Herman 268
heteronomous politics 346
historical materialism 7
bell hooks 127, 268

Herbert Hoover 214
Branko Horvat 140
housing 84
    public housing 86
    squatting 86
Human Sciences Research Council 117,
        118–119, 120, 123
Hutterites 257

I

identity 49. *See also* gender; *See also* class; *See also* race; *See also* kinship
imperialism 3
Industrial Workers of the World 183, 333
intercommunalism 371
International Brigades 194
International Co-operative Alliance 256
International Conference on Democratic Decentralization (Kerala, India) 133
International Longshore and Warehouse Union 252
International Monetary Fund 119, 175, 211, 241
International Noise Conspiracy 316
International Project for a Participatory Society 330
International Workers Association 191
In These Times 325
IRIN 120
Iteration Facilitation Boar 63
Ithaca Hours and Time Dollars 254

J

Michael Rabinder James 51, 53, 55
Jobs with Justice 247
Johannesburg Securities Exchange 120, 121
John J. Cronan Jr. 10
Lionel Jospin 136
Jugoremedija 136
jury system 31

K

Cynthia Kaufman 331
Karl Kautsky 208
Raul Kellerman 156
Robin Kelley 51
Brian Kelly 10
Kensington Welfare Rights Union 251
Kerala experiment 9, 130–134, 278, 303
John Maynard Keynes 206
Keynesian economics 211, 222
    military Keynesianism 242
Mel King 4
kinship 8, 9, 32, 370
    attachment and intimacy 33–34
    caregiving 42–45
    identity 34–36

sex and sexuality 37–41
Helmut Kohl 213
Catherine Komp 307
Pat Korte 10
David Korten 68
Joel Kovel 68, 70, 71
L. Kritzman 185
Peter Kropotkin 14, 16
Paloli Mohammed Kutty 133

L

Land and Freedom 194
Latin American Congress on Recuperated Enterprises 165
Mary Lea 265
La Leche League 36
Kelly Lenora Lee 340
Left Democratic Front (India) 130
lemon socialism 209
V.I. Lenin 25, 184, 188, 190, 191
Leninism 25, 31, 182–193, 224, 349, 361, 369
Gaston Leval 197, 198, 199, 200, 202, 226, 228
Liberating Theory 4, 151–152
Libertarian International 223, 228
Libertarian Municipalism 68, 69
libertarian socialism 14, 223. *See also* anarchism/anarchists
    and reform of capitalism 233–235
    demise of after WWII 229–238
    success in building mass movements 224–228
limited equity housing co-ops 85
Lincoln Center 80
Literary Marketplace 265
Living Wage Resource Center 243
Local Harvest 256
Looking Forward 57, 315. *See also* participatory economics
Loyola University 325
Luiz Inácio Lula da Silva 346
Lyndon Johnson 205

M

Alan Maass 226
Michael MacDonald 116
Mandisi Majavu 9
Malayalam 133
Ernest Mandel 206
markets 19, 95–103, 97, 139, 206, 351
Dave Markland 9
Alice Goldfarb Marquis 80
Nick Martin 340
Karl Marx 191, 206, 207, 276, 289–295
marxism 223
marxism/marxists 4, 191, 192, 231, 349, 374

black Marxism 112
    self-contradiction 192
Massachusetts Institute of Technology 88, 106
G. P. Maximov 186, 189
Matt McBride 10, 323
McDonald's 378, 388
Meetup.com 323
Shreema Mehta 307
Meidner plan 219
Mennonites 257
Mensheviks 183, 187, 225
Robert Michels 208
Midwest Social Forum 324
Slobodan Milosevic 139
Francois Mitterrand 205, 209, 210, 211, 212, 213
Mondragón Bookstore & Coffee House 258, 278–304, 321
    job responsibilities for collective members 279
monist approach 7
Monthly Review publishers 265
William Morris 58
Mothers of Plaza de Mayo 164
multiculturalism 50
    limitations of 50–51
Francisco Murillo 161

N

Ralph Nader 249
nanotechnology 94
Narodniki 225
nationalism 4
National Confederation of Labor (CNT) 194, 202, 226, 228
    Solidaridad Obrera 228
National Cooperative Business Association 254
National Movement of Recuperated Enterprises 165, 333. See also Argentinian self-management
National Public University of Buenos Aires 162
National Welfare Rights Organization 250
National Workers' Union 333
Nicoli Nattrass 117, 118–119
Natural Cycle 258
Antonio Negri 141
neighborhood councils 86, 125, 389
Nested Councils 28, 31, 369
Neuquén Ceramists Union 158, 159, 165
The NewStandard 10, 306–312, 315, 333
    Participatory Decision-Making Process 308–309
    workplace organization 307
New Deal 204, 208, 241

New Left 14, 208, 230, 235, 264
    failure to develop a critique of capitalism 231
New York Post 379
New York Times 379
David F. Noble 94
non-reformist reforms 235–236, 367–368
Nosotros somos asi 194
Alec Nove 206
No Child Left Behind 107
Nuestra Lucha 163. See also Argentinian self-management/Zanon
Julius Nyerere 124

O

Gregg Olsen 222
Oodi Weavers 303
Open University of the Left 325
Oregon Action 251
Organization of the Workers of Sweden (SAC) 9
Organizing Institute 248
George Orwell 194, 228
Jon Osborne 323
Elnor Ostrom 226, 227

P

pan-Africanism 112
Anton Pannekoek 14
Pareton. Life After Capitalism 76, 104, 323
parenting 3
Participative Budget (Brazil) 102
participatory economics 8, 14–24, 147, 195, 278, 355, 370, 380–394, 396–405
    and the environment 56–73
    central features of 15
    groups practicing participatory economics 258. See also Mondragón; The NewStandard; G7 Welcoming Committee, Natural Cycle; South End Press; Z; Arbeiter Ring
    slow acceptance of 20–21
    theory vs. practice 281–298
participatory planning 15, 71, 79, 83, 95, 97, 99, 103, 278, 370, 402. See also participatory economics
    time spent in a parecon 99–102
participatory society 138, 396–405
patriarchy 3, 232
José Peirats 200, 202
C. R. Pennoni 92
People's Plan Campaign 130–134
Cynthia Peters 9
Peter Marcuse 84
Lloyd Philbrook 10, 323
Devan Pillay 117

piquetero movement 346
pluralist approach 7
Justin Podur 9, 173
The Political Economy of Participatory Economics 57
politics 3
Polyculturalism 9, 51
Popular Movement of Neuquén 164
Porter Sargent Publishers 264
post-colonial theory 112–119, 128
Vijay Prashad 51
prefigurative organizing 262
privilege 54
Professional-Managerial Class. *See also* coordinator class
Project for a Participatory Society-U.K. 9, 151
Propagandhi 299
Kurt Prufer 89
Public Interest Research Groups 250

R

race 3, 49
racism 3, 50, 232
Rage Against the Machine 333
Rainforest Action Network 340
Ayn Rand 294
Dennis A. Randolph 91
Nikos Raptis 9
Rata Blanca 163, 164
Ronald Reagan 213
Bernice Johnson Reagon 35
Realizing Hope: Life Beyond Capitalism 92
Redefining Progress 243
referendum democracy 27, 31
remuneration for effort 17, 71, 125, 149, 402
remuneration for effort and sacrifice 15, 140, 150, 288–294, 370. *See also* participatory economics
Marla Renn 10
Representative Democracy 26, 31
Sean Reynolds 324
Rosa Rivera 168
Michel Rocard 212, 213
Rudolf Rocker 14, 16
Franklin Delano Roosevelt 204, 208, 214
Joshua Kahn Russell 10
Russian revolution 182–192, 186, 202
  All-Russian Producers Congress 188
  factory committees 182–187
    Bolshevik policy to suppress 186–187
    Central Soviet of Factory Committees 185
    Practical Manual for the Implementation of Workers' Control of Industry 185
  libertarian socialism within 224–225
  New Economic Policy 189

Red Army 189
soviets 182–184, 357
  Central Soviet of Employees 187
  Workers Opposition 188
  Workers Truth 188
Magnus Ryner 205, 218–222

S

Carlos Saavedra 159
Charles Sackrey 221
Kirkpatrick Sale 28, 68
Anders Sandström 9
Eric Sargent 271
Lydia Sargent 4, 10
John Schall 265
Helmut Schmidt 204
Geoffrey Schneider 221
Juliet Schor 67
Juliet Schor 265
E.F. Schumacher 68
David Schweickart 325
George Scialabba 268
SDS *See* Students For a Democratic Society
Jeremy Seekings 117, 118–119
self-management 3, 83, 86, 122, 138, 380. *See also* Argentinian self-management
  in the Spanish Revolution 195–202
Amartya Sen 51
Serbia 144
Service Employees International Union 248
sexuality 3
Stephen R. Shalom 9, 193, 316, 395
Bill Shatov 183
Simon Fraser University 314
Bart Simpson 315
Paul Singer 102, 104
Marina Sitrin 331
Holly Sklar 4
Theda Skocpol 331
Adam Smith 206
Jorge Sobich 164
social democracy/social democrats 204–262
Social Ecology 68
Social Revolutionary Party 187
solidarity 3
Solidarity Group (Britain) 182
Augustin Souchy 199, 202
South End Press 10, 97, 258, 264–274
  founding of 264–266
  original mission statement 266
  principles for a democratic workplace 266–267
Soviet Union 143
Spanish Revolution 194–202, 223, 226–229, 238
  Levante Collectives 197

John Spargo 191
Spartacus Books 194, 315
Joseph Stalin 189
Stalinism 25
Star Wars 194
Jon Stewart 333
Piotr Stolypyn 225
Karen Struening 43
Students for a Democratic Society 10, 340, 373–379, 376–377, 379
Swedish Employers Association 219
Swedish Labor Federation (LO) 207, 219
Swedish social democratic party (SAP) 219, 221, 222
Syndikalisten 145, 147. See also Central Organization of the Workers of Sweden
System of a Down 333
Mitchell Szczepanczyk 10, 323

T

Megan Tady 307
Frederick Taylor 190
Taylorism 190, 191, 229
Temporary Assistance to Needy Families 250
Sampie Terreblanche 119
Margaret Thatcher 213, 396
The Economist 209
The Institute for Social and Cultural Change 266
Third World liberation movements 229–230, 239
Third World Solidarity 231, 365
Josip Broz Tito 139
Leo Tolstoy 272
Transitional Executive Council 119
Marie Trigona 9
Trilateral Commission 106
  The Crisis of Democracy 106
Flora Tristan 191
Leon Trotsky 188, 190
Mark Twain 272

U

U.S. Department of Treasury 241
Unified Socialist Party of Catalonia (UGT) 194
United for a Fair Economy 242
Teamsters 252
United Steelworkers 252
United Students Against Sweatshops 243
University of British Columbia 314
University of Chicago 324
University of Wisconsin Center for Cooperatives 256
urbanism/cities 3
US Social Forum 10, 332, 363

Peoples' Movement Assembly 363
Utopia 3

V

Vancouver Area Anti-Capitalist Convergence 314
Vancouver Parecon Collective 10, 194, 258, 313–321, 323, 331
Venezuela 6–7
  assessment of Bolivarian revolution 169–180
Vietnam War 365
Omar VillaBlanca 163
Omar Villablanca 159, 164
The Village Voice 268
Carlos Villamonte 158
vision and strategy 6, 275–277, 350–351, 358–362, 396 405
VIVE TV 174

W

Wal-Mart 249
Pat Walker 265
War on Terror 365
Arthur Waskow 54
Philip Watts 136
Tom Wetzel 9, 159, 202
white privilege 125
Tim Wise 129
Kateri Woestman 340
Workers' Party of Marxist Unification (POUM) 194
workers' councils 15, 17, 71, 78, 122, 370, 385, 402. See also participatory economics
  in Spanish revolution 198
Workers' Party (Brazil) 102, 214, 346
World Bank 120, 175
World Economic Forum 136
World Peace Forum 317
World Social Forum 102, 274, 275, 346, 357
World Trade Organization 175, 251
Erik Olin Wright 10
Matt Wuerker 272

X

Malcolm X 369

Y

Yahoo! 356
Joseph C. Yater 94
Yerba Buena Center for the Arts 80
Yugoslavia 138, 143
  "self-management" in 143–144

Z

Z 10
ZNet 273
Z Magazine 271–274

Z Magazine Balkans 136
Z Media Institute (ZMI) 273
Z Strategy and Vision Sessions 25, 48, 330,
    332, 396
Z Video Productions 273
Zanon. *See* Argentinian self-management
Luis Zanon 161
Zapatistas (EZLN) 332, 333, 339, 346, 347,
    352, 353, 357
  Sixth Declaration 347
   Other Campaign 352
Howard Zinn 115

ALSO AVAILABLE FROM AK PRESS

DWIGHT E. ABBOTT—I Cried, You Didn't Listen
MARTHA ACKELSBERG—Free Women of Spain
KATHY ACKER—Pussycat Fever
MICHAEL ALBERT—Moving Forward: Program for a Participatory Economy
JOEL ANDREAS—Addicted to War: Why the U.S. Can't Kick Militarism
JOEL ANDREAS—Adicto a la Guerra: Por qué EEUU no puede librarse del militarismo
ANONYMOUS —Test Card F
PAUL AVRICH—Anarchist Voices: An Oral History of Anarchism in America (Unabridged)
PAUL AVRICH—The Modern School Movement: Anarchism and Education in the United
    States
PAUL AVRICH—The Russian Anarchists
BRIAN AWEHALI (ed.)—Tipping the Sacred Cow
DAN BERGER—Outlaws of America: The Weather Underground and the Politics of Solidarity
ALEXANDER BERKMAN—What is Anarchism?
ALEXANDER BERKMAN—The Blast: The Complete Collection
STEVEN BEST & ANTHONY NOCELLA, II—Igniting a Revolution: Voices in Defense of
    the Earth
HAKIM BEY—Immediatism
JANET BIEHL & PETER STAUDENMAIER—Ecofascism: Lessons From The German
    Experience
BIOTIC BAKING BRIGADE—Pie Any Means Necessary: The Biotic Baking Brigade
    Cookbook
DAN BERGER—Outlaws of America
JACK BLACK—You Can't Win
MURRAY BOOKCHIN—Anarchism, Marxism, and the Future of the Left
MURRAY BOOKCHIN—The Ecology of Freedom: The Emergence and Dissolution of
    Hierarchy
MURRAY BOOKCHIN—Post-Scarcity Anarchism
MURRAY BOOKCHIN—Social Anarchism or Lifestyle Anarchism: An Unbridgeable Chasm
MURRAY BOOKCHIN—Social Ecology and Communalism
MURRAY BOOKCHIN—The Spanish Anarchists: The Heroic Years 1868–1936
MURRAY BOOKCHIN—To Remember Spain: The Anarchist and Syndicalist Revolution of
    1936
MURRAY BOOKCHIN—Which Way for the Ecology Movement?
JULES BOYKOFF—Beyond Bullets: The Suppression of Dissent in the United States
MAURICE BRINTON—For Workers' Power
DANNY BURNS—Poll Tax Rebellion
MAT CALLAHAN—The Trouble With Music
CHRIS CARLSSON—Critical Mass: Bicycling's Defiant Celebration
CHRIS CARLSSON—Nowtopia
JAMES CARR—Bad
DANIEL CASSIDY—How the Irish Invented Slang: The Secret Language of the Crossroads
NOAM CHOMSKY—At War With Asia
NOAM CHOMSKY—Chomsky on Anarchism
NOAM CHOMSKY—Language and Politics
NOAM CHOMSKY—Radical Priorities
STUART CHRISTIE—Granny Made Me an Anarchist
WARD CHURCHILL—On the Justice of Roosting Chickens: Reflections on the Consequences
    of U.S. Imperial Arrogance and Criminality
WARD CHURCHILL—Pacifism as Pathology: Reflections on the Role of Armed Struggle in
    North America
WARD CHURCHILL—Since Predator Came

CLASS WAR FEDERATION —Unfinished Business: The Politics of Class War
HARRY CLEAVER—Reading Capital Politically
ALEXANDER COCKBURN & JEFFREY ST. CLAIR (ed.)—Dime's Worth of Difference
ALEXANDER COCKBURN & JEFFREY ST. CLAIR—End Times: Death of the Fourth Estate
ALEXANDER COCKBURN & JEFFREY ST. CLAIR (ed.)—The Politics of Anti-Semitism
ALEXANDER COCKBURN & JEFFREY ST. CLAIR (ed.)—Serpents in the Garden
DANIEL COHN-BENDIT & GABRIEL COHN-BENDIT—Obsolete Communism: The Left-Wing Alternative
BENJAMIN DANGL—The Price of Fire: Resource Wars and Social Movements in Bolivia
DARK STAR COLLECTIVE —Beneath the Paving Stones: Situationists and the Beach, May '68
DARK STAR COLLECTIVE —Quiet Rumours: An Anarcha-Feminist Reader
VOLTAIRINE de CLEYRE—Voltairine de Cleyre Reader
CHRIS DUNCAN—My First Time: A Collection of First Punk Show Stories
EG SMITH COLLECTIVE—Animal Ingredients A–Z (3rd edition)
HOWARD EHRLICH—Reinventing Anarchy, Again
SIMON FORD—Realization and Suppression of the Situationist International
BENJAMIN FRANKS—Rebel Alliances
YVES FREMION & VOLNY—Orgasms of History: 3000 Years of Spontaneous Revolt
EMMA GOLDMAN (EDITED BY DAVID PORTER)—Vision on Fire
BERNARD GOLDSTEIN—Five Years in the Warsaw Ghetto
DAVID GRAEBER—Possibilities: Essays on Hierarchy, Rebellion, and Desire
DAVID GRAEBER & STEVPHEN SHUKAITIS—Constituent Imagination
DANIEL GUÉRIN—No Gods No Masters: An Anthology of Anarchism
AGUSTIN GUILLAMÓN—The Friends Of Durruti Group, 1937–1939
ANN HANSEN—Direct Action: Memoirs Of An Urban Guerilla
HELLO—2/15: The Day The World Said NO To War
WILLIAM HERRICK—Jumping the Line: The Adventures and Misadventures of an American Radical
FRED HO—Legacy to Liberation: Politics & Culture of Revolutionary Asian/Pacific America
STEWART HOME—Neoism, Plagiarism & Praxis
STEWART HOME—Neoist Manifestos / The Art Strike Papers
STEWART HOME—No Pity
STEWART HOME—Red London
GEORGY KATSIAFICAS—Subversion of Politics
KATHY KELLY—Other Lands Have Dreams: From Baghdad to Pekin Prison
JAMES KELMAN—Some Recent Attacks: Essays Cultural And Political
KEN KNABB—Complete Cinematic Works of Guy Debord
KATYA KOMISARUK—Beat the Heat: How to Handle Encounters With Law Enforcement
PETER KROPOTKIN—The Conquest of Bread
SAUL LANDAU—A Bush & Botox World
JOSH MACPHEE & ERIK REULAND—Realizing the Impossible: Art Against Authority
RICARDO FLORES MAGÓN—Dreams of Freedom: A Ricardo Flores Magón Reader
NESTOR MAKHNO—The Struggle Against The State & Other Essays
SUBCOMANDANTE MARCOS—¡Ya Basta! Ten Years of the Zapatista Uprising
G.A. MATIASZ—End Time
CHERIE MATRIX—Tales From the Clit
ALBERT MELTZER—Anarchism: Arguments For & Against
ALBERT MELTZER—I Couldn't Paint Golden Angels
JESSICA MILLS—My Mother Wears Combat Boots
RAY MURPHY—Siege Of Gresham
NORMAN NAWROCKI—Rebel Moon
MICHAEL NEUMANN—The Case Against Israel
HENRY NORMAL—A Map of Heaven

FIONBARRA O'DOCHARTAIGH—Ulster's White Negroes: From Civil Rights To Insurrection

CRAIG O'HARA—The Philosophy Of Punk

ANTON PANNEKOEK—Workers' Councils

ABEL PAZ (TRANSLATED BY CHUCK MORSE)—Durruti in the Spanish Revolution

BEN REITMAN—Sister of the Road: The Autobiography of Boxcar Bertha

PENNY RIMBAUD—The Diamond Signature

PENNY RIMBAUD—Shibboleth: My Revolting Life

RUDOLF ROCKER—Anarcho-Syndicalism

RUDOLF ROCKER—The London Years

RAMOR RYAN—Clandestines: The Pirate Journals of an Irish Exile

RON SAKOLSKY & STEPHEN DUNIFER—Seizing the Airwaves: A Free Radio Handbook

ROY SAN FILIPPO—A New World In Our Hearts: 8 Years of Writings from the Love and Rage Revolutionary Anarchist Federation

MARINA SITRIN—Horizontalism: Voices of Popular Power in Argentina

ALEXANDRE SKIRDA—Facing the Enemy: A History Of Anarchist Organisation From Proudhon To May 1968

ALEXANDRE SKIRDA—Nestor Makhno: Anarchy's Cossack

VALERIE SOLANAS—Scum Manifesto

CJ STONE—Housing Benefit Hill & Other Places

ANTONIO TELLEZ—Sabate: Guerilla Extraordinary

MICHAEL TOBIAS—Rage and Reason

BOB TORRES—Making A Killing: The Political Economy of Animal Rights

JIM TULLY—Beggars of Life: A Hobo Autobiography

TOM VAGUE—Anarchy in the UK: The Angry Brigade

TOM VAGUE—Televisionaries

JAN VALTIN—Out of the Night

RAOUL VANEIGEM—A Cavalier History Of Surrealism

FRANÇOIS EUGENE VIDOCQ—Memoirs of Vidocq: Master of Crime

MARK J. WHITE—An Idol Killing

JOHN YATES—Controlled Flight Into Terrain

JOHN YATES—September Commando

BENJAMIN ZEPHANIAH—Little Book of Vegan Poems

BENJAMIN ZEPHANIAH—School's Out

CDs

MUMIA ABU JAMAL—175 Progress Drive

MUMIA ABU JAMAL—All Things Censored Vol.1

MUMIA ABU JAMAL—Spoken Word

JUDI BARI—Who Bombed Judi Bari?

JELLO BIAFRA—Become the Media

JELLO BIAFRA—Beyond The Valley of the Gift Police

JELLO BIAFRA—The Big Ka-Boom, Part One

JELLO BIAFRA—High Priest of Harmful

JELLO BIAFRA—I Blow Minds For A Living

JELLO BIAFRA—In the Grip of Official Treason

JELLO BIAFRA—If Evolution Is Outlawed

JELLO BIAFRA—Machine Gun In The Clown's Hand

JELLO BIAFRA—No More Cocoons

NOAM CHOMSKY—An American Addiction

NOAM CHOMSKY—Case Studies in Hypocrisy

NOAM CHOMSKY—Emerging Framework of World Power

NOAM CHOMSKY—Free Market Fantasies

NOAM CHOMSKY—The Imperial Presidency

NOAM CHOMSKY—New War On Terrorism: Fact And Fiction

NOAM CHOMSKY—Propaganda and Control of the Public Mind
NOAM CHOMSKY—Prospects for Democracy
NOAM CHOMSKY & CHUMBAWAMBA—For A Free Humanity: For Anarchy
CHUMBAWAMBA—A Singsong and A Scrap
WARD CHURCHILL—Doing Time: The Politics of Imprisonment
WARD CHURCHILL—In A Pig's Eye: Reflections on the Police State, Repression, and Native America
WARD CHURCHILL—Life in Occupied America
WARD CHURCHILL—Pacifism and Pathology in the American Left
ALEXANDER COCKBURN—Beating the Devil: The Incendiary Rants of Alexander Cockburn
ANGELA DAVIS—The Prison Industrial Complex
THE EX—1936: The Spanish Revolution
NORMAN FINKELSTEIN—An Issue of Justice: Origins of the Israel/Palestine Conflict
ROBERT FISK—War, Journalism, and the Middle East
FREEDOM ARCHIVES—Chile: Promise of Freedom
FREEDOM ARCHIVES—Prisons on Fire: George Jackson, Attica & Black Liberation
FREEDOM ARCHIVES—Robert F. Williams: Self-Defense, Self-Respect & Self-Determination
JAMES KELMAN—Seven Stories
TOM LEONARD—Nora's Place and Other Poems 1965–99
CASEY NEILL—Memory Against Forgetting
GREG PALAST—Live From the Armed Madhouse
GREG PALAST—Weapon of Mass Instruction
CHRISTIAN PARENTI—Taking Liberties
UTAH PHILLIPS—I've Got To know
UTAH PHILLIPS—Starlight on the Rails box set
DAVID ROVICS—Behind the Barricades: Best of David Rovics
ARUNDHATI ROY—Come September
VARIOUS—Better Read Than Dead
VARIOUS—Less Rock, More Talk
VARIOUS—Mob Action Against the State: Collected Speeches from the Bay Area Anarchist Bookfair
VARIOUS—Monkeywrenching the New World Order
VARIOUS—Return of the Read Menace
HOWARD ZINN—Artists In A Time of War
HOWARD ZINN—Heroes and Martyrs: Emma Goldman, Sacco & Vanzetti, and the Revolutionary Struggle
HOWARD ZINN—A People's History of the United States: A Lecture at Reed
HOWARD ZINN—People's History Project Box Set
HOWARD ZINN—Stories Hollywood Never Tells

DVDs

NOAM CHOMSKY—Imperial Grand Strategy: The Conquest of Iraq and the Assault on Democracy
NOAM CHOMSKY—Distorted Morality
STEVEN FISCHLER & JOEL SUCHER—Anarchism in America/Free Voice of Labor
ARUNDHATI ROY—Instant-Mix Imperial Democracy
ROZ PAYNE ARCHIVES—What We Want, What We Believe: The Black Panther Party Library (4 DVD set)
HOWARD ZINN & ANTHONY ARNOVE (ed.)—Readings from Voices of a People's History of the United States

FRIENDS OF AK PRESS

Help sustain our vital project!

AK Press is a worker-run collective that publishes and distributes radical books, audio/visual media, and other material. We're small: ten individuals who work long hours for short money, because we believe in what we do. We're anarchists, which is reflected both in the books we publish and in the way we organize our business: without bosses.

AK Press publishes the finest books, CDs, and DVDs from the anarchist and radical traditions — currently about 18 to 20 per year. Joining The Friends of AK Press is a way in which you can directly help us to keep the wheels rolling and these important projects coming.

As ever, money is tight as we do not rely on outside funding. We need your help to make and keep these crucial materials available. Friends pay a minimum (of course we have no objection to larger sums!) of $25/£15 per month, for a minimum three month period. Money received goes directly into our publishing funds. In return, Friends automatically receive (for the duration of their membership), as they appear, one FREE copy of EVERY new AK Press title. Secondly, they are also entitled to a 10% discount on EVERYTHING featured in the AK Press distribution catalog — or on our website — on ANY and EVERY order. We also have a program where individuals or groups can sponsor a whole book.

PLEASE CONTACT US FOR MORE DETAILS:

AK Press
674-A 23rd Street
Oakland, CA 94612
akpress@akpress.org
www.akpress.org

AK Press
PO Box 12766
Edinburgh, Scotland EH8, 9YE
ak@akedin.demon.co.uk
www.akuk.com